LEGAL TRADITIONS OF THE WORLD

# LEGAL
# TRADITIONS OF
# THE WORLD

## SUSTAINABLE DIVERSITY
## IN LAW

H. Patrick Glenn

OXFORD
UNIVERSITY PRESS

# OXFORD
UNIVERSITY PRESS

Great Clarendon Street, Oxford OX2 6DP

Oxford University Press is a department of the University of Oxford.
It furthers the University's objective of excellence in research, scholarship,
and education by publishing worldwide in

Oxford  New York

Athens  Auckland  Bangkok  Bogotá  Buenos Aires  Calcutta
Cape Town  Chennai  Dar es Salaam  Delhi  Florence  Hong Kong  Istanbul
Karachi  Kuala Lumpur  Madrid  Melbourne  Mexico City  Mumbai
Nairobi  Paris  São Paulo  Singapore  Taipei  Tokyo  Toronto  Warsaw

with associated companies in  Berlin  Ibadan

Oxford is a registered trade mark of Oxford University Press
in the UK and in certain other countries

Published in the United States
by Oxford University Press Inc., New York

British Library Cataloguing in Publication Data
Data available

Library of Congress Cataloging in Publication Data
Data available

ISBN 0–19–876575–4

3  5  7  9  10  8  6  4  2

Typeset by RefineCatch Limited, Bungay, Suffolk
Printed in Great Britain
on acid-free paper by
Biddles Ltd., Guildford and King's Lynn

The manuscript of this book was awarded the Grand Prize of the International Academy of Comparative Law at the XVth International Congress of Comparative Law, Bristol, UK, in August 1998. The Prize was presented by HRH Prince Philip, the Duke of Edinburgh.

For Jane

who wouldn't have written it
quite
the same way

# Contents

# Table of Contents

# List of Abbreviations of Periodicals and Law Reports

| | |
|---|---|
| Am. J. Comp. Law | American Journal of Comparative Law |
| AC | Appeal Cases (law reports) |
| Alberta L. Rev. | Alberta Law Review |
| All ER | All England Reports |
| ALR | Australian Law Reports |
| Am. J. Int. Law | American Journal of International Law |
| Am. J. Juris. | American Journal of Jurisprudence |
| Am. J. Legal Hist | American Journal of Legal History |
| Arab Law Q. | Arab Law Quarterly |
| Arch. philos. dr. | Archives de philosophie du droit |
| Aust. L. J. | Australian Law Journal |
| BGHZ | Entscheidungen des Bundesgericht |
| BLD | Bangladesh Legal Decisions |
| Bol. mex. der. comp. | Boletín mexicano de derecho comparado |
| Boston Coll. Int. & Comp. L. Rev. | Boston College International and Comparative Law Review |
| Boston U. Int. L. J. | Boston University International Law Journal |
| Brigham Young U. L. Rev. | Brigham Young University Law Review |
| Buff. L. Rev. | Buffalo Law Review |
| C. E. | Conseil d'État |
| Calif. L. Rev. | California Law Review |
| Cambr. L. J. | Cambridge Law Journal |
| Can. Bar Rev. | Canadian Bar Review |
| Can. Hum. Rts Yrbk. | Canadian Human Rights Yearbook |
| Can. J. Law and Soc. | Canadian Journal of Law and Society |
| Cardozo L. Rev. | Cardozo Law Review |
| Chicago-Kent L. Rev. | Chicago-Kent Law Review |
| CJQ | Civil Justice Quarterly |
| Clevel. St. L. Rev. | Cleveland State Law Review |
| CLR | Commonwealth Law Reports |
| CMLR | Common Market Law Review |
| Col. L. Rev. | Columbia Law Review. |
| Curr. Legal Problems | Current Legal Problems |
| Dalhousie L. J. | Dalhousie Law Journal |

| | |
|---|---|
| Dalloz | Recueil Dalloz |
| DLR | Dominion Law Reports |
| Duke L. J. | Duke Law Journal |
| *Early Med. Eur.* | *Early Medieval Europe* |
| Eur. Rev. Private Law | European Review of Private Law |
| Gaz. Pal. | Gazette du Palais |
| *Georgia Rev.* | *Georgia Review* |
| Harv. Hum. Rts J. | Harvard Human Rights Journal |
| Harv. L. Rev. | Harvard Law Review |
| Hastings L. J. | Hastings Law Journal |
| Hum. Rts Q. | Human Rights Quarterly |
| Ind. J. Global Legal St. | Indiana Journal of Global Legal Studies |
| Int. & Comp. Law Q. | International and Comparative Law Quarterly |
| Int. Bus. Lawyer | International Business Lawyer |
| *Int. J. Middle East St.* | *International Journal of Middle East Studies* |
| Int. Lawyer | International Lawyer |
| *Int. Lit. News* | *International Literary News* |
| *Int. Pol. Sci. Rev.* | *International Political Science Review* |
| Int. Rev. Law and Econs. | International Review of Law and Economics |
| *Int. Soc. Sci J.* | *International Social Sciences Journal* |
| Islamic & Comp. Law Q. | Islamic and Comparative Law Quarterly |
| Islamic Law and Soc. | Islamic Law and Society |
| J. African Law | Journal of African Law |
| J. Chinese Law | Journal of Chinese Law |
| J. Comp. Law & Int. Law | Journal of Comparative and International Law |
| J. dr. int. | Journal du droit international |
| J. Fam. Law | Journal of Family Law |
| J. Indian Law Inst. | Journal of Indian Law Institute |
| J. Law and Econs. | Journal of Law and Economics |
| J. Legal Hist. | Journal of Legal History |
| *J. Politics* | *Journal of Politics* |
| J.C.P. | Juris-classeur périodique |
| Jewish L. Ann. | Jewish Law Annual |
| Jewish Law Assoc. St. | Jewish Law Association Studies |
| Jur. Rev. | Juridical Review |
| Law & Hist. Rev. | Law and History Review |
| Law & Philos. | Law and Philosophy |
| Law & Society Rev. | Law and Society Review |
| Ld. Raym. | Raymond, Lord (Law Reports) |

| | |
|---|---|
| Legal St. | Legal Studies |
| LQR | Law Quarterly Review |
| McGill L. J. | McGill Law Journal |
| *Med. St.* | *Mediaeval Studies* |
| Melb. U. L. Rev. | Melbourne University Law Review |
| Mich. L. Rev. | Michigan Law Review |
| MLR | Modern Law Review |
| *Mod. Lang. Notes* | *Modern Language Notes* |
| NJW | Neue juristische Wochenschrift |
| NZLJ | New Zealand Law Journal |
| OJLS | Oxford Journal of Legal Studies |
| Or. L. Rev. | Oregon Law Review |
| Osgoode Hall L. J. | Osgoode Hall Law Journal |
| Ottawa L. Rev. | Ottawa Law Review |
| Parker Sch. J. East Eur. Law | Parker School Journal of East European Law |
| *Philos. Soc. Sci.* | *Philosophy of the Social Sciences* |
| PL | Public Law |
| Prax. Jur. Rel. | Praxis juridique et religion |
| QB | Queen's Bench (Law Reports) |
| Rabels | Rabels Zeitschrift für ausländisches und internationales Privatrecht |
| Rev. crit. d.i.p. | Revue critique de droit international privé |
| Rev. dr. int. dr. comp. | Revue de droit international et de droit comparé |
| Rev. dr. McGill | Revue de droit de McGill |
| Rev. gén. dr. | Revue générale de droit |
| Rev. hell. dr. int. | Revue hellenique de droit international |
| Rev. hist. dr. fr. étr. | Revue historique de droit français et étranger |
| Rev. hist. Fac. dr. | Revue d'historie des Facultés de droit |
| Rev. int. dr. com. | Revue internationale de droit comparé |
| Rev. int. dr. econ. | Revue internationale de droit economique |
| Rev. jur. Th. | Revue juridique Thémis |
| *Rev. Politics* | *Review of Politics* |
| Rev. rech. jur. | Revue de la recherche juridique |
| Rev. trim. dr. civ. | Revue trimestrielle de droit civil |
| Rev. univ. dr. de l'homme | Revue universelle des droits de l'homme |
| *S. Atlantic Q.* | *South Atlantic Quarterly* |
| S. C. L. Rev. | South Carolina Law Review |
| S. Calif. L. Rev. | Southern California Law Review |
| *Scientif. Am.* | *Scientific American* |
| SCR | Supreme Court Reports (Can.) |

| | |
|---|---|
| *St. Med. & Renais. Hist.* | *Studies in Medieval and Renaissance History* |
| Stan. L. Rev. | Stanford Law Review |
| *TLS* | *Times Literary Supplement* |
| Tulane L. Rev. | Tulane Law Review |
| U. Calif. Davis L. Rev. | University of California at Davis Law Review |
| U. Pa L. Rev. | University of Pennsylvania Law Review |
| Va. L. Rev. | Virginia Law Review |
| Victoria Univ. Wellington L. Rev. | Victoria University of Wellington Law Review |
| Wayne St. Law Rev. | Wayne State Law Review |
| WLR | Weekly Law Reports |
| *Women's St.* | *Women's Studies* |
| Yale L. J. | Yale Law Journal |
| ZRG | Zeitschrift für Rechtsgeschichte |
| ZvglRwiss | Zeitschrift für vergleichende Rechtswissenschaft |

# List of Biblical Abbreviations

| | |
|---|---|
| Deut. | Deuteronomy |
| Exod. | Exodus |
| Gen. | Genesis |
| Isa. | Isaiah |
| Lev. | Leviticus |
| Matt. | Matthew |
| Rom. | Epistle to the Romans |

# PREFACE

The notion of tradition, after two or three centuries of neglect and opprobrium in the western world, has recently received renewed attention. This appears due in large measure to circumstances internal to western societies, notably that which a recent social science world survey described as a 'postmodern shift' in the last twnty-five years from 'rational-legal authority' to 'self-expression'.[1] Political and social theory has thus turned to tradition as a possible means of maintaining social coherence and identity in liberal, industrialized societies. There has been some reflection of this larger movement in legal writing where, however, the concept, or tradition, of 'rational-legal authority' is profoundly anchored. This book attempts to advance our understanding of tradition in law—or, more precisely, our understanding of legal traditions—for several reasons.

The first is one which appears peculiar to the west (though it pertained as well to the former Soviet Union)—the decline in normative authority of formal sources of law. This phenomenon is not only the object of social science surveys; it is now being recognized explicitly in popular culture. A government-sponsored television commercial in a large, western democracy recently announced that automobile seat-belts would be obligatory in the future and continued: '*It's not just the law*; it makes good sense' [emphasis added]. If formal sources of law, and the law they produce, have become too thin and weak for the tasks they should accomplish,[2] supportive normativity may be found in tradition. This is the project of recent political and social theory; it is here being replicated in law.

A further reason, extending beyond western societies, lies in the necessity of collaboration amongst jurists of all traditions in the resolution of many problems of the world. These may be life-threatening or patrimonial, commercial or gender-related, criminal or environmental—there now appears to be no area of law free of the possibility of extra-jurisdictional complication. Cases may be dealt with by formal methods of choice of law, but inter-traditional understanding may obviate the necessity for expensive and lengthy second-order litigation. Beyond the level of the individual case, there is also the question of the role and influence in the world of particular laws and particular lawyers. The role of human rights in international debate is only one, highly visible, example of this general question. How should we

---

[1] R. Inglehart, 'Changing values, economic development and political change' (1995) 47 Int. Soc. Sci. J. 379 (reporting results of 43-nation World Values Survey in 1990–1).

[2] See B. Oppetit, *Droit et modernité* (Paris: Presses Universitaires de France, 1998) at 7 ('graves dysfonction-nements, marqués par des phénomènes d'indifférence au droit et d'ineffectivité des règles').

think about the general relations amongst laws and lawyers, somehow recognized as different? How do we agree upon the role of whatever we currently understand as law? How do we avoid both dominance and resistance to dominance, and the violence both may entail? How, in the language of the Mexican novelist Carlos Fuentes, do we 'overcome separation'?[3]

Tradition appears today as the most fruitful field of enquiry in addressing these questions. It does not appear to be the product of any particular civilization, yet appears present, explicitly or implicitly, as a formative influence in the law of all of them (including, and to the present day, that of the west). The same cannot be said of the notion of a legal system, the history of which is clearly and exclusively associated with western (and derived Soviet) legal theory, and which now may be thought of as part of the problem rather than as the solution. Systemic thought is an inherent part of what has been described polemically, as 'The Great White Lie of Western Legal Theory'. Its theoretical utility has been further limited by the collapse of the soviet legal system. Similar problems arise with the notion of 'culture' or 'legal culture'. It too appears largely a creation of the western enlightenment,[4] though suffering from a remarkable level of ambiguity. In concentrating on current forms of human thought and activity, moreover, it appears antithetical to whatever normativity may be derived from the past.

Thinking about tradition, however, is not an uncontroversial or simple process. Thinking about a single tradition appears inadequate, since the tradition chosen may be in some manner exceptional, as may be, indeed, all traditions. A single tradition may also have camouflaged its relations with other traditions. Addressing multiple traditions does, however, create problems of its own. How are separate traditions identified? What manner of analysis can be adopted which is appropriate to a number of traditions, yet not exclusive to any one of them? Is a theory of traditions possible? Can one even know a tradition which is not one's own? The organization of this book, and even the titles of its chapters, reflects these difficulties. Multiple traditions are addressed, though a further multiplicity is not excluded and is even acknowledged. Traditions are identified, but not in definitive form, and even the definite article is avoided (grammar permitting). A theory of traditions is contemplated, but not constructed. Learning about tradition is taken to be a process of learning from traditions. Whether this is possible is taken to be a matter of practice. More will be said, particularly after some practice.

Since people may come to this book with different objectives, it can be read in a

---

[3] Address to McGill University, Winter, 1995; and see C. Fuentes, 'The Mirror of the Other' (1992) 254 *The Nation* 408, notably at 409 ('We have too many common problems which demand cooperation and understanding in a new world context, to clash as much as we do').

[4] On both system and culture as concepts derived from western tradition, see below ch. 5, *Revolutions, systems, language and interpretation*.

number of ways. If you are not so much interested in law, but interested in tradition and its relation to society, you can read only the first two chapters and the last chapter. You will pick up some law even in this process, particularly in the last chapter. If your interests are strictly legal (as you understand these things) you can read only the middle seven chapters, and if you are interested only in specific legal traditions, only the chapters relating to them. Alternatively, the seven legal chapters can be read, if you will, horizontally. Each is composed of four parts (dealing respectively with the nature of a particular tradition, its underlying justification, its concept of change, and its relation to other traditions), so the traditions can be read serially with respect to any one or more of these questions. You can also read it from beginning to end, which might present some advantages, since that's the way it was written.

The book attempts to cover a great deal of ground and much is owed, to many. Most immediately, thanks are due to Dean Roberto Santacruz Fernández of the Faculty of Law of the Universidad Autónoma de Puebla and to Jorge Chávez Ramírez, Director of International Relations of the same University, for a warm and spontaneous welcome received in the academic year 1995/6 in Puebla, Mexico. Special thanks are also due to Emma Pacheco, of the UAP Office of International Relations. For the increasingly rare, and much appreciated, enjoyment of a sabbatical year, I owe thanks to Dean Stephen Toope of the Faculty of Law of McGill University. More generally, in a way which can never be adequately repaid, I owe thanks to a remarkable group of colleagues at the Faculty of Law and Institute of Comparative Law of McGill University, who together succeed in creating an environment which is both provocative and collegial. I am also very grateful to Gary Bell, John Brierley, George Bermann, Jane Matthews Glenn, Wael Hallaq, Konstantinos Kerameus, Li Xiaoping, Joshua Shmidman, Stephen Toope, Catherine Valcke, Harro von Senger, Ernest Weinrib, Jeremy Webber, Katherine Young and the several anonymous readers of Oxford University Press for careful readings, sharing of learning, or both. I am also greatly indebted to the editorial staff of Oxford University Press for their patience and professionalism. Research assistants who have provided invaluable assistance include Abdul-Basit Khan, Marie-Pierre Lami, Alissa Malkin, Claudia Pierrot, Laurie Sargent, Marisa Selig, and Ed Vandenburg. I am also grateful for having received the financial support of the Wainwright Trust of the McGill University Faculty of Law and of the Bora Laskin National Fellowship in Human Rights Research. Portions of this book were the object of presentations at the Faculty Seminar programme of the Faculty of Law, Fribourg University, Switzerland; the Graduate Studies Programme, Harvard Law School; the Instituto de Investigaciones Jurídicas of the Universidad Nacional Autónoma de México; the Centre of Private Law of the Russian Federation, Moscow; and the Faculty of Law of the National University of Singapore: and I received valuable comments in each of those places. Over the last ten years I also have learned much from students in the graduate seminar in Legal Traditions at McGill. I received invaluable library assistance from the Law Library, McGill University; the Swiss Institute of Comparative Law, Lausanne, Switzerland; and the Instituto de Investigaciones Jurídicas of Mexico City, and I am much indebted to the cosmopolitan character of those collections.

H. Patrick Glenn
Puebla, Mexico and
Sutton, Quebec
August 1999

# 1

# A THEORY OF TRADITION?
# THE CHANGING PRESENCE
# OF THE PAST

How does one think about the past and about its grip on the present? Some have said that we can either accept the past and its teaching or we can think about it critically. Tradition would therefore exist but everyone would have the option of either being an adherent to it or of being an external critic, free to move on to other concerns. There would thus be a traditional way of thinking and a non-traditional way of thinking. In the same way there would be traditional societies and non-traditional societies (with correspondingly different types of laws), depending on how most people in a society reacted to this question. As well, a theory of tradition might be possible for those who stood back from tradition, critically, gaining theoretical perspective, but impossible for those who chose to remain immersed in a particular tradition, that which has been theirs for all of their lives. No one steeped in the content of a particular tradition, bound to it, could think theoretically of what that meant.

This view of how we can think about tradition has received powerful support, as will be seen, and underlies much popular wisdom in the western world. Traditional societies are thus regularly distinguished from modern, or post-industrial, or even post-modern ones. Traditional thinking is contrasted with progressive or independent thinking. Traditional forms of education are distinguished from new, innovative techniques of education. Traditional people are distinguished from the kind of people it is presumed that most people want to be, at least in the western world.

There are, however, problems with this way of thinking. Karl Popper nicely remarked that 'the rationalist who says such things is . . . very much bound by a rationalist tradition which traditionally says them. This shows the weakness of certain traditional attitudes towards the problem of tradition.'[1] Professor Popper

---

[1] Popper, 'Rational Theory of Tradition' (1969) 120 at 121. Popper goes on, however, to qualify the critical tradition as being a second-order tradition, one which questions the story to be handed on. This appears more problematical, in somehow placing one manner of thought in a superior or controlling manner over others. Might there not also be a second-order tradition of how to accept and work within a tradition? Or is it not preferable to see rationality simply as another first-order tradition, but which invariably would contradict

was relying on historical work which shows that the giving of primacy to human reason in the world is a way of thought which goes back to at least the early stages of Greek philosophy, and some would now say the Egypt of the pyramids.[2] Much of western thought has tended to the rational, but the rest of the world sees this as the leading characteristic of the western . . . tradition. Others have spoken, less charitably, of a 'herd of independent minds'.[3]

Those who have studied the history of attitudes towards tradition locate the origins of a sharp dichotomy between tradition and rationality in the enlightenment of the seventeenth century. As a means of overcoming the inequalities of existing European societies, rooted in tradition, tradition itself had to be overcome, or destroyed, as an operative social concept.[4] Contemporary rationality would then prevail—forever young, as long as one accepted, albeit uncritically, the primacy of the present.

History, with its relativizing effect, tells us, however, that we are all part of a tradition, or traditions. One can perhaps distinguish between individualist or rationalist traditions—there must really be more than one of them—and communal or contextualist traditions—and there are surely more than one of them. They are all, however, traditions, and all allow our predecessors to speak to us, with more—or less—insistence. Western societies, in spite of what is often said, are thus traditional societies, and western law is traditional law. So tradition is a common feature of societies and of laws, and working with tradition allows us to work with a common factor.[5] In any event, western societies are not as hostile to some forms of

many of the others? All traditions would thus rest ultimately on underlying views of the world and the place of human reason in it. This large question will be examined in the context of different traditions, including that of rationality.

[2] See below Ch. 5, Constructing a Tradition; and see Brown, *Rethinking tradition* (1996) at 3 (enlightenment thinkers, in portraying conflict of reason and tradition, 'perhaps failed to recognize the degree to which they were, themselves, rooted in the traditions from which they claimed to have escaped'); Sang-ki Kim, 'Confucian Capitalism: Recycling Traditions' (1993–4) No. 94 *Telos* 18 at 19 ('modernity is ultimately only a part of the larger traditional framework of European civilization—the part pretending to be independent of its historical roots'); W. Everdell, *The First Moderns* (Chicago/London: Univ. of Chicago Press, 1997), notably at 33–5, 351 ff (essence of modernism being notion of ontological discontinuity, first articulated by Greek mathematicians such as Pythagoras who denied irrational numbers, such as the square root of 2, in favour of integers and fractions clearly separate from one another).

[3] The expression dates at least from H. Rosenberg, *The Tradition of the New* (New York: Horizon Press, 1959) at 207.

[4] E. Shils, *Tradition* (Chicago: Univ. of Chicago Press, 1981) at 6; and on the changing tradition of talking about tradition, see Waldman, 'Tradition as Modality of Change ' (1985–6) notably at 318–25 (enlightenment concept prevailing until 1960s; first disturbed by disenchantment with pace and results of development work founded on dichotomy between traditional and modern societies and necessity of transition; now surviving in 'criticized form'); S. N. Eisenstadt, 'Post-Traditional Societies and the Continuity and Reconstruction of Tradition' (1973) 102 No. 1 *Daedalus* 1 ('widespread dissatisfaction' with dichotomy between traditional and modern societies which dominated development studies through 1960s).

[5] For A. Kronman, it is also the distinguishing, identifying feature of human beings. 'Remembrance and fame, the work of conservation, the linkage of the generations . . . together these define . . . a uniquely human world in which neither gods nor animals appear.' Kronman, 'Precedent and Tradition' (1990) at 1065.

tradition as might be thought. In Switzerland, tradition is used to sell the finest of chocolates; in Montreal 'the tradition continues' of the Canadiens winning hockey games; and in the United States it is said, of the product of a well-known southern distillery, 'If it isn't a tradition, it's a very, very, very long fad.' Tradition is here a sign of quality and endurance. Contextual traditions thus survive alongside individualist ones, whichever may be primary in a given context.

# A THEORY OF TRADITION?

Is a theory of tradition then possible? Karl Popper, in the essay previously mentioned, described himself as 'a rationalist of sorts', and the article is entitled 'Towards a Rational Theory of Tradition'.[6] He states in the article, however, that 'the emphasis should be on the word "towards"'[7] and that he does not intend to put forward anything like a 'full theory', choosing rather only to illustrate the kind of questions that a theory of tradition would have to answer, and to outline ideas which might be useful.[7] Why does a rationalist, aware of the traditional character of rationalism, hesitate in constructing a full theory of tradition? Popper himself provided no futher explanation, but reasons for hesitation can be surmised.

Theories are rational constructions, which must first answer to requirements of internal consistency and logic before they are tested for explanatory power in the real world. Theories, and the logic they entail, are part of the tradition of western rationalist thought. As such, a theoretical construct is a creation derived from a particular tradition (though the possibility cannot be excluded that it may also have been developed elsewhere). Now, it is perhaps possible, and even advisable, to be rational about being rational, to be theoretical about western traditions of rationality. Alisdair MacIntyre has done this in writing a chapter on 'The Rationality of Traditions', after examining four western traditions (described as Aristotelian, Augustinian, Scottish and liberal).[8] It is another thing, however, to be rational about non-rational or other-rational traditions or, to put it more precisely, to apply certain forms of logic to ways of thought which follow different forms of logic. This can surely be done; it is the results which should give one pause. They may well be results (though this is not necessarily the case) biased by the imposition of one tradition of thought upon others.

Is it therefore better not to read recent theoretical writings on tradition (largely western in origin) and to reject categorically recent calls which have been made for

---

[6] See Popper, 'Rational Theory of Tradition' (1969) at 120.

[7] Ibid., at 120.

[8] A. MacIntyre, *Whose Justice? Which Rationality?* (1988) at 349–69.

development of a theory of tradition?[9] In studying traditions, legal or extra-legal, there appears to be no initial justification for granting primacy of one over others; equally, there appears to be no initial justification in precluding the particular teaching of any one of them. The western tradition now includes theory on tradition and this theory of one tradition may be useful in the encounter with other traditions. There may well be theory on tradition in other traditions, expressed in different forms of logic. A theory of tradition should therefore not be thought of as a present, or perhaps even future, construction, but rather as a present device, or method, for thinking multiple traditions. It is a method for expanding knowledge and understanding, involving movement from within one tradition to within another, using all of the teaching of both (or all) of the traditions to facilitate this process. Thinking theoretically about tradition means suspending conviction in a given tradition at least to the point of hearing, and learning, from another tradition. It means living, however, briefly, in a 'middle ground', described recently as 'the place in between: in between cultures, peoples, and in between empires and the nonstate world of villages . . . [where] diverse peoples adjust their differences'.[10] It is the process of overcoming separation.

## TRADITION AND TIME

If the importance of tradition has become more widely recognized, further attention will naturally be given to knowing what it is, and how it functions. This is where the lure of theory presents itself. So some tentative theorizing may be useful, before attempting the process of immersion in several legal traditions. If your particular legal tradition is not a theoretical one, you may prefer to turn immediately to the particular traditions.

### PASTNESS

The most obvious and generally accepted element of tradition is what T. S. Eliot has called its 'pastness'.[11] In the English language, this is a very odd and even cumbersome word, which a poet might normally avoid. The problem is in finding an

[9] See, e.g., Izdebski, 'Tradition et changement en droit' (1987) at 841; and for what appears to be a more western variant, calling for a theory of social change, D. Horowitz, 'The Qur'an and the Common Law: Islamic Law Reform and the Theory of Legal Change' (1994) 42 Am. J. of Comp. Law 233 at 240. On the relations between tradition and change see the discussion below, The Changing Presence of the Past.

[10] R. White, *The Middle Ground: Indians, Empires and Republics in the Great Lakes Region* (Cambridge: Cambridge Univ. Press, 1991) at. x.

[11] T. S. Eliot, 'Tradition and the Individual Talent' (1948) at 49. Eliot did speak, however, of a particular 'historical sense', involving not only a perception 'of the pastness of the past, but of its presence'. Loc. cit.

alternative. 'Age' will not do, since although a young age is entirely possible, a young tradition is more problematical. The word 'history' is an obvious candidate, but history, in the view of many, has become a social science and social science generally seeks to avoid normative statements. In the view of many people and of many historians, history is composed of dead people and old facts. This is a respectable intellectual position, but has led to the expression 'You're history' as a means of indicating present irrelevancy.[12] So T. S. Eliot chose 'pastness', an odd, awkward word, probably as a means of indicating that we have to think harder about the past, about how we seize it, and what it may signify in what we call the present, or the future. The notion of 'pastness' also appears to raise interesting questions as to how we think about time.[13]

How much pastness is required? In socialist legal thinking there has been discussion of 'young' or 'recent' tradition, or tradition which was of 'rapid formation'.[14] Two historians recently edited a volume on *The Invention of Tradition*, identifying, notably, the Scottish kilt as an invention of pan-Scottish nationalism, though it had previously existed as a simple garment in some highland areas.[15] If history is, as some say, accelerating, can there be instant traditions? Can you 'invent your own Church,' as was recently proposed in a European newspaper advertisement? Since no one appears able to say that a given measure of time is necessary to constitute a tradition, the answer to these questions might well be yes, though a number of qualifications appear necessary. In the first place, we would have to know the criteria for truly inventing a tradition or, in other words, defining the point of origin of a tradition. The kilt did exist, before additional cultural significance was given to it. In science, the notion of invention is generally accepted, but many say that any given inventor is simply the last participant in a long chain of people who have developed knowledge.[16] Assessing the originality of any human creation may

---

[12] On the emergence of this view of history, in western thought, see Ch. 5, *Changing the idea of change*. Cf. the views of another literary figure, G. K. Chesterton, who remarked: 'Tradition means giving votes to the most obscure of all classes, our ancestors. It is the democracy of the dead. Tradition refuses to submit to the small and arrogant oligarchy of those who merely happen to be walking about. All democrats object to men being disqualified by the accident of birth; tradition objects to their being disqualified by the accident of death.' G. K. Chesterton, 'The Ethics of Elfland' in G. K. Chesterton, *Collected Works*, vol. I. (San Francisco: Ignatius Press, 1986) at 251. On the question of inter-generational relations, see the discussion in Ch. 3, Change and the Natural World.

[13] See below, this Chapter, The Changing Presence of the Past.

[14] Izdebski 'Tradition et changement en droit' (1987) at 841; Granger, 'La tradition' (1979) at 41.

[15] See H. Trevor-Roper, 'The Invention of Tradition: The Highland Tradition of Scotland', in Hobsbawm and Ranger, *Invention of Tradition* (1983) 15, notably at 20; cf., on the limits of 'invention' and the risks of focusing on the novel and neglecting 'residual continuities', C. Hamilton, *Terrific Majesty: the powers of Shaka Zulu and the limits of historical invention* (Cambridge, Mass.: Harvard Univ. Press, 1998), notably at 25–7, with refs.

[16] The notion of invention would itself thus be part of a scientific tradition, often said to have been initiated with the Greek concept of developing some thing from no thing. See E. Severino, *La Tendenza fondamentale del nostro tempo* (Milan: Adelphi, 1988) at 15. There are many claims in the world, however, to the discovery of zero (Mayan, Chinese, Greek, Indian, etc.).

itself take time, such that the instant tradition can only become known as such once time has passed. The instant tradition would thus only be one to which a distinct point of origin could be given, and time (becoming pastness) would be necessary for this process to occur.[17] This would be possible, however, and an exaggerated notion of historical continuity would not preclude, as it might, either the creation of a tradition or its emergence, in identifiable form, over time. You could thus wager, as of now, that you had created a tradition—only the proof would be lacking in the immediate. Traditions do appear to live and die, however, and the young or recent tradition is likely to be one which has received less human support and adherence than an ancient one. The young or recent tradition is thus inherently more fragile than the ancient one. There are likely to be fewer people to remember it and fewer people convinced of whatever normativity it might have. This would not exclude, however, a young tradition with a brilliant future. Nor would even a large and undisputed amount of pastness guarantee survival for the dinosaurs of the world of traditions.

If instant traditions are possible, subject to verification over time, then instant traditions would also be possible in law. The notion of a national legal tradition might be the best indication of this. A national legal tradition could be seen as originating in the creation of a particular state, and since some states are of recent origin, their legal traditions could be seen as recent or new. Yet the notion of a national legal tradition is strongest where the state is very old and, even given some very old states, it has not overcome the concept of legal traditions defined in terms of principles, norms or institutions which extend beyond current political organizations. This is at least the thesis underlying the organization of this book. It will require greater elaboration, and defence, as particular traditions are examined.

## PRESENCE

The past, even as recent as yesterday, may disappear on us. The more past each of us has, the more difficult it is to retain it. So T. S. Eliot again instructs us that 'Tradition cannot be inherited, and if you want it, you must obtain it by great labour.'[18] It is true that human life without recall of the past is scarcely imaginable. It would involve all memory of human accomplishment instantly disappearing.[19] Only hubris would remain, and even this would not be remembered. It is another question, however, of how we remember and what we remember. This is the question, first of all, of how the past is brought into the present.

A present past is one which has been captured, in a way which allows present use and present, further, transmission. How do we capture the past? There is no exclusive method and much to be said about the virtues, and defects, of different

---

[17] See M. Krygier, 'Law as Tradition' (1986) at 239 on the idea of *originating* a tradition.

[18] Eliot, 'Tradition and Individual Talent' (1948) at 49.

[19] Kronman, 'Precedent and Tradition' (1990) at 1062.

methods. There are questions of efficiency, but there are also larger and more obscure questions of the compatibility of various methods with the traditions themselves.

Capturing the past is a question of human communication, since the capture must be in a way accessible to others. Physical objects are a means of communication, and the present science of archaeology has taught us how much information physical objects may contain. Physical objects also contain implicit lessons; they need not be seen as simply inert objects, or artefacts. An ancient clay pot tells us something not only about how clay pots were made, but about how clay pots *should* be made, if they are to last thousands of years. Objects reveal the skills, methods and talents of their makers; they allow us to distinguish the good, the bad and the temporary in means of production. A thing well made will last, and the makers and marketers of things are today well aware of the importance of tradition in maintenance of quality—the good of inanimate objects. Things exist, moreover, not only as a result of human effort, but as a result of what we know as nature. For many, nature is filled with meaning, captured in the drama, or even miracle, of contemporary existence. So a first means or method of capturing the past is in its material deposit, surviving in the present world. Things, of course, do not speak or communicate in a human language, so a particular receptivity is called for in learning of the past from its capture in things. Things may also disappear, and enormous scientific efforts are now being made to ensure future survival of certain objects instructive as to current forms of civilization. Over long stretches of time, or space, objects may be more communicative than any language which we presently know.

Most traditions rely on more than inanimate objects, however, to ensure capture of the past. All legal traditions appear to have relied greatly on the spoken word as a principal means of capture, though the present importance of orality varies greatly.[20] We often therefore speak of oral traditions, but the most important element in an oral tradition is not so much the spoken word as it is human memory. The spoken word, once spoken, must be recalled, and oral traditions are thus subject to all the vicissitudes of human memory. Stories are thus never repeated in exactly the same manner in which they are initially told. Oral traditions, by virtue of their method, or process, are constantly being re-arranged, or are forgotten.[21]

There can thus be no such thing as a static oral tradition. Yet memory is not as limited, fragile and boring a human talent as it is often thought to be today. Medieval concepts of memory referred broadly to all operations of forming, recalling and creating images. It thus included the process of imaging, or imagining, that which had happened, or might have happened, in the outside world.[22] Its devices

---

[20] For recent 'awakening' to orality in western thought, see Ong, *Orality and Literacy* (1982) at 6, 16 ff.

[21] P. Boyer, 'Stuff "Traditions" Made of' (1987) at 62.

[22] M. Carruthers, *The Book of Memory: a study of memory in medieval culture* (Cambridge: Cambridge Univ. Press, 1990).

were many, including entire architectural structures of mnemonic devices,[23] and the human mind was known to possess enormous powers of capture and recall. Entire *books* were learned by mens or mind/heart (the transition is not always from orality to writing), and Aquinas taught that memory was a part of ethics, rather than rhetoric, since it prevented 'subtle and spiritual things' from falling away from the soul.[24] Memory was thus not 'rote', but the process of internalizing that which was worthy of recall. Law worth having and worth keeping, was worth remembering. Instruction in law thus taught the process of internalizing law.

Much content could thus be captured and transmitted with a high degree of fidelity but on the whole, particularly where the memory arts had not been so highly developed, oral traditions retained, and retain, a dynamic character. This is often seen as an advantage. In the dynamic of capture and transmission there is a reflection of the vigour of the tradition itself—always in the minds and necessarily in the discussion of its adherents. Oral tradition also cannot easily be destroyed. It lives as long as memory lives, and memory may be deliberately, aggressively and rebelliously long. It is the ultimate resource of suppressed traditions, which 'snap back like so many bent yet unbreakable twigs'.[25]

In contrast to orality, writing offers to tradition the apparent advantages of physical duration[26] (still more vital where people are dispersed), precision, and detail. The history of communication recorded on physical means of support—a history of some 3500 years—is a history of constant refinement and development, each new stage a testimony to the underlying idea. There appear to be (though the problem may be one of proof) no instances of writing having been suppressed once it had been developed as a technique. Written communication is also independent of memory. That which is written down can be simply looked up; there is no

[23] J. D. Spence, *The Memory Palace of Matteo Ricci* (New York: Penguin, 1985) (on construction of palaces of varying size and structure, appropriately furnished and decorated, to be kept in one's head as storage places for myriad concepts that make up human knowledge), notably at 12, 13 (denigration of memory arts beginning in 16th century and culminating in devastating criticism of Francis Bacon, as models of scientific thinking developed). Current scientific work using positron emission topography (PET) is now suggesting that different parts of the brain are involved in the memory process and that conscious, higher-level thinking is needed in memory search.

[24] Spence, *Memory Palace* (1985), above, at 13; and on the importance of thinking 'memorable thoughts' in oral tradition, a matter of both style and substance, see Ong, *Orality and Literacy* (1982) at 34.

[25] J. Tully, *Strange multiplicity: constitutionalism in an age of diversity* (Cambridge: Cambridge Univ. Press, 1995) at 10, citing I. Berlin, 'The bent twig: on the rise of nationalism' in I. Berlin, *The Crooked Timber of Humanity* (New York: Random House, 1992) 238. On the orality of traditions of rebellion or resistance in England, see E. P. Thompson, *Customs in Common* (1993) notably at 8–15 ('practices and norms are reproduced down the generations within the slowly differentiating ambience of custom . . . the plebeian culture is rebellious, but rebellious in defence of custom. The customs defended are the people's own . . . successive generations stand in apprentice relation to each other.').

[26] 'If you go to the native court and look at the books which clerks wrote twenty years ago or more, they are still as they wrote them. They do not say one thing today and another tomorrow, or one thing this year and another next year. Okoye in the book today cannot become Okonkwo tomorrow. In the Bible Pilate said: "What is written is written." It is *uli* [the juice of the *uli* tree] that never fades.' C. Achebe, *The African Trilogy* (London: Picador, 1988) at 276.

necessity of internalization. Writing is also the principal means of communication of science, and law which aspires to the scientific will find it equally essential.

The virtues of the oral tradition are frequently, however, the vices of the written one. The written word can be destroyed, by manifold means, both human and natural. It may also disintegrate, notably through the effect of internal acids, or moths.[27] It also represents, at least usually, a stationary target, though while the form is fixed, the interpretation never is and 'every reader is a potential radical'.[28] Against non-traditional interpretations, the text cannot answer back. It simply *is* the canon, forever such and as such, forever vulnerable. It may draw support from outside itself, as representing custom or revelation (the reading of one who may not know how to read) but both of these may be known and believed independently of the text. Absent demonstrable adherence to custom, or revelation, the text may be seen more as a point of departure than as a means of continuance. It must survive on its own; it must present, itself, a powerful, detailed argument which convinces on its own terms whomever it may meet. There have been many such glorious texts, and many in law. There have also been many others.

Those who write, being unable to argue, thus assume a major burden. They may choose to write argumentatively, in dialogical form, a method used by many early writers. They may choose to write comprehensively, sweeping into their text the thought and authority of many others, whether acknowledged or not. They may choose to write compellingly, in a way which admits no logical deviation. Yet in the end there is only the text, if the tradition has chosen to exclude the world beyond the text.

The written word is also now acquiring new forms of physical support, and new forms of digital expression. This development of the scientific tradition appears to have major consequences for the preservation of many traditions. Digital forms of expression are ones which quantify language—converting it into a machine-readable code of binary signals. The content of language is of no consequence in this process; the concern of the custodians of digital language is with such questions as capacity of retention, speed of transmission, and so on.[29] In the flood of digital information there are real reasons for what may be described as an increase

[27] E. E. Urbach, *The Sages: Their Concepts and Beliefs*, trans. I. Abrahams (Cambridge, Mass.: Harvard Univ. Press, 1987) at 291, citing Philo ('decisions . . . not inscribed on monuments nor on leaves of paper, which the moth destroys, but on the souls of those who are partners in the same citizenship'); and for the near loss of the tradition of European literacy, see T. Cahill, *How the Irish Saved Civilization: the Untold Story of Ireland's Heroic Role from the Fall of Rome to the Rise of Medieval Europe* (New York: Doubleday, 1995), notably at 193 (absent Irish monasteries and their work of preservation and copying of texts, 'when Islam began its medieval expanson, it would have encountered scant resistance to its plans—just scattered tribes of animists, ready for a new identity').

[28] Pocock, 'Time, Institutions and Action' (1968) 209 at 225; and see L. Wieseltier, *Kaddish* (New York: Alfred A. Knopf, 1998) at 259 ('Tradition is never acquired, it is always being acquired. (Or it is always not being acquired: the world is full of Jews who are not Jewish, Christians who are not Christians, Muslims who are not Muslims)').

[29] On the general failure of information theory and its inability to address 'the issue of meaning', see J. Horgan, 'From Complexity to Perplexity', *Scientif. Am.* (June 1995) 104 at 109.

in capacity and a decrease in content. Of course, there is no decline in the amount of content: there is rather an enormous increase. It is more a question of knowing whether that which should be preserved can still be ascertained, in the enormous flood of electronic signals. It is important to know what should be preserved, and to preserve it, because much digitally stored information is of short and fragile duration. Data banks are deliberately emptied after specified periods of time; physical supports are fragile and unstable; a growing number of records are stored in obsolete and potentially unretrievable formats. Retention is thus particularly indiscriminate and all forms of retention are of potentially short duration. With electronic information systems we have returned in a sense to capture the past through things—things which record the past in a non-human code, and which can be read only through other things or machines. It is a more inanimate form of retention or capture than through human speech or writing; this may have important consequences for the search for law.

Objects, speech (with memory) and writing appear as the major forms of capture of the past, for purposes of tradition. They may exist, or be intended to exist, as exclusive forms of capture; they may also co-exist with others. Objects and writing may be presently explained in speech; speech may be recorded (sometimes over opposition), in writing or on tape or disk. These forms of capture may also co-exist with other, less frequent forms such as art,[30] poetry or song,[31] or ritual (which may tend to art). Ritual appears in the present as the unspoken past, and its own capture and transmission is dependent on other forms. These combinations of forms of capture of the past may be seen as the essential process of immersion or education in a tradition (though each may individually stand as educative); in their more aggressive forms they may constitute proselytizing or universalizing, and there is a major question of the extent to which a vital tradition can simply educate, without proselytizing or engaging in still more vigorous forms of expansion. Education need not be formal and its formalization is closely linked to the type of tradition and the means of capture of the past which it employs. Change in education is thus crucial to maintenance or disappearance of tradition, and the passion generated in educational debate bears witness to its importance. Formal education was a fundamental feature of colonialism.

The presence of the past is thus a variable combination of the means of its capture, in the past, and the means of its articulation or perception in the present.

---

[30] See J. Ribner, *Broken Tablets: the Cult of Law in French Art from David to Delacroix* (Berkeley: Univ. of California Press, 1993), with review esssay by N. Kasirer, 'Larger than Life' (1995) 10 Can. J. Law and Soc. 185; M. L. Cohen, *Law: the Art of Justice* (New York: Hugh Lauter Levin, 1992) (images of legal themes or institutions from different traditions); and on the reciprocal influences of law and art ('le beau droit'), B. Oppetit, *Droit et modernité* (Paris: Presses universitaires de France, 1998) at 195, 196. On preserved symbols of law, in stone, see Ch. 3, *Of sources and structures.*

[31] On memorable phrasing, in rhythmic or poetic patterns, as a mnemonic device, see Ong, *Orality and Literacy* (1982) at 35, 54, 65, 66, and on law expressed in poetic form, see Ch. 8, *Poetic justice* (hindu law) and Ch. 9, *Adat law and chthonic law.*

In law these questions may be the object of institutional regulation (stating formal sources) and the effect given to them may also be regulated (rules as to what is authoritative in the past, including its formal sources). There may, however, be no such formal regulation and the tradition in law may simply be left to continue itself. Whatever method of capture, present perception and regulation is used, there remains the question of how the past may ultimately regulate present conduct, particularly legal actors. Does one follow that which is transmitted, at the critical moment of contemporary decision? How normative is the tradition? This too appears to be a matter of tradition, notably the extent to which rationalist tradition intervenes as an obstacle to continuation of contextual tradition. The foundations of a rationalist tradition, however, may be compatible with certain forms of normativity of tradition.

## TRADITIO

Tradition thus involves the extension of the past to the present. It appears to require thinking about time at least in terms of the past and the present, though there are other ways of thinking about time.[32] There is another dimension of tradition, however, which appears less bound to a particular manner of thinking about time. It is found in the necessity of tradition having been continuously transmitted, in a particular social context,[33] in order for it to be of current relevance. Traditio must have occurred, and between the relevant parties. The transmission of roman law through the process of reception in Europe may be of (some) interest to people who define themselves as Chinese or Mohawk or muslim, and may even influence them in some way, but none would say it constituted part of their tradition, or contemporary culture. It is someone else's tradition, because of the total absence of transmission within their particular social context. Absent historical continuity, reaching down to present adherents, all traditions appear as strange ones and all adherents to them appear as different people. The same result could occur as a result of a radical discontinuity of tradition, as where people in a given place entirely forgot, or abandoned, the elements of their tradition, and adopted another. In such a case, we would probably say not only that the previous tradition was no longer pertinent, but also that the people involved were no longer the same people, or at least that their identity as a group of people had changed. There may also be gaps in available proof of continuity, as where records are deficient in indicating adherence and historical research is necessary to show the continuing pertinence of a particular tradition, thought to have been abandoned. Tradition and its continuity are thus closely linked to the question of identity and to the relations of different people. Tradition must be assessed as a constitutive element of societies or as an

---

[32] See the discussion below, this Chapter, The Changing Presence of the Past, and the discussion relating to individual traditions and their attitude to change.

[33] On the origins of such a social context, see below Ch. 2, Tradition and Identity.

internal element of them. It must therefore be assessed as against other potentially defining criteria such as race or ethnicity. This is a large and vital dimension of tradition, which requires further attention.[34] For present purposes, we need only be aware of the necessity for continuity of tradition in a particular or identifiable social context.

## TRADITION AS INFORMATION: THE CONCEPTUAL BRAN-TUB

That which is brought from the past to the present, in a particular social context, is information. A tradition is thus composed of information, and it would be inappropriate to see it, as mooted by J. G. A. Pocock, as 'an indefinite series of repetitions of an action'.[35] This would be to confuse the results or impact of the tradition, its immediate manifestation, with the tradition itself. If there is a 'traditional way of doing things', the tradition is in the way, and not in the doing itself. Acts or decisions, once they take place, disappear forever if they are not translated into communicable information. In the future one may, or may not, act upon the information, but without it there can be no concept of tradition, only a grim reality of human entropy.

Tradition perceived as information yields further, important questions as to the nature of the information constitutive of tradition. Is tradition composed only of instructions or rules, such that later action may be guided explicitly by them? Are facts necessarily excluded, since the facts of one era tell us nothing about how to act in the next? It may not be possible, in theory, to decide on the type of information constitutive of tradition. It may depend on the tradition. What are perceived as facts in one tradition may be seen as profoundly symbolic and normative in another. The actors in a given tradition will preserve that which may be of future utility, and there may be widely differing views as to what, in a different or later

---

[34]  See below Ch. 2, *Tradition, races and states.*

[35]  Pocock, *Time, Institutions and Action* (1968) at 212; cf., however, the subsequent discussion of traditions as 'complex mental structures' (at 218) and of literacy modifying 'what is taken to be the tradition's content' (at 224). See also Armstrong, 'Nature of Tradition' (1981) at 90 (tradition as 'series of *acts*'); cf., however, at 100 (tradition 'handed on'; 'always involves normative element'); J. Merryman, *The Civil Law Tradition*, 2nd edn. (Stanford: Stanford Univ. Press, 1985) at 2 (tradition a set of 'attitudes', though deeply rooted, historically conditioned). On the western transformation of informal tradition into factual and present 'custom', see below Ch. 3, *Law and the cosmos.* The conclusion that tradition consists of information also dispels the view, derived from the word itself, that tradition consists of the *process* of handing down or traditio. See, e.g., Thapar,'Tradition' (1994) at 8 ('Tradition is defined as the handing down of knowledge or the passing on of a doctrine or technique'). On traditio as a necessary element for the current normativity of tradition, though not as tradition itself, see above, this chapter, *Traditio;* and for the view defended here see A. W. B. Simpson, *Invitation to Law* (Oxford: Blackwell, 1988) at 23 ('law is essentially a tradition, that is to say something which has come down to us from the past').

context, may, or should, prove to be useful. This may be the case from tradition to tradition, and it may also be the case within particular traditions.

The choice of the information to be captured by a tradition is thus fundamental to the tradition itself. Given what has been seen as to the means of capture of the past, however, and of its transmission to the present, it is difficult to see how any tradition can exercise effective control over the process of choice and capture of information. There may of course be attempts. Physical things translative of information may be rigidly controlled. The means of printing or copying may be monopolized. Speech may be qualified as heretical and the sanction of death invoked, as in jurisdictions of western law until the last century.[36] Exercising an effective monopoly over things and means of print is, however, difficult if not impossible; the samizdat has a long history. Effective control of speech and memory is more obviously impossible, and they may always be prayed in aid where more physical means of capture have been made inaccessible. A tradition may invoke more voluntary forms of control, as in the literary tradition of the Byzantine florilegium, consisting entirely of compilation of passages from various sources (the phenomenon is not unknown in law), representing a deliberate refusal to be 'original' and leaving originality to be sought only in the repetition of the formulae and not apart from the repetition.[37] Voluntary adherence to the tradition's means of capture is not necessarily more effective, however, than enforced adherence. In the result, no tradition can exercise full control, in its particular social context, of the capture of present information. Selection and capture is random to some extent, and an analogy has recently been drawn between human transmission of units of information ('memes') and the process of random selection effected by genes in the world of biology.[38] The randomness of the process is now exacerbated by contemporary forms of electronic control of information.

[36] For hanging on grounds of heresy in Scotland at the end of the 17th century and ongoing heresy trials in the 18th, see MacIntyre *Whose Justice? Which Rationality?* (1988) at 243–6 and for the abolition of the inquisition in Mexico in the 19th century, see G. F. Margadant S., *Introducción a la historia del derecho mexicano*, 11th edn. (Naucalpan, Mexico: Editorial Esfinge, 1994) at 126–8.

[37] Pelikan, *Vindication of Tradition* (1984) at 73–4. The repetition was thought of as a means of teasing out the basic assumptions of the tradition—understanding through repetition and consequent reflection.

[38] R. Dawkins, *The Selfish Gene* (Oxford: Oxford Univ. Press, 1976) at 206–9 (citing example of 'Jewish religious laws' propagating themselves for thousands of years); and for the process of transmission of memes, through written and oral means and as affected by, e.g., the law of libel or the 'filters' each of us creates to block out unwanted information, D. C. Dennet, *Darwin's Dangerous Idea: Evolution and the Meanings of Life* (New York: Simon and Schuster, 1995), ch. 12 ('Could There Be a Science of Memetics?'). See also N. Rotenstreich, *Tradition and Reality: the Impact of History on Modern Jewish Thought* (New York: Random House, 1972) at 17 ('The practical problem in tradition is thus that of the relationship between accumulation and selection: how to justify selection within the scope of an accumulated totality'); and see Thapar, 'Tradition' (1994) at 23 ('Traditions are not self-created; they are consciously chosen, and the choice from the past is enormous. We tend, therefore, to choose that which suits our present needs'). The capture is, of course, not only of present contributions to the tradition, but also of past ones where the present sources of information relating to them are failing. Few libraries can today afford to restore their rare books and photocopying may cause further destruction. Which books should be dictated and reproduced, or typed or copied by hand? It is rarely done.

The pool of information captured by the adherents of a particular tradition thus cannot be somehow controlled by the tradition itself. Different levels of understanding, different means of interpretation of existing sources, different opinions, will all contribute to a variety of statements of current elements of the tradition, in one or other of the means of capture. The variety of information captured will increase as the tradition increases in size, and very large, ancient traditions will constitute vast repositories of information. A given tradition emerges as a loose conglomeration of data, organized around a basic theme or themes, and variously described as a 'bundle', a 'tool-box', a 'language', a 'playground', a 'seedbed', a 'rag-bag' or a 'bran-tub.' In the language of modern information theory, a tradition will always include a great deal of noise, not essential for understanding the primary message of the tradition.

From a perspective internal to traditions themselves, there is therefore reason to conclude as to the undefinable or incomplete nature of all traditions. It is of course possible that their future development in all cases will be linear and unchanging, such that the tradition which is now seen to exist will exist unchanged in a decade, a century or a millennium. In some of the criticism of traditions, they have been painted as fundamentally immutable. Yet the structure of a tradition at a given time provides no guarantee that this will be the case. Contemporary chaos theory teaches the fundamental importance of minor variation at the inception of chaotic behaviour. A small initial variation of wind direction, multiplied many times over in effect by other causal factors in weather development, may mean the difference between a local storm or a hurricane. What will happen to a minor doctrinal variation, seen as ingenious, interesting and benign at the time of its formulation, once its full implications are realized over several generations? The fate of present information, and its effect on the future course of a tradition, will depend on the working and processes of the tradition itself.

## MASSAGING TRADITION

There is a story that in the early days of the second world war the British were forced to use light artillery dating from at least the first world war, if not the Boer war, for coastal defence. The guns did not fire rapidly and a time-motion expert was deployed to suggest ways of improving procedures. He watched the gun crews for some time, took slow-motion pictures, but remained puzzled by the performance of two members of each gun crew who, immediately before firing, came rigidly to attention and remained in this pose for three full seconds, extending through discharge of the guns. He eventually showed the pictures to an old artillery colonel and asked whether he could think of any reason for such strange behaviour.

The colonel asked to see the pictures run again. At the end he said, 'I have it. They are holding the horses.'[39]

Everyone can think of similar stories, of conduct which continues because of, well, habit, even though no justification for it can currently be offered. These stories give tradition a bad name, and may well be used for that reason, though they are always a good laugh. Of course, the conduct did change in the artillery story, so we know both that tradition is supported by human inertia and that inertia is insufficient to support tradition over time. Routinization, or inertia, is thus an important device in implementation of tradition which is accepted (artillery officers do not challenge orders) and which must govern detailed and repetitive human conduct. When we see routine being executed in this manner, we do not see, however, the full process of present implementation of tradition. Rather, we see only the results of its having been accepted. We see people acting on the basis of the information constituted by tradition, and here in conformity with the tradition. The full process of implementation, or rejection, of tradition, is more complex.

Why does tradition have to be dealt with and why must a process for dealing with it have to be developed? We could simply forget about it, or say that it is simply history which should stay where it is, in the books. Some attempt to do this, but are never fully successful. The main reason we are constantly addressing tradition appears to be the constraint which it imposes on our lives.[40] Tradition, through its pastness, provides presently available lessons as to how we should act. Tradition tells us how to make good pottery, paint beautiful paintings and write good pleadings. The judgment of many, down through time, confers authority, even legitimacy—at least presumptively—on the lessons of tradition. Even if we do not perceive the lessons provided by tradition, there will be others who do perceive them and who will urge them upon us. So tradition is unavoidable in living our daily lives. Everything is in the process of dealing with it.

Various reactions are possible faced with a multitude of teachings from the past. Compliance is one reaction, and if enough people comply their conception of the tradition will define what that tradition presently is, or at least its primary base of information. Even here there is a process at work, however, since from the bran-tub of information which the tradition contains, the primary or truest teaching of the tradition must first be extracted. In the language of contemporary computer practice, information must often be massaged before it can be put to immediate use. There is a process of refinement and selection which must occur before data can become useful. Noise must be filtered out. In the same way there appears to be a

---

[39] E. Morison, *Men, Machines and Modern Times* (Cambridge, Mass.: MIT Press, 1966) at 17–18, as cited in A. M. Kantrow, *The Constraints of Corporate Tradition: Doing the Correct Thing, Not Just What the Past Dictates* (New York: Harper and Row, 1987) at 86.

[40] 'My natural inclinations impel me to proceed one way; the sastras command me to follow another; why should I follow the latter course in preference to the former?' P. N. Sen, *General Principles of Hindu Jurisprudence* (Allahabad: Allahabad Law Agency, 1984) at 25; and see Postema, 'Moral Presence' (1991).

present process of selection of what a tradition says, even by its most loyal adherents, such that its instructions may be followed.

What is the significance of this process of massaging a tradition, even in the circumstances where there is no recognizable opposition or resistance to the tradition? Assume the tradition is a communal or contextual one, which teaches the primacy of relations between people, as informed by some broader concept of good. Individualism and the primacy of human reason are not part of the tradition. What is the process by which adherents to such a tradition define its present content? Is it a mechanical process or one which is somehow necessarily communal? Is individual human reason not implicated in some way in the process? In remembering a tradition the human mind is at work, with its frailties and its powers. Memory may not be simply 'rote'; it may involve higher, second-order thinking.[41] Copying of prior information may appear simply repetitive, as with the Byzantine florilegium, but subsequent observers search for originality in the process of repetition, not in the content of what is repeated.[42] Rationality is thus present, a constant mole, in the most contextual of traditions. It is the only way in which a tradition may be maintained.

There can also be resistance to the teaching of tradition, however, for a number of reasons. There can be resistance because it appears incoherent, or vague, or contradictory, constituting simply 'a load of ancient lumber'.[43] Or the tradition, and its proponents, may appear corrupt, which raises a very large and difficult question.[44] Or the tradition may be opposed because it justifies and perpetuates inequality and injustice in the treatment of persons (one of the main grounds for opposition to tradition at the time of the enlightenment in Europe, itself linked to notions of corruption). Finally, though no attempt is being made to be exhaustive, the teaching of the tradition may be resisted because it may not appear to be convincing, when examined critically. This last ground of resistance is fundamental, and may be one which subsumes all others. Old teaching simply does not correspond to new circumstances, when present rationality is applied.

What information is relied upon when there is real opposition to the tradition, either on some point of detail or more generally? Take first the smallest form of opposition, one which continues to accept the tradition in its broad outline, but which resists a particular detail or consequence of it. Here the debate is necessarily internal to the tradition. It is the tradition itself, through the bran-tub, which supplies both the justification for opposition and justification for its defeat or accommodation. The opposition, and the majority, will both seek to justify their

---

[41] See above, this Chapter, *Presence*; and see H.-G. Gadamer, *Truth and Method* (New York: Crossroad, 1988) at 250 ('preservation is an act of reason, though an inconspicuous one').

[42] Above, this Chapter, in Tradition as Information: the Conceptual Bran-Tub.

[43] J. T. Harskamp, 'Past and Present in Modernist Thinking' (1984) 24 *British Journal of Aesthetics* 27 at 28, citing M. A. Shee's *Elements of Art* (1804).

[44] See the discussion below, this Chapter, Tradition and Corruption.

position from the information base which they commonly recognize. Here again, however, in the dynamic of opposition and support, it is difficult to see a process which is entirely mechanical or contextual in character. There is strategy in opposition, and in the choice of means, and the individual mind is the source of all strategy of opposition. Traditions do not tell you when or how to resist them, though they may supply much of the authority used in opposition.

Opposition to a tradition may also be more general, though still conducted within the tradition itself, using both its language and its resources (the struggle from within). Here the entire information base of the tradition is likely to be called into play, by both opponents and supporters of the tradition. Old ideas, long dormant, may be resuscitated and given new life. Here the originality and talent of both sides will likely be more evident. The mole of rationality is in danger of losing its cover. However original the play, it remains confined to the context and resources of the tradition.

Some contextual traditions have met opposition of a still broader order. Since the entire tradition is simply old lumber, unjustifiable in present circumstances, it should be entirely and explicitly jettisoned. In the west the argument has extended to the jettisoning even of the notion of tradition itself. Here present rationality is sure enough of its ground to abandon the cover of contextual tradition. The information base of tradition may appear of less importance in this situation, but the reforming rationalist may still have difficulty in avoiding it. Opposition to a particular tradition will inevitably be opposition to what the tradition has claimed, and therefore be defined by the tradition even while opposing it. Proponents of the tradition will argue in its terms; the opponents must reject those terms and give reasons for doing so. Opposition to all tradition, and to the notion of tradition itself, does not necessarily escape this difficulty—there is simply a greater number of traditional positions to be refuted. The information base of tradition thus remains pertinent even to its most radical opponents.

Since radical opposition to tradition is here based on the primacy of human reason, human reason has found more subtle devices than head-to-head opposition, tradition by tradition. It is in the form of the general denial of the authority of the past, while divising 'a mode of authority independent of social continuity'.[45] The past may exist, but it is all fact and fact is all it is. It may be best described in its totality as artefact. You need never address the lessons of the past because there are none, only past lives confined to their own particularity. Only the present and future can be the place of current decisions; only present and future considerations should be operative in the critical, even charismatic, moment of decision. This ultimate strategy of the rationalist, however, encounters further difficulties. One in

[45] Pocock 'Time, Institutions and Action' (1968) at 229; and see S. Steward, 'The Pickpocket: A Study in Tradition and Allusion' (1980) 95 *Mod. Lang. Notes* 1127 at 1129 ('By the historicist's creation of a gap between the present and the past, the integrity of both the past and the present is maintained; tradition is bounded by its pastness and left uncontaminated by the present').

particular is very frustrating. In spite of the insistence of the rationalist on the importance of present constructions, there is a danger that the best of such constructions will be ... remembered. Others will adhere to it as it acquires pastness. The rationalist position thus tends ultimately to self-destruction, the more vigorously and brilliantly it is defended. However rationalist thinking develops, this danger appears necessarily present. In the measure that rationalists do not agree amongst themselves, there will be ongoing debate amongst partisans of various rationalist options, perpetuating the memory of each of them. In the measure that rationalists might eventually agree amongst themselves, and there would be enormous persuasive authority derived from such a consensus, how could their construction fail to attract ongoing adherence, fail to deter encrustations over time, fail to become the tradition of all traditions, at least in the western world?

These problems may be seen as internal to rationalism, inherent in the process of present construction of the rationally justifiable. There is a further problem, however, in the relations between rationality and tradition. Contextual traditionalists have a tendency to place everything in context, and extend this position to rationality itself, even when perceived as primary. Rationality already exists within traditions, they might claim, even though it is often underground. How does one reach the conclusion that there can also be reason outside of tradition? What is the history of this development? What caused it? These are treacherous, though natural, questions. If there is a history of the development of independent rationality, then it itself can be explained in terms of tradition. So, as Karl Popper maintained, rationality is only one of many traditions, characterized by a more explicit recognition of human rationality and by the greater explicit place accorded to it.[46] The biggest conceptual problem with rationalism is that it has been around so long, and has been so successful. It is a conceptual victim of its own success.

If rationality is thus a more or less hidden element in all contextual traditions, then context is the unavoidable companion of all efforts towards free-standing rationality. Each contains its own contradiction, as day and night must co-exist and laughing may be just another form of crying.[47] Everything is in the process.

The necessity of massaging the information of tradition thus extends through the entire range of attitudes towards it. It occurs amongst the most faithful of

---

[46] Popper, 'Rational Theory of Tradition' (1969): see above, introductory text to chapter; and see more recently, for 'archeological excavation' into the tradition of western modernity, B. de Sousa Santos, *Toward a New Common Sense: Law, Science and Politics in the Paradigmatic Transition* (New York/London: Routledge, 1995), notably at p. xi ('European modernity includes many other traditions besides those that ended up consecrated in the modern canon . . . traditions that were gradually suppressed, marginalized or subverted so that the canon could be convincingly canonical').

[47] L. Esquivel, *Como agua para chocolate* (Mexico: Editorial Planeta Mexicana, 1990) at 14 ('a tal grado que durante su niñez Tita no differenciaba bien las lágrimas de la risa de las del llanto. Para ella reír era una manera de llorar'). For further articulation of this theme, particularly developed in Asian tradition, see below Ch. 9, *Limiting religion* and Ch. 10, *Bivalence and multivalence*.

adherents to it, as they seek to perpetuate it; it occurs amongst the most vigorous of opponents to it, as they seek to overcome it; and it occurs between both groups. In the theoretical discussion of tradition, this emerges in the conclusion that tradition never reaches definitive form, but is rather, in the present, a series of interactive statements of information.

## A NETWORK OF TRADITION

Each of us can argue internally, with ourselves, and most people leave plenty of room for internal argument, not taking definitive and life-time personal positions on major issues. It is all we can do to decide on our priorities for the next 24 hours. In our own personal deliberations there are therefore expressions of different points of view, and we may sometimes be of one view and sometimes of another, particularly over a lifetime. We thus massage the information of our particular tradition, or possibly traditions, in order to decide on personal conduct. We must each decide on the constraint which tradition eventually lays upon us. Some of us may readily accept the constraint which tradition represents, and may oppose the idea that individual appreciation is in any way compatible with their tradition; others may resist the restraint more readily, and may agonize over their own choices.[48] In all cases in which a human mind is present, however, there is a process of appreciation of the teaching of the tradition. The massaging of the information may here be an individual process, and may not be clearly evident even to the individual, but it is forever present.

The more obvious massaging of information is that which occurs amongst individual adherents of a tradition, or amongst defined groups of adherents to the tradition. In computer language today the expression LAN is current, indicating a Local Area Network of computer information. In the same way adherents to a tradition, or a group within a tradition, constitute a local area network of information. The network is local because it is not—or at least not yet—universal, and it is a network because the exchange of information is a constant and ongoing process, in which stored information (the pastness) is constantly being juxtaposed with present opinion, itself being retained in some measure for future use. In the computer world LANs are also linked with other LANs, expanding the exchange of information, and in the same way traditions are interconnected, never existing in isolation, as will be seen in the next chapter. For the moment we are concerned

---

[48] On the slow development over time of an explicitly reflective concept of the individual, in the tradition of the west since Augustine, see C. Taylor, *Sources of the Self: The Making of the Modern Mind* (Cambridge, Mass.: Harvard Univ. Press, 1989), notably ch. 7 ('In Interiore Homine') on 'striking difference'—'inward lies the road to God'—between Augustine and Plato, in spite of ongoing commonality.

with the process of exchange of information within a tradition or within and amongst definable groups within a tradition. What are the characteristics of this process?

Those who have discussed a theory of tradition have defined the process in various ways. It may be a 'dialogue', a 'dialectic', a 'conversation', an 'interchange of voices', an 'argument' or a continuing 'controversy'. Other expressions are certainly possible, including that of 'exchange'. The differences in expression may be of consequence. A 'conversation' is different from an 'argument' and both may be different from a 'dialogue'. The forms which human communication may take may be smooth or stormy, explicit or implicit, free or forced. It appears, once again, that much may depend on the tradition. The amount of argument which a tradition generates may depend on the extent to which it purports to constrain human conduct; the amount of conversation it generates may depend on its ambiguity in delineating optional forms of behaviour. Verbal resistance may be valorized in some traditions, actively discouraged in others. In all cases, however, the exchange of information, from person to person, is essential, even if it consists in the giving of orders. There are forms of communication which do not include dialogue, and there are one-sided conversations, but exchange of information is constantly present in all forms of human cohabitation, and rationality is present in some measure in all forms of exchange.

In any theoretical statement of the nature of tradition it therefore seems impossible to state that some forms of information have necessary priority over others, in all traditions, or that some actors in the exchange necessarily have more influence than others. There is no necessary hierarchy in tradition, either in terms of information or in terms of adherents. The informational exchange of tradition is in principle horizontal; deviations towards the vertical will be the product of particular traditions and the reasons which have prevailed in that tradition. The information in a tradition, however, is preserved because of its utility in the tradition; the content of information is important and information is not seen simply as the potential object of digitalization, a purely quantifiable commodity. Human reason being present in all traditions in various amplitudes, the totality of information in the tradition is thus constantly undergoing a process of review, appreciation and ongoing communication. At any moment, given the potentially constraining character of tradition and the process of appreciation of it, some elements of information may generate greater resonance than others amongst the adherents to the tradition. There will always be, however, contrasting or modifying elements of information, as well as adherents to the tradition prepared to defend such information in the process of ongoing exchange. In its most radical form, this may take the form of heresy, treason or sedition and be by way of challenge to the most fundamental tenets of the tradition itself. In such cases, there is a question of whether the challenge is from within or from without the tradition, but the challenge it represents is the same in either case. The undefined or incomplete nature of all traditions[49] thus rests ultimately on the difficulty of concluding as to the existence of absolute or irrefutable knowledge within a tradition, given the ongoing process of exchange. Information exists only alongside other information, available in one form or another; it is always in this sense contingent and comparable. This would not prevent a tradition from concluding, however, that absolute knowledge could exist and should be pursued, or that existing information must be defended, even at great cost.

How to describe the results of this process is a difficult question. Should one speak of a 'dominant' or 'controlling' form of the tradition? This appears inappropriate, since notions of dominance or control do not seem compatible with the exchange of information inherent in an initial concept of tradition. There may be risks in some forms of exchange, but the possibility of exchange is always present. A more qualified form of expression appears appropriate, such as the 'leading' or 'foremost' or 'primary' form of the tradition. This more explicitly acknowledges that priority of place can never be guaranteed as permanent and is subject to constant appreciation and re-evaluation, whether explicity acknowledged or not. The most profound beliefs may wither and die, over time and absent traditio. The conclusion appears important for later discussion of the possibly universalizing or proselytizing character of tradition.[50] If tradition does not exist in apodictic or invariant form, there is less impetus to universalization. Fundamentalism, and violence in pursuit of it, is thus not inherent in tradition, but represents a departure from its most important characteristic. All of this has important consequences for the relation of tradition to the concept of change.

## THE CHANGING PRESENCE OF THE PAST

For centuries in western thought, tradition has been associated with static forms of social order. A traditional society was one which did not change and which was largely impervious to valid reasons for change. Social change was seen, in large part, as both desirable and exceptional, and there may have been good reasons for this view. The default position of human society was thus one of stability. This manner of thought paralleled that which drew a sharp distinction between tradition and rationality, and appears also to have had its origins in the seventeenth century.[51] Rationality and change were thus linked on one side of a dichotomy; on the other side stood tradition and stability, if not downright immobility. In the same way that tradition has been recently re-assessed, however, so has the concept of change been

---

[49] See above, this Chapter, Tradition as Information: the Conceptual Bran-Tub.
[50] See below, Ch. 2, Universalizing: Ruling the World through Truth; and Ch. 10, Reconciling Traditions.
[51] Ch. 5, Constructing a Tradition.

subject to closer examination. Moreover, the revision and broadening of ideas concerning tradition have necessary consequences for the concept of change.

Once tradition is seen as transmitted information, an ongoing bran-tub churned by new generations, with no inherent élites or hierarchy, the linking of tradition with stability becomes less obvious and less defensible. Tradition becomes rather a resource from which reasons for change may be derived, a legitimating agency for ideas which, by themselves, would have no social resonance. The past is mobilized to invent a future.[52] The return to the sources, the process of rolling back or re-volving,[53] may provide grounds both for radical disruption of existing structures and hierarchies and a sense of perpetration of the true, original character of the tradition. Tradition, in all its forms, thus becomes seen as 'procreative of change',[54] 'creative, dynamic and, in a sense, also invented',[55] 'ever afresh and ever fresh',[56] 'a modality of change',[57] 'the means to formulate and legitimize change',[58] 'un facteur de changement',[59] a means by which a civilization 'gradually transforms itself',[60] 'the very stuff that is subject to change'.[61] Different techniques of tradition-driven change may be perceived, such as renewing (bringing forward of ancient practices), maintaining (developing an existing practice in expanded form) and reforming (rethinking of existing traditional formulae).[62] With tradition no longer providing a conceptual strait-jacket for the social world, that social world may be seen in the same terms as the physical world, subject to massive forces of entropy. Thus 'change is the general condition of nature, of societies, and even of individuals, and it requires a special effort to preserve continuity and, if you wish, tradition in the midst of change.'[63] Tradition is thus inherently fragile; only primary or leading

---

[52] A. Touraine, *Pourrons-nous vivre ensemble? Égaux et différents* (Paris: Fayard, 1997) at 49 ('mobiliser le passé pour inventer un avenir'); see also C. Atias, 'Tradition juridique' (1997) at 389 ('La tradition juridique n'est pas conservatrice par principe'); and more generally S. Delany (ed.), *Counter-Tradition: a Reader in the Literature of Dissent and Alternatives* (New York/London: Basic Books, 1971), notably at 3 ('a tradition of opposition to the values of official culture').

[53] On the development of the contemporary, and now devalued, notion of revolution from this position see below Ch. 5, *Revolutions, systems, language and interpretation*.

[54] Friedrich, *Tradition and Authority* (1972) at 39, given 'inherent contradictions' of tradition.

[55] de Sousa Santos, *Toward a New Common Sense* (1995), above, at 373.

[56] Gadamer, *Truth and Method*, above, at 191.

[57] Waldman, 'Tradition as Modality of Change' (1985–6) at 326.

[58] J. C. Heesterman, *The Inner Conflict of Tradition: Essays in Indian Ritual, Kingship and Society* (Chicago/London: Univ. of Chicago Press, 1985) at 1, also at 2 (tradition characterized by 'inner conflict of atemporal order and temporal shift rather than by resiliance and adaptiveness').

[59] Izdebski, 'Tradition et changement en droit' (1987) at 839.

[60] F. Braudel, *A History of Civilizations*, trans. R. Mayne (New York: Penguin, 1993 (orig. French edn. 1963) at 30.

[61] Brown, 'Tradition and Insight' (1996) at 2 (giving islamic examples of revolution in Iran, Sunni revival-ism, islamic feminism).

[62] Waldman, 'Tradition as Modality of Change' (1985–6) at 332, 335; and for the unpredictability of those who move within a tradition, resulting from the transformation of the tradition by its passage from one generation to another, see Munoz, 'Rationality of Tradition' (1981) at 202.

[63] Kristeller, '"Creativity" and "Tradition"' (1983) at 112.

variations may be ascertained, with others waiting in their shadow; it is a question of 'how the argument has gone so far'.[64]

At the same time, tradition does retain a cohesive effect ('They are holding the horses'), where a particular version of it can be maintained, by present effort. Tradition is thus both disruptive *and* cohesive and rarely exclusively one or the other. Parts of society may thus change, while others are preserved. Identity may be preserved, in an ongoing way, while reforms are effected. In this more nuanced and diversified concept of tradition, recent thinking appears to reflect still older thought, in which innovation and continuity were 'inextricably fused'[65] and which maintained that both 'permanent and transitory elements'[66] were necessary for social coherence. Our perception of change in the distant past may, however, be 'foreshortened . . . as in a remote landscape'.[67]

The presence of the past may thus be seen today as changing, and its effect on present society more important, though less predictable. If tradition is thus more important, in the west, it leads to contemplation of other traditions. If the past is of such diversity, moreover, it may be still more diverse when placed in the context of different traditions, which do not all share a constant vision of time, or of the past. Discussion of the past takes place in the context of a larger (potential) discussion of time. Our conception of time may influence both our conception of the past and our conception of social change. The discussion thus far in this chapter has accepted the notion of a past, which is contrasted both with the present and a discernible future. Change occurs within these zones of time, more precisely at the frontier between the past and the present. We *now* change something, which is presently different from what it was. We can contemplate such change in the future, to be realized when it has become the present. This concept of zones of time facilitates our concept of change; the zones of time are the playing fields in which the game of change is played. Absent the fields, the game becomes more difficult.

If time is not conceived in this ongoing, linear manner our concept of change may have to be rethought as well. There are also implications for how we think about tradition itself. If time simply is, and is the same now as others who are born before us and others who are born after us experience it (it is not easy to avoid future and past tenses), then how can we think of anything really changing? We all—those now dead, those now living, those not born—live in the same time; there can be no better life in the future since there is no future; we are all living essentially

---

[64] MacIntyre, *Whose Justice? Which Rationality?* (1988) at 8.

[65] B. Jennings, 'Tradition and the Politics of Remembering' (1982) 36 *Georgia Rev.* 167 at 182.

[66] K. F. Morrison, *Tradition and Authority in the Western Church 300–1140* (Princeton: Princeton Univ. Press, 1969) at 6.

[67] S. Thrupp, *Change in Medieval Society: Europe North of the Alps 1050–1500* (Toronto/Buffalo: Univ. of Toronto Press, 1988) at p. vi (also on the necessity of historical research to determine the extent of past change).

the same lives in a locus which is invariable and shared by all generations.[68] How can we then change something from the way it *was* to the way it is *now*? There may be differences in life—people are different from one another as are other forms of life and nature—but they are all differences within a given, common cadre.

Thinking about time in this manner thus appears to have major consequences for our notion of change. Why do we think one way or another about time? It appears to be derived from what we are taught to think about time, that is, to be part of a tradition. So the western world has constructed, as part of its tradition, a concept of time within which human rationality can be seen as effecting change, making a difference. In the last three to four centuries it was seen that these changes could be effected without any influence of contextual traditions, though this view is now being reconsidered as our concept of tradition has broadened. And as our view of tradition broadens we see that this view of the primacy of the present is itself part of a tradition which has created the notion of a present, as well as that of a past and of a future. We then may have to recognize that other traditions, with other views of time, will probably have other views of change and of its possibility. Adaptability of a 'system' to 'changed' circumstances is thus a criterion of a particular way of thought, as may also be the idea of change of the tradition itself. It may be more appropriate to ask, not, is the tradition responsive to change? but, is the tradition one which recognizes a concept of change?

Our broader recognition of the influence of the past, our recognition that it has had great influence on our present manner of thought, thus allows us to see that even thinking about the past has a past. In non-temporal terms, thinking about the past has had a particular western context. This in turn allows us to see that tradition itself, seen in the west as voices coming from the past, may be seen elsewhere as present voices, though the owners of the voices may be absent. Our expanded notion of tradition leads us to contemplate other communities, and the idea that

---

[68] On theories and ideas of time see D. S. Landes, *Revolution in Time: Clocks and the Making of the Modern World* (Cambridge, Mass.: Harvard Univ. Press, 1983); S. Toulmin and J. Goodfield, *The Discovery of Time* (New York: Harper and Row, 1965); B. Oppetit, 'Les tendances régressives dans l'évolution du droit contemporain' in *Mélanges Holleaux* (Paris: Litec, 1990) 318; F. Ost, 'Les multiples temps du droit' in *Le droit et le futur: Travaux et recherches de l'Université de Paris II, Serie Philosophie du droit—2* (Paris: Presses universitaires de France, 1985) 115. Yet non-linear notions of time are not unknown in western thought. They even represent current scientific orthodoxy which, however, has had little impact on traditional western thinking about time. See, e.g., S. Hawking, *A Brief History of Time: from the big bang to black holes* (Toronto/New York: Bantam, 1988) at 143–53 (laws of science not distinguishing between forward and backward directions of time; time existing simply within space; arrows of time being however perceived and following direction of entropy of universe currently prevailing; reversal of direction of entropy could yield remembering of future rather than past, if humans could then exist); R. Penrose, *The Emperor's New Mind: Concerning Computers, Minds, and The Laws of Physics* (Oxford: Oxford Univ. Press, 1989) at 304 ('Moreover, there is no flow of time at all. We have just 'space-time'—and no scope at all for a future'); H. Price, *Time's Arrow and Archimedes' Point: New Directions for the Physics of Time* (New York/Oxford: Oxford Univ. Press, 1996), notably at 12 (defending 'block universe' view that reality is a 'single entity of which time is an ingredient, rather than . . . a changeable entity set *in* time'). The non-linear view does occasionally surface in popular western culture, however. Thus Sarah, in *The Hustler*: 'A day like any other; people come and people go.'

communities may extend over (our conception of) time. Where communities thus extend through multiple generations (dead, living and yet to be born), change as a concept is improbable.

## TRADITION AND CORRUPTION

Tradition provides advice or models which may be used in living our lives. Most of the tradition which has been captured and retained is aimed at the good or well-being of entire communities, and the largest and greatest of traditions have been directed at very large communities, if not humanity in its entirety. All of these great traditions generate opposition within themselves, aimed at improvement or trans-formation of the tradition. There may also be competing traditions which provide alternative advice or models for the same community. There are other traditions, however, which do not seek to play a major role for an entire community, and do not seek its good or well-being. They are parasitic traditions, living off a larger one and profiting from its adherents in a way antithetical to their welfare and well-being. These are traditions of crime—either generally or in more particular form, such as those of the mafia or of the narcos, and there may be others of more recent generation. Gangs will seek to generate their own traditions, though they may not survive the length of time required for the necessary pastness to be accumulated. There are indications today of a generalized increase of crime and violence in the world, and of increasing organization in their execution; this may constitute an increase in parasitic traditions of crime. Their increase may indicate a decline in influence of larger traditions, or of some of them.

Legal traditions have as one of their main functions the identification and elim-ination of crime and criminal traditions. They do so with some measure of suc-cess,[69] though the task will never be completed. The identification of crime may be seen as a relatively simple or limited process, in spite of its difficulty, because of the antagonism between criminal traditions and larger traditions of good or right. There is a type of crime, however, which has much more profound implications for traditions generally. It is the crime of corruption, which may destroy larger tradi-tions from within. There are also other forms of corruption, institutional or intel-lectual corruption, which are not criminal but which may be equally destructive of tradition.

Corruption is generally thought of as pecuniary corruption and pecuniary cor-ruption (the hook, the bite, la mordida) is usually criminal in character. It may

---

[69] The use of force, in defence of traditions and in response to direct assault, appears common to all traditions and is in no way incompatible with tradition. Its use is more problematical, however, as a means of suppression of dissent.

become so widespread, however, that it is impossible to control by institutions, themselves profoundly affected by it.[70] In some countries positions in law-enforcement agencies are sold, and the purchasers have very good reasons for paying a high price for the purchase. Complex forms of social organization may thus provide increased opportunities for pecuniary corruption, particularly where they are grafted on to other, existing networks of loyalty. Pecuniary corruption is a form of unjustified redistribution of the material resources of a society, a secretive form of inequality. It invariably does great damage to the credibility and effectiveness of traditions of good or right, and it is therefore important to know whether certain traditions are more vulnerable to it or have found effective means to combat it. In the struggle against pecuniary corruption, the hard, internal core of each tradition may be ascertained. If there is none, this will be clearly evident to all who live in the tradition, and to those beyond.

Not all forms of unjustified material advantage constitute crimes, however, and it may be useful to speak more generally of institutional corruption. Institutions play an intermediate role between individuals and accumulated tradition. Their role will be defined by tradition, as will be the role of their members. Legal professions constitute such institutions, as do varying forms of government or institutionalized religion. Institutional corruption occurs when members of institutions take advantage of their institutional role for personal aggrandizement, in ways not prohibited by law but incompatible with their mission. This is the world of privilege and perquisites, of careerism, and of self-perpetuating élites. Here the 'logic of mission'

---

[70] See generally, on the particularities and universality of corruption, T. Gong, 'Corruption and reform in China: An analysis of unintended consequences' (1993) 19 Crime, Law and Social Change 311; A. Etchegoyen, *Le corrupteur et le corrompu* (Paris: Juilliard, 1995); K. J. Meier, ' "I seen my opportunities and I took 'em": Political Corruption in the American States' (1992) 54 *J. Politics* 135; J. Noonan, *Bribes* (Berkeley: Univ. of California Press, 1984); B. Oppetit, 'Le paradoxe de la corruption à l'épreuve du droit du commerce international', J. dr. int. 1987. 5; H. E. Pepinsky, 'Corruption, Bribery and Patriarchy in Tanzania' (1992) 17 Crime, Law and Social Change 25; S. Coldham, 'Legal Responses to State Corruption in Commonwealth Africa' (1995) 39 J. African Law 115; R. Pérez Perdomo and R. Capriles Méndoz, *Corrupción y control: una perspectiva comparada* (Caracas: Ediciones Iesa, 1991); S. Rose-Ackerman, *Corruption. A study in political economy* (New York: Academic Press, 1978); W. Schuler (ed.), *Korruption im Altertum* (München; R. Odenbourg, 1982); M. Borghi, P. Meyer-Bisch (eds.), *La corruption: l'envers des droits de l'homme* (Fribourg: Editions universitaires Fribourg Suisse, 1995); (1996) 149 *Int. Soc. Sci. J.* (theme issue on 'Corruption in Western Democracies'); J.-M. Ghéhenno, *La fin de la démocratie* (Paris: Flammarion, 1995) (ch. 8 'Le veau d'or'); J. Cartier Bresson, *Pratiques et contrôle de la corruption* (Paris: Montchrestien, 1997); C. Fombad, 'Curbing corruption in Africa: some lessons from Botswana's experience' (1999) 51 *Int. Soc. Sci. J.* 242 (outlining experience with anti-corruption agencies). The extent of criminal corruption has now given rise to a voluntary international organization, Transparency International, whose sole objective is to combat it; see http://www. transparency. de; J. Pope (ed.), *National Integrity Systems: The TI Source Book*, 2nd edn. (Washington DC: Transparency International, 1997); and subsequent TI Annual Reports including an annual 'corruption index', rating countries of the world in terms of levels of corruption (see, e. g., *The Economist*, October 3, 1998, at 120). Recognizing the extent of the problem, the states of the Organization for Economic Co-operation and Development (OECD) concluded in 1997 a *Convention on Combating Bribery of Foreign Public Officials in International Business Transactions*, now being implemented in national legislation; as to which see J. Brademas and F. Heimann, 'Tackling International Corruption' (1998) 77 *Foreign Affairs* (No. 5, Sept./Oct.) 17.

is replaced by the 'logic of maintenance'.[71] Tradition may provide means of opposing institutional corruption, though it may also have provided the means for its development. A tradition which teaches nothing but devotion and love, and which rejects institutions as incompatible with those objectives, will itself be a major factor in limiting or controlling institutional corruption. A tradition which encourages the construction of institutions and élites will need to develop second-order means of control. It will need to develop an ethic of institutional or élite life, and effective institutional means of supervision of primary institutions. Absent such protective ethical institutions, the primary tradition may be given effect only in formal terms. Its essential manifestation will be by way of corruption of itself.

The final form of corruption, intellectual corruption, is extremely difficult to define or identify. There appears to be little doubt as to its existence, however, and one identifying feature may be accompanying criminal or institutional corruption. Falsehood or indefensible dogma may be perpetuated, in the preservation of power and interest.[72] Intellectual corruption may also occur by itself, however, and is most generally qualified in terms such as 'dead faith', 'neglect', 'idolatry', 'clichés' or 'wooden language' ('la langue de bois'). We are here close to the dynamic of all traditions, and corruption would entail arbitrary efforts to destroy or eliminate the dynamic. Authority would replace justification, invocation of heresy or treason would replace exchange. Yet much may depend on the tradition, and on fine judgment. A tradition valorizing contingent or historical time, change, and rationality will often see invocation of the past as corrupt, a refusal to follow the primary dictate of present and explicit originality. Heresy will then have little place, though treason and sedition may remain. Traditions defined in terms of constants, whatever they may be, must defend the constants which are the essence of the tradition, or the tradition will no longer exist as such. Much variation and debate may be possible, but heresy (or treason) must exist and all will be in the sanction. Fundamentalism (as it is presently known) may be a form of intellectual corruption, if it invokes an apodictic interpretation of an entire tradition, relying on force or violence as the principal means of response to contrary views, even those from within the tradition itself. Here those accused of heresy may represent a truer version of the tradition than those who make the accusation.[73]

A tradition, in the form of received information, is thus a fragile thing. It bears within itself the seeds of diversity or, more radically, change. It also bears within itself the seeds of corruption, the various forms of human frailty which would convert it to an instrument of perverse and personal ends. All this is the world

---

[71] G. Baum, *Theology and Society* (New York: Paulist Press, 1987) at 234, 235, citing R. Merton, 'Bureaucratic Structure and Personality' in R. Merton (ed.), *Reader on Bureaucracy* (New York: Free Press, 1952) at 361 on ensuing 'goal displacement'.

[72] See, e.g., R. R. Rerether, *Sexism and God-Talk: Toward a Feminist Theology* (Boston: Beacon, 1983) at 15, 16.

[73] J. H. Cone, *A Black Theology of Liberation: The Sources and Norms of Black Theology* (Philadelphia: Lippincott, 1978) at 73.

within, the risks and perils in the internal life of a tradition. There is also the world beyond, the world of other traditions and of the relations between traditions. It too presents its perils.

# GENERAL BIBLIOGRAPHY

Armstrong , D., 'The Nature of Tradition' in D. Armstrong, *The Nature of Mind and Other Essays* (Ithaca: Cornell University Press, 1981) at 89.

Atias, C., 'Présence de la tradition juridique' (1997) 22 Revue de la recherche juridique 387.

Bleckmann, A., 'La tradition juridique en tant que limite aux réformes du droit' in *Rapports généraux au 10e Congrès international du droit comparé* (Budapest: Akadémiai Kiado, 1982).

Boyer, P., 'The Stuff "Traditions" are Made of: On the Implicit Ontology of an Ethnographic Category' (1987) 17 *Philosophy of the Social Sciences* 49.

Brown, D., *Rethinking tradition in modern Islamic thought* (Cambridge: Cambridge University Press, 1996).

Brown, R. L., 'Tradition and Insight' (1993) 103 Yale Law Journal 177.

Eisenstadt, S. N., *Tradition, Change and Modernity* (New York: John Wiley and Sons, 1973).

Eliot, T. S., 'Tradition and the Individual Talent', in *The Sacred Wood: Essays on Poetry and Criticism*, 6th edn. (London: Methuen and Co., 1948).

Fikentscher, W., Franke, H. and Köhler, O. (eds.), *Entstehung und Wandel rechtlicher Traditionen* (Freiburg/Munich: Verlag Karl Alber, 1980).

Friedrich, C. J., *Tradition and Authority* (London: Pall Mall Press, 1972).

Granger, R., 'La tradition en tant que limite aux réformes du droit' Revue internationale de droit comparé 1979. 37.

Hobsbawm, E. and Ranger,T. (eds.), *The Invention of Tradition*, (Cambridge: Cambridge University Press, 1983).

Izdebski, H., 'La tradition et le changement en droit: l'exemple des pays socialistes' Revue internationale de droit comparé 1987. 839.

Kristeller, P. O., ' "Creativity" and "Tradition" ' (1983) 44 *Journal of the History of Ideas* 105.

Kronman, A., 'Precedent and Tradition' (1990) 99 Yale Law Journal 1029.

Krygier, M., 'Law as Tradition' (1986) 5 Law and Philosophy 237.

—— 'The Traditionality of Statutes' (1988) 1 Ratio Juris 20.

Luban (D.), 'Legal Traditionalism' (1991) 43 Stanford Law Review. 1035.

MacIntyre, A., *Whose Justice? Which Rationality?* (Notre Dame, Indiana: University of Notre Dame Press, 1988).

Malek, R., *Tradition et révolution: l'enjeu de la modernité en Algérie et dans l'Islam* (Paris: Sindbad, 1993).

Minogue, K. R., 'Revolution, Tradition and Political Continuity' in King, P. and Parekh, B. C. (eds.), *Politics and Experience: Essays Presented to Professor Michael Oakeshott*, (Cambridge: Cambridge University Press, 1968).

Munoz, L., 'The Rationality of Tradition' (1981) 67 Archiv für Rechts- und Sozialphilosophie 197.

Oakeshott, M. J., *Rationalism in Politics and other Essays* (New York: Basic Books, 1962).

Ong, W. J., *Orality and Literacy: The Technologizing of the Word* (London/New York: Methuen, 1982).

Pelikan, J., *The Vindication of Tradition* (London: Yale University Press, 1984).

Pieper, J., 'The Concept of Tradition' (1958) 20 *Review of Politics* 417.

Pocock, J. G. A., 'Time, Institutions and Action: An Essay on Traditions and the Understanding' in King, P. and Parekh, B. C. (eds.), *Politics and Experience: Essays Presented to Professor Michael Oakeshott* (Cambridge: Cambridge University Press, 1968).

Popper, K., 'Toward a Rational Theory of Tradition' in K. Popper, *Conjectures and Refutations*, 3rd edn. (London: Routledge Kegan Paul, 1969).

Postema, G. J., 'On the Moral Presence of Our Past' (1991) 36 McGill Law Journal 1153.

Rudolph, L. I. and Rudolph, S. H., *The Modernity of Tradition: Political Development in India* (Chicago: University of Chicago Press, 1967).

Shils, E., *Tradition* (Chicago: University of Chicago Press, 1981).

Thapar, R., 'Tradition' in R. Thapar, *Cultural Transaction and Early India: Tradition and Patronage* (Delhi: Oxford University Press, 1994).

Thompson, E. P., *Customs in Common*, (New York: The New Press, 1993).

Waldman, M. R., 'Tradition as a Modality of Change: Islamic Examples' (1985–86) 25 *History of Religions* 318.

Wise, E., 'Legal Tradition as a Limitation on Law Reform' (1978) 26 American Journal of Comparative Law (Suppl.)1.

# 2

# BETWEEN TRADITIONS:
# IDENTITY, PERSUASION AND
# SURVIVAL

Traditions are internally unstable, but the problem of stability is magnified by a tradition's relations with other traditions. The two sources of instability—internal and external—are related to one another, since if a tradition is constituted internally by an exchange of information, it is in some measure open to further exchanges of information, notably those with other traditions. Both internal and external resistance is encountered, and must be answered. Limits on the process of exchange are the product of particular traditions, and may or may not be successful. Over time, the forces of entropy appear overpowering.

The process of exchange between traditions is today accelerating, for a number of related reasons. Increasing awareness in the west of the traditional character of western thought now places western thought beside, and not above, other forms of thought. Increasing juxtaposition with other traditions reveals their own diversity, and measure of internal rationality. It is no longer considered scientifically or intellectually accurate, and therefore no longer politically correct, to speak of 'primitive' or 'advanced' societies or peoples, as western sociology and anthropology traditionally did.[1] Particular practices must be identified, and opposed or defended. At the same time, western society has brought about the material conditions for increased contact amongst traditions.[2] The processes of 'globalization' and

---

[1] This may have been because of the need to provide a standard of comparison for western progress, an empirical (western) means of validating western tradition. On the corresponding growth of cultural relativism as a means of combating 'Eurocentric and racist notions of progress', see A. A. An-Na'im, 'Problems of Universal Cultural Legitimacy for Human Rights' in A. A. An-Na'im and F. M. Deng, *Human Rights in Africa Cross-Cultural Perspectives* (Washington, DC: The Brookings Institution, 1990) 331 at 339; and for similar embrace of cultural relativism as a canon of research method in the social and political sciences, '[a]lmost by way of apology for the racism of the past', T. W. Bennett, 'Human Rights and the African Cultural Tradition' in W. Schmale (ed.), *Human Rights and Cultural Diversity* (Goldbach, Germany: Keip Publishing, 1993) 269 at 275. Compare F. Fernández-Armesto, *Millennium* (London/New York: Bantam, 1995) at 447 (anthropology eventually 'discovering the sufficiency of other cultures, understanding them in their own terms, acknowledging their equivalent wisdom and presenting the western world with their lessons'). On the history of anthropological thought concerning chthonic people, see below Ch. 7, *Western law in the world*; and on scientific views of physical human difference, see below, this Chapter, *Tradition, races and states*.

[2] For the increase in interest in the forms of such contact, see Scollon and Scollon, *Intercultural Communication* (1995).

'development' are accompanied by a process of reaction, as efforts to expand western information more frequently encounter other forms of information.[3] All sides have a sharper sense of identity—strong or weak—and all sides are influenced by the process. They cannot remain what they were. At a time, moreover, of massive efforts to expand the influence of western rationality in the world, western proponents of contextual tradition are increasingly active within the west, often drawing support from external traditions. Within the geographical areas where western tradition has been developed, people of other traditions increasingly settle, facilitated in the process by western means of transportation. Within some of the same geographical areas earlier inhabitants (or more accurately, those who continue their tradition) increasingly insist on their way of life. The branches of humanity bend, but rarely break.

## TRADITION AND IDENTITY

In thinking of the relations between traditions, it becomes necessary to think of the different traditions themselves, and of their separate or distinct identities. Identity is a current preoccupation in the world, though it is probable that without contact between societies, there would be no concern for identity. Each society would simply continue to live out its own existence, untroubled, absent external reflection or challenge, by existential questions. Concern with identity arises from external contact; identity is then constructed by explicit or implicit opposition. The other becomes essential in the process of self-understanding. At the same time the other is an ongoing menace to internal cohesion.

Being in contact with another tradition is itself an interesting notion. To recognize another tradition there are threshold requirements of knowledge and understanding, so it appears that there is no contact between traditions which does not involve exchange of information. The vigour of inter-traditional discussion thereafter may vary according to many factors, and it has been said that even violent debate contains within it the possibility of toleration, since by implication the other is worth arguing with. To direct one's thoughts against someone is to remain within their orbit.[4]

Since tradition is best defined as information,[5] however, the (slightest) contact with another tradition implies a variation in the information base of the initial

---

[3] On the complexity of this process, and on the 'globalizations' presently occurring, see below, this chapter, *Globalizations*.

[4] F. Braudel, *A History of Civilisations*, trans. R. Mayne (New York: Penguin, 1993)(orig. French ed. 1963) at 334.

[5] See above Ch. 1, Tradition as Information: The Conceptual Bran-Tub.

tradition. Its overall identity is no longer what it was, in the sense that the totality of information available to it has expanded. The bran-tub is larger. Given any form of contact between traditions, the overall identity of each becomes non-exclusive; each contains elements of the other, which may find support in the various tendencies in the receiving tradition. In today's world there are therefore no pure identities of tradition. The language of contemporary social science recognizes this in objecting to 'essentialist' conceptions of tradition, or even society. Identities thus become 'contrapuntal'[6] or 'aspectival'[7] the 'inside' and 'outside' are realms which are inter-dependent rather than discrete.[8] Theories of social development which are dif-fusionary (relying on external influence), as opposed to evolutionary (relying on purely indigenous development), appear in the ascendant. Belonging to, or adher-ing to, a tradition in these circumstances becomes less clearly defined. The impre-cise character of the tradition implies imprecision of its members. The other may be (slightly) a part of ourselves. Separateness may be (partly) overcome.

### TRADITION, RACES AND STATES

The identities of traditions are therefore inter-related, in greater or less measure. To what extent, however, is this feature of the identity of traditions related to the identity of other contemporary notions, such as society, culture, legal systems or 'ourselves'? Can there still be separate or pure societies, constituted by something more basic than tradition, such as race, ethnicity, law, or geography? Could such societies possess a character which is not affected by the interdependent nature of tradition? This is the large question of the nature of social identity, upon which an incalculable mass of writing has developed. The problem also emerged in the dis-cussion of traditio in the last chapter, in which it was stated that traditio had to occur within a given social context. Does such a context pre-exist the process of transmission of tradition?

Perhaps the oldest response to the question of social identity is one which paral-lels that which has been given to the question of individual identity. In both cases, it is memory which is constitutive of identity. Persons who have lost their memory no longer know who they are. The thesis goes back at least to Locke,[9] and has been

---

[6] Said, *Culture and Imperialism* (1994) at p. xxv.

[7] J. Tully, *Strange Multiplicity: Constitutionalism in an age of diversity* (Cambridge: Cambridge Univ. Press, 1995) at 11 and 13 (experience of cultural difference *internal* to a culture, experience of otherness internal to one's own identity, this in context of constitutional negotiations between chthonic and western peoples).

[8] S. Fish, 'Change' (1987) 86 *S. Atlantic Q.* 423 at 431, and see 430 (if 'something outside' provoking change, already 'inside').

[9] See generally Perry (ed.), *Personal Identity* (1975), and notably ch. 2 ('John Locke: Of Identity and Diver-sity'); A. O. Rorty, *The Identities of Persons* (Berkeley: Univ. of California Press, 1976); B. Williams, *Problems of the Self: Philosophical Papers 1956–1972* (Cambridge: Cambridge Univ. Press, 1973) at 1 ('Identity of body is at least not a sufficient condition of personal identity, and other considerations, of personal characteristics and, above all, memory, must be invoked').

taken over by social theorists as well.[10] Thus East Germans, on the fall of the Berlin Wall, lost their sense of identity, since they no longer existed in harmony with their own life history.[11] According to this long-held, though not always visible, opinion, tradition would thus underlie all present conceptions of social units or identity. Traditio occurs not within a given social context, but is itself constitutive of the context, which exists when the traditio has been continuous over time, from early adherents to the tradition to present ones. The other would not be a person of different colour, or race, or state, or geography, but would rather be a person of another (though now interdependent) tradition. Since this view runs up against some widely-held present opinions, however, it needs a somewhat fuller defence.

It is possible to see a present society, or minority within a society, as constituted by people of a given colour, or race, or state, or geography. Present characteristics would thus trump tradition as a defining element.[12] We have already seen that there is even some tendency to define tradition as present ritual, as opposed to the information underlying performance of the ritual.[13] In the same way that the information of tradition underlies present ritual, however, so does the information of tradition underlie any present importance accorded to colour, race, state or geography. Why would a society be seen as constituted by people of a given colour or race, when we know that there are other societies constituted according to different criteria? The only explanation for seeing a society constituted in one or another of these particular, present ways, is because there is information which says so. This information is traditional information—the information developed over time which says that some, particular, present characteristics are fundamental in defining social identity. Where does such traditional information exist? It may exist in all traditions. There may be tendencies in all traditions to valorize present characteristics or institutions, even at the expense of the tradition itself. There may also be a tendency for traditions which valorize contingent and historical time, change and rationality, to emphasize current characteristics, to the point where the traditional character of this teaching is forgotten. In all cases, however, the value accorded present features of life is derived from tradition. It is tradition which trumps; it's been around longer.

This view may be tested by examining more closely two widely used present criteria for social identity: race (or ethnicity) and nationality (or statehood). What is the relation of each of them to tradition? The more one examines the concept of

[10] E. Durkheim, *The Elementary Forms of the Religious Life*, trans. J. Swain (London: Allen and Unwin, 1915, 5th impr. 1964) at 422 ('above all it is the idea that it has of itself' which is constitutive of society); J. Fentress and C. Wickham, *Social Memory: new perspectives on the past* (Oxford/Cambridge. Mass.: Blackwell, 1992); A. Touraine, *Pourrons-nous vivre ensemble? Égaux et différents* (Paris: Fayard, 1997) at 48 ('chacun de nous prend conscience de soi comme appartenant à une tradition, une mémoire') and 222 ('la remémoration').

[11] C. Dieckman, *Die Zeit*, 11 Oct. 1991 at 3 ('Warum schaust du hinterher?').

[12] This appears to be less the case with language or religion, since both are more obviously recognizable as traditions, ongoing bodies of information.

[13] See the discussion above, Ch. 1, Tradition as Information: The Conceptual Bran-Tub.

race or ethnicity the more it appears ultimately incapable of playing a major role in social identification. No one is now able to state what race or ethnicity is.[14] Moreover, even colour disappears as a defining element of either of them, in the rainbow of colours of the populations of the world. These colours would exist; it is the grouping or taxonomy of them which has collapsed in science. So race, ethnicity and colour appear not as major, underlying means of distinguishing the world's populations, but as social constructions, varying in importance and intensity over time. What is a social construction? It is information, adhered to by enough people, for long enough, to achieve general recognition. It is a particular result of tradition, though it could also be seen as tradition itself. The question is thus not whether tradition or race is more fundamental; the answer to this question is relatively clear. The important question is the extent to which particular traditions see fit to call

[14] See generally T. Sowell, *Race and Culture: A World View* (New York: Basic Books, 1994), notably at p. xiii (scientific definition of race not attempted, as of little relevance after untold centuries of racial intermixtures); D. A. Hollinger, *Postethnic America: Beyond multiculturalism* (New York: Basic Books, 1995); S. Molnar, *Human Variation: Races, Types and Ethnic Groups*, 2nd edn. (Englewood Cliffs, NJ: Prentice Hall, 1983) at 4 (Darwinian theory led to belief that varieties of human life represented past stages of development), 19 (by end of 19th century scientists realizing no single physical criterion for distinguishing between groups of humans), 24 (race or subspecies an 'artificial construct' to enable mind to 'organize information from the natural world'), 130 (computer taxonomy casting doubt on validity of older taxonomic units) and 183 (racist writings of last century 'sought to describe human society in terms of heredity'); S. J. Gould, *The Mismeasure of Man* (New York: Norton, 1981), notably at 31 (scientific views of race in 18th, 19th centuries developed in societies where little doubt as to propriety of racial ranking); P. Shipman, *The Evolution of Racism: Human Differences and the Use and Abuse of Science* (New York: Simon and Schuster, 1994)(influence of Darwinism, scientific notions of taxonomy in 19th-century anthropology); L. L. Cavalli-Sforza, P. Menozzi and A. Piazza, *The History and Geography of Human Genes* (Princeton: Princeton Univ. Press, 1994) at 17–19 (lists of races appearing in 18th century with origins of taxonomic science, skin colour then playing 'dominant role it still has in the layman's mind'; Darwin, however, concluding that species likely to be one because all races 'graduate into each other', differences unimportant; races 'extremely unstable entities' in hands of modern taxonomists, differences between groups small when compared with that within the major groups, or even within a single population, concept of race 'has failed to obtain any consensus'), and reviewed anonymously in (1995) Scientif. Am. 102 (most alleles found everywhere at some level of frequency; single alleles apparent in nearly all populations; 'On that rock the old and wicked idea of human races foundered utterly. People vary genetically within groups more than they vary from one group to another; most evolution took place during the long time before humans made it to all the continents'); M. Ruhlen, *The Origin of Language: Tracing the Evolution of the Mother Tongue* (New York: John Wiley and Sons, 1994) at 148 (all humans exhibiting very similar cognitive, linguistic abilities, across entire species, no primitive peoples); K. Malik, *The Meaning of Race: Race, History and Culture in Western Society* (New York: New York Univ. Press, 1996), notably at 3 (legal definitions of race tautological, e. g., race as group of people defined by race, legitimating idea that each human being belongs to distinct race); and for the relation of scientific theories of race to western imperialism, see Fernández-Armesto, *Millennium* (1995), above, at 436–8. The concept of ethnicity does not advance that of race. Originally 'ethnos' in Greece designated simply those people who had not adopted the Greek political and social model of the city-state (not adhering to a particular tradition). The larger use of the expression since the 19th century would not be rooted in anything other than social construction. See N. Rouland, S. Pierré-Caps, and J. Poumarède, *Droit des minorités et des peuples autochtones* (Paris: Presses universitaires de France, 1996) at 24–5; and for the construction of the idea of race in western societies, the Greeks themselves refusing a material definition of identity, see E. Hannaford, *Race: the History of an Idea in the West* (Washington, DC/Baltimore: The Woodrow Wilson Center Press/The Johns Hopkins Univ. Press, 1996), notably at 22, 58, 59. For Muhammad's rejection of race see I. Khaldûn, *The Muqaddimah* (Princeton: Princeton Univ. Press, 1967) at 94 ('Every infant is born in the natural state').

upon race (or ethnicity or colour) to play an important role within themselves. To anticipate, the major legal traditions of the world do not appear to do so. Other criteria emerge as more fundamental in all of them. It is difficult, moreover, to conceive a major tradition of the world constructed around such an apparently fragile base. This may not prevent a trans-national, trans-traditional tradition of racism from existing in the world. It exists, however, by way of internal counter-point to, or corruption of, larger and more influential traditions.

Is nationality or statehood a more profound contemporary concept than trad-ition? Both appear historically as creations of the western enlightenment[15] and both, in spite of their contemporary importance in the world, appear rooted in a particu-lar manner of thought or tradition. There are, moreover, many traditional def-initions of states and nationalities, so they also appear as subject to local, traditional criteria of reception. Some states use descent as a primary criterion of membership (the jus sanguinis); others use the territory of birth (the jus soli). These are import-ant differences, and demonstrate important differences as to the nature of a state. Implementation of either of them, in the tangled web of family relations and territorial movement, requires extremely complex, and nationally variable, legisla-tion. The state emerges as the product of a particular tradition and subject to many more. Its present position, moreover, is the object of great, current debate.[16] Received information, or tradition, is the controlling background within which all current states exist.

The conclusion that tradition is the controlling element in determining social identity means that there are no fundamentally different, totally irreconcilable social identities in the world. Each is constituted by tradition and all traditions contain elements of the others. The 'West', as it is usually described, contains some of the 'East'. There are always common elements and common subjects of discus-sion. The French expression 'mixité' thus best describes the common condition of humanity, and notions of societal (or, it may be thought, legal) purity of the nineteenth or early-twentieth century are no longer sustainable.[17] This does not mean, however, that in all traditions all is subject to negotiation. Fernand Braudel has identifed what he called the 'underlying structures' of different civilizations, those elements of a civilization which could not be changed without a fundamental change, or more probably disappearance, of the tradition itself.[18] Moreover,

---

[15] Anderson, *Imagined Communities* (1991).

[16] See below, this chapter, Universalizing: Ruling the World through Truth, and, The State and the New Diasporas, dealing with internal and external challenges to states.

[17] Örücü, Attwooll and Coyle (eds.), *Legal Systems: Mixed and Mixing* (1996); H. Petersen and H. Zahle, *Legal Polycentricity: Consequences of Pluralism in Law* (Aldershot: Dartmouth, 1995), notably T. Wilhelmsson, 'Legal Integration as Disintegration of National Law' at 127 and A.-J. Arnaud, 'Legal Pluralism and the Building of Europe' at 149.

[18] Braudel, *History of Civilizations* (1993), above, at 28, 29 ('A civilization generally refuses to accept a cultural innovation that calls in question one of its own structural elements. Such refusals or unspoken enmities are relatively rare: but they always point to the heart of a civilization').

traditions may absorb foreign elements and contain them, as they contain many internal elements of variance or dissidence.

## PROTECTING IDENTITY

So the identity of a tradition is an elusive concept, and is perhaps best thought of in triptych form. There is the overall identity of the tradition, that which constitutes its total information base and which includes both internal dissenting and external contrasting elements. There is what has been earlier described as the 'leading' or 'primary' version of the tradition, that which, at any given time, appears accepted as its truest version.[19] And there is finally the 'underlying' or 'basic' element or elements of the tradition, those without which no other elements of the tradition could stand. How do different traditions accommodate the notion of change to themselves? It may again depend on the tradition, and on that which is said to change. Change through foreign contact and variation of the entire information base of the tradition may not be seen as change, only as a further complication in implementation of the leading version of the tradition. Or it may not be acknowledged in any way whatsoever. Change may also occur in the leading version of the tradition, whether or not it is acknowledged as such. The teaching would not be as it was before, for whatever reason (new ideas, new understanding of old ones). This type of change can occur consistently with the ongoing character and identity of the tradition, since while some elements change, others are likely to remain constant.[20]

Change to the underlying or basic elements of the tradition is more problematical, since it would appear to bring the tradition to an end. It is possible that this could be done with the assent of all adherents, though it is difficult to provide examples. It is more probable that the basic elements of the tradition slowly lose their force of persuasion, and the tradition declines in vigour to the point of extinction or near extinction.[21] This is likely to occur in tandem with growth in adherence to another tradition, and this in turn may involve the universalizing or proselytizing character of the other tradition.[22] The essential question appears to be whether a tradition can take specific measures to protect its underlying or basic

---

[19] There will always be questions, however, of whether there is any such true version at a given time, and the adherents or participants may disagree profoundly as to the content of the true version. As a defence against this, traditions may expressly adopt the notion of the tradition as presently defined by an agency of the tradition itself.

[20] See above Ch. 1, The Changing Presence of the Past.

[21] Some traditions are now said to be extinct because there are no present adherents, though their information base has been retained. This illustrates why it is difficult to say that a tradition has died. So long as its information is preserved, it may live again, a 'recovered tradition', though this may involve its adoption by a people now different from its original adherents. A tradition may thus exist even without adherents, though in a state of suspended animation. 'Lost identities' are sometimes spoken of in this regard, and Sacco has spoken of 'submerged' law: R. Sacco, M. Guadagni, R. Aluffi Beck-Peccoz, and L. Castellani, *Il diritto africano* (Turin: *UTET*, 1995) at 15, 169.

[22] See below, this Chapter, Universalizing: Ruling the World through Truth.

elements, whether it can specifically protect its identity. Most apparently do, and
the instruments are variously known as heresy, treason or sedition. Their content
varies according to the tradition. It is a more controversial question as to whether a
tradition can restrain its adherents from abandoning it. Are there always the
options of 'voice' and 'exit', or does the identity of some traditions preclude them?[23]
Refusing exit means retaining and internalizing fundamental dissent, increasing the
risk of schism and upheaval. It increases the likelihood of charges of corruption and
self-interest. People may leave in any event. There is no ultimate way of ensuring
adherence to the underlying or basic elements of a tradition. Some would rather
die, which is also de-stabilizing.

Protecting the identity of a tradition by preventing exit is therefore likely to be
controversial in any tradition, and almost certain to attract dissent to itself. Protecting the identity of a tradition by preventing internal dissent or external challenge is
inevitably more controversial. If it is essential to a tradition that it contain more
information than it needs, that its bran-tub is an ongoing source of enrichment and
change, then traditions will not generally seek to freeze their leading or primary
version, or any of the competing versions. This may, however, be done, in granting
apodictic authority to an entire version of a tradition, such that heresy becomes
applicable, not only to challenge to underlying elements, but to any questioning of
any of the elements of the chosen version. This we currently know as fundamentalism, and the growth of violence in pursuit of fundamentalism (in the west, east,
north and south) is therefore ultimately a question of the nature of tradition and its
present capture or interpretation. Why fundamentalism exists is a basic question
going to the notion of tradition, its relation to other notions such as systems or states,
and the extent of universalization or proselytizing in the world. Fundamentalism
may involve the old problem of losing one's identity through protecting it too much.

Tradition is thus essential to understanding any social identity. It is another
question, however, to know whether it is legal traditions which play this constitutive
role or whether other traditions may be identified as more important. This, again,
may depend on the tradition. Creating an identity is an instrumental function.
Some legal traditions may be compatible with this function; others may find it
incomprehensible.


# PERSUASIVE AUTHORITY: CREATING NEW (AND OLD) EPISTEMIC COMMUNITIES


If tradition is information, then the tradition which attracts the most adherence
will be the one whose information is the most persuasive. There is thus a great

[23] Hirschman, *Exit, Voice and Loyalty* (1970).

function of advocacy which the adherents to traditions must perform, in order to ensure their ongoing, albeit interdependent, identity. The information of traditions may be constantly juxtaposed with the information of other traditions, and individuals are constantly faced with the choice (in Greek, hairesis) of information upon which they will rely in living their daily lives. This will be so, it should be recalled, even if they decide to do their own thing, since here they rely on massive amounts of information justifying this conduct. The information of traditions thus represents authority, but it is not necessarily authoritative. Absent instruments of authority, or of dominance or of repression, the authority of tradition is persuasive only. It does not bind, in the sense of somehow automatically ensuring adherence.[24] The great and powerful traditions are those which offer great and powerful, even eternal and ultimately true, reasons for adherence. If there are a number of great traditions, choice amongst them may be very difficult, and habit or inertia may come to play a major part in adherence. This presents its own dangers, since those who adhere through inertia are unable to defend their choice, and are unable to defend their tradition in the face of external challenge.

Traditions, and hence communities, thus come to be defined by the totality of the flow of information in the world, including its quality and meaning. In the past the flow of information from tradition to tradition was largely that of formal learning (translatio studii), since contact between traditions was less frequent. Evolutionary (autonomous) or multiple-independent theories of social development thus enjoyed considerable support. Today such theories have become extremely hard to defend, at least in contemporary contexts, since it has become very difficult to identify any tradition which maintains itself through exclusively internal reflection and debate. All of the legal traditions to be discussed here, which cover the greater part (if not the totality) of the world's population, are in constant contact with one or more of the other legal traditions.[25] There is thus a possibilty of transmission and exchange of all forms of tradition, and of all or most of their content. Formal learning is now accompanied by other forms of diffusion.

There is thus a new dynamic in the processes by which the past is captured, and communicated in the present.[26] Modern means of communication facilitate advocacy on a mass scale. The advent of computer technology, linked with modem-driven means of transmission, has given rise to the apparently new concept of an epistemic community.[27] An epistemic community is one linked by modern means of communication, in a way which allows it to transcend existing communities,

[24] See L. Munoz, 'The Rationality of Tradition' (1981) 67 Archiv für Rechts- und Sozialphilosophie 197 at 203 (tradition as 'retroprojection'; 'we choose what we say determines us and we present ourselves as heirs of those we have made our ancestors').

[25] On the reasons for this increase in contact, see the discussion at the beginning of this chapter.

[26] See above Ch. 1, *Presence*, for means of capture and transmission of tradition, in the context of each tradition.

[27] Haas, 'Epistemic Communities' (1992). See, however, for epistemic communities in philosophy, S. Haack, *Evidence and Inquiry: Towards Reconstruction in Epistemology* (Oxford: Blackwell, 1993) *passim*, notably at 190–2. The origins of the expression may not now be traceable; no one's contribution is recognizable as original.

notably states. This is an exciting development, for many kinds of people, and particularly for the legal professions.[28] Written traditions have thus acquired a new mobility. As well, oral traditions have found new and powerful means of external expansion in modern forms of audio-visual communication. Chthonic peoples[29] now present their tradition to the entire world, with immediacy, and in a way which allows the immediacy to be preserved for future distribution. Chthonic tradition changes in this process, but much of it is made known to others. There is also new communication amongst chthonic peoples.

The concept of an epistemic community appears to be a new and interesting idea. It is, however, simply an old and good one, presented in a different environment. If tradition is information, and if information is the formative element in all social identities, then the adherents to traditions have always constituted epistemic communities. This is what they primarily and fundamentally are, though we have often taken the teaching of individual traditions (for example, states, religion) to be the constitutive element of identity. The notion of an epistemic community is a welcome one, since it describes current technological reality in the world, and also describes a wider and older reality. The information of a tradition exists in a network. If it is communicated by modem through multiple and interconnected LANs, it remains a tradition. And traditions must still persuade by their content, which cannot be confused with their means of transmission.

Modern means of communication are therefore powerful aids to distribution of persuasive authority, and powerful aids to expansion or reinforcement of traditions. There is another dimension to them, however, which is less supportive of established traditions. Though many object to their dominating influence, they may be liberating at the individual level, and this is particularly true of contemporary computer technology. States now find that information is a largely uncontrollable commodity. It probably always has been, but the existence of national, state monopolies on many forms of communication succeeded in camouflaging this for some time. States now recognize, however, that they cannot control individual computer transmissions, and that fundamental policy objectives, such as protection of personal information held in computer banks are now possible only at the level of inter-governmental co-operation. Even this is questionable. If states, and the traditions they represent, are unable to control the diffusion of information by computer, no other tradition is likely to be able to do so either. Nor is it possible even to oversee the information transmitted.[30] So traditions are now even less capable

---

[28] See below Ch. 5, *European identities*.

[29] See below Ch. 3, *Chthonic peoples, states and human rights* and on the notion of 'secondary orality', orality sustained by modern means of communication and itself contributing to a rediscovery of orality, see W. Ong, *Orality and Literacy: The Technologizing of the Word* (London/New York: Methuen, 1982) at 3, 11, 136, 137.

[30] See H. P. Glenn, 'Les nouveaux moyens de reproduction: papier, sonores, audiovisuels et informatiques, Rapport général,' (1986) Travaux de l'Association Henri Capitant des amis de la culture juridique française, Journées néerlandaises, vol. xxxvii 33 at 51 (information analogous to liquid, penetrating even by capillary attraction); Information Highway Advisory Council (Canada), *Connection, Community, Content: the*

than they were historically of controlling the information circulating among the adherents to a tradition, or amongst adherents to different traditions. Western rationality and individuality appears here to have given themselves a major boost, or at least to have given other traditions reason to multiply their efforts of persuasion.

The increasing freedom of communication may have different impacts, however, on different traditions, whether legal or other. Some may never have sought to control information, and new forms of communication may present no problem for them, only advantages. Others may have created informational élites or informational monopolies, and these may be severely threatened, both qualitatively and quantitatively. Others may rely on institutions, whose information base can no longer be protected as in the past. Some traditions may rely on concepts of heresy or treason or sedition; these will now be more difficult to detect and identify. Many forms of activity will thus now come to enjoy the advantage enjoyed by western scientists, whose freedom of communication has been largely unrestricted for centuries. This has many potential implications for lawyers, whose identity has been largely submerged into those of other traditions within which they function. Thus there are lawyers identified as being lawyers of particular countries, or of particular religious legal traditions, as opposed to simply being lawyers. Legal information has been the object of various types of control by traditions within which lawyers function, or more spontaneously by legal traditions themselves. If legal information is to enjoy new freedom, such controls will decline in importance. There will be new patterns in the flow of legal information.

Given new and very effective means of communication, further questions arise as to the best means of persuasion and the types of information to be communicated. The capacity of the new means of communication means that large amounts of very detailed information may be transmitted, and the specialization inherent in many aspects of western tradition is thereby facilitated. At the same time, so is the transmission of specialized information to non-specialists within and without the tradition. New specialists may be created, even where a given tradition had not previously lent itself to specialization. The general increase in information may facilitate persuasion and argument at more precise levels of human activity and difference.[31] Smaller pieces of tradition may confront one another. There need not be judgment on the totality of a tradition each time it is encountered. New means of communication may also constitute active means of education and instruction.

*Challenge of the Information Highway* (Ottawa: Ministry of Supply and Services, 1995) at 49 ('problems of enforcement related to jurisdictional boundaries'); N. Negroponte, *Being Digital* (New York: Vintage Books, 1995) at 55, 56 ('There is simply no way to limit the freedom of bit radiation, any more than the Romans could stop Christianity.').

[31] For a positive view of the relations between comparative law and specialization (too often seen as narrowing and exclusive), see H. Patrick Glenn, 'Comparative Law and Specialization' in Swiss Institute of Comparative Law, *The Responsiveness of Legal Systems to Foreign Influences* (Zürich: Schulthess, 1992) 315.

Existing institutions of education may be transformed into electronic ones. The electronically equipped mosque is already in existence.

Acceleration of contact amongst traditions will increase the necessity for evaluation across traditions. It raises the question of commensurability of traditions.

## COMMENSURABILITY: OF APPLES AND ORANGES

One of the most well-known pieces of popular wisdom in the English-speaking world is that you cannot compare apples and oranges. Difference implies isolation. Yet how do we know there is such difference if comparison has not somehow, already, taken place? Think of apples and oranges and how you can actually compare them. There are obvious criteria of roundness, acidity, colour, sweetness, fibre-content, specific gravity, price, pit/seed content, fruitiness, and so on. Why do people say you cannot compare things, that they are incommensurable, when they are so obviously comparable or commensurable? There are some very broad currents of thought lurking behind this question. Notions of incommensurability are well known in the west and are therefore part of western, rational tradition.[32] If two things, or societies, or scientific paradigms, are incommensurable, then you cannot conclude anything about their respective merits. They simply *are* (simple existence, as a concept, being a clear indicator of western thinking). To put it in another, more recognizable, way, they are simply facts and facts do not provide any normative instruction. Absent normative instruction from whatever is incommensurable, we are left to our own devices, and notably our own reflective processes. So the current debate on what is incommensurable appears to be only another reformulation of

[32] For incommensurability in science, see Kuhn, *Structure of Scientific Revolutions* (1962); and in philosophy Rorty, *Philosophy and Mirror of Nature* (1979); and for comment on Kuhn and Rorty, Haack, *Evidence and Inquiry* (1993), above, at 182–94. These authors need to be carefully read on the characteristics of incommensurability. It is here taken to mean that which is incomparable, as a way of simplifying the discussion. The word is derived from the Latin com and mensurabilis, indicating a means of common measure, and historically originated from Greek mathematics, where Pythagoreans determined that the proportional lengths of the diameter and side of a regular pentagon could not be expressed in terms of integers or whole numbers, concluding as to the absence of a single scale of measure. This idea of mathematical incommensurability overthrew older views that all could be expressed in integers, but has itself been overtaken by the development of real numbers, expressed in decimals. The mathematical example suggests a general proposition that initial incommensurability will yield to greater precision of information. For discussion see R. Chang (ed.), *Incommensurability, Incomparability and Practical Reason* (Cambridge, Mass.: Harvard Univ. Press, 1997) (notably at 1, 255 on the Pythagoreans); D. Pearce, *Roads to Commensurability* (Dordrecht: D. Reidel, 1987); H. Sankey, *Rationality, Relativism and Incommensurability* (Aldershot: Ashgate, 1997); H. P. Glenn, 'Are Legal Traditions Incommensurable?' (forthcoming); H. P. Glenn, 'Commensurability and Translatability' (forthcoming, Am. J. Comp. L.); and for opposition to the notion of incommensurability (though on grounds which deny our cognitive ability to appreciate difference outside of language and which therefore reduce difference to the inconsequential or the ineffable) see Davidson, 'Idea of a Conceptual Scheme' (1972–3)

(some) western attitudes toward the past, now actualized towards the present, which says that there isn't any existing teaching which should impede our individual, charismatic, rational, decision-making.[33] The argument for incommensurability would be simply the argument for the past as 'history'; though now it is the present which must be off-loaded. It is a form of closure. If the past is dead, so is the present. And the future will have to be still-born.

Notions of incommensurabilty are closely linked to other, important features of western thought, that is, other, linked elements of the tradition. If neither past nor present has any lessons, then, some have concluded, anything goes, and a sub-strain of anarchistic rationalism or solipsis has developed.[34] More positively, and there has been great resonance of this idea in the west, notably in western legal theory, we can set aside all of the encumbering, existing variations of western and other thought, and constructively, rationally, create a just society.[35] We simply need to place ourselves in a world notionally free of prior or present teaching, constrained only by principles of logic and fair debate (as we understand them), and agreement will be reached. In the previous chapter we saw how this position is itself wrapped in tradition, of long standing and comparable to other traditions, and how, if successful, it would generate a tradition of all traditions. The notion of incommensurability thus does not somehow represent an epistemologically superior position. It is part of a larger western context, which itself exists alongside other contexts in the world. To understand the idea of incomparability, you have to compare it with other ideas.

In general the argument of present incommensurability has been less successful in the west than the idea of the past being composed of old facts. People object to being confined to a particular way of thought which by definition cannot have influence outside itself. They object to being buried alive, and tend to announce that declarations of their demise are premature. In the west, therefore, there is challenge to this more extreme variant of western tradition, which is contextualized and made to respond to internal objection. This phenomenon illustrates a more

---

[33] See above Ch. 1, Massaging Tradition.

[34] See notably P. Feyerabend, *Science in a Free Society* (London: NLB, 1978) (reason a tradition like all others; all incommensurable and simply are; none qualifiable as good or bad, except relatively, and little to choose amongst them); Feyerabend, *Against Method* (1978).

[35] The most visible and persistent proponents of this idea have been Rawls, in his *Theory of Justice* (1971) and Habermas, in *Theory of Communicative Action* (1984, 1987) and *Moral Consciousness and Communicative Action* 1990). Neither author now takes a categorical position, however, on the irrelevance of context. On the epistemological background of these positions see Nagel, *View from Nowhere* (1986); and for articulation at the level of legal theory, R. Alexy, *A Theory of Legal Argumentation* (Oxford: Clarendon Press, 1989). The maxim 'Comparison n'est pas raison' perhaps says it all. It is, however, a very French maxim. See, for French criticism of French universalism, Rouland, Pierré-Caps and Poumarède, *Droit des minorités* (1996), above, at 13, 21–3 ('*La propension à l'universalisme ne serait-elle pas d'autant plus facile lorsqu'elle s'accompagne de la volontaire ignorance des différences?*') (itals in orig.); and for the view that Habermas' theory of communicative action 'starts out by excluding about four-fifths of the world population', B. de Sousa Santos, *Toward a New Common Sense: Law, Science and Politics in the Paradigmatic Transition* (New York/London: Routledge, 1995) at 507.

general one, that the argument of incommensurability assumes static and distinct social identities or traditions, whereas in reality they are all composed of variants and even contradictions, some of which parallel positions which exist outside the tradition and which are known within it. The notion of incommensurability is thus incompatible with the fundamental nature of all traditions, which live as a flow of communicable and communicated information. What the proponents of incommensurability would ultimately have to establish is the impossibility of human communication, radical untranslatability, and this is denied by all human experience, and possibly by the very idea of being human.[36]

Given the failure of the argument of incommensurability, we are all left within communicable traditions. All criteria of judgment are contained within existing traditions (including rationalist ones, which may leave more room for manoeuvre); all views or places to stand or perspectives are from within a particular (inter-dependent) tradition. There is no view from nowhere, no possibility of judgment from without a tradition, in reliance on ultimate, non-traditional criteria. Human reasoning inevitably becomes comparative reasoning, all criteria standing beside others, all methods co-existing with others.[37] Denial of this would be simply closure; it could not be ignorance because there is no ignorance today sufficiently immense as to preclude minimal knowledge of the existence of other views, and even of other traditions. Knowing only one's own tradition is partly knowing others. In evaluating different versions of morality, or of law, we therefore do what we do with apples and oranges. We compare them with criteria drawn from themselves, with internal criteria.[38] This is where the action is. There is no tertio comparationis; it is all internal debate, which is what gives it its sense. Would you compare apples and oranges in terms of their compatibility with international human rights norms? You could, but the internal criteria provide you with what you need in order to reach any conclusion you might want to reach.

Comparative reasoning thus permits and facilitates judgment. It does so in a way which precludes irreconcilable difference or conflict. Knowledge of all criteria

---

[36] On the translatability of philosophical languages, and the importance of knowing as many as possible of them, see J. Randal Jr., *How Philosophy Uses its Past* (New York: Columbia Univ. Press, 1963) at 69.

[37] C. Taylor, *Sources of the Self: The Making of the Modern Identity* (Cambridge, Mass.: Harvard Univ. Press, 1989) at 72 ('Practical reasoning . . . is a reasoning in transitions. It aims to establish, not that some position is correct absolutely, but rather that some position is superior to some other. It is concerned, covertly or openly, implicitly or explicitly, with comparative propositions'); A. Jonsen and S. Toulmin, *The Abuse of Casuistry: A History of Moral Reasoning* (Berkeley/Los Angeles/London: Univ. of California Press, 1988) at 341 ('Practical reasoning in ethics is not a matter of drawing formal deductions from invariable axioms, but of exercising judgment—that is, weighing considerations against one another'); C. Atias, 'Présence de la tradition juridique' (1997) 22 Rev. rech. jur. 387 at 389 ('c'est toujours par comparaison avec le passé . . . que le juriste détermine sa position').

[38] See Kuhn, *Structure of Scientific Revolutions* (1970) at 145 (absent a scientifically or empirically neutral system of language or concepts, alternate tests and theories 'must proceed from within one or another paradigm-based tradition'); T. S. Eliot, 'Tradition and the Individual Talent' in T. S. Eliot, *The Sacred Wood: Essays on Poetry and Criticism*, 6th edn. (London: Methuen, 1948) 47 at 50 ('a comparison, in which two things are measured by each other').

will be shared to some extent, and we may profit from this if our own knowledge of them is sufficiently large (this assumes, of course, minimal education in other traditions). The less information we have, the more conflictual every situation will appear. Not only is contextual judgment possible, the judgment based on criteria of existing traditions, juxtaposed with other criteria, is the only judgment which can possibly exist. What you see is what you get. You cannot wait, given all these different opinions, for the ultimate response to be somehow revealed. There is no ultimate response[39] or, which may be the same thing, there can only be a number of them.[40] Choosing the relatively better solution is a final solution, and you must choose it. Where two traditions are present, you necessarily stand in both of them to do so.

There is a further version of the incommensurability argument which should be raised, which is based on the variety of languages of the world. It is the argument of untranslatability or, if you will, the falsity of all translations ('traduire c'est trahir'). This argument may loom large in traditions where law is expressed in formal, written language, or where it has been revealed in a particular language. Information here would be frozen into its original means of expression; it could be extracted only at the cost of deformation. While this argument is a version of the incommensurability argument, limited here to language, it clearly exists in more than one tradition. People everywhere (since we lost the one, great mother of all languages) have realized that learning languages is a difficult, time-consuming process. Most have also realized that it is unlikely that traditional languages will be abandoned in favour of a single universal language. So there is some justification in feeling that information in languages you do not know is locked up on you. Reading a translation is not the real thing.

Like the incommensurability argument, however, the untranslatability argument exaggerates the difficulties in human communication. It also exaggerates the importance of the text. The most recent cognitive science now assures us that thought, and thus information, may exist prior to and independently of language;[41]

---

[39] On this conclusion in contemporary western moral philosophy, see Williams, *Ethics and Limits of Philosophy* (1985); and for similar conclusions in science, D. C. Dennett, *Darwin's Dangerous Idea: Evolution and the Meanings of Life* (New York: Simon and Schuster, 1995) at 502–5 ('time-pressured decision making is like that *all the way down* . . . The mistake that is sometimes made is to suppose that there is or must be a single (best or highest) perspective from which to assess ideal rationality').

[40] As the contents of this book should indicate, this is not in any way meant to be an anti-religious statement, only a statement of the human condition. The human (non-divine) condition does not permit ultimate responses, though it can develop final ones. See the discussion in subsequent chapters of notions of 'legal truth'—res judicata, chose jugée, Rechtskraft, cosa juzgada, cosa guidicata and the reasons for their absence in certain legal traditions. On reconciling multiple ultimate responses, see below Ch. 10.

[41] S. Pinker, *The Language Instinct: How the Mind Creates Language* (New York: Harper Perennial, 1995) at 19 (language not 'an insidious shaper of thought'), 48, 57, 58 (if language depended on words, how could new words be coined, how could translation be possible); L. Weiskrantz, 'Thought Without Language: Thought Without Awareness?' in J. Preston (ed.), *Thought and Language* (Cambridge: Cambridge Univ. Press, 1997) 127 (reporting on pre-verbal infants, adults who have lost language capacity); for parallel islamic teaching, see L. Gardet, 'Kalam,' in E. van Donzel, B. Lewis and C. Pellat, *The Encyclopaedia of Islam*, new edn. (Leiden: E. J.

it is therefore not co-extensive with language, and may be rendered in multiple languages. There will of course be variations, and good and bad translations. This kind of noise we encounter, however, even in our own language. Some people are just impossible to understand. So differences in language are obstacles to under-standing and communication, but not insuperable ones. The translation industry in the world stands as testimony to this; the untranslatability argument, like the incommensurability argument, emerges (only) as a variant in western tradition. If you don't like translations, moreover, you can always learn the other language. Then you will stand in two traditions twice over, substantively and linguistically. Modern literature has provided us with the model of the person who speaks several languages, and *at the same time.*[42]

## UNIVERSALIZING: RULING THE WORLD THROUGH TRUTH

If a body of information is so persuasive that large numbers of people have gath-ered around it, over vast periods of time, shouldn't more people know about it? Already we have seen that advocacy was necessary for the emergence of a major tradition. Is not more of the same a good idea? Should we not extend the benefits of our truth, or truths, to others, so they may also benefit? If they do not at first realize the benefits, should we not make them available to them anyway?

It appears to be very easy for a tradition to become a universalizing force. Again, however, it should be recalled that a tradition is information, and information itself (as distinct from how it is used) is not dominating. It may give advice, but we always have to decide what to do. We always have to decide exactly how the advice applies to our particular problem. Tradition is persuasive authority; in itself it lacks authoritativeness.

So it is possible to consider tradition as a major contribution to domination in the world, or as entirely innocent. This suggests that we have to think a little harder about what is going on. If the way we act is always in function of one tradition or another, even when we do our own thing (a rationalist tradition), then tradition as information cannot be entirely divorced from the way it is used. How it is used may

Brill, 1978), vol. IV, 468 at 470 ('It is not true that there can be no speech without letters and sounds. Internal speech, "the discourse of the soul"... is a reality'); Khaldûn, *Muqaddimah* (1967), above, at 31 ('the word that expresses what is in the mind'); and for law prior to articulated language see R. Sacco, 'Mute Law' (1995) 43 *Am. J. Comp. Law* 455 at 460. Cf. J. Derrida, *Of Grammatology*, trans. G. C. Spivak (Baltimore/London: Johns Hopkins Univ. Press, 1976) 158 ('There is nothing outside of the text [ il n'y a pas de hors texte]').

[42] U. Eco, *Il nome della rosa* (Milan: Bompiani Grandi Tascabili, 1984) at 54, 55 ('Salvatore parlava tutte le lingue, e nessuna . . . E tuttavia, bene o male, io capivo cosa Salvatore volesse intendere, e così gli altri').

depend on how it says it should be used, explicitly or implicitly, and we must contemplate traditions as inducements to domination. It may be the case that not all traditions are inducements to domination. A tradition which teaches self-effacement appears innocent enough, but then we have to ask whether it teaches that *everyone* has to be self-effacing. The major question appears to be the extent to which a tradition teaches truths, or a truth, which must be respected, and by everyone. If it teaches this, then it will also teach, explicitly or implicity, that its truth should dominate. Now, there may be traditions which have such teachings, or (and this appears more likely) there may be such teachings within traditions, but there is something in this idea which is not entirely compatible with tradition as we have been discussing it. A tradition is a bran-tub of information. It necessarily contains varying and even conflicting views. It is today always in contact with other traditions, such that its information base is even larger and still more diffused. So the essential nature of tradition should mean that it is innocent of domination, since it is tolerant of different views. Domination would be thus the corruption of tradition and not its implementation. It's just people who have been somehow corrupted who act in a dominating way. Corruption, however, is a large enough concept to present several variations.[43]

Corruption which is criminal in character may constitute a means of domination, and some criminal traditions have become dominating in some parts of the world. They do so underground, in ways which are largely unknown except through rumour and anecdote, and which most of us do not wish to emulate. So domination through the tradition of criminal corruption can be resisted as well as we know how; we know enough about it to condemn it with confidence. In dealing with societal domination, however, we are more frequently dealing with corruption which cannot be (relatively easily) categorized as criminal, or even institutional. It is the much more elusive notion of intellectual corruption of a tradition. It is the process of closing down the dynamic of a tradition, such that it speaks with only one voice and all others are stilled. Since there is only one voice to be heard, silence must be created for it and the zone of silence must be constantly enlarged. The quieter it is in a room the more you hear the noise outside, which can be very disturbing for clear understanding of a single voice. Traditions which are great and large have of course become great and large because they provide an over-arching means of reconciling different views. So their dynamic has become almost impossible to shut down. All that can occur is that some major feature of the tradition is taken as apodictic, by some adherents to the tradition, who then undertake to universalize it. For them, there is only one means of mediating the one truth. We have already encountered this phenomenon in discussing fundamentalism.[44] Fundamentalism need not always be accompanied by violence. There are subtler forms of fundamentalism, and some may be irresistible to even the majority of members

---

[43] See above Ch. 1, Tradition and Corruption.     [44] Ibid.

of a tradition. Fundamentalism, and ensuing efforts of domination, emerge not as corruption of particular traditions—they faithfully reflect major elements of teaching of their particular tradition—but as corruption of what we understand as tradition, the gathering together of diverse elements into a larger, but still coherent, identity.

Another way of saying this might be to say that within all traditions, and therefore within all humanity, there are accompanying traditions of tolerance and intolerance. Thus even traditions of tolerance could be intolerant in their teaching of it. Even traditions using a concept of 'thin' standards, applicable abroad, as opposed to 'thick' standards, applicable at home, may be intolerant in the application of their 'thin' standards.[45] They may not look so thin elsewhere. Do adherents to a tradition have to occupy themselves with application of any of their standards, abroad? Or with its application to non-adherents, anywhere?

The toleration of the pluralist is thus very demanding. On the one hand it means resisting the tendency to authority, always being willing to see one's advice turned down, always being willing to be a loser. On the other hand it means never giving up the struggle, never giving in to the internal desire for closure, for stability. It means continuing to learn and to test the learning, while continuing to make the decisions that have to be made. Toleration is not easy, which may be why there is a tradition of intolerance.

Do some types of tradition lend themselves more easily to intolerance and domination, or to an accompanying tradition of intolerance and domination? Religious traditions teach one large truth, yet many religions appear to be tolerant ones. Rationalist traditions appear as tolerant ones, since they tolerate multiple efforts of rationality. Yet rationalist tradition has developed systemic thought, with its implications of boundaries and conflict.[46] A tradition of toleration may be the most difficult of all to understand, since it has to operate over other traditions, and in function of their respective relations.

## GLOBALIZATIONS

Globalization, or world domination, is usually thought of as a single process. The problem with this analysis of the state of the world is that there are a number of globalizations going on. It is not just the spread of western technology, open markets and human rights. There is also, for example, globalization in the form of islamization. The percentage of people in the world who are muslim has been rising, and Professor Braudel estimated in the 1960s that it was then closer to 15 per

---

[45] See this notion of 'thick' and 'thin' standards in Walzer, *Thick and Thin:* 1994, notably at 10–12 and 60, 61 ('thin' standards defined by western concepts of 'minimal rights' of 'abstract individuals').

[46] On the tendency to domination of biological systems richest in information see R. Margalef, *Perspectives in Ecological Theory* (Chicago: Univ. of Chicago Press, 1968) at 16, 17.

cent than its historical position of under 10 per cent.[47] In absolute terms this then represented some 400 million people, the population (very roughly) of the United States of America and western Europe combined. Estimates of the islamic population of the world now approach (or go beyond) 900 million and 16 per cent of the world's population.[48] Counting is becoming more difficult. Many more parts of the world, including North America and Europe, are now subject to islamic influence. While globalization has been going on above, islam has been expanding on the ground. It is persuading more people than it did in the past. There is also a process of easternization, said in management circles to be replacing an exhausted process of westernization, as western techniques of management and organization are replaced by those of Asia.[49] There may still be further forms of world domination ahead, presently unperceived.

So the process of globalization represents something more than expanding western influence encountering local and particular forms of resistance. This might be seen as normal, and globalization and particularization (or fragmentation) are often presented as necessarily concurrent phenomena. It is the old story of the vicious dog, who bites when attacked. The world is too complicated, however, to be caught in a single dichotomy of a growing 'us' and many, smaller, 'thems'. It is rather the case that each tradition, or at least each of the major ones, has within it the potential to globalize, to be used for purposes of domination in a way which suppresses, by manifold means, variant opinion. There now appear to be three main candidates in a race to globalize: the west, islam and Asia. No one is able to foresee the result of such a race, and some argue that other traditions, notably the chthonic one, hold the key to human and ecological survival. So we may not be heading for a single, cosmopolitan, world culture, since *a* cosmopolitan culture implies that somebody's culture is cosmopolitan, while those of others are not.[50] In thinking about 'globalization' we may be caught in ways of thought that grew out of the colonialism of the eighteenth and nineteenth centuries. The world is out there, and you can make it a place of your culture or civilization or system (read tradition) if you are more vigorous than the others. The reactions are just particular ones. We may, however, be reaching the limits of expansion of traditions. They may

---

[47] Braudel, *History of Civilizations* (1993), above, at 61 (representing data in 1962).

[48] See S. Huntington, *The Clash of Civilizations and the Remaking of World Order* (New York: Simon and Schuster, 1996) at 84, 85 (placing islamic population at 4.2% of world population in 1900).

[49] R. Kaplinsky and A. Posthuma, *Easternization: The Spread of Japanese Management Techniques to Developing Countries* (Ilford/Portland, Oreg.: F. Cass, 1994); and Ch. 9, *Easternization.*

[50] On hellenistic and notably stoic origins of cosmopolitanism (involving 'one law') see Kristeva, *Strangers to Ourselves* (1991) at 56–9 (concentric circles of human arrangements being compressed together so that all absorbed into ourselves); and on the enlightenment version, ibid., at 122, 123 ('A new cosmopolitanism is being born, no longer founded on the unity of creatures belonging to God, as Dante conceived, but on the universality of a self that is fragile, casual, and nevertheless virtuous and certain'). For the enlightenment view that radically different societies cannot live in peace, necessitating imposition of the western peace, see J. Goldsmith, *La Trampa*, trans. M. J. Margariños de Mello (Mexico: Plaza and Janes, 1995) at 164. Compare the notion of the Iroquois peace, Ch. 3, *Universalizing the chthonic?*

all have to develop explicit teaching of their own as to the terms of co-existence with other traditions. Some have already done so, though refinement may be, as always, required. If this is what is occurring, the west will have played an important part in it, since western means of communication will have played an essential role. They will have been used, however, to sustain other visions of the world than that of the west, just as the western concept of the state came to be turned against colonial powers. A major, recent review of world history concluded that 'initiatives' towards global supremacy will be of briefer and briefer duration, suggesting some form of international equilibrium.[51] This information should be made known. It might do something to the arms trade.

The present state of the world may thus illustrate some of the emerging teaching on traditions. Since traditions are composed of information, they are as difficult to suppress as information. Traditions do not ultimately triumph over one another; there are almost always adherents hanging on, waiting for the moment of rejuvenation. If all the adherents die, the information is not lost, and someone may some day make it theirs. They may see themselves as, and they may be, descendants of the original adherents. There is nothing 'determined or automatic' about hegemony, and it can never be 'an all-embracing domination upon the ruled'.[52] Persuasion is ultimately all that is worthwhile and persuasion involves the meeting, and mutual respect, of traditions. If the traditions are going to survive, there is no justification for efforts to destroy them, and particularly by force.

Globalization, in whatever form, implies the extension of traditions beyond the states in whose form they may have crystalized, as 'frozen accidents',[53] at any given time. States of immediately cognate traditions may bind together in some supranational form, in an effort to catch up to their own, constitutive traditions. We know this as regionalization and, as there are multiple globalizations, so there are multiple regionalizations. Regionalization takes the form of formal structure, however, and is of necessarily limited extent. States exist both as impetus to regionalization (to capture dwindling control over the real world) and as major impediments to it (in insisting on their existing structures and forms of rationality).[54] Regionalization is thus not the threat to individual traditions which globalization might be, but both serve to weaken considerably the authority of individual states. The tradition which created the state is losing its grip; there are wider fora in which traditions may be given effect. At the same time, however, there are still smaller fora, within the state,

---

[51] Fernández-Armesto, *Millennium* (1995) above, at 708, 709.

[52] E. P. Thompson, *Customs in Common* (New York: The New Press, 1993) at 86, 87.

[53] The phrase is that of M. Gell-Man, in *The Quark and the Jaguar: Adventures in the Simple and the Complex* (New York: Little, Brown, 1994) at 134, 228 (quark as basic element of matter combining, in frozen accidents, to create complex structures such as jaguar; common elements of universe composed of 'mutual information').

[54] See W. Davey, 'European Integration: Reflections on its Limits and Effects' (1993) 1 Ind. J. Global Legal St. 185, notably at 217 (European integration succeeding thus far because of 'high degree of commonality' yet 'serious constraints on integration').

and the state sees its hegemony decline both from external, globalizing forces and from internal, divisive ones (though the two may overlap). The state, as frozen accident, is beginning to melt, though the process may be a very long one.

## THE STATE AND THE NEW DIASPORAS

The state may be explained by the ascendance, in the west, of a tradition of individualized, constructive rationality. This is not the place to explore the historical process, but there was bitter resistance, in the west itself, to the ascendancy of this form of rationality. The resistance was that of people we now think of as having belonged to the same political community (the state extended backwards into time, the present altering the past in its choice of information), who objected both to the decline in their other-rational way of life and, moreover, to the growing role of people formally designated as lawyers.[55] The important point appears to be that a state (or national legal 'system') is only an institutionalized recognition of the ascendancy of a particular tradition at a particular time, which is unlikely to have obliterated other, competing traditions even within its territory. The state being, however (or so goes the argument), the culmination of rational agreement, it is ideally expressed in universal terms and in terms which, depending on the state, tend to the 'monological', that is, they tend to exclude forms of information which are not in rational form, as it is understood.

What are the problems with all of this? There are first of all many states, or multiple forms of universal rationality. While rationality is meant to be universal, and rational agreement always the goal, the rational tradition has created or exacerbated a principle of formal legal disharmony in the world, which then has to be overcome by other means.[56] Conflicts of laws are the least disruptive forms of such underlying disharmony; states, of the rational, western tradition, appear as capable of war amongst themselves as other forms of social identity. Second, the state, as a formal institution, becomes the ultimate arbiter of its own membership[57] and thus

---

[55] See, e.g., for resistance to the reception of roman law in what we now know as Germany, G. Strauss, *Law, Resistance and the State: The Opposition to Roman Law in Germany* (Princeton: Princeton Univ. Press, 1986); and Ch. 5, *Roman law and law in Europe*. Resistance was as great in France, though both in the name of regional traditions and in the name of an emerging tradition of royal (central) authority.

[56] For both formal and informal methods of harmonization, see H. P. Glenn, 'Harmonization of law, foreign law and private international law' (1993) 1 Eur. Rev. Private Law 47.

[57] In public international law the principle is clearly established that it is for each state to decide who are its own nationals. On varying criteria for membership, see above, this Chapter, *Tradition, races and states*. State determination of conditions of entry is widely known and debated; less widely known is state control of conditions of departure (exit), which may include denial of loss of nationality. See below Ch. 5, *Protecting identity*.

becomes a major obstacle to freedom of movement in the world and individual, rational choice in movement. Third, the state's internal instrument of rationality, constitutional law, becomes the arbiter of other forms of rationality which may continue to exist or emerge within it. There are increasingly expressed opinions that western constitutional law, as it has existed until now, is unable to do so. The exclusivity of its sources, the logic at its disposal, would make it more an instrument of repression of other traditions than an adequate means of reconciling them. This would be in no way the fault of constitutional lawyers, who sometimes accomplish near miracles, but the fault of elevating one tradition into a position of institutional dominance over others. The system of the state cannot tolerate the possibility of other systems within it; this is the nature of systemic thinking. The system necessarily controls the inter-acting elements which compose it.

States do not all share these problems in equal degrees, however, since no state is identical to any other. Some states hardly exist; they really are no more than ongoing, daily plebiscites of the peoples who compose them.[58] Others are confederal or consociational, explicitly preserving in legal form some social identities within themselves. Others are more committed to philosophical and legal statements of equality (though none have succeeded in creating it) and recognize only individual citizens, accommodating diversity only, and if absolutely necessary, through multiple levels of legislative authority. To the extent that all of these forms of states rely on their own authority as paramount over all others, on the primacy of secular constitutional law and national forms of identity, they are all today experiencing the same internal problems. They are the problems of the new diasporas. The new diasporas all involve a view from somewhere else.

## THE VIEW FROM SOMEWHERE ELSE

The word diaspora comes to us, in the west, from the Greek . . . diaspora. It means dispersion, and has historically been associated with the dispersion of jewish people from their historic homeland in Palestine.[59] The word dispersion directs our attention to a point of departure, the place where dispersion begins. Dispersion occurs outward, from here. Yet the word diaspora is now coming to have, not another meaning entirely, but another sense. It is dispersion from the other end of it—a looking back to the coherent point of departure, an effort to resist the entropy which has already occurred, an effort to deny the outward journey. It is a view, here, from somewhere else. Many, if not most of us, can look back on some form of

---

[58] Even though Renan would have had all states as merely 'un plebiscite de tous les jours'. Renan, 'Qu'est-ce que une nation' at 904.

[59] See below Ch. 4, A Tradition Rooted in Revelation; and for other diasporas in the world see R. Cohen, *Global diasporas: an introduction* (Seattle: Univ. of Washington Press, 1997); R. Cohen, 'Diasporas, the Nation-State, and Globalisation' in W. Gungwu (ed.), *Global History and Migrations* (Boulder, Colo.: Westview, 1997) at 117.

diaspora. It is usually only a question of the extent of memory, of our ability to recall our tradition. Jewish people remember the diaspora well; this is why they are jewish people. Some may have recently emigrated, and remembering is an entirely personal, and relatively easy, enterprise. Others have more difficulty in remembering. Long-standing settlers, of whatever tradition, in states of immigration, may remember the tradition of the place from which their ancestors came, with varying intensity. The intensity today appears to be increasing. Those who were there when the settlers arrived, and their descendants, see the dispersion, and arrival, of the settlers more clearly. They may describe themselves as aboriginals. Yet the term is only a relative one, relative to the later settlers, and relative to their own arrival, which often was still further away, in time and often in space.

A dispersion is to a geographical place, a territorial home. Yet all those who can remember a dispersion may attempt to re-create an original home, based on the information they have available and given the limits of local circumstance. They may find support in others who share the same memory of the same information. So in current states, more or less monological, people seek to identify themselves distinctively from all the others, more or less presumed to be all the same, just (according to various forms of western thought) citizens, or even bodies or machines for thinking (and much western philosophy and science of mind seeks to prove the essentially mechanical character of the process of thought).[60] In all the sameness, people ask who they are, and the answer can only come from the past. There is something about rationality that makes people reach for their scrapbooks. For those who have always, in memory, been part of the rational tradition—a tradition of the present—personal, present characteristics may be used for identification. This too is part of the tradition. Gender or sexual preference thus become fundamental; their particular tradition must be sought; the past is looked to for support and explanation. There are therefore reasons for the historical work now being done in these fields. It has to be done. Otherwise one may be locked into a present identity, or *be* only a passing preference. As usual, the past is a great ally here as well, even if its teaching had become faint, once you learn how to read it.

Different traditions thus assert themselves, or re-assert themselves, within a particular, crystallized form of tradition—the state. While the state may be melting, it still may shatter, and enormous efforts are now being made to find ways of accommodating multiple identities (traditions) within something which still qualifies as a state—which still controls a territory and provides a minimal level of support and protection to its citizens. The state appears today a more flexible concept than it did

---

[60] See F. Crick, *The Astonishing Hypothesis: The scientific search for the soul* (New York: Scribner, 1994), notably at 3 ('"You"... are no more than the behaviour of a vast assembly of nerve cells and their associated molecules') and 281 (for useful, annotated suggestions for further reading); D. Dennett, *Consciousness Explained* (Boston: Little, Brown 1991); and for opposing views, still within the scientific–philosophical tradition, R. Penrose, *The Emperor's New Mind Concerning Computers, Minds and The Laws of Physics* (Oxford: Oxford Univ. Press, 1989); D. Chalmers, *The Conscious Mind* (Oxford: Oxford Univ. Press, 1996).

in the past and this may flow from recognition that traditions are never entirely incompatible with one another; that information is constantly flowing between them; that their adherents always overlap to some extent. So a state could be seen as a place of overlapping traditions—some now say, at least, an intercultural place—where what is common can be a platform for common effort, while what is not common can be left alone, for inevitable further discussion. The state would thus not impose a unilateral vision of the world, but be a place, a territory, of reconciliation of traditions. There might then be citizens, tout court, and hyphenated citizens, but this happens anyway.[61] As they say in management, turn your necessities into strengths. Loyalties may be multi-directional, as identities overlap. Citizenship may be national, transnational[62] or, within states, differential.[63]

How does a state do all of this, to survive? All of the options are open. One clear indication of this is the new, interactive character of public law. Once seen as the untouchable nucleus of local sovereignty, the public law of each state has had to learn about co-operation with other states, and now voluntarily looks abroad for solutions conceived as domestic. The distinction between foreign and domestic, or international and domestic, has thus become difficult to draw.[64] So the variable character of relations previously seen as international may come to be replicated internally, to the extent we can still perceive the internal. We may see more internal choice of law; we may see more in the way of personal laws (most legal traditions do not include legislators, so their recognition is not obviously conflictual); we may see more explicit, legal recognition of social identities (that is, traditions); we may see state support of a broader range of identities and traditions.

If the means of comparison and reconciliation are to be drawn from the traditions themselves, however, it is better first to consult the traditions. Does this mean, the sceptic may ask, that we are locking ourselves into the same old attitudes, that it's just another case of back to the future? It seems impossible to deny this entirely, but it can't be the same old future, not all over again.

---

[61] Braudel, *History of Civilizations* (1993), above, at 27 ('Unity and diversity, after all, coexist uneasily. We have to take them as they come').

[62] Bauböck, *Transnational Citizenship* (1994).

[63] W. Kymlicka, *Liberalism, Community and Culture* (1989) at 151.

[64] See, e.g., X. Prétot, commenting on C. E., 19 Apr. 1991, Dalloz 1991. II. 399 ('Cette double décision illustre, si besoin était, la perméabilité, on ne peut plus nette depuis quelques années, de la jurisprudence administrative à la norme internationale'); A. C. Aman, Jr., 'Indiana Journal Global Legal Studies: An Introduction' (1993) 1 Ind. J. Global Legal St. 1 at 2.

# GENERAL BIBLIOGRAPHY

Anderson, B., *Imagined Communities: Reflections on the origins and spread of nationalism*, rev'd ed. (London/New York: Verso, 1991).

Bauböck, R., *Transnational Citizenship: Membership and Rights in International Migration* (Aldershot: Edward Elgar, 1994).

Bernstein, R. J., 'The Varieties of Pluralism' (1987) American Journal of Education 509.

Davidson, D., 'On the Very Idea of a Conceptual Scheme' (1972–3) 47 Proceedings of the American Philosophical Association 5; reproduced in D. Davidson, *Inquiries into Truth and Interpretation* (Oxford: Oxford University Press, 1984) at 183.

Devine, P., 'Relativism' (1984) 67 *The Monist* 403.

Dowty, A., *Closed Borders: The Contemporary Assault on Freedom of Movement* (New Haven: Yale University Press, 1987).

Feyerabend, P., *Against Method: Outline of an Anarchistic Theory of Knowledge* (London: Verso, 1978).

Garver, E., 'Why Pluralism Now'? (1990) 73 *The Monist* 388.

Gellner, E., *Nations and Nationalism* (Oxford: Blackwell, 1983).

Haas, P. M., 'Epistemic Communities and International Policy Coordination' (1992) 46 *International Organization* 1.

Habermas, J., *The Theory of Communicative Action*, trans. T. McCarthy, 2 vols. (Boston: Beacon Press, 1984, 1987).

—— *Moral Consciousness and Communicative Action* (Cambridge, Mass.: MIT Press, 1990).

Hirschman, A. O., *Exit, Voice and Loyalty: Response to Decline in Firms, Organizations and States* (Cambridge, Mass.: Harvard University Press, 1970).

Kristeva, J., *Strangers to Ourselves*, trans. L. S. Roudiez (New York: Columbia University Press, 1991.

Kuhn, T. S., *The Structure of Scientific Revolutions* (Chicago: University of Chicago Press, 1962).

Kymlicka, W., *Liberalism, Community and Culture* (Oxford: Clarendon, Press 1989).

MacIntyre, A., *Whose Justice? Which Rationality?* (Notre Dame: Notre Dame University Press, 1988).

Nagel, T., *The View from Nowhere* (New York: Oxford University Press, 1986).

Örücü, E., Attwooll, E. and Coyle, S., *Studies in Legal Systems: Mixed and Mixing* (The Hague/London/Boston: Kluwer Law International, 1996).

Perry, J. (ed.), *Personal Identity* (Berkeley: University of California Press, 1975).

Rawls, J., *A Theory of Justice* (Cambridge, Mass.: Belknap Press, 1971).

Renan, E., 'Qu'est-ce que une nation?' in *Oeuvres Complétes* vol. 1 (Paris: Calmann–Lévy, 1948).

Rorty, R., *Philosophy and the Mirror of Nature* (Princeton: University of Princeton Press, 1979).

Rudolph, Kurt., 'Heresy' in M. Eliade (ed.), *Encyclopedia of Religion*, vol. 6 (New York: Macmillan, 1987).

Said, E.W., *Culture and Imperialism* (New York: Vintage, 1994).

Scollon, R. and Scollon, S., *Intercultural Communication: A Discourse Approach* (Oxford/Cambridge: Blackwell, 1995).

Sowell, T., *Race and Culture: A World View* (New York: Basic Books, 1994).

Taylor, C., 'The politics of recognition' in A. Gutmann (ed.), *Multiculturalism and the politics of recognition* (Princeton: Princeton University Press, 1994) 25.

Walzer, M., *Spheres of Justice: A Defence of Pluralism and Equality* (New York: Basic Books, 1983).

—— *Thick and Thin: moral argument at home and abroad* (Notre Dame: Notre Dame University Press, 1994)

Williams, B., *Ethics and the Limits of Philosophy* (Cambridge, Mass.: Harvard University Press, 1985).

Zolo, D., *La Cittadinanza: Appartenenza, identità, diritti* (Rome/Bari: Editori Laterza, 1994).

# 3

# A CHTHONIC LEGAL TRADITION: TO RECYCLE THE WORLD

Peoples subjected to European domination in recent centuries have often been identified, and identified themselves, in opposition to the Europeans who moved in with them. They have been variously known as 'aboriginals', 'natives' or 'indigenous peoples'.[1] There are, however, problems with these designations. They may be, in particular cases, inaccurate, to the extent that the peoples designated have themselves come from elsewhere, and hence after an imprecise 'beginning'.[2] The expressions are also not used consistently, since European peoples, who have been where they are for a very long time, are never designated as 'aboriginal' or 'native'. There is also great resistance to the terminology in Asia, where western colonialism had less lasting effect than elsewhere.[3] In all instances, moreover, even where the usage

[1] The expression 'indian', as applied to peoples outside of, and unconnected to, the state of India, is still more problematical, resting on the historical error of Columbus as to where he had arrived (eventually in Spanish 'las indias occidentales', for the Americas generally, though in English the expression 'West Indies' (now lacking precise political significance) has been limited to a number of Caribbean islands). As to the expression 'indian', consider your reaction if you continued to be described as a 'Saturnian' because visitors from space thought they had landed on Saturn and not Earth.

[2] For the ongoing scientific debate as to the origins of human population in North America, see L. Cavalli-Sforza, P. Menozzi, A. Pizza, *The History and Geography of Human Genes* (Princeton: Princeton Univ. Press, 1994) at 303–8 ('In summary, there is little [scientific] agreement about the first occupation of the Americas'). Scientific conclusions based on migration from elsewhere to North America are also challenged by North American chthonic people. On the some 260 million chthonic people of the world, representing 4–5% of the world's population, see B. Goehring, *Indigenous Peoples of the World: an Introduction to their Past and Future* (Saskatoon: Purich Publishing, 1993) notably at pp. vi–viii (80% of world chthonic population would be found in north, east and south Asia, 7% in South America, 6% in North America, 4% in Africa, 3% in Australia/Oceania and 0.1% in northern Europe); Schulte-Tenckhoff, *La question des peuples autochtones* (1997).

[3] See B. Kingsbury, 'The Applicability of the International Legal Concept of "Indigenous Peoples" in Asia' in J. R. Bauer and D. A. Bell, *The East Asian Challenge for Human Rights* (Cambridge: Cambridge Univ. Press, 1999) 336, notably at 340 (concept a product of European colonial settlement; inapplicable to those parts of Asia where no substantial European settlement), 350 (impossibility in much of Asia of determining prior arrival; either all or no present inhabitants to be treated as 'indigenous'); A. Béteille, 'The Idea of Aboriginal People' (1998) 19 *Current Anthropology* 187, notably at 189 (on Asian population diversity; slow but continuous movements of population in India over very long periods of time; 'impossible to disentangle history from mythology in the available accounts of migration').

may be most accurate, the expressions tell us little about the people themselves or their way of life. They are simply other, differentiated only by existence in time and place. Should we not know more about people before we begin to draw fixed social boundaries?

European domination was most extensive when the peoples encountered were few in number or lacked strong institutional means of resistance, or both. The domination, and settlement, was most extensive and lasting in the Americas and Australasia. It was extensive, though less enduring, in Africa, India and south-east Asia. It was less extensive, and less enduring, in China and in islamic territories. We learn something about traditions, and their power of immediate resistance, from this pattern of expansion of European traditions, and people. The people there when the Europeans arrived, in a definitive manner, appear not as walled up behind a tight and exclusionary social wall, but as just folks, living their lives and not unhappy with them, unstructured though they may have been through European eyes. So we could call these people 'folk', and their law 'folk law', and this has been the conclusion of the Commission on Folk Law and Legal Pluralism, whose work is immensely valuable.[4] Yet 'folk' is perhaps too general and uninformative a descriptor. In our unguarded moments, we are all folks, and the notion of volk law has had a distinguished career in Europe, as the law of European Völker and as perceived by such a brilliant lawyer as von Savigny. Folk law is also perilously close to folk lore. So the best description for the law we want to talk about is apparently that used by Edward Goldsmith in describing people who live ecological lives by being chthonic, that is, by living in or in close harmony with the earth.[5] To describe a legal tradition as chthonic is thus to attempt to describe a tradition by criteria internal to itself, as opposed to imposed criteria. It is an attempt to see the tradition from within, in spite of all problems of language and perception.

[4] The Commission on Folk Law and Legal Pluralism was created in 1978 under the general sponsorship of Unesco. Its membership, now at about 350 persons representing all regions of the world, is open to persons having 'serious and substantial scholarly or practical commitment to or involvement in the field of folk law and legal pluralism'. It is currently administered through the Institute of Folk Law, Catholic University, Nijmegen, The Netherlands. Work on chthonic law is also done in North America by the Native Law Centre of the College of Law of the University of Saskatchewan, and by the Tribal Law and Policy Program of the University of Arizona College of Law. For a survey of current work and institutions dealing with chthonic law from the perspective of legal anthropology and legal pluralism, see Rouland, *Anthropologie juridique* (1988) at 17–22, 95, 102–19.

[5] E. Goldsmith, *The Way: an Ecological World View* (London: Rider, 1992) from the Greek kthonos, or earth, in French chthonien or chtonien, as in autochtone (or in English the rarely used autochthonous). Attempting to describe the tradition internally in this manner would be without prejudice, however, to claims based on prior title, which may properly be described as aboriginal. It may also track some chthonic language, as the Maori 'tangata whenua', translated by J. G. A. Pocock as 'people of the land', and as entailing 'more than a linear sense of time . . . [rather] a relationship with the cosmos so close and exclusive as to contain both space and time within itself'. J. G. A. Pocock, 'Law, Sovereignty and History in a Divided Culture: The Case of New Zealand and the *Treaty of Waitangi*' (1998) 43 McGill L. J. 481 at 493, 499.

# A TRADITION EMERGES

There was no point of origin of a chthonic legal tradition. There was no recorded revelation; no dramatic rupture from other traditions; no single, literally unforgettable achievement. A chthonic legal tradition simply emerged, as experience grew and orality and memory did their work. Since all people of the earth are descended from people who were chthonic, all other traditions have emerged in contrast to chthonic tradition. It is the oldest of traditions; its chain of traditio is as long as the history of humanity.[6]

Chthonic people have recently been telling the world a great deal about their tradition, and it is now evident that it is a tradition which contains a great variety of information. Some might say the information is so varied that it is impossible to speak of a single tradition. We must reconcile within a single tradition lives as diverse as those of northern Inuit and southern Polynesians; practices as distinct as farming and hunting; beliefs as heterogeneous as theism and animism; structures as opposed as monarchy and democracy. Yet amongst such human diversity the tradition also tells us there are constants, those characteristics which tell us what a chthonic person *is*. How do we know what they are?

## OF SOURCES AND STRUCTURES

The most evident feature of a chthonic legal tradition has been its orality.[7] The teaching of the past is preserved through the informal, though sometimes highly disciplined, means of human speech and human memory. This may appear highly unreliable and vulnerable to external influence, until we remember that the tradition appears to have preserved that which it says to preserve for hundreds of thousands of years. So it is a tradition which is not overly preoccupied with voluminous detail, that which human memory really cannot master. It does not want its people looking things up. This does not exclude transmission of detail, such as

---

[6] The tradition would be of some 2 million years duration. Hunting and gathering were the exclusive means of subsistence for all but the last 10,000 years of it, during which time farming and herding were developed. See Wesel, *Frühformen des Rechts* 1985) at 71.

[7] R. Sacco, 'Mute Law' (1995) 43 Am. J. Comp. Law 455 at 456 ('law existed and operated efficiently in the absence of either lawgivers or lawyers') and 460 (law existing also prior to articulated language); Jenness, *Indians of Canada*, (1963) at 125 ('There were no written laws, of course; merely rules and injunctions handed down by word of mouth from an immemorial antiquity, and more temporary taboos operative during the lifetime of an individual'); and for the compatibility of the idea of a single tradition of orality with the teaching of modern anthropology, see Wesel, *Frühformen des Rechts* (1985), above, at 34, 35 (distinguishing different forms of chthonic social organization, based on hunting and gathering, farming and herding, or hierarchical structures immediately preceding the development of urban life); and for the complex 'unity' of African law, given its orality, A. N. Allott, *Essays in African Law* (London: Butterworths, 1960) at 64, 66.

words of ceremony[8] or techniques of life, but only that amount of detail manageable by human means of recall. So the most obvious and perhaps most important element of a chthonic legal tradition is that it rejects formality in the expression of law, though the reasons for this may not be immediately clear. There has, however, been implicit and in some cases very explicit resistance to efforts to write down chthonic law. That which does exist in written form has been written by European colonial administrators, by anthropologists or comparative lawyers,[9] or very exceptionally by chthonic peoples themselves, perhaps most frequently in an effort to describe their law to external observers.[10]

The insistence on orality appears related both to form and to substance. If no one is allowed to write down the law, no one can enjoy the privileged role of scribe, and no one can subsequently write large, ongoing commentaries and themselves become sources. The law is vested in a repository in which all, or most, share and in which all, or most, may participate.[11] Transmission of the tradition is through the dynamic process of oral education, in daily life, and the dialogical character of the tradition is a matter of daily practice, for all ages of people. The orality and communal nature of the traditio (the tradition can never be read, alone) are powerful inducements to consensus. So ideally the important information is learned by all, with the help of many, and all become able to assist in the ongoing process. This is an ideal description, however, since we know that dissent emerged, in irrecuperable form, and entire new traditions were generated, or created, by people rejecting, in whole or in part, the chthonic world. The tradition appears to have developed no

[8] For elaborate oaths of office see González Galván, 'Una filosofía del derecho indígena (1997) at 533 ('la palabra vale'); for the general refusal of chthonic tradition to articulate precise norms, however, see Sacco et al., Il diritto africano (1995) at 71–3 (precise norms requiring precise statement of relevant facts; chthonic tradition refusing notion of isolated and precise 'facts').

[9] See, e.g., J. Vanderlinden, Coutumier, manuel et jurisprudence du droit Zande (Brussels: Editions de l'Institut de Sociologie, 1969); and for the process of redaction of chthonic law in Africa, and African resistance to it, Rouland, Anthropologie juridique (1988) at 201, 202 (questioning whether writing constituting a 'progress'), 354–6; E. Cotran, 'African Law' (1974) at 157, 158 (task of redactor that of separating 'rules of law' from 'social custom'); T. W. Bennett, Human Rights and African Customary Law (Cape Town: Juta, 1995) at 61, 62; and for controversy on the process of redaction, Sacco et al., Il diritto africano (1995) at 63, 127. Cf. the western notion of 'custom' and the transformative European process of redaction of customs, below, this Chapter, Law and the cosmos, and Ch. 5, Law's expansion.

[10] See, for such an example, The Great Law of Peace of the Longhouse People: Iroquois League of Six Nations (Rooseveltown, NY: Akwesasne Notes, Mohawk Nation, 5th printing, 1977). Law appears also to have been inscribed in monumental stone, for symbolic purposes, by the Aztecs, Maya and Babylonians, though here the normative effect of the symbols may be overshadowed by artistic effect. The Maya had developed books of paper, derived from the bark of trees, though few have survived. On Aztec written law, a mixture of pictorial expression and phonetic transcription, see J. A. González Galván, 'El derecho consuetudinario indígena en México,' in J. E. Ordóñez Cifuentes (ed.), Cosmovisión y prácticas jurídicas de los pueblos indios (Mexico: Instituto de investigaciones jurídicas, 1994) 73 at 75 ff.

[11] For the essentially egalitarian character of chthonic society, and notions of factual as opposed to institutional inequality, see Wesel Frühformen des Rechts (1985), at 81–4; also 84 ff. on conflicting anthropological reports on equality of treatment of men and women.

specific means of combating or avoiding this.[12] Exit was available to all those for whom the tradition was entirely or partially unacceptable. It appears to remain so today. Even a tradition which greatly limits the information it transmits cannot avoid the flowering of opinion. It may even be the most vigorous stimulant of it. The substance of its information appears so essential, however, that it survives as a living tradition in spite of all dissent, in spite of all defections, and in spite of all alternatives.

A tradition which is oral in character does not lend itself to complex institutions. So the tradition faces less danger of pecuniary and institutional corruption, offering fewer positions of prestige and authority. In such a wide world of chthonic peoples, however, there were, and are, important differences in the development of institutions. The most common feature appears to be a council of elders, individual people who, by their assimilation of tradition over a longer period of time, often speak with greater authority. There is no guarantee of this, no process of screening out those faltering with age, but it appears to have been generally held to be true. This has been referred to as gerontocracy, but it may be preferable to see it as an expression of a link with past generations.[13] Councils of elders may be supplemented, or even replaced, with chiefs, but rule by chiefs is also necessarily a consultative form of rule.[14] Chiefs have no armies and can continue to function only to the extent that they generate consensus. The elders could prevent this from happening. Where chiefs became kings, as in the Aztec world, they functioned with a 'curia regis'.[15] In Africa and the Americas forms of legislation are reported as having existed, though this may have been only a description of the formal deliberations of a council.[16]

Dispute resolution was usually informal, and while 'alternate' dispute resolution occasionally existed it is here in the form of courts and formal adjudication.[17] There

[12] This did not preclude the development of punishment for violation of the unwritten norms of the community, and the punishment could extend to banishment. There appears to have been no contemplation of sanction, however, for voluntary departure.

[13] On the inter-generational nature of the community, see below, this Chapter, Change and the Natural World; and on the notion of 'necrocacy', or government by the dead, Goldsmith, *Way* (1992), above, at 109.

[14] T. W. Bennett, 'Human Rights and the African Cultural Tradition' in W. Schmale (ed.), *Human Rights and Cultural Diversity* (Goldbach, Germany: Keip Publishing, 1993) 269 at 272 (approved form of decision-making by consensus).

[15] G. F. Margadant S., *Introducción a la historia del derecho mexicano*, 9th edn. (Mexico: Editorial Esfinge, 1994) at 27; for African forms of kingship see Sacco et al., *Il diritto africano* (1995) at 97–102 (divine character based on Egyptian model); and on the necessarily limited power of chthonic kings, given lack of resources to bind allegiance, J. Roberts, *History of the World* (London/New York: Penguin, 1995) at 463.

[16] Schott, 'Triviales und Transzendentes' (1980) 165 at 297; M'Baye, 'African Conception of Law' (1975) at 150; Allott, 'African Law' (1968) at 135; Rouland, *Anthropologie juridique* (1988) at 310–12; and for the Aztecs, Margadant S., *Introducción a la historia del derecho mexicano* (1994), above, at 23.

[17] Informal sources suggest informal procedures, since if there are no definite rules which must be applied, there is no need for formal institutions charged with their application. Yet there is no need to think in terms of a double dichotomy, 'formal sources and formal courts' versus 'informal sources and informal dispute resolution', since various combinations are entirely possible. In the common law, no one knew what law the jury applied, yet the jury functioned in a highly formal setting. Variable combinations of formality of sources and structures appear probable in the variety of the chthonic world.

appears to have been no distinct judiciary in the Pacific or northern North America, though the Aztecs again differed with a system of permanent judges and formal appeals.[18] In Africa informal types of arbitration co-existed with more formally established courts.[19] There is no fixed line between chthonic and non-chthonic people. Some information is common to both. Procedure was also informal and the reconciliation of interests required a slow, careful determination of the circumstances of a case, described as a process which was neither confusing nor alienating, with a primary goal of reconciliation rather than adjudication.[20] This does not preclude procedural sophistication. Among the Dinka of Africa the closest relative or best friend of a disputant assumes responsibility for presenting the position of the adversary.[21] In general the system of dispute resolution is open and immediately accessible.[22] There are no de facto barriers of cost and no de jure barriers of preliminary screening or permission, such as those of both roman law and common law throughout most of their history. The law also is immediately applicable, by adjudicators and preferably by the parties themselves. This suggests what is known in the west as 'substantive law'. There is here, however, nothing immediately analogous to what is known in the west by this expression—no formal sources, no sharply delineated rules, only shared information on the way to live a life.

## ON WAYS OF LIFE

Chthonic ways of life recall in many ways those of European peoples prior to the major events, known as renaissances or enlightenments, of the twelfth, and again of the seventeenth and eighteenth, centuries. In some ways they may suggest future, and even present, ways of European life. Thus there appears to be relatively little recognizable chthonic law of obligations (contract and tort),[23] in the same way that continental law was lacking in these fields and had to be supplemented by roman

[18] Margadant S., *Introducción a la historia del derecho mexicano* (1994), above, at 34.

[19] Cotran, 'African Law' (1974) at 159–60; Allott, 'African Law' (1968) at 134.

[20] Bennett, 'Human Rights and African Cultural Tradition' (1993), above, at 272; Cotran 'African Law' (1974) at 160; Allott, 'African Law' (1968) at 145; Sacco et al., *Il diritto africano* (1995) at 73.

[21] R. D. Schwartz, 'Human Rights in an Evolving World Culture,' in A. A. An-Na'im and F. M. Deng, *Human Rights in Africa: Cross-Cultural Perspectives* (Washington, DC: Brookings Institution, 1990) 368 at 375.

[22] For the 'right to a trial' in Akan justice in west Africa see K. Wiredu, 'An Akan perspective on Human Rights' in An-Na'im and Deng, *Human Rights in Africa*, above, 243 at 252 ('modern misdeeds, on the part of certain governments both inside and outside Africa, of imprisoning citizens without trial would have been inconceivable in a traditional Akan setting, not only because there were no prisons but also because the principle of such a practice would have been totally repugnant to the Akan mentality').

[23] Cf., however, for differing views on the extent to which aboriginal rights in Canada included, and have always included, a right to market fish commercially, *R. v. Van der Peet* (1996) 137 DLR (4th) 289 (majority of Supreme Court of Canada deciding that evidence of practice of marketing fish insufficient to justify inclusion in evolutionary concept of aboriginal rights); for North American Huron trading practices, B. Trigger, *Children of Aataentsic* (1976) at 168–76; and for chthonic African conceptions of contract (including guarantee), Rouland, *Anthropologie juridiques* (1988) at 267–81; Cotran, 'African Law' (1974) at 162; Sacco et al., *Il diritto africano* (1995) at 85–9.

law, and the common law of England had to be stimulated by the court of the chancellor (again drawing on the Romans). The people living close to the land, and from it, it is rather the land itself, its harvests, and the personal relations of the people who live upon it, which is the object of what we can discern of chthonic law.

Chthonic family law, like chthonic law in general, is characterized by informality.[24] Marriage, divorce and adoption are not in a domain of institutional control, of church or state, and while publicity and reputation may in some manner be constitutive of status, this appears more by way of communal life than by way of fundamental requirement. In Inuit practice, adoption is thus effected by present declaration of the future parents; insistence on form is equivalent to infanticide in the Arctic.[25] Marriage and divorce are generally consensual; in the language of contemporary civil law they are 'privatized' institutions of the family, and always have been.[26] European and non-chthonic North American law has been moving steadily in this direction for decades, with due deference to national variations.[27] On the arrival of the French in the pays d'en haut, above the North American Great Lakes, chthonic people were repelled by French practices, notably prohibition of divorce, corporal punishment of children and prudish attitudes towards the human body.[28] There are fewer grounds of social antagonism today. It is true, however, that western law does not allow concurrent polygamy, while there are indications of a resurgence of this in some chthonic societies, notably in Africa with the receding of European influence.[29]

Living close to the land and in harmony with it means limiting technology which could be destructive of natural harmony. So there is no incentive for the development of complex machines, and no way of accumulating wealth through their use. There is therefore little reason to accumulate personal or movable property.[30] For the same reason there is no reason to accumulate land; there is nothing to be done to it or with it, except enjoy its natural fruits. Chthonic notions of property are

---

[24] Informality does not exclude, however, complexity, as to which see Rouland, *Anthropolgie juridique* (1988) 212 and following, on variety of parental relations and their significance; Wesel *Frühformen des Rechts* (1985), ch. 8, on family relations, notably patrilinear and matrilinear ones, and social organization.

[25] In contemporary Canadian case law see *Casimel v. Insurance Corporation of British Columbia* (1993), 106 DLR (4th) 720 (chthonic, informal adoption recognized for purposes of claim for no-fault benefits, review of prior cases).

[26] Yet divorce has been described as difficult to obtain in African law, since it involved an arrangement between the families assisted by clan elders. Cotran, 'African Law' (1974) at 163.

[27] See below, Ch. 5, *The centrality of the person and the growth of rights.*

[28] B. Trigger, interview on *Children of Aataentsic* in *Le Devoir*, Montreal, 30 Sept. 1991, p. B1.

[29] In contrast, there are fewer current reports of matrilinear forms of chthonic social organization, though this existed often in the past, notably where polyandry was current or there was at least a general liberty in sexual practices. Given difficulty in establishing a male line (father), only the matrilinear method of organization was possible. Children would grow up in the mother's home, take her name, and not know their father. Nor would a father know his children. Patrilinear modes of kinship emerge with stabilized forms of cohabitation. For polyandry in India in the early 20th century (and which has not disappeared entirely today), see W. Markby, *Hindu and Mahommedan Law* (Delhi: Inter-India Publications, 1906) (1st repr. 1977) at 26–8.

[30] Wesel, *Frühformen des Rechts* (1985), above, at 95–9.

therefore those of a chthonic life, and the human person is generally not elevated to a position of domination, or dominium, over the natural world. The movable or personal property of a person was that which the person used in their daily life; no further aggregations were necessary; no law of successions was vital to prevent disputes concerning the partition of movable things on death. Land, of course, could be effectively occupied, and western notions of adverse possession or pre-scriptive acquisition are suggestive of some form of ownership developing over time, even in chthonic societies. This is now a very current question in the Americas and Australasia, and an interesting process is occurring whereby chthonic use of land is being recast into various western concepts of property, at the insistence of chthonic peoples. According to evidence of chthonic law which has convinced high courts, the chthonic use of land consisted of communal or collective enjoyment, with no formal concept of property crystallizing this loose relationship between groups of people and the soil upon which they lived.[31] It could be used for hunting, farming, for limited forms of excavation (for example, soapstone for carving), and possibly (the question is crucial for much mineral exploration) other uses. There is no right of alienation. Until very recently this concept of property was conceptually controversial in the west, since it implied (partial) abandonment of the concept of individual ownership. In many jurisdictions of western law it is, however, a long-established concept (the Allmend or communal pasture in Swiss law—was allen gemein ist,[32] the ejido incorporated into Mexican law[33]) and recalcitrant jurisdic-tions now have recognized the manifold possibilities of property law to reflect different legal traditions. In Canada the Supreme Court borrowed from civil law terminology to decide a chthonic claim coming from a common law province, referring to a chthonic 'community . . . usufruct' over land, cognizable by com-mon law jurisprudence.[34] Here too western law sees some of its own ideas, either of

---

[31] Rouland, *Afrique juridique* (1988) at 254–9; Cotran, 'African Law' (1974) at 163; Allott, 'African Law' (1968) at 154 (noting different possible forms of personal entitlement, e. g., on clearing bush, though 'community aspect . . . would also make itself felt at every stage'); Sacco et al., *Il diritto africano* (1995) at 81–5, 200; Bennett, *Human Rights and African Customary Law* (1995), above, at 131 ff. (arguing African land holding not com-munal since chiefs exercised powers of allotment, though all members had access and no succession to land in informal law).

[32] See L. Carlen, *Rechtsgeschichte der Schweiz*, 3rd ed. (Berne: Francke Verlag, 1988) at 61; and for general European antecedents in the form of collective forms of seisin, below Ch. 5, *Roman law and law in Europe*.

[33] See M. R. Massieu, *Derecho agrario* (Mexico: Universidad Nacional Autónoma de México, 1990) at 61–7 ('social patrimony' of land); J. L. Ibarra Mendivil, *Propriedad agraria y sistema político en México* (México: El Colegio de Sonora, 1989) ch. 6.

[34] See *Calder* v. *Attorney-General of British Columbia* (1973) 34 DLR (3d) 145 at 175; the language of usufruct appears to have first been used by the Supreme Court of Canada in *The St. Catharines Milling and Lumber Company* v. *The Queen* (1887) 13 SCR 577 at 604 ('so familiar in Roman law') and was used subsequently by the Judicial Committee of the Privy Council in *Amodu Tijani* v. *Secretary, Southern Nigeria* [1921] 2 AC 399 at 402–4; for comment see K. Lysyk, 'The Indian Title Question in Canada: An Appraisal in the light of *Calder*' (1973) 15 Can. Bar Rev. 450. On the underlying concept of title see Slattery, 'Understanding Aboriginal Rights' (1987); and for acquisition of property rights by 'prescription immémoriale' in New France, see A. Émond, 'Existe-t-il un titre indien originaire dans les territoires cédés par la France en 1763?' (1995) 41 Rev. dr. McGill 59. In Australia a similar view was reached in *Mabo and Others* v. *State of*

the past (as will be seen)[35] or of the present.[36] The boundary between bodies of law is once again difficult to establish. The Aztecs are also spoilers once again; they appeared in many ways to have preferred individual forms of entitlement to things.[37]

If the private law of obligations was unnecessary, it was and remains otherwise for the law of crime. Yet in a communal society lacking formal institutions there is little place for individual responsibility or institutional control. So crime becomes the responsibility of civil society, in the form of the groups, clans or families which make it up. Injury to a member was an injury to the group; injury caused by a member was the responsibility of the group. In the absence of formal courts (in most instances), reparation was by negotiation between groups, and by means either of payment or equivalent punishment. Absent negotiated agreement, there remained the blood feud, a powerful incentive to agreement. These are not refined instruments, and require investment of time and effort by members of the community to resolve radical anti-social conduct. Yet the role of criminal law was not great. There was to all intents and purposes no law of theft or burglary;[38] no law of drugs; no organized crime; no money laundering; no white collar crime; no fraud. The list could go on. Crime was a serious social wound, usually involving physical violence. It required the attention of the entire community and the objective was not to punish, but to restore community. If damage had been caused by an individual, the community would gather round, to deliberate sanction and rehabilitation. The 'sentencing circle' is now being deployed by some western courts in cases involving chthonic people.[39]

---

*Queensland (No. 2)* (1992) 107 ALR 1, 175 CLR 1; and for comment R. Lumb, 'Native Title to Land in Australia: Recent High Court Decisions' (1993) 42 Int. & Comp. Law Q. 84; C. Edwards, 'Australia: Accommodating Multi-culturalism in Law' in E. Örücü, E. Attwooll and S. Coyle, *Studies in Legal Systems: Mixed and Mixing* (The Hague/London/Boston: Kluwer, 1996) 53 at 66 ff.; H. Coombs, *Aboriginal Autonomy: Issues and Strategies* (Cambridge: Cambridge Univ. Press, 1994), notably ch. 17 ('The Mabo decision: a basis for Aboriginal autonomy'); B. Atwood, *In the Age of Mabo: History, Aborigines and Australia* (St. Leonards, Australia: Allen and Unwin, 1996). For the south Pacific, see notably P. Donigi, *Indigenous or Aboriginal Rights to Property: A Papua New Guinea Perspective* (Utrecht: International Books, 1994). In Africa the most frequently used expression appears to be 'customary land'. See P. McAuslan, 'Land Policy: A Framework for Analysis and Action' (1987) 31 J. African Law 185. As to the notion of chthonic law constituting 'custom' see below, this Chapter, *Law and the cosmos*.

[35] See below Ch. 5, *Roman law and law in Europe*.

[36] Such as, again, the Swiss Allmend (above, this paragraph), which has come all the way from the past (though the Swiss are less chthonic than they were) and more recent types of inalienability derived from lease or marital status.

[37] Margadant S., *Introducción a la historia del derecho mexicano* (1994), above, at 26.

[38] For the insignificance of theft even in Inuit society, where personal belongings were essential to survival, see Wesel *Frühformen des Rechts* (1985), above at 122, 123.

[39] See R. Green, *Justice in Aboriginal Communities: Sentencing Alternatives* (Saskatoon: Purich Publishing, 1998), dealing also with community sentencing panels, sentence advisory committees; cf., however, for illegal use of a sanction of banishment decided upon by chthonic people using such a circle, *R. v. Taylor* (1995) 132 DLR (4th) 323.

# THE WEB OF BELIEFS

Since there are no (well, few) formally designated actors in chthonic law there is no one whose activity can readily be designated as law. Law is thus not command, nor decision, and can be found only in the bran-tub of information which guides all forms of action in the chthonic community.[40] Does everything in the tradition constitute law? Western lawyers would probably say no to this question; chthonic people would probably not be very interested in trying to answer it. If law is somewhat differently defined, as sanction, the 'system' of sanctions is still too irregular to permit identification of what is law. There are no formal enforcers of sanctions; if a sanction is not applied now there may be larger, more important sanctions in some other world. So the law that we know is in there, in the chthonic tradition, is all mixed up with other things—how to cook, how to catch rabbits and deer, how to behave to one's family (in a very large sense), how to be honourable. We can't be too precise about this. *It just doesn't matter.* If we take law simply as some sort of social glue, among others and of whatever composition, chthonic peoples have it. If pressed, they can produce it, and even convince supreme courts of it, but there is something not quite chthonic in the process.

Chthonic law is thus inextricably interwoven with all the beliefs of chthonic people and is inevitably, and profoundly, infused with all those other beliefs. If there is chthonic law, and there is, you cannot understand it without understanding other things. There is no separation of law and morals, no separation of law and anything else. It's the old hidden ball play. Your side has to fan out to see what's going on. Moreover, if law is all mixed in with other important messages, it may not be appropriate to see it as just custom, just doing things over and over, just repetition. There may be more to chthonic law than simple custom, at least as some people presently understand it.

## LAW'S DOMAIN

Law may be indistinguishable from all else in the chthonic world, but it is not co-terminous with all else. Nor is it controlling over all else. Law has its place. This is an interesting phenomenon, given what we have seen of what we think we can call a chthonic legal tradition. The legal or adjudicative process is completely open; there is nothing to keep it from being inundated with complaints or procedures. Some notion of legislation was known, in some places at least, but legislation is almost

---

[40] 'Dinka law is not a dictate of the Augustinian sovereign, with coercive sanctions. Rather, it is an expression of the collective will of the community, inherited from the ancestors, generally respected and observed, sanctioned largely through persuasion or, if need be, spiritual curse as an ultimate resort.' F. Deng, 'A Cultural Approach to Human Rights among the Dinka,' in An-Na'im and Deng, *Human Rights in Africa:* (1990), above, 261 at 269.

imperceptible. So law had its place, and was kept in its place, not through formal obstacles or meta-rules, but simply by the ongoing presence, and vitality, of all else in the chthonic world. Religion was important in this (and will be returned to) but it was not an institutionalized religion. There were no courts or bailiffs; no restraining power. So religion in a sense was everywhere, but nowhere. Other forms of life simply had their own autonomy and were expected to function. They had their own regulatory mechanisms, which included persuasion and maybe a little self-help. Law was for when something went really wrong, or for external display. Even then it was likely to be all mixed up with other things—the trial with the meeting, the ownership with the use, the sanction with the healing.

So in being meshed with all else in society law does not get to call all the shots. It is too busy on the ground to reach a commanding position. Still more, its content is necessarily dictated by all else in the society. There are no distinct actors to give it formal content. The communal usufruct extends to the hunting and fishing that was actually done; extending it beyond this requires some fancy argument.[41] There is no way it can be turned into an abstract, western-style notion of full ownership, a right to use and abuse. Contemporary sociology would conclude that culture here controls the law, but chthonic societies did not function in terms of culture. They functioned in terms of tradition. So the nature of chthonic law—its source in the bran-tub—is a huge obstacle to legal ambition. The tradition gives everything its place, including that of law. If you want to change this, you have to put something into the tub, and see if it develops over time, with the help of others. There's not much you can do, yourself, to make a difference.

### REASON'S DOMAIN

Since law has its place, as defined by all else, there are important implications for present human rationality. Everyone knows the rationality is there. Everyone knows it can't somehow be gotten rid of, or suppressed. So it too will have to be given its place. There seems to be a number of ways of doing this.

Some forms of innovation (let's not talk just yet about 'change') seem to be acceptable. Agriculture emerged as something distinct from hunting and distinct from gathering. Someone must have noticed seeds actually growing. It was a small step, but an important one, to place seeds in the ground to grow.[42] Someone must have realized a sharp instrument was more effective than a blunt one, stone more resistant than wood. The wheel, too, seems to have been invented, many times over. It had to be re-invented because it kept getting forgotten, or put away. So innovation was possible, as a vehicle for rationality, but there were also evident limits. If

---

[41] This would not preclude evolution in use, however, compatible with the tradition, as to which see above, *On ways of life.*

[42] For the process of transition to agriculture occurring in the 9th and 8th millennia BC, and with possible reasons such as ecological change, see Wesel *Frühformen des Rechts* (1985), above, at 189.

you didn't like them, you had to leave. Yet there were other avenues for agile minds in the chthonic tradition. You had to work with it, in a way which continued to generate consensus, and the tradition didn't always say exactly what you wanted it to say. So interstitial rationality emerges, that which acknowledges the fragility of all traditions and seeks to use the resources of the chthonic one to prevent its dissolution. The sophistication of much of this thinking has been the object of recent writing.[43] Yet the inventiveness in working with the tradition is always, and only, the continuation of the tradition. The moment of decision is not charismatic and creative; even the actor will be at pains to show the reliance on existing knowledge. The notion of invention, of creation, is submerged in the long line of intellectual forebears. We are all add-ons to what has gone before; we cannot know ourselves the importance of what we may do. We decide, for reasons perhaps not yet entirely clear, not to invoke, or create, a tradition of present, autonomous rationality.

This restrained view of the importance of current events has important con-sequences for the concepts of chthonic law. Most importantly, since the present individual is submerged in the past and the wider community, there is no indi-vidual power—or potestas—to obtain the object of the individual will. There are no rights.[44] Even if rights are looked at as simple interests protected by law (a modern variant), then the law does not protect purely individual interests. This is evident in the law of the family (infants possibly excepted, but the community is interested in its members), the law of property, the law of crime. There are enor-mous obstacles to integrating a concept of rights into the chthonic tradition. The tradition stands four-square against it, on all fronts. You would have to work with the concept of rights to smuggle it into this intellectual fortress. Law is linked to everything else; how can it turn around the individual? 'It is because of the need to have someone blow out the speck of dust in one's eye that antelopes go in twos.'[45]

Chthonic law will therefore protect you, but you have few means of protecting yourself against it. You appear to have no negative rights, as a member of the community. Outsiders are worse off, so cannibalism is common, following justified violence.[46] Nor can you rely on any embedded notion of equality to escape the role which the tradition accords you. If no one can create the tradition, no one can escape its teaching and the roles it defines, except by departure (and there may be

---

[43] Levi-Strauss, *Pensée sauvage* (1962); C. Achebe, *The African Trilogy* (London: Picador, 1988); and on the situational, non-abstract type of thought found in oral traditions (hammer, saw, hatchet and log all placed together when requested to place similar objects together, refusal to recognize abstract concept of tool), see W. Ong, *Orality and Literacy: the Technologizing of the Word* (London/New York: Methuen, 1982) at 51–2; and on analogy as 'the essence of African adjudication', Allott, 'African Law' (1968) at 144.

[44] See M'Baye, 'African Conception of Law' (1975) at 138–9 (African law 'ignorant of law as a weapon placed in the individual's hands', Africans giving 'no importance to individual rights').

[45] Wiredu, 'Akan perspective on Human Rights' (1990), above, at 247.

[46] For well-documented and grisly examples in North America, see White, *The Middle Ground* (1991) at 4–6, 231, 501.

no place to go). This represents a classic problem that no one, anywhere, has solved. How can a communal form of organization avoid disequilibrium, and inequality, of social role? The chthonic legal tradition is perhaps the most democratic, or open, of all communal forms of social organization, yet it has not avoided differentiated and permanent roles. The woman is thus seen largely in terms of productive and pro-creative potential (though respected and guaranteed support).[47] Over time, some, even many, will find a static role intolerable. Why don't more leave? Why does the tradition continue to exert authority?

## LAW AND THE COSMOS

If you put this question to a chthonic person the reply may not satisfy you entirely. It may be formulated in ambiguous terms, such as a 'principle of respect' or 'a need for harmony'. If you persist you may find the discussion turning towards the religious, but it may not be the kind of religion western people are used to discuss-ing. Even if it is theistic, there is no church, no structure of implementation.[48] It may, however, be polytheistic (many gods) or even animistic (many, many gods, wherever you look).[49] Whatever the type of religion, and there are many in the chthonic world, the religion is regarded as a constant presence; hence the absence of formal structures. The forest is a church; the hunt, or harvest, a gift of god(s). The unstructured character of chthonic religions means the natural world is their best embodiment. The natural world is sacred; it may be more than a gift of god, it may be the gods themselves. There is no such thing (and this theme will be met again, in other traditions) as a secular world, or simple facts of nature. So the chthonic legal order is not simply compatible with chthonic religion; it is shot through with it. It is a divine legal tradition, and the role one plays is a divine role. This is not easily refused. It may take the unsettling effect of a still more divine order.

There are two large conclusions flowing from this teaching, which have been seen as highly relevant to current debate in the west. They relate to the environment and to animals. If the natural world is divine, it is not something to be chopped down,

---

[47] See, on the role of women in African and native American religions (and hence law), J. O'Connor, 'Rereading, reconceiving and reconstructing traditions: feminist research in religion' (1989) 17 *Women's St.* 101, notably at 114–17, notably on institutions of tradition to 'placate and sooth'; Hay and Wright, *African Women and the Law* (1982); Bennett, 'Human Rights and African Cultural Tradition' (1993), above at 273; Bennett, *Human Rights and African Customary Law* (1995), above, at 80 ff. (noting at 83 that position of women in Africa 'probably better' before colonization than now); and on 'the inequities inherent in the logic of the lineage system and its stratification on the basis of descent, age, and sex', Deng, 'Cultural Approach to Human Rights among Dinka' (1990), above, 261 at 273; cf., however, on conflicting anthropological reports on the equality of treatment of women and men in chthonic societies, Wesel, *Frühformen des Rechts* (1985) at 84 ff.

[48] On theistic chthonic orders see Schott, 'Triviates und Transzendentes' (1980) at 292 (God Nawen of Bulsa in Africa); Deng, 'Cultural Approach to Human Rights among Dinka' (1990), above, (God Nhialic of Dinka) at 264.

[49] Animism teaches that there are spirits in all natural things, animate and inanimate. If a tree has a soul, can it be denied standing? See the discussion below, *Chthonic topics.*

dug up, extracted and burned, or dumped upon. Would you do such things to your god or, if you don't have a god, to yourself? Chthonic law is thus environmentally friendly, in a way which most ecological debate in the west does not fully reflect. It is not just green; it is dark green. You don't have simply to repair damage to the environment; you and your kind have to live entire lives which accord as much respect to natural things as to yourself. Do unto all things as you would have them do unto you. Thus, if we are to have 'an ecological world-view . . . the inspiration must come from the world-view of vernacular societies, in particular from the chthonic world-view . . . the overriding goal of the behaviour pattern of an eco-logical society must be to preserve the critical order of the natural world'.[50] The laws of nature are neither descriptive nor positive; they are normative, and there is a moral duty to obey the law.[51]

Since animals are part of nature, they too enjoy its sanctity. There is no neces-sity of founding their entitlements on utilitarianism (their interest in not suffer-ing)[52] or on some extended notion of rights.[53] Nor can they be disentitled for their lack of speech, tradition and culture. They may have had it;[54] if not, the human tradition encompasses both human and animal life. The chthonic tradition thus avoids both mistreatment of animals for scientific purposes and the ferocious (western) debate as to how to criticize it. The west may not have to accept the chthonic world to change its treatment of animals, but its traditional position (for the last few centuries) is incapable of standing as a universal one, given the chthonic view.

If chthonic law carries all these heavy, if implicit, messages, how accurate is it to describe it as customary law? It depends on our concept of custom, but since at least the writings of Locke in the seventeenth century, our concept of custom has not been a very charitable one. This is reflected in recent western concepts of law, which come very close to eliminating custom entirely as a source of normativity. Custom became, with Locke, 'the *de facto* habits acquired by engaging in the practices and institutions of one's society, from the most primitive and least reflective to the most

---

[50] Goldsmith, *Way* (1992), above, at pp. xvii, xviii; and for one of many statements of the sacred character of the chthonic world, J. Olson and R. Wilson, *Native Americans in the Twentieth Century* (Urbana/Chicago: Univ. of Illinois Press, 1986) at 16 (soft moccasins used so as not to disturb the 'mother' of everything).

[51] For an opposed position of modern positivism see, e.g., J. Raz, 'The Obligation to Obey the Law,' in J. Raz, *The Authority of Law: Essays on Law and Morality* (Oxford: Clarendon Press, 1979) 233 at 233 ('there is no obligation to obey the law'); and for rigid chthonic controls over hunting, to prevent waste, see Goldsmith, *Way* (1992), above, at 256, 257.

[52] See P. Singer, *Animal Liberation*, 2nd edn. (New York: New York Review/Random House, 1990).

[53] See R. Regan, *The Case for Animal Rights* (Berkeley: Univ. of California Press, 1983). For the reasons why animals do not have rights, in traditional western rights theory, see Ch. 5, *The centrality of the person and the growth of rights*.

[54] S. Cohen, *The Intelligence of Dogs: Canine consciousness and capabilities* (New York/London: Free Press, 1994) at 46, for African story of how the dog decided to stop speaking, to avoid obvious duties of messenger. For the elephant world, see J. Masson and S. McCarthy, *When Elephants Weep: the Emotional Lives of Animals* (London: Jonathan Cape, 1994). Animals may also be seen as the ancestors of particular clans or bands of chthonic people.

civilised and enlightened'.[55] Earlier we saw a tendency to turn tradition into its present manifestation—the 'fact' of human adherence which, if repeated, appears as habit.[56] Tradition is just doing things over and over again. The same can be said of custom,[57] and both therefore lack rational justification and are cast out of the rational tradition. The rational tradition does this, however, by divorcing custom from its justification, from the reasons and information which lead to its ongoing performance. People who engage in explicitly rational activity are never said to be engaging in customary activity, even though millions do it every day and without really thinking about the thinking they are doing. So we should think of custom as the outcome of a particular tradition, the result of a process of massaging pre-existing information and deciding how to act. It is therefore the result of an entirely respectable mental process, and where it exists there is necessarily very persuasive pre-existing information to explain and justify it. Chthonic law is customary law in this sense; it is not customary law in the way customary law is (now) traditionally thought of. Perhaps it is better to just think of it as chthonic law.

## CHANGE AND THE NATURAL WORLD

You therefore adhere to chthonic tradition and to chthonic law because you believe the world, which is your world, depends on it. The past is normative because that which has lived in the past must be preserved. It must be preserved because it is sacred. The chthonic legal tradition is therefore profoundly conservationist. This suggests what has become known as 'immutable' tradition and 'hostility to change', but we should be becoming wary of accepting traditional designations of other traditions. What is the attitude of chthonic law to whatever it is which is called change?

Earlier it was suggested that the notion of change requires a particular notion of time, one which allows us to say that a particular thing has changed from what it

---

[55] Tully, *Strange Multiplicity* (1995) at 88, 89, citing Locke's *An essay concerning human understanding* (1690) and *Thoughts concerning education* (1694). For (rare) western dissents from traditional (post-Lockean) western views of custom, see C. Geertz, *Local Knowledge* (New York: Basic Books, 1983) at 208 (Adat law *not* custom; 'mischief done by the word "custom" in anthropology, where it reduced thought to habit, is perhaps only exceeded by that which it has done in legal history, where it reduced thought to practice'); O. Correa, 'La teoría general del derecho frente al derecho indígena' (1994) Crítica jurídica 15 at 21 (better to abandon concept of custom in dealing with chthonic law, use concepts of written and unwritten law). For western development of the concept of custom, see below, Ch. 5, *Law's expansion*.

[56] Above, Ch. 1, Tradition as Information: the Conceptual Bran-Tub and Ch. 1. Massaging Tradition.

[57] With precise consequences in law, such as the exclusion of 'customary law' from the reach of private international law as being simple repetition of facts, unless 'converted' into norms. See, e.g., Miaja de la Muela, *Derecho Internacional Privado*, vol. I (Madrid: 1954) at 292 ('nacido de una repetición de actos') as cited in C. Arellano García, *Derecho Internacional Privado*, 11th edn. (Mexico: Editorial Porrua, 1995) at 901.

was then to what it is now. This is usually referred to as a linear, or contingent, or historical notion of time.[58] It is a notion of time which is clearly predominant in the western world, where time is sliced up and counted in uncountable ways, and particularly in law. Another notion of time would see it, however, not as a race or as a flowing commodity, but as an envelope, an environment, which simply surrounds us as we live. Time would thus not be going anywhere; there would be no future identifiable as such; nor would there be a past—of dead, irrelevant time—since time is always with us. There is much writing which suggests that the chthonic notion of time has been predominantly this latter one of time standing still.[59] Here again, however, there is probably much variation in the chthonic world,[60] so we cannot be too affirmative in constructing definitive attitudes. Yet much of the teaching of the chthonic tradition is explicitly or implicitly supportive of a non-linear concept of time. What are the implications of this for change?

If time simply surrounds us, so there is no past and no future, then a first conclusion is that there is no valid temporal distinction between the dead, the living, and the yet to be born. The dead may be dead, but they are not dead and gone, disappearing somehow into the folds of past time, or into heaven, or into hell. You may therefore communicate with the dead, since they are still here, and in the chthonic world there are ceremonies for communication with the dead, strongly disapproved of by western religions. And the yet-to-be-born are simply yet to be born. It is not that their day has not yet arrived; all days are their days as they are our days. It is simply that they cannot now give voice to whatever they might want to say. So the conservationist chthonic legal tradition is also a tradition of inter-generational equity. The community is composed without regard to the accidents of birth and death. It includes the ancestors, and the successors.[61] This is a profound reinforcement of the conservationist character of the tradition, since we now know

[58] Above, Ch. 1, The Changing Presence of the Past.

[59] Goldsmith, *Way* (1992), above, at 108; F. Ost, 'Les multiples temps du droit' in *Le droit et le futur: travaux et recherches de l'Université de Paris II, Serie Philosophie du droit—2* (Paris: Presses universitaires de France, 1985) 115, 119–21; White, *Middle Ground* (1991) at 442; Ong, *Orality and Literacy* (1982), above, at 98 (in oral tradition, past not felt as 'an itemized terrain, peppered with verifiable and disputed "facts" or bits of information'; rather 'resonant source for renewing awareness of present existence'; Olson and Wilson, *Native Americans in Twentieth Century* (1986), above, at 17–18 (notion of 'expanded present'); and for the compatibility of a chthonic notion of time with that of contemporary science, see above, Ch. 1, The Changing Presence of the Past.

[60] Goldsmith, *Way* (1992), above, at 103 (differences among vernacular societies); S. Pinker, *The Language Instinct* (New York: Harper Perennial, 1995) at 63, challenging Whorf's description of Hopi concept of time, particularly given Hopi use of descriptors of time, such as days, seasons, etc. Yet anyone living on this earth will distinguish this day from the one which preceded, separated by night. The larger question appears to be whether, taken together, the days, nights, etc., are going anywhere, or whether every year it is just the same old routine—day, night, etc. One can think of days, without thinking of time in an historical, linear manner. For Mayan use of 20-year markers, in monument form, see Roberts, *History of World* (1995), above, at 466.

[61] Goldsmith, *Way* (1992), above, at 110; and for consequences in law see David and Brierley, *Major Legal Systems* (1985) at 550 (land belonging to past, present and future generations, hence inalienable): M'Baye 'African Conception of Law' (1975) at 142 (death affects body only, not soul which continues to live; death only passing from material to superior immaterial life, funerals therefore featuring rejoicing).

there are present members of the community (though not yet born) for whose benefit the natural world must be preserved. We are not simply making our own decisions about the environment; we also act as surrogate for all those whose dependency on the natural world will come about once we have died. These are not stakeholders. They are not people who stand outside a thing declaring their interest in it, which could be transferred to something else. They are an inextricable, sacred part of the sacred whole. To destroy the environment is thus to commit a double wrong—to that which is immediately destroyed, and to all that which may be dependent on it, wherever this occurs in the envelope of time. Environmentalists in the western world have been much impressed with the idea of inter-generational obligations; it is an idea which speaks to all traditions.[62]

Where is the change in all of this? You can find it if you really want to. There is change in going from a living being to a dead being. There is change from night to day, summer to winter, warm to cold. There is a change from hunting to farming, as a means of subsistence. It's always a different river you step into. If you look at the world this way, however, you are not looking at it the chthonic way. Of course the seasons vary. You may even say the world dies every winter. Yet it must be made to re-live and all have an obligation to make it re-live. The world must be re-cycled. What is important is that it continue to be the world and continue to support all the beings that seek to live within it. So chthonic lives can be different from one another, and a given life can be different in one season from what it was in a previous season, but if the life is in harmony with the world, not inexhaustibly depleting it, there is no change in the life of the world. Those yet to be born will find it as supporting as we have found it. The rest is simply the normal process of existence. To call it change is simply myopic.

So there is a great deal of flexibility in chthonic existence,[63] though it is not seen as change because the perspective is different. The nature of the tradition very much controls the perception of change. Things may not be the same, but this is normal and not anything drastic enough to give a name to. The chthonic tradition is therefore not seen as unduly restrictive by those who adhere to it. If they need to live another kind of life they are perfectly free to do so. There are limits, but the limits are for everyone's benefit, and so the tradition says.

---

[62] See, e.g., E. B. Weiss, 'Our Rights and Obligations to Future Generations for the Environment' (1990) 84 Am. J. Int. Law 198; H. Ph. Hooft, 'On Justice between Generations with the Environmental Context' in Pre-prints, 17th World Congress of Philosophy of Law, Bologna, 1995, vol. III, at 120 (concept of sustainable society with clear implication of an equitable sharing of resources with future populations 'is on its way to becoming a fundamentally new starting point for the definition of social and economic aims'); and generally G. Brundtland, *Our Common Future* (Oxford/New York: Oxford Univ. Press, 1987).

[63] Slattery, 'Understanding Aboriginal Rights' (1987) at 747, 748; Trigger, *Children of Aataentsic* (1976) at 841 (Huron people never in 'equilibrium'; 'change' more rapid after 1000 AD); A. N. Allott, 'The Changing Law in a Changing Africa' (1961) 11 Sociologus (n. s.) 115; Allott, 'African Law' (1968) at 140 ('impression one derives is not that of unthinking adherence to immutable principle but precisely the reverse'); Goldsmith, *Way* (1992), above, at 110, 116; and on the evolutive character of aboriginal rights, *R. v. Van der Peet* (1996) 137 DLR (4th) 289.

What about changing the tradition, or seriously changing the real world? What about innovation? What happens then in the chthonic tradition? What does it do to people who advance such ideas, or projects? Its adherents will clearly try to hang on to them, through discussion within the terms of the tradition. The stirring of the bran-tub will be more intense. There are real problems of appreciation here, and endless range for interpretation. What projects are ultimately sufficiently dangerous for the world to be outside the tradition? To what extent would the tradition be changed by acknowledging them? There is here no real difference between the teaching and the world; the word and the being. They all teach; they are all sacred. So in all instances it is a question of trying to determine their limits, given that the tradition is not one of detail. It says to preserve the world, but it does not present a permissible depletion rate of given natural resources. If soapstone is OK, what about bronze, then gold, then oil? The tradition only survives by constant decisions, based on previous decisions, and hence previous information.

So the best view appears to be that the tradition has a fundamental core—the sacred character of the world—which cannot change. If this changes, by change of word or by change of deed, then the chthonic tradition and the chthonic people no longer exist. It is not that the tradition is immutable; it is simply vulnerable. It is open to endless debate as to its interpretation and application; it can be rejected in its most fundamental teaching and disappear. This theme will be a recurring one for many, if not all, traditions. The chthonic tradition has been rejected many times, by those within it who wished to create a better way, and by those within it who perceived an alternative, existing, better way. So the tradition cannot simply tell its members what it has always told them; it has to show why other ways are not better ways.

## CHTHONIC WAYS AND OTHER WAYS

The chthonic way is thus an unstructured one, which literally seeks to blend into the surrounding landscape. This is why people adhering to chthonic ways offered only sporadic resistance to western expansion when it occurred. Put differently, chthonic peoples did not have a sharp, and institutionalized, sense of their own identity when western people arrived amongst them. They knew who they were, in the sense of having a social memory, a tradition,[64] but the sense of identity in relation to the other, a self-consciousness, had not fully developed, absent contact. Many of the names of chthonic peoples thus are simply the equivalent of 'human

---

[64] For memory as constitutive of identity, see above, Ch. 2 *Tradition, races and states.*

being', such as Apache, Comanche, Khoi-khoi, Egyptian, Bantu and Roma.[65] Humanity emerges as an abstract concept only as the boundaries of social knowledge expand. Humanity is the sum of us and them. For this to occur, however, the knowledge had to develop that there is a difference between us and them. Criteria of social differentiation had to emerge.

Recent critics of chthonic claims have referred to them as hyper-romantic and marked by racism or racialism, with identity being transmitted by blood line. This is an important question, but the process of identification appears to have been much more complex. We have some record of arguments used to maintain the coherence of chthonic peoples, faced with varying forms of western proselytism. The westerners put the general proposition that traditional practices were not innate but were transferable from one people to another. Chthonic people could thereby become western (and the reverse must hold as well). The response of chthonic people was not one based on race, or at least not exclusively. There was rather a full barrage of all the arguments that could be thought of—a mixture of merits and loyalties. A Peoria chief put the case for traditional medicine: 'Has this man who has come from afar better medicines than we have, to make us adopt his customs? His fables are good only in his own country; we have ours, which do not make us die as his do.'[66] A Kaskaskia elder was more concerned with loyalty: 'Leave their myths to the people who come from afar, and let us cling to our own traditions.'[67] There is no explicit call to race in these statements, only substance (the medical debate goes on today, with even more vigour) and identity, though undefined. Anthropologists tell us that some conception of identity based on birth was operative, but tempered in major ways by possibilities of adoption and, more importantly, by residence (many groups' names being those of place).[68] We also know that identity based on birth is only presumptive, since exit has been massively practised and without apparent sanction. So the charge of racism seems inaccurate, though race, whatever it is, is never entirely excluded in encountering others. The defining criterion of identity appears rather the information people chose to adhere to, which is mostly substantive but partly definitional. Race occupies no great place in the process, since it possesses very little persuasive power and has no substantive content. The 'white man' and the 'redskins' had and have their place in popular

---

[65] J. Rüsen, 'Human Rights from the Perspective of a Universal History' in Schmale, (ed.), *Human Rights and Cultural Diversity* (1993), above, 28 at 41.

[66] White, *Middle Ground* (1991) at 59.

[67] Ibid.

[68] N. Rouland, 'Les fondements anthropologiques des droits de l'homme', 25 Rev. gén. dr. (1994–5) at 37 (highest expression of chthonic identity found in territorial rights); Hoebel, *Law of Primitive Man* (1961) at 295; Wesel, *Frühformen des Rechts* (1985) at 213 (first sense of identity that of inhabitant of village), 219; for use of territory in definition of south-east Asian adat groups, see below, ch. 9, *Adat law and chthonic law*; for current scientific attitudes towards criteria for human grouping, see the discussion above, ch. 2, *Tradition, races and states*; and for the importance of geography in recognizing human groups, absent scientific possibility of doing so by a single physical criterion, S. Molnar, *Human Variation: Races, Types, and Ethnic Groups*, 2nd edn. (Englewood Cliffs, NJ: Prentice-Hall, 1983) at 131.

culture—they exist as counterpoints or corruptions of the informational means of identity used in the real debate. So too do notions of 'native', 'aboriginal', or 'indigenous peoples' tell us little about why chthonic people should remain chthonic, given western, islamic or other alternatives. The means of identification used by chthonic people themselves consisted of the most persuasive information they could assemble. The tradition had to continue to convince, or the people would lose their identity.[69]

So chthonic law, as inextricably linked with all parts of chthonic tradition, plays in part an instrumental role of identification of chthonic peoples. It does so, however, in the most abstract and general way, since it allows great flexibility on the ground, in permitting manifold forms of social organization (the transition from one to another not even constituting 'change') and in enforcing a generalized respect for the natural world only in an imprecise and unstipulated manner. Law is also defined communally and over time, so this partially instrumental character of chthonic law is not subject to immediate control by any particular individuals or particular groups.

## CHTHONIC AND OTHER IDENTITIES

There are no pure chthonic traditions in the world today. Since the expansion of western and islamic traditions, all chthonic peoples have recently seen their total information base expand, incorporating western or islamic ideas, or both. So in the absence of pure chthonic traditions there are no purely chthonic people (and the same may be said of many other types of people today). The great debate is as to the extent to which the 'new' information will have an impact on previously leading versions of the tradition, sway its people from their previous identity in some measure, or even displace the core information or belief of the tradition. So with the increase in means of communication between traditions,[70] we are now benefiting from an intense debate between chthonic and non-chthonic people, and between people within their particular traditions, as to the respective merits of chthonic and non-chthonic information.

The exchange of information with the chthonic tradition is facilitated by the open character of the tradition. Lacking precise institutional definition, and lacking exclusive sources, it is unable to define itself in such a way as to preclude entry of non-chthonic information. It is true that the tradition is defined in terms of chthonic information, as transmitted by chthonic people, but this is simply what a tradition is. The chthonic tradition appears to have developed no more precise means of protecting itself from the influence of outside information. So not only

[69] 'Tradition was the storehouse of a tribal people's *knowledge of themselves as a people* and a guide to how they should act' (emphasis added). White, *Middle Ground* (1991) at 57.

[70] See above, Ch. 2, Persuasive Authority: Creating New (and Old) Epistemic Communities, and on chthonic use of the Internet to argue their case, below, this Chapter, *Chthonic peoples, states and human rights*.

could western settlement occur, absent adequate institutional opposition, but western proselytizing could occur in such a way that there was always an audience for it. Colonial education also did much to eliminate chthonic forms of education, and hence to eliminate the traditio of chthonic tradition.[71] Spontaneous syncretism is everywhere the order of the day. A 'middle ground' is created—a 'place in between'.[72] Yet the continuing existence of chthonic tradition indicates that openness and vulnerability are not the dominant criteria in the ongoing life of a tradition. Much more would appear to depend on what the tradition says.

## THE STATE AS MIDDLE GROUND

The greatest indicator of the interdependent character of chthonic identity today is the state. There are now no chthonic peoples in the world who do not live within a state, which is a non-chthonic construction. Yet if the state is in crisis today this is at least partly due to its losing its grip on chthonic peoples, who never made it entirely their own and now appear less convinced of its virtues. Within states the relation of chthonic tradition to the western tradition of the state (however it may have been received within a particular territory) is complex and variable. Two basic models are evident. On the one hand there is the state constructed by western powers in colonized territories, which persists following withdrawal of western authority. On the other hand there is the state constructed by western powers in the process of permanent settlement in colonized territories, which persists as an ongoing instrument of western authority.

Africa and south-east Asia present examples of the first model of present chthonic–state relations. There appears to be no uniform pattern between the two. In south-east Asia the state appears to prosper, at least to the extent that it is a vehicle in the expanding south-east Asian economies. Yet here the relation is not simply chthonic–state; it is also trilateral, since both exist in a wider context of Asian tradition, which appears to place its own more definitive stamp on both. In Africa the contrast between (declining) western tradition and chthonic tradition is more evident. Even at the height of colonial power, there was no effort to eliminate the chthonic legal tradition, or traditions. Personal laws were maintained by both English and French imperial authority. In the English model imperial control was indirect and existing law continued to prevail, except to the extent it was specifically displaced by English legislation, and this occurred usually only in the domains of criminal and public law. French rule was more direct, and a specific option was

---

[71] Goldsmith, *Way* (1992), above, at 285 ('The colonial powers sought to destroy the cultural patterns of traditional societies largely because many of their essential features prevented traditional people from subordinating social, ecological and spiritual imperatives to the short-term economic ends served by participation in the colonial economy . . . the young were deprived of that traditional knowledge which alone could make them effective members of their societies').

[72] White, *Middle Ground* (1991) at p. x, distinguishing the middle ground from a process of acculturation in which a dominant group is largely able to dictate conduct to a subordinate group.

available for chthonic peoples to opt for French law, including private law.[73] Inevitably, some did. In both models, however, the effect of the arrival of European law was not automatically detrimental to chthonic tradition. European courts could be used for purposes of enforcing chthonic ways, and there are reports of chthonic tradition being considerably reinforced by the provision of state-derived means of sanction.[74]

Today the state persists, and in terms of formal, state law, African states can be divided between those following, in broad terms, common law models (generally in east Africa) and those following civil law ones (more specifically French, and generally in west Africa). Some, such as Cameroon, share both. 'And so, in law, the quest for morally appropriate institutions eventually incorporates at least some of what is imported.'[75] Yet the state in Africa is not the institution it is elsewhere. It is corrupt in a debilitating way (more on this later) and exists as a kind of 'pays légal', distinct and distant from the mass of people, who look, absent a viable alternative, to old ways as means of sustenance. Yet the old ways are not what they were, debilitated by labour migration, partial industrialization, urbanization, and more generally by both capitalism and christianity.[76] The 'middle ground' may here resemble more a 'no-man's land' and there is growth of parasitic traditions of crime. Traditions can speak to one another, and exchange information, but there can also be a process of mutual destruction. The colonial experience was not a happy one during its life; its residue may be still more disquieting. Yet there are signs of both vigour and tolerance in contemporary Africa, though the ground be often barren and dry.

[73] P. Gannagé, 'La pénétration de l'autonomie de la volonté dans le droit international privé de la famille,' Rev. crit. d. i. p. 1992. 425 at 433, with references; Sacco et al., Il diritto africano (1995) at 206, 207.

[74] See, e.g., Schott, 'Triviales und Transzendentes' (1980) at 293 (British arrival in Ghana strengthening the hand of chthonic leaders, co-opted by British) and 295 (chthonic traditions enforced in British courts). Western-style courts have even been seen as constitutive of 'customary' law, and in the measure that such law was articulated as specific and positive rules, this may have been in some measure the case. See, for discussion, Bennett, 'Human Rights and African Cultural Tradition' (1993), above, at 274, 275 (though, '[p]resent scepticism is due in large part to a greater awareness of the intellectual biases of previous generations of scholars'); M. Chanock, Law, Custom and Social Order: the Colonial Experience in Malawi and Zambia (Cambridge: Cambridge Univ. Press, 1985), notably at 8–10, 22 and passim, for relations between English law and African 'customary' law; M. T. Sierra, 'Indian Rights and Customary Law in Mexico: A Study of the Nahuas in the Sierra de Puebla' (1995) 29 Law & Society Rev. 227 (also on chthonic peoples astutely picking and choosing between chthonic and western law); W. J. Mommsen and J. A. de Moor (eds.), European Expansion and Law: the Encounter of European and Indigenous Law in 19th-and 20th-Century Africa and Asia (Oxford/New York: Berg Publishers, 1992), notably at 3–7 on 'interaction' and 'unequal bargains' between European and indigenous law.

[75] D. Horowitz, 'The Qur'an and the Common Law: Islamic Law Reform and the Theory of Legal Change' (1994) Am. J. Comp. Law 543 at 578; this would follow attempts to return to 'frozen tradition' (citing A. Memmi, The Colonizer and the Colonized (1965) at 137); and see G. Kouassigan, Quelle est ma loi? Tradition et modernisme dans le droit privé de la famille en Afrique noire francophone (Paris: Editions Pedone, 1974). The influence of western law is evident in estimates that Africa today would contain only some 14 million 'autochtonous' people, out of a total population of some 400 to 500 millions. See Rouland, Pierré-Caps and Poumarède, Droit des minorités (1996) at 15, 16.

[76] See generally Bennett, 'Human Rights and African Cultural Tradition' (1993), above, at 274; though for the remarkable resilience of chthonic law in Africa, Sacco, et al., Il diritto africano (1995) at 169, 197.

The second model of chthonic–state relations are provided by the Americas and Australasia, where the European presence was in the form of permanent settlement. Here the variations have much to do with the European legal traditions which European settlers carried with them. The common law was the least explicit about chthonic peoples, and even where English common law was received by the effect of statute, common law judges were still called upon to decide the extent of its displacement, if any, of chthonic law for chthonic people. There are no uniform responses to this question, which is fitting for a case-law tradition,[77] though the massive character of European settlement has generally been debilitating for chthonic law, particularly when combined with the notion, prevalent in North America north of Mexico, of the 'reservation' (separate land) for chthonic peoples.[78] Civil law powers, such as Spain and France, were more systematic in incorporation of metropolitan law into non-metropolitan territories, or to put it into civilian terms, all are entitled to the benefit of metropolitan law.[79] This did not

---

[77] For the existence of what is close to a principle of personal laws for chthonic people in Canada, the result of the work of common law judges, see H. P. Glenn, 'The Common Law in Canada' (1995) Can. Bar Rev. 261 at 277.

[78] Black Elk spoke in these terms: 'Up on the Madison Fork the Wasichus had found much of the yellow metal that they worship and that makes them crazy, and they wanted to have a road up through our country to the place where the yellow metal was . . . They told us that they wanted only to use a little land, as much as a wagon would take between the wheels; but our people knew better. And when you look about you now, you can see what it was they wanted . . . [T]hey have made little islands for us and other little islands for the four-leggeds, and always these islands are becoming smaller, for around them surges the gnawing flood of the Wasichu; and it is dirty with lies and greed . . . [M]y father told me what his father told him, that there was once a Lakota holy man, called Drinks Water, who . . . said: 'When this happens, you shall live in square gray houses, in a barren land, and beside those square gray houses you shall starve.' *Black Elk Speaks: Being the Life Story of a Holy Man of the Aglala Sioux (as told through J. G. Neihardt)* (Lincoln Nebr./London: Univ. of Nebraska Press, 1988) at 99, 100; and see H. Robertson, *Reservations are for Indians* (Toronto: James Lorimer, 1970); W. Canby Jr., *American Indian Law in a Nutshell* (St. Paul, Mich.: West Publishing, 1988) at 16–19 (US policy of removal of chthonic peoples from settlement territories and creation of reservations); R. Clinton, N. Newton and M. Price, *American Indian Law: Cases and Materials*, 3rd. edn. (Charlottesville, Va.: The Michie Company, 1991) at 146, 147, and see 1201 ff. (useful comparative surveys of treatment of chthonic peoples in Canada, New Zealand, Australia, Brazil, Venezuela, Nicaragua and South Africa); R. Cooter and W. Fikent-scher, 'Indian Common Law' (1998) 46 Am. J. Comp. Law 287 (pt. 1) and 509 (pt. 2) ('distinctively Indian' social norms pervading tribal courts); and for the practice of reservations in the world, with 'all its ambiguity', see Rouland, Pierré-Caps and Poumarède, *Droits des minorités* (1996) at 375 ff.

[79] Hence much of the western legal theory now relied upon by chthonic peoples in the Americas and Australasia has its roots in Spanish legal and theological writing, notably that of Vitoria, who insisted that rights granted by papal authority to the Spanish crown could not be extended beyond the goal of christianization and that chthonic peoples were as entitled as Spanish authority and Spanish settlers to ownership of land in the Americas. On the ground, however, this did not always occur, and the brutality of the Spanish conquest provoked continuing re-evaluation of the theoretical foundations of colonialism. On Vitoria, see Margadant S., *Introducción a la historia del derecho mexicano*, (1994), above, at 60; Cumming and Mickenberg, *Native Rights in Canada* (1972) at 14, 15, with references; Williams, *American Indian in Western Legal Thought* (1990) at 97–108 (Vitoria's defence of indian rights under natural law not emancipating, however, indians from guardianship of christian Europeans; Spain could still conquer and colonize indians of Americas for refusing to hear the truth of the christian religion); Rouland, Pierré-Caps and Poumarède, *Droits des minorités* (1996) at 114–16; A. Pagden, *Lords of all the World: Ideologies of Empire in Spain, Britain and France c. 1500–c. 1800* (New Haven/London: Yale Univ. Press, 1995) at 46–52.

mean total displacement of chthonic law, though it existed henceforth within a civilian legislative cadre, and inevitably suffered decline in this formal enclosure. 'Indian law' in latin America is not the law of chthonic people; it is all the law of the metropolitan power relating to the territory of the new Indies, and chthonic law is a very small part of it, usually existing contra legem and in rural areas, such as Chiapas in Mexico.[80] Again, however, European institutions support in some measure chthonic tradition, and chthonic people in the United States, Canada, Australia and New Zealand have been skilful in using independent courts as fora for affirmation of their tradition. The clearest air for inter-traditional legal exchange is thus in a guaranteed middle ground, if this can be found. What are some examples of the current exchange of chthonic and western legal information?

## CHTHONIC TOPICS

The influence of chthonic thought on the environmental debate in the west has already been noted. The response has been at many levels: philosophical,[81] economic[82] and legal.[83] No winner has yet been declared. What chthonic thought represents is a radical alternative, intellectually coherent and with thousands of years of experience and application. All other shades of green become tested against it, in terms of feasibility and results. The externalities of western thought can therefore no longer be ignored. This traditionally neglected area of the western tradition has now become perhaps its most vulnerable feature. If the world is transformed into an ozone-depleted junk–yard, it may not be the immediate result of any rational construction, but the responsibility will rest somewhere.[84]

The chthonic concept of the legal relations between human beings and land is also one which has generated enormous reflection in the western world. The use of

[80] See A. Burguete Cal y Mayor, 'Autonomía indígena' in *V Jornadas Lascasianas, Etnicidad y derecho un diálogo postergado entre los científicos sociales*, (Mexico: Instituto de investigaciones jurídicas, 1996) 57.

[81] See L. Ferry, *Le nouvel ordre écologique: l'arbre, l'animal et l'homme* (Paris: Grasset, 1992) (chthonic view still anthropomorphic, since consists in humans stating what nature wants; much of nature savage and inharmonious; preference for indirect duties, towards nature).

[82] See E. F. Schumacher, *Small is Beautiful: a Study of Economics as if People Mattered* (London: Blond & Briggs, 1973); J. E. Cohen, *How Many People can the Earth Support?* (New York/London: W. W. Norton, 1995); for diversity of economic views, however, see J. Simon (ed.), *The State of Humanity* (Oxford/Cambridge, Mass.: Blackwell & The Cato Institute, 1995), notably at 7 ('all aspects of material human welfare are improving in the aggregate'), 642 ('The material conditions of life will continue to get better for most people, in most countries, most of the time, indefinitely').

[83] The concept of environmental law is one which has emerged only in the last quarter of this century, and is now taught and practised in both national and international forms. The classic article is C. Stone, 'Should Trees have Standing?—Toward Legal Rights for Natural Objects' (1972) 45 S. Calif. Law Rev. 450.

[84] 'The whole attitude of using technology as a method of fighting the world will succeed only in destroying the world, as we are doing. We use absurd and uninformed and shortsighted methods of getting rid of insect pests, forcing our fruit and tomatoes to grow, stripping our hills of trees and so on, thinking that this is some kind of progress. Actually, it is turning everything into a junk heap.' A. Watts, *The Philosophies of Asia* (Boston/Rutland, Vt/Tokyo: Charles E. Tuttle, 1995) at 57.

western courts to affirm and protect chthonic use of land has already been noted;[85] it has become an inextricable dimension of contemporary chthonic land use. More generally, recognition of multiple forms of ownership and use of land—of pluralism in legally defined relations with the soil—has emerged as a technique in itself for long-term maintenance of the earth. Chthonic law may be recognized, but regulated in a western manner to prevent over-use. Formal western systems of ownership can be used in urban areas, but should not be overextended to disrupt chthonic use in rural areas (creating inequities) or to attempt regulation of ongoing development of the 'informal' sector (the unofficial market, controlled by practice and use, in urban peripheries).[86]

Chthonic thought in matters of crime and criminal repression also provides an ongoing alternative to western practices of determination of individual guilt and incarceration. The costs of prisons are enormous, and accelerating. Chthonic people don't have any. The Cree do not have a word for guilt.[87] Yet chthonic people, in many instances, are the principal occupants of prisons. How much violence and crime must be perpetrated in western societies before someone decides to try something else? The process has already begun, at least in small measures. The sentencing circle is one example, at least for chthonic peoples.[88] Reconciling different views of criminal conduct was a necessary process on the arrival of European peoples in chthonic territories.[89] The necessity appears to be re-emerging.

## CHTHONIC PEOPLES, STATES AND HUMAN RIGHTS

The most vigorous contemporary discussion generated by the revival of chthonic legal tradition concerns the relations of chthonic peoples to state structures. This inevitably puts into question the state structures themselves. It also raises the question of rights for chthonic people. The constitutional debate on the legal position of chthonic peoples is intense, since it is in the nature of western constitutionalism to formally define all relations of power and authority within the state. The process is not incremental, as with the common law process of recognizing, in precise cases, application of chthonic law. It is rather global (all problems must be resolved) and charismatic (in a present document). There are now some two to three million people in the world seeking some form of constitutional recognition of their existence, as a group, and some form of self-government.[90] How can self-government be assured, within a state? The eighteenth- and nineteenth-century notions of an

---

[85] Above, this Chapter, *On ways of life.*

[86] See McAuslan, 'Land Policy' (1987), above, notably at 195–201, on notion of overlapping circles of land use, each presenting advantages but none capable of exclusive dominion.

[87] T. Chalifoux, 'A Need for Change: Cross-cultural Sensitization of Lawyers' (1994) 32 Alberta L. Rev. 762.

[88] See above, this Chapter, *On ways of life.*

[89] White, *Middle Ground* (1991) at 75–83, on reconciling chthonic and French concepts of murder and its punishment/reparation.

[90] Tully, *Strange Multiplicity* (1995) at 3.

indivisible sovereignty are here in question, and vigorous pleas are now being made 'of the need to retrace our steps, recover the arguments' by which more ancient forms of constitutionalism allowed recognition, consent and continuity of peoples.[91] The position of chthonic peoples, and chthonic law, represents the most vivid argument in favour of 'differential citizenship'.[92] Chthonic peoples do not represent the new diasporas; they are arguing on the basis of a prior claim. Present constitutions, it is therefore said, must be shaken out, to become more inclusive, less conflictual, more accommodating of cultural diversity through deployment of a wider range of constitutional devices. The development of a specialized tribunal in New Zealand for adjudication of chthonic land claims is an example of a looser form of constitutional structure.[93]

Contemporary state structures in the west are dominated by notions of rights, either embedded in primary constitututional documents or as fundamental concepts of legal thinking generally. Rights have become the object of international declarations.[94] Since all chthonic peoples dwell in territories of established states, their enjoyment of rights follows as a logical consequence of the existence of state structures which surround them. Yet the responses to this question vary widely, and there is much to be said for each of the responses. It may be that each response is entitled to some recognition, in variable manner and depending on national and chthonic particularities. Where constitutional documents impose a monolithic form of rights analysis, chthonic opposition is founded on the particular, and distinct, form of chthonic law. Rights analysis is here not protective and enabling; it is rather a form of cultural and legal domination.[95] Use of rights analysis by chthonic peoples would thus constitute 'an instrument for the recognition of historical

[91] Ibid. at 184 ('a contemporay constitution . . . should be seen as an activity, an intercultural dialogue, in which the culturally diverse sovereign citizens of contemporary society negotiate agreements'). The ancient constitutions are not necessarily those of the western world; the Hurons had confederacy, and chthonic peoples generally had many forms of alliance.

[92] W. Kymlicka, *Liberalism, Community and Culture* (Oxford: Oxford Univ. Press, 1989) at 151, arguing principally in terms of constitutional recognition of chthonic peoples and (at 147) in terms of 'a continuum of possibilities, involving greater or lesser guarantees of power for aboriginal people, and greater or lesser restrictions on the mobility and political rights of non-aboriginal people'.

[93] See P. McHugh, *The Maori Magna Carta: New Zealand Law and the Treaty of Waitangi* (Auckland: Oxford Univ. Press, 1991); P. McHugh, 'The Constitutional Role of the Waitangi Tribunal' (1985) NZLJ 224; I. Kawharu, *Waitangi: Maori and Pakeha Perspectives of the Treaty of Waitangi* (Auckland: Oxford Univ. Press, 1989); K. Keith, 'The Roles of the Tribunal, the Courts and the Legislature' (1995) 25 Victoria Univ. Wellington Law Rev. 129; A. Sharp, *Justice and the Maori*, 2nd edn. (Auckland/Oxford: Oxford Univ. Press, 1997).

[94] On the emergence and present status of rights in western thought, see below, Chs. 5 & 7.

[95] See, e.g., M. E. Turpel, 'Aboriginal Peoples and the *Canadian Charter*: Interpretive Monopolies, Cultural Differences' (1989–90) 6 Can. Hum. R. Yrbk 3, notably at 4 ('objective . . . to call into question the cultural authority of the *Canadian Charter*), 20 ('The legal textual and interpretive context in which collective rights would have to be advanced is so foreign to Aboriginal people, so abstract and removed from their own social or political context, that simply making a claim requires accepting the dominant cultural and conceptual framework') and 30 ('the conceptions of law are simply incommensurable'). On the notion of incommensurability, however, here used outside a purely western context, see above, Ch. 2, Commensurability: Of Apples and Oranges.

claims of cultural difference . . . the *only* (or last) resort'.[96] Elsewhere there is more reception to rights implementation. This appears particularly the case in Africa, where rights proponents advance two distinct theses. The first would see rights, and the means of their implementation, as essential instruments in the struggle against political regimes which are arbitrary, despotic and corrupt. Of these characteristics, corruption appears most frequent. Its existence may have something to do here with the laying of state structures over existing familial or tribal loyalties, which continue to prevail over the apparently arbitrary even-handedness of the state.[97] Rights here are western in character, formalized in documents and requiring vigorous judicial intervention for their protection. The argument is that you cannot adopt the western tradition in part only; its corruption requires western means of correction.[98] A second thesis would draw on the increasing ambiguity of rights discussion in the west, to find at least collective rights ('intersubjective' or 'polysubjective')[99] which would in many instances be superior to particular western rights.[100] The totality of chthonic tradition could thus serve the goal of human dignity as effectively as a western code of human rights.[101] In some instances the sacred

[96] Turpel, 'Aboriginal Peoples and the *Canadian Charter*' (1989–90), above, at 33; cf., however, for the view that 'Aboriginal rights' would constitute 'a set of norms that are fundamentally intercommunal, created not by the dictation of one society, but by the interaction of various societies through time', see J. Webber, 'Relations of Force and Relations of Justice: The Emergence of Normative Community between Colonists and Aboriginal Peoples' (1995) 33 Osgoode Hall L. J. 623, notably at 626; and generally the discussion of interaction between European and 'indigenous' laws, above, this Chapter *The state as middle ground*.

[97] Sacco, 'Mute Law' (1995), above, at 463 ('They feel righteous. If caught, they feel like martyrs'); Moore, *Social Facts and Fabrications* (1986) at 315 ('supplies and services are distributed in anything but impersonal evenhanded ways . . . unofficial activity can undermine the legitimacy and effectiveness of the official political system'); R. Pérez Perdomo, 'Justice in Times of Globalization: Cause and Prospects for Change' in Inter-American Development Bank, *Justice and Development in Latin America and the Caribbean* (Washington DC, 1993) 131 (judges left to debt collection in over-regulated, developing state; generally of poor quality; still further tendency to corruption).

[98] See, for example, C. Welch Jr., 'Human Rights in Francophone West Africa' in An-Na'im and Deng, *Human Rights in Africa* (1990), above, at 203, 209–212 (for African countries adhering to international human rights instruments); C. Nchama, *Développement et droits de l'homme en Afrique* (Paris: Publisud, 1991); F. Ouguergouz, *La Charte africaine des droits de l'homme et des peuples: une approche juridique des droits de l'homme entre tradition et modernité* (Paris: Presses universitaires de France, 1993); E. El-Obaid and K. Appiagyei-Atua, 'Human Rights in Africa—A New Perspective on Linking the Past to the Present' (1996) 41 McGill L. J. 819; and for the use of human rights in the new South African democracy, Bennett, *Human Rights and African Customary Law* (1995), above, notably on means of reconciliation with informal law.

[99] González Galván, 'Una filosofía de derecho indígena' (1997), above, at 535 (including rights to practise chthonic religion, to practise chthonic medicine, to learn chthonic languages); J. Ordóñez Cifuentes, 'Conflicto, Etnicidad y Derechos Humanos des los Pueblos Indios' (1994) 14 Crítica Jurídica 57, notably at 76 ('El derecho a sus derechos').

[100] R. Howard, 'Group versus Individual Identity in the African Debate on Human Rights' in An-Na'im and Deng, *Human Rights in Africa* (1990), above, at 159, with extensive references to literature on African perspectives on human rights; J. Silk, 'Traditional Culture and the Prospects for Human Rights in Africa' in ibid., at 290.

[101] Bennett, 'Human Rights and African Cultural Tradition' (1993), above, at 270, 271 (citing African authors; right to life broader than in west, since entails an obligation to feed and shelter); Silk, 'Traditional Culture' (1990), above, at 292 ('values that are consistent with and supportive of human rights').

character of chthonic law can be invoked with the same effect as invocation of rights, as in the current chthonic Internet campaign against inclusion of chthonic peoples in the human genome project (the human body, as 'sacred', requires protection; lack of protection will likely lead to discrimination).[102] The debate suggests an overlapping field of potential agreement between western rights analysis and chthonic law. Neither, however, could entirely displace the other.

## UNIVERSALIZING THE CHTHONIC?

Chthonic peoples are not now known in the world as aggressive or dominating peoples. If they are, they are less so than others. Often idyllic portraits are made of inter-chthonic relations. The nature of the chthonic tradition is broadly supportive of this non-universalizing character of the chthonic tradition, at least by aggressive means. War and conflict do not appear to be compatible with the natural order, or at least a peaceful and harmonious version of it. And since chthonic peoples have not constructed the institutional means of resisting expansion by other traditions, they are likely to be equally ill-equipped to undertake systematic expansion. Again, however, there is no unanimity within the large tradition. The Iroquois peace was one intended to be extended to the entire North American continent.[103] Other traditions have also known the idea of an aggressive form of peace. And even unwritten traditions can be taken as apodictic, in their totality. Yet most chthonic people think the argument that the world should be preserved is a self-evident one; and that those who do not accept it will eventually bear the burden of not accepting it.

# GENERAL BIBLIOGRAPHY

Allott, A. N., 'African Law' in Derrett, J. (ed.), *An Introduction to Legal Systems* (London: Sweet and Maxwell, 1968) at 131.
—— *New Essays in African Law* (London: Butterworths, 1970).
Bennett, T., *A Sourcebook of African Customary Law for Southern Africa* (Cape Town: Juta, 1991).
Bohannan, P. *Justice and Judgment among the Tiv* (London/New York: Oxford University Press, 1957).
Borrows, J., 'With or Without You: First Nations Law (in Canada)' (1996) 41 McGill Law Journal 629.

---

[102] See, e.g., http://bioco9.uthscsa.edu/natnet/archive/nl/hgdp.html or http://www.niec.net/ipcb/resources/index.html——and for a range of web sites dealing with issues concerning chthonic peoples, see http://conbio.rice.edu/nae

[103] On the possibility, in particular instances, of the autochtonous person of today being the conqueror of yesterday, see Rouland, Pierré-Caps and Poumarède, *Droits des minorités* (1996), above, at 432.

Cotran, E., 'African Law' in International Association of Legal Science (K. Zweigert and U. Drobnig, eds.), *International Encyclopedia of Comparative Law*, vol. II, ch. 2 (Tübingen/ The Hague/Paris: J. C. B. Mohr/Mouton, 1974) at 157.

Cumming, P. and Mickenberg, N., *Native Rights in Canada*, 2nd edn. (Toronto: Indian–Eskimo Association of Canada & General Publishing Co. Ltd. 1972).

David, R. and Brierley, J. E. C., *Major Legal Systems in the World Today*, 3rd edn. (London: Stevens & Sons, 1985), Pt. Four, Title IV ('Laws of Africa and Malagasy').

de Deckker, P. (ed.), *Coutume autochtone et évolution du droit dans le Pacifique sud* (Paris: L'Harmattan, 1995).

Deloria Jr., V. and Lyde, C. M., *American Indians, American Justice* (Austin: University of Texas Press, 1983).

Dickason, O. P., *Canada's First Nations: a History of Founding Peoples from Earliest Times* (Toronto: McClelland & Stewart, 1992).

Elias, T. O., *The Nature of African Customary Law* (Manchester: Manchester University Press, 1956).

Gluckman, M., *The Ideas in Barotse Jurisprudence* (New Haven: Yale University Press, 1965).

González Galván, J. A., *El estado y las ethnias nacionales en Mexico. La relacion entre el derecho estatal y el derecho consuetudinario* (Mexico: Instituto de Investigacciones Juridicas, 1995).

—— 'Una filosofía de derecho indígena: desde una historia presente de las mentalidades jurídicas' (1997) 89 Boletín Mexicano de Derecho Comparado 523.

Hamnett, I., *Chieftainship and Legitimacy: an anthropological study of executive law in Lesotho* (London: Routledge & Kegan Paul, 1975).

Hay, M. and Wright, M. (eds.) *African Women and the Law: Historical Perspectives* (Boston: Boston University Press, 1982).

Hoebel, E. A., *The Law of Primitive Man: a Study in Comparative Legal Dynamics* (Cambridge, Mass.: Harvard University Press, 1961).

Hooker, M., *Legal Pluralism: an Introduction to Colonial and Neo-colonial Laws* (Oxford: Oxford University Press, 1975).

Jenness, D., *The Indians of Canada*, 6th edn. (Ottawa: National Museum of Canada, 1963).

Kuper, A., *The Invention of Primitive Society: Transformations of an Illusion* (London/New York: Routledge, 1988).

Levi-Strauss, C., *La pensée sauvage* (Paris: Plon, 1962).

Llewellyn, K. and Hoebel, E., *The Cheyenne Way: Conflict and Case Law in Primitive Jurisprudence* (Norman: University of Oklahoma Press, 1941).

Malinowski, B., *Crime and Custom in Savage Society* (London: K. Paul, Trench & Trubner & Co., 1926).

M'Baye, K., 'The African Conception of Law' in International Association of Legal Science (K. Zweigert & U. Drobnig, eds.), *International Encyclopedia of Comparative Law*, vol. II, ch. 1 (Tübingen/The Hague/Paris: J. C. B. Mohr/Mouton, 1975) at 138, with extensive bibliography at 157, 158.

Moore, S. F., *Law as Process: an Anthropological Approach* (London: Routledge & Kegan Paul, 1978).

—— *Social Facts and Fabrications: 'Customary' Law on Kiliminjaro, 1880–1980* (Cambridge: Cambridge University Press, 1986).

Morse, B. and Woodman, G., *Indigenous Law and the State* (Dordrecht: Foris, 1988).

Popisil, L., *Anthropology of Law—A Comparative Theory* (New York: Harper & Row, 1971).

Radcliffe-Brown, A. R., *Structure and Function in Primitive Society* (New York: Free Press, 1952).

Renteln, A. D. and Dundes, A., *Folk Law: Essays in the Theory and Practice of* Lex Non Scripta (New York: Garland Publications, 1994).

Rouland, N., *Anthropologie juridique* (Paris: Presses universitaires de France, 1988).

Rouland, N., Pierré-Caps, S., and Poumarède, J., *Droit des minorités et des peuples autochtones* (Paris: Presses universitaires de France, 1996).

Sacco, R., Guadagni, M., Aluffi Beck-Peccoz, R. and Castellani, L., *Il diritto africano* (Turin: UTET, 1995).

Schott, R., 'Triviales und Transzendentes: Einige Aspekte afrikanischer Rechtstraditionen unter besonderer Berücksichtigung der Bulsa in Nord-Ghana' in W. Fikentscher, H. Franke, and O. Köhler, (eds.), *Entstehung und Wandel rechtlicher Traditionen* (Freiburg/ Munich: Verlag Karl Alber, 1980), 265.

Schulte-Tenckhoff, I., *La question des peuples autochtones* (Brussels/Paris: Bruylant/LGDJ, 1997).

Slattery, B., 'Understanding Aboriginal Rights' (1987) 66 Canadian Bar Review 727.

Snyder, F. G., 'Colonialism and Legal Form—the creation of "customary law" in Senegal' in (1981) 19 Journal of Legal Pluralism 49.

Trigger, B., *The Children of the Aataentsic: a History of the Huron People to 1660* (Montreal/ Kingston: McGill-Queen's University Press, 1976).

Tully, J., *Strange multiplicity: constitutionalism in an age of diversity* (Cambridge: Cambridge University Press, 1995).

Wesel, U., *Frühformen des Rechts in vorstaatlichen Gesellschaften* (Frankfurt: Suhrkamp, 1985)

White, R., *The Middle Ground: Indians, empires and republics in the Great Lakes region, 1650–1815* (Cambridge: Cambridge University Press, 1991).

Williams Jr., R. A., *The American Indian in Western Legal Thought: the Discourses of Conquest* (New York/Oxford: Oxford University Press, 1990).

Woodman, G. and Obilade, A., *African Law and Legal Theory* (New York: New York University Press, 1995).

# 4

# A TALMUDIC
# LEGAL TRADITION:
# THE PERFECT AUTHOR

Jewish people have maintained their identity for thousands of years, and talmudic law has played a very large part in this process. Talmudic law represents one of the oldest, living, legal traditions in the world; after chthonic law, it may be the oldest, depending on one's view of the current status of hindu law.[1] This means that it was one of the earliest to separate itself, in a definitive and lasting way, from chthonic law. Others which did so, perhaps even earlier, have since lost their grip.[2] The talmudic legal tradition continues, however, with great vitality, and is now also attracting interest from outside itself, in western legal theory.

Is there a starting point of the talmudic legal tradition? This is not an easy question to answer. There were jewish people, and jewish law, long before Moses,

---

[1] See below, Ch. 8. The jewish calendar begins with the creation of the world (fixed by genealogy back through Genesis), and 2000 AD is the equivalent of 5760 in the jewish calendar. In secular matters, however, jewish tradition uses christian dating, accompanied by designation of whether the date is before the common era (BCE) or within it (CE). For the long history of jewish people, see S. Grayzel, *A History of the Jews*, revd. edn. (New York: Meridian, 1984); P. Johnson, *A History of the Jews* (London: Phoenix, 1995).

[2] The best-known example is probably the code of Hammurabi, king and creator of the Babylonian empire, some 1800 years BCE. Hammurabi's code largely suffered the fate of Babylon itself, lost to the Persians (today's Iranians, mutatis mutandi) around 500 BCE, though the code's information survives, notably in engraved slab form in the Louvre in Paris. For the extensive literature on Hammurabi's code, see B. Jackson, 'Evolution and Foreign Influence in Ancient Law' (1968) 16 Am. J. Comp. Law 372 at 373, notes 10–12; and for the surviving texts of the time, M. Roth (ed.), *Law Collections from Mesopotamia and Asia Minor*, 2nd edn. (Atlanta, Ga.: Scholars Press, 1997). In contrast, we have lost almost all of the information of early Egyptian law; ibid, at 383, n. 60 (no code surviving though references to one; some records of litigation), though see A. Schiller, 'Coptic Law' (1931) 43 Jur. Rev. 211, for later christian, coptic law (600 AD—1000 AD), itself having partly received ancient Egyptian law); P. G. Monateri, 'Black Gaius: a Quest for the Multicultural Origins of the "Western Legal Tradition"' (forthcoming, Hastings L. J. and accessible at http://www.gelso.unitn.it/card-adm/pigi/blackgaius/bg.htm); and see B. Lewis, *The Middle East: 2000 Years of History from the Rise of Christianity to the Present Day* (London: Weidenfeld and Nicolson, 1995) at 244, 245, for general phenomenon of loss of middle-eastern learning ('lost, forgotten and literally buried'). Early Greek law has left more traces: M. Gagarin, *Early Greek Law* (Berkeley/Los Angeles/London: Univ. California Press, 1986); D. MacDowell, *The Law in Classical Athens* (Ithaca, NY: Cornell Univ. Press, 1978); R. Sealey, *The Justice of the Greeks* (Ann Arbor: Univ. Michigan Press, 1994), notably at 32, 33 and 37 for Greek law (nomos) marking transition from Hittite law as pious hope or moral resolve to 'prescriptive rule'; accord N. Lemche, 'Justice in Western Asia in Antiquity, or: Why no Laws were Needed!' (1995) 70 Chicago-Kent L. Rev. 1695.

and they worshipped the same God (Yahweh[3] or Jehovah) which jewish, christian and islamic people worship today. It is not likely that the revelation of God's word to Moses, on Sinai in the thirteenth century BCE, completely changed the existing law of jewish people.[4] It did, however, transform it, and add to it, and constitute it as divine law. So the revelation to Moses of the will of God gave to jewish law at least a new beginning; it could not be the law of old and it could not be observed as the law of old. Revelation changed understanding of the world; a new covenant had been undertaken.[5] Law subsequently would have to be in its name.

## A TRADITION ROOTED IN REVELATION

Talmudic law is thus rooted in the word of God as revealed to Moses, now found in the first five books of the Hebrew Bible (constituting the Pentateuch—Genesis, Exodus, Leviticus, Numbers and Deuteronomy). Here we first encounter the language of the sources of talmudic law, which are not always clear if you are meeting them for the first time.[6] These first five books of what the christian world knows as the Old Testament constitute the Torah. The word Torah, however, has other uses than that which refers simply to the Pentateuch. Generally, it means divine wisdom, and therefore refers also to the totality of divine teaching,[7] since the beginning of the world and relating to all things subject to the divine will, which doesn't leave much out. So you have to pay attention to the way the word Torah is used. It may mean almost everything; it may refer more specifically to what is also called the 'written Torah' (the Pentateuch).

Tradition being what it is, even religious tradition, things always get more complicated over time. So the written Torah generated comment and explanation, by

---

[3] Yahweh would be a later derivation of the original Yhwh, ancient hebrew being written without vowels, and would be an archaic form of the verb to be. So in telling Moses who he was God may have been saying simply 'I am who I am'. See T. Cahill, *The Gifts of the Jews* (New York: Doubleday, 1998) at 108–10.

[4] On legal practices antedating the Revelation at Sinai, see Elon, *Jewish Law*, vol. I (1994) at 95 ff.; Dorff and Rosett, *Living Tree* (1988) at 7, 16–20 (ancient Habiru—Abraham and kin—wandering in Mesopotamia; coming to Canaan (Palestine); acquiring name Israelites, children of Israel—Israel another word for Jacob), 425, 426 (pre-revelatory practices retained in talmudic teaching). The word 'jew' is simply a modification of the word 'judean', referring to the southern kingdom of the people, itself named after a son of Jacob.

[5] Deut. 34: 10: 'Since then, no prophet has risen in Israel like Moses, whom the Lord knew face to face.' At the same time, advice was given as to determining the false prophet, one who could not inspire tradition. Deut. 18: 22: 'If what a prophet proclaims in the name of the Lord does not take place or come true, that is a message the Lord has not spoken. The prophet has spoken presumptuously. Do not be afraid of him.'

[6] For a useful glossary, see R. Goldenberg, 'Talmud' in Holz *Back to Sources* (1984), 129 at 137–9; and for a chronological guide, N. Rakover, *Guide to the Sources of Jewish Law* (Jerusalem: Library of Jewish Law, 1994).

[7] Goldenberg, 'Talmud' (1984), above, 129 at 129, 130. This wider concept of Torah naturally includes the rest of the Hebrew Bible, completed in written form around the 4th-century, BCE.

the sages, and the tradition of talmudic law became more developed. Perhaps the greatest period of jewish history extended from Moses through David and Solomon (builder of the First Temple in the tenth century BCE), to the time of Babylonian rule in the sixth century BCE (when the First Temple was destroyed). Through this whole time people studied the written Torah, talked about it and remembered its teaching. An oral tradition developed, alongside the written one. This oral tradition was not simply hearsay. It began with Moses himself, explaining the written Torah, and the chain of traditio was recorded along with the methods of learning (by heart) through multiple repetitions by the teacher.[8] Since the oral teaching began with Moses it had to have a status equal to that of the written teaching. The oral tradition was also divine, and the written Torah even served as a mnemonic device for recalling the fuller explanation of what had become known as the 'oral Torah'. So we now have three Torahs altogether, all representing the divine will—an all-encompassing Torah, a written Torah, and an oral Torah. Things get still richer. We are closing in on the Talmud.

   The jewish people lost what we would today call political sovereignty in the 6th century BCE, to the Babylonians, and did not recover it until 1948 CE. The Babylonians were replaced by others, notably the Greeks, and then by the Romans. The diaspora began with the Babylonians. In the first years of the common era the failed insurrection against the Romans occurred, and the Second Temple was destroyed in 70 CE (except for one remaining wall, now a wall of lament, the wailing wall). The diaspora accelerated. The means of oral traditio of the teaching were weakening; if it was remembered, it would likely be in increasingly fragmented and diverse form. A decision of enormous importance was taken (and there may have been some Greek or Roman influence in its taking):[9] the oral tradition had to be written down. Thus began the massive accumulation of texts in the talmudic tradition.


## THE WRITTEN WORDS

Beside the written Torah we now have an oral Torah, which has become written. It is still often referred to as the oral Torah, but is more frequently, in the tradition, referred to as the Mishnah, which may be intended to make things simpler. The word Mishnah comes from a root which means 'to study' and it is therefore a

---

[8] For the method, see Maimonides, *Introduction to the Talmud*, trans. and annot. Z. Lampel (New York: Judaica Press, 1975) at 35 (first repetition to first recipient, who then awaits to hear second repetition to second recipient, etc.).

[9] See E. Urbach, *The Sages: Their Concepts and Beliefs*, trans. I. Abrahams (Cambridge, Mass.: Harvard Univ. Press, 1987) at 290, indicating that the concept of a higher oral (unwritten) law may have been contributed to by Greek thought; the notion of extensive written transcription of law was also highly developed in the Greek and Roman worlds. The main reason for writing down the oral tradition may, however, have been simply mnemonic; nobody could remember all that had been said; and the diaspora limited the possibility of bringing together those who remembered parts of it. See Steinsaltz, *Essential Talmud* (1976) at 32, 33; Elon, *Jewish Law*, vol. I (1994) at 226.

written and extended study of the (original) written Torah, the Pentateuch. The Mishnah began to be planned following the fall of the Second Temple in 70 CE; it was completed around 200 CE.[10] As a written exposition of law it invited more written exposition (we are now approximately 1500 years after Moses, or one and a half times the duration, thus far, of the common law). The oral interpretation and discussion of the Mishnah went on, however, for some three hundred years, through the declining years of roman law and the Roman empire, and the rise of christianity. There were many questions put as to the meaning of the divine trad-ition, and many opinions expressed, including those of persons who had become learned in the intricacy of the teaching. So the accumulated, learned opinions, themselves not derived directly from Moses, began to have great weight in the ongoing application of the law. Their consensus was irresistible (the divine will was here most evident); their differences were also instructive, and the tradition had to retain a record of them (until the divine will became more clearly understood). So, as with the Mishnah, as the opinions grew in number so grew the necessity to record them. This happened, of course, not once but twice, though both recordings bear the name of Talmud.

The Jerusalem Talmud ('Talmud', too, means study) was composed in the fifth century CE (so about a century before Justinian's Codification). It is in the form of a commentary (lawyers tend to do this) on the primary text, the Mishnah, but it also sets out the Mishnah, for convenience, as the object of the commentary. Strictly speaking, the Talmud (also Gemarah (study) in aramaic, used frequently) is the commentary, but the entire book (Mishnah and Talmud/Gemarah) has become known, by usage, as the Talmud. The Jerusalem Talmud was the first effort of recording valuable opinions on the written and oral Torahs. It was followed by what is generally regarded as a more refined effort, a century or two later (that is, at the same time or somewhat later than Justinian), the Babylonian Talmud. It has been said that study of the Babylonian Talmud is 'more challenging, but also more gratifying' than study of the Jerusalem Talmud, which is 'often just obscure'.[11]

The Talmud, in its two forms, is thus the basic book of law of the talmudic legal tradition. By the time of its writing almost two millennia of legal discussion had occurred, and the Talmud is the repository of all that was considered worthy of retention, on both sides of many issues. There is also much in it which may not be

---

[10] B. Lifshitz, 'The Age of the Talmud', in Hecht et al. (eds.), *History and Sources of Jewish Law* (1996) at 169; *Gordis, Dynamics of Judaism* (1990) at 62; for controversy on the dating, however, see Elon, *Jewish Law*, vol. I (1994) at 227, with refs.; and for a view that the Mishnah even continued as oral tradition down to its incorporation in the Talmuds, see Hoenig, *Essence of Talmudic Law and Thought* (1993) at 31–3; D. Akenson, *Surpassing Wonder; the Invention of the Bible and the Talmuds* (Montreal/Kingston: McGill-Queens Univ. Press, 1998) at 296, 297.

[11] Goldenberg, 'Talmud' (1984), above, at 136; and on differences between the two Talmuds, see Elon, *Jewish Law*, vol. III (1994) at 1095. The Babylonian Talmud is taken as the more authoritative. The two Talmuds are not the exclusive source of the oral tradition, however, and further portions of it are found in other collec-tions, notably the Tosefta and the Midrashe Halakhah, as to which see P. Segal, 'Jewish Law during the Tannaitic Period' in Hecht et al. (eds.), *History and Sources of Jewish Law* (1996) 101 at 120, 121.

law (more on this later), but everyone was obliged to study it. You can remember all of this by a little phrase—'mitzvat talmud Torah' ('talmud' and 'Torah' are in alphabetical order)—the duty of studying (talmud, and by means of the Talmud), the Torah. When the Talmud was written they stopped writing it, but no one signed off and no one is known as the author. So, as they say, 'The Talmud was never completed'[12] or, as the French say, a door was closed but a window was opened. The Talmud was not meant to end the debate, but to provide means for its continuance, within the tradition. This is an enormously powerful idea, rich in religious and legal significance and we will return to it as well. For now, you'll just have to take it on faith.

### THE WRITTEN WORDS PROLIFERATE

The Talmud is the most important single element in the bran-tub of the talmudic legal tradition. It contains a great deal of varying opinion, but did not purport to exclusivity. So both before and after its writing, there were other means of contribution, in writing, to the accumulating tradition. Legislation was one means, and the Great Assembly (of elders), the Sanhedrin, functioned as a source of many ordinances once the monarchy of the time of the First Temple had ended.[13] The tradition thus recognizes a notion of 'the law of the land', which has consequences both within the tradition and for its relations with other traditions.[14] Nor has it been possible to constrain the impulse to restate the law, incorporating later opinion. There has thus been a phenomenon of subsequent commentaries, even called codes, which have assumed great importance in the ongoing application of talmudic law. These began as early as the eighth century; the most famous are those of Maimonides in the twelfth century and Joseph Caro in the sixteenth century (known today as the most authoritative of the codes).[15]

The process of application of the law also generates a written record, most notably in the form of responsa, the written opinions of those learned in the law, formulated in response to questions of all sorts, not necessarily from those involved in disputes. The responsa are forms of advice; they are, however, of great authority and have been a vital factor in maintaining talmudic law as a living tradition over so

---

[12] Steinsaltz, *Essential Talmud* (1976) at 47.

[13] Elon, *Jewish Law*, vol. III (1994) at 558 ff.; Steinsaltz, *Essential Talmud* (1976) at 15. The Sanhedrin ceased to function following the destruction of the Second Temple, in 70 CE. There is now opposition to its re-creation, as a religious legislative institution, in Israel. Legislation is here seen as the preserve of an institution of the (western) state. For the positions, see Rackman, *Modern Halakhah* (1995) at 6; and for the subjection of the kings of Israel to rabbinic law, see M. Greenberg, 'Rabbinic Reflections on Defying Illegal Orders: Amasa, Abner, and Joab' (1970) 19 *Judaism* 30; Rackman, *Modern Halakhah* (1995) at 101.

[14] See the discussion of the notion of the 'law of the land', below, this chapter, *Talmudic law and jewish identity*.

[15] On the two codes, see Elon, *Jewish Law*, vol. III (1994), ch. 34 (Maimonides), 36 (Caro); and on the debate on codification of talmudic law, Dorff and Rosett, *Living Tree* (1988) at 396 ff.

many years.[16] Those who wrote, and write, the responsa are the rabbis, an office formalized around the time of the fall of the Second Temple (70 CE), and whose function is contemplated even by the written Torah itself.[17] The official character of the office, eventually salaried,[18] led to an increase in the number of scholars and to elevation of their status. The time of creation of the rabbis was also a time of increasing individualization of the scholarly tradition, contributions no longer being anonymous.

The talmudic tradition is thus one which is defined by its sources, which are both divine and written and in no way dependent on what is called elsewhere decisional law or case law or jurisprudence. The tradition has been usefully described as a large, inverted pyramid,[19] with the written Torah at the base, extending upwards to the (written) oral Torah, the Mishnah, then to the Talmud, then to the codes and responsa, and on to current contributions. Yet if the pyramid is inverted, and the Talmud is never finished, the upper reaches of the pyramid simply continue to grow; the base of revelation bears greater and greater weight as the tradition continues. It is, moreover, the law of jewish people wherever they live. This may be in the form of state-authorized personal law, largely in matters of family law, in states such as Israel or Morocco or others which know the concept of personal laws. It is also applied in secular states, by rabbinical courts, to all problems of jewish people, whenever the authority of rabbinical courts is invoked.

## APPLYING DIVINE LAW

A written law tends to precision in expression, though the number of expressions may be riotous. So there is some tendency to precision in institutions, or at least to have institutions, such that the written law has some guaranteed means of application. Talmudic law has thus long known formal courts,[20] though the religious character of the law is often reflected in their composition. The usual court had three members, all rabbis or ordained judges, enjoying immunity in the exercise of

---

[16] Elon, *Jewish Law*, vol. III (1994), ch. 39, notably at 1458 (responsa more authoritative than codes); Goldenberg, 'Talmud' (1984), above, at 160; D. Feldman, *Marital Relations, Birth Control and Abortion* (New York: Schocken Books, 1968), ch. I, 'The Structure of Jewish Law', at 17, 18; Dorff and Rosett, *Living Tree* (1988) at 303 ff., notably at 305 (written responsa emerging only in eighth century, CE).

[17] Deut. 17: 9: 'Go to the priests, who are Levites, and to the judge who is in office at that time. Inquire of them and they will give you the verdict'; Steinsaltz, *Essential Talmud* (1976) at 13, 14, 25; Dorff and Rosett, *Living Tree* (1988) at 139–42.

[18] Sherwin, *In Partnership with God* (1990) at 43.

[19] B. W. Holz, 'Introduction: On Reading Jewish Texts,' in Holz (ed.), *Back to Sources* (1984) at 13. The tradition of positive law is also often formulated as a pyramid, though here the pyramid is right side up and all descends from a narrow, and presumed, point of departure. If you prefer to think about law in terms of comparative pyramids, why is one right side up and one inverted, when the point of origin is in both cases the narrow point? Perhaps the inverted pyramid is more miraculous and leads us higher; the right-side-up directs our attention to the ground, and its form of reality, where we all live. Metaphor has its place in all traditions.

[20] See Exodus 18: 26: 'They served as judges for the people at all times. The difficult cases they brought to Moses, but the simple ones they decided themselves.'

their functions. Alternatively, the parties could agree to a panel of three lay people, who enjoyed, however, no immunity of function.[21] As in islamic law and the common law, there was no appeal and the absence of appellate courts continues today. There were, however, high courts in the form of a Small Sanhedrin, for capital offences, and the Grand Sanhedrin itself, which sat as first-instance court in matters of broad importance. The Sanhedrin's prestige gave its decisions great importance and provided a unifying force, though no notion of strict precedent or stare decisis existed.[22] The Sanhedrin was presided over by two sages, one its president, the other the head of the law court, the bet din (literally the house of law). The Sanhedrin ceased to exercise its judicial function in the early years of the common era.

The institution of the bet din continues to function around the world, however, wherever there is a jewish population. It is composed of three rabbis, who may have particular competence for the type of dispute, exercising a strong moral authority and having as one of their major objectives the restoration of harmony between the parties. The procedure is expeditious, and judgment may be given in a matter of weeks after only two or three appearances of the parties. Representation by lawyers is not excluded, though has never been encouraged. The parties agree to abide by the decision of the court. There are some indications of increasing use of the bet din, which may be invoked by non-jewish parties if the other party is jewish, as a preferable alternative to civil litigation. The law they apply covers the entire field of what is known in western private law, and is highly developed in commercial matters, reflecting christian exclusion of jews from farming and holding of land.[23] Lacking formal state authority its judges are now sometimes referred to as decisors, an ancient and traditional English word, now being revived, to indicate a person having authority to decide regardless of their not occupying an official position.[24]

The effect of a judgment of a bet din is indicated to some extent by the absence of courts of appeal. If a party is convinced that an initial judgment is erroneous, their remedy is to ask the court to correct it. Since the court is still available, there is no

[21] Steinsaltz, *Essential Talmud* (1976) at 164. The court of lay members resembled in many respects what we know as arbitration today, though in some cases exercised a more independent authority. On the debate, remarkably similar to that of contemporary western law, on the advantages and disadvantages of informal systems of arbitration, see D. Novack, 'Religious Human Rights in Judaic Texts' in J. Witte Jr. and J. D. van der Vyver, *Religious Human Rights in Global Perspective* (The Hague/Boston/London: Martinus Nijhoff, 1996) 175 at 197 (tendency of later authorities to urge arbitration, though legal rulings could 'pierce the mountain'); Steinsaltz, *Essential Talmud* (1976) at 204; Dorff and Rosett, *Living Tree* (1988) at 293–8.

[22] Dorff and Rosett, *Living Tree* (1988) at 372.

[23] See C. Roth, 'The European Age in Jewish History (to 1648)', in L. Finkelstein (ed.) *The Jews: Their History, Culture and Religion*, 3rd. edn., vol. I (New York: Harper and Row, 1960) 216 at 217, 227, 229 (jews barred from holding christian or other slaves, effectively barring them from farming; subject to ecclesiastical tithes if land owned; eventually formally forbidden to hold land); Grayzel, *History of Jews*, (1984), above, at 276, 277 (adding inability of jewish people to take religious oath of allegiance in feudal regimes). For the influence of talmudic commercial law on the development of the common law, see below, Ch. 7, *The secreted law*.

[24] Dane, 'Yoke of Heaven' (1994), at 386, n. 24 (expression even 'in vogue').

need for a court of appeal. Put another way, the notion of res judicata (chose jugée, Rechtskraft) has little or no place in the thinking, and the truthful solution has been considered of greater value than that of efficiency and stability.[25] Criminal cases, however, could only be re-opened by the accused, and in all instances resort could be had only to the original court and not another court. There were therefore some limits. If there is no doctrinal notion of res judicata, what place could there be for precedent or stare decisis?[26] There are not even regular collections of decisions, though the responsa of those consulted are now generally preserved.[27]

## THE DIVINE LAW APPLIED

We thus see a procedural and adjudicative structure which is open, as is the case in the chthonic tradition, and in which no formal barriers or obstacles limit access to officials of the law. The law applied can thus be thought of as 'substantive', as opposed to procedural, and talmudic law as substantive law occupies the same position in the tradition as does substantive law today in the civil or common laws. It can be thought of as defining the precise obligations of the parties. It is probably inaccurate, for reasons to be seen, to think of it as defining their rights.

Western and islamic lawyers will recognize in talmudic law almost all the private law they know themselves, though some later fields such as copyright may be formally absent from the original texts. There is also much law which western lawyers do not know as law, such as that relating to diet, hygiene and ritual. In the field of traditional private law, however, the sources are rich and varied—in family law, successions, property, obligations and crime. The particularity of talmudic law is not so much in its substance, but in its methods.

Family law is largely consensual in character, the religion exercising no formal or bureaucratic control over familial relations. Marriage is thus effected by present words of consent, though ceremonies take place and, by usage, a rabbi is usually present. The parties complete a marriage contract—the ketubah—which sets out in detail their patrimonial relations.[28] The traditional matrimonial regime has been one in which the administration of the wife's property during the marriage is the responsibility of the husband; it is close if not identical to the regime of use and administration (Nutzen und Verwaltung) of many European countries prior to recent reforms. Since marriage is consensual children born out of wedlock are not

---

[25] Bazak, 'Res Judicata and Authority of Arbitrators' (1992); M. Chigier 'The Doctrine of Res Judicata' (1988) 8 Jewish L. Ann. 127, notably at 134 (though jewish law 'fully aware' of the doctrine).

[26] Elon, Jewish Law, vol. III (1994) at 978–86; Stone, 'In Pursuit of Counter-Text' (1993), at 828, n. 79 ('no precedential value'); H. Ben-Menahem, 'Postscript: The Judicial Process and the Nature of Jewish Law' in Hecht et al.(eds.), History and Sources of Jewish Law (1996) 421 at 430 (if decision published, authority attaches as a responsum rather than from judicial determination).

[27] For talmudic reluctance to publish decisions, addressed in principle to the parties, concrete, specific and non-doctrinal in character, see B. Jackson, 'Jewish Law or Jewish Laws?' (1988) 8 Jewish L. Ann. 15 at 25.

[28] See Epstein, Jewish Marriage Contract (1927); Naamani, 'Marriage and Divorce in Jewish Law' (1963); Dorff and Rosett, Living Tree (1988) Pt Two, 'Marriage' at 442 ff.

seen as illegitmate.[29] Polygamy is authorized by the texts; it was, however, the object of a rabbinical ban, perhaps influenced by christian practice, and is now generally obsolete.[30] Divorce law is controversial, since the divorce (or get) is granted by the husband; this is usually done in proceedings before a bet din, but the husband's consent remains essential.[31] Where the parties have first divorced in a civil ceremony the husband may withhold consent as a means of leverage in property or other settlements. Civil courts are increasingly seized with requests for injunctive relief against husbands, raising large questions as to the relations between religious and secular law.[32] Family relations are strengthened, however, by the law of inheritance, which does not recognize a principle of free testamentary disposition.[33]

The law of obligations is profoundly marked by its private character. Since money may be the object of gift, and replaced by other money, parties are free to allow their obligations to be governed by the law of the land (recalling western choice of law in matters of contract) and the courts have extensive and liberal powers to re-order the patrimonial relations of the parties.[34] In a general way the law of obligations recalls that of Rome, or even of the early common law. Contracts are contracts, individual in character and not all subsumed into a general, consensual part. So there are contracts of sale, partnership and employment, while form, symbol, and even traditio (of the thing exchanged) are fundamental to their existence.[35] The law of civil wrongs is exactly that, and in the law of wrongs caused by fire, ox or other it is possible to see the same mental processes at work which led to similar categories in the agricultural

---

[29] Steinsaltz, *Essential Talmud* (1996) at 130. Illegitimacy may attach, however, to issue of specific, prohibited relations.

[30] Ibid., at 133; cf., for the ongoing legality of bigamy for yemenite jews in certain circumstances, Falk, 'Jewish Law' (1968) at 40.

[31] Fishbane, 'Image of the Human and Rights of Individual' (1988) 17 at 28; Gordis, *Jewish Tradition in Modern World* (1978) ch. 10 ('Women's Status in Marriage and Divorce').

[32] M. Mielziner, *The Jewish Law of Marriage and Divorce in Ancient and Modern Times, and its Relation to the Law of the State*, 2nd rev. edn. (New York: Bloch, 1901); Glenn, 'Where Heavens Meet' (1980), with refs; S. Glick, 'The Agunah in the American Legal System: Problems and Solutions' (1992–3) J. Fam. Law 885 (reform judaism accepting, however, civil divorce); D. Novak, 'Modern Responsa: 1800 to the Present', in Hecht et al. (eds.), *History and Sources of Jewish Law* (1996) 379 at 384; Dorff and Rosett, *Living Tree* (1988) at 523–63. Some jurisdictions now allow a civil court to require undertakings that religious obstacles to divorce have been removed, prior to granting the civil divorce.

[33] Steinsaltz, *Essential Talmud* (1976) at 161.

[34] Ibid., at 145 ff.

[35] As to a requirement of consideration, see B. Lifshitz, 'Consideration in Jewish Law—A Reconsideration' (1988) 8 Jewish L. Ann. 115 ('two views emerge'; in classical sources no insistence on abstract concept of consideration; consideration may nevertheless be seen in many modes of acquisition); M. Elon, 'Contract' in Elon (ed.), *Principles of Jewish Law* (1975) at 246, 247 (no generic term for concept of contract, given 'preference for a concrete rather than an abstract terminology', consideration nevertheless of importance in creation of particular contractual ties); A. Levine, *Free Enterprise and Jewish Law* (New York: Ktav Publishing House/ Yeshiva Univ. Press, 1980) at 34–6 ('Voluntary exchange does not acquire legal force in Jewish law until it becomes objectively evident that the parties involved have firmly resolved to conclude the arrangement at hand'); J. Kary, '"Ask Me Ever So Much and I Will Give It. . . ": A Biblical Era View of Contracts' (1996–7) Ottawa L. Rev. 267 (notion of obligation arising from receipt of gift, as a responsibility to reward gratuitous generosity).

worlds of Rome and England. The religious character of the law is evident by what is known in the civil law world as the natural obligation—the debt unenforceable in law but which should be paid and, if paid, which cannot be recovered. As in roman law, no sharp or structural division is made between delict and crime. The teaching is largely the same for both, though sanctions may be monetary or corporal. Theft gives rise largely to civil sanctions of restoration of property and fine.[36]

# THE TALMUD AND REVELATION

So now we have courts and judges, written sources of law, marriage, divorce, contracts, crime—all growing roughly out of the same geographical basin that gave us roman law. This looks pretty straightforward after all, once you get used to the time-span and some kind of religious beginning. There is now also a territorial base, at least to some extent, in the state of Israel.[37] If you want to learn a little more of the talmudic legal tradition, however, you will begin to experience its particularity and the profound and ongoing role which jewish faith continues to play in its operation. It doesn't (for example) have the same role as western law, it doesn't read like western law, it isn't studied like western law and ultimately it is not structured like western law. So we have to look beyond some immediate similarities and try to understand some profound differences. This might not be easy, in what is here an inevitably cursory way. You might be better off spending twenty or thirty years at it, or more, from inside. Mitzvat talmud Torah.

## HALAKHAH AND AGGADAH

The Talmud and the Torah contain a great deal of information, and much of it is what people would call legend, or even myth, and philosophy, as well as law. The law is known in the tradition as halakhah (the way or path to walk); the rest is aggadah. So we have a separation here, which is formally recognized, and in this the tradition also distinguishes itself from the chthonic tradition. It is not, however, the separation of law and morals as is known in the west; halakhah does not have the same role as law; aggadah does not have that of morals; and both have something in common which law and morals do not.

To start with the common element, from which all else flows, halakhah and aggadah both have their ultimate source in divine will, in revelation. In a sense it is an incomplete separation, not the clean break some would make between law and morals, since the same source inspires them both and it is unlikely they can be seen

---

[36] Steinsaltz, *Essential Talmud* (1976) at 155, 163.
[37] On religion and law in Israel, however, see below, this Chapter, *Talmudic law and jewish identity*.

as conflicting. We have already seen the idea of natural obligation in talmudic law;[38] this may be seen as a recognition of the limits of formal institutions and formal sanctions, and the obligation of divine will exists regardless of the limits of formal institutions. In the talmudic tradition you of course do not act outside the law—that is illegal—but you are also expected to act 'inside the law',[39] that is, to do what halakhah may not require but which aggadah does. There are ultimate sanctions.

Of the two, moreover, it is law which is vastly more important. The jewish tradition is a normative or legal tradition in much the same measure as it is a religious tradition. The two have become fused in the idea that the divine will best expresses itself in legal norms, which have sanctions, leaving relatively little outside the reach of the law, or halakhah. The divine character of the norms, and the love of study, have pushed talmudic law to cover almost all of life,[40] in a way that western law can probably never reach. So the non-jewish (or non-islamic) reader has first to get used to the idea that law is almost everywhere, both in the relations between the person and God (and hence in matters of prayer, food, hygiene, ritual) and in the relations between the person and others. Rabbinical courts have now lost much of their authority to sanction much of this law. It is still, however, law, and some authors rejoice that it is now only love of God and not a power to punish which should motivate compliance.[41] Law could expand because it was God's law and once expanded it retains, in its entirety, the perfection of God. So talmudic law has a Perfect Author, which no human intelligence is ever going to be able to fault. The Talmud is never completed, and will go on being written by generation after generation, because all that is said in the name of the Talmud is contained in original divine intention. Nothing is new; all is discovery. 'Of course every interpretation that ever will be was known at Sinai, was intended by God.'[42] And since the law is God's, obedience to it is an affirmation of love of God; the place left for ethics is necessarily reduced, though the law is profoundly infused with ethics. People have spoken of theocracy.[43]

---

[38]  Above, this Chapter, *The divine law applied.*

[39]  Steinsaltz, *Essential Talmud* (1976) at 199, 202; and generally A. Lichtenstein, 'Does Jewish Tradition Recognize an Ethic Independent of Halakha?' in M. Fox (ed.), *Modern Jewish Ethics* (Columbus, Ohio: Ohio State Univ. Press, 1975) at 62, repr. in Golding, *Jewish Law and Legal Theory* (1993) at 155.

[40]  Goldenberg, 'Talmud' (1984), above, at 130; Steinsaltz, *Essential Talmud* (1976) at 95; Novack, 'Religious Human Rights in Judaic Texts' (1996), above, at 181 ('whole tendency of the normative Jewish tradition to expand rather than contract the range of the law').

[41]  Dane, 'Yoke of Heaven' (1994) at 377, 378, n. 3, with refs.

[42]  Holz (ed.), *Back to Sources* (1984) at 15; and see Urbach, *Sages* (1987), above, at 313, citing calculation that whole universe is one three-thousand-and-twentieth of the Torah; Steinsaltz, *Essential Talmud* (1976) at 5, citing dictum 'Turn it and turn it again, for everything is contained in the Torah'.

[43]  C. Taylor, *Sources of the Self: the Making of the Modern Identity* (Cambridge, Mass.: Harvard Univ. Press, 1989) at 269.

## TALMUD AND TORAH

The Torah is the divine law, as revealed, and the Talmud is, as stated earlier, 'not derived directly' from Moses.[44] Yet we now understand that the Talmud, and all else, is contained implicitly in the Torah and thus partakes of the divine. So the Talmud is much broader than the Torah, but it is not somehow lesser in importance, simply because its immediate authors appear as human. It is all law and all of it is divine. God is very subtle in this, and obviously understands a lot about tradition. Some have said that talmudic law is above all a tradition; it is therefore not some presumed point of departure which is important, but rather the accumulating character of the tradition, which itself is the source of the ongoing normativity, whatever may have existed near (or even at) the beginning. Put more brutally, revelation may or may not have occurred, the important thing is whether a lot of people, in an ongoing manner, have taken it as occurring. Talmudic law can therefore be studied as, say, sociology, or as a somewhat looser form of positive law, or even as economics.[45]

God appears, however, to have already answered this question as to the role of ongoing tradition. It is already part of the fold, and cannot be seen itself as uniquely constitutive. It is derived from and legitimated by the Torah, while itself explaining and giving effect to it. Some, within the tradition, have even said that the Talmud transcends the Torah, such that God himself is bound by it.[46] Yet all is still divine will. So, in informational terms, the relation of the two has been described in terms of feedback; each informs the other.[47] Revelation cannot be read out of the picture by the ongoing force of tradition, since the tradition has been scripted by the Perfect Author. Yet the tradition itself is essential, as tradition, for the divine will to be done. This too is foreseen. So this tradition, as a divine tradition, has a beginning. Revelation trumps tradition. If you remove the beginning, you wind up with something else. Some have said you don't even then have tradition, just nostalgia.

## THE STYLE OF THE TEXT

Written law in the west is associated either with declaratory ('La propriété est . . . ') or imperative ('It is forbidden to . . . ', 'All persons shall . . . ') styles of text. It has

[44] Above, this Chapter, *The written words.*

[45] See, e.g., though not literally, Dane, 'Yoke of Heaven' (1994) with refs. (invoking, notably (at 356) the argument that revelation is itself inadequate to ground halakhah since christians have also accepted the Hebrew Bible, as the Old Testament; written law also not self-explicating, oral law must direct explication (359)).

[46] Urbach, *Sages* (1987), above, at 304, 305; the Talmudic source is Bava Metzia 59a–b, in which Rabbi disputes with a Heavenly Voice, saying 'It is not in Heaven', to which God eventually replied, laughing with joy, 'My children have defeated Me. My children have defeated Me.' On a similar debate in islamic law, in which the primacy of subsequent tradition over scripture has been maintained, see below, Ch. 6, *Ijma, the hadith and revelation.*

[47] Y. Leibowitz, 'Religious Praxis: The Meaning of Halakhah' in E. Goldman (ed.), *Judaism, Human Values, and the Jewish State* (1992) 3, 12, as cited in Dane, 'Yoke of Heaven' (1994) at 384, n. 21; and on the previously noted concept of the written Torah serving as mnemonic device for the oral, Steinsaltz, *Essential Talmud* (1976) at 33.

been said that these are exclusionary styles, since they allow no explicit internal argument, only frontal attack (by illegal action or, in some instances, constitutional challenge) or deconstruction (the exclusive meaning is really no meaning). The talmudic style is neither declaratory nor imperative. It has been described as 'argumentative',[48] but this must be understood in the sense of a rather relaxed and ongoing kind of argument, the kind that friends keep going over time, to see if anyone can better their position from the last time round. So there is no single text, no single author, but many texts and many authors, and they do not speak serially, one after another, each the author of a chapter. They speak, as it were, all at once, on the page, each giving their view on the particular point under discussion, with even the layout of the page reflecting the growth outward over time of opinion on a central text, the Mishnah, centrally located on the page.[49] Moreover, the sages often speak in the present tense, as though they're still here. *And nobody tells you what the rule really is.* It's just in there somewhere (that's why you're allowed to ask for a responsa). So when it is said that the Talmud was never finished, this is not just an abstract proposition. It couldn't be finished, in the sense of a finished, normative product, because the discussion is still going on, and the Talmud just captures the discussion as it has gone thus far. It is, of course, too late to get your argument into the physical text of the Talmud; they stopped actually writing it a millennium and a half ago. If you were there, though, you could have gotten your oar in and since you could then there is no reason why you can't now. So you can write a responsa or a code or commentary, and you will also be creating the talmudic tradition, as it was intended.

Before you write a new code or commentary, however, in the talmudic tradition, you have a lot of existing Talmud to learn. And you have to learn it, to be taken seriously, the way it was meant to be learned, that is to say, not just by studying it, with a yellow marker, but by actually joining in the discussion and re-creating it, with the old students of the Talmud, those on the page, and with the new ones, other than yourself. So learning the Talmud is not a process of reading, as it is usually understood; it is rather a process of 'interactive reading',[50] interaction in discussion with those who have been at it a long time and interaction in discussion with those like you, who are just starting or are somewhere in the process. Studying the Talmud makes a lot of collective noise; it happens formally in yeshiva, rooms where groups split up into twos and threes and each group works through a text, someone always talking, someone always questioning, the texts coming alive as they

---

[48] Goldenberg, 'Talmud' (1984), above, 129 at 157 (also 'a terribly frustrating book . . . everything is fascinating . . . nothing can be trusted'); cf., however, Dorff and Rosett, *Living Tree* (1988) at 230 (even Gemarah form of reporting by the 'winners').

[49] See, for the layout, Goldenberg, 'Talmud' (1984), above, at 140, 141; and for the 'interactive' character of the text, implicitly telling historians to 'go away', see Akenson, *Surpassing Wonder* (1998), above, at 379, 612.

[50] Holz (ed.), *Back to Sources* (1984) at 16. On the late (10th-cent.) development of silent reading as a general phenomenon in the western tradition, however, see A. Manguel, *A History of Reading* (New York: Penguin, 1996) at 43 ('rumbling din' of libraries of Carthage and Rome).

get support, or lose it. You don't learn the Talmud by reading about it, as you are now doing, or even by reading about it from a teacher who is learned in it, as you could do. You learn it by doing it. '[T]he student must participate intellectually and emotionally in the talmudic debate . . . becoming, to a certain degree, a creator.'[51] And as the Talmud was never completed so is there never an end to its study; '[O]ne never says goodbye.'[52]

The Talmud therefore includes the voices of many and is open to all. It follows that its language is not intimidating, that its categories and concepts are those of everday life, that it appears deliberately to avoid abstraction in expression. If all of life is to be ruled by law, for all adherents to the tradition, the law must be immediately accessible. There are many dimensions, however, to this simplicity of expression. If all of life is to be ruled, then all the situations of life must be recognizable in the law; more accurately, the law begins to resemble the situations of life and to itself dissolve into a reflection of existing life. When is the time for evening prayer? Well, when *could* be the time for evening prayer? There is sunset, the evening meal, the end of the first watch, midnight (that is, before the next day), or before the light of dawn. And there are opinions in favour of each of these. So here we all deliberate. There's lots of law, but we also have to decide. Moreover, the categories which do exist cannot be taken, well, literally. If there is liability for the damage of the ox, you cannot really believe that an ox is an ox.[53] So we combine the endless variations of life with the use of simple but really technical models and we discover very intricate forms of reasoning.

## THE STYLE OF REASON

There is great mental agility required for talmudic reasoning. All the opinions have to be dealt with; all the potential cases, and variations, have to be considered; there's usually no time to retreat and write—the written tradition is applied most frequently in oral study and debate. So again, as with the chthonic tradition, we find what is perhaps best described as interstitial rationality, that which acknowledges the fragility of all traditions and seeks to use the resources of the present one to prevent its dissolution.[54] Unlike the chthonic tradition, however, the talmudic tradition leaves clear tracks; much of what has gone before is recoverable in writing. So there is enormous escalation in detail; the interstitial rationality is no longer

---

[51] Steinsaltz, *Essential Talmud* (1976) at 9.

[52] Hoenig, *Essence Talmudic Law and Thought* (1993) at 169.

[53] Steinsaltz, *Essential Talmud* (1976) at 147, citing an unidentified sage, and arguing, at 229, that '[T]he great advantage of employing such models, as opposed to abstract concepts, lies, *inter alia*, in the ability constantly to supervise the validity of methods of demonstration . . . [A]bstract thought . . . cannot be defined except by use of similarly abstract terms, we can never know whether they constitute a departure from the subject or are still relevant'; and generally on the Talmud's casuistic style, Elon, *Jewish Law*, vol. I (1994) at 79, ibid., vol. III at 1073–8.

[54] Above, Ch. 3, *Reason's domain*.

something you use whenever you have to, with what you can remember. It is now a life's work, and requires great natural gifts of recall and analysis. There is enormous rationality within the tradition; it bristles with personal accomplishment. What is most important, however, is that the rationality is within the tradition. The mole risks losing its cover, but stays within its chosen terrain.[55]

There is thus a particular style of rationality which emerges within the tradition. It is not a systematic type of rationality. The existence of the texts, their inspiration, and the disparate forms of life which they address, resist the systematizing impulse.[56] There is resistance to system most of all because the Talmud resists simple and apparently satisfactory forms of proof, which could establish elements of the system, capable of systemic interaction. There can be no system if nothing is established, all is constantly swirling in the exchange of opinion.[57] There can be no one to systematize. There is discipline of thought in all of this but it is polyvalent, tolerating contradiction. It also tolerates what western lawyers call equity; the law is only an external framework and people have also to act according to other criteria.[58] If you are a very good talmudic lawyer you can try to make it clearer, try to make it more explicitly rational, try to push outwards the boundary of the tradition. Maimonides did this in the twelfth century (the timing is probably important, a lot was then going on). He wrote a brilliant commentary, or code, setting out the law and leaving out the opinions on which it was built. What then happened? Maimonides was not purporting to start a new tradition, but to provide new impetus to an old one. He did this by eliminating much of the evidence of the tradition, by attempting to reduce it to the text he produced. He demonstrated, to use a contemporary phrase, 'mere brilliance'.[59] So the tradition pulled him back in; it contextualized the effort of visible rationality. Maimonides was criticized for arrogance; his code is now viewed as one of a number, dependent on its predecessors and on the comments it has itself attracted.[60]

---

[55] On rationality as the mole in contextual traditions, see above, Ch. 1, Massaging Tradition.

[56] G. Scholem, 'Revelation and Tradition as Religious Categories in Judaism' in G. Scholem, *The Messianic Idea in Judaism* (New York: Schocken, 1971) 282 at 289 ('Not system but *commentary* is the legitimate form through which truth is approached'); Abécassis, 'Droit et réligion' (1993) at 28 ('la justice ne peut se réduire à des règles et à des systèmes'; also cannot obtain perfection, purity, clarity); Gordis, *Dynamics of Judaism* (1990) at 63 (while western thought based on logic of relevance and coherence, Talmud adheres to logic of association, not unlike free-association techniques of modern psychoanalysis).

[57] On concepts of system, see below, Ch. 5, *Revolutions, systems, language and interpretation*; and on pilpul (dialectical reasoning) being incapable of accepting simple proof, continually searching for incontrovertible evidence, Steinsaltz, *Essential Talmud* (1976) at 231.

[58] A. Weingort, 'Ethique et droit dans la tradition du judaïsme' Rev. hist. dr. fr. étr. 1990. 463 at 470 ('Justice, oui, mais on doit y associer la miséricorde, le ra'hamim'); and on living 'inside the law', above, *The divine law applied*.

[59] J. Gordley, 'Mere Brilliance: The Recruitment of Law Professors in the United States' (1993) 41 Am. J. Comp. Law 367, notably at 383.

[60] Dorff and Rosett, *Living Tree* (1988) at 368, 369, 372; Goldenberg, 'Talmud' (1984), above, at 162 ('no code has brought that history [of talmudic law] to an end'); and on the 'fierce debate and sharp critical reaction' following Maimonides' Code, Elon, *Jewish Law*, vol. III (1994) at 1215; C. Leben, 'Maïmonide et la codification du droit hébraïque' Droits 1998. 113 at 122 ff.

In modern language, we would say that the talmudic tradition is one of inter-pretation. There are very interesting features to this interpretation, beyond those already noted. The process of Midrash, or interpretation, is a recognized one, and there are provisions in the Mishnah itself relating to deduction, analogy and things that most lawyers know about.[61] The formal provisions are swamped, however, by the sources themselves and the process which flows more directly from them. The process itself seems to control the discussion of methods of interpretation. Are earlier sources (more sacred) or later sources (more learned) to be preferred? There is authority . . . for both propositions.[62] You are allowed, moreover, to deduce 'the possible from the impossible'.[63] Is male religious conversion valid without circum-cision of the penis? Well, women can be converted without circumcision of the penis. Is this a valid argument? 'Although it is impossible, it is an impressive piece of evidence.'[64] The tradition builds in ways which do not always follow certain types of reasoning.

## THE INDIVIDUAL IN THE TALMUD

The chthonic tradition is one which resists individual powers or entitlements, in the form of rights, because of the higher form of obligation owed to the cosmos. Individuals are much more evident in the talmudic tradition, which has recorded individual opinions, with their authors' names, for more than a thousand years. Yet there is no language of rights in the Talmud, no single word which conveys the same bundle of prerogatives as does the word 'right' and its equivalences in western languages.[65] The word which dominates is rather mitzvah, as in bar mitzvah (on reaching the age of obligation) or, once again, mitzvat talmud Torah. The first obligation is to study the Torah, through the Talmud, to know one's remaining obligations. In performing one's obligations, one shows one's love of God. Where is the place for right or individual prerogative in this? You can, it is true, always look at the other end of an obligation and find someone entitled to its benefit, and you can always call this person a holder of a right. You could, but the talmudic tradition doesn't. It does place the human person in a

---

[61] See B. W. Holz, 'Midrash,' in Holz (ed.), *Back to Sources* (1984) at 177; Steinsaltz, *Essential Talmud* (1976) ch. 27 on *Midrash* (Halakhic Exegesis); Gordis, *Dynamics of Judaism* (1990) at 86; D. Halivni, *Midrash, Mishnah, and Gemara* (Cambridge, Mass., London: Harvard Univ. Press, 1986); Elon, *Jewish Law* vol. I (1994) at 283 ff.; Segal, 'Jewish Law during Tannaitic Period' (1996), above, at 108 ff.; Dorff and Rosett, *Living Tree* (1988) at 145 ff. Midrash usually refers to exegesis of biblical texts, but may also extend to that of other sacred texts, such that the 'gemara sections of the Talmud are a kind of Midrash on the Mishnah'; Holz (ed.), *Back to Sources* (1984) at 178.

[62] Feldman, *Marital Relations* (1968) above, at 14; Stone, 'Pursuit of Counter-Text' (1993) at 853.

[63] Steinsaltz, *Essential Talmud* (1976) at 228.

[64] Ibid., at 229.

[65] Novack, 'Religious Human Rights in Judaic Texts' (1996), above, at 177; Weingort, 'Ethique et droit dans la tradition du judaïsme' (1990), above, at 465; Hoenig, *Essence of Talmudic Law and Thought* (1993) at 72 (emphasis on duty rather than rights since talmudic law is theocentric).

privileged position in the universe, so you can argue that the value of the person, the ultimate justification for rights, exists in the Talmud, and this is probably true.[66] You might go on then to say that rights therefore implicitly exist in the Talmud, and of course there have been some who have said this.[67] So the notion of rights does exist somewhere in the entire bran-tub of the talmudic tradition, as it does in all traditions today. There is a very vigorous argument, however, as to whether rights can have any larger hold than this in the world of the Talmud.[68]

Since the place of rights is not firmly established in talmudic thinking, neither is that of equality. Again, if all roles are divine, all should be accepted with joy. But what, precisely, does the talmudic tradition say about role? Probably as much, precisely, as it does about anything else. There may be opinions which are given precedence over others, but if you need another opinion, you can probably find one. It has been said, however, that if you argue that women have rights of partici-pation in jewish life which are equal to those of men, you are assuming a double burden. You have to make a general case for rights (a difficult one) and a particular case for women. So the traditional argument, the one within the tradition, for equal participation of women, is one which uses the resources of the tradition.[69] Who needs rights? They may just provoke more opposition. Are women prohibited certain forms of participation? It is true there is an obligation imposed on fathers to educate sons in the Talmud, but does this mean women are excluded?[70] Once again, the tradition is being worked over. The role of women historically may be a 'male construct'; there would then be nothing divine about present practices.[71] This would mean you could change things.

---

[66] Novack, 'Religious Human Rights in Judaic Texts' (1996), above, at 177 (absence of language of rights not implying non-existence of ideas and values for which they stand).

[67] Fishbane, 'Image of the Human and Rights of the Individual' (1988) at 19, citing Gen. 9:6 'for in the image of God has God made man'.

[68] See the discussion below, this Chapter, *Talmudic example?*

[69] Cover, 'Obligation' (1987) at 67, 68 (arguing in terms of 'the law, properly understood').

[70] Steinsaltz, *Essential Talmud* (1976) at 138, 139. On women's roles see J. O'Connor, 'Rereading, reconceiv-ing and reconstructing traditions: feminist research in religion' (1989) 17 *Women's St.* 101 at 108–10; Naamani, 'Marriage and Divorce' (1963); Grajevsky, 'Quelques réformes des droits de la femme juive' (1963); Epstein *Jewish Marriage Contract* (1927); Gordis, *Dynamics of Judaism* (1990) ch. 11 ('Women's Role in Religious Life'); Rackman, *Modern Halakhah* (1995), ch. 63; P. Strum, 'Women and the Politics of Religion in Israel' (1989) 11 Hum. Rts Q. 483; M. Meiselman, *Jewish Woman in Jewish Law* (New York: KTAV/Yeshiva Univ. Press, 1978); R. Biale, *Women and Jewish Law* (New York: Schocken, 1984), notably at 33, 34 on teaching of Torah to women.

[71] Fishbane, 'Image of the Human and Rights of the Individual' (1993) at 27. Some would have women officiating and fully participating in synagogues until approximately 300 BCE.

# TALMUD, THE DIVINE WILL AND CHANGE

Concepts of change are profoundly influenced by the tradition within which they exist. So the chthonic tradition doesn't really have a concept of change, since the changes the tradition tolerates don't really matter—they are simply the ongoing phenomenon of life, compatible with the tradition. That which counts, the cosmos, is maintained for later arrivals, unprejudiced by any notion of passage of time. Things begin to shift, however, with the Talmud, though nothing is abrupt. God is there, the Perfect Author, and if it is true that all which is written has been foreseen, so all which comes to pass has been contemplated. '[I]f the world changes, the Word has been prepared for all contingencies from the outset.'[72] As the Talmud can be a work of ongoing *creation*, under divine auspices, so too can change occur within the world, under divine control. 'God is never on sabbatical', and there can therefore be no fatal rupture between past and present.[73] Historical or contingent time, and change, can therefore now exist, but they are built right in. If historical time does exist, moreover, it exists within 'a special, timeless sphere of revelation, in which all generations were, as it were, gathered together'.[74] So change does not occur at the level of human relations with God; it occurs at the level of relations of humans with one another and with the world, and here all is controlled by talmudic obligation.

Why talmudic tradition developed this way, departing in some ways from chthonic tradition while adhering to it in others, is profoundly anchored in jewish religion. In this religion, we find for the first time the statement that 'in the image of God has God made man',[75] so we now know that human beings are not simply part of the cosmos, they occupy a special relation to divinity in the cosmos. The jewish religion is rather sparing, however, in terms of the consequences of this special relation. The biblical texts are reticent in terms of salvation and there is relatively little reassurance of life after death.[76] You could, however, as a reflection yourself of God, move towards an understanding of the divine word; you could move towards being something like God, even if you could never arrive. In doing so you use to the utmost your human talents and rationality, themselves a reflections of God's,

---

[72] J. Goldin, 'Of Change and Adaptation in Judaism' in J. Goldin, *Studies in Midrash and Related Literature* (ed. B. Eichler and J. Tigay) (Philadelphia/New York/Jerusalem: The Jewish Publication Soc., 5748/1988) 215 at 222.

[73] Ibid., at 221.

[74] G. Scholem, 'Tradition and Commentary as Religious Categories in Judaism,' in A. Cohen (ed.), *Arguments and Doctrines* (New York: Harper and Row, 1970) 303 at 306; yet for 'this marvelous new concept of time' as a great gift to western thought see T. Cahill, *The Gifts of the Jews* (New York: Doubleday, 1998), above, at 127–32, 251.

[75] Gen. 9: 6, and see above, this Chapter, *The style of reason*, for talmudic conclusions.

[76] For talmudic 'refusal to compete with the Christians' in relation to life after death, see Akenson, *Surpassing Wonder* (1998), above, at 362, 363 and 383–9.

though infinitely paler. You can change yourself, over time, through dedication to God. So one tradition moves slowly away from another, on the ground of necessary recognition of human particularity, still within a divinely inspired world.

Talmudic thought is thus compatible with a notion of change of the world, though does little to really encourage it. Creation is a hard act to follow. The sages thus displayed little interest in either scientific speculation or what we know as philosophy, and it has been said that this was so because of the 'correlation between the world and Torah, the latter forming part of the essence of the natural world and not merely constituting external speculation on it'.[77] If you need to be scientific for purposes of the Talmud, so be it.[78] Beyond that, there is no real place to stand.

### OF SCHOOLS, TRADITIONS AND MOVEMENTS

Change and significant difference do not instantly appear, however, as soon as the new tradition has formed around the revelation. The process appears to have taken a relatively long time. Some have said that the Sanhedrin played an important role, during its existence, in ensuring coherence within the tradition. Yet coherence is not stagnation, and the tradition had to offer means of acknowledging human efforts to realize divine will. So there was legislation near the end of the second century BCE to improve the status of women in marriage.[79] There was also resort to divine will to evade the letter of the law, even known as evasion of law, so that a rabbi could marry three hundred times to provide inexpensive food to those who would otherwise hunger.[80] The technical models of the Talmud, moreover, continue to provide ongoing means of argument in situations perceived as novel, today notably in bioethics.[81]

Major differences within the tradition, and changing views of it, seem to have crystallized, however, with the disappearance of the Sanhedrin.[82] The historic schools of Shammai and Hillel emerged, the latter taking views said to be more

---

[77] Steinsaltz, *Essential Talmud* (1976) at 7.

[78] For talmudic, clinical investigation, see ibid. at 97–100; cf., however, for sporadic outbursts of jewish scientific activity, e.g., in contact with islam from the 13th to 15th centuries, or from mid-19th to mid-20th centuries (Albert Einstein, Niels Bohr), C. Singer, 'Science and Judaism' in Finkelstein (ed.), *The Jews* (1960), above, at 1376, notably at 1381, 1383.

[79] Steinsaltz, *Essential Talmud* (1976) at 23.

[80] Silberg, *Talmudic Law and Modern State* (1973) at 22, 23.

[81] For traditional talmudic argument applied to the euthanasia debate, relying on talmudic concept of terefah (person suffering from fatal disease) and responsa in tragic choice cases (whether one can smother coughing child to save others from escaping pursuers; whether one can bury those not entirely dead to escape killing of self), see Sinclair, *Tradition and Biological Revolution* (1989). Cf. Fishbane, 'Image of the Human and Rights of the Individual' (1988) notably at 17 (on 'the absolute and uncompromisable worth of human life', though defending historical diversity of opinion in halakic literature as strongest argument against legal dogmatism); and more generally F. Rosner and J. Bleich, (eds.), *Jewish Bioethics* (New York/London: Sanhedrin Press, 1979).

[82] Urbach, *Sages* (1987), above, at 299 ('The proud of heart increased, the disputes multiplied in Israel and became two Torahs').

'lenient',[83] and eventually becoming the accepted or leading version of the tradition. Here are institutionalized forms of difference; one would change the teaching of the other, if not the entire tradition. Once again, however, revelation reels them both in. So some of the most famous words of the talmudic tradition are those which reconcile, within a single, ongoing tradition, the apparently conflicting schools of Shammai and Hillel. '[T]hese and these [both] are the words of the Living God.'[84] In the notion of 'These and these' there is affirmation of the conciliatory, multi-valent character of the tradition. One cannot say of the Torah, 'this is good and this is not'; all views within the Torah are sacred and all must be accepted.[85] This does not prevent, however, the ongoing exercise of judgment within the tradition.

Diversity within the tradition did not end with the decline of the school of Shammai. Today the world of the Talmud contains great diversity of thought, probably more than ever before in its history. There are thus 'traditions' within the tradition, themselves reflecting both internal and external influence. The sephardic tradition originated in the Babylonian community; with the diaspora it took root in Spain and Africa, and moved on from there. It has been influenced by Arab thought. The ashkenazi tradition originated in the Palestinian community; it then took refuge in Italy, and elsewhere in Europe, in the first years of the common era. Here as well there has been great subsequent movement. The sephardic tradition, like the Babylonian, may be more pluralist and de-centralized than the ashkenazi and Palestinian.[86]

If the multiplicity of talmudic 'traditions' has much to do with geography, the existence of so-called 'movements' has more to do with what some would call ideology. In the world there are orthodox jews (all halakhah is binding, including the later codes); conservative jews (the Talmud itself is binding); and reform jews (all is persuasive, given contemporary rationality).[87] The task of reconciliation is rendered more difficult by concentration of reform and conservative jews in the United States and Europe; orthodox jews in Israel. Some have drawn pessimistic conclusions.[88] And the story is told of the jew stranded on the desert island who built two synagogues—one to go to and one to stay away from. The differences between the movements are not simply on points of detail in substantive law; they relate to the entire normativity of the tradition and its interpretation. If some

[83] Dane, 'Yoke of Heaven' (1994) at 369. Jesus would have been a member of Hillel's school.

[84] *Babylonian Talmud*, Eruvin 13b; discussed and cited in Stone, 'Pursuit of Counter-Text' (1993) at 828; Steinsaltz, *Essential Talmud* (1976) at 6; Abécassis, 'Droit et religion' (1993) ('Les deux thèses expriment les deux la parole du Dieu vivant').

[85] Steinsaltz, *Essential Talmud* (1976) at 6.

[86] See the discussion of recent research into comparative dimensions of the traditions, in Stone, 'Pursuit of Counter-Text' (1993) at 848; and on the notion of 'jewish laws' as opposed to 'jewish law', Jackson, *Essays* (1975); and on the variety of jewish 'practice,' Falk, *Introduction, Jewish Law* (1968) at 40.

[87] For more subtle differentiations, see N. Totenstreich, *Tradition and Reality: the Impact of History on Modern Jewish Thought* (New York: Random House, 1972) at 112–14; Dane, 'Yoke of Heaven' (1994) at 354, 358, 359; Gordis, 'Jewish Tradition in Modern World' (1978) at 152; Sherwin, *In Partnership with God* (1990) at 42, 43.

[88] D. Vital, *The Future of the Jews* (Cambridge, Mass.: Harvard Univ. Press, 1990).

would put reform jews nearly without the tradition, orthodox jews are criticized for monolithic and static views, repudiating the nature of talmudic dialogue.[89] There are intimations of corruption in both these sets of charges, intimations of abandonment of essentials.

## TALMUD AND CORRUPTION

Corruption is a delicate and fleeting subject. The most difficult to ascertain is intellectual corruption, the disengagement of the mind and reliance on formulae, often accompanied by force. There is, in this, nothing itself which would justify adherence by others, no present contribution to the life of the tradition. Reform jews do not appear to represent so much a corruption of the tradition as, in some individual cases, its near abandonment, and we will see that the tradition (at least presently) provides no specific means to prevent this. The discussion of corruption of the tradition appears more acute with respect to certain ultra-orthodox, marginal versions of it, those which would preclude all present debate, vest absolute authority in enforcers of the true tradition, and resort to violence in protection of it.[90] The tradition, inevitably, has some information which might be used to support this view, notably the law relating to the rodef or pursuer of the jewish people, invoked recently to justify the murder, by a jewish person, of the Prime Minister of Israel.[91] Again, we may be encountering the possibility of all traditions being affected in their ongoing existence by meta- or second-order traditions of tolerance or intolerance. Even a tradition as internally tolerant as the talmudic one may find itself invoked as an instrument against others.

Of the more precise forms of corruption, criminal and institutional, there appears no debilitating form of the former in the talmudic tradition. There is just crime, with which the tradition deals, as it should. There are famous charges of institutional corruption, however, in the form of the attacks by Jesus and his disciples against the priests, scribes and rabbis. The priests would have enlarged the borders of their garments, sought the uppermost rooms at feasts (we again see the use of technical models in the tradition, here used by the new christians).[92] Yet

---

[89] Sherwin, *In Partnership with God* (1990) at 42, 43 (orthodox jews cannot account for plurality of halakhah views; cannot reject external models while continuing to use them, e.g., salaried rabbinate).

[90] On ultra-orthodox thought, see M. Friedman, 'Life Tradition and Book Tradition in the Development of Ultraorthodox Judaism' in H. Goldberg (ed.), *Judaism Viewed from Within and From Without* (Albany: State Univ. of New York Press, 1987) at 235 (notably on adoption of more stringent standards by young); Dane, 'Yoke of Heaven' (1994) at 374, n. 102.

[91] The din rodef would allow the killing of the tyrant of the jewish people, here said to be an elected prime minister. On the general law of the rodef, see Rackman, *Modern Halakhah* (1995) at 84; M. Finkelman, 'Self-Defense and Defense of Others in Jewish Law' (1987) 33 Wayne St. Law Rev. 1257. Cf., however, on the invalidity, according to talmudic law, of terrorist acts by the jewish 'underground', Rackman, *Modern Halakhah* (1995) at 98 ff., notably at 102.

[92] See Matt. 23: 1; and for elucidation of the ancient charges, W. Barklay, *By What Authority* (Darton: Longman and Todd, 1974), ch. 2 ('Authority in the Old Testament: the Authority of Tradition').

priests and rabbis were unsalaried at this time, and most today would not criticize some advantage drawn from a life's work. The salaries did in fact later materialize, and living within salaries is no form of corruption. Jesus also attacked the entire intellectual tradition of the Talmud, for its legalism and reach into everyday life. Here Jesus' words have been brought into contemporary form by the New International Version of the New Testament, and they have perhaps still wider significance today. In previous versions he is reported as saying: 'Beware of the scribes.' Today it has become 'Beware the teachers of the law.'[93] So with Jesus we see the emergence of a still later tradition, with profound legal significance. This is but one instance, however, of the relations between talmudic law and other legal traditions.

## TALMUDIC LAW AND STATE LAW

The law of the jewish people may be seen as originally chthonic, in its form prior to Moses. The revelation granted to Moses gave a new beginning to the tradition, and also allowed it to define itself differently from the earlier, chthonic tradition. Some of these differences, notably with respect to the place of the individual, have been noted, along with ongoing commonalities.[94] To the extent that jewish people now became other than chthonic people, it is because of the effect of revelation, and its subsequent inspiration of a talmudic tradition which gave primacy of place to law. So from this point the identity of the jewish people became more precise, and more legally dependent. From one of many chthonic peoples, the jewish people came to be one inspired by revelation and governed by law rooted in revelation. Talmudic law has thus been, given its place in the tradition, a major defining element of jewish identity. Absent a territory or state, it has been said, the text itself became a homeland.[95] Others are those who do not bind themselves by talmudic law.

---

[93] Mark 12: 38. For a contemporary response to Jesus, who had plans incompatible with the Talmud, see Goldenberg, 'Talmud' (1984), above, at 130 (scribes attacked as pettifogging, self-righteous hypocrites, religious style open to corruption, since unending interpretation, yet scribes considered scriptures a source of infinite wisdom, saw no better way to spend lives than in study).

[94] See above, this Chapter, *The individual in the Talmud* and discussion in Talmud, the Divine Will and Change.

[95] Holz (ed.), *Back to Sources* (1984) 15, at 17, citing G. Steiner on the text as homeland; and see Steinsaltz, *Essential Talmud* (1976) at 267 ('no Jewish community could survive for long without the ability to study Talmud', itself requiring constant renewal and innovation, requiring active participation). Yet if the text is the homeland, it is a homeland of almost infinite doctrinal possibilities, given the disparity of talmudic thought. So the instrumental use of law, as an instrument of identification, is diluted by the impossibility of linking identification with particular rules or with a maker of particular rules.

## TALMUDIC LAW AND JEWISH IDENTITY

Jewish identity, like other identities, is thus ultimately defined by recall and use of information, or memory. It is true that there is great controversy on the question of jewish identity, largely in relation to constituting the members of the state of Israel. And talmudic law did admit the transmission of jewish identity through the maternal line.[96] More importantly, it admitted it, and still does, through conversion, though the orthodox movement resists mightily conversions effected by the reform movement. So if you agree to make the Talmud your law, you may become jewish, assuming jewish identity.[97] And you may also leave the jewish community, through no longer adhering to its law, though at this point the boundaries of personal identity are not sharply defined.[98] When it could apply physical sanctions, talmudic law used notions of both treason and heresy,[99] yet neither of these could be invoked for simple departure from the community, simple neglect of the law. Today notions of excommunication and shunning are still in use in some measure, controlled by state law of tort or delict, yet these do not prevent departure; they give example to those who would remain within the community.[100]

Jewish identity, in the form of reliance on the Talmud, was partly in function of the reactions of others. Seeing its importance, those opposed to talmudic teaching banned its teaching or burned the Talmud on a number of occasions through the

[96] England, 'Law and Religion in Israel' (1987) at 193–6 ('Who is a Jew?'); Steinsaltz, *Essential Talmud* (1976) at 136 (where marriage mixed, child jewish only if mother jewish); Gordis, *Dynamics of Judaism* (1990) at 204–9 (controversy over change to patrilineal descent by reform judaism); D. Sinclair, 'Jewish Law in the State of Israel' in Hecht et al. (eds.), *History and Sources of Jewish Law* (1996) 397 at 404–6.

[97] See, e.g., Lewis, *Middle East* (1995), above, at 32 (Greeks and jews differed from other definitions of difference based on birth and blood; barriers could be crossed or even removed; by beginning of christian era 'Hellenized barbarians and Judaized gentiles were a common feature in many Middle Eastern cities'). On conversion in ancient jewish law, notably on the obstacle of male circumcision, then a 'gruesome prospect', see D. Daube, *Ancient Jewish Law* (1981), Lecture I at 1, notably at 11; and more generally J. Rosenbloom, *Conversion to Judaism: From the Biblical Period to the Present* (Cincinatti: Hebrew College Press, 1978); J. Cohen, *Intermarriage and Conversion: A Halakhic Solution* (Hoboken, NJ: KTAV Publishing House, 1987); S. Lerner, 'Choosing Judaism: Issues Relating to Conversion' in R. Geffen (ed.), *Celebration and Renewal: Rites of Passage in Judaism* (Philadelphia/Jerusalem: Jewish Publication Soc., 5753/1993).

[98] Talmudic teaching includes a notion of apostasy, without apparent discussion of sanction for the act of apostasy itself, though the Supreme Court of Israel has determined, in a majority opinion, that the apostate can no longer benefit as a jew from the Law of Return, 1950. See *Rufeisen v. Minister of the Interior* in A. Laudau (ed.), *Selected Judgments of the Supreme Court of Israel* (Jerusalem: Ministry of Justice, 1971) at 1; B.-Z. Schereschewsky, 'Apostate', in Elon (ed.), *Principles of Jewish Law* (1975) at 378, 379; M. Corinaldi, 'Continuing Apostasy According to Halakha and the Law of Return' (1996) 8 Jewish Law Assoc. St. 43.

[99] Dane, 'Yoke of Heaven' (1994) at 361, with refs.; Stone, 'Pursuit of Counter-text' (1993) at 872; Greenberg, 'Rabbinic Reflections on Defying Illegal Orders' (1970) above.

[100] Broyde, 'Forming Religious Communities and Respecting Dissenter's Rights' (1996) 203 at 208–10, noting that vast numbers have distanced themselves from the Talmud yet are under no danger of excommunication (at 212). Excommunication appears to have been rarely used for simple statements, given the great diversity of opinion in the Talmud; it was invoked, however, for opposition to concrete decisions. See, for an example, Steinsaltz, *Essential Talmud* (1976) at 27; and generally Elon, *Jewish Law*, vol. I (1994) at 10–13.

centuries.[101] Jewish people also came to live in 'compulsory communities', those formed in response to 'organized pressure' of states or other communities.[102] They were also expelled, at various times from the thirteenth through the eighteenth centuries, from England, France, Spain, Portugal, Lithuania, and many specific towns and regions in Germany, Italy, Slovakia and the Czech Republic. All of this did not eliminate, but reinforced, a sense of identity. The oral tradition, at least, can be maintained, even if all the books are burned. Today the identity of jewish people appears to have overcome the threat of external aggression, though the state of Israel may never be entirely secure. Some maintain, however, that there are more serious threats from within, given the alternatives of other traditions.

## TALMUDIC RETREAT?

As a tradition, talmudic law relies on talmudic sources and not external ones. Since the Talmud has never been formally completed, however, the contributions of present generations continue to expand its stock of information. So the Talmud has no formal technique for effecting closure to the outside world; in such a riot of opinion the idea is even difficult to contemplate. People who are jewish can thus seek to integrate external ideas into talmudic thought, or they can simply act according to external thought. In both cases the total identity of jewish tradition, and jewish people, is altered. Already the development of the tradition showed elements of Greek, Roman and Arab thought.[103] With the diaspora into the western world, western thought became unavoidable.

The first block of western information which created difficulties for the talmudic tradition, however, was that of christianity. In the criticism by Jesus and his disciples of the talmudic tradition there is more than a desire for reform. Paul concluded

---

[101] See, for detailed enumeration of burnings, Hoenig, *Essence Talmudic Law and Thought* (1993) at 112–21; for Paris in 1242, N. Rouland, S. Pierré-Caps, J. Poumarède, *Droit des minorités et des peuples autochtones* (Paris: Presses universitaires de France, 1996) at 68; and for the role of the Crusades in the pattern of violent anti-semitism beginning in the 11th century, see R. Cohen, *Global diasporas: an introduction* (Seattle: Univ. of Washington Press, 1997) at 8; N. Davis, *Europe: a History* (London: Pimlico, 1997) at 358 (crusaders 'ravaged' countries through which they marched; in 1096 killed up to 8,000 Jews in passage through Rhineland, first of Europe's pogroms).

[102] Gordis, 'Jewish Tradition in Modern World' (1978) at 242 (compulsory community later evolving into ghetto). The word 'ghetto' appears derived from the old Italian word for a foundry—gietto—which was the most evident landmark in the area in Venice which was assigned to Jews.

[103] For Greek influence see Urbach, *Sages* (1987), above; Jackson, 'Evolution and Foreign Influence' (1968), above at 376; Gordis, *Dynamics of Judaism* (1990) at 123; for Roman, Rouland, Pierré-Caps, Poumarède, *Droit des minorités* (1996), above, at 67 (use of roman legal language in Hebrew); B. Jackson, 'On the Problem of Roman Influence on the Halakhah and Normative Self-Definition in Judaism', in E. P. Sanders (ed.), *Jewish and Christian Self-Definition*, vol. II, *Aspects of Judaism in the Graeco-Roman Period* (Philadelphia: Fortress Press, 1981) at 157; and for Babylonian, Jackson, *Essays* (1968) at 373, n. 10–12 (indicating initial thesis of direct Babylonian influence being supplanted by that of parallel, independent development; this view itself now seen as probably going 'too far').

that 'Christ is the end of the law'[104] and in the description of Jesus the jew as a new Moses there is the implication of a new covenant in law, overtaking the old as had that of Moses had overtaken the old.[105] Christianity proposed the end of law, in return for eternal salvation and life after death. These are major new proposals, but they built on what was known and accepted, notably the same God. So there would be a new world free of legal constraint and a later world in company with one's existing God. Many found the new proposals irresistible, and for them it was the end of talmudic law. Christianity therefore withdrew from the talmudic legal tradition vast numbers of potential adherents. Others, however, and this is our present concern, were unconvinced, either of the christian path to life after death or of a world without law (and in the latter case at least there is some proof they were right). So in the entanglement of jewish and christian theological and legal debate in the first years and centuries of the common era, we see the fragmenting of the older tradition and the partial emergence of the new. Neither could be distinct from the other. The new teaching of christianity accepted the Hebrew Bible, yet its proponents remained perplexed by ongoing adherence to the old law. So the burning of the Talmud in later centuries can be seen as part of a religious project to wipe the slate clean, sooner or later. Yet how could the Talmud be made to disappear if its foundation, the written Torah, was preserved by christianity itself? In recent writings on jewish and christian faiths, taken together, there is recognition of both commonality and diversity and mutual continuing existence.[106] What is true for theology appears true for law.

The entanglement of western and talmudic legal thought continues in the survival of talmudic law in the structures of western (and other) states. Secular state structures have provided both a means of protection of the jewish tradition, and the attraction of an alternative tradition. The dilemma is no less acute in the state of Israel, where the rabbinate has been formally incorporated into state structures, though talmudic law is applied only in matters of personal status and family law.[107] The state emerges, as elsewhere, as the guarantor of religious freedom and the ultimate arbiter of secular–religious relations. To reform jews, impressed with nine-

---

[104] Rom. 10: 4.

[105] Urbach, *Sages* (1987), above, at 302, 308; Dorff and Rosett, *Living Tree* (1988) at 235 ('mainstream' christian position following Paul that Jesus brought an end to covenant of law; 'hebrew christians' lasting only to 5th century). Cf., however, for the new covenant as fulfilling, rather than abolishing, talmudic law, A. Watson, *Jesus and the Law* (Athens, Ga. and London: Univ. of Georgia Press, 1996) at 8, 101, 102 (citing Matt. 5: 17, 'Do not think that I have come to abolish the Law or the Prophets; I have come not to abolish them but to fulfil them'); and for the 'wide variety of attitudes' found in the Gospels towards talmudic law, D. Piattelli and B. Jackson, 'Jewish Law During the Second Temple Period' in Hecht et al. (eds.), *History and Sources of Jewish Law* (1996) 19 at 37.

[106] See, e.g., E.-W. Böckenförde and E. Shils, *Jews and Christians in a Pluralistic World* (New York: St. Martin's Press, 1991).

[107] England, 'Law and Religion' (1987) at 192, 196, 197; Elon, *Jewish Law*, vol. IV (1994) at 1652 ff.; Dorff and Rosett, *Living Tree* (1988) at 564, 565; D. Sinclair, 'Jewish Law in the State of Israel' in Hecht et al. (eds.), *History and Sources of Jewish Law* (1996). Jewish law is also influential, however, in the creation of contemporary legislation in Israel. Elon, *Jewish Law*, vol. IV (1994) 1627 ff., with examples.

teenth and twentieth century concepts of rationalism, it has also provided another form of identity, in nationality, and maintaining talmudic tradition has been ultimately perhaps more problematical in a climate of official tolerance than in one of official hostility.[108] Yet there is also a 'turning back', and the emergence of neo-orthodoxy is the most visible and controversial evidence of this.

The relations between state and talmudic law exist also at more precise levels, notably in the working of the talmudic concept of the 'law of the land', or 'the law of the state is law' ('dina de malkhuta dina').[109] As in western choice of law, talmudic law can incorporate into itself norms which are not formally derived from its own sources. This has occurred, for example, in areas such as housing or rent control and copyright; it has been mooted for conflict of interest rules for legal counsel.[110] As in choice of law theory, the ultimate reasons for doing so are controversial. Can talmudic law have 'gaps'? It may be more appropriate to think in terms of deliberate incorporation, as suggested by the name of the doctrine itself. The decision to incorporate or not must still be made, however. Equity and equality in application of state law have been suggested as major criteria in deciding on incorporation.[111]

Talmudic law is criticized in contemporary states, however, precisely on these grounds of equity and equality. Notably in the United States, legal traditions which do not explicitly ensure equality of opportunity and participation have been criticized for failing to meet formal western ideals of individual equality.[112] So we see adherents to western law here taking the initiative, requiring the talmudic tradition to justify itself in terms of criteria which are at least partially external to the tradition. There are indications this justification is being undertaken.[113] This must be done if, more generally, talmudic law is to serve as a model or example for western law.

---

[108] B. Wasserstein, *Vanishing Diaspora: the Jews in Europe since 1945* (Cambridge, Mass.: Harvard Univ. Press, 1996) (citing high rates of intermarriage, low fertility, ignorance of hebrew); Vital, *Future of Jews* (1990), above; yet for the possibility of maintenance of cultural identity compatible with incorporation into the modern state, see R. Breton, W. W. Isajiw, W. E. Kalbach and J. G. Reitz, *Ethnic Identity and Equality* (Toronto: Univ. of Toronto Press, 1990) notably at 261 (jewish people ranking highest of surveyed groups in both 'ethnicity as a basis of social organization' and 'degree of incorporation' into Canadian society), 263 ('Cultural retention does not necessarily retard or impede incorporation; it may facilitate it'). Jewish legal identity in the modern state is also facilitated by any loosening of constitutional models to accommodate cultural diversity. See the discussion concerning chthonic peoples, above, Ch. 3, *The state as middle ground*.

[109] S. Shilo, 'Equity as Bridge' (1991); J. I. Roth, 'Crossing the Bridge to Secular Law: Three Models of Incorporation' (1991) 12 Cardozo Law Rev. 753; A. Fuss, 'A Question of "Comity" in Rabbinic Law' (1993) 7 Jewish Law Assoc. St. 59; L. Landman, *Jewish Law in the Diaspora: Confrontation and Accommodation* (Philadelphia: Dropsie College for Hebrew and Cognate Learning, 1968); S. Shilo, 'Dina de-Malkhuta Dina' in Elon (ed.), *Principles of Jewish Law* (1975) at 710; Elon, *Jewish Law*, vol. I (1994) at 64 ff.; Dorff and Rosett, *Living Tree* (1988) at 515 ff. (notably on recognition, or not, of civil divorces).

[110] Shilo, (1991) at 741, 744, 746.

[111] Ibid. at 739, 743.

[112] M. Minow, 'Interpreting Rights: An Essay for Robert Cover' (1987) 96 Yale L. J. 1860.

[113] See above, this Chapter, *The individual in the Talmud*.

TALMUDIC EXAMPLE?

How can a legal tradition so ancient, so religious, provide a model or example in contemporary states, which see themselves as secular? The answer is coming from adherents to contemporary western law and adherents to the idea of contemporary states, though it is entirely possible that the individual people most actively engaged in the debate are both jewish and western in their adherence to laws. The mingling of the traditions means a mingling of the adherents, which in turn influences the relations of the traditions. So we are seeing two major arguments made, in reliance on talmudic law, which are profoundly critical of western law yet from within western law. One argument concerns rights; the other the entire concept of law.

Talmudic law is aware of the concept of rights, as an element on the periphery of its base of information. The tradition itself did not enunciate a doctrine of individual entitlement but rather a doctrine of individual obligation, or mitzvah. Yet, the argument goes, if you look at obligation from the perspective of the person to whom it is owed, you have rights and, moreover, the analysis of obligation in terms of rights is preferable, since it accords due place to individual interest, or power, and constitutes a unique instrument for ensuring both equality and progress.[114] These are the arguments which have given rights doctrine such a pre-eminent place in the world, and nowhere are they heard more persistently than in the states which have given official recognition to them, now growing in number. Yet, the Talmud now says, as it always has, this is not all the debate. Perhaps the most distinguished critic of rights doctrine, in the name of the Talmud, was Robert Cover in the United States. Rights, said Cover, are 'indifferent to the vanity of varying ends' and are 'singularly weak in providing for the material guarantees of life and dignity'.[115] They can also be waived, which is not the case of obligation. Rights also are accompanied by a propensity to violence and are enforced by the state, a 'monstrous and powerful collective engine' with its 'almost unique mastery of violence'. A world of obligation, on the other hand, is not an empty or vain world. Obligations 'strongly bind and locate the individual [and] make a strong claim for substantive content.' If there is a right to education, we still have to look for someone to provide it. If there is an obligation to educate, as there is in the Talmud, we need look no further. So we have here an argument which does not accept the usual rhetoric of rights, nor their self-evident character, and offers something said to be better, and even older and better. Here too the Talmud would distinguish itself from the chthonic tradition; instead simply of an obligation to preserve the world, we owe obligations to do justice and help the oppressed. 'Cease to do evil. Learn to do good.'[116] Obliga-

---

[114] Ibid.

[115] Cover, 'Obligation' (1987) at 66–71, Rights doctrine would be more successful, however, with respect to the so-called negative rights, of expression or due process. For the claimed superiority of chthonic law in guaranteeing life and the support necessary for it, see above, Ch. 3, *Chthonic peoples, states and human rights*, and for Asian criticism of violence and sanction as a means of enforcing law, below, Ch. 9, *Limiting fa*.

[116] Isa. 1: 16, 17, in the version cited by Taylor, *Sources of Self* (1989), above, at 269.

tions trump rights; they're what you need, if you have rights, to have rights respected.

So the talmudic tradition is enriching western thinking on how rights can be justified, or criticized. More generally, it is enriching western thinking on how law can be conceived. Again in the United States, it is said that the academy is suffering a 'loss of confidence in the moral and intellectual basis of authoritative and supposedly neutral legal interpretation and in liberal political theory generally' and would now be seeking 'alternative models'.[117] Now, this might simply be a crisis in the academy (and there are many of them) or it might be something larger and of still greater concern. We have seen indications for greater concern coming from serious studies of individual conduct in the western world in the last quarter-century.[118] So talmudic law in the United States would be being reinterpreted to provide a requisite 'counter-model' for US law, while its incorporation into US legal thinking would also be redefining US legal theory. There is another middle ground here, though it is an 'often hidden encounter'.[119] Talmudic law would be appreciated now as a 'valuable and distinct tradition',[120] one which would be 'anti-hierarchical, egalitarian [well, almost] . . . communitarian, . . . written in a feminist voice (though not by females), based on reciprocal obligations, rather than rights' and which could maintain social coherence and identity even with a 'radically inconsistent and plural understanding' and 'a radically diffuse system of authority'.[121] Of course, it does all this because of God, and faith in God, so it might not work in a secular state. Can a tradition be borrowed only in part, while leaving out something fundamental to it? It wouldn't be the first time. Large differences do not yield incommensurability.

## A UNIVERSAL TALMUD?

The Talmud does not teach that it must be universalized. Salvation may be achieved outside of it and there is no need for others to convert to it. They may not even be particularly welcome.[122] The history of jewish religion and talmudic law has been

---

[117] Stone, 'Pursuit of Counter-Text' (1993) at 818.

[118] R. Inglehart, 'Changing values, economic development and political change' (1995) 47 Int. Soc. Sci. J. 379 (reporting results of 43-nation World Values Survey in 1990–1).

[119] Stone, 'Pursuit of Counter-Text' (1993) at 814; and see also at 821, on interpreting of the jewish tradition in light of particular concerns. On the notion of 'middle ground', see above, Ch. 3, Chthonic and other identities.

[120] And no longer one to be submerged in the construction of a national tradition. On earlier notions of legal acculturation and a unitary judaeo-american legal tradition, see J. Auerbach, Rabbis and Lawyers: The Journey from Torah to Constitution (Bloomington: Indiana Univ. Press: 1990).

[121] Stone, 'Pursuit of Counter-Text' (1993) at 818, 819 and 828, on 'anarchy of legal interpretation'; and see I. M. Rosenberg and Y. L. Rosenberg, 'Advice from Hillel and Shammai on How to Read Cases: Of Specificity, Retroactivity and New Rules' (1994) 42 Am. J. Comp. Law 581.

[122] See the discussion in England, 'Law and Religion' (1987) at 194, of orthodox resistance to conversions effected by the reform movement.

one of preservation, not conquest or aggression. The state of Israel may pursue some aggressive policies, but the state of Israel is not coterminous with jewish religion or talmudic law. 'Do not mistreat an alien or oppress him, for you were aliens in Egypt.'[123] 'When an alien lives with you in your land, do not mistreat him. The alien living with you must be treated as one of your native-born. Love him as yourself, for you were aliens in Egypt.'[124] So before the Greeks we have here a kind of cosmopolitanism, a recognition of the element of commmonality in us and them, gained through much experience of difference.[125] If the Talmud is to be used to justify aggression, this will have to be by way of defence, against external aggression. This, however, like the Iroquois peace, is a broad notion, and may be used with fatal results, however exceptional it may be.[126]

# GENERAL BIBLIOGRAPHY

Abécassis, A., 'Droit et religion dans la société hébraïque' (1993) 38 Archives de philosophie du droit 23.

Bazak, J., 'Res Judicata and the Authority of Arbitrators and Law Courts to Amend or to Change their Award in Jewish Law' (1992) 6 Jewish Law Association Studies 1.

Broyde, M. J., 'Forming Religious Communities and Respecting Dissenters' Rights: A Jewish Tradition for a Modern Society' in J. Witte, Jr. and J. van der Vyver, Religious Human Rights in Global Perspective (The Hague/Boston/London: Martinus Nijhoff, 1996) at 203.

Cohen, B., Jewish Law and Roman Law: A Comparative Study (New York: Jewish Theological Seminary, 1966).

Cover, R., 'Obligation: A Jewish Jurisprudence of the Social Order' (1988) 5 Journal of Law and Religion 65.

Dane, P., 'The Yoke of Heaven, the Question of Sinai, and the Life of Law' (1994) 44 University of Toronto Law Journal 353.

Daube, D., Ancient Jewish Law: Three Inaugural Lectures (Leiden: E. J. Brill, 1981).

Dorff, E. N. and Rosett, A., A Living Tree: the Roots and Growth of Jewish Law (Albany: State University of New York Press, 1988).

Elon, M., (ed.), The Principles of Jewish Law (Jerusalem: Keter Publishing House, 1975).

—— Jewish Law: History, Sources, Principles, trans. B. Auerbach and M. Sykes, 4 vols. (Philadelphia/Jerusalem: The Jewish Publication Society, 5754/1994).

Englard, I., 'Law and Religion in Israel' (1987) 35 American Journal of Comparative Law 185.

Epstein, L. M., The Jewish Marriage Contract: a Study in the Status of the Woman in Jewish Law (New York: Jewish Theological Seminary of America, 1927).

---

[123] Exod. 22: 21.

[124] Lev. 19: 33–4.

[125] For the inevitable limits on 'foreign' activity, however, see Rouland, Pierré-Caps, Poumarède, Droit des minorités (1996), above, at 41 (non-jewish people unable to hold real property, not benefiting from prohibition of interest). On such rules in islamic and western societies, see below, Ch. 6, Jihad.

[126] See the discussion of the concept of the rodef, or pursuer of the jewish people, above, Talmud and corruption.

Falk, Z. W., 'Jewish Law,' in J. Derrett (ed.), *An Introduction to Legal Systems* (London: Sweet & Maxwell, 1968) at 28.

—— *Introduction to Jewish Law of the Second Commonwealth* (Leiden: Brill, 1972–8).

Fishbane, M., 'The Image of the Human and the Rights of the Individual in Jewish Tradition' in L. Rouner (ed.), *Human Rights and the World's Religions* (Notre Dame: University of Notre Dame Press, 1988) 17.

Friedell, S. F., 'The "Different Voice" in Jewish Law: Some Parallels to a Feminist Jurisprudence' (1992) 67 Indiana Law Journal 915.

Glenn, H. P., 'Where Heavens Meet: The Compelling of Religious Divorces' (1980) 28 American Journal of Comparative Law l.

Golding, M. (ed.), *Jewish Law and Legal Theory* (New York: New York University Press, 1993).

Gordis, R., 'Jewish Tradition in the Modern World: Conservation and Renewal' in A. Jamison (ed.), *Tradition and Change in Jewish Experience* (Syracuse: Department of Religion, Syracuse University, 1978).

—— *The Dynamics of Judaism: a Study in Jewish Law* (Bloomington: Indiana University Press, 1990).

Grajevsky, A. L., 'De quelques réformes des droits de la femme juive à travers les ages' Revue internationale de droit comparé 1963. 55.

Hecht, N., Jackson, B., Passamaneck, S., Piattelli, D. and Rabello, A. (eds.) *An Introduction to the History and Sources of Jewish Law* (Oxford: Institute of Jewish Law, Boston University School of Law/Clarendon Press, 1996).

Hoenig, S., *The Essence of Talmudic Law and Thought* (Northvale, NJ/London: Jason Aronson, 1993).

Holz, B. W. (ed.), *Back to the Sources: Reading the Classic Jewish Texts* (New York: Summit Books, 1984).

Jackson, B., *Essays in Jewish and Comparative Legal History* (Leiden: E. J. Brill, 1975).

Naamani, I. T., 'Marriage and Divorce in Jewish Law' (1963) 3 Journal of Family Law 177.

Rackman, E., *Modern Halakhah for Our Time* (Hoboken, NJ: KTAV, 1995).

Rakover, N., *Guide to the Sources of Jewish Law* (Jerusalem: Library of Jewish Law, 1994).

Rotenstreich, N., *Tradition and Reality: the Impact of History on Modern Jewish Thought* (New York: Random House, 1972).

Roth, J. I., 'Responding to Dissent in Jewish Law: Suppression versus Self-Restraint' (1987) 40 Rutgers Law Review 31.

Sherwin, B. L., *In Partnership with God: Contemporary Jewish Law and Ethics* (Syracuse: Syracuse University Press, 1990).

Shilo, S., 'Equity as a Bridge between Jewish and Secular Law' (1991) 12 Cardozo Law Review 737.

Silberg, M., *Talmudic Law and the Modern State* (New York: Burning Bush Press, 1973).

Sinclair, D., *Tradition and the Biological Revolution: the Application of Jewish Law to the Treatment of the Critically Ill* (Edinburgh: Edinburgh University Press, 1989).

Steinsaltz, A., *The Essential Talmud*, trans. C. Galai (New York: Basic Books: 1976).

Stone, S. L., 'In Pursuit of the Counter-Text: The Turn to the Jewish Legal Model in Contemporary American Legal Theory' (1993) 106 Harvard Law Review 813.

Warburg, R. F., 'A Bibliographic Guide to *Mishpat Ivri*: Books and Articles in English' (1986) 1 National Jewish Law Review 61.

# 5

# A CIVIL LAW TRADITION: THE CENTRALITY OF THE PERSON

Chthonic and talmudic traditions offer constants, which have served to give them definition and identity throughout their existence. The constants—the sacred character of the cosmos, the Torah—reduce other circumstances of life to the status of the non-consequential, or to that of object of obligation. A civil law tradition had to grow out of all of this, and it was not an easy thing to bring about. There was ferocious resistance to the creation of something new, and above all to the *idea* of creating something new. And since the civil law tradition is not one which is rooted in a single, revelatory, text, there could be no immediate point of departure, no jump start which would mean that suddenly, a new tradition had arrived, displacing others and creating a space (space is important to the civilian tradition) of its own. European people have been chthonic people for most of the existence of what we know as Europe. If they were to have a particular legal tradition they could not adhere to the talmudic one, nor remain chthonic. A tradition would have to be constructed. The process, and struggle, lasted more than two millennia, and isn't over yet.

We know the history of continental or civil law largely as a history of two periods, that of roman law and that of modern continental law, beginning with the 're-discovery' of roman law in the eleventh century AD. Things didn't, however, happen like this. There wasn't somehow a break, a 'dark' age (as the still unavoidable western language puts it).[1] From whenever roman law began, to the present, there has been a major, and ongoing, discussion (maybe argument would here be

---

[1] For the mildly less pejorative notion of the 'Middle' ages, see J. Roberts, *History of the World* (London/New York: Penguin, 1995) at 472 ('wholly Eurocentric usage, meaning nothing in the history of other traditions . . . embodies the negative idea that no interest attaches to certain centuries except their position in time . . . first singled out and labelled by men in the fifteenth and sixteenth centuries'); and see, for the view that 'the traditional picture of early medieval law, as presented in the early 20th-century legal histories, and indeed still accepted by many modern experts on the legal changes of the 12th and 13th centuries, cannot be maintained', W. Davies and P. Fouracre, *The Settlement of Disputes in Early Medieval Europe* (Cambridge: Cambridge Univ. Press, 1986) at 228, and defending supporting views, at 214 (that medieval dispute resolution not arbitrary but historically comprehensible), 222 ('irrational' means of proof only used in last resort and usually as ritualized version of community decisions), 228 ('procedures, however rough, were workable, and made some sense to the people that used them') and 240 ('[b]y the standards of most of the world, all European societies are violent' and medieval procedures 'only way for legal institutions to make an impact on societies perpetually riven by antagonism and oppression').

more appropriate) as to what European law should be. The argument didn't stop when roman law became less visible; it was simply that other conceptions of law became more ascendant with the decline in Roman authority. Roman law was always there. It was not a ghost;[2] it had simply lost a lot of its re-creative ability and resonance. It had lost, for a while, its ability to convince people. So if we are to try and find a civil law tradition, we have to be aware of all the arguments, of everthing in the bran-tub. There are leading characteristics today of a civil law tradition—codification is the most obvious of them—but these are present characteristics, and we cannot cast them backwards as having always constituted the leading version of the tradition. There have been too many stops and starts, too many reversals and recommencements, to conclude as to a constant tradition. This tells us already something about change in continental law. Maybe change *is* the tradition; but then many wouldn't agree with that.

## CONSTRUCTING A TRADITION

Just 3,000 years ago Europe was a very chthonic place. The population density was greater than it was, say, in the Americas, but ways of life were probably not much different. The action (to be western about it) wasn't in Europe, it was further south and east. The Egyptians had already built the pyramids; Babylon was becoming one of the seven wonders of the world. So there were models down there of how you could build some thing out of no thing (didn't they need the idea of zero to do all that?). The Greeks must have known about these efforts, hence the great argument today about whether Greek philosophy was all Greek or whether it too built on things already known.[3] Eventually some people in Europe, more particularly in Rome, began to think that all this fancy thinking had consequences for law (lawyers have always had to adjust their law to the societies they live in). So things began to happen in Rome which were identifiable as legal. But they didn't write a civil code; they did things very slowly (again, there is no clear line between the chthonic and the non-chthonic).

There was a lot of internal debate in Rome (from its founding in the eighth

---

[2] Cf., on the 'ghost story' of roman law, Vinogradoff, *Roman Law in Medieval Europe* (1968) at 13.

[3] M. Bernal, *Black Athena: The Afroasiatic Roots of Classical Civilization*, vol. I, *The Fabrication of Ancient Greece 1785–1981* and vol. II, *The Archaeological and Documentary Evidence* (New Brunswick, NJ: Rutgers Univ. Press, 1987, 1991); cf. R. Lefkowitz and G. M. Rogers, *Black Athena Revisited* (Chapel Hill, NC: Univ. of North Carolina Press, 1996); and for the debate in law, which would see roman law as derived from prior, and more sophisticated, Egyptian or Middle Eastern models, R. Yaron, 'Semitic Elements in Early Rome' in A. Watson (ed.), *Daube Noster: Essays in Legal History for David Daube* (Edinburgh/London: Scottish Academic Press, 1974) at 343; J. Gaudemet, *Les naissances du droit* (Paris: Montchrestien, 1997); P. G. Monateri, 'Black Gaius: a Quest for the Multicultural Origins of the "Western Legal Tradition"' (forthcoming in Hastings L. J. and accessible at http:/www.gelso.unitn.it/card-adm/pigi/blackgaius/bg.htm).

century BC) between those of high rank and those of lower rank. So eventually they tried to placate people by writing down on tablets (after a formal type of delibera-tive process) some very elementary principles of how to resolve disputes. These Twelve Tables (around 450 BC, or after the fall of the First Temple, the time of the unwritten Torah) are often seen as the beginning of roman law and the beginning of civil law, but they were really just a peace-making endeavour, in a given city at a given time. A lot of important things had already happened (like pre-Socratic philosophy) and a lot more had to follow, if any distinct tradition was to emerge. It was just work, work, work, over centuries, and no prospect of overall consensus.

## SOURCES AND INSTITUTIONS

There were no sources of law in the chthonic tradition. What would a source of law be? If there was to be a source, in the present, there would be a legitimate means of change or destabilization, a threat to the world which had to be re-born. So first you have to insinuate the idea of a source of law into the way people think about how their lives should be governed. This means a gradual process; you *could not* simply create sources of law, as such. They would be seen as illegitimate. So the tradition of roman law does not grow out of something called legislation, still less codification. There was occasional legislation, as there was in other communities which retained their chthonic character, but it was for exceptional questions, of general import-ance. Today we would call it public law, but it was a very limited form of public law, one with little or no impact on the lives of individual people. The law of the people had to grow rather out of institutions in which people somehow participated them-selves, conferring legitimacy by the participatory character of the process. This is what the chthonic tradition did, though in the weakest form of institutional framework.

There have been two major instances in the world of creating institutions to facilitate the growth of legal tradition through widespread public participation. One instance was that of roman law; the other was that of the common law. They both did it differently, but they both looked to public participation in an insti-tutional framework to develop law. You couldn't just do it; all you could do was provide a possible point of departure, and watch for a few centuries.

Even then, the Romans didn't just create a system of courts, and invite people to go to them. Their initiatives were much more limited, and cautious. They didn't create a (potentially disruptive) group of professional judges; they simply let one of their nobles or patricians (the iudex) decide an individual case, in a kind of benevo-lently amateur way. And since these were patricians, not just anyone could get access to them, as judges. Access had to be controlled by an official, the praetor[4] (another patrician), who on assuming office each year could set out, in an edict, the

[4] The word appears to be derived from prae, before, as a prior control. On roman procedures, see Jolowicz, *Historical Introduction to Study Roman Law* (1972), chs. 13 and 23; Buckland, *Text-book Roman Law* (1963), chs. 13–15; Kaser, *Roman Private Law*, (1968), Pt Seven.

kind of cases which could properly be heard. And for most of roman legal history when someone complained legitimately to the praetor, the praetor would formulate the case the iudex had to decide. This was known as formulary procedure, and if you are a common law lawyer and it sounds something like the writ system, you are right (more later). Only at the end of the period of Roman authority, in the fifth century AD (when nobody was really minding the store) were the courts opened up; what was previously an extraordinary procedure of directly seizing the iudex became the rule. Just getting in front of a judge, directly and with no official screening, took a thousand years.

So there was no legislation and the judges were rank amateurs. Even if the question to be decided got set up for them (by the praetor), how could they be expected to decide it? The help had to come from somewhere, and it had to be loyal and reliable. So a monopoly was created in interpreting the law (determining true meaning) in the hands of the College of Pontiffs, the priests. Alan Watson has recently said that '[O]ne cannot exaggerate the importance for subsequent legal development in the whole of the Western world' of this decision.[5] From the developing expertise of the pontiffs and their successors, the jurisconsults (they were only consultants and couldn't decide anything), comes the entire idea of law as learning, in written form and according to rigorous requirements of reasoning. The writing started on papyrus rolls, during the time of the empire; the rolls then became leaves, eventually bound into volume (codex) form.[6]

## SUBSTANTIVE, SECULAR LAW

Roman law thus found its origins in advice given, by jurisconsults, with respect to particular cases or disputes. The law which emerged looks very much like life, as did the law of the Talmud. There is a law of persons, or the family, which reflects Roman family life, with the paterfamilias, the wife and children, and the slaves. Marriage is constituted by present intent to live as man and wife, though became the object of various forms of celebration. It was rigorously monogamous; concubinage existed but its offspring was not legitimate, following the maternal line and not entering the family of the father. Legitimation was possible, notably through subsequent marriage. Adoption too was possible and various forms of tutelage or guardianship existed. Since marriage was consensual so, in general, was divorce, on the part of husband or wife.[7]

[5] A. Watson, 'From Legal Transplants to Legal Formants' (1995) 43 Am. J. Comp. Law 469 at 472 (importance of concept of interpretation, exclusion of 'foreign' arguments (as from foreign religion), exclusion of economic considerations and well-being of parties).

[6] Honoré, 'Justinian's Codification' (1974) at 859.

[7] See Jolowicz, *Historical Introduction to Study Roman Law* (1972) at 235 (with indications of efforts by Augustus to remedy high rates of divorce, largely unsuccessful). Women were subject to various forms of guardianship, but the reasons for this were characterized by Gaius as 'specious' and it has been said that 'women were not necessarily so gravely disadvantaged in comparison with men'. See J. Gardner, *Women in Roman Law and Society* (Bloomington: Indiana Univ. Press, 1986) at 5, 21, 263–4.

As with the Talmud, things could be owned, and we now see multiplication of criteria for organizing the world of things. They could be patrimonial things or extra-patrimonial things; common things or sacred things; principal things or accessorial things; corporeal things or incorporeal things. The categorizations went on and on.[8] Ownership was essentially private, though there were things that looked like trusts, in which someone had to look after the property of another.[9] Many forms of jus existed short of ownership, notably the hypothec, the civilian equivalent of the mortgage.[10] Deposit existed, and has given its content to the common law of bailment.[11] Contracts, again, were contracts (in the plural) and there was no general, consensual concept.[12] So there are real contracts (requiring transfer of the thing); verbal contracts (solemn words); literal contracts (in writing); and, in certain instances, consensual contracts (sale, lease, partnership, mandate (agency)). Delictual conduct is sanctioned, though there is no general principle of liability, whether of fault or negligence or some stricter form. Liability exists when the conditions of liability are met, according to the objective descriptions of how damage is caused (burning, breaking or rendering property, disabling a limb, etc).[13] Liability can only be described as objective. There is also a law of quasi-contract, recognized as such, and this more than two millennia ago.

So roman law became an object of admiration, because the jurisconsults were able, so convincingly, to state conditions for governance of complex personal relationships. There were highs and lows in roman legal history; the period of the classical jurists, those whose opinions have lasted longest, ran from the first century BC to the middle of the third century AD. Gaius wrote his famous Institutes, or hornbook, near the end of this time. From then on things ran down; by the middle of the fifth century AD there was such a mass of opinion that a law of citations was passed (to *create* order): Papinian, Paul, Gaius, Ulpian and Modestinus were to be treated as authoritative; in case of conflict the majority would prevail; Papinian would prevail in the event of a tie.[14] Later in the century Rome had fallen; Justinian, presiding in the eastern remains a half-century later, ordered a compilation of

[8]   See Buckland, *Text-Book Roman Law* (1963) ch. 5; Kaser, *Roman Private Law* (1968) Pt Three, §18.

[9]   Giving rise to the classic thesis, notably of Bacon and Blackstone, that the trust had roman origins. See D. Johnston, *The Roman Law of Trusts* (Oxford: Oxford Univ. Press, 1988). For other explanations, see below, Ch. 7, *The practice of comparison.*

[10]   While the mortgage is traditionally constituted by transfer of ownership of the property to the creditor, with a guaranteed right of redemption on payment, the hypothec is a pure security device and does not require transfer of ownership in its entirety.

[11]   Largely through the decision of Holt C. J. in *Coggs v. Bernard (Barnard)* (1703) 2 Ld. Raym. 909.

[12]   W. Buckland and A. McNair, *Roman Law and Common Law: a Comparison in Outline*, 2nd edn. by F. H. Lawson (Cambridge: Cambridge Univ. Press, 1965) at 265.

[13]   See Kaser, *Roman Private Law* (1968) at 214, 215.

[14]   Prof. Honoré describes this, however, as a reflection of Latin revival in the 4th century, along with establishment of a new university in Constantinople, where law had its place. Honoré, 'Justinian's Codification' (1974) at 862. See generally, on the jurists, Dawson, *Oracles of Law* (1968), ch. 2 ('The Heritage from Roman Law'), §§. 3 and 4; Jolowicz, *Historical Introduction to Study Roman Law* (1972) at 374–94, 451–3.

laws. It was pulled together in three or four years, finishing in 533 AD, paralleling in time the Babylonian Talmud.[15] This main compilation of Justinian was called the Digest or the Pandects (from Greek, meaning all is included), yet it left out a lot. If it consisted only of opinions of jurists, gathered together with no systematic design, it also represented a choice of opinions. There was inclusion, and also much exclusion.[16] When it was finished, it was very finished. Justinian prohibited all further comment on it;[17] it was a very different book from the Talmud.

## ROMAN LAW AND LAW IN EUROPE

The Romans took their law with them, all over Europe, as far north as what we now know as Germany and as far west as the British Isles. So a lot of people knew about roman law in Europe, but it was the law of the conqueror and not always loved as such. When the Romans were eventually driven out they essentially took their law with them, and the old chthonic law, which everyone still remembered, became once again the law of the lands. So there is here a re-assertion of a different tradition in law, taken with full knowledge of the alternatives. The re-assertion was not a fleeting thing; it essentially drove roman law off the European territorial map for centuries, except for some rudimentary versions of it in Italy and the south of France. Even when roman law was 're-discovered' in the eleventh century, the opposition went on for more centuries and has not disappeared today.

We already know a lot about the chthonic law that prevailed over roman law at this time. It was mostly unwritten; it didn't say much about contracts or obligations; its family and succession law kept large families together, since many members were necessary for many tasks; its property law looked mostly to communal use rather than any formal or individual concept of ownership.[18] The legal notion was seisin (saisine, gewehr) and this was often joint or collective in nature ('le foin à

---

[15] The authoritative study is Bluhme, 'Die Ordnung der Fragmenten in der Pandektentiteln' (1820) 4 ZRG 257.

[16] 1,528 books of classical authors were reduced to approximately ⅟₂₀th of their volume. Honoré, 'Justinian's Codification' (1974) at 877, 878.

[17] See S. P. Scott, *The Civil Law*, vol. II (Cincinatti: The Central Trust Co., 1932), Second Preface to the Digest or Pandects, para. 21, at 196; *The Digest of Justinian*, trans. A. Watson, vol. I (Philadelphia: Univ. of Pennsylvania Press, 1985), p. xlix. Justinian also solemnly prohibited making jokes about the law professors who would come to teach it, though sanctions were not set out. Scott, above, this note, First Preface to the Digest or Pandects, para. 9, at 188; *Digest of Justinian*, above, this note, pp. liii, liv. There was also a short textbook for law students. See *Justinian's Institutes*, trans. P. Birks and G. McLeod, with Latin text of P. Krueger (Ithaca, NY: Cornell Univ. Press, 1987).

[18] See above, Ch. 3, and for a new review on the age (in law, ethnicity and other matters), *Early Medieval Europe*, first vol.: Longman, 1992, containing articles such as P. Amory, 'The meaning and purpose of ethnic terminology in the Burgundian laws' (1993) 2 *Early Med. Eur.* 1. Under Roman influence, continental chthonic law also came to be written, from the 5th or 6th century; see *The Laws of the Salian Franks*, trans. K. F. Drew (Philadelphia: Univ. of Pennsylvania Press, 1991), and for similar developments in England, below, Ch. 7, n. 1.

l'un, le regain a l'autre, ou les arbres à l'un, l'herbe à l'autre').[19] The Allmend of contemporary Swiss law was a kind of general, European model.[20] Feudalism bound the law, and its people, to the soil; it also allowed élites to develop and social inequality to become flagrant. Christianity had spread throughout Europe by now; Augustine in the sixth century had begun to teach the necessity of inner reflection and spirituality; Aquinas in the twelfth was to allow for a certain measure of human flowering and creation, linking christianity to Greek philosophy.

Roman law came crashing back in the tumultuous events of the eleventh to thirteenth centuries in Europe. In a very short space of time, the state and the church were separated, universities begun, legal professions created, legal proof radically reformed, roman law revitalized and Greek philosophy unearthed; the common law began its own, particular, uncommon history. Maimonides also wrote his reforming version of the Talmud. Why this all happened so fast had much to do with the Arabs, who were already occupying a large part of the Mediterranean basin, including Spain. They too had certain ideas about law. Whatever the ultimate reasons, this first European renaissance marked a further challenge to the primacy of chthonic law and very interesting things then took place, a rare combination of different traditions.

Recall that legal procedures of the chthonic tradition were essentially open ones; there were no barriers such as the praetor of roman law or (later) the chancellor (keeper of the writs) of the common law. Recall also that roman law had abandoned such barriers with the adoption of the so-called extraordinary procedure around the end of its reign (c 450 AD). Both traditions therefore had notions of what could be called substantive law; whether written or unwritten it addressed substantive obligations, and perhaps even rights. And since substantive law existed, there was general agreement that judges had to get the facts right, so the substantive law would be applied where it was meant to be applied. Procedure had to be investigative (which is not what the common lawyers call it).[21] There also had to be courts of appeal, since a substantively erroneous decision was illegal, according to criteria external to the decision itself. It *had* to be quashed.[22] So there was a certain underlying harmony in continental Europe in the eleventh century. If the time had come

---

[19] A.-M. Patault, *Introduction historique au droit des biens* (Paris: Presses universitaires de France, 1989) at 134; and see, more generally, for the commonality of European concepts of seisin, F. Joüon des Longrais, *La conception anglaise de la saisine du xiie au xive siècle* (Paris: Jouve, 1924), notably at 43. Teutonic forms of landholding, prevailing in England prior to the Norman conquest, included folcland, the land of the people; see K. Digby, *An Introduction to the History of the Law of Real Property with Original Authorities* (Oxford: Clarendon Press, 1875) at 3.

[20] See above, Ch. 3, *On ways of life*.

[21] On continental civil procedure, using the German model, see B. Kaplan, A. von Mehren and R. Schaefer, 'German Civil Procedure' (1958); J. Langbein, 'German Advantage in Civil Procedure' (1985); and on the designation of different types of procedure, see below, this Chapter *Constructing national law*.

[22] The expression is that of A. Tunc, in 'La Cour judiciaire suprême: Enquête comparative; Synthèse,' Rev. int. dr. comp. 1978. 5 at 23 ('Une décision est conforme à la loi, et elle doit être maintenue, ou contraire à la loi, et elle doit être cassée. Elle *doit* être cassée: il serait choquant qu'elle subsiste').

to engage in a major debate on the type of law to have, everyone agreed that the debate should be about the type of *substantive* law to have, given that procedures or courts or institutions should be open. In common law language, there was never any real question of a closed writ system. In modern language, nobody could raise issues of alleged incommensurability between European chthonic and roman law. In the absence of conceptual or institutional barriers, and under immediate external challenge by a highly civilized Arab world, Europe had to get its legal act together. Christianity no longer appeared as a major obstacle to this; since the fourth century it had been developing its own form of legality within the church (later known as canon law[23]) and by the twelfth century major legal works were being written by canonists, notably Gratian.[24] Canon law was to take its place beside roman law in the slow overturning of the chthonic tradition in Europe.

This did, however, take a long time, since if roman law could be looked at as a base of legal learning, much of it had a peculiarly Roman look, requiring recasting for the modern Europe. So the great, new universities, with law and theology as their primary disciplines, took on the tasks of adapting roman law to the new ways. Roman law eventually served as the base for the construction of European, continental law. This process took centuries, and there is much intellectual ambiguity in the process. For centuries, those who wrote the glosses on roman law seemed more talmudic than civilian. They were more interested in questions (quaestiones) than answers; more interested in accumulating opinions than choosing among them; more interested in debate than action. They may have seen themselves as reviving a more ancient tradition, that of rhetoric.[25] Their intellectual leader, in Italy, was Bartolus, and for centuries it could be said 'siamo tutti Bartolisti'.[26] A new substantive law was being created, however, in general language which could be applied anywhere in Europe. It became known as a common law or ius commune (there

---

[23] The word 'canon' is from the greek 'kanon', meaning measuring rod or rule.

[24] Whose *Concordance of Discordant Canons*, written around 1140, has been described as 'the first comprehensive and systematic legal treatise in the history of the West'; see Berman, *Law and Revolution* (1983) at 143. Canon law has now become the internal law of the roman catholic church, paralleled by the 'ecclesiastical' law of the church of England and varying forms of internal ordering of other churches. On the processes of successive codifications of canon law (1500, 1917, 1983) and the formal structure of the catholic church (thus replicating much secular, western law), see J. Gaudemet, *Le droit canonique* (Paris: Cerf/fides, 1989); P. Valdrini (ed.), *Droit canonique* (Paris: Dalloz, 1989); J. Hite and D. Ward, *Readings, Cases, Materials in Canon Law* (Collegeville, Minn.: The Liturgical Press, 1990), Pt IB (citing notably J. Taylor, 'Canon Law in the Age of the Fathers' 43 at 43, 'a law, and a true law at that, comparable to the legal system of any nation', and 48, on the development of 'Christian Halakhah' as christian teaching moved away from the talmudic); R. Helmholz, *The Spirit of Canon Law* (Athens, Ga.: Univ. of Georgia Press, 1996); Ius ecclesiae: Revista internazionale di diritto canonico; Wieacker, *Private Law in Europe* (1995), ch. 4 ('Canon Law and its Influence on Secular Law').

[25] For the rhetorical tradition, and for parallels with the mos italicus, see T. Viehweg, *Topics and the Law*, 5th edn., trans. W. Cole Durham Jr. (Frankfurt: Peter Lang, 1993) notably at 53, 54. And for the parallel with the talmudic page, glosses developing around the central text, as the Talmud on the Mishnah, see van Caenegem, *Historical Introduction to Private Law* (1992) at 51; and for the talmudic page, above, Ch. 4, *The style of the text*.

[26] See W. Rattigan, 'Bartolus' in J. MacDonell and E. Manson, *Great Jurists of the World* (London: John Murray, 1913) at 45, with refs.

have been two in Europe, both particular in themselves) and slowly began to exercise influence, in persuasive manner, in the different parts of Europe.[27] This process of reception, like that of the concept of the state later in the world, varied according to the locale. It was most influential in germanic countries, understanding themselves as descendants of the first Roman empire and the second (Holy) Roman empire (that of Charlemagne). It met resistance from the kings of France, who didn't quite see themselves in the same new empire as the German princes. It was resisted everywhere in the name of the old law, the chthonic law, itself often seen as inspired by God. 'Juristen, böse Christen' went the germanic, religious, and customary denigration of the new, rationalizing, roman lawyers.[28] In seeking to take the church back to its roots, a revolving, Luther also attacked the lawyers. 'The real reason you want to be lawyers', he said, 'is money. You want to be rich.'[29] This theme too is still with us.

## CONSTRUCTING NATIONAL LAW

The tradition of rationality in law, however, was on a roll. There was so much good thinking going on, such a 'chaos of clear ideas', that more had to be begotten. Those exercising political power were not insensitive to certain features of the new thought. The royal ordonnances of Louis XIV in the seventeenth century were the first indications of a centrally directed, national law on the continent. The notion of teaching French law, as French law, had emerged already in the sixteenth century,[30] and in the same century legislation was used to create French as a national language in France, even though it was then spoken by only a minority of the population. France's codification of private law, under Napoleon in 1804, was the world's first systemic, rational codification of law.[31] Germany's, of 1900, advanced systemic legal thought still further. Then all of Europe, including eastern Europe and Russia, had to have their codes. It was an idea whose time had come, the culmination of a long struggle, a long tradition.

[27] On the slow and massive growth of the literature of a continental common law, see Coing (ed.), *Handbuch der Quellen* (1973–7).

[28] See generally Strauss, *Law, Resistance and State* (1986); and more generally on dissent in Europe, R. Moore, *The Origins of European Dissent* (Oxford: Basil Blackwell, 1985); J. Scott, *Domination and the Arts of Resistance* (New Haven, Conn.: Yale Univ. Press, 1990) (resistance and domination as inseparable companions, citing Ethiopian proverb, at p. v, that '[w]hen the great lord passes the wise peasant bows deeply and silently farts'); E. P. Thompson, *Customs in Common* (New York: The New Press, 1993) at 102 (agrarian custom never 'fact', but lived environment of practices, inherited expectations, rules).

[29] Strauss, *Law, Resistance and State* (1986) at 183.

[30] T. Carbonneau, 'The French Legal Studies Curriculum: Its History and Relevance as a Model for Reform' (1979–80) 25 McGill L. J. 445 at 448–52 ('Louis XIV's reform of legal education').

[31] On the French codification, and codes in general, see C. Szladits, 'Civil Law System' (1974) 15 at 67 ff.; Herman and Hoskins, 'Perspectives on Code Structure' (1980); R. Batiza, 'Origins of Modern Codification of the Civil Law: The French Experience and its Implications for Louisiana Law' (1982) 56 Tulane L. Rev. 477; H. P. Glenn, 'The Grounding of Codification' (1998) 31 Univ. Calif. Davis L. Rev. 765 (codes now responding to local circumstances, no longer 'natural law codes', examples from Quebec, Russia, Vietnam).

Today chthonic law is hard to find in Europe. When Savigny became famous in Germany for defending an 'historical school' of jurisprudence, he meant, not the old chthonic (volk) law, but the old roman law—the old, roman, common law of Europe as opposed to new national codifications.[32] Moreover, the procedures and institutions of continental Europe, and latin America, all reflect the existence of written law. Since it exists it must be enforced, and judges have to actively establish the facts which justify its application. Common lawyers call this, pejoratively, an 'inquisitorial' type of procedure.[33] It really isn't called anything in the civil law world; it's just the type of procedure you have to have, given everything else. The judge is presumed to know the law (jura novit curia) and has to apply it, where it should be applied.[34] The judges also have to be resident judges; written law will not wait for judges riding (or even flying) on circuit. The courts, which could reflect chthonic law or, if you will, custom, are not formally recognized as sources of law, though this appears to be changing, once again. So chthonic law is now thought of, in Europe, largely as existing elsewhere in the world, and debate with it is in terms of debate with another tradition, one which has essentially lost its grip in Europe, but which now re-enters from without. The opposition to the rational tradition in law is today found in opposition to its further expansion, to the European level. This raises very large questions of legal identity, and the relation of still differing traditions in Europe; are there to be others in law in Europe, or only others in law outside of Europe?[35]

# THE RATIONALITY OF THE CODES

So we now have in place the visible elements of what we know as a civil law tradition—codes of law, large resident judiciaries, procedure which is controlled by the judge (let's call it investigative), denial of judicial law-making, historical prestige

---

[32] Which he defended as contemporary, modern, roman law, in his 8-vol. treatise, *System des heutigen römischen Rechts*, published 1840–49. Savigny was, however, a pandectist, and himself did much to prepare the ground for codification, in spite of his opposition to it. Traditions pick and choose where they will, and even over the opposition of those they choose. More recently, on the roman tradition, see Zimmerman, *Law of Obligations* (1990); and for its continuing influence in contemporary codifications, H. Ankum, 'Principles of Roman Law Absorbed in the New Dutch Civil Code' in A. Rabello (ed.), *Essays on European Law and Israel* (Jerusalem: The Harry and Michael Sacher Institute for Legislative Research and Comparative Law, 5757–1996) at 33.

[33] And civilians, correspondingly, tend to see 'adversarial' procedure of the common law as 'accusatorial'. The neutral, non-pejorative expressions would be 'investigative' and 'adversarial'. On changes in the procedure of the common law world, enhancing the role of the judge and bringing it closer to the civilian model, see below, Ch. 7, *Common law and nation-states*.

[34] See J. A. Jolowicz, 'Da mihi factum dabo tibi jus: A problem of demarcation in English and French law' in *Multum Non Multa: Festschrift für Kurt Lipstein* (Heidelberg/Karlsruhe: C. F. Müller, 1980) at 79.

[35] See below, *European identities*.

of law professors (pace Jesus, on the 'teachers of the law'.)[36] Some of this is relatively old, say a thousand years (resident judges, investigative procedure, law professors); some of it is quite recent (codes, denial of judicial law-making).[37] There has therefore been a lot of movement even in the fundamentals of the tradition. The movement is even larger if we consider the whole sweep of the tradition, from the Twelve Tables to the present. What can we say about underlying features of the tradition, given all the diversity it presents?

## LAW'S EXPANSION

Most of the history of civil law tradition is inextricably linked with that of chthonic legal tradition. The history, however, is one of expansion of the civil law, with the notable exception of the five hundred years or so following the fall of Rome, when chthonic law re-asserted itself. The role of civil law expanded first in Rome. From a time of very rigid and formalistic procedures in the early empire, with essentially only chthonic law to be applied, the civil law grew and grew, both substantively and procedurally. It became substantively adequate to deal with an entire range of societal problems, and eventually, after a thousand years, the courts were simply thrown open to everyone. A formulary system of procedure had become too restrictive for an expansive substantive law.

From the time of its rediscovery, roman law continued to expand, though once again it had to prevail over persistent adherents to chthonic ways. It did so from its established positions in universities and in central political authority. Part of its success came from co-opting chthonic law. The so-called customs of the regions (notably the Custom of Paris) were written down; their content could then be found in writing; if the writing was changed, the content was changed.[38] When the writings came to be called ordonnances or codes, the creative power of the writer, or legislature, became more evident. The law could expand to the extent of the creative power. The most striking example is article 1382 of the French civil code, which simply says that anyone causing damage to another by their fault must compensate for the damage. Gone are the particular wrongs of roman law, gone the notions of objective liability born out of particular cases of damage. In their place is a principle of stoic philosophy, of enormous explanatory power and capable of reaching to all features of social life. In Germany the law of delict under the 1900

---

[36] See above, Ch. 4, *Talmud and corruption*.

[37] For the use of case law throughout French legal history, until the revolution, see Dawson, *Oracles of Law* (1968) ch. 4 ('The French Deviation'), notably at 337 ('a tabulation would surely show that beween 1600 and 1750 France had far outstripped England in the use of case law').

[38] On the process, see H. P. Glenn, 'The Capture, Reconstruction and Marginalization of "Custom"' (1997) 45 Am. J. Comp. Law 613; and more generally, J. Gilissen, *La Coutume* (Turnhout, Belgium: Brepols, 1982), with references; van Caenegem, *Historical Introduction to Private law* (1992) at 35–45, 68; and on early European views of legislation as simply the statement of that which already bound, susceptible to recall by change in 'custom', J. Kelly, *A Short History of Western Legal Theory* (Oxford: Clarendon Press, 1992) at 139, 185, 186.

civil code was more particularized, notably in refusing liability for so-called moral or non-patrimonial damage. Savigny probably had something to do with this, arguing that law should not be extended to human sentiment. Yet case law has subsequently recognized a right to privacy, and deliktsrecht has as much potential reach in Germany now as in France.[39]

The growth of formal law necessarily implies a decline in other forms of social cohesion, or glue. The chthonic tradition is largely eliminated; religion and religious morality have their place, but not in public life (so separation of church and state becomes formally recognized in some, though not all, jurisdictions); the small, local ways of life—of community, work and play—become subject to legal control and inevitably wither, though contemporary sociology of law has done much to bring them back to legal life. In the absence of institutional barriers (formulary procedure), law can go essentially where it wants to go, so the texts multiply. There are not only civil codes; there are penal codes, commercial codes, urban codes, codes of administration, of forestry, of taxation, of *sport*, and they all have their implementing regulation, spiralling deductively down and down and down. The law becomes specialized;[40] in its reach it becomes nearly talmudic, though there are major differences in its expression.

## LAW'S EXPRESSION

As secular, civil law expands, its language changes. This has something to do with humanism, and humanist (or explicit) rationality. The Talmud governs nearly everything, yet never abandons its technical models drawn from everyday life, its almost folksy intricacy. For reasons still to be guessed at, this style ultimately became unsatisfactory for a civil law tradition. It was not that the Romans had problems with it; their law was, to use a tricky word, casuistic,[41] and in the extreme.

---

[39] Since a 1954 decision of the Federal Supreme Court (Bundesgerichtshof) reported at BGHZ 13, 334.

[40] For the allegedly regressive character of modern civil law, abandoning general norms in favour of regulation of particular classes, groups and interests, in specialized form, see B. Oppetit, 'Les tendances régressives dans l'évolution du droit contemporain' in *Mélanges Holleaux* (Paris: Litec, 1990) 317; and for the same tendency more generally in western law, B. Rudden, 'Civil Law, Civil Society, and the Russian Constitution' (1994) 110 LQR 56 at 67 ('It is the case that in many countries the law is to some extent returning from contract to status where, for reasons of public policy, certain classes are singled out and protected from themselves as well as from others: for instance, residential tenants, borrowers who use their homes as security, workers, and consumers').

[41] Casuistry (from the latin casu, or case) was originally the theological discipline of resolution of individual or particular cases, and was certainly inherent in talmudic learning, though there largely taken for granted. It acquired a more distinct profile in the christian west, often with a 'sinister application' (Oxford English Dictionary), as being opposed to reasoning from 'first principles'. See A. Jonsen and S. Toulmin, *The Abuse of Casuistry* (Berkeley/Los Angeles/London: Univ. of California Press, 1988), and the discussion below, Ch. 10, *Bivalence and multivalence*. On the shift in style of expression of law, from the conditional, story-telling ('If someone steals a sheep . . .') to the relative, categorical ('Whoever steals a sheep . . .'), as indicating a 'generalizing, systematizing thrust', see D. Daube, *Ancient Jewish Law: Three Inaugural Lectures* (Leiden: E. J. Brill, 1981), Lecture III ('The Form is the Message'), notably at 73.

It was formulated at a very low level of abstraction, close to the level of daily events. This explains why the law of contracts was in plural form; there were many kinds of deals, and the law had to follow the deals, not vice versa. The same could be said of the law of delicts (plural again) and family relations. Chthonic ways are here hanging on, in Rome; the ways of life are making their imprint on the law, even if it is now being expressed by experts. We are in a middle ground again. In the questioning style of the Bartolists, now developing roman law once again, there remains some of this stylistic modesty. Questions are more important than answers (which may change); understanding is more important than coherence; social contact is more important than precision. Yet the Bartolist style, or tradition, did not maintain itself; it became unconvincing over time, and yielded, as has been noted,[42] to declaratory or imperative styles ('La propriété est . . . '; 'It is forbidden to . . . '). In the thinking which in the west has become known as the philosophy of law, there is a philosophy which says that law is command, of a sovereign. Most people now think this is rather simple and inadequate as a philosophy of law, but it may not really have been a philosophy, just observation of what law was becoming, in expression. Joseph Caro's talmudic code, in the sixteenth century, also left out much law no longer applied, going, in this, even beyond Maimonides.[43]

In the world of the civil law, however, there are still many forms of expression of law. The French civil code is relatively untechnical; its language is not far from everyday life, its structure not complex. It was drafted largely by practitioners, with a sense of the literary. In its combination of simplicity and beauty of language with conceptual reach, it has been widely emulated in the world. Some say that it had to realize a compromise between the more roman south of France and the more chthonic north of France. The German civil code was later; the pandectists, including Savigny, had had another century to refine their ideas. It is probably the most abstract of the civil codes, with a general, introductory part applicable to all else, which seeks to explain basic concepts such as capacity, consent or declarations of will, for later application. Nobody reads this for the fun of it. It has been called, in an uncomplimentary way, 'professors' law' (Professorenrecht) and viciously parodied within Germany.[44] It too, however, has its attractions and virtues and has been much emulated, notably outside of the civil law world and in the United States.[45]

---

[42]  See above, Ch. 4, *The style of the text.*

[43]  On these talmudic codifications, see above, Ch. 4, *The written words proliferate.*

[44]  See, in English translation, R. von Jhering, 'In the Heaven of Legal Concepts' in M. Cohen and F. Cohen, *Readings in Jurisprudence and Legal Philosophy* (New York: Prentice Hall, 1951) at 678–89 (heaven of juridical concepts difficult to enter, Savigny nearly refused entry; heaven filled with living juridical concepts and machines—hair-splitting machine, fiction machine, dialectic-hydraulic interpretation press, dialectic drill for getting to bottom of things, dizzying path of dialectical deduction).

[45]  See S. Riesenfeld, 'The Influence of German Legal Theory on American Law: The Heritage of Savigny and His Disciples' (1987) 37 Am. J. Comp. Law 1, notably at 6 ('The thought pattern of the modern common law legal architects and that of the modern Pandectists merge in Llewelyn; that is all that can be said, but it says a lot').

In abandoning casuistic expression, in favour of technical and abstract expression, law became difficult to learn. So the people who brought the change about, the university professors, were not free of self-interest. Yet the civil law cannot be explained in terms of a conspiracy of self-interest. There were more profound reasons for developing the codes, and their rationality of expression. They relate to the value of the human person, and the need for extricating the human person from much of the social fabric which had come to envelop the human person. There were reasons for overcoming the chthonic tradition, in Europe.

## THE CENTRALITY OF THE PERSON AND THE GROWTH OF RIGHTS

If you were born into the fourteenth or fifteenth centuries in Europe the mathematical chances were very good that you would be a kind of slave. You probably wouldn't be called a slave (there were many other expressions),[46] but your life would be one of obligation, not to a cosmos you loved but to a lord you might not. In short, the chthonic tradition had become one in which the cosmos was preserved, but some people did most of the work and for the advantage of a few. There was even a great deal of advantage. In this situation of gross social inequality, some people felt aggrieved, and did not feel there was anything universal or necessary about the state of things. If it was the chthonic tradition, it had become corrupt, stratified and hierarchical. From within the tradition, living within it, people became convinced of this, and reached out to another tradition to improve their lot.

Enlightenment thinking portrayed traditional thought as constraining and necessarily immutable. Yet the inherent vulnerability of the chthonic tradition is best demonstrated by the success of enlightenment thinking itself. Traditions don't have any grip in and of themselves; they persuade or don't, depending on current efforts of persuasion. In Europe there was increasingly little to be said in favour of the ancien régime; even the judges (and there were large numbers of them) were corrupt. If they didn't buy their offices to make money from them, they sold sub-offices, to make money from them. In Bordeaux, when the revolution came, they guillotined about half the judges of the great court, or Parlement, of the region.[47] There was corruption in the single, great church.[48] The social fabric was one

---

[46] As, in English, 'serf', from the Latin 'servus' (or slave), or 'villein'. Slavery or serfdom persisted in Europe into the 19th century, ending elsewhere in Russia in 1861, the United States in 1865 and Brazil in 1888. J. M. Roberts, *A History of Europe* (New York/London: Allen Lane/Penguin, 1996) at 130, 220, 325.

[47] Dawson, *Oracles of Law* (1968) at 370, n. 22; in 1573 the Duke of Alva wrote from Flanders that '[t]here is no case before a court, whether civil or criminal, which is not sold like meat in the butcher's shop'. F. Braudel, *The Mediterranean*, trans. S. Reynolds (New York: HarperCollins, 1992) at 494.

[48] For the variety of 'secondary functions' in the church (the ethic of maintenance) and opportunites for careerism on the part of 'lawyers, pen-pushers and politicians', see E. Cameron, *The European Reformation* (Oxford/New York: Clarendon Press/Oxford Univ. Press, 1991) at 21, 30 (Luther's view of 'swarm of parasites' in Church, 'as the wolves lie in wait for the sheep') and 36 (heretical 1539 view that 'better that priests should marry than go after other men's wives').

which people wanted to tear up. They wanted to tear themselves away from it, s'arracher.[49]

This enormous project required a larger one in its place. The existing law was relational and obligational. People were stuck in their existing relations to one another, often hierarchical, and that's where the law said they had to stay. So not only did the law have to be changed, there had to be overpowering reasons to change it. These reasons were found, not only negatively in the charges of corruption, but positively, in human nature and the divine recognition of it given by the judaeo-christian tradition. Working this out is a very long story, reaching back to the idea of the Old Testament (as it is now known in the west) that individuals are created in the image of God[50] and to the philosophical idea of nominalism, that individual things, and hence individuals, may be all that the world is composed of.[51] Since human beings (unlike animals, or trees) are created in the image of God, and possess powers of reason which are a reflection of God's, they may act in the world as delegates or lieutenants of God. They may exercise dominion over things, as does God over the world,[52] and they have the power (or potestas) to ensure they receive their due. The jus of roman law, which could be seen as a bilateral statement of legal relation,[53] now becomes formulated as unilateral entitlement, and law becomes the earthly sanction to ensure that such entitlements are respected. Law becomes

[49] On the human talent being that of tearing oneself out of patterns and instinctive behaviour (s'arracher), see L. Ferré, *Le nouvel ordre écologique: l'arbre, l'animal et l'homme* (Paris: Grasset, 1992) at 49. It is another thing to say, however, that there is a human talent for tearing oneself out of tradition. It didn't happen in the enlightenment and never has, though humans have options as to the traditions they chose, and some are more flexible than others. On the ancestry of the tradition which came to prevail at the time of the enlightenment, see below, *Law as reason's instrument.*

[50] See above, Ch. 4, *The individual in the Talmud.*

[51] The history of the debate has been set out at length by M. Villey. See M. Villey, 'La genèse du droit subjectif chez Guillaume d'Occam' (1964) 9 Arch. phil. dr. 97; and more generally Villey, *Pensée juridique moderne* (1975); Villey, *Droit et droits de l'homme* (1983); cf. B. Tierney, 'Villey, Ockham and the Origin of Individual Rights' in J. Witte Jr. and F. Alexander, *The Weightier Matters of the Law: Essays on Law and Religion* (Atlanta, Ga.: Scholars Press, 1988) at 1; B. Tierney, *The Idea of Natural Rights: Studies on Natural Rights, Natural Law and Church Law* (Atlanta, Ga.: Scholars Press, 1997) (identifying notions of subjective right in 12th century commentaries on Gratian); and on the parallel development of notions of rights and revolution, see Glenn, 'Revolution and Rights' (1990) at 9.

[52] And so Locke in the English-speaking world was careful to point out, continuing the tradition, that human property is essentially given to humanity by God. He then got to the important part (or so the subsequent version of the tradition has had it), that humans were also commanded 'to subdue the earth', J. Locke, *Two Treatises of Government*, ed. M. Goldie (London: J. M. Dent, 1993) at 130; and for the prior historical development of the notion of the human person as delegate of God, M.-F. Renoux-Zagamé, *Origines théologiques* (1987) notably at 109, 191–5; and a partial English version in M.-F. Renoux-Zagamé, 'Scholastic Forms of Human Rights' in W. Schmale, *Human Rights and Cultural Diversity* (Goldbach, Germany: Keip Publishing, 1993) 121; W. Pannenberg, 'Christliche Wurzeln des Gedankens der Menschenwürde' in W. Kerber (ed.), *Menschenrechte und kulturelle Identität* (Munich: Kindt, 1991) at 61.

[53] See Villey, 'Genèse du droit subjectif' (1964), above, at 106; Tuck, *Natural Rights Theories* (1971) at 7–9 (notably with respect to the jus of having to receive water from a neighbour's land); cf., however, for a more subjective view of roman law, G. Pugliese, '"Res corporales", "res incorporales" e il problema di diritto soggettivo' in *Studi in onore di Vincenzo Arangio-Ruiz*, vol. III (Naples: Jovene, 1953) at 223.

subjective and in becoming subjective it generates rights. Le droit (or law) in French gives rise to le droit subjectif (or rights). In property law this meant the individual ownership of roman law had to become an exclusive form of ownership, so communal forms of ownership were prohibited and the trust was essentially rendered impossible in continental law (though some limited forms persist in germanic jurisidictions).[54] Contract becomes the result of the meeting of autonomous wills;[55] if nominate or particular contracts persist they are all now consensual in origin. There can be no notion of consideration, or bargain, as the basis of contract. Delictual obligation becomes fault-based (as in France) or right-based (as in Germany); gone are the old, specific cases of liability. There is no ox-which-is-not-an-ox to be found.[56] The law of the family will eventually become more consensual, more private.[57] Rights of course are not absolute. This is official teaching; law controls the conditions of their exercise and the manner of their exercise.[58] They may be seen as general standards, the content of which is always to be defined.[59] They are, however, a powerful instrument for bringing about basic conditions of human dignity. In the context of Europe, they unquestionably did a great deal. Their development is also very specific to the conditions of Europe and to the religion which prevailed, and largely continues to prevail, in Europe. This part of the tradition may not, however, always be remembered. There is nothing illogical about forgetting the reasons for reaching a conclusion, and then arguing from the conclusion. You are just choosing what to take out of the bran-tub.

Once rights exist, and everyone has them without regard to birth or race or wealth (which were the things which then most concerned people), then there is

---

[54] On property law developments, which reach back to papal bulls of the 12th century, see Renoux-Zagamé, *Origines Théologiques* (1987), above; Renoux-Zagamé, 'Scholastic Forms of Human Rights' (1993); and for the impact of the property debate on the notion of trusts, below, Ch. 7, *The practice of comparison.* The trust may be re-appearing, however, in continental law, given back by the common law in spite of difficulties in reconciling underlying property concepts. See A. Gambaro, 'Trust in Continental Europe' in A. Rabello (ed.), *Aequitas and Equity: Equity in Civil Law and Mixed Jurisdictions* (Jerusalem: The Harry and Michael Sacher Institute for Legislative Research and Comparative Law, Hebrew Univ. of Jerusalem, 1997) at 777, notably at 787 ('trust rush'); M. Cantin Cumyn, 'L'avant-projet de loi relatif à la fiducie, un point de vue civiliste d'outre-atlantique,' Dalloz 1992. I. 117; C. Larroumet, 'La fiducie inspirée du *trust*' Dalloz 1990. I. 119; and on the historical differences, V. de Wulf, *The Trust and Corresponding Institutions in the Civil Law* (Brussels: Bruylant, 1965); C. Witz, *La fiducie en droit privé français* (Paris: Economica, 1981).

[55] A. Rieg, *Le rôle de la volonté dans l'acte juridique en droit civil français et allemand* (Paris: LGDJ, 1961).

[56] On the ox in talmudic obligational law, see above, Ch. 4, *The divine law applied* and *the style of the text.*

[57] See V. Frosini, *Il diritto nella società tecnologica* (Milan: Giuffrè, 1981) at 126–31; and for convergence of national family laws in this direction, F. Rigaux, 'Le droit comparée comme science appliquée' Rev. dr. int. et dr. comp. 1978. 65 at 65; J. B. D'Onorio, 'La protection constitutionnelle du mariage et de la famille en Europe' Rev. trim. dr. civ. 1988. 27; and for broader comparison, Glendon, *State, Law and Family (1977).*

[58] For inter-dependency of rights and obligations in medieval thought, see J. Coleman, 'Medieval Discussion of Human Rights' in Schmale, *Human Rights and Cultural Diversity* (1993), above, 103, notably at 110; also tracing origins of rights theories from John of Paris in the 12th century and Ockham in the 14th, as predecessors to Locke and Hobbes in the 17th (at 115–18).

[59] See, e.g., M. Delmas-Marty, *Pour un droit commun* (Paris: Seuil, 1994) at 120 (rights as resting on notions 'weakly determined').

also a notion of social equality which is afoot. And since people have the power, in rights, to resist oppression, there is also a guarantee of human liberty. So all the great concepts of western civilization come together in a kind of package, and at the base is the centrality of the person, now a rather abstract concept even if seen originally as a divine representative of the jewish and christian God. And then, once the theoretical package is in place, you have to look around and see if it is being applied properly, or whether the tradition is neglecting someone or something. If it is, someone will point it out, either from within the tradition, or from without, or both. To make sure the theoretical package is doing what it should, however, you need means of implementation, and you have to be very rational about such a large undertaking.

## LAW AS REASON'S INSTRUMENT

The full realization of the consequences of the judaeo-christian tradition, for law, were enormous. Not only, in the christian version, was the human person the centre of the world, as God's delegate and because of the sharing in God's power of reason, but this could itself be known because of human reason,[60] with the aid of revelation, and human reason could be put to work to fulfil God's instructions. The religious rationalists, such as Descartes, Grotius, Pufendorf and Locke, developed from this the foundations for human law which were lacking in the chthonic tradition. The Bible also said 'Give to Caesar what is Caesar's, and to God what is God's',[61] so there was explicit authorization in the scriptures for the construction of human law which could exist as human law.[62] Its inspiration and authorization were religious, but its development was a matter of human reason (as defined somewhere). The change in the expression of law thus follows from the necessity of placing explicit human rationality above the interstitial rationality of the chthonic or talmudic traditions. And this place for explicit rationality follows from the necessity of ensuring that humanity would subdue the world and not be subdued by it. So law, after about a millennium and a half of discussion, comes to be recognized as having a human goal, a human instrumentality. There had to be rights, and there had to be codes to ensure their respect.

What does it mean to be rational in law? The lawyers of the enlightenment did not simply invent contemporary legal rationality. They went, or revolved, a long way back, to the Greek (or maybe Egyptian) tradition of rational enquiry. What did this mean, and what are its consequences today for legal traditions? It appears to mean essentially two things. The first is that human construction is possible; from

[60] M.-F. Renoux-Zagamé, 'Scholastic Forms of Human Rights' in Schmale, *Human Rights and Cultural Diversity* (1993), above, 121 at 134, 135.

[61] Matt. 22: 21.

[62] See generally F. Braudel, *A History of Civilizations*, trans. R. Mayne (New York: Penguin, 1993) at 333, 334: 'Western Christianity was and remains the main constituent element in European thought—including rationalist thought, which although it attacked Christianity was also derivative from it.'

no thing can be developed some thing.[63] So if religion authorized human creation, Greek thought said that it was also possible. Second, the means of creation is through logical thought, and logic is embodied in that which, since Aristotle, is known as the law of non-contradiction, or sometimes the law of the excluded middle. This is not really complicated, though sometimes it is made to appear so. Aristotle said that what you really can't do, what nobody will let you get away with in argument, is affirming at the same time two things which contradict themselves. Put the other way, between two contradictory things there is no middle (it's excluded). You heard this as a child—you can't have your cake and eat it too. And everbody now knows this. There is no middle ground, between contradictory things.[64] If you want to put it in a formula you can put it as '[A] or [not A]'. '[A] *and* [not A]' would be having your cake and eating it too. So once you know that two things are contradictory, once they have been defined and boundaried so that you know they are contradictory, that's it. You have irreconcilable difference, or separation, or possibly incommensurability, or quite possibly conflict (the reason we have a notion of conflicts of law is because laws defined as different are seen as conflicting). But what you do now have is precision, since you have a notion of consistency, and consistency is what allows you to build, as opposed to simply wandering around amongst the differences.

Deductive thought follows from this form of logic; given a point of departure, you can reach further conclusions which are derivable from it (or entailed by it, some might say), in a consistent manner. So by the time of the pandectists, this manner of thought had become highly developed, and the pandectists developed it still further in law.[65] This is why the German civil code is the way it is. It is a very logical construction, according to certain principles of logic. The German civil code is very Greek, which may also be why it has been very influential in Greece. So rationality in law is very logical, according to the logic of having to choose between contradictory things. Does this means it's universal? Well, it doesn't sound quite

[63] See, on this as a fundamental, though ancient, feature of contemporary life, E. Severino, *La tendenza fondamentale del nostro tempo* (Milan: Adelphi, 1988). And on the continuing reception of Greek thought into European thought, through the Roman, itself seen as a means of renewal rather than an original contributor, see R. Brague, *Europe: La voie romaine*, 2nd edn. (Paris: Criterion, 1993) at 36–40, 97–112 (notion of multiple re-naissances), 114, 123–5, 142 (content of Europe to be that of being a container, open to that outside itself); and on the Greek concept of expanding knowledge, K. Popper, 'Back to the Presocratics' in K. Popper, *Conjectures and Refutations*, 3rd edn. (London: Routledge & Kegan Paul, 1969) at 151. For the specific influence of Greek and notably stoic thought on Roman lawyers, see Kelly, *Short History of Western Legal Theory* (1992), above, at 45–52.

[64] On the serious problem, however, of someone eating half their cake, see below, Ch. 10, *Bivalence and multivalence*.

[65] On the logical structure of what would become pandectist thought, initiated by Christian Wolff in the early 18th century, see Herman and Hoskins 'Perspectives on Code Structure' (1980) at 1019, also giving examples, at 999, 1000 of deductive method employed (if right to private property axiomatic, servitude strictly construed against owner of dominant land); Wieacker, *Private law in Europe* (1995) at 218, 253–5, 296.

compatible with the 'These and these' of the talmudic tradition,[66] and the chthonic tradition is able to tolerate a lot of different ways of life. So we seem to have come back to a notion of toleration again, and its relation to different ways of thinking about the world. Western logic does not appear to be the only way of thinking about it, in law or in anything else.

Once you are thinking logically, however, in the Greek (or Egyptian) way, you can build things, from pyramids to temples to large philosophic or legal constructions. Using law as the instrument of reason, you can also construct a modern state, which is essentially built upon formal, written law. So in some places in the civilian tradition people speak about the 'State of law' rather than the rule of law, since law is inextricably linked with the modern state: it created the state; it depends on it for its enforcement; it guarantees the continuing efficacy and integrity of the state. The formal construction of the state is very important for the ongoing development of legal institutions. As states develop, and develop into democratic institutions, functions of legislation and execution develop, and separate themselves from the more rudimentary form of government which is dispute settlement. So we now have the separation of the state from the church, and the separation of distinct powers within the state.[67] If the judiciary is well thought of, and protected, it may achieve independence in this process. There are problems, however, with the notion of judicial independence in the civilian tradition. Given the ancien régime, nobody wants a 'gouvernement des juges', so the primacy of the codes, and legislation in general, is reinforced by ongoing scepticism towards, and even surveillance of (through control of the career structure) the civilian judiciary. It's also hard to even see the judiciary, behind the mountain of cases. If everyone has pre-defined rights (which do not in any way depend on judicial determination), then their violation may exist prior to judgment, and the judicial function is largely one of verification of claims of violation of pre-existing rights, and remedying the violations. Given a world of pre-existing rights, there is no judiciary in the world which can catch up

[66] See above, Ch. 4, *Of schools, traditions and movements* ('These and these' contradictory statements of schools of Hillel and Shammai both representing Talmud). The position of the talmudic tradition was reached in part because of its refusal to accept definitive proofs (above, Ch. 4, *The style of reason*); on European acceptance of forms of proof, allowing further deduction, see Herman and Hoskins 'Perspectives on Code Structure' (1980), at 998, 999.

[67] The separation of powers is generally more thorough in civilian jurisdictions than in common law ones, and this has much to do with the place of the judiciary. The civilian teaching would have the executive fulfilling its functions in a separate and independent manner, and the judiciary could not reach beyond its own separate powers to impede those of the executive. There are still larger problems with judicial control of legislation. So generally the private law courts do not exercise administrative law functions; these are the domain of specialized courts of the executive (the French tradition) or of an entirely separate structure of purely administrative courts, separate both from private law courts and from the executive (the later, German tradition). Yet in some parts of the civil law world, the teaching has yet to be followed (it requires expenditure, for a new institution), so traditional courts continue to do much of the work of judicial control (Denmark, Mexico, others). Yet the institutional distinction between public and private law has now made its appearance in English law; see below, Ch. 7, *Formal limits and informal accommodation*. Thus the notion of the state is differently received, even in the tradition of its creation.

with the claims, and the backlog of cases in the civil law world rises with even more regularity than it does in the common law world.[68] Rights brought people out of the ancien régime; the problem now is where to go with them, and finding a vehicle to do it with.

So we find a civilian tradition of explicit rationality in law. It's been developing for a very long time and its greatest moments may now be over (those of the great codifications). There are now a lot of problems close to the ground, which the great theory does not specifically address. There are evident points of vulnerability in the civil tradition, which are attracting criticism from within (those standing in line in the courts) and from without. Some speak, a little dramatically, of the end of the state.[69] Yet the civilian tradition has immense resources; its constructions are truly remarkable for their normative and explanatory force. It has rendered possible a remarkable flowering of human activity. Can it continue to change the world? Can it change itself to renew itself?

## CHANGING THE WORLD AND CHANGING THE LAW

Chthonic law didn't really talk about change; it could happen, on the ground, but that was just the life of the world. Talmudic law explicitly contemplated it, as well as ongoing human creation, but wrapped it in the blanket of God's love, and his ultimate authority. The Roman lawyers had behind them Greek thinking, which looked at change as a process of transformation of things, which could or could not happen, depending on one's philosophy and the actual conditions of the world. So change is now coming closer to you and me; we can understand it, all of it, and have a part in it. In roman law there is a controlled notion of changing the law; there does not yet appear to be a notion of changing the world through law. Yet since law is now separating itself from the world, this is becoming a conceptual possibility.

### THE SELF-DENIAL OF ROMAN LAW

How do you make law but not allow law to change the world, given that these are now becoming separate things? There doesn't seem to be much doubt that the

---

[68] For the growth of the case-load in France, see E. Tailhades, *La modernisation de la justice: rapport au premier ministre* (Paris: La documentation française, 1985), notably at 36 (deficit of cases before French courts of appeal increasing from 100,000 in 1971 to more than 300,000 in 1983); and more recently J.-M. Coulon, 'Réflexions et propositions sur la procédure civile: Rapport à M. le Garde des Sceaux' Gaz. Pal. 17–18 Jan. 1997, at 2, notably at 3 (volume of cases now such that administration of justice in France likely to be paralysed, at level of courts of appeal, by 2000).

[69] J.-M. Ghéhenno, *La fin de la democratie* (Paris: Flammarion, 1995), ch. 1 ('La fin des nations').

Romans made their law, and knew they were making law.[70] They also made very good law, which lasted a long time. In method, structure and philosophy, however, the Roman lawyers turned away from changing the world; their making of law was only in the form of human intelligence applied to its formulation; essentially it remained a product of the world and its activities. So roman law was casuistic in expression; it was limited by formulary procedure for almost all of its history; there were no professional or salaried jurists; a large place was given to interpretation and the art of the controversia; the structure of the praetor's edict was chaotic, as was that of the Digest of Justinian;[71] there was no articulated, or applied concept, of system.[72] In short there was no machinery[73] or tradition for effecting major and radical change in law, and therefore none for transforming the world. Yet the Romans left a notion of changing the law; the praetor could change the edict; the procedure of the legis actio changed to that of formulary procedure, which itself gave way to extraordinary procedure; the jurists re-worked the substantive law; there were legal fictions to disguise the changes going on.[74] That was all the change there was, however; law did not expand any further.

## CHANGING THE IDEA OF CHANGE

The changes of the first western renaissance (of the eleventh to thirteenth centuries) arguably did not go beyond the Roman limits of legal change. They took place in a context of chthonic law and were major in that context, but they remained within the Roman cadre. Forms of proof could be changed; roman law itself could be used, in written form, to generate further writing; specialists in law could emerge (though with the idea of 'professing' law, for formal and systematic remuneration, we are already moving beyond the Romans); courts could be opened to all comers (though not yet in the British Isles, with its uncommon law). These changes exhausted everyone for centuries. Half a millennium later it was time to test the limits of change, through reason, using law as instrument.

[70] Watson, *Law Making in Later Roman Republic* (1974); W. Gordon, 'Legal Tradition, with particular reference to Roman Law' in N. MacCormick and P. Birks, *The Legal Mind: Essays for Tony Honoré* (Oxford: Clarendon Press, 1986) 279 at 282; M. Humbert, 'Droit et religion dans la Rome antique' in *Mélanges Felix Wubbe* (Fribourg: Editions de l'Université de Fribourg, 1993) 191 at 199 (law created by professionals) and 192 (profound division separating 'prédroit' or chthonic law, prior to Twelve Tables, and subsequent formalist law, or jus humanum; traditional view also that religion and law kept separate in Rome, though this questioned).

[71] Watson, *Spirit of Roman Law* (1995) 472.

[72] J. Gaudemet, 'Tentatives de systématisation du droit à Rome' (1986) 31 Arch. phil. dr. 11, notably at 15, 28 (by 1st century BC transition to works more 'constructed' than previously, due to discovery of Greek thinking, with refs.; yet ultimately unsystematic throughout history); A. Cock Arango, 'El Derecho Romano se formo a base de realidades objetivas no por teorias o sistemas' in *Studi in onore di Vincenzo Arangio-Ruiz* (Naples: Jovene, 1953) at 31.

[73] Gordon, 'Legal Tradition' (1986), above, at 283.

[74] On the fictions of roman law, see J. Hadley, *Introduction to Roman Law* (New York: Appleton, 1907) at 94–6.

To change something you first have to isolate or separate it from everything else, so you can work on it (and this includes the state, which needs precise boundaries) and you need a concept of historical time in which this can happen (change from then to now). The time part seems to have come both from the Greeks[75] and from christianity; in the resurrection of Christ christianity began its separation from the jewish tradition,[76] and in life after death it created a point of future salvation, something towards which life and time could be directed. So now was different from the state of salvation, which came later, in a discernible future, and what we do now will affect that future state. In deferred gratification there is a notion of the future, and contingent time. The remaining problem was with respect to the objects of change, which had to be separated out from the sacred matrix in which the chthonic and talmudic worlds had embedded them. This large task appears to have been effected by the discovery of facts, and law played a major part in this, according at least to a non-lawyer, who appears not very happy about it. Alisdair MacIntyre tells us that the notion of a fact was invented in the seventeenth century, and is derived from the legal and Roman notion of the factum (as in non est), the formal document in law representing solemnized reality, that which the law would presume to be true (at least for the limited purposes of law).[77] Once you let loose the notion of verifiable reality, however, outside of law, you have facts, and they exist simply as observable phenomena, outside of any matrix in which they might arguably exist, according to non-factual (non-observable or, to be fancy again, metaphysical) assertions.[78]

[75] See L. Schulz, 'Time and Law. How the Life-World Acceleration Affects Imputation in Criminal Law' in (1998) Rechtstheorie, Beiheft 18, 405 at 410 (at beginning of Attic philosophy, concept of repetition of time replaced by concept of linear, unlimited stream of time in which given possibilities to be realized); C. Taylor, Sources of the Self: The Making of the Modern Identity (Cambridge, Mass.: Harvard Univ. Press, 1989) at 463 (objectified view of world produced by disengaged reason involves a spatialization of time, seen as a series of discrete moments, between which certain causal chains can be traced). For the manner in which linear, temporal legal systems use time for allocation of rights (e.g., in registration of security interests), see J.-L. Bergel, Théorie générale du droit, 2nd edn. (Paris: Dalloz, 1989) 122 ff. ('Le temps dans le droit'); and more generally P.-A. Côté and J. Frémont, Le temps et le droit (Cowansville, Quebec: Yvon Blais, 1996); G. Winkler, Zeit und Recht (Vienna/New York: Springer-Verlag, 1995) (emphasizing public law). On the compatibility of this western tradition of time with the views of contemporary science, however, see above, Ch. 1, The Changing Presence of the Past.

[76] On the movement of talmudic tradition towards historical, contingent, time, commencing with the notion of Creation yet hesitant over salvation, see above, Ch. 4, Talmud, the Divine Will and Change.

[77] A. MacIntyre, Whose Justice? Which Rationality? (Notre Dame, Notre Dame Univ. Press, 1988) at 357; and for tracking of the idea of fact from law to history to science, in the Anglo-American tradition, see B. Shapiro, 'The Concept "Fact": Legal Origins and Cultural Diffusion' (1994) 26 Albion 1, repr. in D. Sugarman (ed.), Law in History: Histories of Law and Society, vol. II (New York: New York Univ. Press, 1996) at 245.

[78] On western science not simply as a neutral method of acquiring knowledge but as a distinctive metaphysics, constructing a view of the world 'as if we were not here' (itals in orig.) yet not contradicting religion since growing out of it, see B. Appleyard, Understanding the Present: Science and the Soul of Modern Man (New York: Doubleday, 1993) at 191; and on traditional styles of scientific thinking, A. Crombie, Styles of Scientific Thinking in the European Tradition (London: Duckworth, 1994). For the importance of scholastic, abstract Latin in the development of western science, see W. Ong, Orality and Literacy: The Technologizing of the Word (London/New York: Methuen, 1982) at 113, 114.

We can talk about the role of lawyers in this. You can make a good argument that lawyers didn't discover facts and that they were more interested in law. What they did with law simply provided a model for what could be done with the rest of the world. They did turn law into fact, and dead fact at that, with the notion that roman law wasn't really normative for Europe but was only the law of the Romans, a particular people at a particular time who made their particular law. This legal development occurred in France, notably through the work of Cujas in the six-teenth century, and it is important that the French at this time were concerned with getting out from under the re-generated roman law (those German princes again).[79] So from precise political circumstances we see a major philosophical shift emerging (or at least one taken later to be a major philosophical shift; perhaps at the time Cujas just didn't like German princes). With Cujas, as they say, the mos italicus (the Bartolists) gave way to the mos gallicus (the Cujadists), and the entire idea of the past, even the legal past, having no normativity, is articulated.[80] So with the object-ivization of law, the extracting of it from any natural, religious or even societally relevant background,[81] law can become an object of major change and creation. There are no restraints any more, nothing beyond human law which can limit its development, or limit its growth. It is simply the product of human creativity, a fact of human invention. So you can say that it must have been the scientists who turned the rest of the natural world into facts, the lawyers being only interested in law. The problem with this is Francis Bacon, generally thought to be the main impetus in the development of modern science, who was also, of course, a lawyer (sympathetic to the Crown and, in England, to the civilians).[82] He was also, appar-ently, a corrupt lawyer, someone who didn't really understand the idea of law as limit (all those gifts of silver that didn't affect his judgment), so it is possible to conclude that the modern world of science is really the work of a corrupt lawyer. Which is perhaps why they say that when the world comes to an end, there'll be a lawyer at the closing.

So what the French lawyers and the scientifically inclined meant to bring about was the separation of mind from matter. Matter was just matter, and so we, in the

---

[79] See C. Phillipson, 'Cujas' in MacDonnell and Manson, *Great Jurists of World* (1913), above, 45 at 83, with refs.

[80] See van Caenegem, *Historical Introduction to Private Law* (1992) at 56 (roman law reduced to 'the state of an academic relic, a historical monument, a dead law for scholarly study only').

[81] Thus the need to develop 'a mode of authority independent of social continuity'. J. Pocock, 'Time, Institutions and Action: An Essay on Traditions and their Understanding' in P. King and B. Parekh (eds.), *Politics and Experience: Essays Presented to Professor Michael Oakeshott* (Cambridge: Cambridge Univ. Press, 1968) 209 at 229; and see Roberts, *History of World* (Penguin, 1995), above, at 550 (emergence of 'the idea that a sovereign, legally unrestrained lawmaking power was the characteristic mark of the state').

[82] See D. Coquillette, *Francis Bacon* (Stanford: Stanford Univ. Press, 1992), notably at 12, 38, 39, 75, 239 (on familiarity with civil law, including English civilian writing, views on universal law), 222 (on modern research confirming Bacon's confession to taking of bribes); J. de Montgomery, 'Francis Bacon' in MacDonnell and Manson, *Great Jurists of World* (1913), above, 144, notably at 145 (first three years of study in France, returning to Gray's Inn), 158 (pleader for codification), 148–51 (drawn into 'network of corruption that surrounded the whole judicial system').

west, have all learned that it is mind over matter (though some are now teaching that mind too is only matter).[83] And law too is only matter, that thrown up by each particular society. The efforts of Bartolus and Baldus to overcome the 'separatorum separata ratio'[84] take a real beating, which is to go on for centuries, so that Carlos Fuentes can be complaining about it today.[85] Carlos Fuentes, it turns out, is a Bartolisti, one of the twentieth- (and hopefully twenty-first) century.[86] With the separation of mind and matter, you have not only the possibility of separate laws, but also the possibility of separate disciplines of philosophy of law and sociology of law, neither of which exist in the other legal traditions of the world, at least not as separate disciplines, based on the idea that you can be legal by just thinking, with no factual base, and that you can be legal by just looking at facts, with no normative base. We have here the ideas that law needn't have anything to do with life, and that life needn't have anything to do with law (or normativity). We have moved some way from the chthonic and talmudic worlds,[87] though there has never been a moment of total rupture or transition, only ongoing shifts in perspective, each building on the earlier. Nor has the newer tradition succeeded in eliminating the older ones, which keep watch on the new ways, always ready to provide advice, if any problems crop up. They can provide advice since communication is assured, by the incremental, dialogical character of the development of one tradition from others.

## POSITIVE LAW AND POSITIVE SCIENCE

Much of what has occurred in western science and law in the last three centuries or so has been the working out of the idea that you can change both the world and the law, since they are simply positive objects or constructions. The two ideas are very closely related to one another, and their interdependence is perhaps most evident in the idea that you cannot use the law to prevent changing the world. You can't prevent scientists from changing the world since it's just a fact, with no normative significance, though we now may be seeing some changes in this idea, partly from the ongoing influence of the chthonic tradition. The underlying position is still

---

[83] See above, Ch. 2, *The view from somewhere else*.

[84] F. Calasso, *Introduzione al diritto commune* (Milan: Giuffrè, 1970) at 73, cited by M.-F. Renoux-Zagamé, 'La méthode du droit commun: Réflexions sur la logique des droits non codifiés' Rev. hist. fac. dr. 1990. 133, at 148.

[85] See above, Preface.

[86] Ibid.

[87] The fusing of law and the world is implicit in the entire chthonic tradition; with talmudic law the union is brought about, at least in large measure, by talmudic law's expression, making it look and sound like life, above, Ch. 4, *The style of the text*. In both cases, acting according to law is therefore just living naturally. Why ask people whether they want to obey the law, or not, when you can just presume that they will, since it's their law? Nor did talmudic thinking really encourage scientific development. See above, Ch. 4, Talmud, the Divine Will and Change.

strong, however; so long as law is just positive (or posited, or made) law, then it can't really have any hold on people engaged in other, similarly positive, activities. You can't really think of the work of scientists as a challenge to lawyers to do something about it; there is a real unity in the basic perspectives of both groups. So while the scientists construct a newer positive world, while observing and learning from the actual one, the lawyers construct newer positive law, as the instrument of human rationality. The idea of law as command was perhaps the first abstract formulation of this idea,[88] but the idea of positive law has subsequently been the object of profound and sympathetic development, remarkably also in the common law tradition, which thus is becoming more common. Posited law would be ultimately grounded in a presumed basic norm,[89] authorizing present institutions to formally create law, and masking contact with other traditions or historical origins (and continuity). Roman law could thus be 'decanted' into the French civil code and essentially lose its identity as roman law, and French law thereby would lose its recognizable affiliation with roman law.[90] Or positive, formally created law would be ultimately based on its social acceptance, itself a fact, so as to not depend entirely and exclusively on formal utterance. This subtle joinder of formal and informal positivism, which is that of H. L. A. Hart, has given still more bite to the idea of positive law—it even has a faint whiff of the chthonic and talmudic in it, in the necessarily social character of law.[91] Yet here law comes from fact, it has lost its inherent normativity, from nature or divinity. So if the facts change, and people start disobeying the law, in a large and regular manner, there are some major problems in bringing them back under it. The teaching of present sociology, as

---

[88] Formulated in England in the mid-19th century by John Austin, though after extended immersion in German legal theory and preceded in formulation, if not publication, by the work of Jeremy Bentham. See J. Austin, *The Province of Jurisprudence Determined* (New York/Cambridge: Cambridge Univ. Press, 1995); and for Austin's immediate departure for Bonn on nomination to his position at the University of London, J. Austin, *Lectures on Jurisprudence*, 5th edn., ed. R. Campbell (New York: James Cockcroft, 1875) at pp. vi, vii (Austin already had conceived a 'profound admiration' for great jurists of Germany).

[89] H. Kelsen, *Pure Theory of Law*, trans. M. Knight, from 2nd German edn. (Gloucester, Mass.: Peter Smith, 1989) notably ch. 5 ('The Dynamic Aspect of Law', s. 34 ('The Reason for the Validity of a Normative Order: the Basic Norm') and s. 35 ('The Hierarchical Structure of the Legal Order'), constituting the Kelsenian pyramid of norms. On the inverted pyramids of talmudic and islamic tradition, see above, Ch. 4, *The written words proliferate*, and below, Ch. 6, *The shari'a: sources*; and on the history of pyramidical concepts of law in western legal thought, J. Vanderlinden, *Comparer les droits* (Diegem, Belgium: Kluwer/Story-Scientia, 1995) at 260.

[90] See Carbonnier, 'Usus hodiernus pandectarum' (1982) at 110 (roman laws 'transvasées dans des articles de la codification') and 107 (current need for more direct form of reception, of limited nature, 'des gorgées de droit prises de temps en temps, selon la soif, à l'antique fontaine').

[91] H. L. A. Hart, *The Concept of Law*, 2nd edn. (Oxford: Clarendon Press, 1994), notably at 116 ('There are therefore two minimum conditions necessary and sufficient for the existence of a legal system. On the one hand those rules of behaviour which are valid according to the system's ultimate criteria of validity must be generally obeyed, and, on the other hand, its rules of recognition specifying the criteria of legal validity and its rules of change and adjudication must be effectively accepted as common public standards of official behaviour by its officials').

simple fact,[92] has some disturbing implications for law as simple fact. One response to this is to create more law, and there is much evidence today of an acceleration in legal production.[93] We do not know what the eventual effect of this will be.

## REVOLUTIONS, SYSTEMS, LANGUAGE AND INTERPRETATION

The contemporary civil law tradition manifests itself in many ways, and the idea of positive law is only one of them, though all are related. French law, as a major contributor to the tradition, has also given to the world the notion of revolution, now not as a revolving to an earlier, presently disruptive tradition, as it was originally thought to be, but as a sharp and creative break with the past. We know from historical research on the origins of the French civil code that much of it was not at all new, and it is probably impossible to think of a radically new departure in law,[94] yet the word 'revolution' has now become one of the most over-used words in the western world and in all western languages, and law has some part in this. A revolutionary tradition has come to exist, and this is not an oxymoron.

Contemporary positive law has also been thought of as systemic law and, since it can be changed so easily, even as multiple, successive systems, each new one replacing the previous one as changes occur.[95] This tells us already that the notion of system, as a unity of presently interacting elements, is undergoing strain. It is still used in other disciplines, notably in biological ones, where it arguably had its

[92] See, on present adherence to rational–legal authority, R. Inglehart, 'Changing values, economic development and political change' (1995) 47 *Int. Soc. Sci. J.* 379, discussed above, Preface.

[93] See, on inflation of norms, B. Oppetit, 'L'eurocratie ou le mythe du législateur suprême' Dalloz 1990. I. 73.

[94] For a detailed argument, rejecting the possibility of intellectual disentanglement from previous law, see Glenn, 'Law, Revolution and Rights' (1990) at 9 (idea of revolution only possible with notions of fixed positive law and institutions, which are capable of being target of revolution, impossibility of revolting against a milieu); and on the idea of revolution representing the 'fallacy of mistaking the part for the whole', K. Minogue, 'Revolution, Tradition and Political Continuity' in King and Parekh (eds.), *Politics and Experience* (1968), above, 283 at 305; or as 'depending on the extent of the field that we take in at a single view', P. Shrecker, 'Revolution as a Problem in the Philosophy of History' (1969) 8 *Nomos* (*Revolution*) 33 at 49 (storming of Bastille illegal change under fundamental law of French monarchy, legitimate and legal action under the fundamental law of France); and for the failure of the Soviet revolution to eliminate civil law, M. Jankowski, 'Le droit romain en Union soviétique' Rev. his. dr. fr. et étr. 1990. 43.

[95] J. Raz, *The Concept of a Legal System: an Introduction to the Theory of Legal System*, 2nd edn. (Oxford/ New York: Clarendon Press/Oxford Univ. Press, 1980); and for the origins and development of legal system building, W. Krawietz, *Recht als Regelsystem* (Wiesbaden: Franz Steiner Verlag, 1984), notably at 65 ff. Systemic thought is highly dependent on aristotelian or binary logic and notions of consistency, since a system is thought of as inherently coherent, to function as a system. Contradictory elements are those without the system, which defines itself by exclusion of contradictory elements. On the relation of different 'legal systems', including those said to be 'open' ones, to one another, see below, this Chapter *European identities*. On systems thought generally, in law and science, see T. Barton, 'The Structure of Legal Systems' (1992) 37 Am. J. Juris. 291 (notably for history of concept of system); C. Grzegorczyk, 'Évaluation critique du paradigme systémique dans la science du droit' (1986) 31 Arch. phil. dr. 281, notably at 301 (idea of system finally not very rich or productive (not 'féconde') but necessary if law positive and rational).

scientific beginnings,[96] yet recently it has become highly elastic in character,[97] given emerging scientific views of a fundamentally chaotic or non-linear physical world. In concentrating our attention on current elements of a system, systemic thought concurs with positive law in declaring social continuity as largely irrelevant to normativity. Yet if you say that the system can tolerate catastrophe, in the form of widespread non-conformity, the notion of system here fulfils no evident function or utility, other than a purely formal one. There are however, denials of the systemic character of western thought, most notably by the French codifiers, who insisted that their code, particularly in its simplicity and its retention of non-roman French law, avoided systematic thinking.[98] Even those who advance a tradition are not convinced, entirely, how far they advance it, or should advance it.

Contemporary informal positivists, those who practise the sociology of law, have put forward the notion of culture as a substitute for that of system. Culture appears to be a present, ill-defined, all-inclusive system, which may present some advantages over the notion of system, but again appears as a particularly western construction which in no way advances any idea of normativity.[99]

[96] C. von Linne (Linnaeus), *Systema naturae* (London: Trustees of the British Museum, 1956) (1st edn. 1735, founding taxonomic methodology) and on contemporary autopoietic (self-referential or self-reproducing) systems in biology, yielding an autopoietic theory of law, H. Rottleuthner, 'Les métaphores biologiques dans la pensée juridique' (1986) 31 Arch. phil. dr. 215, explaining biological background to autopoietic theory of law, as developed notably by N. Luhmann. See G. Teubner (ed.), *Autopoietic Law: A New Approach to Law and Society* (Berlin: Walter de Gruyter, 1988); G. Teubner, *Law as an Autopoietic System* (Oxford/Cambridge Mass.: Blackwell, 1993).

[97] For concepts of systems which would accommodate even catastrophe, see I. Ekeland, *Mathematics and the Unexpected* (Chicago: Univ. of Chicago Press, 1988) at 88–90, 106; and for system in the social sciences which would tolerate even the most 'strategic, innovative or rebellious choice-making,' see S. F. Moore, 'History and the Redefinition of Custom on Kilimanjaro' in J. Starr and J. Collier, *History and Power in the Study of Law: New Directions in Legal Anthropology* (Ithaca NY/London: Cornell Univ. Press, 1989) 277 at 287, 288, with further refs.

[98] R. Sève, 'Système et Code' (1986) 31 Arch. phil. dr. 77 at 82 (Thus Cambacérèces: 'loin de nous la présomption d'avoir inventé une théorie ou un système. Un système! Nous n'en avons point . . . la nature est le seul oracle que nous ayons envisagé'). In *Les grands systèmes de droit contemporain*, 10th edn., (Paris: Dalloz, 1992) with C. Jauffret-Spinosi (English-language 3rd edn., (London: Stevens, 1985) with J. E. C. Brierley), to which this volume owes a great deal, Prof. David thus uses the notion of 'legal systems' sparingly and more as a didactic device to underscore similarities and differences (at 20, 21, of the English edn.), in spite of the title of the book. The notion of a 'major legal system' appears limited to the civil law, the common law, and socialist law, and it is true that the notion of system has played, or did play, an important role in all three of these. Other laws are described under the heading 'Other Conceptions of Law and the Social Order'. Throughout, the notion of 'legal family' is used more frequently than that of 'legal system'. The notion of 'legal family' is also used in Weir's translation of Zweigert and Kötz, *Introduction to Comparative Law* (1998), in rendering the original German 'Rechtskreis', literally 'law circle'. Cf. U. Mattei, 'Three Patterns of Law: Taxonomy and Change in the World's Legal Systems' (1997) 45 Am. J. Comp. Law 5 at 14 ('legal systems never *are*. They always *become*'); and for increasing reluctance to speak of a legal system in France, where law is increasingly perceived as a method of dispute resolution or a juxtaposition of solutions, see B. Oppetit, *Droit et modernité* (Paris: Presses universitaires de France, 1998) at 113, n. 1.

[99] For 'culture' as a German response to French 'universalism' see M. Sahlins, *How Natives Think: About Captain Cook, for example* (Chicago/London: Univ. of Chicago Press, 1995) at 10–14, with refs. (though now 'in the twilight of its career, and anthropology with it'); also at 10 on coining in France in 1750s of expression

With law expressed formally, in formal language, it is also natural to conclude that law is language. In this, some western and civilian theories of law have followed other western intellectual trends, which have given major importance to language as a controlling element in individual and societal development.[100] Interpretation could then become subjective, less the collective search for a meaning taken to be true than imposition of meaning by the recipient of the text. Yet here too there is ongoing challenge, notably in cognitive science affirming the primacy of human thought (we always have still to decide what to do, in a way uncontrolled by language)[101] and in the idea that the civil law is the result of a process of collective, and learned, deliberation. If there is no Perfect Author, there are at least authors, whose ongoing arguments require ongoing response.[102] The notion that legislation and its interpretation are simply means of continuing the discussion, and not in any way means of bringing it to an end or limiting its breadth, is brilliantly represented in recent continental writing.[103] Interpretation, in the sense of search for the truest of meanings, would thus remain at the heart of the civilian tradition, as it was in the time of Rome. This would explain the enduring quality of much of the civil law. It is difficult to improve on it, and all its implications have yet to be discovered.[104] So if the civil law retains a large interpretative, as opposed to creative, dimension, what is the effect of this on its relations with other legal traditions?

'civilization'; and more generally F. Barnard, 'Culture and Civilization in Modern Times' in P. Wiener (ed.), *Dictionary of the History of Ideas: Studies of Selected Pivotal Ideas*, vol. I (New York: Charles Scribner's Sons, 1973) at 613, notably at 613, 614 (notions of both 'culture' and 'civilization' gaining currency in 18th century Europe, by mid-20th century 164 definitions of 'culture' catalogued); for protest against the notion of culture as 'no matter what manner of acting' see Brague, *Europe* (1993), above, at 133; and as 'failing to identify any particular factors that can be seen to be making a difference' R. Cotterell, 'The Concept of Legal Culture' in D. Nelken (ed.), *Comparing Legal Cultures* (Aldershot/Brookfield, Vt./Singapore/Sydney: Dartmouth, 1997) 13 at 20; and for 'civilization' as a concept of universal history developed during western colonialism, see below, Ch. 7, *Western law in the world.*

[100] Above, Ch. 2, Commensurability: Of Apples and Oranges; and on civilian discussion of law and language, see *Le langage du droit* (1974) 19 Arch. phil. dr.; J.-L Sourioux and P. Lerat, *Le langage du droit* (Paris: Presses universitaires de France, 1975).

[101] Above, Ch. 2, Commensurability: Of Apples and Oranges.

[102] On the Perfect Author of talmudic tradition, and the resulting interpretive process, see above, Ch. 4, *Talmud and Torah,* and *The style of the text.*

[103] See Atias, *Épistémologie juridique* (1985); Rémy, 'Éloge de l'exégèse' (1982).

[104] On the adages of French law, see H. Roland, *Adages du droit français,* 3rd edn. (Paris: Litec, 1992); and on the continuing validity of particular adages or maxims, E. Putman, 'Sur l'origine de la règle: "Meubles n'ont point de suite par hypothèque",' Rev. trim. dr. civ. 1994. 543: H. P. Glenn, 'A propos de la maxime "Nul ne plaide par procureur"' Rev. trim. dr. civ. 1988. 59. The notion of a tradition of jurists (Juristentradition), distinct from the legal tradition itself and acting as a means of traditio, is defended in H. Izdebski, 'La tradition et le changement en droit: l'exemple des pays socialistes,' Rev. int. dr. comp. 1987. 839 at 879.

## CIVIL LAW AND COMPARATIVE LAW

Identities have always been problematical in Europe. There have been lots of them, and we see here the importance of the chthonic in grouping people according to their local ways. Think of all those tribes with odd names that somehow brought down the Romans. Yet all of them were chthonic, and all were European, and most eventually came to be followers of a single church. So we seem to have people adhering at the same time to small and larger groupings, adhering both to particular and more universal types of information, and being both Burgundian and catholic, or Bavarian and germanic, or Roman and pan-European. Prior to the state we seem to be faced with this interplay between the particular and the general, so chthonic ways engaged first with roman law, then with canon law, then with the renewed roman law. Historically Europe seems to say you can have more than one identity. Then we had the state, but now European states and the people in them are interacting with a new type of pan-European law. So in the complexity of European society, all packed into a relatively small space, we have a remarkable and ongoing process of exchange between traditions, and many demonstrations of the interdependency of identities. The process began, as a recognizable one, even before the Romans. Then it accelerated.

### EUROPEAN IDENTITIES

Knowing who you were in Europe used to be relatively simple, say 3,000 years ago. Being European didn't matter much, because if you travelled by foot it was a pretty big place and you didn't meet many people who weren't European. There wasn't much that could be looked to in a formal way which was pan-European either, and there was notably no European church. So identity was created, as it was elsewhere in the chthonic world, initially by a combination of birth and residence,[105] then by ongoing adherence to the ways of the community into which one had initial entry. In Europe the number and proximity of these peoples was such, however, that they may have worked out ways of regulating legal relations between them, in the form of a rough choice of law rule which said that the personal law of people went with them wherever they went.[106] At least we know that this existed during the time of the Romans, when chthonic people became subjugated to them; it is not clear when it may have begun. So the unwritten traditions had regular contact with one another, but they had so much in common that there was no major problem of

---

[105] See above, Ch. 3, Chthonic Ways and Other Ways.

[106] H. Batiffol and P. Lagarde, *Droit international privé*, 7th edn., vol. I (Paris: LGDJ, 1981) at 10; and on the continuing application of personal laws, see L. Stouff, 'Étude sur le principe de la personnalité des lois depuis les invasions barbares jusqu'au xiie siècle' (1894) Revue bourguignonne 1–65, 273–310.

conflict,[107] and any influence of one on another would remain well within the range of chthonic options.

The relations between traditions become more complex, and recognizable as such, with the growth of roman law. Roman law was actually composed of two kinds of law, and the law we have been discussing to date was only one of them, the civil law (jus civile) applicable to Romans themselves (who of course knew who they were, since roman law said a lot about it, without excluding change in identity). There was another law, though it was still under the umbrella of Rome and its empire, for people who were not Roman—the jus gentium, or the law of people generally. So what the Romans did was to simplify their legal relations with other people. They didn't try to track any diversity of local law; they just said, 'Other people are different from us so they will all be governed by non-roman law, which we say has the following characteristics.' In doing this, the Romans didn't simply impose the civil law on the rest of the world; they actually appear to have synthesized in a very interesting way the law they met in different parts of Europe and the Mediterranean. So we have here a form of what later came to be called comparative law, though it was really not then recognized as such and didn't have any formal method. The lawyers dealing with inter-traditional problems just used the law that seemed appropriate,[108] and the law that slowly developed this way began to exercise a certain influence on the civil law itself, again in an entirely informal manner. To put it in modern terms, roman law didn't recognize any real problem of conflicts of laws, and didn't develop any law for dealing with them. They just used the law that was available, in a very rough way, admitting two general kinds of law, each open to the other. They had to be open to the other since there was no way of effecting closure. Chthonic law can't be closed; the roman law of the jurists had no mechanism for radical change; hence no mechanism for anything as radical as closure. The Roman notion of the jus gentium didn't eliminate particular identities, however. People said, 'If the Romans want to build a general law for non-Roman people, they are free to do so, but I'm still a Burgundian.' So we now have three types of legal tradition to deal with—the chthonic, the ius gentium and the ius civile—and three types of identity, though some operative only according to the context.

In a way, things got simpler with the end of Roman authority and even with the re-emergence of roman law. People thought of themselves, as before, as Burgundians or Bavarians, but there wasn't any alternative. And when roman law began its growth into a common law of Europe it did provide a larger notion of European

[107] See Vinogradoff, *Roman Law in Medieval Europe* (1968) at 126 ('Medieval people had no strong sense of historical diversities').

[108] In doing this they may have been emulating Greek practice, in which use was made of the law of another city, where appropriate, and with no great ado. See R. Bauman, 'Comparative Law in Ancient Times' in A. Tay (ed.), *Law and Australian Thinking in the 1980s* (Sydney: Organizing Committee of the 12th International Congress of Comparative Law, 1986) 99; K. Assimakopoulou, 'Comparative Law in the History of Greek Law' (1986) 39 Rev. hell. dr. int. 323 at 325.

identity (so the late twentieth-century European student exchange programme could be named Erasmus, after the pan-European, conciliatory humanist of the sixteenth century). But we now are back to only two identities, the local and the European, not the three which existed in Roman time. We already know that there was a lot of toing and froing between local law and modern, Europeanized, roman law, a lot of resistance by chthonic tradition to modernization by rational, roman tradition; and we already largely know which tradition prevailed. The result of this process, the adhering of people to modern, rational law, was the creation of new identities in Europe, those of nation-states, the people of which could be identified by their citizenship. The people became neither local, nor European, but some-where in between.

The construction of states, and citizenship as a means of adherence to them, implied the disappearance of other forms of identity, at least as defined by law.[109] So law as reason's instrument now becomes very instrumental. Not only is it formally defined to exclude other solutions, other voices, in terms of substantive solutions, but it also now has the function of binding people together within a single territory, creating an identity which previously did not exist. It no longer is possible to be citizen of a city; attachment to a region, to a former area of chthonic law, could retain only nostalgic importance. The domicile of origin retained some importance in Swiss law, though now in terms of a canton of origin, and there were areas of derecho foral or chthonic law in Spain, but the state set out to eliminate legal particularity and made a very good job of it.[110] It unified the law of the peoples and lands falling within its defined territory (how this was done also had implications for comparative law, which we're getting to). The result of this process of unifying law, which swept through all of Europe, was a new phenomenon of legal disunity in Europe. Law becomes 'territorial zersplittert'.[111] While there had usually been some form of legal commonality in Europe in the past (chthonic, canon, roman—old or new), each state now purported to occupy the legal field. Each created its own unity (with codes tending to universal expression) but the combination was destructive of any larger unity. So we see here the general effect of systemic thinking in law. Systems require boundaries; these are the boundaries of the states. Systems require consistency; this is provided by exclusivity of sources. Systems conflict; the science of European private international law comes into being, a formal law of all formal laws which is also, necessarily, national in character. Some states even require that it

---

[109] Even here, however, as catholics, most Europeans remained subject to canon law as the law of their church. This had become, however, a private matter, largely separate from the formal world of state law.

[110] Though the instability of states gave rise to a new type of particularity, that resulting from the overlapping of state laws, itself contributing to local forms of identity, as in Alsace–Lorraine; see H. P. Glenn, 'The Local Law of Alsace–Lorraine: A Half Century of Survival' (1974) 23 Int. & Comp. Law Q. 769.

[111] H. Coing, 'Die Bedeutung des Rechts in der neureren Geschichte Europas' in W. Fikentscher, H. Franke and O. Köhler (eds.), Entstehung und Wandel rechtlicher Traditionen (Freiburg/Munich: Verlag Karl Alber, 1980) 755 at 760.

be mandatorily applicable by the judge, so that in inter-state relations the parties are not free to submerge differences in formal law by common accord.[112]

This era of radical separation of European laws and European identities was, however, of relatively short duration, no more than a century and a half, if we take the French civil code of 1804 as its origin. By the mid-twentieth century the European Community was under way, as was the construction of a new European law. This began in terms of formal law, the construction of a new and larger European legal rationality. It is evident that there are now limits to this process, even with the enormous legislative production of Brussels. Legislative unification in Europe was successful in the eighteenth and nineteenth centuries because the new rationality was overtaking the residues of the chthonic world in law. Now a new unification, a new rationality, must overcome existing unifications, existing rationalities.[113] Already the process of European legal unification has given way to European harmonization, which accords some measure of autonomy in implementation of European directives. The process of *informal* harmonization, the informal generation of a new ius commune, proceeds even more rapidly. The legal professions have been released from narrow, territorial anchors, to float more freely over Europe;[114] private international law has already lost its primacy of place in the

---

[112] On the obligatory character of private international law rules and the current process of harmonization of European law see, however, Glenn, 'Harmonization' (1993) 1, arguing for a presumption of harmony, rather than of conflict, of European laws.

[113] For the immense literature on European legal unification and harmonization, see G. Kegel, *Internationales Privatrecht*, 6th edn. (Munich: C. H. Beck, 1987) at 66; De Witte and Forder (eds.), *Common law of Europe and future of legal education* (1992); R. Schulze, 'Le droit privé commun européen' Rev. int. dr. comp. 1995. 7, notably at 10, 11, on 'general principles of law' and 'common traditions'; J. Taupitz, *Europäische Privatrechtsvereinheitlichung heute und morgen* (Tübingen: J. C. B. Mohr (Paul Siebeck), 1993); A. Hartkamp, M. Hesselink, E. Hondius, C. Joustra and E. du Perron *Towards A European Civil Code*, 2nd edn. (Nijmegen/The Hague: Ars Aequi Libri/Kluwer, 1998); P. Legrand Jr., 'Against a European Civil Code' (1997) 60 MLR 44; J. Basedow, 'The renascence of uniform law: European contract law and its components' (1998) 18 Legal St. 121, with further refs. at n. 14; P. de Vareilles-Sommières, *Le droit privé européen* (Paris: Economica, 1998); F. Werro (ed.), *New Perspectives on European Private Law* (Fribourg: Editions Universitaires Fribourg, 1998); and for the emergence of pan–European, civil law–common law treatises, see H. Kötz and A. Flessner, *Europäisches Vertragsrecht*, vol. I by H. Kötz (Tübingen: J. C. B. Mohr, 1996); C. von Bar, *Gemeineuropäisches Deliktsrecht*, vol. I (Munich: Beck, 1996). A non-legislative, persuasive, statement of principles of European contract law has also been formulated; see O. Lando and H. Beale (eds.), *Principles of European Contract Law Part I: Performance, Non-performance and Remedies* (Dordrecht/Boston/London: Martinus Nijhoff, 1995). On the limits and extent of legal unification generally, see H. Kötz, 'Rechtsvereinheitlichung—Nutzen, Kosten, Methoden, Ziele' RabelsZ. 1986. 1; P. Behrens, 'Voraussetzungen und Grenzen der Rechtsfortbildung durch Rechtsvereinheitlichung' RabelsZ. 1986. 19; R. David, 'The International Unification of Private Law' in International Association of Legal Sciences (K. Zweigert and U. Drobnig, eds.), *International Encyclopedia of Comparative Law*, vol. II, (Tübingen/The Hague/Paris: J. C. B. Mohr (Paul Siebeck)/Mouton, 1971), ch. 2, at 5: Glenn, 'Harmonization of Private Law Rules Between Civil and Common Law Jurisdictions' in International Academy of Comparative Law, XIIIth International Congress General Reports (Cowansville, Quebec: Yvon Blais, 1992) at 79.

[114] See generally R. Goebel, 'Professional Qualifications and Education Requirements for Law Practice in a Foreign Country: Bridging the Cultural Gap' (1989) Tulane L. Rev. 443; R. Bain, G. Endreo and J. Simpson, 'Le libre établissement des juristes en Europe (mythes et réalités)' JCP 1988. I. 3324; G. Gornig, 'Probleme der Niederlassungsfreiheit und Dienstleistungsfreiheit für Rechtsanwälte in den Europäis chen

rational ordering of laws.[115] There is also the work of the European courts, those of the European Union and of the European Convention on Human Rights. They are generating a European jurisprudence (the return of the judges). There is also talk of a different form of legal logic, one more tolerant of difference, more 'fuzzy' (non-aristotelian) and capable of conciliating different particular European laws in a larger European cadre.[116] The European activity has led to a new, European identity or citizenship,[117] alongside that of states (putting the rest of us into the long line in the airports). The city has also emerged as a new field of inter-traditional activity, the result of massive population movement in the world, having possibly its greatest effect in Europe. Islam is back.[118] So we see the people of Europe identifying themselves with their large cities, which have their own intricate law; with their states, which increasingly play a kind of mediating role between the local and the continental; and with their Europe, which is Europe because it cannot eliminate all the others.[119] They are torn between these identities, though will defend any of them against external challenge. There is also a resurgence of local regional identity—the Basques, the Corsicans, the Flemish, the peoples of eastern Europe, who have no recent memory of a modest state—insisting that states justify themselves, resisting application to them of the tradition of constructive rationality in law, resisting

Gemeinschaften' NJW 1989. 1120; H. P. Glenn, 'Private International Law and the New International Legal Professions' in *Mélanges von Overbeck* (Fribourg: Presses de l'Université de Fribourg Suisse, 1990) at 31. The professional organizations have followed, creating a new code of conduct for cross-border activities of the lawyer. See Council of the Bars and Law Societies of the European Community (CCBE), *Cross Border Practice Compendium* (Deventer, Netherlands: Kluwer, 1991).

[115] The role of private international law depended on the existence of complete and systemic national legal orders. See H. Batiffol, *Aspects philosophiques du droit international privé* (Paris: Dalloz, 1956) at 16, 24; Krawietz, *Recht als Regelsystem* (1984), above, at 51 (on notion of legal system of legal systems, System von Rechtssystemen). Even in public law, however, the national has now become blurred with the European. See notably X. Prétot, commenting on C. E. 19 Apr. 1991, Dalloz 1991. II. 399 ('Cette double décision illustre, si besoin était, la perméabilité, on ne peut plus nette depuis quelques années, de la jurisprudence administrative à la norme internationale').

[116] Delmas-Marty, *Pour un droit commun* (1994), above, at 158 (on 'controlled sovereignty', 'relative European primacy' and 103, 108 (on relations between non-hierarchical systems); M. Delmas-Marty, *Le flou du droit* (Paris: Presses universitaires de France, 1986); F. Ost, 'La jurisprudence de la Cour européenne des droits de l'homme: amorce d'un nouveau "jus comune"?' in De Witte and Forder, *Common Law of Europe and future of legal education* (1992) at 683. On fuzzy or multivalent logic, see the discussion below, Ch. 10, *Bivalence and multivalence.*

[117] C. Closa, 'The Concept of Citizenship in the Treaty of European Union' (1992) 29 CMLR 1137; and for the theoretical debate, D. Zolo, *La cittadinanza: Appartenenza, identità, diritti* (Rome/Bari: Editori Laterza, 1994).

[118] See J.-Y. Carlier and M. Verwilghen, *Le statut personnel des musulmans: droit comparé et droit international privé* (Brussels: Bruylant, 1992).

[119] See E. Morin, *Penser l'Europe* (Paris: Gallimard, 1987) at 48, 49 ('L'Europe n'est en fait l'Europe que parce qu'il n'y a pas d'Europe en droit'); C. Varga, 'European Integration and the Uniqueness of National Legal Cultures' in de Witte and Forder (eds.) *Common law of Europe and future of legal education* (1992) at 721; and on the emerging European principle of subsidiarity—of leaving regulation to the lowest possible level—see G. Bermann, 'Taking Subsidiarity Seriously: Federalism in the European Community and the United States' (1994) 94 Col. L. Rev. 331.

tradition from within. Outside Europe, in the newer civil law world, the regional claims are more clearly related to chthonic law as, again, in Chiapas.[120] There is more and more occasion for conversation, and the occasional argument. This is inevitable in convincing people that they have more than one identity, but Europe may be (again) leading the world in this. It may be a little confusing, but it's way ahead of ethnic cleansing.

## PROTECTING IDENTITY

Chthonic law did little to protect the identity of its groups. People could come and go, but there were lots of reasons out there for not going very far. Talmudic law had concepts of both treason and heresy but they were of limited application, given the riot of opinion the tradition expressly authorized (and they were used chiefly at the level of disobedience to decision, rather than at that of doctrinal dissent). Both traditions would let their people go, or exit, and in the contemporary world this has happened to a considerable degree. There are variations in this according to the practices of states, and some have made it difficult for chthonic peoples to escape a chthonic identity.[121] Yet the mixité of the populations of latin America shows the absence of internal restraint on exit. The civil law world also has known heresy, treason and sedition, though the first has disappeared with the rights of expression born of the enlightenment. Scientists can no longer be killed for their pursuit of science.[122] The inquisition lasted longest in Mexico, until the nineteenth century, but charges of heresy were not made against chthonic peoples (at least from the sixteenth century). Jews and foreigners enjoyed no immunity.[123] Treason and sedition are still with us, however, and there is no requirement of war for their invocation.

The state in the tradition of the civil law will also allow its people to leave and

---

[120] Where the Mexican government has resisted the idea of 2 'systems' of law within the Mexican state. Here we have some real difficulties of communication, and the notion of system has a lot to do with it. In particular, we appear to have a corrupt, formal system (according to the current President of Mexico, who seems to be trying to do something about it) refusing to recognize or deal with an honest, informal system. Then again, it may be that the informal system is being used as a front by marxists, who would establish a corrupt, marxist system of their own (on corruption in socialist law, see below, Ch. 9, *Asian corruption*). Theory will only take you so far; then you have to get a closer look at what's really going on.

[121] See above, Ch. 3, *The state as middle ground*, on the notion of 'reservations' for chthonic peoples.

[122] See, for the last public hanging for heresy in Scotland in 1697, subsequent unsuccessful heresy trials, and 'target' of Archibald Pitcairn, physician and teacher of medicine, MacIntyre, *Whose Justice? Which Rationality?* (1988), above, at 243–5; for torture in Holland as late as the mid-18th century see M.-S. Dupont-Bouchard, 'Criminal Law and Human Rights in Western Europe (14th–18th Centuries). The Example of Torture and Punishment. Theory and Practice' in Schmale, *Human Rights and Cultural Diversity* (1993), above, 183 at 186, 187; and for burning of the 'last heretic' in Poland in late 18th century, see Roberts, *History of World* (1995), above, at 649.

[123] G. F. Margadant S., *Introducción a la historia de derecho mexicano*, 10th edn. (Naucalpan: Editorial Esfinge, 1994) at 126–8.

many have, to the benefit of newer worlds.[124] Whether they are allowed to lose their
citizenship, by simple choice, is a little trickier. Some states have no general provision for loss of nationality, though don't appear to punish the attempt.[125] There
would therefore be no civil apostasy.[126] Protection of identity is accomplished rather
by keeping people out. Since the state is territorial, and law is territorial, people can
become subject to state law, and benefit from it at least to some extent, just by
getting in. So, in the face of state-generated means of mass transport, we now see
contemporary civil law states erecting enormous and vastly efficient barriers to
access to national territory on the part of others.[127] In Europe there is also collaboration amongst states in doing so; the wagons are gathered round. Here the state,
constructed as an instrument for advancing human liberty and choice, becomes a
suppressor of both, in terms of movement of people. Constitutional guarantees of
people are not interpreted as being of universal application; only people on the
inside benefit from them. There is a lot of complicated debate about whether
airports are inside or outside. This is a vulnerable area for the tradition of states;
there may even be some incoherence, some slip between the philosophy and the
practice. Much criticism is generated, and not only from the outside. The territorial
barriers mean that rules for acquisition of nationality have become less consequen-
tial. They differ considerably from state to state (different local traditions again)
and the usual contrast is between France (citizenship by choice) and Germany
(citizenship by birth). This is too simple a comparison, however. To exercise your
choice to become French you first have to get in; if you get into Germany they have
made it easier, recently, to become German. And in both places so many do get in
that there are long-standing, foreign, resident populations, generating a language of
necessary 'integration'. So we seem to be dealing with an idea of the integrated
other—the neighbour still kept at arm's length. European state identities are now
also subject to intermingling, given European citizenship and freedom of movement within Europe, for Europeans. So identities do get a lot of protection in the
civil law world, particularly the constructed ones. They're the most fragile. They
depend on formal law, and have to be protected by formal law.

[124] Restrictions on movement were imposed by socialist civilian jurisdictions, however. See A. Dowty,
*Closed Borders: the Contemporary Assault on Freedom of Movement* (New Haven/London: Yale Univ. Press,
1987).

[125] R. Bauböck, *Transnational Citizenship: Membership and Rights in International Migration* (Aldershot/
Brookfield, Vt.: Edward Elgar, 1994) at 123; and for historical inability to abandon one's citizenship in France,
see C. Wells, *Law and Citizenship in Early Modern France* (Baltimore/London: Johns Hopkins Univ. Press,
1995) at 97.

[126] On this concept, see below, Ch. 6, *The umma and its protection*.

[127] On the complexity of these national regimes, see H. P. Glenn, *Strangers at the Gate: Refugees, Illegal
Entrants and Procedural Justice* (Cowansville, Quebec: Yvon Blais, 1992), notably at 12, 13 on the relation
between complexity and admissibility.

## THE SCIENCE OF COMPARISON

Comparison is at the heart of the relations of traditions to one another. So in chthonic times, and roman times, a lot of it went on. There was, literally, no avoiding it. There was also a lot of contact between the civil and canon laws, given that both were studied in the universities at the same time, such that you became (and often still do, if you want to get that far) a doctor of laws (both of them). They even published student textbooks on how to study the two together.[128] With the growth of systematic thinking, however, the idea began to take hold that comparison also had to be systematic. If systems were to be built, systematic comparison was essential to the construction, and thereafter to their refinement. So the process of comparison, the intellectual process of keeping traditions in touch with one another, itself became subject within the civil law tradition to the characteristics of the tradition itself. If the civil law was to be rational and systematic, things could get all mixed up again by just allowing other ideas or concepts to wander in. The tradition's definition of system could be called an open one, but it had to be a controlled openness.

The first instances in the world of forced or hyper-comparison come in the sixteenth century, when the ideas of Cujas take hold. Other legal systems (and particularly past ones) have no inherent normativity, or immediate lessons to provide, but they can be mined for good ideas in the construction of the present one. So the Cujadists were intensely interested in roman law, but were perhaps most interested in what could be taken over from it, in the form of formally sanctioned French law. Soon the 'customary' law of France also came to be mined, as an alternative to roman law (the notion of a common law of France emerges, as one of a necessary synthesis of the various 'customs').[129] Bodin caressed the idea of constructing a universal law, based on comparison, but what he really meant was informed rationality.[130] So we end up with what might otherwise appear to be a perverse idea, that of comparing laws on the assumption that each people has a particular law and that particularity can be better constructed through comparison. Comparison here has been co-opted to the rationalist effort. The tradition is being consistent with itself.

So thereafter comparative law has a formal, structured place in civil law thinking. Since its uninhibited practice can be destabilizing, there are prohibitions on certain uses of it. Even roman law suffers this ignominy. In Spain roman law is formally

---

[128] On a 1491 student guide to the utriusque iuris methodus, see Coing (ed.), *Handbuch der Quellen*, vol. I (1973) at 352.

[129] J.-L. Thireau, 'Le comparatisme et la naissance du droit français,' Rev. hist. fac. dr. 1990. 153 at 160, 177 ('pour dégager un droit commun coutumier que l'on substituerait au droit romain'), though roman law's good parts could be retained (at 188, 189); more generally, for the phenomenon as one of 16th-century humanism in Europe, see A. Wijffels, 'Arthur Duck et le *ius commune* européen' Rev. hist. fac. dr. 1990. 193 (including also the English romanists).

[130] J.-L. Thireau, 'comparatisme et naissance du droit français' (1990), above, at 169.

prohibited; in France claims of illegality can no longer be based upon it.[131] The practice necessarily develops of exclusion of foreign sources in judicial practice; this follows almost necessarily from the restriction of local sources to legislative ones, though there are some variations in national practice. The positive side of ongoing comparative law is as an aide in legislative reform, but since this suppletive function isn't always invoked, and often depends more on politics than on law, the comparativists take refuge in science. They raise their discipline to an autonomous one, beyond even legislatures, by taking on the task of studying the positive laws of the world and, scientifically, almost biologically, categorizing them. Comparative law becomes taxonomic, and large volumes are written with the purpose of classifying the laws of the world, and developing criteria of classification, of separate and distinct existence.[132] However removed this exercise was from the practice of law, and the ongoing justification of tradition, it did make available to the civil law world information on other legal worlds. It was a kind of bottled-up information, as though it were in a contemporary museum of modern law, but it was available. So there was a kind of lurking threat to the rationalist tradition in the growth of the nineteenth-century scientific tradition of comparative law, when most of the current societies and associations of comparative law were born. The information and thought of the other just wouldn't go away. And while the formal restrictions on the use of foreign sources continue largely to prevail in Europe, notably in France, recent detective work has shown that the comparisons are made anyway, behind the scenes.[133] So the traditions just do go on talking to one another, however you try to limit the process.[134] It's tough to control information.

What is going on in terms of present exchange of information? The civil law is taking a beating in terms of ecology (absolute rights of property are incompatible

---

[131]   Carbonnier, 'Usus hodiernus pandectarum' (1982) at 109, 110.

[132]   See, most recently, L. -J. Constantinesco, *Traité de droit comparé*, 3 vols. (Paris: LGDJ/Economica, 1972, 1974, 1983); for a tabulation of taxonomic efforts, concluding that western comparison too limited by a single manner of conceiving law, Vanderlinden, *Comparer les droits* (1995), above, at 328, 417; and for recent criticism of the static character of the taxonomic effort, Mattei, 'Three Patterns of Law' (1997), above; B. de Sousa Santos, *Toward a New Common Sense: Law, Science and Politics in the Paradigmatic Transition* (New York/London: Routledge, 1995) at 273 (classifications 'tell us more about the ideology of Eurocentred comparative law than about the ideology of the different legal families', yet given present 'intense legal transnationalization' enterprise of legal comparison 'more relevant and urgent' than ever, wealth of knowledge of comparatists 'cannot be dismissed out of hand'), 325 (indigenous struggles for legal autonomy illustrate extent to which comparative law has 'ignored deep-rooted legal traditions and legal cultures governing the social life of millions of people throughout the world').

[133]   M. Lasser, 'Judicial (Self-) Portraits: Judicial Discourse in the French Legal System' (1995) 104 Yale L. J. 1325 at 1370 (work of judges of French Cour de cassation including search for 'any appropriate foreign (usually European) legislative norms or judicial solutions'); and for more open use of persuasive authority across states of civil law tradition, see H. P. Glenn, *Droit québécois et droit français: communauté, autonomie, concordance* (Cowansville, Quebec: Yvon Blais, 1993); Glenn, 'Persuasive Authority' (1987).

[134]   And for non-taxonomic, issue-specific comparative law, see the major undertaking of the International Association of Legal Science, the *International Encyclopedia of Comparative Law*, under the successive direction of K. Zweigert and U. Drobnig, of the Max-Planck-Institut für ausländisches und internationales Privatrecht in Hamburg, Germany.

with it), animals (Descartes said they were simply soulless machines, but people tend to find them warm and beautiful and make them members of their families), economic inequality (possessive individualism, and growing percentages of wealth in decreasing percentages of people[135]; the islamic tradition often provides comparative comment on this feature of the western world) and refugees (islam once again). Yet the historical influence of the civil law in the world has been unmistakable, and much of the emulation has taken place out of simple admiration, notably that which took place in the common law world. On the other hand, much of the influence flowed from the colonization process, which raises the delicate issue of the relation of law to political dominance.

## CIVIL LAW IN THE WORLD

You really can't get away from the idea that the civil law tradition is somehow associated with dominance. The romans dominated, then the national civilians dominated (so out went the chthonic ways), then the world became a zone of influence of civil laws, as the colonization process occurred.[136] The western religions appear to be clearly proselytizing ones, but is the same true for western laws, notably of the civilian tradition? Is their rationality necessarily universal in ambition, in spite of the lack of universality in Europe itself? Are westerners essentially fundamentalists, such that their ways are so true that they have to be followed elsewhere? These seem like questions which are worth pursuing, if we are to understand the relations of traditions to one another, but it is difficult here to avoid talking about western law in general. The common law tradition is also present in many parts of the world, and that also came about largely through colonization. So we should probably, for this reason alone, start thinking about the common law and the civil law as representing some of the same ideas, compared with other traditions. We can then talk about a universalizing western law (don't forget about human rights) once we've brought the common law tradition into the discussion. Before the common law got under way, however, islamic law began its accumulation of information.

---

[135] See *Die Zeit*, 31 Oct. 1997, 8, 9 ('The Unjust Society', with statistics).
[136] So the civil laws of Europe became dominant, or extremely influential, in all of latin America, Africa, eastern Europe and Russia (before, and even during, socialist law) and exercised more limited but still important influence in Japan, China, and south-east Asia. Yet today there is a relative decline in influence, as other traditions criticize, and re-generate themselves.

# GENERAL BIBLIOGRAPHY

Arnaud, A.-J., *Les origines doctrinales du Code civil Français* (Paris: LGDJ, 1969).

Atias, C., *Epistémologie juridique* (Paris: Presses universitaires de France, 1985).

Bell, J., Boyron, S. and Whittaker, S., *Principles of French Law* (Oxford: Oxford University Press, 1998).

Berman, H., *Law and Revolution: The Formation of the Western Legal Tradition* (Cambridge, Mass.: Harvard University Press, 1983).

Brierley, J. E. C. and Macdonald, R. (eds.), *Quebec Civil Law: an Introduction to Quebec Private Law* (Toronto: Emond Montgomery, 1993).

Buckland, W., *A Text-Book of Roman Law from Augustus to Justinian*, 3rd edn. rev. by P. Stein (Cambridge: Cambridge University Press, 1963).

Carbonnier, J., 'Usus hodiernus pandectarum' in R. Graveson, K. Keuzer, A. Tunc and K. Zweigert (eds.), *Festschrift für Imre Zajtay* (Tübingen: J. C. B. Mohr, 1982) 107.

—— *Droit civil*, 20 edns., 4 vols. (Paris: Presses universitaires françaises, 1955–96).

Certoma, G., *The Italian Legal System* (London: Butterworths, 1985).

Cohn, E. J, *Manual of German Law*, 2nd edn., 2 vols. (London/Dobbs Ferry, NY: British Institute of International and Comparative Law/ Oceana, 1968, 1971).

Coing, H. 'Zur Geschichte des Begriffs "subjektives Recht"' in *Das subjecktive Recht und der Rechtsschutz der Persönlichkeit*, Arbeiten zur Rechtsvergleichung No. 5 (Frankfurt/Berlin: A. Metzner, 1959) at 7.

—— (ed.) *Handbuch der Quellen und Literatur der neueren europäischen Privatrechts-geschichte*, 3 vols. (Munich: C. H. Beck'sche Verlagsbuchhandlung, 1973–7).

David, R. and Brierley J. E. C., *Major Legal Systems in the World Today*, 3rd edn. (London: Stevens, 1985), Pt One ('The Romano-Germanic Family').

Dawson, J., *The Oracles of the Law* (Ann Arbor: Univ. of Michigan Law School, 1968).

de Witte, B. and Forder, C. (eds.), *The common law of Europe and the future of legal education* (Deventer, Netherlands: Kluwer, 1992).

Dickson, B., *Introduction to French Law* (London: Pitman, 1994).

Ebke, W. and Finkin, M. (eds.), *Introduction to German Law* (The Hague/London/Boston: Kluwer, 1996).

Esser, J., *Grundsatz und Norm in der Richterlichen Fortbildung des Privatrechts*, 4th edn. (Tübingen: J. C. B. Mohr, 1990).

Fromont, M. and Rieg, A. (eds.), *Introduction au droit allemand*, 3 vols. (Paris: Cujas, 1977, 1984, 1991).

Gény, F., *Méthodes d'interprétation et sources en droit privé positif* (Paris: LGDJ, 1919).

Glendon, M., *State, Law and Family: Family Law in Transition in the United States and Western Europe* (Amsterdam/New York: North-Holland, 1977).

—— Gordon, M. W. and Osakwe, C., *Comparative Legal Traditions* (St Paul, Mich.: West Publishing, 1994), Pt II ('The Civil Law Tradition').

Glenn, H. P., 'Harmonization of law, foreign law and private international law' (1993) 1 European Review of Private Law 47.

—— 'Law, Revolution and Rights' in W. Maihofer and G. Sprenger, *Revolution and Human Rights, Proceedings of the 14th IVR World Congress, Edinburgh, 1989* (Stuttgart: Franz Steiner Verlag, 1990) at 9.

—— 'Persuasive Authority' (1987) 32 McGill Law Journal 261.

Herman, S. and Hoskins, D., 'Perspectives on Code Structure: Historical Experience, Modern Formats, and Policy Considerations' (1980) 54 Tulane Law Review 987.

Honoré, A. M., 'The Background to Justinian's Codification' (1974) 48 Tulane Law Review 859.

Jhering, R., *Law as a Means to an End*, Modern Legal Philosophy Series, vol. V, trans. I. Husik (Boston: Boston Book, 1913).

Jolowicz, H. F., *Historical Introduction to the Study of Roman Law*, 3rd edn. rev. by P. Stein (Cambridge: Cambridge University Press, 1972).

Kaplan, B., von Mehren, A. and Schaefer, R., 'Phases of German Civil Procedure' (1958) 71 Harvard Law Review 1193 & 1443.

Kaser, M., *Roman Private Law*, 2nd edn., trans. R. Dannenbring (London: Butterworths, 1968).

Koschaker, P., *Europa und das römisches Recht*, 4th edn. (Munich: C. H. Beck, 1966).

Langbein, J., 'The German Advantage in Civil Procedure' (1985) 52 University of Chicago Law Review 825.

Lawson, F. H., *A Common Lawyer Looks at the Civil Law* (Ann Arbor: University of Michigan Press, 1953).

Lawson, F. H., Anton, A. and Brown, L., *Amos and Walton's Introduction to French Law*, 3rd edn. (Oxford: Oxford University Press, 1967).

Lewis, A. and Ibbetson, D., *The Roman Law Tradition* (Cambridge: Cambridge University Press, 1994).

Mancini, G. F., 'Politics and the Judges—the European Perspective' (1980) 43 Modern Law Review 1.

Merryman, J. H, *The Civil Law Tradition, 2nd edn.* (Stanford: Stanford University Press, 1985).

—— Clark, D. and Haley, J., *The Civil Law Tradition: Europe, Latin America, and East Asia* (Charlottesville, Va: The Michie Co., 1994).

Nicholas, B., *An Introduction to Roman Law* (Oxford: Clarendon Press, 1962).

Rémy, P., 'Éloge de l'exégèse' (1982) 7 Revue de la recherche juridique 254, repr in (1985) 1 Droits 115.

Renoux-Zagamé, M.-F., *Les origines théologiques du concept moderne de la propriété* (Geneva: Droz, 1987).

Sawer, G., 'The Western Conception of Law' in International Association of Legal Science (K. Zweigert and U. Drobnig, eds.), *International Encyclopedia of Comparative Law*, vol. II, ch. 1 (Tübingen/The Hague/Paris: J. C. B. Mohr (Paul Siebeck)/Mouton, 1975) 14.

Schlesinger, R., Baade, H., Herzog, P. and Wise, E., *Comparative Law*, 6th edn. (Mineola, NY: Foundation Press, 1998).

Strauss, G., *Law, Resistance and the State: the Opposition to Roman Law in Reformation Germany* (Princeton: Princeton University Press, 1986).

Szladits, C., 'The Civil Law System' in International Association of Legal Science (K. Zweigert and U. Drobnig, eds.), *International Encyclopedia of Comparative Law*, vol. II, ch. 2 (Tübingen/The Hague/Paris: J. C. B. Mohr (Paul Siebeck)/Mouton, 1974) at 15.

Tuck, R., *Natural Rights Theories: Their Origin and Development* (Cambridge/New York: Cambridge University Press, 1979).

van Caenegem, R., *An Historical Introduction to Private Law*, trans. D. Johnston (Cambridge: Cambridge University Press, 1992).

Villey, M., *La formation de la pensée juridique moderne*, 4th edn. (Paris: Montchrestien, 1975).

—— *le Droit et les droits de l'homme* (Paris: Presses universitaires de France, 1983).

Vinogradoff, P., *Roman Law in Medieval Europe* (Cambridge/New York: Speculum Historiale/Barnes & Noble, 1968).

von Mehren, A. and Gordley J., *The Civil Law System*, 2nd edn. (Boston/Toronto: Little, Brown, 1977).

von Savigny, F. K., *Vom Beruf unserer Zeit für Gesetzgebung und Rechtswissenschaft* (Hildesheim: Georg Olms Verlagsbuchhandlung, 1967) (repr. of 1814 edn.).

Watson, A., *Law Making in the Later Roman Republic* (Oxford: Clarendon Press, 1974).

—— *The Making of the Civil Law* (Cambridge, Mass.: Harvard University Press, 1981).

—— *The Spirit of Roman Law* (Athens, Ga./London: University of Georgia Press, 1995).

Wieacker, F., *A History of Private Law in Europe: with particular reference to Germany*, trans. T. Weir (Oxford: Clarendon Press, 1995).

Zimmermann, R., *The Law of Obligations: Roman Foundations of the Civilian Tradition* (Cape Town/Wetton/Johannesburg: Juta, 1990).

Zweigert, K. and Kötz, H., *Introduction to Comparative Law*, 3rd edn., trans. T. Weir (Oxford: Clarendon Press, 1998), chs. B. I ('The Romanist Legal Family') and B. II ('The Germanic Legal Family').

# 6

# AN ISLAMIC LEGAL TRADITION:
# THE LAW OF A LATER
# REVELATION

By the time Muhammad, the later Prophet, began to hear the voice of God, or Allah,[1] there were many kinds of law around him. He was born in the late sixth century CE (as it then was), about thirty-five years after the completion of Justinian's Digest and around the time of the writing (not completion) of the Babylonian Talmud. The Jerusalem Talmud had been written a century or two before. Muhammad was born south of all of this, in Mecca, in what we know as Saudi Arabia, about 700 miles from Jerusalem down the Red Sea. This land had not been part of the Roman empire, but the law school in Beirut was functioning, until about this time, and its graduates would be around until into the next century. So roman law was known, as was talmudic law, since jewish people were here and there, abiding by their law.[2] Some would later come to Muhammad for resolution of their disputes. These were all thought of as semitic, or middle eastern peoples (all are descendants of Sem, son of Noah)[3] and the concept of land boundaries here was weak, if not absent entirely.[4] So people moved around, with their law, and different laws were known.

The notion of written law was therefore firmly implanted in the world by the time of Muhammad. Written law had not displaced chthonic law, however, in Arabia (from the Arabic 'arab', or nomad), so the law to which many of the people of Muhammad had been loyal was a particular variant of that cosmos-loyal ethic

[1] A contraction of 'Al Ilah', 'the God'.

[2] For a jewish monarchy in the south-western corner of Arabia, resulting from conversion to judaism of the king of the Himyarites, see B. Lewis, *The Middle East: 2000 Years of History from the Rise of Christianity to the Present Day* (London: Weidenfeld & Nicolson, 1995) at 45; and for jewish people constituting 'a significant part of the population that accepted Islam in its formative centuries' see M. Hodgson, *The Venture of Islam: Conscience and History in a World Civilization*, vol. I, *The Classical Age of Islam* (Chicago/London: Univ. of Chicago Press, 1974) at 316, 317.

[3] The people of Mecca claimed descent from Abraham through Ishmael and the tradition stated that their temple, the Ka'bah, had been built by Abraham for the worship of the One God. M. M. Pickthall, *The Meaning of the Glorious Koran: an Explanatory Translation* (New York: Penguin/Mentor, undated) at p. ix.

[4] For the introduction of the western idea of land boundaries in Arabia, in combination with development of the petroleum industry, see H. Liebesny, 'English Common Law and Islamic Law in the Middle East and South Asia: Religious Influences and Secularization' (1985–6) 34 Clevel. St. L. Rev. 19 at 31.

which simply tells people of their way to live.[5] Because of all of this, islam has been described as a 'successor civilization',[6] though it is probably more exact to think of all civilizations, other than the chthonic, as successor civilizations. Islam is more evidently a successor civilization, however, because so many others had been established, in close proximity, at the time of its emergence. To believe you are the Prophet of a new way of life, in these circumstances, might be seen as presumptuous, and it is reported that Muhammad asked the advice of his wife Khadijah (he only had one wife, until her death) as to whether he should make known that which had been revealed to him.[7] She encouraged him, and so a third revelation, of great legal consequence, was made known to the world.

## A TRADITION ROOTED IN LATER REVELATION

Jews, christians and muslims worship the same God, whose teaching has been revealed through three Prophets—Moses, Jesus and, latest in time, Muhammad. Being latest in time did not mean that all which had preceded could be swept away, or abrogated,[8] since the earlier revelations are also the word of God. The relations between the revelation to Muhammad and the earlier revelations are thus conditioned by the ongoing, looming presence of God and by the nature of the revelation to Muhammad. It was not a revelation like the others. That which had been made to Moses was relatively concise and limited in time, though rich in meaning. Jesus' teaching of the word of God was through his own words, which the Gospels reported in diverse fashion. God revealed his teaching to Muhammad, however, word for word, over a period of some twenty-three years, from his time in Mecca to his later, triumphal, retreat to Medina.[9] As it was revealed, word for word, it was written down, by others, on pieces of leather, bits of pottery, palm-leaf stems and

[5] See Rahim, *Muhammadan Jurisprudence* (1911) 2–16 ('Customs and Usages of the Arabs before Islam'), particularly on family law; Schacht, *Introduction to Islamic Law* (1964), ch. 2 ('The Pre-Islamic Background', with acknowledgement of developed forms of commercial law); Khadduri, *War and Peace* (1955) at 20–2; Fyzee, *Outlines*, (1974) at 6 ff.; Hodgson, *Venture of Islam* (1974), above, at 103 ff. ('The World before Islam'); and for 'camel nomadism' in centuries preceding Muhammad, Lewis, *Middle East* (1995), above, at 42.

[6] F. Braudel, *A History of Civilizations*, trans. R. Mayne (New York: Penguin, 1993) at 41, notably with respect to its relations with judaism and christianity. There was also, however, the question of relations with the pre-islamic, Arabic world.

[7] Pickthall, *Meaning of Glorious Koran* (undated), above, at x, xi; Stowasser, *Women* (1994) at 87, 122; for Muhammad's subsequent wives, however, see M. Ruthven, *Islam in the World* (London: Penguin, 1984) at 85–7.

[8] On the islamic debate on abrogation see below, *Jihad*, and on the earlier christian–jewish discussion (Paul advocating abrogation of talmudic law), above, Ch. 4, *Talmudic retreat?*.

[9] 'The Prophet did not have anything to do with its words; it was revealed to him as it is now read.' Doi, *Shari'ah* (1984) at 48. Muhammad was thus 'the final Prophet. Through him . . . God spoke his last message to mankind.' J. Roberts, *History of the World* (London/New York: Penguin, 1995) at 317.

even bones (including camel ribs).[10] It was a written word from the beginning, in rich profusion (over 6,000 verses) and it said itself, in the very beginning, that the Lord 'teacheth by the pen'.[11] So the sacred book, the Koran, is, literally, 'the Reading', and since Muhammad could not read, the revelation to him was a reading by one who could not read. If you are not a muslim, you may not believe this, but there are more and more people who do believe it, and particularly after they have read 'the Reading'. The Koran convinces those who read and study it because, it is said, it is an inimitable work, which no human hand could have written. So even if you are not born into the tradition you may become convinced by it, and of Muhammad's role in revealing it, by reading.

Reading the Koran is a major undertaking, however, and particularly if you are most interested in its law. There is not really much law in it, most say, involving some 500 of the 6,000–odd verses, and they are just scattered around, in no particular, evident order. Nor is the rest of the Koran in any evident order, even though it was fixed on the instructions of Muhammad himself, who indicated to his scribes the place of all the different texts, such that they could eventually be brought together by his successors. So the Koran has some law, but not much, and it's hard to find. It was, however, an inspiration, a source, of further law, and once completed the working-out of all its implications could begin.

### THE SHARI'A: SOURCES

Islamic law also has its pyramid of sources, and it is probably best to think of this pyramid, like that of the Talmud, in inverted form.[12] At the miraculous, all-sustaining point is the Koran itself, upon which all is built. The further sources then develop and spread beyond it, each dependent on its predecessor and each ultimately on the Koran. The process of developing the law and its further sources took centuries, and islam too, like judaism and christianity, counts time. Since we can't really speak here of BC/AD, or BCE/CE, the accepted tradition is (as so often) a combination of traditions. The islamic era began in its first century, which was the seventh of the common era, so it is the first/seventh century.[13] Thereafter you just add six (to go from islamic to common) or substract six (to go from common to

---

[10] A. M. de Nola, *L'Islam: Storia e segreti di una civiltà* (Rome: Newton & Compton, 1998) at 58; Aldeeb Abu-Sahlieh, *Introduction à lecture juridique*, Texte à l'intention des étudiants de l''Institut de droit canonique de l'Université de Strasbourg (Lausanne: 1986) at 8; Rahim, *Muhammadan Jurisprudence* (1911) at 19.

[11] 96: 4. Unlike Jesus, Muhammad is not reported as accomplishing miracles nor rising from the dead; the revelatory character of his words rests upon the words themselves. I. Khaldûn, *The Muqaddimah* (Princeton: Princeton Univ. Press, 1967) at 73 ('It is itself the wondrous miracle. It is its own proof.').

[12] On religious and secular pyramids of law, see above, Ch. 4, *The written words proliferate.*

[13] More precisely, the retreat of Muhammad, the Hijra, to Medina in 622 CE marks the beginning of the islamic era and the islamic calendar. It is the year (anno) of the Hijra, and subsequent years within islam are numbered from this year and designated AH. The relation of western to islamic years is not constant, however, because of differences in the lengths of the calendars. For a table of parallel years, see Calder, *Studies Early Muslim Jurisprudence* (1993) at 12.

islamic). Thus the fouth/tenth century, the fourteenth/twentieth century, and so on. It's both easy, once you get the hang of it, and important, once you consider the alternatives.

The totality of islamic law is known as the shari'a and shari'a, like halakhah, means the way or path to follow.[14] The notion of a way of life was also vital in chthonic thought, so we find in all of these traditions an effort to explain their importance, through their name or concept, in the daily life of people. We learn immediately from this designation something about normative reach. The substance of the shari'a is found in the corpus of fiqh or fikh, sometimes referred to in western writing as the 'science' of islamic law or jurisprudence, though its literal meaning is simply that of 'understanding'.[15]

What is it you have to learn and understand in islamic law, beyond the Koran? That which flows immediately from it can be seen as comment, or explanation, and the comment or explanation which naturally enjoys the greatest authority is that of the Prophet himself. In this, islamic law parallels talmudic law, since both have known formal written revelations, and less formal, or oral, development of the Prophet's revelation. Jesus, on the other hand, just talked, and christianity has been described as a religion of 'feeble juridical intensity' (though it is certainly not feeble in juridical consequences).[16] So in talmudic law there is the Pentateuch, the written revelation of Moses, and the oral tradition, or Mishnah, derived originally from Moses himself. In the same way, in islam, there is the Koran, and then the explanations and conduct of the Prophet in living and explaining the Koran. These constitute the Sunna, literally the path taken or trodden, by the Prophet himself, and the content of the Sunna is found in hadith, or traditions,[17] statements which have been passed on in a continuous and reliable chain of communication, from the Prophet himself, to present adherents. A hadith necessarily contains two parts: the normative statement itself, and then, as proof of legitimacy, the detail or chain (isnad) of

[14] On halakhah as way, see above, Ch. 4, *Halakhah and aggadah*. The word 'islam' means submission to divinity and 'muslim' is a derivation from it.

[15] Fiqh is thus variously described as knowledge of the self and that which is against the self, as that which is permissible or required, or as that which is permissible or forbidden. Rahim, *Muhammadan Jurisprudence* (1911) at 48, 49. Hence the study of the sources of law or understanding, usul al-fiqh.

[16] The phrase is that of Prof. Y. B. Achour, of Tunis, in the oral presentation of his paper 'Nature, raison et révelation dans la philosophie du droit des auteurs sunnites', del. to 17th World Congress of Philosophy of Law (IVR), Bologna, 1995.

[17] The noun hadith is derived from the verb hadatha, 'to be new' (as in hebrew, hadash): A. Guillaume, *The Traditions of Islam* (Oxford: Clarendon Press, 1924) at 10. We know what is new to us by its means of communication, here in the form of speech, later by other means of communication. The news brings the new, but it is new only to the hearer and is already part of a larger base of information, which the west knows as a tradition. So in western languages the notion of tradition has been largely captured by the *process* of transmission, or traditio, which inadequately reflects the (often revelatory) newness to the recipient of the information transmitted. Use of the word 'tradition' to translate 'hadith' is widespread, but properly controversial. Could western thought have been the same if someone had thought of a word indicating the 'revelatory new' to describe existing information and teaching, seen from the perspective of the new acquirer of it? For criticism of translation of 'hadith' as 'tradition', see Hodgson, *Venture of Islam* (1974), above, at 64.

the traditio which it has followed.[18] A hadith could thus be judged, not in terms of its wisdom[19] but in terms of its reliability (sound, fair, weak), and eventually much learning accumulated on how to judge and classify the tens of thousands, if not hundreds of thousands, of hadith reported.[20] Choosing amongst reported hadith became an essential dimension of fiqh. There had been controversy over whether it was permissible to write down hadith received directly from the Prophet[21] and many were not written down in spite of their legitimacy; others, and the tradition admits this, were simply invented. The necessity and process of choosing amongst them are profoundly important in islamic law (for reasons we'll get to).[22]

Just as talmudic law could not be supported solely on the written Torah and the Mishnah, and went on to the Talmud, so islamic law went on to a still more explicit source, more evidently human in origin, in the form of doctrinal consensus, or ijma.[23] There are therefore real parallels in the development of islamic and talmudic law, in spite of differences in content and further development. Ijma is thus the third level of the pyramid, as is the Talmud. In the notion of ijma, however, we find something different, at least on first impression and perhaps ultimately, from the ongoing conversation, or argument, of the Talmud.

Ijma is constituted by a common religious conviction,[24] but commonality, or consensus, is difficult to establish and, once established, may resist its own dissolution. Consensus can be established only through debate and discussion, and there appears to be widespread agreement that for at least a century after the Prophet the process of debate and individual reasoning (ra'y) was intense.[25] As the western experience was also later to illustrate, however, rational debate does not

[18] See Guillaume, *Traditions of Islam* (1924), above; M. Maulana, *A Manual of Hadith* (London: Curzon Press, 1977); Pearl and Menski, *Muslim Family Law* (1998) at 6; Coulson, *History of Islamic Law* (1964) at 63; Doi, *Shari'ah* (1984) at 24, 25, 45, 49, 53, giving examples of chains of hadith ('According to Bukhari (chapter 30, Tradition 26) "Abdan related to us (saying): Hisham related to us saying: Ibn Sirin related to us from Abu Huraria from the Prophet . . . that he said . . . "') and identifying the 6 canonical collections of hadith, at 52–4.

[19] Though a hadith contrary to the Koran or to other traditions created problems. For reconciliation of hadith, see below, *Ijma, the hadith and revelation*.

[20] The criteria relate to the number of reports of the hadith, the interrupted or uninterrupted nature of the transmission, the reputation of the reporters, and any evident political motivation in the content of the tradition. See generally Guillaume, *Traditions of Islam* (1924), above, at 86, 87; G. Juynboll, *The Authenticity of the Tradition Literature* (Leiden: E. J. Brill, 1969) at 7; Doi *Shari'ah* (1984) at 57 (notably on 'broken' traditions).

[21] Guillaume, *Traditions of Islam* (1924), above, at 15–17, giving hadith in support of inscription.

[22] Below, *Ijma, the hadith, and revelation*.

[23] Parallel (though not identical) notions in western law are those of the communis opinio doctorum of the late middle ages, the various Restatements of US law and the herrschende Meinung of contemporary German law. For comparison of ijma with the former two, see P. Owsia, 'Sources of Law under English, French, Islamic and Iranian Law—A Comparative Review of Legal Techniques' (1991) 6 Arab Law Q. 33 at 41.

[24] Coulson, *History of Islamic Law* (1964) at 77; and on establishing consensus, Rahim, *Muhammadan Jurisprudence* (1991) 115–36; W. Hallaq, *A History of Islamic Legal Theories* (Cambridge: Cambridge Univ. Press, 1997) at 75 ff.; Weiss, *Spirit of Islamic Law* (1998) at 122–6.

[25] See, e.g. Noth, 'Die Sharia' (1980) at 428 (original diversity of opinions illustrated by schools, emergence of which prevent monopolization of law).

yield a general consensus but, at most, pools of consensus, each relying on prior legitimating authority and present explication and refinement. In the islamic experience this occurred through the emergence of different schools of law, and even different movements in islam, such that in implementing the notion of ijma it becomes necessary to think of a consensus in plural form. There is more to be said about this, but it is driven in large part by the enormous effect of a particular hadith, a particular statement of the Prophet, which states that 'My people cannot agree to error'.[26] Agreement, once reached within some level of the islamic community, is sanctioned by the highest of authority, and its legitimacy as a source of law can be surpassed only by the Koran itself and by the Sunna. So ijma is recognized as the third source of islamic law, in general form, though its manifestation has been plural. In this we see something like the schools and movements of talmudic law, which crystallized in spite of the fluidity and tolerance (commonality not being required) of the Talmud itself. In the notion of religiously sanctioned consensus, however, there are still further consequences, which have to do with the notion of change in islamic law.[27]

The leading or primary statement of sources in islamic law lists a fourth (after the Koran, the Sunna and ijma), which is that of qyas, or analogical reasoning.[28] This will appear surprising to western lawyers, who are not used to seeing forms of reasoning or logic categorized formally as sources of law. They may inspire or facilitate the functioning of forms of law, but cannot themselves be seen as sources. Western sources are now known, however, as positive or formal ones (which automatically excludes individual reasoning) while islamic sources are not positive or formal, though they are mainly written. It is therefore necessary to state the type of reasoning which can be used to complement existing sources, recognizing that they may well require complementing. Talmudic law makes no such broad, permissive statement as to types of reasoning, and many types have been used. The importance of the islamic position is not simply to authorize individual reason, in the form of analogy, but apparently to exclude more affirmative forms of reasoning.[29] So in the definition of islamic sources we are beginning to see not only the shape of the sources themselves, but necessary preclusion of other sources, or potential means of change. Consensus, once established, is religiously sanctioned, reducing the prospect of a varied consensus; individual reasoning is a source of law, but only in analogical form. Those islamic sources which are authorized, however, provide a great deal of written law, which calls for some form of institutional implementation.

[26] On the hadith, see A. Brohi, 'Die Rechtsideen in Islam' in May, *Islamischem Rechtsdenken* (1986) 13 at 22, 23 (giving as sources Ibn Maga, *Sunan*, Cairo, 1953, vol. II at 1303; at-Tirmidi, *Sunan*, Cairo, 1964 ff., Pt 3, at 315); Doi, *Shari'ah* (1984) at 65; Coulson, *History of Islamic Law* (1964) at 77, 78.

[27] See below, *Re-opening the door of endeavour*.

[28] Hallaq, *Islamic Legal Theories* (1997) at 83 ff., with refs.

[29] For disagreement in the islamic community, however, on the use of more affirmative forms of human reason, see below, *Re-opening the door of endeavour*.

## QADI JUSTICE AND MUFTI LEARNING

The qadi, or judge, is the most internationally known figure of islamic law, and this is due largely to disparaging remarks made by common law judges on the allegedly discretionary character of the qadi's function.[30] These remarks were made at a time of greater confidence in a process of judicial law-making and judicial law-applying than is presently the case in the common law world, and few would today deny the existence of substantial powers of individual appreciation and disposition on the part of trial court judges. The function of the qadi is to resolve disputes in accordance with islamic law, and the process is characterized by a high degree of integrity and impartiality.[31] The place of the qadi in the islamic tradition is not the same, however, as the place of the judge in the common law tradition, so there are different perspectives on the judicial process and the judicial decision. The common law appears to have moved somewhat closer to the islamic perspective in recent years, and in this may be returning to an earlier perspective of the common law itself.

Qadi dispute resolution takes place in what has been described in the west as a 'law-finding trial' (Rechtsfindungsverfahren),[32] so the notion of simple application of pre-existing norms, or simple subsumption of facts under norms, is notably absent from the overall understanding of the judicial process. It is understood as a dynamic process, one in which all cases may be seen as different and particular, and for each of which the precisely appropriate law must be carefully sought out. The law of each case is thus different from the law of every other case, and all parties, and the qadi, are under an obligation of service to God to bring together the objectively determined circumstances of the case and the appropriate principles of the shari'a. Since the parties are so obliged, they are not free to obstruct in any way the judicial process, and are rightly seen as partners of the qadi in the law-seeking process. The process is not adversarial, in common law language, but neither is it investigative in the formal manner of civil law procedure. There is even relatively little procedural law,[33] so it has been said that 'legal decision-making ... has emphasized compromise and the concrete facts of the particular case over

---

[30] For examples, see J. Makdisi, 'Legal Logic and Equity in Islamic Law' (1985) 33 Am. J. Comp. Law 63 at 63–5 (describing resulting image of islamic judiciary, diplomatically, as 'truly mistaken'). Much of the blame for this may be laid upon Max Weber. See his Economy and Society: An Outline of Interpretive Sociology (New York: Bedminster Press, 1968), notably vol. III at 976 ('Kadi-justice knows no rational "rules of decision" ... whatever').

[31] On the qualifications for appointment as qadi, and the appointment process, see A. Falaturi and R. May, 'Gerichtsverfahren und Richter im traditionellen islamischen Recht' in May, Islamischem Rechtsdenken (1986) 47 at 55, 56, 63, 64; Milliot and Blanc, Droit musulman (1987) at 537; Doi, Shari'ah (1984) at 11–13; Schacht, Introduction to Islamic Law (1964) at 188, 189; Khadduri, Islamic Conception of Justice (1984) at 145, 146.

[32] Falaturi and May, 'Gerichtsverfahren' (1986), above, 47 at 50. For the notion of 'law-finding' in continental legal history, notably in Germany, see G. Strauss, Law, Resistance and the State: the Opposition to Roman Law in Reformation Germany (Princeton: Princeton Univ. Press, 1986) at 48.

[33] Noth, 'Die Sharia' (1980) at 431; and for the procedure, involving invitations by the qadi to argue or present proof, Milliot and Blanc, Droit musulman (1987) at 559–61.

adherence to broad principle or application of universal abstract norms'.[34] This sounds a lot like earlier views of the common law process; there is also something reminiscent of modern case-management, pre-trial conferences, and even obligatory mediation. Legal representation was not an inevitable part of this process, but recent practice has apparently not found it incompatible with any fundamental principle of the procedure.[35] Since it is the parties themselves who are under an obligation to bring about an understanding of the case compatible with the knowledge of God, there is great emphasis on oral testimony, and written proof is in principle excluded, though may be admitted in exceptional cases or to support oral testimony.[36]

Once reached, the decision of the qadi is simply given, with no written reasons and often with no explicit reasons of any kind. By this point the parties, partners in the process, are expected to understand what is going on, and why. Absent reasons, there is no system of case-reporting.[37] Absent case reports, there is no operative notion of precedent, still less of any stricter concept of stare decisis. As in talmudic law, the notion of res judicata is also, necessarily, weak.[38] Islamic law (like talmudic law and the common law) knew no courts of appeal; the remedy of a losing party was to return to the deciding qadi.[39] Where there has been no relief from the initial judgment, execution is however possible, though a judgment contrary to islamic law (according to extra-judicial criteria) cannot change the status of the parties in the eyes of God.[40] You can win, but still lose, eventually. If you adhere to the tradition, this is to be taken into account. It is something like having to act 'inside the law'.[41]

---

[34]  Cammack, 'Islamic Law in Indonesia's New Order' (1989) at 73.

[35]  Falaturi and May, 'Gerichtsverfahren' (1986), above, at 73; islamic justice, however, is in principle 'absolutely free' with 'no fees and no costs', I. al Faruqi and L. al Faruqi, *The Cultural Atlas of Islam* (New York/London: Macmillan/Collier Macmillan, 1986) at 269. For emergence of profession of advocate only in 19th century, see Lewis, *Middle East* (1995), above, at 188.

[36]  Lewis, *Middle East* (1995), above, at 124; Pearl and Menski, *Muslim Family Law* (1998) at 18.

[37]  Though some civilian-style reporting, i.e. skeletal, of cases occurs in some islamic countries, at least with respect to decisions of courts understood as secular. See I. Edge, 'Comparative Commercial Law of Egypt and the Arabian Gulf' (1985–6) 34 Clevel. St. L. Rev. 129 at 140 (French reporting model; Egyptian decisions most influential and best reported; law firms build own collections of reports).

[38]  Milliot and Blanc, *Droit musulman* (1987) at 562 (all decisions can be revised by judge who gave it, or by another judge); and for Muhammad's instructions to the judge that 'you should not feel prevented by your first judgment from retracting', see Khaldûn, *Muqaddimah* (1967), above, at 173. On the absence of a strict concept of res judicata in talmudic law, see above, Ch. 4, *Applying divine law.*

[39]  Liebesny, 'English Common Law and Islamic Law' (1985–6), above, at 20; Anderson, *Law Reform in Muslim World* (1976) at 13; Coulson, *History of Islamic Law* (1964) at 163; Falaturi and May, 'Gerichtsverfahren' (1986), above, at 90, 91; Khadduri, *Islamic Concept of Justice* (1984) at 146. Cf., for appeal to the caliph through a single magistrate or radd in moslem Spain, Milliot and Blanc, *Droit musulman* (1987) at 547 .

[40]  Falaturi and May, 'Gerichtsverfahren' (1986), above, at 88; Weiss, 'Theory of Ijtihad' (1978) at 206.

[41]  See, for this talmudic notion, above, Ch 4, *Halakhah and aggadah*; and for the idea of the muslim person reaching the Truth 'which resides within the sacred forms and injunctions of the Law', often associated with sufi teaching within islam, see S. Nasr, 'Islam' in A. Sharma, *Our Religions* (San Francisco: HarperSanFrancisco, 1993) 425 at 465, 477.

As an adjudicator the qadi neither contributes to the development of the law nor stands among those most learned in it. So, as in the civil law, there is a large place for expertise outside of the courts. Here the mufti, or jurisconsult, appears to play a role remarkably similar to that of the roman jurist or contemporary European law professor (in providing Gutachten or opinions to courts). Free of formal responsibility, yet possessed of immensely useful knowledge and great analytical ability, the mufti comes to be the most effective means of bringing vast amounts of law to bear on highly particular cases. The opinion of the mufti, the fatwah, is often filed in court as a means of assisting deliberation. Thereafter, as recent work has shown,[42] fatwahs were not simply discarded or buried in archives; they were the object of collections and even systematic incorporation into the large doctrinal works, or furu. So there is a major question as to whether islamic law is simply, as often affirmed, an ideal statement as to how people should live and what courts should do, without any real contact with actual practice. The contact is not evident in any ascertainable end product of court practice, but exists in the actual working-process of the lawyers. There is feedback between holy law and the real world.

In the life of islamic law, however, there is a remarkable lack of institutional support. In this, islamic law remains closest to its immediate predecessor, Arabic chthonic law. It is true that the qadi occupies a formal, institutional position, but beyond this islamic law is simply sustained by the islamic community. There is no islamic legislator (though there are now state legislators in islamic jurisdictions), no appeal or supreme courts (they too come with the state), nothing equivalent to a Grand Sanhedrin, and no institutionalized, hierarchical church.[43] The imam is a prayer leader, the muezzin the caller to prayers in each community. Those learned in islamic law are not authorized or licensed in any way; they simply become learned and become known as such.[44] So legal authority is in a very real sense vested in the private, or religious, community and not in any political ruler. In the second/eighth century there was some movement to unify islamic law through legislation.[45] It failed, and there have been conceptual problems with the idea of an islamic state

[42] Hallaq, 'From *Fatwas* to *Furu*' (1994); Hallaq, 'Model *Shurût* Words and the Dialectic of Doctrine and Practice' (1995) 2 Islamic Law & Soc. 109. On the particular importance of fatwahs in the shi'ite tradition in islam (e.g., that which was pronounced against the author Salman Rushdie for writings judged to be blasphemous), see below, *Of schools and schism*; and on the general role of the mufti, Schacht, *Origins of Muhammadan Jurisprudence* (1964) at 73–5; M. Masud, B. Messick and D. Powers (eds.), *Islamic Legal Interpretation: Muftis and their Fatwas* (Cambridge, Mass./London: Harvard Univ. Press, 1996), notably B. Messick, 'Media Muftis: Radio Fatwahs in Yemen' at 310 (opinions of contemporary muftis broadcast daily to a national listening audience).

[43] S. Haider (ed.), *Islamic Concept of Human Rights* (Lahore: The Book House, 1978) at 69; Noth, 'Die Shariâ' (1980) at 419; Weiss, *Spirit of Islamic Law* (1998) at 15, 16.

[44] A. Brohi, 'Die Rechtsideen', (1986), above, at 27; Calder, *Studies Early Muslim Jurisprudence* (1993) at 164 ('reputation and . . . status [gained] . . . informally as a result of personality and public perception'); Hallaq, *Islamic Legal Theories* (1997) at 117–23, 144–7 (notably on overlapping roles of the mujtahid, the person learned in law, and the mufti, the mujtahid of good character whose legal opinions are accepted as a matter of public office); Weiss, *Spirit of Islamic Law* (1998) at 128, 133, 134.

[45] Coulson, *History of Islamic Law* (1964) at 52.

forever after.[46] Islam is meant to provide a personal relationship with God. There are relatively few possibilities of institutional corruption.[47] This is part of the attraction of islam.

## SUBSTANTIVE SHARI'A

Everybody outside of islam has heard bits and pieces of islamic law. They are usually rather spectacular bits and pieces, viewed from another tradition. The bulk of islamic law does not appear as spectacular, however, and the spectacular parts are subject to all kinds of exceptions and restrictions. This is not to say that western newspaper reports on islamic law are necessarily inaccurate, but there is a great deal of law which is not reported, and it's not the spectacular parts that are bringing in the conversions. Those are based on other arguments.

The law of the family and the law of succession in islam are profoundly marked by the Arabic chthonic law which Muhammad encountered, and by his reaction to it. In general, it's private, consensual law, since there has been no organized church, or state, to stipulate conditions and administer them. Marriage is by mutual consent, though ceremonies may be added,[48] and there is a formal type of temporary marriage in the shi'ite tradition.[49] In some parts of the islamic world the parties may be very young, under 13.[50] There are obvious economic motives for this, but in

[46] See below, *Subtle change* (for relations with secular authority generally); *Contrapuntal exchange, with islams* (for relations with state structures).

[47] Cf., however, Braudel, *History of Civilizations* (1993), above, at 100 ('Furthermore, like all societies, Islam has its plutocrats, few in number but all the more powerful for that. Beliefs and traditions often serve as pretexts whereby the privileged defend their own interests, keeping in being some societies that are truly "medieval" as in Yemen, feudal as in Iran [under the Shah of Iran], or archaic as in Saudi Arabia—despite, or perhaps even because of, its oil'); Aldeeb Abu-Salieh, *Musulmans face aux droits de l'homme* (1994) at 253–5 (detailing remarkable levels of spending by particular Arab leaders). On the dramatic decline in governmental expenditure on palaces, services, stables and special secretariats in Iran following the fall of the Shah, see J.-P. Digard, 'Shi-isme et Etat en Iran' in O. Carré (ed.), *L'Islam et l'Etat en Iran* (Paris: Presses universitaires de France, 1982) 4 at 84; and on corruption in islamic states, as elsewhere, often being a matter of 'putting one's family first,' Ruthven, *Islam in World* (1984), above, at 178, 179. On the notion of doctrinal corruption, however, which some see in the notion of immutable texts, of apparently human origin, see the discusssion of ijtihad, below, *Re-opening the door of endeavour.*

[48] M. Khadduri, 'Marriage in Islamic Law: The Modernist Viewpoints' (1978) 26 Am. J. Comp. Law 213 at 213, 214; D. El Alami and D. Hinchcliffe, *Islamic Marriage Divorce Laws of the Arab World* (London/The Hague/Boston: CIMEL/Kluwer Law International, 1996) (with texts of contemporary national laws); Cammack, 'Islamic Law in Indonesia's New Order' (1989) at 59; Milliot and Blanc, *Droit musulman* (1987) at 298, 299.

[49] Amin, *Islamic Law* (1989) at 75; S. Haeri, *Law of Desire: Temporary marriage in Shi'i Iran* (Syracuse: Syracuse Univ. Press, 1989); Aldeeb Abu-Salieh, *Musulmans face aux droits de l'homme* (1994) at 169. The notion of temporary marriage is defended as being preferable to informal sexual relations, though the argument has not prevailed in orthodox islam.

[50] Amin, *Islamic Law* (1989) at 81, citing North Yemen, Pakistan, Bangladesh; Aldeeb Abu-Salieh, *Musulmans face aux droits de l'homme* (1994) at 161–3; and for fuller discussion, indicating that such arranged marriages may in some cases give rise to criminal liability by state law, L. Carroll, 'Marriage–Guardianship and Minor's Marriage at Islamic Law' (1987) 7 Islamic and Comp. Law Q. 279.

the past they were more evident, since chthonic arabic law knew the bride sale. Muhammad changed this, providing that the wife alone was to receive any payment by the husband or his family.[51] As in earlier talmudic law, marriage is potentially polygamous, up to four wives being permitted.[52] There is controversy about this in islamic debate,[53] and Muhammad's monogamous first marriage has been cited by Benazir Bhutto, recently Prime Minister of Pakistan, whose husband is conspicuously monogamous. Polygamy has been abolished by legislation in Tunisia; elsewhere this has not been accepted as possible.[54] A wife may be allowed to stipulate by contract for a monogamous marriage, however, and the abusively polygamous husband (one unable to provide support) may be sanctioned.[55] Divorce has historically been by the husband's pronouncement in the form of the talaq, well known in western jurisdictions with islamic populations.[56] Here again Muhammad improved things, creating a delay or waiting period prior to divorce becoming effective.[57] The consensual character of the marriage also provides relief, permitting agreement on the possibility of divorce by mutual consent. Judicial divorce is also possible in many jurisdictions.[58] Adoption does not exist in islamic law. This has been justified in terms of the obligation of all muslims to care for children and, in western scholarship, in terms of the Prophet's later marriage to the divorced wife of his adopted son.[59] The general obligation of care and support of children is a serious argument in islamic law, which is profoundly supportive of people in need, but adoption has been given legislative authority in some jurisdictions.[60] Islamic law limits disposition by will to one-third of property; the law relating to the remaining fixed shares, and intestacy in general, is complex. Women do not share equally with men and generally receive only half the succession of a male heir in the same

[51] Coulson, *History of Islamic Law* (1964) at 14. Muhammad's views on women and marriage are being raised a lot these days. There are some large questions lurking behind this about sources of law, and the role of women in them. See below, *The individual in the shari'a* and *Contrapuntal exchange, with islams*.

[52] Khadduri, 'Marriage in Islamic Law' (1978), above, at 214 ff.

[53] Nasir, *Status of Women*, (1994) at 26–8; Aldeeb Abu-Salieh, *Musulmans face aux droits de l'homme* (1994) at 166–9; Stowasser, *Women* (1994) at 121.

[54] For Tunisia, see art. 18 of the 1956 Tunisian Personal Status Law ('Polygamy is prohibited') in El Alami and Hinchcliffe, *Islamic Marriage Divorce Laws* (1996), above, at 242, 239 ('The justification given for this is that it is humanly impossible to treat two wives with absolute equity and equality; on this basis it is forbidden for a man to take more than one wife').

[55] Ibid., at 26, 27.

[56] On its modalities, see Schacht, *Introduction to Islamic Law* (1964) at 163, 164; Milliot and Blanc, *Droit musulman* (1987) at 350 ff.; and for its 'accommodation' in western law, Y. Meron, 'L'accommodation de la répudiation musulmane' Rev. int. dr. comp. 1995. 921; for common origins of talmudic and islamic repudiation in Deut. 24: 1, Aldeeb Abu-Salieh, *Musulmans face aux droits de l'homme* (1994) at 178, 179.

[57] Coulson, *History of Islamic Law* (1964) at 14.

[58] Nasir, *Status of Women* (1994) at 74 ff.; Amin, *Islamic Law* (1989) at 79.

[59] Coulson, *History of Islamic Law* (1964) at 13.

[60] Amin, *Islamic Law* (1989) at 75; and for widespread practice of adoption inconsistent with law, Milliot and Blanc, *Droit musulman* (1987) at 415–17.

degree. This is defended (defence implying criticism) in terms of the male obligation of support.[61]

In recognizing both private property (in Arabic, milk) and state or communally-
owned property, islamic property law broadly parallels that of the west.[62] Moreover,
in recognizing a type of charitable foundation, the waqf (used notably to establish
educational institutions, including law schools), islamic law recognizes overlapping
forms of entitlement to land, familiar to common law lawyers in the form of the
trust, though largely driven out of the civil law in recent centuries by the notion of
individual dominium over property.[63] Yet the use of land, and property generally, is
placed in a broader social context in islamic law than it is in western law. There are
parallels with earlier western law,[64] in that absolute ownership of property is seen as
vested ultimately in God,[65] such that individual ownership, while respected, is subject to the larger obligation 'that in all wealth all sections of society have a right to
share,' and more particularly, that 'those in need have a right in the property of
those who are better off'.[66] These moral obligations appear to be the source of the
islamic tax on wealth, the zakat, criticized, however, for generating relatively little
revenue.[67] Combined with the koranic admonition against waste and prodigality,[68]

---

[61] M. Khan, *Islam and Human Rights*, 4th edn. (Tilford: Islam International Publications, 1989) at 52; and
see generally N. J. Coulson, *Succession in the Muslim Family* (Cambridge: Cambridge Univ. Press, 1971); J.
Makdisi, 'Fixed Shares in Intestate Distribution: A Comparative Analysis of Islamic and American Law' [1984]
Brigham Young. L. Rev. 267; Milliot and Blanc, *Droit musulman* (1987) at 475 ff, notably at 480 for testaments;
Aldeeb Abu-Salieh, *Musulmans face aux droits de l'homme* (1994) at 141–6; and cf. D. Powers, *Studies in Qur'an
and Hadith: The Formation of the Islamic Law of Inheritance* (Berkeley/Los Angeles/London: Univ. of California Press, 1986), arguing that law actually given by Muhammad different from that subsequently developed,
notably in giving much greater latitude for testamentary succession.

[62] R. Debs and F. Ziadeh, 'Der Begriff des Eigentums im islamischen Recht', in May, *Islamischem
Rechtsdenken* (1986) at 93; C. Mallat, *The Renewal of Islamic Law: Muhammad Bager as-Sadr, Najaf and the
Shi'i International* (Cambridge: Cambridge Univ. Press, 1993) at 114; Rahim, *Muhammadan Jurisprudence*
(1911) at 12 (individual ownership prevailng even in pre-islamic Arabia, though usually limited to movables),
261–79 (for substance of property law); and on the debate between the schools on private versus collective
forms of ownership, Khadduri, *Islamic Concept of Justice* (1984) at 138 (view favouring private ownership
prevailing).

[63] For the waqf, see Rahim, *Muhammadan Jurisprudence* (1911) at 303–10; and on the relations, and there
appear to have been relations, between the waqf and the trust, see below, Ch. 7, *The practice of comparison*.

[64] See M. -F. Renoux Zagamé, *Les origines theologiques du concept moderne de la propriété* (Geneva; Droz,
1987), notably at 155, 191, 193 (tracing divine concession of world to human beings).

[65] Khan, *Islam and Human Rights*, (1989), above at 49, citing 2: 108, 3: 190; Mallat, *Renewal of Islamic Law*
(1993) at 114.

[66] Khan, *Islam and Human Rights* (1989), above, at 49, 56; Aldeeb Abu-Salieh, *Musulmans face aux droits de
l'homme* (1994) at 218–31; and see Mallat, *Renewal of Islamic Law* (1993) at 114 on the moral values of wealth-
sharing, and 117 on religion alone, not science, being capable of creating 'a new perception of . . . interests and
a concept of profit and loss which goes beyond . . . the mere commercial or material context'.

[67] *The Economist*, 6 Aug. 1994, at 9; Aldeeb Abu-Salieh, *Musulmans face aux droits de l'homme* (1994) at 229,
230 ('marginalisation de la zakat').

[68] 6: 142 ('and be not prodigal. Lo! Allah loveth not the prodigals'), and for hadiths on the Prophet's
admonition in favour of kindness to animals, see M. Khan, *Islam and Human Rights*, (1989), above at 47
(prohibition of beating, or branding animal on face).

islamic law may be seen as environmentally friendly, yet it is said that 'we have failed to date in practising those general relevant guidelines.'[69]

The law of obligations and commercial law is also impressed with this broader ethic of the Koran, and the means of implementation are here more precise, and arguably more effective. The law of contract has been described as 'consensual, [though] not promissory',[70] requiring exchange of grants, or words of past connotation, reflecting the pre-islamic era in which sales consisted of unilateral conveyances.[71] Yet the substantive law of obligations is largely overshadowed in commercial matters by the general prohibition of riba (interest, or usury, depending on the interpretation). So the market of the islamic world is not an entirely free market, in spite of the volume of trade. It must live within the broader law of the Koran, which generally prohibits speculation and the unfair distribution of risk.[72] Translated to the world of banking, this means that banks (where islamic banking has been introduced, since its appearance in Egypt in 1963) cannot simply charge interest on loans but must take equity in the financially-supported enterprise, sharing the risk of loss and the possibility of profit. There are highly developed commercial vehicles for doing so, notably a variety of types of partnership agreement (mudarabah, musharakah), though historically no corporate form of business organization.[73] Islamic finance is thus neither socialism (which eliminates markets)

[69] Amin, *Islamic Law* (1989) at 73, citing also provisions on necessary purity of water, and concluding, at 74, that the islamic world has 'fallen far behind the industrialized countries in this field'.

[70] B. Zysow, 'The Problem of Offer and Acceptance: A Study of Implied-in-Fact Contracts in Islamic Law and the Common Law' (1985–6) 34 Clevel. St. L. Rev. 47 at 76; and see Schacht, *Introduction to Islamic Law* (1964) at 145 (on conclusion of contracts of gift with no counter-value or consideration, in Hanafi law); on mistake, J. Makdisi, 'An Objective Approach to Contractual Mistake in Islamic Law' (1985) 3 Boston U. Int. L. J. 325.

[71] Zysow, 'Problem of Offer and Acceptance' (1985–6), above, at 76; and see Chehata, 'Islamic Law' (1974) 138 at 139, 140 (contract founded not on autonomy of will but on notion of 'equivalence of performances' and this notion of mutuality inherent in prohibition of interest and requirement of sharing of risks).

[72] For the discovery of 'Islamic economics' (in the Shi'ite tradition), see Mallat, *Renewal of Islamic Law* (1993) at 113 ff., notably at 161 on the prohibition against ribah; C. Mallat, *Islamic Law and Finance* (London: Graham & Trotman, 1988); and for the absence of a general principle of liberty of contract (though measure of freedom within certain types of contract), Schacht, *Introduction to Islamic Law* (1964) at 145.

[73] See N. D. Ray, *Arab Islamic Banking and the Renewal of Islamic Law* (London/Dordrecht/Boston: Graham & Trotman, 1995) (with description in ch. 2 of medieval and modern forms of islamic contracts and indicating, at 80, 81, differences within islam on contemporary banking practices); A. Saeed, *Islamic Banking and Interest: a Study of the Prohibition of Riba and its Contemporary Interpretation* (Leiden/New York/Cologne: E. J. Brill, 1996) (arguing for new ijtihad in developing islamic banking practices); F. Vogel and S. Hayes, III, *Islamic Law and Finance: Religion, Risk and Return* (The Hague/London/Boston: Kluwer Law International, 1998) (also arguing for renewal of islamic commercial techniques); H. Alqabid, *Les banques islamiques* (Paris: Economica, 1990); S. A. Meenai, *The Islamic Development Bank: a case study of Islamic co-operation* (London/New York: Kegan Paul International, 1989) (on islamic equity financing of development); A. von Sponeck, 'Islamization of Economic Laws and the Riba Judgment in Pakistan: An Overview in Comparison with the Law of Iran' (1994) 14 Int. & Comp. Law Q. 77; Q. Abbas, 'The Legality of Interest Payments,' *Int. Lit. News*, July 1992, 17; Amin, *Islamic Law* (1989) notably at 105–19; Aldeeb Abu-Salieh, *Musulmans face aux droits de l'homme* (1994) at 245–8 (criticizing islamic system as yielding higher rates of return than western system; mudarabah representing type of partnership developed in west to avoid prohibition of usury). It follows that banks cannot pay fixed interest to depositors, yet they are entitled to pay them a share in the bank's profits, and do

nor capitalism (which liberates them). It is another way of thinking. *The Economist* magazine, not known for its islamic tendencies, has said that it 'may be better'.[74]

The islamic law of crime is known more for its sanctions than for its content. The most well known text is 5: 38 of the Koran: 'As for the thief, both male and female, cut off their hands.' Now, this is pretty straightforward, even if you are skilled in deconstruction, and has generated great debate, both within (of course) and without the tradition. Many hands have also been cut off, and in recent years. If you want to steal something in an islamic jurisdiction, you should think carefully about it. Yet there is no way of knowing, for certain, whether you would lose one, or both, of your hands, if found guilty of theft. How does the argument go? Those for cutting off argue the impossibility of overturning a part of the Koran without systemic effect; the interpretive principle that God means what God says; deterrence; the impossibility of concluding that deprivation of liberty is less cruel or less damaging; acceptance by islamic peoples; the failure of western criminology and methods of deterrence;[75] and the appropriateness of the measure in an islamic society, 'where all motives for crime have been abolished'.[76] Those opposed to cutting have been both more casuistic, and more imaginative. Thus the measure should be used, and actually only is used, in 'extreme and hardened cases' where there are elements of aggravation, any measure of extenuation or uncertainty justifying relief;[77] and, perhaps most interestingly, the notion of cutting off hands should be seen as capable of secondary meanings—cutting off is to limit or close down; hands are metaphors for power or capacity. The expression would be a type of model, in the same way that cutting out the tongue can be seen as simply

---

so. Depositors, it has been found, can live with this. For similar western reasoning, approved by Aquinas, which drew a 'crucial moral difference between loan and *societas* [partnership]' resting on the sharing of risk, see A. Jonsen and S. Toulmin, *The Abuse of Casuistry* (Berkeley/Los Angeles/London: Univ. of California Press, 1988), ch. 9 ('Profit: The Case of Usury'), notably at 185 ff. Western thought began to tolerate interest as an exception to the general prohibition of usury, specifically where a debtor had caused damage through failure to repay in time, preventing re-use of the monies loaned. Roman law allowed this, providing for payment of the difference between the 2 positions (quod inter est) of the creditor. The exception became generalized from the 15th century, when a theory of interest arose from the exception, justifying interest not merely at the end of the loan but from its creation. See J. Noonan, *The Scholastic Analysis of Usury* (Cambridge, Mass.: Harvard Univ. Press, 1957).

[74] *The Economist*, 4 Apr. 1992 at 49; and see *The Economist*, 6 Aug. 1994 at 17 (of Islam Survey) ('new left . . . should now be looking to Islam with an interested gleam in its eye').

[75] See notably Amin, *Islamic Law* (1989) at 52–5; Doi, *Shari'ah* (1984) at p. ii ('no legal system deriving its sustenance only from human intelligence can cure our society of the evils of criminality and exploitation'); and generally D. Forte, 'Islamic Law and the Crime of Theft: An Introduction' (1985–86) Clevel. St. L. Rev. 47 (concluding, interestingly, that 'there are limits to our subjecting the rationality of the Islamic law of theft to a modern, systematic analysis' (at 53), a view not consistently defended even within islam; also comparing islamic law to western infliction of death penalty for theft until 18th century and to Chinese practice of 'slow slicing' (at 50)).

[76] Mallat, *Renewal of Islamic Law* (1993) at 116; cf., for the cutting off of hands in pre-islamic, Arab law, Rahim, *Muhammadan Jurisprudence* (1911) at 7.

[77] Khan, *Islam and Human Rights*, (1989), above, at 74; M. S. Al-Ashmawy, *l'islamisme contre l'islam* (Paris/Le Caire: La Découverte/Al-Fikr, 1987) at 99 (citing hadith urging clemency in case of doubt).

requiring enforced silence, thus allowing both adherence to the Koran and measures other than mutilation.[78] The ox-which-is-not-an-ox here casts its shadow.[79]

# SHARI'A AND REVELATION

Islamic law therefore represents a highly developed and complex legal tradition.[80]
Revelation doesn't provide, explicitly, all the answers nor stop the discussion and
argument. The talmudic example has already demonstrated this. The argument,
moreover, doesn't simply turn on particular points of substantive law, given revelation, or on the types of reasoning permissible in this process. It goes to the entire
relationship between revelation and the derived corpus of law, over an extended
period of time. So if you are muslim you can't simply fall back on revelation and
say nothing else; there is an ongoing necessity of justification of Muhammad's
revelation as source of law, given the weight of social practice it must support, and
there are challenges both internal and external. The Koran itself, of course, is the
first justification, and further justification is found in the teaching of the great
jurists. The jurists of the classical period of islam,[81] however, never had to address
western arguments based on concepts of human rights, since western law was itself
not then formulated in terms of human rights. Nor had western academic research
been directed towards islam, as has now become the case. So the work of islamic
lawyers is now directed not only towards the internal working out of the shari'a, but
also towards ongoing justification of the entire islamic legal enterprise.

## SHARI'A AND KALAM

The shari'a shares with talmudic law an extraordinary reach into the daily lives of
its adherents. Fiqh has thus been described as a 'composite science of law and
morality', and this must be understood not as a joint administration of the two
separate concepts but as a fusion, or composition, of (almost all of) both.[82] So fiqh,
like halakhah, extends not only to civil and criminal law as they are known in the
west, but also to etiquette, food, hygiene and prayer.[83] Is there then nothing outside

---

[78] Khan, *Islam and Human Rights*, (1989), above, at 75.

[79] On such technical models in talmudic law, see above, Ch. 4, *The divine law applied* and *The style of the text*.

[80] For the notion of complex traditions, see D. Armstrong, 'The Nature of Tradition' in D. Armstrong, *The Nature of Mind and Other Essays* (Ithaca: Cornell Univ. Press, 1981) 89 at 90, 102, 103 and the discussion below, Ch. 10, *Complex traditions*.

[81] From the 3rd/9th to the 6th/12th centuries.

[82] Coulson, *History of Islamic Law* (1964) at 83.

[83] Ibid.; Brohi, 'Die Rechtsideen' (1986), above at 19; Hallaq, 'Logic of Legal Reasoning' (1985–6) at 81 (islamic law 'all-encompassing'). For flexibility of sanctions, however, depending on the type of conduct involved, see below, *Subtle change*.

of shari'a, nothing equivalent to the reduced field of aggadah in talmudic learning, no residual field of internal conscience? Of course there is, though it doesn't have a neat, collective name. There are islamic variants of all fields of human activity, and that which perhaps comes closest to law, in terms of normativity, is the philosophical theology known as kalam.[84]

The shari'a owes its importance, however, to the preference it has received over kalam as a means of giving effect to God's will. In the third/ninth century there was a great debate between the proponents of kalam and those of the shari'a, and, '[t]o put it in simple terms, law won out over philosophical speculation'.[85] So there is life outside of law, but not much, and those parts of the Koran recognized as other than law do not have much to do with (legal or moral) notions of obligation. Of course, when law is so broad, it cannot be enforced in its totality by worldly means. So you can find equivalents of the civil law's natural obligation, or talmudic law's 'living inside the law', in the islamic world as well. As we've seen, a decision of a qadi may be enforced, though if it is contrary to divine law it will be ever so, and you may be inclined to act accordingly.[86]

### IJMA, THE HADITH, AND REVELATION

As in talmudic law, revelation is explicated and given effect by human means, and in both traditions the product of human effort has been prodigious. If the legal content of the Koran consists of some 500 verses, the work of the jurists now fills libraries.[87] So, as in talmudic law, it is an easy thing to say that the real law is that which has been produced by human jurists, which both provides the essential human regulation and legitimates, after the fact (as they say), the revelation. This view appears well represented in western scholarship on islam, and it is scholarship of the highest order. It provides information on islam which islam itself has not been very interested in providing, so we now benefit both from islamic statements of the eternal teaching of the Koran, and more particular studies of how an islamic legal tradition actually appears to have developed, given the necessity of legal development beyond the Koran. These various statements may not be contradictory, but they can certainly be taken as contradictory (divine law in principle but human law in practice).

Western scholarship on islam has concentrated on three crucial features of the

---

[84]  See G. Makdisi, 'Guilds of Law' (1985–86) at 7.

[85]  Ibid., at 6, 7 (law preferred as middle road between philosophical speculation and 'exaggerated fideism'); Malek, *Tradition et révolution* (1993) at 46; M. Fakhry, *A History of Islamic Philosophy*, 2nd edn. (New York: Columbia Univ. Press, 1983), notably at 203, 204 (spirit of theological enquiry inspired by Greek philosophy 'not completely snuffed out', jurists thereafter unable to continue 'pure' form of early jurists and exegetes); Brown, *Rethinking tradition* (1996) at 13 ff.; Weiss, *Spirit of Islamic Law* (1998) at 25–30 (kalam eventually seen as 'handmaiden to jurisprudence'; relying on aristotelian, deductive logic, though distinguishing between its own theological reflection and 'falsafa', from Greek philosphia).

[86]  See above, *Qadi justice and mufti learning*.

[87]  R. Arnaldez, 'La loi musulmane' (1993) at 85.

development of islamic law: the historical process of establishing the hadith, as proof of the Sunna; the development of ijma; and the theoretical relation between ijma on the one hand and the Koran and the Sunna on the other.[88] It is impossible to do justice to the extent of this western scholarship, but the general effect is to demonstrate the particularity and contingency of the entire process, which lasted some three or four centuries following Muhammad. Thus the real beginning of islamic law, as law, has been said to be some one hundred years after the death of the Prophet, when non-formal and administrative practices began to be formally expressed by jurists in doctrinal form. Ijma is the product of schools of law, and the schools emerged with specific teaching only at this time.[89] It was also during the ensuing century that the sacred character of the Sunna would have been articulated, notably by the great islamic jurist al-Shafi, such that both the importance of the Sunna, and the actual choice of particular hadith, is not entailed by the Koran but is the fruit of subsequent doctrinal development.[90] Finally, given the result of the historical work, the divine character of both Sunna and ijma has been challenged. Ijma itself, 'as a juristic principle . . . is none the less the self-asserted hypothesis of Muslim jurisprudence' and it is this self-asserted hypothesis, or ijma, which 'guarantees the validity of the Tradition [Sunna]'.[91] Thus, the 'precise identification' of the bulk of islamic law 'with the terms of the divine will was artificial'.[92] So while some western historical scholarship may be compatible with islamic teaching, this cannot be said for all of it, and islamic law has been challenged by this research in a way not paralleled in talmudic law. How can islamic lawyers respond to this careful examination of their own doctrinal past?

Two types of answer have been made by islam to the challenge of contemporary western scholarship: the first is based on the nature of revelation in general; the second is based more particularly on the circumstances of islam. The first answer is

---

[88] For a 4th issue, the effect of non-islamic law on its formulation, see below, *Contrapuntal exchange, with islams.*

[89] See generally Schacht, *Origins of Muhammadan Jurisprudence* (1950) notably at 138 ff.; Pearl and Menski, *Muslim Family Law* (1998) at 9 (qualifying Schacht's view as 'heretical'); Calder, *Studies Early Muslim Jurisprudence* (1993) notably at 198, 199 (theory of Schacht 'both flexible and convincing' though reservations as to historical periods and influence of 'normative and virtuoso patterning').

[90] Coulson, *History of Islamic Law* (1964) at 56, 61 (Sunna still a form of compromise between independent human reason (ra'y) and literal reading of many hadith; hadith became subject to criteria of validity, reason in form of ijma legitimated); Anderson, *Law Reform in Muslim World* (1976) at 8; and on the process of selecting legitimate hadith, and proof of the falsity of many of them, see Guillaume, *Traditions of Islam* (1924), above; Juynboll, *Authenticity of Tradition Literature* (1969), above, notably at 100 (all muslim theologians agree forgeries took place) and ch. 8 (on forgeries for political reasons, to legitimate succession to Muhammad); G. Juynboll, *Muslim tradition* (Cambridge: Cambridge Univ. Press, 1983), notably at 9, 10 (hadith literature not 'standardized' until end of 1st/7th century); Brown, *Rethinking tradition* (1996) at 87 ff.; A. Walker, *The Caliphate* (New York: Barnes and Noble, 1966) at 12, 46; Doi, *Shari'ah* (1984) at 54–7 (Bukhari accepted 7,397 hadith of some 600,000 reported); Hallaq, *Islamic Legal Theories* (1997) at 60–8.

[91] Coulson, *History of Islamic Law* (1964) at 77; and on the struggle between 'the people of hadith' and the 'legists', see I. Lapidus, *A History of Islamic Societies* (Cambridge: Cambridge Univ. Press, 1988) at 104.

[92] Coulson, *History of Islamic Law* (1964) at 85.

one which has already necessarily been given, and by talmudic lawyers. God has heard all this before, and now gives the same answer, since it is the same God. As a Perfect Author, all forms of human implementation of God's word are already scripted, so historical scholarship can't *prove* anything. If it is accurate, it simply illustrates God's script; if it is not accurate, well, it's just history, that can be argued with, as history. So saying ijma is everthing, legitimating all else, is 'at best an oversimplification and, in the final analysis, an inversion of cause and effect . . . [since] such a consensus [of ijma] is automatically ensured in advance as a logical consequence of the . . . primary sources'.[93] If you've read the Koran, and believe it, there is no threat in historical research. It is therefore said, with pride, 'We are a people who follow, not invent.'[94] So islamic law, like talmudic law, can hold its primary source subject to the interpretive power of a later source. The Torah is subject to talmudic interpretation; the Koran is subject to the explanation of the Sunna, as determined by ijma.[95] There can also be contradiction in various forms of human understanding, so there is a need to reconcile different reports of Sunna, different hadith.[96] None of this would challenge the basic script.

A second type of answer is more particularly related to islam. One variant of this is to challenge the claims of historical research, to show an underlying parallel between classical teaching and actual practice. This has been done recently in show-ing the importance of fatwahs in legal development, and how their incorporation into doctrinal law was something which was taking place in the century following the Prophet's death, such that the legal consequences of the Koran were immedi-ately appreciated and immediately put into practice. Islamic law was not, in reality, an afterthought.[97] More generally, the particular history of islamic law, different from that of the Talmud, can be seen as flowing from the different nature of the koranic revelation. It was a much fuller, textual revelation than those which pre-ceded it, so there was correspondingly less room (though still much room) for human development. This could occur through consensus ('My people will never

[93] Owsia, 'Sources of Law' (1991), above, at 40; al Faruqi and al Faruqi, *Cultural Atlas* (1986), above, at 276 ('createdness' argument already dealt with in islam and rejected in 3rd/9th century); Hallaq, *Islamic Legal Theories* (1997) at 76; and for denial of historical approach generally in islam, see Pearl and Menski, *Muslim Family Law* (1998) at 13.

[94] R. Charles, *Le droit musulman* (Paris: Presses universitaires de France, 1965) at 8.

[95] Coulson, *History of Islamic Law* (1964) at 57; Walker, *Caliphate* (1966), above, at 12; and for the talmudic relations, see above, Ch. 4, *Talmud and Torah.*

[96] Coulson, *History of Islamic Law* (1964) at 58; A. A. An-Na'im, 'Problems of Universal Cultural Legitimacy for Human Rights,' in A. A. An-Na'im and F. Deng, *Human Rights in Africa: Cross-Cultural Perspectives* (Washington DC: Brookings Institution, 1990) 331 at 358; Doi, *Shari'ah* (1984) at 54.

[97] Hallaq, 'From Fatwas to Furu' (1994); and for the notion of sunna as even pre-existing the Prophet, Hallaq, *Islamic Legal Theories* (1997) at 3, 11; for development of islamic law of succession in a 'continuous manner' from the time of the Prophet, though with shifts of direction, see D. Power, *Studies in Qur'an and Hadith: The Formation of the Islamic Law of Inheritance* (Berkeley/Los Angeles/London: Univ. of California Press, 1986), notably at 8; for further challenge to the accuracy of the historical work of J. Schacht, see M. Al Azami, *On Schacht's Origins of Muhammadan Jurisprudence* (Riyadh/New York: King Saud University/John Wiley and Sons, 1985); Pearl and Menski, *Muslim Family Law* (1998) at 13 (with refs).

agree to error'), but not through ongoing individual effort (according to the leading form of the tradition). So of course the good hadith had to be separated from the bad, since there were bound to be many. Absent consensus, how else could one get something into the law? Even if western history is accurate, the practice was part of islam, with its later revelation.

## ISLAMIC TEXTS AND ISLAMIC REASON: THE ROLE OF IJTIHAD

All the law known at the time of Muhammad was casuistic in expression. Roman law dealt with specific cases; talmudic law reflected the instances of daily life; chthonic law slowly built its base of information from the experience of past and present lives. Islamic law did not depart from this pan-traditional tradition. Given the importance of islamic law in the daily life of individuals, the need for its immediate understanding by large numbers of people, it is doubtful if any other form of expression could have been chosen. The process of incorporation of fat-wahs into the great doctrinal works is entirely compatible with, and contributes to, this general form of expression. So reading islamic law is like reading any form of casuistically expressed law, and lawyers from many traditions will feel immediately at home when confronted with an islamic text. A classic piece of islamic reasoning on what is known as non-contractual rent is as follows:

The result is that if someone tills someone else's land without his permission, even by way of unauthorized use, then [the following applies]: If the land was private property and the proprietor reserved it for agricultural use [on a sharecropping basis], the customary rate of sharing, if there is one, is taken into account; if there is no such custom and he [viz., the landowner] reserved it for the purpose of farming it out, the entire crop falls to the cultivating peasant, who becomes responsible for the fair rent to the proprietor; if not [that is, if the land was not prepared for the purpose of being farmed out] and the land diminishes in value [as a result of its cultivation], the cultivator owes the diminution of the value. If it did not diminish in value, he owes nothing; if it is a waqf and a custom [about rates of crop-sharing] exists and [this custom] proves to be more beneficial to the waqf [than the fair rent], then it is the custom that is legally relevant; otherwise the fair rent [applies]. This rule holds also if the land is the property of an orphan or belongs to the Sultan . . .[98]

Religiously-inspired law doesn't read like religion; it reads like law, and the manner of expression is closely related to the type of reasoning profoundly anchored in islamic legal thought.

The nature of islamic legal rationality flows from the ascendancy of law over kalam (the more speculative, theological philosophy) in islamic society and the inclusion of analogical reasoning (qyas) as an authorized source. More affirmative,

---

[98] Cited in B. Johansen, 'Casuistry: Between Legal Concept and Social Praxis' (1995) 2 Islamic Law & Soc. 135 at 141–2 (square brackets by Johansen); and for casuistic nature of islamic texts and reasoning, see Chehata, *Islamic Law* (1974) at 138.

western, deductive forms of reasoning are therefore in principle excluded. If law is distinct from kalam, more faithful to the primary texts, it cannot then transform itself into a new, legal form of kalam. It is possible, again, to see both divine inspiration and particular social circumstance in development of the tradition. aristotelian logic was known, and severely criticized as incompatible with koranic learning.[99] So, as the organization of the Koran itself is chaotic, so the structure of islamic law cannot be made systematic, in any western sense. The intellectual tools are not available, or at least not authorized by the leading statement of the tradition. Still, it has been said that islamic lawyers have been 'less successful than common lawyers in resisting the influence of logic on law',[100] and the sheer volume of islamic law suggests creation somewhere in the process. This was most evident in the century following the Prophet, when individual reason (ra'y) and intellectual effort (ijtihad) are widely recognized as having prevailed. In the two subsequent centuries the schools developed major doctrinal statements of law, and minor forms of deduction were used in this process (alcohol is forbidden, beer is alcohol . . .). With the completion of the great works, however, and the compilations of the hadith, further human invention appeared incompatible with the divine nature of law and the implementation which had already occurred (again, 'My people will never agree to error'). So somewhere between the third/ninth and seventh/ thirteenth centuries, something occurred which has dominated general discussion of islamic law ever since. It is referred to as the 'closing of the door of endeavour', more precisely the elimination of ijtihad (endeavour, or effort—it's a very important word) and affirmative forms of rationality, in the ongoing life of islamic law.[101] Constitutional lawyers will recognize here the difficulty of binding one's successors, and the remarkable feature of the closing of the door appears to be its informal character. People, or at least a large number of people, simply came to agree that given the nature of the tradition, further effort had become incompatible with it. This never happened in talmudic legal history, but talmudic legal history is different. Precisely why it happened in islam has been the object of enormous specula-

---

[99] Arnaldez, *La loi musulmane* (1993) at 87; Fakhry, *History of Islamic Philosophy*, (1983), above, notably at p. xix (for Greek inspiration of speculative theology or kalam opposed by jurists); Weiss, *Spirit of Islamic Law* (1998) at 67, 68 (outlining opposition even to analogical reasoning, seen as leading to more general rules and categories which would allow subsequent deduction or subsumption, this being an objectionable 'expression of human initiative'); and for an extensive bibliography comparing western and islamic rationalities, see Makdisi, 'Legal Logic and Equity' (1985), above, at 67.

[100] Hallaq, 'Logic of Legal Reasoning' (1985–6) at 80.

[101] On the process, see Pearl and Menski, *Muslim Family Law* (1998) at 14, 15 (with summary of conflicting views); Coulson, *History of Islamic law* (1964) at 72, 80–2; Fyzee, *Outlines* (1974) at 98; F. Rahman, *Islamic Methodology in History* (Karachi: Central Institute of Islamic Research, 1965) (door never formally closed; later writers looked back and determined had been closed; process of gradual contraction); Weiss, 'Theory of ijtihād' (1978) at 208 (more 'accident of history than a requirement of theory . . . doctors reached an immutable consensus of opinion that further *ijtihād* was unnecessary and untenable'); Malek, *Tradition et revolution* (1993) at 48; J. Thompson and R. Reischauer, *Modernization of the Arab World* (Princeton: D. Von Nostrand and Co., 1966) at 40, 41.

tion, since at approximately the same time the islamic sciences which had provided so much stimulation to the west (al-Djabr (algebra), al-Khwārizmi (algorithms), mathematics in general, medicine, astronomy) were also closing down.[102]

In the result, however, for centuries the dominant form of thought in islamic law has been taqlid, or imitation. Taqlid is probably the most discreet form of interstitial rationality, that of deliberate and explicit self-effacement. It recalls the Byzantine florilegium, the deliberate copying of previous forms of text, originality detectable only in the ordering and manner of reproduction.[103] Since law involves more than the copying of texts, however, the rationality of islamic law has never been effaced, only denied the luxury of any form of hubris. Innovation can be detected, on careful examination;[104] the categories of casuistic thought may yield unexpected flexibility;[105] even deliberate efforts of taqlid involve introspection and an exercise of conscience.[106] Individuality is always present in some measure.

## THE INDIVIDUAL IN THE SHARI'A

The limits on human reason in developing the law and the limits on market activity are, however, indications of the place of the individual in the totality of the islamic legal tradition. The purely subjective is proscribed; law does not contemplate an individual potestas; in the legal language there is no word corresponding to that of 'right', in the subjective sense.[107] There is little doubt, however, of the general importance of the individual in the tradition. In language remarkably similar to that used in the development of the doctrine of rights in the civil law, human beings are described as 'vice-regents', 'successors', 'deputies' of God on earth.[108] The

---

[102] See, for the importance of loss of the Mediterranean and resulting insulation, Braudel, *History of Civilizations*, (1993), above, at 84, 85; and for the effect of the loss of Baghdad to the Tartars in the 13th century, Coulson, *History of Islamic Law* (1964) at 81; Doi, *Shari'ah* (1984) at 69. Internal reasons cannot be discounted, however, since the Mediterranean, and Europe in general, were not then providing much stimulation, and the fall of Baghdad came very late in the process. On the importance of 'internal causes' and the notion that the material sources of divine will had been fully explored, see Coulson, *History of Islamic Law* (1964) at 81. Closing the door not only prevented in large measure the development of new law, but also prevented the exercise of ijtihad to deconstruct the old, and is therefore closely related to development of the doctrine of heresy; see below, *The umma and its protection*. On the decline of islamic science, see T. Huff, *The rise of early modern science: Islam, China, and the West* (Cambridge: Cambridge Univ. Press, 1993) at 48.

[103] See above, Ch. 1, Tradition as Information: the Conceptual Bran-Tub.

[104] J. Makdisi, 'Formal Rationality in Islamic Law and Common Law' (1985–6) notably at 109.

[105] See below, *Subtle change*.

[106] Weiss, 'Theory of Ijtihad' (1978) at 207.

[107] The word haqq is used in ways compatible both with a western concept of right and a western concept of obligation, in much the same way that jus was used in roman law. See Geertz, *Local Knowledge* (1983) at 188, 189; and on the ambiguous concept of jus in roman law, see above, Ch. 5, *The centrality of the person and the growth of rights*.

[108] See Khan, *Islam and Human Rights* (1989), above, at 49; Mallat, *Renewal of Islamic Law* (1993) at 124; and 35: 39 ('He it is who hath made you regents in the earth'), 95: 5 ('Surely we created man of the best stature'). On the human person as delegate of God in the civil law tradition, see above, Ch. 5, *The centrality of the person and the growth of rights*.

entire structure of islamic law would be directed to ensuring justice for the individual person and mutual respect, and the treatment of the shari'a would make 'the aristocracies of birth, race, wealth, language . . . all suspect as disrespectful of persons'.[109] If rights had become necessary as a means of levering people out of arbitrary hierarchies in Europe, islam rejects hierarchy, even in religion, and rights are both unnecessary and potentially disruptive of mutual obligation.

In 'giving priority to human welfare over human liberty',[110] however, islamic law does not purport to guarantee equality of treatment of all persons. Perhaps it should, and perhaps this is its ultimate objective. But perhaps full equality is impossible, and ultimately incomprehensible,[111] and perhaps a notion of formal, legal equality should not be used to mask the substantive, material injustices which islam has set itself to eliminating. So we find efforts to justify formal inequalities (notably those of women and non-islamic peoples) by collective goals (the old story). There are indications, however, that islamic people, and even Muhammad, may not have convinced themselves entirely of this, and that the insistence of western arguments in favour of formal equality are having some effect. This, however, necessitates change of islamic law, a question which is larger than any particular legal question.

## IJMA AND CHANGE

As a later revelation of an ongoing God, the Koran confirmed both the importance of the human being (in the image of God, vice-regent on earth), life after death[112] (as developed in christianity) and a notion of time flowing towards eventual salvation. So change, as a concept and as a reality, is clearly possible in this context, now far removed from the chthonic one. Islam is different from both judaism and christianity, however, in its attitude towards potential change and its control of it. While christianity eventually set people free in the world of Caesar to effect the changes they would make (at least after Gallileo), judaism wrapped the world in a blanket of obligation, such that science was essentially uninteresting and the notion of talmudic science is a kind of oxymoron.[113] Islam can be seen as combining the

[109] Doi, Shari'ah (1984) at 9.

[110] Ibid.

[111] On the definitional problem in western law, see P. Westen, 'The Empty Idea of Equality' (1982) 95 Harv. L. Rev. 537 (recalling aristotelian counsel to treat like things alike, unlike things unalike; no criteria for identifying like and unlike things; if criteria found, concept of equality superfluous); M. Minow, Making All the Difference: Inclusion, Exclusion and American Law (Ithaca, NY/London: Cornell Univ. Press, 1990) at 20 ('when does treating people differently emphasize their differences and stigmatize or hinder them on that basis? and when does treating people the same become insensitive to their difference and likely to stigmatize or hinder them on that basis?').

[112] M. Mughal, 'Islamic Concept of Human Rights' in Haider (ed.), Islamic Concept of Human Rights (1978), above, at 69.

[113] See above, Ch. 4, Talmud, the Divine Will and Change.

two attitudes. The world is a sacred one. 'Facts are normative: it is no more possible for them to diverge from the good than for God to lie.'[114] Yet the human being must pursue knowledge, of all kinds, as a sacred mission. A hadith says that knowledge must be pursued even in far-off Cathay,[115] and the flowering of islamic science was in part due to knowledge and use of both Greek and Indian texts. So at the time of the first Crusades, beginning in the fifth/eleventh century, islamic science stood far beyond anything existing in Europe, though admittedly there was little development of history as a major branch of knowledge.[116] There was therefore a question of whether the islamic blanket of obligation could take the strain of ongoing, strenuous, scientific enquiry, and in the result the door of endeavour was softly closed, in law as well as in science. The knowledge required by the Prophet's word had been accumulated. Change thereafter would have to be muted. There were, of course, people who did not agree with this, and the debate continues with great vigour today, within the tradition. So change can still occur. It can occur as a result of the diversity of opinion—reflected in the relations of schools of law and different concepts of islam; it can occur through subtle techniques of change, within the range of permissible endeavour; and it can occur (this is the great debate) through re-opening of the famous door.

## OF SCHOOLS AND SCHISM

Differences within the islamic community, and differences in the information its members adhere to, are so widespread and institutionalized that some now speak of islams.[117] This may be the best way to recapture the dynamic of all traditions, recognizing the shared differences, the diverse forms of commonality which all traditions represent. In islam the differences are institutionalized in the form of schools of law (madhahib), which have existed since the first century of islam. There were originally perhaps hundreds of them (generally attached to mosques as living and teaching facilities), though some were far more prestigious than others, and by the fifth/eleventh century only four had survived.[118] The oldest are those of the cities of Medina and Kufa, eventually known, after their greatest teachers, as the

---

[114] Geertz, *Local Knowledge* (1993) at 189.

[115] Khan, *Islam and Human Rights*, (1989), above, at 47.

[116] For islamic science, see Huff, *Rise of early modern science* (1993), above, arguing for the importance of law and forms of corporate organization in promoting or dampening scientific endeavours; and for history in islam, Mallat, *Renewal of Islamic Law* (1993) at 2 ('relative irrelevance of the historiographic tradition', leaving much room for western historical research); though for 14th-century islamic world history see Khaldûn, *Muqaddimah* (1967), above.

[117] See, e.g., 'A. 'Azmah, *Islams and Modernities* (London/New York: Verso, 1993).

[118] G. Makdisi, 'Guilds of Law' (1985–6) at 6; and see, more generally, Coulson, *History of Islamic Law* (1964) at 36–53, 71–3; Pearl and Menski, *Muslim Family Law* (1998) at 16, 17; Brohi, 'Die Rechtsideen' (1986), above, 13 at 24; Arnaldez, 'La loi musulmane' (1993) at 88; Doi, *Shari'ah* (1984) at 27; Afchar, 'Muslim Conception of Law' (1975) at 90–3.

Maliki and Hanafi schools. They were firmly established by the end of the second/ eighth centuries; both had known an initial period of ra'y or creativity, though the Medina/Maliki school, as that of the Prophet's own city, was known as slightly more conservative than the Kufa/Hanafi school. The teaching of the great jurist al-Shafi'i, who died in the early third/ninth century after formulating the divine character of the Sunna, gave rise to a third school, seen eventually as occupying a middle position. A literalist tradition (back to the sources again) grew out of the teaching of Imam Hanbal, who died in the middle of the third/ninth century.[119] These were schools of law in the same way that we know schools or faculties of law today, the difference being that their teaching was and is the primary source of law. Their teachers have a common enterprise and responsibility in the recognized corpus of law they profess.

So talking about islamic law is a bit like talking about US law. They are both very general expressions and, to solve a problem, you have to know which school's law is applicable, or which state law. In contrast to the United States model, however, the law of each school applies as a result of personal adherence and not territorial supremacy.[120] So you may find people of different schools almost anywhere in the world, though there are areas in which some schools are more present than others. The oldest of the schools, the Kufa/Hanafi school, has the greatest number of adherents and has spread north and east into what we know as Israel, Syria, Lebanon, Jordan, Turkey, Iraq, Afghanistan, the muslim south-west of the former Soviet Union, and on into India and Pakistan. It is also present in Sudan and east Africa. Its long-standing historical companion, the Medina/Maliki school, went west, and is now prevalent in northern and western Africa, and northern Nigeria. The later Shafi'i school went further east (though it is present also in Egypt, where al-Shafi'i died) and prevails in the islamic communities throughout south-east Asia. The Hanbali (originally literalist) school has long held sway in Saudi Arabia. The schools differ both in terms of substantive law and in terms of sources of law. Grounds of divorce thus vary from school to school; there are important differences in the extent of the prohibition of riba, or interest/usury.[121] The differences result from the different hadith adopted by them in the first centuries of the islamic era, and the particular forms of ijma which they had developed. The two oldest schools, the Hanafi and Maliki, which taught prior to the canonization of the Sunna, remain

---

[119] A further literalist school, the Zahiri, which denounced even analogical reasoning, became extinct, though its teaching is still known and discoverable, a sub-tradition in suspended animation. See Coulson, *History of Islamic Law* (1964) at 71, 73.

[120] Such at least is the islamic teaching. Legislation in given states may claim exclusive application, and may incorporate the law of a single school.

[121] Coulson, *History of Islamic Law* (1964) at 96, 79 (the Koran prohibited inequality in exchange of 6 basic commodities, including gold and silver, and the question is how far the prohibition can be extended, by analogy; the Hanafi school extends it to all fungible commodities sold by weight or measure; other schools limit it to various forms of food).

attached to a wider range of techniques of legal reasoning,[122] though concur in the proscription of ijtihad.

How does islamic doctrine deal with the division within itself, and how is this question related to change within islam? God has again already given the answer, in recognizing the validity of polyvalent forms of reasoning. 'These and these' in judaism brings openly conflicting schools into the range of reconcilable difference;[123] the muslim equivalent, even more articulate, is the doctrine of ikhtilaf, or diversity of doctrine, expressed in endless metaphors of trees and branches, rivers and seas, threads and garments, and formally sanctioned in another of the great hadith: 'Difference of opinion among my community is a sign of the bounty of God.'[124] You may wonder how this relates to 'My people will never agree to error', but if you are thinking in this conflictual and contradictory manner it is essentially your problem, not God's. If you read some more Koran, and think about it, you will eventually reconcile notions of difference and consensus.[125]

Since the two notions, of difference and consensus, are inherently reconcilable, within islam, it follows that adherence to one or another school is not necessarily a lifetime decision, and the differences which islam tolerates are ones which people may freely use, notably by changing schools when the need presents itself. Put in western language, there is no notion of conflict of laws or fraude à la loi or evasion of law, within islam; exit from a given school to another is always possible, even if it appears issue-driven.[126] Moreover, since individual choice of school is possible, legislative re-statement of islamic law is not obliged to follow a system of personal law, but may adopt the teaching of a single school for a given territory, or pick-and-choose amongst the rules of the school to achieve a preferred synthesis (the process of takhayyur).[127] Since there's lots of information in islam, you have a lot to choose

---

[122] The Hanafi school accepts the notion of istihsan, sometimes referred to as juristic preference, which allows choice between competing sources of law. It has often been seen as a form of equity, in law, though the analogy with equity has been challenged. See J. Makdisi, 'Legal Logic and Equity' (1985), above. The Malaki school accepts the notion of istislah, or deciding according to the 'public interest', a horse potentially as unruly as that of 'public policy'. On both concepts, see Pearl and Menski, *Muslim Family Law* (1998) at 15; Doi, *Shari'ah* (1984) at 81, 82; Hallaq, *Islamic Legal Theories* (1997) at 107–13.

[123] See above, Ch. 4, *Of schools, traditions and movements*.

[124] See generally Coulson, *History of Islamic Law* (1964) at 86–9, 102 (doctrine originating, explicitly, in late 3rd/9th century, alleviating earlier polemical and intolerant attitudes); Noth, 'Die Scharīa' (1980) at 420 (differences more end point of an initially common way than expression of irreconcilable difference); Doi, *Shari'ah* (1984) at 85, 86 (no differences 'as far as the basic principles of Islam are concerned'); Owsia, 'Sources of Law' (1991), above, at 33.

[125] There is, of course, an easy, textual answer, that consensus is required only for the source of law which is ijma, while difference between schools also results from differences in the hadith which they recognized. More generally, however, there is a notion of a wider consensus, that of all islam (or all judaism) which both tolerates and envelops difference.

[126] Thompson and Reischauer, *Modernization* (1966), above, at 40; Coulson, *History of Islamic Law* (1964) at 182, 183 (citing acceptance of the doctrine by state courts in India, in case where party unable to marry by Shafi'i personal law declared conversion to Hanafi school and marriage held valid); A. M. di Nola, *L'Islam: storia e segreti di una civiltà* (Rome: Newton and Compton, 1998) at 96.

[127] Noth, 'Die Scharīa' (1980) at 429; Coulson, *History of Islamic Law* (1964) at 182–93.

from, though we are still speaking of information which can be broadly qualified as orthodox. There is other information in the entire bran-tub, both non-orthodox islamic and western.

Thus far the discussion has turned, for purposes of roughing out the terrain, on the leading or primary version of an islamic tradition. The schools dealt with are orthodox, or sunni schools, so-called for their adherence to the hadith recognized by them as supporting the Sunna (hence by appellation the true or leading version of the tradition). There were, and are, still wider differences in the islamic community, and the difference which gave rise to schism and war in the first/seventh century concerned the manner of designation of the successor of the Prophet. It was a profound religious and political difference and in no way confined to particular legal questions. There were those who felt the successor could simply be chosen, in a quasi-democratic process; others, who have been called the 'legitimists' of islam, the shi'ites, were of the view that succession was by divine right. The choice was between the companions of the Prophet or his family.[128] Those for family formed the party (shi'a) of Ali (son-in-law of the Prophet), but lost the struggle for immediate power. Thereafter they continued to adhere to the descendants of Ali (the imams of the shi'itc tradition), who were twelve in number. Hence the dominant tradition *within* the shi'ite tradition is that of the imamites or 'twelvers'.[129] Now when the last of the divine sources died, it might be thought that the forces of loyalty (some might say inertia) would take over, and that the door of endeavour would also softly swing shut in the shi'ite tradition. If you have been following the so-called Iranian revolution, however, you will know that shi'ism represents perhaps the most vibrant and affirmative group within islams. This came about because of the divine character of leadership in the shi'ite view of the world. If there were no more immediate successors to the Prophet, there still had to be an imam, one best suited to the task and one authorized to do all in his power to represent the will of God. So divinity here authorizes *ongoing* endeavour, at least until a new Prophet arrives.[130] Ijtihad is obligatory, though since it is in the name of God, it must be limited to the most learned and able of interpreters. So here aristotelian

---

[128] See, on the entire question, Hourani, *History of Arab Peoples* (1991) at 61, 158, 181 ff.; Lewis, *Middle East* (1995), above, at 62–7; Walker, *Caliphate* (1966), above, at 55 ('legitimists'); Tabataba'i, *Introduction to Shi'i Law* (1984), ch. 1; Digard, 'Shi-isme et Etat en Iran' (1982), above; Coulson, *History of Islamic Law* (1964) ch. 8; Afchar, 'Muslim Conception of Law' (1975) at 93–6.

[129] On the further sub-traditions of shi'ism, see Pearl and Menski, *Muslim Family Law* (1998) at 17; Coulson, *History of Islamic Law* (1964) at 106; and for the 4 canonical collections of hadith recognized by shi'ites, as descending from the Prophet and the imams, see Tabataba'i, *Introduction to Shi'i Law* (1984) at 5 (constituting the equivalent of the 6 canonical collections in the sunni world).

[130] See Digard, 'Shi-isme et Etat en Iran' (1982), above, at 70, on the need to 'combler la vide', and 71 on the great power of the shi'ite imams; Doi, *Shari'ah* (1984) at 80 (on presumed 'infallible' character of imams); Tabataba'i, *Introduction to Shi'i Law* (1984) at 6–11 (on ongoing use of 'reason' as a source of law, even 'pure reason') and Foreword (unnumbered) on 'long continuous tradition of innovation'; Mallat, *Renewal of Islamic Law* (1993) at 30; Coulson, *History of Islamic Law* (1964) at 106; and for computerization of islamic doctrine at the University of Qom in Iran, *Die Zeit*, 23 Sept. 1994 at 17.

deduction is not only permitted but encouraged,[131] and 'orthodox' sources of consensus and analogy have little or no place. It is the thought processes of the imam
which matter, originally a single one but now expanded to six, given the burden of
the office, and designated by the honorary title of ayatollah since the early twentieth
century.[132] Like the sixteenth to eighteenth century civilians, the shi'ites used comparative law as an adjunct source in this process, and the shi'ite legal tradition is
perhaps best seen as a combination of sunni law (or, to be more precise, of law
derived from some of the sunni schools) and more autonomously derived shi'ite
principles.[133] In all of this it is the imams (ayatollahs) who play an almost exclusive
role as source of law and provider of opinions (fatwahs). So there is an extremely
dynamic tradition within islam, as well as a less dynamic tradition. And there is the
possibility of changing from one to the other.[134] People have to stay convinced for
the relations between orthodox and unorthodox to remain stable.

## SUBTLE CHANGE

Most sunni jurists remain adherents to the limits of change of sunni law, however,
which means working with sources of law now seen as fixed (whether they are
immutable is another and different question). In this, however, they are like lawyers
of most traditions, who prefer to advance arguments rooted in authority rather
than something they think up on their own (though there are exceptions). So the
law which is practised is often assumed to be fixed, for a present case, whether it is
or not, and those who practise law know there is a great deal of room for manoeuvre between any 'norm' and any set of 'facts' to which it might apply. If cases
can go one way or another, then at the level of individual cases there is always the
possibility of radical, 180-degree change, and many ways of bringing this about. In
jurisdictions which have a notion of appeal, this happens with interesting regularity
in about a third of all cases appealed. So while an islamic tradition is one in which
the notion of stability is taken further than perhaps in any other, in its working it
can no more guarantee stability, or precise and constant results, than can any other
legal tradition. What are the elements of instability, or subtle change, in the working of islamic law?

---

[131] Tabataba'i, *Introduction to Shi'i Law* (1984) at 29 ('Rational argument is accepted on the basis of aristotelian
deduction, which brings certainty *according to the principles of that logical system*') (emphasis added), and 31,
33 and 40 on opposition to deductive methods in shi'ite law by those more loyal to hadith, consensus and
analogy (sunni teaching within shi'ism); Weiss, 'Theory of Ijtihad' (1978) at 211 (on 'greater capacity of the
human intellect to derive legal knowledge').

[132] Digard, 'Shi-isme et Etat en Iran' (1982), above, at 71.

[133] Tabataba'i, *Introduction to Shi'i Law* (1984) at 46, on al-Shaykh, 4th/11th-century author of the 'first
notable work of comparative law among Shi'is' and 43 on 'mixture' of shi'ite expositions of law.

[134] Thompson and Reischauer, *Modernization* (1966), above at 40 (change possible amongst all schools
mentioned, including shi'ite); cf. Fyzee, *Outlines* (1974) at 78, 79 (change possible to 'any other Sunnite
school'). Change across the orthodox/unorthodox border, however, would be inevitably less frequent than
change occurring even with respect to particular transactions among the sunni schools.

There appear to be two basic types of instability in islamic practice. One is in the working of the tradition itself, in the inevitable fluidity of its concepts, techniques and structures. The other is found in a process of renunciation of immediate application of these concepts and structures, in favour of some form of (freer) delegated authority. To take the latter process first, islam has always admitted some form of secular legal authority. Some would say it had to, since so little of it is in the form of public law. Variously described as state policy (siyasa), secular law (kanun), or the complaints jurisdiction (mazalim), secular rulers can therefore make law, as they see fit. The limit, of course, is that they must stay within the permissible limits of islamic tradition.[135] So here we have one of the classic problems of law everywhere, deciding whether given rules are in conflict or whether there is a discernible element of compatibility. It's much like deciding whether state or provincial laws are compatible with a paramount federal law, and nobody has ever called this a simple process. Prior to the twentieth century the secular power was not used that much; since then it has been used a great deal[136] (there may be western influence here, but it may also be a process of the religion itself shifting to more secular concerns, entirely compatible with the reach of islamic legal tradition). So if you are rationally inclined, within a sunni tradition, you can legislate or help to bring legislation about. God is the ultimate legislator, but much can be done in God's name, and if there are already major differences in the articulation of God's word, who is to decide, and by what criteria, that you have gone just a little too far? Even if you just re-state the teaching of a school, there is a process of masking the original law (as the French 'decanted' roman law).[137] Taken to its extreme, legislation could be seen as repealing islamic law, and this has been said to have occurred in the Tunisian abolition of polygamy.[138] On the other hand, if judicial authority cannot change the effect of divine law (and you had better realize this),[139] then legislation may be inherently limited in the same way, so though it's on the books, there is a supreme form of review. The legislative process was clearly in the ascendancy for most of the fourteenth/twentieth century. The outlook today is more obscure.

An islamic tradition may also tolerate local, informal tradition, where it is com-

---

[135] A. Amor, 'La place de l'Islam dans les constitutions des Etats arabes. Modèle théorique et réalité juridique', in G. Conac and A. Amor, Islam et droits de l'homme (Paris: Economica, 1994) 13 at 13; Brohi, 'Die Rechtsideen' (1986), above, at 20.

[136] See David and Brierley, Major Legal Systems (1985) at 473 ff.; for the process up to 1976, Anderson, Law Reform in Muslim World (1976); for attempts to create 'compromise' legislation, see Coulson, History of Islamic Law (1964) at 153; and for the interdependence of state and islamic law, K. Bälz, 'Die "Islamisierung" des Rechts in Ägypen und Libyen: Islamische Rechtsetzung im Nationalstaat' RabelsZ 1998. 437.

[137] For the French process, in the language of Prof. Carbonnier, see above, Ch. 5, Positive law and positive science; and for the acute character of the problem in relation to hindu law, see below, Ch. 8, Hindu law in India (process of 'expropriation' of hindu law).

[138] See above, Substantive shari'a.

[139] On the limited notion of stare decisis in islamic law, see above, Qadi justice and mufti learning.

patible with islamic teaching. This is not an independent source of islamic law, but islamic tolerance of other sources of law, and has been described as being of fundamental importance in the territorial expansion of islamic law.[140] So what has been usually described as usage (urf) or custom (adat), that is, informal, local traditions,[141] have retained great importance in Indonesia, India and Africa.[142] While islamic law may not be changed by this process, it may become inoperative or desuet as a result of changes in informal tradition amongst even adherents to islam. Islamic law says a great deal about slavery, but does not require it, so as the practice of slavery disappeared the islamic law of slavery became an inoperative part of islamic tradition.

If you look back into the tradition itself, to its own working instruments, you will find ways of changing the result of your case from those of previous cases (not that the cases control in any way). Analogy can move in different directions;[143] the extent that ijma may still be alive (the door closed on it, but it is a source, and ijma is more than individual initiative), there is no formal statement of its requirements (consensus of whom, in what form, and so on);[144] the inherent casuistry of islamic thought has been said to enlarge the judge's margin of action;[145] different schools authorize such ambiguous concepts as juristic preference (istihsan) and the public interest (istislah).[146] There is also enormous flexibility in the formulation of islamic law in a non-binary fashion. Conduct is not divided into only two classes, permitted or prohibited. It falls into one of five classes: compulsory, rewarded, indifferent,

---

[140] M. Alliot, 'Über die Arten des "Rechts-Transfers"' in W. Fikentscher, H. Franke and O. Köhler (eds.). *Entstehung und Wandel rechtlicher Traditionen* (Freiburg/Munich: Verlag Karl Alber, 1980), 161 at 166.

[141] On the conflation of practice and tradition, to the prejudice of the normative content of the tradition, see above, Ch. 1, Tradition as Information: the Conceptual Bran-Tub and, in the context of chthonic law, Ch. 3, *Law and the cosmos.*

[142] See the discussion on the relations between islamic and other traditions, below, *The islamic diaspora*; and on the place of urf and adat in islamic thinking, E. Graf and A. Falaturi, 'Brauch/Sitte und Recht in der traditionellen islamischen Jurisprudenz' in May, *Islamischem Rechtsdenken* (1986) 29 at 31; K. Ephroz, 'Custom as a Source of Muslim Law—A Study of its Importance' in S. Gupta, *Personal Laws* (Delhi: Commercial Law Publications, 1983) at 31; Anderson, *Law Reform in Muslim World* (1976) at 11 (notably on reliance on commercial traditions even in violation of islamic prohibition of riba; prevalence of chthonic traditions in many islamic jurisdictions of Africa, such as Morocco, northern Nigeria); Milliot and Blanc, *Droit musulman* (1987) at 140 (on custom in north Africa).

[143] Noth, 'Die Scharīa' (1980) at 428.

[144] See, for various techniques of ijma, M. Shabbir and K. Ephroz, 'Does Muslim Law In India Need To Be Reconsidered' in Gupta, *Personal Laws* (1983), above, at 43 (can only look back and say ijma exists); Doi, *Shari'ah* (1984) at 67; Thompson and Reischauer, *Modernization* (1966), above, at 39; and on the restricting effect of al-Shafi's teaching on ijma, Coulson, *History of Islamic Law* (1964) at 80 (as infallible effect of existing ijma spread, use of individual reasoning or ijtihad slowly contracted).

[145] Johansen, 'Casuistry' (1995), above, at 154, 155 (legal concepts not of universal and uniform legal consequences, but vary according to geography, fields of law; analogy with quaestiones disputatae of civil law (the Bartolisti tradition, here in islam); graded transitions from the central core of one concept to that of another, allowing accommodation of high degree of social differentiation).

[146] See above, *Of schools and schism.*

disapproved and forbidden.[147] There is flexibility within the categories, further flexibility in the determination of their boundaries. And since that which is not prohibited is (more or less) permitted, then parties are free to adjust their conduct in a way which is tolerated. So husbands can grant their wives a power of divorce,[148] and more generally parties can set up transactions which might be seen as shams, evasions, fictions or just plain tricks (all of the expressions are used to translate the notion of hiyal) so as to remain formally outside the range of prohibited conduct. Riba is prohibited between you and me, but if you need a loan and I have money you can sell me your watch, and agree at the same time to buy it back at a later date, for a higher price (the double sale). You get the cash you need; I have the watch as security; and the watch is only security, which you can get back by paying the agreed-upon price.[149] You can get away with this in Hanafi and also in Shafi'i law; Maliki law, however, concerned with real intentions, repudiates tricks (though apparently not change of school to avoid the repudiation). As for Hanbali thinking, tricks or stratagems are not even countenanced. If you are really at a loss for something to argue, there is also a floating notion of the 'circumstances of revelation', which would limit texts to the circumstances prevailing at the time of revelation. There is, however, as you might expect, no agreement on its scope.[150]

## RE-OPENING THE DOOR OF ENDEAVOUR

Everybody in islam knows about the door of endeavour that has been closed, and it is a mighty metaphor, which has had enormous influence.[151] Of course, there never was a door, and there never was a closing (that anyone could see, or hear) but everyone can instantly seize what a closed door means. It is a silent but effective barrier, and you can never know what will be on the other side if you open it and go through. So the proponents of the closed door argue not only that God's will has been fulfilled in existing teaching, but that the re-opening of the door would raise fundamental questions about the future direction and even identity of islam.[152] Yet the controversy within islamic legal thought on this subject in the last century has

---

[147]   Doi, *Shari'ah* (1984) at 59, with consequent range of sanctions; Brohi, 'Die Rechtsideen' (1986), above, at 25; Cammack, 'Islamic Law in Indonesia's New Order' (1989) at 59; Khadduri, *Islamic Concept of Justice* (1984) at 143; Coulson, *History of Islamic Law* (1964) at 83 (this manner of extension of law far into that which is often seen as morality, leaving little beyond); Weiss, *Spirit of Islamic Law* (1998) at 18–22.

[148]   See above, *Substantive shari'a*.

[149]   See David and Brierley, *Major Legal Systems* (1985) at 469; Coulson, *History of Islamic Law*, (1964) at 140, 141; and on the controversy within islamic thinking over hiyal, Khadduri, *Islamic Concept of Justice* (1984) at 152, 153.

[150]   Arnaldez, 'La loi musulmane' (1993) at 86, and see below, *Jihad*, with respect to its application to this notion.

[151]   See above, *Islamic texts and islamic reason: the role of ijtihad*.

[152]   See Noth, 'Die Scharia' (1980) at 430 (who is to point the direction of the shari'a, without the force of taqlid?).

been described as 'violent'.[153] Some say the door should be re-opened,[154] at least for the least precise of the koranic injunctions;[155] others say it is already open,[156] or even never closed.[157] How can this happen, or how did it happen? A rationalist tradition has always been represented in islam; it is now bringing out both technical arguments as to how the process can occur and substantive arguments as to why it must occur. The re-opening can occur because there never was any formal process of closing; the door just swings in the wind, and can open as easily as it closed. Collective ijtihad, moreover, would be nothing other than ijma, a constantly valid source.[158] That islam can remain islam, with ijtihad, would be indicated by the renewal of islamic banking, and the entire notion of islamic economics developed in shi'ite islam.[159] The necessity for re-thinking of islam in modern circumstances (some even refer to 'modernization', though this appears to miss the mark) would be necessary and justified by the need to resist colonialization and non-islamic influence. So the internal arguments are closely related to the external arguments, and nobody today can say whether the shari'a, in the totality of its primary sources, is immutable. Given a doctrine of immutability, the argument (and it is more than a conversation) is going on.

## ISLAMS AND THE WORLD

As the talmudic revelation gave rise to a notion of jewish people, distinct from their chthonic ancestors, so the islamic revelation, and adherence to it, generated a community recognizable as islamic. It is a community because it recognizes a way to follow, the shari'a, and acts with sufficient commonality to be identifiable, given

[153] Coulson, *History of Islamic Law* (1964) at 203; and see, for the history of efforts to revive ijtihad, extending back to the 17th century, Brown, *Rethinking Tradition* (1996) at 22 ff., 43 ff. (on scripturalists, who would free interpretation of the Koran from the hadiths) and 109 (contemporary 'revivalists' who would preserve the sacred character of hadith while subjecting them to contemporary scrutiny).

[154] Brohi, 'Die Rechtsideen' (1986), above, 13 at 23; M. Arkoun, *Pour une critique de la raison islamique* (Paris: Maisonneuve & Larose, 1984), notably at 38; and for major authors taking this position in Egypt and India, Coulson, *History of Islamic Law* (1964) at 203; Shabbir and Ephroz, 'Muslim Law In India' (1983), above at 42, citing M. Iqbal; Hallaq, *Islamic Legal Theories* (1997), ch. 6 ('Crises of Modernity: Toward a New Theory of Law'), distinguishing between islamic religious utilitarians and islamic religious liberals.

[155] Doi, *Shari'ah* (1984) at 38, 39 (thus acceptable for notions of war, peace, jihad, booty, relations with non-muslims; inacceptable for detailed injunctions in field of crime).

[156] Arnaldez, 'La loi musulmane' (1993) at 89 (opened in 19th century).

[157] See W. Hallaq, 'Was the Gate of Ijtihad Closed?' (1984) 16 *Int. J. Middle East St.* 3, repr. in Edge, *Islamic Law and Legal Theory* (1996) at 287; and for a Bangladesh judicial decision refusing to admit closing of the door (and rejecting Privy Council decision having so affirmed), see *Rahman* v. *Begum* (1995) 15 BLD 34. I am grateful to Dr Werner Menski for this reference.

[158] Shabbir and Ephroz, 'Muslim Law in India' (1983), above, at 42, citing M. Iqbal.

[159] See above, *Substantive shari'a*.

comparison. The identity of an islamic community, and more generally of a concept which has been described as 'orientalism' has been the object of great recent controversy, largely due to the writings of Edward Said. Said has attacked the notion of a monolithic islam as being an invention of western thought, largely for purposes of establishing its own identity and superiority, given a dehumanized and static presentation of islamic life.[160] Before Said, however, western historians were pointing out the 'insidious fragmentation' of islamic identity and islamic territory, and the pull of geography and local life on a widely dispersed islamic people.[161] So the debate about whether there is an islam, or whether there are islams, or whether there is just a slightly diverse form of human life, largely depends on the information you choose to look at. If you look at the Koran, and accept a notion of binding taqlid (which would have much of the effect of western law, in terms of binding people to particular substantive provisions, here seen as perpetual), then there is an islam. If you look at the dynamic of islamic law, including the different schools, shi'ite law and the national and expatriate versions of the shari'a, you will tend to a notion of islams. If you lump all semitic people together, or all religious people together, islam won't count for much; it's just cause for (yet) another group of fundamentalists. So identities are not fixed, and to the extent they exist they are interdependent. Islamic identity, however, is particularly complex. It arrived late, had to create its own place in the world, and has relations with everybody else. Current revisionist arguments also raise major concerns about future identity. Yet it is difficult to quarrel with the general conclusion of Professor Hourani that by the end of the fourth/tenth century, there existed an 'elaborated system of ritual, doctrine and law clearly different from those of non-Muslims' yielding 'an identity . . . the community of believers (the umma)'.[162] So an identity emerges from differences; its existence depends on their perception.

## THE UMMA AND ITS PROTECTION

Since the Prophet urged the faithful to seek knowledge everywhere,[163] it is doubtful if early muslim jurists chose the path of deliberate ignorance of existing law, whether chthonic, roman, talmudic or other (now petrified). All were well known, and easy to find. So there has been an ongoing debate, with subversive undertones, about whether islamic law is *really* islamic or whether it is just a pastiche of everything

[160] E. Said, *Orientalism* (New York: Vintage, 1979).

[161] Braudel, *History of Civilizations*, (1993), above, at 95, 96, and 76, 77 ('Muslim thought is intimately linked with that of . . . volatile cabals . . . was both one and many, universal and regionally diverse'); Lewis, *Middle East* (1995), above, at 73 (great radical movements in islamic empire all movements within islam and not against it).

[162] Hourani, *History of Arab Peoples* (1991) at 47, 57. Individual islamic identity would flow from islamic identity of the father in the case of a mixed marriage between an islamic man and a non-islamic woman; the islamic woman cannot marry outside the religion; Weiss, *Spirit of Islamic Law* (1998) at 151.

[163] See above, Ijma and Change.

else.[164] There would be an example even here, even in religious law, of Alan Watson's thesis that borrowing of law is the primary instrument of law's development.[165] This argument closely parallels that concerning the relation between revelation and ongoing tradition, and their relative primacy, and some of the same protagonists are involved. Thus, for some, ongoing tradition would be the real source of islamic law, regardless of revelation, and revelation could not have provided the corpus of the law, which had to come from elsewhere, through a process of islamization. The latter would represent the same kind of constructive borrowing, the same kind of 'decanting' that is so well known in western law.[166] So the origins of islamic law would be found not in the Koran and the Sunna, but in the 'raw material of the existing customary [chthonic] law and administrative practice'.[167] Others would extend the list of contributors to roman, byzantine, persian, and talmudic law, the latter contention being supported by the existence of the isra'iliyat, hadith in which the talmudic influences are discernible.[168] Others admit the contact but deny the influence.[169] Influence was certainly possible, and even direct incorporation, since the underlying character of chthonic, talmudic, later

[164] An echo of this debate occurs with respect to the islamic religion as a whole, some pointing out overlap of scripture with judaism and christianity, others calling for their abrogation by the Koran. The debate has important consequences for the status of non-islamic people in islamic law. See below, *Jihad*.

[165] A. Watson, *Legal Transplants: An Approach to Comparative Law*, 2nd edn. (Athens, Ga.: Univ. of Georgia Press, 1993).

[166] See above, *Subtle change* and Ch. 5, *Positive law and positive science*. The process would have been greatly facilitated in the islamic world, as in Europe, by insistence on conversion to local language. Greek was the language of early Arab administration, but was replaced by Arabic in 100/700 when Greek officials were told that their 'present employment had been withdrawn by God', ending a long linguistic modus vivendi. Braudel, *History of Civilizations*, (1993), above, at 72.

[167] Anderson, *Law Reform in Muslim World* (1976) at 8; Schacht, *Origins of Muhammadan Jurisprudence* (1950); Calder, *Studies Early Muslim Jurisprudence* (1993); Coulson, *History of Islamic Law* (1964) at 39; B. Tibi, 'The European Tradition of Human Rights and the Culture of Islam' in An-Na'im and Deng, *Human Rights in Africa* (1990), above, 104 at 126.

[168] See generally Arnaldez, 'La loi musulmane' (1993) at 83; Hallaq, *Islamic Legal Theories* (1997) at 113; Pearl and Menski, *Muslim Family Law* (1998) at 7, 8, 493 (on debate on whether waqf has pre-islamic roots, with refs.). On possible roman influence, compare J. Schacht, 'Foreign Elements in Ancient Islamic Law' (1950) 32 J. Comp. Law & Int. Law 9, and S. Fitzgerald, 'The Alleged Debt of Islamic to Roman Law' (1951) 67 LQR 81, both reproduced in Edge, *Islamic Law and Legal Theory* (1996) at 3, 13; and P. Crone, *Roman, provincial and Islamic Law* (Cambridge: Cambridge Univ. Press, 1987) (also on Greek, other oriental influence, though, at 2, islamic tradition 'armed to the teeth against imputations of foreign influence'). For possible talmudic influence, see J. Wegner, 'Islamic and Talmudic Jurisprudence: The Four Roots of Islamic Law and their Talmudic Counterparts' (1982) 26 Am. J. Legal Hist. 25; A. Geiger, *Judaism and Islam* (New York: KTAV Publishing, 1970) notably at 64–70 (though 'few borrowings' of moral and legal rules); on the isra'iliyyat, Juynboll, *Authenticity of Tradition Literature* (1969), above, at 14; Stowasser, *Women* (1994) at 22, 23 (influence of isra'iliyyat declining in importance with rise of islamic legal science, though continuing to be influential with respect to Koranic women figures); and on the hadith, 'Narrate from the Israelites and there is no harm', Doi, *Shari'ah* (1984) at 28, 29.

[169] Brohi, 'Die Rechtsideen' (1986), above, at 18, giving examples of parallel texts between Old Testament and Koran, with comment by Falaturi, at 27 on controversial character of the subject; and see Calder, *Studies Early Muslim Jurisprudence* (1993), at 209–214, notably at 213 ('media were not funnels, permitting the integral passage of a particular item from insular culture to insular culture . . . no question of an integral system being transferred, of books or texts of codes being specifically translated for this purpose').

roman and islamic law is everywhere the same. Law is substantive, directly available to parties and adjudicators, administered in essentially open adjudicative or court structures. The procedural and judicial restrictions of early roman law, or the common law, are absent. So there is clear evidence, according to many people, that a substantial part of the substance of islamic law is the same as other laws.

What conclusion should islamic and other people draw from this? Well, it may just be the old debate about history again, and much of the islamic reaction has been simply to deny the history.[170] Yet even if the history is true, and it is at least plausible, there doesn't seem to be much of a problem for the essentials of islamic law. The question thus wouldn't be one of originality (a western concept), but of revelation. Muhammad would never have claimed to have abolished the old Arabian law, only to have moved it along in the appropriate direction.[171] So much of the old law could stay, but there were significant reforms of the status of women.[172] And that which stayed, or was even brought in from elsewhere, wasn't copied but revealed, as true law. Like the old, pre-revelation jewish law, it acquired a new status through revelation, and existed thereafter not in its old garb, but as the law of God. Revelation doesn't only trump tradition; it would also trump the process of constructive borrowing. Lawyers aren't constructively borrowing; God is revealing.[173] So there is law common to the islamic tradition and other traditions (and this is no small conclusion). In islamic law it would be, however, more clearly law.

An islamic community is therefore distinguishable by its adherence to islamic teaching, which itself is distinguishable. Since the teaching contains much (or some) of what is taught outside it, such that the boundaries of the teaching are difficult to trace precisely, it might follow that the boundaries of the islamic community are difficult to trace precisely. To the extent there are 'statistical' muslims,[174] (something like non-practising christians, and God knows there are many of them), this is true, but islam has been more concerned with the boundaries of, and protection of, its community than have other faiths and other laws. It is not entirely clear why this is so, and the subject is highly controversial today, but if you are muslim

---

[170] Falatur, comment on Brohi, 'Die Rechtsideen' (1986), above, at 27; David and Brierley, *Major Legal Systems* (1985) at 463.

[171] Guillaume, *Traditions of Islam* (1924), above, at 11 (Prophet 'careful to depart as little as possible from the path of his forefathers', appears even as restorer of ancient faith); Schacht, *Introduction to Islamic Law* (1964) at 11 (aim 'not to create a new system of law'); Anderson, *Law Reform in Muslim World* (1976) at 10, contrasting accommodating sunni view with more radical shi'ite position on creation of distinct islamic texts.

[172] Schacht, *Introduction to Islamic Law* (1964) at 13; Pearl and Menski, *Muslim Family Law* (1998) at 4, 5 (succession opened to women, dower payable to wife, talaq controlled by waiting period, polygamy limited to 4 wives, with obligation of equal treatment); Lapidus, *History Islamic Societies* (1988), above, at 30 (Koran introducing 'new freedom and dignity to individual family members'); Fyzee, *Outlines* (1974) at 6 (noting view of Sir James Colville that position of islamic wife superior to that of English wife until early 20th century); above, *Substantive shari'a*.

[173] E. Klingsmüller, 'Entstehung und Wandel rechtlicher Traditionen im islamischen Recht' in Fikentscher, (1980), above, 375 at 376 on older law being 'religiös sanktioniert'.

[174] Cammack, 'Islamic Law in Indonesia's New Order' (1989) at 54, referring to Indonesian population.

you must pay some attention to the consequences of disloyalty, either in the form of heresy or apostasy (from the Greek apostasis, to stand off or desert).

Revelation bears a larger burden in islamic thought than it does in either judaism or christianity. There is precious little law in the christian world which has been revealed, and while all the Talmud is revelation there's a lot of debate about what it says. Islamic law, however, is all revelation and, though it is casuistic, it speaks with a declarative or imperative voice, and not argumentative ones. So if you do anything wrong you are, more clearly than elsewhere, violating God's instructions.[175] And if you challenge the system it's even worse. So though both judaism and christianity used heresy, and killed for it, they both now live without it (though they may kill for treason, its secular equivalent, and punish sedition). Islam has not reached this stage, and may never. It's different, and knows why it's different, in a way that those who do not follow the way may not fully appreciate. Still, the doctrine of heresy developed out of the original conflict between sunnis, shi'ites and a third dissenting sect, the kharijites, and is not profoundly anchored in the Koran. As toleration (ikhtilaf) grew between the schools and sects, the killing for heresy declined, and it could decline again, overtaken by bridging forms of thought. In the same way the 'former burning question' as to who was to be considered an unbeliever (kafir) gave way to a tolerant solution: disbelief would attract sanction only if an essential element of islam was denied.[176] Yet islamic concepts of heresy are useful to civic authority in islamic countries, and this may prolong its life (the government of Sudan killed a prominent exponent of ijtihad for heresy in the 1980s; a leading theoretician of islamic economics was killed in Iraq around the same time). Sanctioning heresy is also closely linked to the ongoing human rights debate, with and within islams.[177]

Apostasy is closely linked to heresy, since by leaving the faith you challenge it and may provide a model for others. Of the major, complex legal traditions, islam is the only one with an operative concept of apostasy, which appears curious in that it is also the religious and legal tradition which is attracting the most new members. Neverthless, exit is out, and the Koran is here, again, terribly precise. 'If they [the hypocrites] turn back (to enmity) then take them and kill them wherever ye find them'.[178] The debate goes on, however, since the concept may have been entailed by the emergency conditions of Muhammad's struggle (the doctrine of the circum-

---

[175] Coulson, *History of Islamic Law* (1964) at 80 ('Once formed the ijma was infallible; to contradict it was heresy, and the possibility of its repeal by a similar ijma of a later generation, though admitted in theory, was thus highly unlikely in practice'); Brohi, 'Die Rechtsideen' (1986), above, 13 at 23; D. Arzt, 'The Treatment of Religious Dissidents under Classical and Contemporary Islamic Law' in J. Witte Jr. and J. van der Vyver, *Religious Human Rights in Global Perspective: Religious Perspectives* (The Hague/Boston/London: Martinus Nijhoff, 1996) at 387; Doi, *Shari'ah* (1984) at 39 (if ruler fails to apply Koran, is 'a rebel', since 'violates a human right or overlooks a principle of justice and equality') (on islamic notions of human rights, see below, *Contrapuntal exchange, with islams*).

[176] Schacht, *Introduction to Islamic Law* (1964) at 131.

[177] See below, *Contrapuntal exchange, with islams*.

[178] 4: 89.

stances of revelation)[179] and there is another part of the Koran which says 'No compulsion is there in religion',[180] usually taken to refer to involuntary conversion to islam, but recently explored for its application to apostasy.[181] There is also, again, the human rights argument, and in its light the sanction for apostasy has been referred to, within islamic debate, as a 'problem'.[182] The sanction, moreover, would only be applied in cases of formal conversion to another religion. No religion and no religious law can effectively police, in this life, intensity of belief. Islam may have learned this from the western inquisition. Martyrs tend to win, over time.

## CONTRAPUNTAL EXCHANGE, WITH ISLAMS

As elsewhere, western colonialism, and local opposition to it, led to adoption of the western concept of the state in islamic territories. So the political shape of islamic thought (though not the religious or the legal) is in recognizable western form, at least in general outline. Within the islamic world there is therefore a constant exchange between islamic ideas and ideas which are linked to the western concept of the state. There are islamic intellectuals and less islamic intellectuals. And in discussion with the non-islamic world, particularly the west, there is the same contrapuntal exchange, to which is now added the contribution of islamic people in western states. Relations between the traditions have been described as 'porous',[183] in spite of the passion which has often characterized them, and this was so when islamic civilization was at its height, passing on ideas to the west,[184] and remained so when the flow of ideas shifted in the other direction.[185] From the western perspective the debate centres on constitutionalism, human rights and equality. From the islamic perspective it is one of recognition of God's word, international social justice and community. There may never be a winner.

[179] D. Little, 'The Western Tradition,' in D. Little, J. Kelsey and A. Sachedina, *Human Rights and the Conflicts of Culture: Western and Islamic Perspectives on Religious Liberty* (Columbia: Univ. of South Carolina Press, 1988) at 30, and on the larger doctrine, Arnaldez, 'La loi musulmane' (1993) at 86. The defection of the 'hypocrites' has been said to have been the chief cause of the loss of muslim life in the battle of Uhud, shortly after the Prophet's arrival in Medina.

[180] 2: 256.

[181] A. Sachedina, 'Freedom of Conscience and Religion in the Qur'an' in Little, Kelsey and Sachedina, *Human Rights and Conficts of Culture* (1988), above, 53, notably at 66, 67 and 86 ('much concurrence regarding the underlying commitment of Islam and the West in respect to religious liberty').

[182] Amin, *Islamic Law* (1989) at 57.

[183] Horowitz, 'Qur'an and Common Law' (1994) at 244.

[184] For islamic contributions to western law see below, Ch. 7, *Of judges and judging* and *The practice of comparison*; for islamic contributions to western science, above, *Islamic texts and islamic reason: the role of ijtihad*; and for the drinking of the 'black liquid' of coffee (qahwa), Lewis, *Middle East* (1995), above, at 162, 163.

[185] On islamic fundamentalist views of science as both western and evil, refusing to recognize the major contribution of islamic science to western thought, see A. Mayer, 'The Dilemmas of Islamic Identity' in L. Rouner, *Human Rights and the World's Religions* (Notre Dame: Univ. of Notre Dame Press, 1988) 94 at 104. Here the contemporary western self masks the distant islamic one, from an islamic perspective. In the same way, the contemporary western view of islamic law, as religious law, tends to mask the role of religion in the creation of western law.

Public law has become a large part of western legal traditions, though it has been described as a 'pious hope' in islamic law by western observers.[186] Perhaps it is best seen as a pious certainty, since given islamic belief an unjust ruler will eventually be sanctioned, though not on this earth. The idea of an islamic state is therefore a challenging one for islamic thinkers. It is, however, part of the renewal of islamic law, led most evidently, though not exclusively, by shi'ite scholars.[187] There is as yet no model of the islamic state, however, and the most successful of western institutions is that of the 'least dangerous' branch, secular courts.[188] These have generally been structured to include even courts of appeal, and in many places have taken over the work of the qadi. The notion of a secular court is not totally alien to islamic thought, however, and often existed in the domain of the urf (informal tradition, outside islam) or in the complaints jurisidiction (mazalim) of the sovereign.[189]

Concern with the islamic state has been said to contribute to 'an islamic tradition of human rights'.[190] Some have gone further, to argue that the existence of the state necessarily implies the existence of human rights, as the two have often developed in parallel fashion in the west.[191] As western state models have not been replicated in islamic countries, however, western models of human rights have not been directly received, though there has been a noteworthy effort to reformulate islamic principle in the language of human rights, and to justify variance. Thus there are a number of islamic declarations of human rights (never formally incorporated into state laws)[192] and a vast literature, islamic and western, on reconciliation of human rights

---

[186] David and Brierley, *Major Legal Systems* (1985) at 474; and on the notion of 'de facto' rulers, Coulson, *History of Islamic Law* (1964) at 82, 83.

[187] See generally Digard, 'Shi-isme et Etat en Iran' (1982), above, at 64 (2 traditions within shi'ism, one opposed to, one supporting secular power, thus monarchists and anti-monarchists, constitutionalists and revolutionaries, democrats and Khomeyniists); Mallat, *Renewal of Islamic Law* (1993) notably Pt. One 'Islamic law and the constitution'; Hourani, *History of Arab Peoples* (1991) at 162 ; Amor, 'La place de l'Islam (1994), above, at 13; M. Hermassi, 'De la théorie de l'"Etat en Islam' in Conac and Amor, *Islam et droits de l'homme* (1994), above, at 28; Walker, *Caliphate* (1966), above, notably at 47 ('unrestricted power in the hands of the ruler', possible inheritance from persian monarchy); Tibi, 'European Tradition of Human Rights and Culture of Islam' (1990), above; and on the notion of national identity competing with that of muslim identity, Malek, *Tradition et révolution* (1993) at 49, 50 (nation most rational of modes of being for a people).

[188] The phrase is that of Alexander Hamilton, in the 78th FEDERALIST, 'The Judges as Guardians of the Constitution'. See A. Bickel, *The Least Dangerous Branch: The Supreme Court at the Bar of Politics* (New York: Bobbs-Merrill, 1962), at p. viii.

[189] Falaturi and May, 'Gerichtsverfahren' (1986), above, at 61; Pearl and Menski, *Muslim Family Law* (1998) at 17.

[190] Tibi, 'European Tradition of Human Rights and Culture of Islam' (1990), above, at 112.

[191] A. Mayer, *Islam and Human Rights: Tradition and Politics*, 2nd edn. (Boulder, Colo./San Francisco and London: Westview Press and Pinter Publishers, 1995) at 10. The argument cannot be understood in formal terms, since English law, e.g., has not been sympathetic to the concept of rights; see below, Ch. 7, *Right reason*. Within a common law tradition there are therefore arguments as to how best one can bring about respect for human values, a debate which in general terms is similar to the one carried on between western human rights advocates and islamic lawyers.

[192] On islamic human rights instruments, see Aldeeb Abu-Salieh, *Musulmans face aux droits de l'homme* (1994).

with islamic teaching.[193] What is common to both sides of the debate is the primary place to be given to respect for the human person.[194] The difference is in whether a formal concept of rights is the most effective instrument for doing so. Islamic lawyers challenge the effectiveness of rights doctrine, pointing out widespread and flagrant violations in countries which accept the existence of rights,[195] regionalization and nationalization of what are said to be universal norms,[196] and the need for 'social arrangements that are in the common interests'.[197] Western lawyers insist on individual liberty and individual equality, the need for effective court sanctions, and the need for proportionate and non-arbitrary forms of punishment. There are no bad arguments in the lot. So human rights are partially taken over by islamic declarations, but then made subject to the shari'a. They emerge as group rights, a notion itself developed in western jurisdictions,[198] socialist legal doctrine,[199] and chthonic and environmentalist notions of inter-generational rights.[200] Islam in this context appears as a particular variant of a larger, pan-traditional way of thinking.

The human rights debate exists in more acute form with respect to the status of women, since the Koran provides that 'Men are in charge of women, because Allah hath made the one of them to excel the other, and because they spend of their

---

[193] See S. Aldeeb Abu-Sahlieh, 'Muslims and Human Rights: Challenges and Perspectives' in W. Schmale (ed.), *Human Rights and Cultural Diversity* (Goldbach: Keip Publishing, 1993), at 239; Aldeeb Abu-Salieh, *Musulmans face aux droits de l'homme* (1994); Amin, *Islamic Law* (1989); A. A. An-Na'im, 'Human Rights in the Muslim World: Socio-Political Conditions and Scriptural Imperatives' (1990) 3 Harv. Hum. R. J. 13 (notably on need for cross-cultural approach and working with islamic sources, rather than imposition of western concept); Conac and Amor, *Islam et droits de l'homme* (1994), above, (notably at 5 on search for 'points de convergence et . . . zones de rupture' in order to 'dépasser la polémique'); Haider (ed.), *Islamic Concept of Human Rights* (1978), above; Khan, *Islam and Human Rights*, (1989), above; Little, Kelsey and Sachedina, *Human Rights and Conflicts of Culture* (1988), above; Rouner, *Human Rights and World's Religions* (1988), above, (Pt. Two; Islam, with articles by M. Farhang, N. Keddie & A. Mayer).

[194] On the common doctrinal base for this idea see above, *The individual in the shari'a*.

[195] See R. Hassan, 'Rights of Women Within Islamic Communities' in Witte, and van der Vyver, *Religious Human Rights in Global Perspective* (1996), above, 361 at 361–3, with refs. The best example, uncited, would be a number of latin American countries, where classic rights doctrine is standard fare in law schools. The islamic argument also echoes recent criticism by advocates of the talmudic tradition in the USA. See above, Ch. 4, *The individual in the Talmud*.

[196] See Aldeeb Abu-Salieh, *Musulmans face aux droits de l'homme* (1994) at 23 (stating position of islamic jurists).

[197] Doi, *Shari'ah* (1984) at 8.

[198] See, e.g., W. Kymlicka, *Multicultural Citizenship: a Liberal Theory of Minority Rights* (Oxford: Clarendon Press, 1995, notably ch. 3 ('Individual Rights and Collective Rights'), with extensive bibliography.

[199] See, e.g., art. 5 of the the Fundamentals of Civil Legislation of the former Soviet Union: 'Civil rights shall be protected by law, except as they are exercised in contradiction to their purpose in socialist society in the period of building communism. In exercising their rights and performing their duties, citizens and organisations must observe the laws and respect the rules of socialist community life and the ethical principles of the society building communism', in V. Grebenikov (ed.), *Rights of Soviet Citizens: Collected Normative Acts* (Moscow: Progress Publishers, 1987) at 34, 35.

[200] On the parallels, see B. Weiss, 'Our Rights and Obligations to Future Generations for the Environment' (1990) 84 Am. J. Int. Law 198, at 205, and on inter-generational rights and obligations, see above, Ch. 3, *Law and the cosmos* and Change and the Natural World.

property (for the support of women)'.[201] Yet being 'in charge' is not itself a legal code, so improvement in the status of women is part of the larger debate on the immutability of ijma (with its more precise rules) and the ongoing effect of the hadith 'My people can never agree to error'. Ongoing improvement of the status of women is said to be inherent in the Koran, since this was its effect in relation to pre-islamic Arabian law.[202] There were also differences in treatment from school to school,[203] such that islamic law reform drawing on the ijma of the schools could have as its 'primary purpose ... the amelioration of the position of women'.[204] Reform is also possible within existing texts, as by allowing women on marriage to contract for wider options. So within islam there is much to say about the equality of the sexes, in the same way that talmudic law is here being re-appraised.[205]

These debates have had islamic thinkers responding to western ideas. Western ideas have also had to respond to islamic ideas, though this has happened more in informal debate in the so-called 'developing countries' than in western literature. Islamic ideas of social justice have here had profound impact. Amongst impoverished people, faced with mobile capital always on the alert for lower wages in a 'global economy' (global for whom?), the idea of communal aid and assistance is enormously powerful.[206] There are no windows of opportunity in such lives, only

[201] 4: 34; and for current exegesis of the text see B. Stowasser, 'Gender Issues and Contemporary Quran Interpretation' in Y. Haddad and J. Esposito, *Islam, Gender, and Social Change* (New York/Oxford: Oxford Univ. Press, 1998) at 30.

[202] See above, *Substantive shari'a*; Mayer, 'Dilemmas of Islamic Identity' (1988), above, at 110; Pearl and Menski, *Muslim Family Law* (1998) at 4; Falaturi and May, 'Gerichtsverfahren' (1986), above, at 64 (on differing opinions on women as qadi, de facto refusal); Hassan, 'Rights of Women' (1996), above, at 361 (Koran interpreted in terms of equality of men and women, each protector of other). More generally, see J. O'Connor, 'Rereading, reconceiving and reconstructing traditions: feminist research in religion' (1989) 17 *Women's St.* 101 at 117; N. R. Keddie, 'The Rights of Women in Contemporary Islam' in Rouner, *Human Rights and World's Religions* (1988), above, at 76 (notably at 92 with respect to 'more profound study than before of the Qur'an and of Islamic laws and traditions so as to find better Islamic bases for an egalitarian position'); Nasir, *Status of Women* (1994) at 26; S. Iqbal, *Woman and Islamic Law* (Delhi: Al-Asr Publications, 1988); Esposito, *Women in Muslim Family Law* (1982); Stowasser, *Women* (1994) (notably Pt One for Koranic attitudes to women in sacred history prior to Muhammmad: women of Noah, Lot, Abraham; women in lives of Moses; Bilqis, Queen of Sheeba; Mary); M. Afkhami, *Faith and Freedom: Women's Human Rights in the Muslim World* (Syracuse: Syracuse Univ. Press, 1995), notably the essays in Pt One ('Women, Islam and Patriarchy'); Haddad and Esposito, *Islam, Gender and Social Change* (1998), above; N. Othman, 'Grounding Human Rights Arguments in Non-Western Culture: *Shari'a* and the Citizenship Rights of Women in a Modern Islamic State' in J. Bauer and D. A. Bell, *The East Asian Challenge for Human Rights* (Cambridge: Cambridge Univ. Press, 1999) 169, notably at 177 ff. for debate in Malaysia: and for amelioration to the status of women in Arab countries down to 1990, see R. A. Beck-Peccoz, *La modernizzazione del diritto di famiglia nei paesi arabi* (Milan: Giuffrè, 1990) at 84–152 ('Le riforme').

[203] Pearl and Menski, *Muslim Family Law* (1998) at 8 (Kufa/Maliki qadis more tolerant than Medina/Hanafi ones).

[204] Coulson, *History of Islamic Law* (1964) at 190.

[205] Above, Ch. 4, *The individual in the Talmud*.

[206] See J. Goytisolo, 'Out of Stagnation: Parallels between old Spain and Islam today', *TLS*, 3 Feb. 1995, at 3 ('Islam confers on those excluded from the benefit of the new ecumenical dogma of the West (ultraliberalism, monetarism, untrammelled trade, the planet as Global Shopping Centre) a consciousness to identify with ... [an] Islamist system ... more tolerable than the oppressive regimes by which they are now governed').

need. The Koran would free people to compete, but the type of competition is also set out in the Koran: 'So vie one with another in good works.'[207] The general concept of islamic social justice prevails, moreover, over state interests, and this manifests itself particularly with respect to refugees. 'Those who entered the city and the faith before them love those who flee unto them for refuge, and find in their breasts no need for that which hath been given them, but prefer (the fugitives) above themselves though poverty become their lot.'[208] To some 15 million refugees in the world, this has more attraction than applying sanctions to airlines for the flying of undocumented aliens. It is also attractive to liberal western migration theorists[209] and to western refugee advocates, so there is again some meeting of islamic and western minds. There has also been recognition in the west of the wisdom of islamic equity financing for international development—partnership rather than debt.[210]

Islamic tradition, however, has not exchanged ideas only with the west. Much of the inspiration for shi'ite re-thinking of the shari'a's regulation of economic activity was to meet the 'communist appeal to redress the "social balance"'.[211] Islamic thinking could not be outflanked on the left while defending its different path against the right. There has also been (peaceful) exchange with talmudic law,[212] which is appropriate given a common allegiance. There is information of great value in each tradition on the recuperative ability of revelation and the bridging of institutionalized difference.

## THE ISLAMIC DIASPORA

Islamic populations are now spread widely throughout the world, both as a result of earlier expansion of islamic civilization and as a result of contemporary patterns of migration and conversion. The exchange between islamic law and other laws thus often takes place beneath a constitutional umbrella of a host state, while the identification of the umma becomes less precise, as host state laws displace, in variable measure, application of the shari'a. This is the case even in islamic lands, such as Turkey, where non-islamic law may have displaced in large measure the shari'a. It

---

[207]  5: 48.

[208]  59: 9; and see Khan, *Islam and Human Rights*, (1989), above, at 83 ('Islam does not contemplate any restriction on freedom of movement and residence, whether within a State or beyonds its borders').

[209]  See, e.g., J. Carens, 'Aliens and Citizens: The Case for Open Borders' (1987) 49 *Rev. of Politics* 251, reprinted in W. Kymlicka (ed.), *The Rights of Minority Cultures* (Oxford: Oxford Univ. Press, 1995) at 331.

[210]  See above, *Substantive shari'a*. Again, the philosophy of islam has met with approval by *The Economist* magazine. See 6 Aug. 1994, at 17, 18 (possibility of more relaxed 21st century between the 2 'cousins' if westerners 'reopen their minds' to sense of 'belonging together', such that west 'may have a better chance of solving its own problems').

[211]  Mallat, *Renewal of Islamic Law* (1993) at 9, 11.

[212]  See Y. Meron, 'La rencontre contemporaine entre le droit juif et le droit musulman' Rev. int. dr. comp. 1984. 59.

has been said that 'it is difficult to have an over-all picture of the laws of Muslim countries',[213] and this is the case because no single circumstance dictates the importance of the shari'a in a given state. A territory may or may not have once been under islamic authority; its population may contain a majority or a minority of muslim people (of varying historical prerogatives and political significance); the influence of chthonic or western traditions may be more or less important, and this may depend in part on highly variable colonial experiences. There is also a current process of formal revival, as in Sudan and Pakistan. However, in states in which the shari'a is not the law of the land (as it is in Saudi Arabia, Iran, Sudan, Pakistan), two broad models are evident.

In the first model, islamic law is guaranteed a formal status as the law of islamic people (though often limited to certain matters). In India, which was under islamic rule for centuries prior to English colonization, islamic law thus remains the personal law applicable to the muslim minority, in matters of family law and succession. Its place was assured by legislation in 1937, which at the same time stopped the growing ascendancy of local custom over shari'a, host state legislation here reinforcing the (remaining) role of islamic law.[214] Elsewhere, as in Africa, an islamic personal law may dominate in a given region, such as northern Nigeria.[215] Here islamic law is often conflated with 'native law', and both chthonic and islamic traditions distance themselves from western sources of law.[216] The same coexistence of multiple traditions is evident in south-east Asia, where islamic law of

[213] David and Brierley, *Major legal Systems* (1985) at 479.

[214] See Gupta, *Personal Laws* (1983), above; Pearl and Menski, *Muslim Family Law* (1998) at 33, 36–8; Fyzee, *Outlines* (1974) at 58, 65 (noting 'amphibious communities' between islamic and hindu law). Under the Mughal emperors of India, islamic law of the Hanafi school was the law of the land (hindu law being reduced to exceptional and personal application). The British did not recognize the ongoing primacy of islamic law, and reduced it to the status of a personal law, while introducing European notions of legal sources and jurisdiction (in 1853) of British courts. See Liebesny, 'English Common Law and Islamic Law' (1985–6), above, at 20. The muslims began their expansion into Pakistan and India as early as the 8th century; by the late 17th century Mughal control extended throughout both countries. 'Muslim adventurism was at first of the smash-and-grab variety; systematic conquest was not attempted until late in the twelfth century: the first enduring Muslim state, the Sultanate of Delhi, was not founded until 1206'. F. Fernández-Armesto, *Millennium* (London/New York/Toronto/Sydney/Auckland: Bantam, 1995) at 105.

[215] Anderson, *Law Reform in Muslim World* (1976) at 6.

[216] See ibid., notably at p. xi, 2, 3 (example of wills being drawn according to 'Muhammadan customary law'); N. Rouland, *Anthropologie juridique* (Paris: Presses universitaires de France, 1988) at 347, 348 (on creation of 'droit coutumier islamisé,' facilitated by links of Maliki school with chthonic, pre-islamic Arabian and Bedouin law); R. Sacco, M. Gaudagni, R. Aluffi Beck-Peccoz and L. Castellani, *Il diritto africano* (Turin: UTET, 1995) at 106, 112 (relation between chthonic and islamic law key to legal reality in Africa); and for a similar phenomenon in south-east Asia, see M. Hooker, *A Concise Legal History of South-East Asia* (Oxford: Clarendon Press, 1978) at 112, 113 (commingling of islamic law and adat law); Z. bin Zakaria, 'The Legal System of Malaysia' in ASEAN Law Association, *ASEAN Legal Systems* (Singapore/Malaysia/Hong Kong: Butterworths, 1995) 77 at 84 (muslim law of marriage and divorce adopted in different types of adat law in Malaysia); Ruthven, *Islam in World* (1984), above, at 265 (expansion of islam due in large measure to assimilation of many local deities to Allah).

both majority and minority islamic populations co-exists with local chthonic tradi-tions, notably adat law in Malaysia and Indonesia, and western law.[217]

The second model is that of most western states, which are marked by exclusivity of state sources of law, and hence deny in principle the existence of personal laws, whether chthonic, islamic or other. Western states vary amongst themselves, how-ever, and there are important differences with respect to any principle of separation of church and state, and important differences with respect to the primacy of purely legislative sources of state law. So countries with no formal separation of church and state, and no principle of legislation as an exclusive source of law, may come to recognize non-state law in some measure.[218] And even in countries such as France, where the separation of church and state is of the highest constitutional order, and where the role of legislation is of (theoretically) exclusive importance, constitutional law may come to protect in some measure islamic practices (and by inference islamic law, since all islamic practices are rooted in islamic law).[219] In all western states, moreover, religious tribunals may function in a private manner for their adherents, and there are indications that shari'a adjudicators are increasingly active in settlement of the disputes of muslim people in these states.[220] Islamic law may therefore play an important role in the lives of islamic people living in the west, whether or not it is recognized by the state.[221] The role of islamic minorities in the west is of theoretical interest not only to western lawyers; there are major questions on the islamic side as to the extent to which islamic law can authorize adherence by

[217] See Hooker, *Islamic Law in South-east Asia* (1984); M. B. Hooker, 'The Law Texts of Muslim South-East Asia' in M. B. Hooker (ed.), *Laws of South-East Asia*, vol. I, *The Pre-Modern Texts* (Singapore: Butterworths, 1986) at 347; Horowitz, 'Qur'an and Common Law' (1994).

[218] As has occurred with respect to chthonic land claims in Australia and Canada, and in some measure with respect to chthonic family law; see above, Ch. 3, *On ways of life*. There is greater resistance, however, to recognition of religious law. For ongoing, and representative, refusal to recognize islamic divorce of persons domiciled in England, see L. Collins (gen. ed.), *Dicey and Morris on the Conflict of Laws* (London: Sweet and Maxwell, 1993), vol. II at 726.

[219] See C. E., 27 Nov. 1989, Gaz. Pal., 8–9 Dec. 1989 at 21; C. E., 27 Nov. 1996, J. C. P. II. 22808 (prefects may prohit wearing of religious apparel, notably hijab, though only in cases of risk to public order).

[220] For shari'a dispute resolution in the UK see Pearl and Menski, *Muslim Family Law* (1998) at 77–80; and for creation of a shari'a council in Montreal (said to be a 'North-American first'), see *The Gazette*, 20 Feb. 1994 at A-3.

[221] See generally S. Poulter, *English Law and Ethnic Minority Customs* (London: Butterworths, 1986), and review by W. Menski (1988) 37 Int. & Comp. Law Q. 218 suggesting 'continuation of various forms of ethnic customary divorce in the UK, about which we know, so far, precious little'; Pearl and Menski, *Muslim Family Law* (1998), ch. 3 ('Muslim Law in Britain', arguing for an 'English shari'a', 'angrezi shariat'); for the muslim debate in the UK on whether to press for formal recognition of islamic law, see D. Pearl, 'Islamic Family Law and Anglo-American Public Policy' (1985–6) 34 Clevel. St. L. Rev. 113 at 126; and more generally, S. Aldeeb Abu-Salieh, 'L'impact des droits musulmans sur un droit "laic". Le cas de la Suisse', Prax. juri. rel. 1991. 18; Aldeeb Abu-Salieh, *Musulmans face aux droits de l'homme* (1994) at 392–401; S. Aldeeb Abu-Salieh, 'Conflits entre droit religieux et droit étatique chez les musulmans dans les pays musulmans et en Europe', Rev. int. dr. comp. 1997. 813; J. Syrtash, *Religion and Culture in Canadian Family Law* (Toronto: Butterworths, 1992). For islamic recognition of western personal laws in islamic jurisdictions, see below, *Jihad*.

muslim people to non-islamic law.[222] That they do adhere to local state law, while retaining an islamic identity, says a great deal about the contemporary status of jihad in islamic law.

## JIHAD

Islam colonized much of the world with the same instruments the west was later to use: religious zeal, commercial vigour and military force.[223] The notion of jihad is often said to be behind all of this—but the word does not mean war, only effort or striving, so there is a (traditional) doctrinal ambiguity in islamic thought about what the notion of jihad might justify. In the same way the west (even using the word 'war') has argued about holy wars, then just wars, then trade wars. It is clear enough that the Koran, as later revelation, preaches conversion. 'And there may spring from you a nation which invites to goodness' is the most frequently cited text,[224] yet it is accompanied by the equally famous 'There is no compulsion in religion'.[225] So it has been said that the interpretation of jihad as religious war 'is wholly unauthorized by the Qur'an and can only be extracted therefrom by quoting isolated portions of different verses'.[226] Still, picking and choosing in the information base of a tradition is common practice, and this is precisely what the jurists of islam were generally required to do. So religious wars were undertaken, in the name of jihad, though the practice appears to have coincided with that of islamic

[222] See generally K. A. El Fadl, 'Islamic Law and Muslim Minorities: The Juristic Discourse on Muslim Minorities from the Second/Eighth to the Eleventh/Seventeenth Centuries' (1994) 1 Islamic Law & Soc. 141, notably at 165–75, on the differences (again) between islamic schools (Hanafi school more territorial, others more personal); 178, on reticence of islamic jurists to deal specifically with cases of conflict between islamic law and local state law ('practical compromises were inevitable, and Muslim jurists may have realized that any attempt to control or regulate behavior was bound to be ignored by muslim minorities living in different historical situations'); and 179, muslim minorities 'should maintain a separate identity'; Pearl and Menski, *Muslim Family Law* (1998), at 2–65 (notably on more flexible views of Hanafi and Shafi'i schools, though no 'uniform juristic guidance available' in islamic law); and see, for resolution by courts in Arabic countries of questions of personal status of muslims who are nationals of foreign secular countries through application of islamic law and not through application of the foreign national law, R. A. Beck-Peccoz, 'Cittadinanza e appartenenza religiosa nel diritto internazionale privato. Il caso dei paesi arabi' (1993) 9 *Teoria politica* 97.

[223] Though there is much debate on the primary motives and on the most effective means. For 'a universalism implicit in Muhammad's teaching and actions,' see Hourani, *History of Arab Peoples* (1991) at 22; and for use of force followed by rapid adherence of conquered peoples, Lewis, *The Middle East* (1995), above, at 55, 57 ('true wonder' of Arab empire arabization and islamization of conquered peoples); cf. Doi, *Shari'ah* (1984) at 444 (Jihad 'never been fought for mere territorial gain and colonialism' though 'to spread what they considered to be the truth wherever they were invited by the rulers or oppressed people of distant lands').

[224] 3: 103; and on the notion of the 'missionary Jihad' see Doi, *Shari'ah* (1984) at 437; Maulana, *Manual of Hadith* (1977), above, at 253; T. W. Arnold, *The Preaching of Islam: A History of the Propagation of the Muslim Faith* (Lahore: Ashraf Printing Press, 4th repr. 1979).

[225] 2: 256.

[226] Arnold, *Preaching of Islam* (1979), above, at 451; and see Khadduri, *War and Peace* (1955) at 56 (jihad 'not necessarily' war and fighting). For hadith on jihad see Maulana, *Manual of Hadith* (1977), above, ch. 19.

ascendancy, from the first/seventh to the eighth/fourteenth centuries, and to have declined as both doctrine and practice thereafter.[227]

The extent of any aggressive form of jihad is controlled, moreover, by another well entrenched doctrine of islamic thought, which is that of a special status accorded to jews and christians (and hindus are assimilated to them), the other 'people of the book', sharing the same God with muslims.[228] These peoples are known also as the dhimmi, whose status is derived from a fictional contract (the dhimma, for residence in return for taxes) and 'it is right to point out the similarities with concepts both in Roman and in Jewish law'.[229] So historically jews have been better off under muslim than under christian rule,[230] a position which has varied only in recent centuries, and through changes in thought in the west. Today it is said that the dhimmi are 'excluded from the specifically Muslim privileges, but on the other hand they are exempt from the specifically Muslim duties' while (and there are here clear parallels with western public and private law treatment of aliens—Fremdenrecht, la condition des étrangers), '[f]or the rest, the Muslim and the dhimmi are equal in practically the whole of the law of property and of contracts and obligations'.[231] The juridical notion of the dhimmi is possible, however, only because of a wider religious toleration, in the Koran and under islamic thinking, of the other major (western) religions. While there has been debate in islam as

---

[227] M. Khadduri, *The Islamic Concept of Justice* (Baltimore: Johns Hopkins Press, 1984) at 165–9 (notion of religious war formulated by Shafi in late 2nd/8th century, after initial period of tranquility, notion of defensive jihad dominating from 8th/14th century); M. Khadduri, *War and Peace in the Law of Islam* (Baltimore: Johns Hopkins Press, 1955) at 58 (jihad as notion of just war); B. Ye'or, *The Dhimmi: Jews and Christians under Islam*, trans. D. Maisel, P. Fenton and D. Littman (Rutherford/Madison/Teaneck and London/Toronto: Fairleigh Dickinson University Press and Associated University Presses, 1985) at 161, citing 4th/10th century text of al-Qayrawani ('We Malikis maintain that it is preferable not to begin hostilities with the enemy before having invited the latter to embrace the religion of Allah except where the enemy attacks first'); Aldeeb Abu-Salieh, *Musulmans face aux droit de l'homme* (1994) at 377–80; and for jihad activities, Noth, 'Die Scharîa' (1980) at 435, and more recently in shi'ite history, Digard, 'Shi-isme et Etat en Iran' (1982), above, at 71.

[228] Pearl and Menski, *Muslim Family Law* (1998) at 7 (notably on hindu assimilation, this being possible, presumably, because of hindu religious texts and hindu tolerance of multiple, single gods, as to which see below, Ch. 8, *Time and Brahman*); Ye'or, *Dhimmi* (1985), with juristic texts from 161; Khadduri, *War and Peace* (1955) at 175 ff.; N. Rouland, S. Pierré-Caps and J. Poumarède, *Droit des minorities et des peuples autochtones* (Paris: Presses universitaires de France, 1996) at 116–35.

[229] Pearl and Menski, *Muslim Family Law* (1998) at 7; and see S. Herman, 'Legacy and Legend: The Continuity of Roman and English Regulation of the Jews' (1992) 66 Tulane L. Rev. 1781.

[230] See M. R. Cohen, *Under Crescent and Cross: The Jews in the Middle Ages* (Princeton: Princeton University Press, 1994); Rouland, Pierré-Caps and Poumarède, *Droit des minorities* (1996), above, at 65 (Arab conquest of Spain in 711 as liberation); E. Schochetman, 'Jewish Law in Spain and the Halakhic Activity of its Scholars before 1300' in N. Hecht, B. Jackson, S. Passamaneck, D. Piatelli & A. Rabello (eds.) *An Introduction to the History and Sources of Jewish Law* (Oxford: Institute of Jewish Law, Boston University School of Law/Clarendon Press, 1996) 271 at 272. Islamic recognition of non-islamic personal laws within islamic jurisdictions has been described as 'unique in all the legal systems history has known'. See al Faruqi and al Faruqi, *Cultural Atlas* (1986), above, at 268. For western refusal to recognize religious personal laws, see above, *The Islamic diaspora*.

[231] Schacht, *Introduction to Islamic Law* (1964) at 132, 143; Cf., criticizing inequality of treatment on human rights grounds, with no discussion of western treatment of aliens, Mayer, 'Dilemmas of Islamic Identity' (1988), above, 94 at 143.

to whether Muhammad's revelation abrogated the earlier ones, the Koran itself used the language of confirmation and toleration. 'And unto thee have We revealed the Scripture with the truth, confirming whatever Scripture was before it . . . For each We have appointed a divine law and a traced out way.'[232] Where islamic law became prominent in lands other than those of people of the book, its toleration of local custom (urf) also allowed continuance of local practice[233] and, again, there was no compulsion in religion.

So for this variety of reasons, jihad has come to be seen today more in the literal sense of the Koran, an obligation to spread the word of the Prophet and an obligation to defend the faith against outside aggression.[234] The debate within the islams is therefore as to the extent of external challenge and the appropriate means of response. The latter have become more violent since the creation of the Muslim Brotherhood in the 1960s in Egypt, a time when expansion of western law and western legal technique in islamic lands was probably at its height.[235] Islamic thought also makes effective use of the Leninist idea that imperialism is a necessary feature of capitalism, so the need for defence is given some air of necessity. If jihad is now a defensive war, its appropriateness (and its measures) requires some appreciation of the external challenge. This comes from the west, from the combined resources of civil and common law traditions.

---

[232] 5: 48, and for non-abrogation see F. Rahman, *Major Themes of the Qur'an* (Chicago: Bibliotheca Islama, 1980) at 167, 170 (citing also the 'unheeded' invitation of 3: 64 'O People of the Scripture! Come to an agreement between us and you . . .'); Brohi, 'Die Rechtsideen' (1986), above, at 17, 18 (giving examples of parallel language in Old Testament, Koran); Hourani, *History of Arab Peoples* (1991) at 21 (jews, christians, zoroastrians, muslims 'in the early centuries . . . remained more open to each other than they were later to be'). Muhammad would have recognized only in Medina that jews and christians were likely not to follow him, and there recognized them as communities. F. Rahman, *Major Themes of the Qur'an* (1980), above, at 163–5; Hourani, *History of Arab Peoples* (1991) at 18. For abrogation, however, see Arnaldez, 'La loi musulmane' (1993) at 83, 84 (though earlier revelations right for the time and God not in error); and further references in Graf and Falaturi, 'Brauch/Sitte und Recht in der traditionellen islamischen Jurisprudenz' (1986), above, at 32. Proponents of abrogation, however, have the jewish-christian teaching to overcome (Paul's advocacy of abrogation not followed, and understandably, by jews; see above, Ch. 4, *Talmudic retreat?*), as well as the special status conferred on other followers of the Book). A doctrine of non-abrogation also provides a means of conciliation with later prophets, such as that of the islamic Ahmadiyya movement, with some 10m. adherents following prophet Ahmad of the late-19th century, and pursuing a persuasive but not aggressive evangelism.

[233] See above, *Subtle change*; Alliot, 'Rechts-Transfers' (1980), above, at 166.

[234] See R. Peters (trans. and annot.), *Jihad in Mediaeval and Modern Islam: the chapter on jihad from Averroes' Legal Handbook 'Bidayat al Mudjtahid' and The Treatise 'Koran and Fighting' by the late Shaykh Al-Azhar, Mahmud Shaltut* (Leiden: E. J. Brill, 1977), notably at 31–8; Doi, *Shari'ah* (1984) at 437; Little, Kelsey and Sachedina, *Human Rights and Conficts of Culture* (1988), above, at 84.

[235] On re-islamization as an effort towards re-equilibrium, see Graf and Falaturi, 'Brauch/Sitte und Recht' (1986), above, at 45; N. R. Keddie, *An Islamic Response to Imperialism: Political and Religious Writings of Sayyid Jamal al-Din 'al-Afghani'* (Berkeley/Los Angeles/London: Univ. of California Press, 1968); R. Patel, *Islamisation of Laws in Pakistan?* (Karachi: Paiza Publishers, 1986); and on the 'anti-islamic tradition' in the west, see A. Hussain, *Western Conflict with Islam: Survey of the Anti-Islamic Tradition* (Leicester: Volcano Books, 1990), notably at 66 (impossible to understand anti-western feeling in muslim world without understanding anti-islamic tradition in west).

## GENERAL BIBLIOGRAPHY

Afchar, H., 'The Muslim Conception of Law' in International Association of Legal Science (K. Zweigert and U. Drobnig, eds.), *International Encyclopedia of Comparative Law*, vol. II, ch. 1 (Tübingen/The Hague/Paris: J. C. B. Mohr (Paul Siebeck)/Mouton, 1975) at 84.

Aldeeb Abu-Sahlieh, S. A., 'Introduction à la lecture juridique du Coran' (1988) 65 Revue de droit international et de droit comparé 76.

—— *Les Musulmans face aux droits de l'homme: religion & droit & politique* (Bochum: Dr. Dieter Winkler, 1994).

Aldeeb Abu-Salieh, S. A., see Aldeeb Abu-Sahlieh, S. A.

Amin, S. H., *Islamic Law and its Implications for [the] Modern World* (Glasgow: Royston Ltd., 1989).

Anderson, J. N. D., *Law Reform in the Muslim World* (London: Athlone Press, 1976).

Arab Law Quarterly (The Hague: Kluwer).

Arnaldez, R., 'La loi musulmane à la lumière des sciences coraniques' (1993) Archives de philosophie du droit 83.

Brown, D., *Rethinking tradition in modern Islamic thought* (Cambridge: Cambridge University Press, 1996).

Calder, N., *Studies in Early Muslim Jurisprudence* (Oxford: Clarendon Press, 1993).

Cammack, M., 'Islamic Law in Indonesia's New Order' (1989) 38 International & Comparative Law Quarterly 53.

Charles ,R., *Le droit musulman*, 4th edn. (Paris: Presses universitaires de France, 1972).

Chehata, Ch., 'Islamic Law' in International Association of Legal Science (K. Zweigert and U. Drobnig, eds.), *International Encyclopedia of Comparative Law*, vol. II, ch. 2 (Tübingen/The Hague/Paris: J. C. B. Mohr (Paul Siebeck)/Mouton, 1974) at 138.

Coulson, N. J., *A History of Islamic Law* (Edinburgh: Edinburgh University Press, 1964) (with extensive further bibliography at 242 ff.).

—— 'Islamic Law' in J. Derrett (ed.), *An Introduction to Legal Systems* (London: Sweet and Maxwell, 1968) at 54.

David, R. and Brierley, J. E. C., *Major Legal Systems in the World Today* (London: Stevens & Sons, 1985), Pt. Four, Title I ('Muslim Law').

Diwan, P. and Diwan, P., *Muslim Law in Modern India*, 6th edn. (Allahabad: Allahabad Law Agency, 1993).

Doi, A. R. I., *Shari'ah: The Islamic Law* (London: Ta Ha Publishers, 1984).

Edge, I., *Islamic Law and Legal Theory* (Aldershot/Singapore/Sydney: Dartmouth, 1996).

Esposito, J. L., *Women in Muslim Family Law* (Syracuse: Syracuse University Press, 1982).

Fyzee, A. A. A., *Outlines of Muhammadan Law*, 4th edn. (Delhi/Bombay/ Calcutta/Madras: Oxford University Press, 1974).

Geertz, C., *Local Knowledge* (New York: Basic Books, 1983).

Hallaq, W. B., 'The Logic of Legal Reasoning in Religious and Non-Religious Cultures: The Case of Islamic Law and the Common Law' (1985–6) 34 Cleveland State Law Review 79.

—— 'From *Fatwas* to *Furu*: Growth and Change in Islamic Substantive Law' (1994) 1 Islamic Law and Society 29.

—— *A History of Islamic Legal Theories: An Introduction to Sunni Usul al-Fiqh* (Cambridge: Cambridge University Press, 1997).

Hooker, M. B., *Islamic Law in South-East Asia* (Singapore: Oxford University Press, 1984).

Horowitz, D. L, 'The Qur'an and the Common Law: Islamic Law Reform and the Theory of Legal Change' (1994) 42 American Journal of Comparative Law 233.

Hourani, A., *A History of the Arab Peoples* (Cambridge, Mass.: Harvard University Press, 1991).

Islamic Law and Society (Leiden: E. J. Brill, thrice yearly).

Khadduri, M., *War and Peace in the Law of Islam* (Baltimore: Johns Hopkins Press, 1955).

—— *The Islamic Concept of Justice* (Baltimore: Johns Hopkins University Press, 1984).

Khadduri, M. and Liebesny, H. J., *Law in the Middle East*, vol. I, *Origin and Development of Islamic Law* (Washington, DC: The Middle East Institute, 1955).

Lev, D., *Islamic Courts in Indonesia: A study in the political bases of legal institutions* (Berkeley: University of California Press, 1972).

Linant de Bellefonds, Y., *Traité de droit musulman comparé*, 2 vols. (Paris: Mouton, 1965).

Makdisi, G., 'The Guilds of Law in Medieval Legal History: An Inquiry into the Origins of the Inns of Court' (1985–6) 34 Cleveland State Law Review 3.

Makdisi, J., 'Formal Rationality in Islamic Law and the Common Law' (1985–6) 34 Cleveland State Law Review 97.

Malek, R., *Tradition et révolution: L'enjeu de la modernité en Algérie et dans l'Islam* (Paris: Sinbad, 1993).

Mallat, C., *The Renewal of Islamic Law: Muhammad Baqer as-Sadr, Najaf and the Shi'i International* (Cambridge: Cambridge University Press, 1993).

May, R., *Beiträge zu Islamischem Rechtsdenken*, Vol. II, Studien zu nichteuropäischen Rechtstheorien (Stuttgart: Franz Steiner Verlag, 1986).

Milliot, L. and Blanc, F. -P., *Introduction à l'étude du droit musulman*, 2nd edn. (Paris: Sirey, 1987).

Nasir, J. J., *The Status of Women Under Islamic Law and Under Modern Islamic Legislation*, 2nd edn. (London/Dordrecht/Boston: Graham & Trotman, 1994).

Noth, A., 'Die Scharîa, das religiöse Gesetz des Islam—Wandlungsmöglichkeit, Anwendung und Wirkung', in W. Fikentscher, H. Franke and D. Köhler (eds.). *Entstehung und Wandel rechtlicher Traditionen* (Freiburg/Munich: Verlag Karl Alber, 1980).

Pearl, D. and Menski W., *Muslim Family Law*, 3rd edn. (London: Sweet & Maxwell, 1998).

Peters, R. (trans. and ann.), *Jihad in Mediaeval and Modern Islam* (Leiden: E. J. Brill, 1977).

Rahim, A., *Muhammadan Jurisprudence* (Lahore: All-Pakistan Legal Decisions, 1958 repr. of 1911 edn.).

Rayner, S. E., *The Theory of Contracts in Islamic Law* (London: Graham and Trotman, 1991).

Rosen, L., *The anthropology of justice: law as culture in Islamic society* (Cambridge/New York: Cambridge University Press, 1989).

Salem, N. A., *Unlawful Gain and Legitimate Profit in Islamic Law: Riba, Gharar and Islamic Banking* (London/Dordrecht/Boston: Graham & Trotman, 1992).

Schacht, J., *The Origins of Muhammadan Jurisprudence* (Oxford: Clarendon Press, 1950).

—— *An Introduction to Islamic Law* (Oxford: Clarendon Press, 1964).

Stowasser, B., *Women in the Qur'an, Traditions, and Interpretation* (New York/Oxford: Oxford University Press, 1994).

Tabataba'i, H. M., *An Introduction to Shi'i Law: a bibliographical study* (London: Ithaca Press, 1984).

Tyan, E., *Histoire de l'organisation judiciaire en pays d'Islam* (Leiden: E. J. Brill, 1960).

Weiss, B., 'Interpretation in Islamic Law: The Theory of *Ijtihad*' (1978) 26 American Journal of Comparative Law 199.

—— *The Spirit of Islamic Law* (Athens, Ga./London: University of Georgia Press, 1998).

Ye'or, B., *The Dhimmi: Jews and Christians under Islam*, transl. D. Maisel, P. Fenton and D. Littman (Rutherford/Madison/Teaneck/London/Toronto: Fairleigh Dickinson University Press & Associated University Press, 1985).

Zweigert, K. and Kötz, H., *Introduction to Comparative Law*, 3rd ed., trans. T. Weir (Oxford: Clarendon Press, 1998), ch. 22.

# 7

# A COMMON LAW TRADITION:
# THE ETHIC OF ADJUDICATION

If islamic law entered a crowded field, in the first/seventh century, there was even more law, including islamic law, four centuries later, when the Normans set out across the channel, with territory in mind. The British Isles had known chthonic law, then roman law, then chthonic law again[1] (repeating in this the model of much of the continent), while the law of the christian church was increasingly present in civil life.[2] The commercial law of Europe was also emerging, in the (then) borderless world of trade,[3] while roman law (later described by Goethe as a 'diving duck'[4]) was re-surfacing. So there was no absence of law for the regulation of civil life in England, and no evident space for the emergence, still less creation, of a new and particular legal tradition.[5]

[1] Perhaps in slightly romanized form, since the Roman example has been seen as influential in the writing of the laws of Aethelberht, in the 7th century. See Baker, *Introduction to English Legal History* (1990) at 2, 3. The Roman occupation had lasted for nearly the first 4 centuries AD. See W. Senior, 'Roman Law in England before Vacarius' (1930) 182 LQR. 191. For the intervening 'pagan' legislation ('if an offensive word can be used inoffensively') in the Kingdom of Kent, see H. Richardson and G. Sayles, *Law and Legislation from Aethelberht to Magna Carta* (Edinburgh: Edinburgh Univ. Press, 1966) (quotation at 1; arguing against Roman influence).

[2] Largely in the form of roman law prior to the emergence of a distinct body of canon law, but discernible in its use by the church in England prior to the arrival of the Normans. See Senior, 'Roman Law in England' (1930), above, at 193–6 (also for Anglo-Saxon bishops sitting as members of local courts prior to creation of separate ecclesiastical tribunals by Normans, fulfilling promise to papal authority). Early jurisdiction of ecclesiastical courts extended to matters of family law and succession, but also to more general forms of conscience-based, ecclesiastical remedy. See R. Helmholz, 'The Early Enforcement of Uses' (1979) 79 Col. L. Rev. 1503; S. Devine, 'Ecclesiastical Antecedents to Secular Jurisdiction over the Feoffment to the Uses to be Declared in Testamentary Instructions' (1986) 30 Am. J. Legal Hist. 295; H. Coing, 'English Equity and the Denunciatio Evangelica of the Canon Law' (1955) 71 LQR 223; and for Norman initiation of ecclesiastical courts, Hudson, *Formation of English Common Law* (1996) at 48–50 (noting much evidence of co-operation between ecclesiastical and lay courts).

[3] See R. van Caenegem, *An Historical Introduction to Private Law*, trans. D. Johnston (Cambridge: Cambridge Univ. Press, 1992) at 83, 84 (commercial law constructed 12th–15th centuries; written compilations emerging by 1150s); though for borough commercial fairs held in boroughs in Anglo-Saxon times, see Kiralfy, *Potter's Historical Introduction to English Law*, (1958) at 187.

[4] See P. Stein, *Roman Law and English Jurisprudence Yesterday and Today* (Cambridge: Cambridge Univ. Press, 1969) at 3, citing J. P. Eckermann, *Conversations with Goethe*, trans. J. Oxenford (London: Everyman's Library, 1930) at 313.

[5] For the lack of specificity of English law prior to Norman development of it, see van Caenegem, *Birth of English Common Law*, (1988) at 89, 110; and on the variants of seisin, saisine and gewere prevalent both in the British Isles and on the continent, F. Joüon des Longrais, *La conception anglaise de la saisine du XIIe au XIVe siècle* (Paris: Jouve, 1924) at 43. Debate thus turned on whether the law was more roman or germanic. See Kiralfy, *Potter's Historical Introduction to English Law* (1958) at 631, with refs.

R. C. van Caenegem has therefore concluded that the best explanation for the existence of a common law tradition is the historical accident, or chance, of the military conquest of England by the Normans. By 'chance' he means simply circumstances for which we can give no adequate explanation, and certainly no legal explanation.[6] As a result of this historical accident, the first identifiable, modern state came into being in Europe, with defined (though largely geographical) boundaries and a central government. Given all of this, the Normans came to the conclusion that something could be *done* in the sense of developing a legal order responsive to Norman, as well as local, needs. Surrounded by animosity and strange languages, however, there were evident limits on what they could bring about. So, again, it does not appear possible here to speak of the creation of a tradition, but only of a birth, a small but important event, which would allow subsequent development to occur. The development was of a tradition we now know as that of the common law, but it was also, from a larger, European perspective, the development of a particular law, particular from the European circumstances from which it developed.

# BIRTH AND DEVELOPMENT

The Norman, francophone heads of state of England put together the basic ingredients of the common law in about a century and a half after the conquest of 1066. If you put yourself in their place, and think what you would have done in the circumstances, you might have brought about the same results. There were obvious limits on what any clear-headed monarch might then do. On the other hand, in the eleventh and twelfth centuries many avenues were opening up in European law, and there were intellectual temptations to be enjoyed, or avoided. The result, we now know, was a cautious sampling of the new ideas (from the continent) while adapting them to the necessities of legal, political and social life among the franci and the anglici of England. The most famous analogy is that of an inoculation with roman law, generating immunity to it thereafter.[7] It might be just as accurate to think of a jump start, or a booting-up.

### OF JUDGES AND JUDGING

The only avenue for a Norman legal order, common to the realm, was through a loyal judiciary. This immediately marks off a common law tradition from all others.

---

[6] van Caenegem, *Birth of English Common Law* (1988) at 106, 107.

[7] H. Brunner, 'The Sources of English Law', in *Select Essays in Anglo-American History*, vol. II (Boston: Little, Brown, 1908) 7 at 42 (rendering the national law immune against 'destructive infection' of roman law).

There was here no loyal chthonic people, no available revelation, no corpus of learned, indigenous doctrine. So, as monarch, you could not rely on God, the people, or your own legislation. You needed a corps of loyal adjudicators, able to bring a newer, more efficient and modern king's peace to the different parts of the realm. Of course, you couldn't name patricians, or nobles, to the judicial task, as did the Romans. Your nobility could only speak French; their's, of England, couldn't be trusted (to the extent they had survived). So some kind of permanent judicial officer was required, who could work in a controlled and efficient manner. The only choice for filling such an office, moreover, was that of priests, who could read and write and who were often already trained in canon (and civil) law.[8] Given that they could read and write, they could be given precise written instructions for the particular case (a paper trail), such that a priori and, if necessary, a posteriori control could be exercised over their activities. There couldn't be many of them, or they would cost too much (to the royal purse or to hapless litigants). And it would be wise to co-opt the population into their work, so if actual decisions were left to the local folks (they could be sworn, or jurés) then the judges could just get the right questions asked in a number of cases, and be off to another town. Nor would there be, in principle, anything obligatory about proceeding in a royal court, as opposed to all the others, thick on the ground and often still using older means of proof (fire, water and all that).[9] So the faster, more efficient, more rational royal courts, using local knowledge, could just quietly insinuate themselves into the landscape, without costing too much, and subject (in the beginning at least) to some form of royal audit, just to know what was going on.

One can look at the development of this judiciary, and this judicial process, in two ways. The usual way is to look at what actually happened, and the best version of this holds that a process of 'judicialization' of royal disposition of complaints to the crown occurred.[10] First everyone came to the king, and his council, who then began referring things to the chancellor, who then began to ensure that things were properly looked at by some type of judge. The judges had to be who they were, since there wasn't anybody else, and the procedure was just right, for the post-conquest circumstances. So local circumstances (even if accidental in origin) and intelligent local response seem essential in the birth of a common law tradition. Yet if you step

---

[8] See H. Cohen, *History of the English Bar and Attornatus to 1450* (London/Toronto: Sweet and Maxwell/ Carswell, 1929) at 151; R. Turner, *The English Judiciary in the Age of Glanvill and Bracton, c. 1176–1239* (Cambridge/New York: Cambridge Univ. Press, 1985) at 88–107; Plucknett, *Concise History of Common Law* (1956) at 232–6 (cautioning, however, that not all clerical judges were canonists); Hudson, *Formation of English Common Law* (1996) at 133, 134 (noting 'constant rearrangement'), 150, 229.

[9] Cf., however, for defence of these techniques in the context in which they were used, above, Ch. 5, in introductory text; and for explanation of their use in English context, Hudson, *Formation of English Common Law* (1996) at 72, 77 ('no headlong rush for the supernatural', overall use 'seems to have been acceptable'). For the optional jurisdiction of the royal courts see ibid at 116, 139, 140 (though King 'inviting claimants to come to him').

[10] van Caenegem, *Birth of English Common Law* (1988) at 34.

back a little, and consider that all of this was going on while many of the same things were going on all over Europe, it also seems inspired by some larger patterns of western thought. There was a renaissance at this time throughout Europe (and the growth of islamic faith and science seem responsible in some measure for it).[11] Everywhere written forms of law were gaining ascendancy over chthonic ones; everywhere legal professions were being developed; everywhere there was abandonment of 'non-rational' forms of proof; everywhere there was the new teaching that human intelligence and law were compatible with one another, most evidently in the teaching of roman law. So the common law seems to emerge as both common and particular to England, and common and particular to Europe. If 'modernization' is a European process, the common law was the first to do it, in its own way, but as part of a larger process.

English judges, as professional judges, were different from the amateur Roman ones. Yet the manner of judging was eerily similar to that of Rome.[12] In both cases the actual decision, the law-finding, was the work of amateurs: the judge or iudex in Rome, the jury in England. In both cases they acted on the basis of instructions, from the praetor in Rome, from the judge in England. And in both cases the complaint had to go through a process of screening: to conform to the praetor's edict in Rome, to be within the categories of written royal commands or writs which could be used to start up the royal procedures in England. The English

[11] See, for islam as the 'great threat of the age', leading to western christianity developing 'an aggressive intransigence almost as a defensive reflex; it was a sign of its insecurities', J. M. Roberts, *A History of Europe* (New York: Allen Lane/Penguin, 1996) at 105–7, 119, 145, 146, 160; and for islam providing 'the single greatest stimulus to what was eventually called "Europe"', all Christians living earlier 'in Islam's shade', N. Davies, *Europe: a History* (London: Pimlico, 1997) at 266; on the general influence of the Crusades, and islamic influence through Spain and Sicily, see E. J. Passant, 'The Effects of the Crusades upon Western Europe', in J. Tanner, C. Previté-Orton and Z. Brooke, *The Cambridge Medieval History*, vol. V (Cambridge: Cambridge Univ. Press, 1926) 320, notably at 331 (for influence of muslim scholars of Spain, translations from Arabic of Greek philosophy); W. Watt, *The Influence of Islam on Medieval Europe* (Islamic Surveys, No. 9) (Edinburgh: Edinburgh Univ. Press, 1972), notably at 29 (most Europeans not aware of islamic character of what they were adopting), 60, 61 (by twelfth century most Arab works of merit translated into Latin), 79 (turn to Greek philosophy partly inspired by European assertion of distinction from islam), 85 ff. (list of English words derived from Arabic, e.g., admiral, alcohol, alcove, banana, coffee, cotton, etc.); for the existence of muslim centres of higher education in the 3rd/9th and 4th/10th centuries, prior to the founding of western universities, see B. Lewis, *The Middle East: 2000 years of History from the Rise of Christianity to the Present Day* (London: Weidenfeld and Nicolson, 1995) at 190, 191; and for still earlier Chinese centres of higher learning, see below, Ch. 9, *Asian time and space*. Transmission of Greek learning to the west occurred largely through translation from the Arabic, facilitated in large measure by jewish translators, as to which see R. Brague, *Europe, la voie romaine*, 2nd edn. (Paris: Criterion, 1993) at 55, 56, 87–91; and for islamic legal texts included in these 12-century translations, M.-T. d'Alverny, *La connaissance de l'Islam dans l'Occident médiéval* (Aldershot/Brookfield Vt.: Variorum, 1994) at V 591–600, VI 238–45; C. Burnett, *The Introduction of Arabic Learning into England* (London: British Library, 1997), notably at 58–60 on arabic influence on Henry II (principal architect of common law institutions) and at 61 ff. in creation of Oxford University.

[12] Pringsheim, 'Inner Relationship between English and Roman Law' (1935).

judicial process, based on writs, may well have been an original construction.[13] The roman-continental procedure being used in the eleventh and twelfth centuries was the later, extraordinary procedure, in which open courts were simply seised of complaints and applied substantive law. English lawyers knew of this procedure, and one even wrote a book on it,[14] but there is no written trace of English legal knowledge, at this time, of the earlier roman formulary procedure. Either it was known, and influenced the English procedure, or this Roman/English way is just the only way to do it, the only way to set up institutions which will, over time, generate a tradition in law.

The other major influence on English legal institutions in these formative years appears to be islamic.[15] To develop the teaching necessary for the new legal professions, working in the royal courts, English lawyers eventually developed the Inns of Court, for centuries charged with instruction in the common law while legal instruction in Oxford and Cambridge was limited to roman law. The earliest inns, however, were attached to churches, as the madhahib were attached to mosques. The madhahib reached the height of their development, physical and intellectual, in the fifth/eleventh century, that of the Norman conquest of England. The first Crusade began in 1095; by the middle of the next century there were three famous schools or inns in London, attached to churches, pre-dating the Inns of Court, the Inns of Chancery and the earliest colleges in Oxford.[16] Two of the surviving Inns of

[13] Yet see, for prior development of Anglo-Saxon royal writs, and for parallel Norman procedures of requenoissants, van Caenegem, *Birth of English Common Law* (1988) at 31, 82, 97; and on the English notion of 'recognitions' (formal answers given by sworn jury to question of fact), R. C. van Caenegem, *Royal Writs in England from the Conquest to Glanvill: Studies in the Early History of the Common Law* (London: Selden Soc./ Professional Books, 1972) at 51. On the procedure of the writs, the forms of action, see below, *Lawyers' law: pleading to issue.*

[14] See the reference to the work on roman procedure by William Longchamp, 'King Richard's viceroy and the true rule of England' in G. Woodbine, 'The Origins of the Action of Trespass' (1924) 33 Yale L. J. 799 at 813.

[15] On the following, see G. Makdisi, 'The Guilds of Law in Medieval Legal History: An Inquiry into the Origins of the Inns of Court' (1985–6) 34 Clevel. St. L. Rev. 3; and more generally G. Makdisi, *The Rise of Colleges: Institutions of Learning in Islam and the West* (Edinburgh: Edinburgh Univ. Press, 1981), notably at 287 (western developments roughly a century after those of islamic world, 'to resist admitting influence would be to continue the medieval attitude toward Islam').

[16] Makdisi, 'Guilds of Law' (1985–6), above, with references. The origins of the Inns of Court themselves have been traced to the 1340s; see J. H. Baker, *The Third University of England: the inns of court and the common-law tradition* (London: Selden Soc., 1990) at 7, 9, and there is widespread agreement on the existence of prior inns. See R. Roxburgh, *The Origins of Lincoln's Inn* (Cambridge: Cambridge Univ. Press, 1963) (origins of Inns of Court themselves may be associated with reforms of legal education of Edward I, notably Order in Council of 1292); H. Ringrose, *The Inns of Court* (London: Paul Musson, 1909) at 2 (prohibition of clergy acting in temporal courts led to settling of students in hostels or inns in 1207); D. Barton, C. Benham and F. Watt, *The Story of Our Inns of Court* (London: G. T. Foulis and Co., 1924) at 4, 7 (in twelfth and thirteenth centuries schools of law in London under clerical control, extant records inadequate to trace development to organized institutions); R. Pearce, *A History of the Inns of Court and Chancery* (Littleton, Colo.: Fred B. Rothman, 1987) at 1 (seminaries for study of law in time of Stephen, 1135–54); P. Brand, 'Legal Education in England before the Inns of Court' in J. Bush and A. Wijffels, *Learning the Law: Teaching and Transmission of Law in England 1150–1900* (London/Rio Grande, Ohio.: Hambledon Press, 1999) 51, notably at 57 (for prohibition in 1234 of teaching of 'laws' in London).

Court, moreover, the Inner Temple and the Middle Temple, were, according to tradition, closely associated with the Order of the Knights Templar, founded in Jerusalem in 1120. There they had quarters near the Aqsa Mosque near the site of the (destroyed) Temple of Solomon, hence their fuller name of the Poor Knights of Christ and the Temple of Solomon.[17] They established themselves in England in 1128, and not long after their property came to the lawyers. Thus, '[t]he origin of the inn as an institution of learning in the Christian West is historically connected with London and Paris; the inns of these two cities are in turn connected historically with the Holy City of Jerusalem. This type of inn, born in Baghdad and the eastern Caliphate, had moved westward to other great cities, including Jerusalem and cities throughout Spain and Sicily.'[18] The Normans were also in Sicily, conquering Palermo in 1072 and governing this 'brilliant civilization . . . [which] combined the best of the Latin, Arabic and Greek traditions'[19] until the end of the next century. They allowed islamic law to continue to be applied under their rule, and could not have been ignorant of its institutions.

LAWYER'S LAW: PLEADING TO ISSUE

The common law grew slowly in the plenitude of laws and legal institutions of medieval England. It did so by the accretion of learning around the royal commands, given by the chancellor, for the resolution of individual disputes. Each writ gave rise to a particular procedure to be followed, appropriate for the type of dispute. If you are not a common law lawyer, and even for many who are, the writs and forms of action are a world filled with darkness, complexity and, more recently, boredom. They are slowly losing their grip. But you can't really understand a common law tradition without understanding their broad outlines and function. They were all there was; outside the writs, there was no common law, no way to state a case or get before a judge. They also allowed the judge to attain, and maintain, priority of place in the hierarchy of common law institutions.

---

[17] On the Temples of Jerusalem, see above, Ch. 4, A Tradition Rooted in Revelation.

[18] Makdisi, 'Guilds of Law' (1985–6), above, at 14, and making the larger claim, at 9, that the islamic schools developed the medieval scholastic method (sic et non, dialectic and disputation, generally attributed to Abelard in the twelfth century).

[19] Berman, Law and Revolution (1983) at 410, 413 and 415 (for Norman creation in Sicily of competitive civil service examinations, possibly inspired by Chinese example, reported by muslim or jewish travellers); Watt, Influence of Islam (1972), above, at 21, 25 (Roger of Sicily bringing islamic knowledge of world geography to west; also initiating use of paper to replace Egyptian papyrus, relying on Arabian refinement of Chinese techniques); and for the full, swashbuckling story, J. J. Norwich, The Normans in Sicily: the magnificent story of the 'other Norman Conquest' (London: Penguin, 1992), notably at 7 (importance given by nordic Normans to law), 52, 53 (islamic control of Sicily from 9th century tolerant of other religious traditions), 190–3, 442 (islamic law continued to be applied by islamic courts during reign of Roger II, Norman king of Sicily, in multiracial, polyglot, harmonious society; Roger 'genuinely admired' muslim civilization), 364 (Roger taught by Greek and Arab tutors), 464, 518 (Roger surrounding himself with leading scientific advisers of Europe and Arab world, personally spoke Arabic; Arab group largest of advisers; Sicily then the 'cultural clearing-house of three continents'); P. Aubé, Les Empires normands d'Orient (Paris: Perrin, 1991), notably at 167, 168 (on Norman respect for existing laws, particular respect for muslims).

A writ took the form of instructions from the Crown to a royal officer (usually the sheriff, hence the classic expression, 'The King to the sheriff, greetings . . .') indicating what the sheriff had to do to advance investigation of a dispute. It might command the sheriff to require a defendant to appear and show cause; to seize property unless a defendant justified the keeping of it; to empanel a jury; and so on. Maitland described each writ, with its accompanying form of action, as a 'pigeon-hole'. A plaintiff had to choose amongst them; there was no changing in mid-litigation (even if the case was filled with surprises) and it might well be that no writ was available. 'Where there is no remedy there is no wrong.'[20] So the common law came to be composed of a series of procedural routes (usually referred to as remedies) to get before a jury and state one's case. The jury enjoyed a monopoly on what we today call substantive decision-making. The system of writs (there were about 50 of them by the middle of the thirteenth century; six centuries later only another 25 or so had been added) profoundly influenced contemporary common law procedure and the judicial role, as well as substantive law.

In contemporary language the common law was therefore a law of procedure; whatever substantive law existed was hidden by it, 'secreted' in its 'interstices', in the language of Maine.[21] The procedure was, and is, unique in the world and may be today the most distinctive feature of the common law. Chthonic law had no trials, and little procedure; roman law used no jury; neither talmudic nor islamic law used (much) representation, and parties were expected to collaborate more than contest; in contemporary civil law it is the judge who investigates. In the common law world all came together to produce something radically different. The judge's function was not to decide the case; that was left to the jury. Yet the judge had things to decide, notably whether the case which emerged fell within the chosen writ; other-wise the court was without jurisdiction (choice of writ was not only binding, it contained all the royal authority which had been granted). Originally the jury knew all about the case (local knowledge, local law), so the task of lawyers was to argue about whether the verdict they wanted from the jury fell within the writ ('pleading to issue'). When witnesses eventually came to be necessary, the lawyers continued to plead to issue, and now brought forth the facts they needed, within the writ. The judge had no responsibility of finding 'objective' fact; nor did the lawyers.[22] There was no external law stating with precision the facts to which it applied. Since the

---

[20] Maitland, *Forms of Action* (1954) at 4, 5. Writs could also be addressed to feudal lords, requiring that justice be done in the feudal court (the writ of right). Ibid. at 6.

[21] H. S. Maine, *Dissertations on Early Law and Custom: lectures delivered at Oxford* (London: John Murray, 1883) at 389.

[22] Today the adversarial form of procedure is defended as the best means of ascertaining fact, though it never had this function originally. The argument is an indication of how far the common law has moved towards civilian thinking, in the sense of having to get the facts right in order to apply pre-existing law correctly. The civil law world has long accepted the necessity of getting the facts right, and has never allowed party presentation of them. Now both traditions are asking the same question, but there is a lot of conflictual rhetoric (e.g., 'inquisitorial' vs. 'accusatorial' procedures; cf. 'adversarial' and 'investigative'), discussed above, Ch. 5, *Constructing national law*.

members of the jury had day jobs, and were usually illiterate, the argument and proof had to be made orally, in what came to be known as a trial (as in the old trial by ordeal, but now radically made over). The trial is a dramatic event, and one in which the judge plays a commanding, but distant, role, as befitting a source of law. Freed from the burden of finding fact, advised on law and fact by the barristers (themselves eventually benefiting from judge-like treatment, enjoying immunity of function), the judge could concentrate on the general contours of the writs, the general contours of the law. Judicial rulings, by a very small number of royal judges working out of Westminster on circuit,[23] eventually came to define the ambit of the writs, encrusting themselves slowly, with no notion of stare decisis, on the skeletal language of the royal commands. There were only first-instance judges, no courts of appeal. The judges worked out themselves what was to be allowed. It was better not to suggest that they had erred.[24] And the jury, of course, could not.

## THE SECRETED LAW

If you made it through all that your writ required, and the jury believed you, you would win your case. So it is possible to say that the procedure implied a substantive law, on the merits; it was simply that no one other than the jury knew what it was. They were the law-finders. The writs were fundamental, however, since they determined when you could get to the jury, and they became the best available indicators of a secreted, substantive law. They indicated when a truthful, aggrieved party might obtain relief; they intimated obligation. Gradually, the great writs began to fill entire fields of human activity, which other lawyers (civilian, islamic, talmudic, hindu) recognized as fields of substantive law. There was a writ of novel disseisin (you have to get used to the old, now distorted, law French[25]—it means nouvelle dissaisine, for protection of those recently dispossessed of their land). It

[23] The technical expression is that of nisi prius. The case would be heard at Westminster, unless before (nisi prius) the royal judge came to the local assizes (sittings, as in assises) on the regular judicial itinerary or circuit.

[24] Notably because there were few criteria external to them to conclude that they had. There were, of course, exceptional possibilities for doing so, notably by alleging error of law on the face of the record (of the trial), such that subsequent review (by a group of first-instance judges sitting together—the Court of Exchequer Chamber—was possible. But since there was no written substantive law, there could be no error in its application. The jury, then as now, worked in strange and wondrous ways. The absence of courts of appeal in the common law, talmudic law and islamic law is therefore founded on quite different reasons. In religious traditions, there is law beyond the judges, but no judges with a final say, so the only remedy is to return to your judge, to ask for correction of error. In the common law there is no (written) law beyond the judges, so those (even) of first instance have a final say, and along with the jury on the merits. Given the prominence of the judge in the common law, the finality of their decision came to have fundamental importance in the emergence of common law conceptions of positive law, in spite of the judge's protests. See the discussion below, this Chapter, *Right reason*, and *Changing thought*.

[25] As to which, see J. H. Baker, *Manual of law French*, 2nd edn. (Aldershot: Scolar Press, 1990); J. H. Baker, 'The Three Languages of the Common Law' (1998) 43 McGill L. J. 5 (comparing use and influence of English, French and Latin in common law history).

came to be supplemented, and even largely displaced, by a writ of ejectment (here, later, from the Latin), available for those not seised of land but having a contract of lease. There were no writs of family law; this was the domain of ecclesiastical law (and there was no divorce, adoption or legitimation until their legislative adoption in the nineteenth and twentieth centuries). There were writs for the control of other courts, a precursor of modern administrative law (more later).[26] There were particular writs of debt and covenant (both for liquidated sums of money, the latter available only in case of covenant under seal), which was about all the potential for commercial law there originally was. And there was the mother of all writs, trespass, originally for assault (un assaut) or battery (une batterie) involving direct application of force. It would gradually extend to the entire field of obligations, still showing the signs of its original compass.[27]

The writs thus reflected, above all, an agrarian, non-commercial, even chthonic society. The society would take on feudal structures, but this only meant giving structure to chthonic ways of life and not providing great impetus for legal change. The writs were indigenous creations, and the scholarship eventually devoted to them was complex and original, another form of interstitial rationality. Its complexity, and particular vernacular, provided a certain impermeability to exchange with other legal traditions, notably the roman and civilian. Yet the 'immunity' of the common law from civilian (and other) influence has been exaggerated (the later insular character of national law being early demonstrated in this first prototype). There were lots of other laws in England, and they influenced the common law both in its creation and thereafter. So the old, chthonic law got a new and vigorous means of enforcement and the re-surfaced roman law made perhaps its first real conquests in the new Europe. As revelation provided new garb for old law in other traditions, so the common law lawyers approved other ideas in limited and qualified form. Roman law was widely known. Lanfranc of Pavia, William the Conqueror's 'right-hand man', argued for the compatibility of roman and pre-conquest law.[28] A Lombard civilian, Vacarius, taught roman law extensively in the twelfth century.[29] Bracton used roman notions of real and personal actions to create

---

[26] See infra, *Formal limits and informal accommodation.*

[27] See the discussion of various forms of trespass on the case, infra, *Changing secreted law.*

[28] Pollock and Maitland, *History of English Law* (1898) at 77.

[29] F. de Zulueta and P. Stein, *The Teaching of Roman Law in England around 1200* (London: Selden Soc., 1990), notably at p. xxiii (Vacarius' main text, the Liber Pauperum, designed for those, still with us today, who 'could not face, or could not afford, the full texts'). On the influence of Vacarius and the role of roman law between 1150 and 1250, notably in relation to the works of Glanvill and Bracton, see W. Holdsworth, *Some Makers of English Law* (Cambridge: Cambridge Univ. Press, 1966) at 20, 21 (roman law as *ratio scripta* and not *jus scriptum*; decline of the influence of Bracton from the fourteenth century because practitioners became incapable of understanding roman law); G. Keeton, *The Norman Conquest and the Common Law* (London: Ben, 1966) at 71 ff.; P. Vinogradoff, *Roman Law in Medieval Europe* (Cambridge/New York: Speculum Historiae/Barnes & Noble, 1968) at 97; P. Stein, *The Character and Influence of the Roman Civil Law* (London/Ronceverte, W. Va.: Hambledon Press, 1988) at 167–85; Kiralfy, *Potter's Historical Introduction to English Law* (1958) at 632–5; van Caenegem, *Birth of English Common Law* (1988) at 101 (notaby on the 'non-automatic' character of the use of roman law); Q. Breen, 'The Twelfth Century Revival of the Roman Law'

notions of real and personal property, concepts unique to the common law.[30] Old, shared concepts of seisin were rejected as common law courts individualized, relations between land and its masters, in keeping with new civilian and canonical teaching.[31] The writ of novel disseisin would have its origins, for some, in the actio spolii of canon law, itself derived from the Roman interdict unde vi.[32] Until the end of the thirtheenth century efforts were made to link the writ of right to the notion of proprietas and the possessory assizes to that of possession.[33] So there was never a reception of roman law in England, in the sense of an incorporation en bloc of roman rules, as occurred in Germany. Yet there are many identifiable Roman ideas in the common law, worked over, massaged and put to work in different ways and in different language. Once this process has started, there is a certain, underlying compatibility, in spite of differences. Between a writ system and continental, substantive law, there is no fundamental incommensurability. Nor is there incommensurability between a writ system and revealed law. So talmudic law in turn exercised great influence on the development of the common law from the eleventh century. The common law was, in its origins, largely a law of land. Excluded, however, from farming and land-holding, jewish people had turned to commerce, and the resulting, talmudic, commercial law was highly developed. When English commerce began to emerge, talmudic practices, known because of jewish-gentile commercial relations, were a natural model for common law development.[34]

(1945) 24 Or. L. Rev. 244 at 282 ff; Woodbine, 'Origins of Action of Trespass' (1924), above, at 812–15; F. Wieacker, 'The Importance of Roman Law for Western Civilization and Western Legal Thought' (1981) 4 Boston Coll. Int. and Comp. L. Rev. 257 at 260; H. Berman, 'The Origins of Western Legal Science' (1977) 90 Harv. L. Rev. 894 at 899.

[30] Vinogradoff, *Roman Law in Medieval Europe* (1968), above, at 14, 15; and see D. Seipp, 'Bracton, the Year Books, and the "Transformation of Elementary Legal Ideas" in the Early Common Law' (1989) 7 Law and Hist. Rev. 175. Glanvill's earlier treatise has recently been described, in thought and form, as 'more in accord with the sensibilities of Angevin-age continentals and continentally trained Englishmen than with native forms': B. O'Brien, 'The Becket Conflict and the Invention of the Myth of Lex Non Scripta' in Bush and Wijffels, *Learning the Law* (1999), above, 1 at 15.

[31] The result left the way open for Equity's intervention and creation of the trust. See the discussion below, this Chapter, *The practice of comparison*.

[32] Vinogradoff, *Roman Law in Medieval Europe* (1968), above, at 98, 99; Woodbine, 'Origins of Action of Trespass' (1924), above, at 807. Prof. van Caenegem does not agree, for chronological reasons, but admits that the roman law of property would have influenced the development of basic concepts. van Caenegem, *Birth of English Common Law* (1988) at 387–90.

[33] See van Caenegem, *Royal Writs* (1972), above, at 311.

[34] See generally J. Rabinowitz, 'The Influence of Jewish Law on the Development of the Common Law' in L. Finkelstein, *The Jews: Their History, Culture and Religion*, 3rd edn., vol. I (New York: Harper and Row, 1960) at 823, detailing reliance on talmudic models in matters of execution against land (the statute of elegit), recognizance, general release ('from the beginning of the world', reflecting the jewish calendar), warranty of real property, dower, mortgage, conditional or penal bonds, trial by jury (initially by consent, as with the talmudic lay tribunal; language of 'putting oneself' on the jury found in talmudic records) and possibly even in the notion of the supremacy of the 'law of the land'. For acknowledgement of the talmudic influence, see E. H. Burn, *Cheshire's Modern Law of Real Property*, 12th edn. (London: Butterworths, 1976) at 804, n. 2 (chapter omitted in subsequent edns.).

# A COMMUNAL LAW

A country can be conquered militarily but should not be governed militarily. So the Normans incorporated the local jury into the working of their new, modern, royal courts. Yet the common law they set in motion was communal in many other ways. Even given military conquest (some were to say legal conquest is another thing),[35] it was not a brutal case of imposition of a conqueror's law. This came to be thought of as a possibility in later times, when law was only writing, but in the eleventh century you just couldn't think in terms of creating a new 'system' of law, or effecting legal change in large batches. How could you get rid of all the local, informal traditions, nesting here and there in the countryside? And with what? The process of insinuating a common law into a vigorous, and not very friendly, society, was a major undertaking, to be pursued on many fronts.

## FORMAL LIMITS AND INFORMAL ACCOMMODATION

The common law was very much held in check by its originators. Its courts did not lay claim to large areas of exclusive jurisdiction, though they were available if people chose to use them. More obviously, the writ system limited the reach of the common law to that which received royal approval. So other sensibilities could be protected by the old and always useful technique of inertia, and there is much evidence that the congealing of the process of granting writs was due to pressure by feudal lords, who had their own courts to protect. So like roman law, but unlike all the others, there were formal, internal limits on the growth and reach of the common law, limits which its judges rightly felt incapable of overcoming. They had authority which was royal, beyond it they had nothing, and there was much which was evidently beyond it. Like the jus commune of Europe, the common law of England was therefore suppletive law and not binding law. Its judgments were of course binding, once jurisdiction had been invoked, but there was no sense of binding everyone in the kingdom with a corpus of fixed rules. This would have obvious consequences for any identity to be derived from the existence of a common law.

Since the common law was necessarily and formally limited, it left much room for other types of law and other types of social glue. In this it had little in common with talmudic law or islamic law, nor for that matter with chthonic law. So the separation of law and morals is not simply a philosophical construction in common law history; it was just the way things were and in large measure had to be. Nor could morality inform and flesh out the common law once it came into being, as it was arguably to do in the civil law; the procedural thicket was protection not only

---

[35] See below, this Chapter, *Right reason.*

against roman law but against invocation of higher orders. There wasn't even much place for law professors. Jesus would have approved.[36]

So the old chthonic law continued to be applied as in the old pre-conquest Hundred Courts, now in the local, feudal courts and by juries in the royal courts. Local people couldn't object much to royal justice if they themselves controlled the decisions, and reliance on local ways gave needed legitimacy to the royal process. With the new relations between popes and kings extending throughout Europe from the eleventh century, formal ecclesiastical courts assumed jurisdiction over matters of family law, successions, even defamation, without transgressing any necessary jurisdiction of royal courts. Thereafter relations between ecclesiastical and common law courts were remarkably amiable, a process facilitated by clerics sitting as common law judges.[37]

Royal courts did, however, throw a web of 'natural' justice over the assembly of courts and institutions of the realm. Since they were available, they could be approached in the event of miscarriage of justice, or excess of jurisdiction, elsewhere. Their intervention in such cases would present no threat, however, to the competence of the other tribunal, nor to the law it applied. Indeed, supervision can be seen as reinforcing the true law and the true jurisdiction of the supervised court. The foundations of the present administrative law jurisdiction of common law courts is found in this process. As a result the common law courts still remain more distant from the merits than the administrative law courts of continental jurisdictions. The supervisory power was eventually to extend far beyond occasional prohibitions addressed to ecclesiastical authority, and to the full range of state agencies, but there remains a healthy respect for first-instance adjudication in the entire process of common law review ('deference' is what they now call it).[38] Much of the

[36] On Jesus and the teachers of the law, see above, Ch. 4, *Talmud and corruption*.

[37] On the level of civility and mutual respect, see W. R. Jones, 'Relations of the Two Jurisdictions: Conflict and Cooperation in England during the Thirteenth and Fourteenth Centuries' (1970) 7 St. Med. & Renais. Hist. (O. S.) 77; W. Bassett, 'Canon Law and the Common Law' (1978) 29 Hastings L. J. 1383 at 1407 ff.; and on the process of 'compromise' in tricky situations, such as clerical common law judges having to participate in condemnations to death, see R. H. Helmholz, 'Conflicts between Religious and Secular Law: Common Themes in the English Experience, 1250–1640' (1991) 12 Cardozo L. Rev. 707, notably at 718 (the clerics simply withdrew; judges can always recuse themselves). Relations were also facilitated by frequent appearance by ecclesiastical lawyers in common law courts, acting as witnesses on points of spiritual law (ibid., at 723) and by the general type of process followed in ecclesiastical courts, which placed great emphasis on conciliation and particularity of cases, submerging any notion of formal rules (which could conflict with other formal rules) in the endless possibilities of 'factual' resolution of cases, recalling the islamic process (see above, Ch. 6, *Qadi justice and mufti learning*), as well as that of the common law itself (see below, this Chapter, *Right reason*). On the ecclesiastical procedure, see C. Donahue, 'Roman Canon Law in the Medieval English Church: Stubbs vs. Maitland Re-Examined After 75 Years in the Light of Some Records from the Church Courts' (1974) 72 Mich. L. Rev. 647 at 705. Ecclesiastical adjudicators, of course, had the same problems of mutual accommodation as common law judges, notably with local, chthonic law. See, e.g., H. Pryce, *Native Law and the Church in Medieval Wales* (Oxford: Clarendon Press, 1993).

[38] On review of ecclesiastical courts see Helmholz, 'Early Enforcement of Uses' (1979), above; R. H. Helmholz, 'The Writ of Prohibition to Court Christian before 1500' (1981) 43 Med. St. 297; G. B. Flahiff, 'The Writ of Prohibition to Court Christian in the Thirteenth Century' (1944, 1945) 6, 7 Med. St. 261, 229; for expansion of

reserve of common law judges may have been due to the paucity of their ranks; but then this itself may have been due to a larger vision of the necessity of common law reserve. For whatever reason, there was great reserve, even to the extent of leaving room for the emergence of still further courts, notably those of Admiralty and Equity. Their later emergence is profoundly related to the notion of change in a common law tradition.[39]

## COMMUNAL RELATIONS

The communal character of the common law manifested itself in ways other than use of the jury and accommodation with other institutions. It reached into the manner of expression and functioning of the common law itself. Since the common law was limited and distinct from morality, its limits were in large measure societal limits, though formally (and negatively) expressed by the lacunae of the writs. The common law, and the other laws, had their place, and while it could not be said that this flowed from some explicitly recognized principle, it worked itself out in the play of different institutions and in relations with the chthonic, feudal world. The common law therefore had to express itself in terms of its surrounding society. To do otherwise would be to risk non-recognition, and non-acceptance. It had to reflect the society to be recognized as a part of it. Expressed otherwise, expressed in autonomous terms or roman terms, it would fail the test of discreet insinuation. So, even today, the common law is often expressed in language so historical in character as to be closer to talmudic or islamic law than to civil law. It could not, and did not, subsequently modernize itself, in terms of overall expression.

So there is still a law of torts (the plural is important) since there were no general principles of liability in England, only given wrongs, as in talmudic, roman and islamic law. The writ of trespass covered harm *directly* caused, which is different from harm *intentionally* caused, since there is immediate communal sense of directness, though little of intention. Other torts concerned fire, or trespass by cattle (direct enough, if you know cattle) or escape from land of dangerous commodities. It has subsequently proven difficult in the extreme to push the law of torts to the fields of non-patrimonial or purely economic damage. To the extent a law of contract developed,[40] it had to emerge *from* the facts it had to regulate, a natural conclusion from what had actually happened, so if the parties had paid for something, provided consideration, it followed they should have it. Juries could work

the review power to state agencies, notably and initially over sewer commissions, see L. Jaffe and E. Henderson, 'Judicial Review and the Rule of Law: Historical Origins' (1956) 72 LQR 345; and for the emergence of a continental private law/public law distinction in English law, see J. Allison, *A Continental Distinction in the Common Law: an Historical and Comparative Perspective on English Public Law* (Oxford: Clarendon Press, 1996) (distinction argued as inappropriate for traditional common law jurisdiction, lacking developed theory of state, systemic sense of law, separation of judiciary from administration, and investigative procedure).

[39] See below, this Chapter, *Changing secreted law*.
[40] On the process, see below, ibid.

with these ideas; they already knew them. They couldn't be given instruction in the normative effect of acts of will.

Land was not owned in the common law, but held and enjoyed. It still is, at least in formal expression. So there has never been, in the common law, an absolutist, legal concept of human mastery over land, no notion of dominium or ownership. Use of land is defined in relational terms, all land being 'held' from the initial grantor, the Crown, in a way permitting indefinite enjoyment and succession. If you buy a house in the common law world today (unbelievable though this is to civilian lawyers) you become, not the owner, but the holder of a fee simple (fief simple), the highest form of free holding of land the feudal system allowed. It defined your *relations* with others in holding land. And the notion of seisin is still alive, the old, direct, God-given form of enjoyment and use, long after its disappearance (as saisine, gewere) in the romanized world. Common law judges thus took the common law along paths readily recognizable. If they could not find the way, they would not decide. Absent clear enough law, beyond themselves, there was no obligation to decide, so they didn't.[41]

### RIGHT REASON

Juries didn't leave any record of how they thought, but there is written evidence of the judicial rationality used in the common law, in the process of defining the boundaries of the writs. Coke, in his struggle with the Crown in the seventeenth century (and Francis Bacon appears here again) spoke of 'the right reason of the law'[42] and by this did not mean the emergent legal rationality of Bacon and the Cujadists,[43] but an 'artificial perfection of reason,' one 'gotten by long study, observation and experience' and derived 'from many succession of ages', such that no one should presume out of 'private reason . . . to be wiser than the law, which is the perfection of reason'.[44] So right reason is rooted in a contextual tradition, an interstitial rationality, which moves within existing principles and categories and

---

[41] See, on the judicial non-decision, Baker, 'English Law and Renaissance' (1985) at 58 ('If, after all that, they still had qualms—they did nothing. Judicial inaction was not seen as a dereliction of duty, as it would be today, because it encouraged and helped parties to settle their differences when the merits were balanced').

[42] Co. Litt., f. 183b. Coke borrowed the expression from Cicero, while bending it to his purpose. For Cicero, 'a true law namely right reason . . . is in accordance with nature, applies to all men and is unchangeable and eternal.' *De Republica* III, xxii.

[43] On the role of the continental-trained Bacon in advancing both science and civilian thinking, see above, Ch. 5, *Changing the idea of change*. Bacon sided with the Crown and civilian thinking, and said that the judges of the common law should be 'lions, but yet lions under the throne, being circumspect that they do not check or oppose any points of sovereignty.' Coke was not impressed. On the drama of the times see C. D. Bowen, *The Lion and the Throne: the Life and Times of Sir Edward Coke (1552–1634)* (Boston: Little, Brown, 1957); D. Coquillette, *Francis Bacon* (Stanford: Stanford Univ. Press, 1992), notably at 195 for Bacon's use of the lions metaphor and for the famous passage cited above as an addition in 1625 to earlier work; and for continuing efforts of rational deduction of law, from basic features of human life, J. Finnis, *Natural Law and Natural Rights* (Oxford: Clarendon Press, 1980).

[44] Co. Litt., f. 97b.

without imposing conclusions broader than those already, and explicitly, authorized. It is qiyas, analogical reasoning, legitimated by consensus, or ijma,[45] as in
islamic law (though here in no way conclusive, or definite). There were obvious
reasons for this rationality being that of the common law. It flowed from its own
manner of expression, necessarily rooted in societal phenomena, and from the
absence of any higher authority (intellectual or positive) justifying more far-
reaching forms of deduction and construction. There were only the judges, law-
seekers and law-finders themselves, but whose decisions could not bind, could not
serve as points of departure, since there were so few of them, and all were colleagues. Who could 'bind' a colleague, of equal talent, equal authority?

So the common law grew through the accumulation of precedent, though no
concept of stare decisis—binding authority attaching formally to each decision—
could possibly have existed throughout most of its history.[46] Cases were part of a
body of common experience, to be used in further reasoning, but in no way constituting unalterable law. There was a notion of res judicata, once the jury had spoken,
but not much more. The common law process, and common law rationality, had
much in common with the ecclesiastical process, and the commonality of their
processes facilitated relations one with the other. Neither set of judges elevated their
work to the level of fixed rule; neither proceeded thereafter by way of ineluctable
deduction from their own previous work; neither placed much premium on uniformity of result. Case reporting in the common law world reflected this situation; it
was haphazard in the extreme, and the expression 'chaos with an index' has been
used.[47] If cases were reported, the reports usually ended with '. . . and so to judgment'. Nobody, beyond the parties, cared who won.[48] Nor did the judge's rationality
impinge on local, chthonic law. It even served to perpetuate it, in the form of jury
verdicts, and ran with it in the societal formulation of the writs. So the common law
set itself up as the law of the realm, pre-dating even the conquest (which was only
military) and re-inforced itself by this process of intellectual self-denial.[49]

A law of relations, of mutual obligations, is not a law which concentrates its
attention on the legal powers or interests of the individual. It is not a law of rights,
and the notion of the subjective right (as they say in civilian language) played little
or no role in the history of the common law in England. The existence of rights in

[45] See above, Ch. 6, *The shari'a: sources* and *Subtle change.*

[46] See G. J. Postema, 'Roots of our Notion of Precedent' in Goldstein (ed.), *Precedent in Law* (1987) at 22;
more generally, with ref., M. Lobban, *Common Law and English Jurisprudence* (1991); Lieberman, *Province of
Legislation Determined* (1989).

[47] The expression is that of Sir Thomas Holland, cited by N. Marsh, Review (1981) 30 Int. & Comp. Law Q.
486 at 488. The remark parallels Alan Watson's description of the praetor's edict and the Digest of Justinian as
'chaotic'. See above, Ch. 5, *The self-denial of roman law.*

[48] See T. F. T. Plucknett, *Early English Legal Literature* (Cambridge: Cambridge Univ. Press, 1958) at 103, 104
('What the judgment was, nobody knew and nobody cared').

[49] On denial of conquest in law (and change only in the person of the king) as a doctrine of the common
law, see J. G. A. Pocock, *The Ancient Constitution and the Feudal Law: a Study of English Historical Thought in
the Seventeenth Century,* 1st edn. (Cambridge: Cambridge Univ. Press, 1957) at 16, 17, 68, 69, 126.

English law has been denied well into the twentieth century,[50] and resistance in contemporary England to a bill of rights, or a right to privacy, is explained as much by unease with rights in general as it is to unease about their entrenchment or love of the reporting habits of the English press. Even with the incorporation of the European Convention on Human Rights into English law, the courts will not be able to strike down primary legislation, being authorized only to issue declarations of incompatibility between particular laws and Convention rights.[51] The English experience thus did not parallel the continental one, in which rights were developed as an important instrument in overcoming feudal hierarchy. The English judiciary might have had something to do with this, since they were never the object of physical attack (except for the odd brickbat, which the contempt power expeditiously dealt with). They were never seen as part of a hostile and distant autocracy in the way, say, the French judiciary was.[52] It was not a perfect judiciary, and its status was to change, but it had done a remarkable job of staying out of trouble, and advancing the idea of a common law. Rights were not necessary in doing this, and would even have presented a jarring, discordant note in the process of faithfully reflecting the society. There was inequality in all of this, and in the beginning villeiny (another word for another kind of slavery), but the society had lots of instruments other than law to bring about change in itself. And the common law could itself be altered in ways contributing to equality, liberty and right, without renouncing its explicitly communal character.

## INCREMENTAL CHANGE

A common law tradition, with the judge as its leading figure, thus emerged in the first century and a half following the Norman conquest. It is a tradition still recognizable today, at least in terms of the ongoing importance of the judge and judicial decisions. Yet like the ship of the Argonauts rebuilt in its entirety, there are few constituent parts of the original structure still remaining.[53] It's still the same ship and it's still the

---

[50] F. H. Lawson, ' "Das subjektive Recht" in the English Law of Torts' in *Selected Essays*, vol. I (Amsterdam/New York: North-Holland, 1977) 176 at 179, 182; G. Samuel, ' "Le droit subjectif" and English Law' (1987) 46 Cambr. L. J. 264 at 267, 286. This all in spite of the political declarations of the Bill of Rights of 1689.

[51] Lord Irvine of Lairg, 'The Development of Human Rights in Britain under an Incorporated Convention on Human Rights' [1998] P. L. 221 at 225. Cf., however, indicating the contemporary importance of international and European human rights instruments, C. McCrudden and G. Chambers, *Individual Rights and the Law in Britain* (Oxford: Clarendon Press, 1994).

[52] On violence against the French judiciary during and following the French revolution, and the entire (abhorrent) notion of a 'gouvernement des juges' see above, Ch. 5, *The centrality of the person and the growth of rights* and *Law as reason's instrument*.

[53] The analogy is that of Sir Matthew Hale, who insisted, unlike Coke, on the ability of the common law to change and adapt. See P. Stein, 'Legal History: The British Perspective,' Rev. hist. dr. fr. étr. 1994. 71 at 74.

common law, but a twelfth-century English lawyer would find many surprises in the contemporary world of the common law, both in its society of origin, and beyond.

## CHANGING SECRETED LAW

Both roman law and twelfth century continental law were accustomed to a limited concept of change. Roman law had changed, more precisely it had *been* changed, by Roman lawyers, and in the pan-European renaissance of the eleventh and twelfth centuries much of the old, chthonic law had also been changed. The common law took part in this process, and the Normans must have had a sense they were changing things in their reforms of the administration of justice. There was as yet no concept of changing the world, of the world as inanimate fact awaiting re-shaping, but law at least was amenable to some measure of re-forming. So we are again some distance from the chthonic world, while in the idea of a common law somehow autonomous, unto itself, any restraints of religion became rather margin-alized. Lawyers were likely to be religious people, but they practised religious law in the ecclesiastical courts, not in those of the Crown. Still, the chthonic world was very much present in the common law mind (which had to worry about local juries and occasionally about local courts). And there were all those other jurisdictions to keep in mind—nice people in all of them but not likely to disappear by the stroke of a pen. So while the Roman lawyers exercised a kind of self-denial in the extent of change they wrought, the common lawyers exercised a kind of necessary self-denial. The place they had was one of many, and it might take, say, eight hundred years to bring about a unified court system.[54] Inertia is not the best way to describe this state of affairs; it has more to do with equilibrium. And while the common law judges, with the prestige, wealth and cunning of the national government behind them, were ascendant forces, they had to tread rather softly. So change in the law could occur, recognized as such and brought about from within by the lawyers and judges, but it was necessarily incremental change.

Internal incremental change came about in the expression of the law and in its avoidance. There were many tricks and fictions, in the islamic manner. To avoid the (then) prohibition of interest, living security (le gage vivant) was used (the lender kept the land used as security, and the profit from it). The dead security (mortgage) came later, with the allowance of interest, such that borrowers could just pay the interest and keep the fruits of the land for themselves. Fictions were many; they overcame territorial limitations of the court (so Harfleur, in France, became notionally situate in the county of Kent) as well as the rigidity of the writs (to sue with the newer and more flexible writ of ejectment, confined to leasehold relations, a disseised owner could invent a lease, and bring action in the name of the famous tenant, John Doe). The fictions maintained existing law (which must be a good

---

[54] See below, this Chapter, *Changing fundamentals: procedure.*

thing), yet let everyone avoid it, for reasons considered entirely acceptable by every-one, including the judges. There were no more rigorous schools around to criticize them.[55] Categories of law were also recognized as of variable content. The fee simple of today is far from what it originally was, and now in effect is hard to distinguish from civilian ownership. And within the writs there was case, more precisely the action on the case, the action brought using the writ of trespass, alleging trespass, but alleging also that the circumstances of the particular case constituted a trespass, of sorts, so that trespass could extend to such civil wrongs as common law judges thought the common law should extend to. First, there was simple trespass, for direct infliction of damage (delict, if you wish to think civilly and in terms of intention), then trespass on the case for damage inflicted indirectly (the tree left on the road struck by the carriage, quasi-delict), then trespass on the case for an obligation assumed (indebitus assumpsit), such that by the sixteenth century the common law had gotten around to contractual obligation, at least where consider-ation existed, though breach of contract still exists as a kind of tort and lacks the independence of civilian notions of contract.[56] What the common law refused, or could not countenance, other courts would often pick up. If they responded to a petition for change, the common law did not have to. This too was a manner of change of the common law—contemplated by it, but left to others.

## CHANGING FUNDAMENTALS: PROCEDURE

Roman formulary procedure survived for about eight centuries; so did the writs and forms of action. If you have formal law, that people know they can get to, with formal sanctions, maybe this is the length of time which limited or restricted institutions can last. By then the differential in treatment—some get in, some don't, which is not the same thing as winners and losers—becomes too abrasive a phe-nomenon in society. Someone will start complaining in intelligent fashion, not about particular cases, but about general inadequacies. If the institutions outside the law are not capable of bearing the load they used to, law has to become open, neutral in access (at least formally) so old privileges are not automatically perpetu-ated. We don't seem to know who did the complaining in Rome; maybe the switch to open courts (extraordinary procedure becoming ordinary) was just somebody's pet project. In England the complainer was Jeremy Bentham, who complained about almost everything in England, and particularly about the courts. He even wanted to codify the common law, overstating, like all good reformers, the possible objectives of reform. If you couldn't codify the substantive law, as they did in

---

[55] On the fictions see L. Fuller, *Legal Fictions* (Stanford: Stanford Univ. Press, 1967).

[56] So in principle you could always allege tortious grounds of liability in case of breach of contract (choice of writ is the plaintiff's; breach of contract is a tort), as well as contractual grounds, though this is now beginning to be questioned, as it long has been in the civil law world (option or cumul). On the growth of assumpsit, see A. W. B. Simpson, *A History of the Common Law of Contract: the Rise of the Action of Assumpsit* (Oxford: Clarendon Press, 1975).

France, because there wasn't any, the only thing left was the procedure. This was the heart of the common law and if there were problems they were necessarily here. So the idea of changing the law, in some kind of fundamental way, necessarily meant changing the procedure, changing the writs and forms of action. This was done, of course, incrementally, over a half century, and in the dry, neutral-sounding language of procedure. Nobody would dream of talking about a revolution here, yet the effect on the common law was far greater than the effect of the political revolutions of France and the United States on the laws of those countries.[57]

The reforms essentially did three things. The first, in 1832, was to eliminate the requirement of a formal grant of a writ by the chancellor's office to inititate an action. Since the chancellor's office by now gave out writs almost as a matter of course, this really meant that action was conceptually freed from existing law. Whatever the possibilities of winning or losing, on whatever claim, suit could be brought. So the courts of the common law became open for the first time, as those of the continent had been for centuries and where it had become common practice to speak of a *right* of action. The substance of the right now existed in England, though nobody talked about it in these terms. After the practice of private issuance of writs (now just summonses to a defendant to appear, in standard form) had become established, the next step, in the mid-nineteenth century, was to tidy up. In the old pleadings you always had to state your writ and your form of action, that in which the action 'sounded', and the formal necessity of stating one's form of action had not been abolished by the new accessibility of the courts. People could sue, but their counsel still had to say, in writing and up front, before all the facts were known, on what ground they would eventually win. This was difficult, often impossible, and amendment a strange and mistrusted concept. So after open courts we got open pleading, or fact pleading ('code pleading' in the US, where by now there were codes of civil procedure), so people could just state their case (as in the old action on the case) and expect the law (now necessarily substantive, awaiting application, and no longer secreted) to be applied. And since now all manner of fact could be pleaded, in search of law, the jury could not really be expected to handle everything and became optional. It also became, very rapidly, highly exceptional in civil cases (except, again, in the US, where it had been constitutionally protected).

So from the mid-nineteenth century, common law judges had to decide cases, that is, decide cases on the merits (as we can now say) and by application of substantive law. Where they got the law from, and how they did it, is the whole story of the emergence of substantive common law. Part of the story is borrowing law from elsewhere (even God did this)[58] but another part is the famous process of converting old procedural rules into new substantive law. In Maitland's wonderful

[57] Thus in the USA the forms of action survived well into the nineteenth century and began to be abolished only from the New York Field Code of 1848.

[58] See, for islamic revelation of law previously known, above, Ch. 6, *The umma and its protection*; and for the common law process, below, this Chapter, *The practice of comparison*.

language, 'The forms of action we have buried, but they still rule us from their graves.'[59] This wasn't just sleight of hand. If you think of the writs and forms of action as a kind of visible mould, shaping though concealing the secreted law, removal of the mould leaves the revealed substance beneath. Where you could previously get to the jury, and win if they believed you, it can now be said that you are entitled as a matter of substantive law (or more probably, that the defendant is obliged towards you as a matter of substantive law). So though the procedural reforms are fundamental in the history of the common law, they also provided a bridge between the old processual world and the new substantive world. The new substantive law bears all the marks, and uses much of the language, of the old writs. The judges still needed to borrow, however, because the writs only went so far. And since judges were now deciding cases, the possibility of judicial error had become possible, on the merits, in the process of matching now distinct concepts of fact and substantive law. So a court of appeal, like those of the continent, was required, and created in 1875. You even had two levels of appeal, again as on the continent, since, with permission, you could go beyond the Court of Appeal to the House of Lords. Not only were the relations between law and procedure essentially those of the civil law world, so now the structure of courts of general jurisdiction assumed the same three-level structure as that of continental courts (with the old, lush jungle of first-instance courts being largely fused as well).

These fundamental, incremental reforms did not otherwise affect the role of the judge or the role of the barrister in the litigation process. Procedure remained adversarial, with the barrister enjoying great latitude in the conduct of litigation. While the judge now had to pronounce on the totality of a case, it remained true that the judge assumed no immediate responsibility for the adducing of evidence, nor for the overall management of litigation. So the judicial role was essentially limited to the trial process, and any incidental preliminary motions, and did not involve any more active participation in a case. Some now justify this in terms of judicial objectivity and impartiality, but the need for justification has emerged only since the nineteenth century reforms. Some century and a half after the reforms, their full effect has not yet been felt, and the role of the judge and counsel in litigation is now the object of profound debate, and further reform.[60]

Through all of this, however, the formal status of the judge remained what it had been since the Act of Settlement of 1701, when judicial nominations ceased to be made at the pleasure of the Crown and became quam diu se bene gesserint or during good behaviour.[61] This is perhaps the single most important element of the common law tradition, towards which it built in the first six centuries, and which has sustained it thereafter. Nomination quam diu se bene gesserint means that a

---

[59] Maitland, *Forms of Action* (1954) at 2.
[60] See below, this Chapter, *Common law and nation-states*.
[61] See Lederman, 'Independence of Judiciary' (1956); S. Shetreet, *Judges on Trial: a Study of the Appointment and Accountability of the English Judiciary* (Amsterdam: North-Holland, 1976).

judge cannot be dismissed except by nearly impossible procedures (joint addresses to the two legislative Houses) and this has never occurred in England, nor indeed in much of the common law world. With judicial nomination coming closer to the end of a legal career than its beginning, there is no control of the career of a judge (as on the continent) and no effective means of dismissal. There are further elaborate guarantees of maintenance of salary, depending on the common law jurisdiction. In England there is also no present means of discipline of superior court judges, who also enjoy civil immunity in the exercise of their functions.[62] There is no prise à partie in the common law.

Why a common law tradition came to incorporate a formal principle of the independence of its judges is a large and interesting question. The principle exists, in such form, in no other tradition, so it is very much the product of everything in the history of the common law, which singled out the judge and the judge's decision as of fundamental importance, and this since the arrival of the Normans. There were also immediate political reasons, and the independence of the judiciary was clearly part of the overall constitutional struggle, and negotiations, of the seventeenth century, when the judges allied themselves with Parliament against royal executive authority. Beyond the historical reasons, however, it should be pointed out that the independence of the common law judiciary was acquired at an interesting time. It was the time of the enlightenment, a time of unleashing of all the forces of human creativity, imagination and talent. In the social and political world this meant giving direction to all things, yet here, in the common law judiciary, was creation of an institution incapable of direction (even higher judges could do nothing with lower, tenured judges). Moreover, in enlightenment thought, enlightened debate could yield consensus, and the judge could be part of this (largely political) process and need not enjoy any particular status. This is largely the position of judges elsewhere in the world, even in parts of the common law world, yet ultimately the common law, in creating an independent judiciary, hedged its bets on the enlightenment and on the prospects for rational consensus. Judges beyond the process of reasoned debate might still be necessary; if this turned out to be so, there would be still greater need for their independence, since in an enlightened, less contextual world, there would be still greater pressure for particular decisions to be made, vital interests to be protected. Yet the independent judge is free to pursue the law, and need enforce, as enforcer, no one else's law. So independent judges come to apply the law, not because they are bound to, in any positive, legal sense (they are not bound to do anything, including the deciding of cases) but because they commit themselves to an ethic of independently administering justice, within the cadre of the law. They are freed to be law-seekers, and not law-appliers. They are self-disciplining loose cannons, dangerous for systems.

---

[62] For variations in the common law world, however, see below, *Common law and nation-states.*

## CHANGING THOUGHT

Legal thought in the common law world was profoundly impressed with the need for integration with society, so doctrinal initiatives were few and the more impressive when they existed, as in the case of Bracton and Littleton in the thirteenth and fifteenth centuries, then Coke again in the seventeenth century and Blackstone in the eighteenth. This judicial and doctrinal restraint was entirely compatible with chthonic and religious thought, so necessity also had the advantage of virtue. The internal growth of the common law, however, and the upheaval of the nineteenth century, could not have occurred without important intellectual shifts. On the continent, the major shift which occurred was that of the enlightenment, best typified by Cujas in the sixteenth century (roman law as fact, to be mined in constructing law of France, using comparative law as instrument)[63] and this was also, by and large, the century of the extension of the common law writ of trespass to contractual obligation, so a lot of thinking was going on in the world of writs. Professor Baker situates the source of English innovative thinking in the Inns of Court, from the period between 1490 to 1540 (even just a bit ahead of Cujas) and the process was one of a 'seemingly universal desire for more detailed law', which 'may have something to do with Renaissance humanism'.[64] Coke thereafter wrote *on* Littleton, and the shift is one towards the deductive, the filling out in more systematic manner of the implications of the old law. Comparative law also was taking place in England, with extensive research and writing on relations between common, civil and ecclesiastical law.[65] A lot of information was floating around for potential use. By the eighteenth century Blackstone's full statement of the common law purported to reproduce much of the old law, much of the inherently legitimate 'custom of the realm', but the enterprise was profoundly marked by systematization, roman classifications and a sense of law being national.[66] Blackstone was ambiguous about many things, but not about the idea of setting out the law.[67]

By the nineteenth century English thought had developed a large measure of compatibility with that of the continent. If Bentham's project of codification was

---

[63] See above, Ch. 5, *Changing the idea of change.*

[64] Baker, 'English Law and Renaissance' (1985) at 46.

[65] See generally D. Coquillette, *The Civilian Writers of Doctors' Commons: Three Centuries of Juristic Innovation in Comparative, Commercial and International Law* (Berlin: Duncker & Humblot, 1988); B. Levack, *The Civil Lawyers in England, 1603–1641: a Political Study* (Oxford: Clarendon Press, 1973); on the influence of Henry Spelman and John Selden on the 'flowering' of 17th-century literature, 'under the belated influence of continental humanism', see Stein, 'Legal History', above, at 73; and for ongoing influence of continental university training on English lawyers, J. Woolfson, *Padua and the Tudors: English Students in Italy 1485–1603* (Toronto/Buffalo: Univ. of Toronto Press, 1998), ch. 2 ('Students of Law').

[66] On subsequent autonomous statements of English law by doctrinal writing, avoiding 'incursions into both history and other legal traditions' and concealing 'the historical origin of much of what they transmit as homespun law', see A. W. B. Simpson, 'Innovation in Nineteenth Century Contract Law' (1975) 91 LQR 247 at 256, 257.

[67] See Cairns, 'Blackstone' (1984), notably at 350–1, on Roman influence; yet on the subtlety of Blackstone's writing, see A. Alschuler, 'Rediscovering Blackstone' (1996) 145 U. Pa L. Rev. 1.

simply an impossibility, the *general* idea of national, positive, constructed law now received a great deal of support, subject to ongoing resistance to the role of logic as a common law instrument. The common law itself, however, could develop its own form of logic—a type of compromise—notably through the emergence of stare decisis, the idea that each decision of the court would represent a rule of law, somewhat similar to an article of a code, such that a system of positive rules could exist in England, the faithful, indigenous counterpart of the continental versions of the same underlying idea. So the nineteenth century saw two important ideas emerge, that of judges actually making law (and binding law at that)[68] and of systematic, doctrinal treatises explicating the law of the judges.[69] There was a lot of ambiguity in this, since if judges are free and make law there are some problems with them being bound by pre-existing law. Yet there was enough coherence for people to begin to think of a common law 'system'[70] and English legal philosophy, which had come to exist, arguably made advances on continental theories of pure and positive law.[71] Case law could be shown to be every bit as systematic as legislation. There have been a lot of changes in common law theory and practice since the nineteenth century peak of legal construction, while stare decisis, notably, is not what it was.[72] Yet the rationalist tradition became firmly anchored in the common law in the nineteenth century, if not earlier in the sixteenth. More recently, this last century has been defined as 'a century of change', the change being an 'intellectual transformation' resulting from 'an interaction between the literature of the law and legal education' such that the 'paradigm of the common law as solely judge-made, so far as it survives, has become grossly misleading'.[73] The emphasis is here on doctrinal contribution to the law; there is now also legislation, as to which more must be said.[74]

The common law, like the civil law, is therefore broadly compatible with contemporary science. Both are seen as positive endeavours, and the physical world has lost much of its sacred character. Francis Bacon may have been continental-trained,

[68] For stages in the growth of stare decisis, including the notion of 'binding' law, through the 19th century, see J. Evans, 'Change in the Doctrine of Precedent during the Nineteenth Century' in Goldstein (ed.), *Precedent in Law* (1991), above, at 45–54, 68; and more generally R. Cross and J. W. Harris, *Precedent in English Law*, 4th edn. (Oxford: Clarendon Press, 1991), notably at 24, 25 (precedents not being followed as late as 1869). At the same time, the judgments of the courts lengthened considerably. See J. L. Goutal, 'Characteristics of Judicial Style in France, Britain and the USA' (1976) 24 Am. J. Comp. Law 43 at 58, 61–5.

[69] See A. W. B. Simpson, 'The Rise and Fall of the Legal Treatise: Legal Principles and the Forms of Legal Literature' (1981) 48 U Chi. L. Rev. 632.

[70] See J. Raz, *The Concept of a Legal System: an Introduction to the Theory of Legal System*, 2nd edn. (Oxford/New York: Clarendon Press/Oxford Univ. Press, 1980), contributing equally to the civilian debate on the same theme, discussed above, Ch. 5, *Revolutions, systems, language and interpretation*.

[71] See notably Hart, *Concept of Law*, (1994), also discussed in the context of civilian theory of positive law, above, Ch. 5, *Positive law and positive science*.

[72] See below, this Chapter, *Common law and nation-states*.

[73] Birks, 'Adjudication and interpretation in common law' (1994) at 159.

[74] See below, this Chapter, *Common law and nation-states*.

but he was an English lawyer.[75] So too is there a current idea of the law as language, and vast attention given to the impact of this idea on the process of interpretation.[76] And since the common law can now be thought of systematically, revolution against the definable system is also a conceptual possibility. The common law has therefore known revolution, which brings us to relations within the larger world of the common law, and with the larger world.

## COMMON LAW AND UNCOMMON LAW

A common law tradition must today be highly flexible and accommodating if it is to continue to provide some measure of commonality to the diverse legal orders which have been associated with it, at one time or another. From an islamic or talmudic perspective, there may appear to be schools of common law scattered about the world and, as in other complex, major traditions, some measure of internal tolerance is necessary to maintain an overarching tradition. So, as there may be islams, so there may be common laws, though neither idea is uncontroversial. And since a common law tradition has diversified internally, its relations with other legal traditions have also intensified. There are therefore the ever-present questions of identity and exchange, though there are also major questions of domination and corruption, which coincide with similar questions concerning the civil law and its relations with the world.

### COMMON LAW AND NATION-STATES

The common law expanded throughout much of the world as a result of the British empire, and this process of military, economic and legal domination must be returned to. The result, however, was a kind of embedding of common law thinking in a large number of diverse societies around the world, many of whom are now loosely knit together in the Commonwealth and the Commonwealth Lawyers'

---

[75] See above, Ch. 5, *Positive law and positive science*.

[76] See P. Goodrich, *Reading the Law: A Critical Introduction to Legal Method and Techniques* (Oxford/New York: Blackwell, 1986); S. Fish, *Is there a Text in this Class? The Authority of Interpretive Communities* (Cambridge, Mass.: Harvard Univ. Press, 1980); J. B. White, *Heracles' Bow: Essays on the Rhetoric and Poetics of Law* (Madison, Wis: Univ. of Wisconsin Press, 1985); D. Klinck, *The Word of the Law: Approaches to Legal Discourse* (Ottawa: Carleton Univ. Press, 1992); O. Fiss, 'Objectivity and Interpretation' (1981–2) 34 Stan. L. Rev. 739; and for common foundations of civil and common law attitudes towards interpretation of legislation, P.-A. Côté, 'L'interprétation de la loi en droit civil et en droit statutaire: communauté de langue et différences d'accents' (1997) 31 Rev. jur. Thémis 45 (both civil and common law adopting principle of strict interpretation of texts derogating from a jus commune); R. Zimmermann, '*Statuta sunt stricte interpretanda?* Statutes and the Common Law: A Continental Perspective' [1997] Cambr. L. J. 315 (arguing for more liberal, collaborative principles of interpretation, as prevailing in contemporary German law).

Association, neither of which, however, is co-extensive with the common law world. What has happened, generally, is the marriage of the idea of a common law with that of multiple nation-states, and the marriage has been at times a difficult one. Yet a common law tradition lived with many legal orders during its development in England, so it may still be possible to speak of a single common law tradition, since the tradition demands far less in terms of compliance than do other traditions, notably islamic. So one can speak of islams, since deviations from such a demanding tradition are so important, yet a single common law tradition, since deviations don't matter much. The demands of the state may fit within a common law environment; they are much more difficult to square with the breadth and sanctity of islamic law. Yet the idea of a single common law tradition has been sorely tried, by national affirmation and national identities.

The diversity of opinion on the nature of a common law tradition in the world may be rooted in the ambiguity of the position of the common law in England. At some point an identifiable common law tradition had developed, though its relation with an English identity is far from clear. R. C. van Caenegem has concluded that 'because the Common Law had become part and parcel of her political constitution, an element of her national conscience and the foundation of her social order, England became an island in the Romanist sea'.[77] England, of course, with Scotland and Wales, was already an island, and the statement falls short of concluding that the common law was constitutive of English identity. Moreover, a common law tradition, with all those judicial loose cannons, could not play the same identifying role as other legal traditions, which extended to much more of life and often by way of previously given rules or principles. If you adhere to chthonic, talmudic, islamic or civil law, you have a pretty good idea of what this means, substantively. Adhering to a common law tradition was more difficult to do, if only because the common law was so wraith-like for much of its existence. And today the idea of British nationality is much more amorphous and diverse than that of European civil law countries,[78] and much less important for resolution of private law problems, domicile being the preferred criteria for application of different national laws in matters of personal status, family law, matrimonial property law and successions. The common law, though identifiable, is a weak identifier. It can float around the world, but in so doing it provides little reinforcement for national identities. There is therefore the same tendency as has existed in the civil law world (there in terms of the jus commune) for the common law to be nationalized for purposes of national identity. Unlike chthonic, talmudic or islamic law, western law is controllable and may be given national direction. This is what makes it what it is. Controlling judges, however, is a more difficult process than controlling legislation. Nationalizing the common law means doing something with common law judges, doing something to the tradition itself.

[77] van Caenegem, *Birth of English Common Law* (1988) at 105.
[78] L. Fransman, *British Nationality Law and the 1981 Act*, 2nd edn. (London: Fourmat, 1989).

This has happened most evidently, and deliberately, in the United States of America. Law in the United States is generally seen as adhering to a common law 'family',[79] but today this is far from obvious. In many respects US law represents a deliberate rejection of common law principle, with preference being given to more affirmative ideas clearly derived from civil law. These were not somehow reinvented in the United States but taken over directly from civilian sources in a massive process of change in adherence to legal information in the nineteenth century.[80] The entire process replicated the use of comparative law and foreign law which occurred in the process of national legal construction in continental Europe— Cujas in the new world. This was evident in substantive law, most particularly in the reception of the idea of rights, but still more evident in terms of structures and sources of law. Thus the common law was reconceptualized as a local, official product, as a 'means of fitting the common law into an emerging system of popular sovereignty'.[81] State judges could therefore not be independent, in the English sense (a denial of the claims of popular sovereignty), and a general pattern of judicial election emerged (though now reduced considerably in importance by subsequent reforms). State court citation patterns subsequently show a concentration on local law which closely parallels continental concepts of exclusivity of local sources.[82] And since each state had their judges and their common law, it followed in a federal

---

[79] David and Brierley, *Major Legal Systems* (1985) at 397 ff. Useful overviews of US law are found in Morrison (ed.), *Fundamentals of American Law* (1996); Levasseur, *droit des états-unis* (1990); A. E. Farnsworth, *An Introduction to the Legal System of the United States*, 3rd edn. (Dobbs Ferry, NY: Oceana 1996).

[80] See, as part of the expanding literature on the subject, P. Stein, 'The Attraction of the Civil Law in Post-Revolutionary America' (1966) 52 Va L. Rev. 403; W. Brison, 'The Use of Roman Law in Virginia Courts' (1984) 28 Am. J Legal Hist. 135; M. Hoeflich, *Roman and Civil Law and the Development of Anglo-American Jurisprudence in the Nineteenth Century* (Athens, Ga.: Univ. of Georgia Press, 1997); M. Hoeflich, 'John Austin and Joseph Story: Two Nineteenth Century Perspectives on the Utility of the Civil Law for the Common Lawyer' (1985) 29 Am. J. Legal Hist. 36; M. Hoeflich, 'Roman Law in American Legal Culture' (1992) 66 Tulane L. Rev. 1723; R. Helmholz, 'Use of the Civil Law in Post-Revolutionary American Jurisprudence' (1992) 66 Tulane L. Rev. 1649; J. Stychin, 'The Commentaries of Chancellor James Kent and the Development of an American Common Law' (1993) 37 Am. J Legal Hist. 440; J. Langbein, 'Chancellor Kent and the History of Legal Literature' (1993) 93 Col. L. Rev. 547; M. Reimann (ed.), *The Reception of Continental Ideas in the Common Law World* (Berlin: Duncker & Humblot, 1993); E. Wise, 'The Transplant of Legal Patterns' (1990) 38 Am. J. Comp. Law (Suppl.) 1. For continuation of the process well into the twentieth century see S. Riesenfeld, 'The Influence of German Legal Theory on American Law: The Heritage of Savigny and His Disciples' (1989) 37 Am. J. Comp. Law 1 (notably on highly abstract notion of 'secured transactions', alien to prior common law thinking).

[81] Horowitz, *Transformation of American Law* (1992) at 20, citing the 1798 essay of J. Root, *On the Common Law of Connecticut*. State law reports also emerged at the same time, as official repositories of state common law. On the process of 'Americanization' of the common law see Nelson, *Americanization of Common Law* (1975) and on its 'instrumentalization' see Horowitz, *Transformation of American Law* (1992).

[82] See J. Merryman, 'Toward a Theory of Citations: An Empirical Study of the Citation Practice of the California Supreme Court in 1950, 1960, and 1970' (1977) 50 Calif. Law Rev. 381, notably at 394–400 (citations to other state courts only some 10% of all citations; non-US citations less than 1%); L. M. Friedmann, R. A. Kagan, B. Cartwright and S. Wheeler, 'State Supreme Courts: A Century of Style and Citation' (1981) 33 Stan. L. Rev. 773; W. Manz, 'The Citation Practices of the New York Court of Appeals, 1850–1993' (1995) 43 Buff. L. Rev. 121, notably at 153 (citations to foreign authority 25. 7% of citations in 1850, less than 1% in 1950, 0% by 1993).

structure that the federal government should also have its judges, and even its own common law. Madison's argument prevailed that '[a] government without a proper executive and judiciary would be the mere trunk of a body, without arms and legs to act or move'.[83] Judges thus became seen both as formal participants in government and as necessarily attached to legislative authority. A federal common law is not seen as a conceptual problem, and for much of the history of US law it was seen to exist even in so-called diversity cases, involving citizens of different states, which could be removed from state courts and given to federal judges for decision.[84]

Legislation in the United States has also assumed civilian proportions and often receives civilian treatment. Codes of civil procedure and criminal law exist in many states; California, the largest state, has a civil code. Legislation, moreover, receives a broad, liberal interpretation, in keeping with civilian doctrine, and this purposive form of interpretation has now returned to English law.[85] Even adversarial procedure is now declining in importance. Under the massive, civilian-style case-load, leaving the conduct of litigation in private hands is seen as creating unnecessary delay and expense, so the 'case management' judge has emerged, drawing closer to the civilian judge's management of procedure (le juge de la mise en état). 'Case management' is now also being implemented elsewhere, notably in common law Canada and, most recently, England.[86] The case-load is also the malady which has most affected the notion of stare decisis. Given open courts, and millions of decisions, it turns out to be very difficult to say that each represents a rule of law. The same problem has also surfaced in England, where it has been said that the notion is finally self-destructing, since all decisions must be reconciled in attempt-

---

[83] See J. Elliot (ed.), *Debates on the Adoption of the Federal Constitution at the Convention held in Philadelphia* (1907) at 158, 159, as cited in H. A. Johnson, 'Historical and Constitutional Perspectives on Cross-Vesting of Court Jurisdiction' (1993), 19 Melb. U. L. Rev. 45 at 51, n. 32.

[84] *Swift v. Tyson*, 41 US (16 Pet.) 1 (1842). The decision was later reversed, in *Erie R. R. Co. v. Tompkins*, 304 US 64 (1938), not so much on the ground of the irreducibility of the common law, but so as not to impinge on state sovereignty, and state control of common law in state matters. On federal common law beyond the context of diversity cases, see M. A. Field, 'Sources of Law: The Scope of Federal Common Law' (1986) 99 Harv. L. Rev. 883 (though restraint exercised in its development). For the resistance of other common law jurisdictions to the idea of a federal common law, see below, this section. Cf., for a civilian jurisdiction's codification of it, the Mexican Código civil para el Distrito Federal en materia Común y para toda la República en materia Federal.

[85] See *Pepper v. Hart* [1992] 3 WLR 1032 (HL) (allowing reference to Hansard record of Parliamentary debate). Simply giving legislation its 'plain meaning'—the historical attitude of the common law—has therefore become highly controversial in the US, in spite of its recent re-appearance in certain judgments of the US Supreme Court.

[86] See the report of Lord Woolf, *Access to Justice, Final Report* (London: HMSO, 1996), yielding new Civil Procedure Rules in 1999; commented on critically by A. Zuckerman, 'Lord Woolf's Access to Justice: Plus ça change. . .' (1996) 59 MLR 773 (underlying problem of cost and delay caused by financial incentives to lawyers to complicate litigation; case management inadequate to entirely remove such incentives; German model of fixed fees according to value of litigation proposed); and on the relation of case management to the adversarial system, contrasting 'procedural justice' (dispute resolution) with 'substantive justice' (ascertaining truth), see J. A. Jolowicz, 'The Woolf Report and the Adversary System' (1996) 15 CJQ 198.

ing harmonious statements of law.[87] Decisions must be batched, to ascertain their drift, to see if there is a jurisprudence constante.[88] Stare decisis appears now, with hindsight, as a quick fix, the starch necessary to make the new substantive common law take hold. The actual cases, the decisions, now fade, necessarily, in importance. So the problems of the civil law are also becoming the problems of the common law, and there is much greater room for collaboration and mutual understanding, even given the magnitude of the problems.

Still, common law thinking retains a vital place in US law. Federal judges are independent; and federal courts exercise major powers of supervision and control over state courts (diversity jurisdiction, removal by defendants of cases involving diversity or federal questions to federal courts, Supreme Court review on constitutional grounds, necessary adherence by state court judges to guarantees of Bill of Rights, as federally interpreted). So the concept of the common law as state politics, as local, political consensus, is hedged. There is still a distant judiciary to call in aid, as in the old practice. And cases are thought to be important, subject to systematic reporting (now by computer, and including first-instance decisions) in a way historically unthinkable in the civil law world. And the old idea of a trans-national 'Anglo-American' law is not dead, even if its practice at the judicial level is faint indeed.[89] So to the extent that a common law tradition is best represented by the place given to independent adjudication, it is still present in the United States

The particular genius of US law, however, has been its constructive combination of elements of both civil and common law. Grant Gilmore observed that US lawyers were 'convinced eighteenth-century rationalists', in the French tradition, while at the same time, US law would represent 'the arrogation of unlimited power by the

---

[87] J. A. Jolowicz, 'Décisions de la Chambre des Lords' (1979) at 525 (law thus found not in single decison but in many); Atiyah and Summers, *Form and Substance in Anglo-American Law* (1987) at 121, 122 (asking 'what is left of *stare decisis*?'). The formal weakening of stare decisis occurred in England in 1966, with the Practice Statement of the House of Lords that it would no longer be bound by its own decisions, the practice followed since 1898. See Practice Statement (Judicial Precedent), [1966] 1 WLR 1234; [1966] 3 All ER 77; and for the prior practice, *London Street Tramways Co.* v. *London County Council* [1898] AC 375. Yet the real decline of the concept is in its practice, in the reduced normative force of first instance courts, courts of appeal and supreme courts. A Commonwealth judge has written that '[t]he attraction of precedent is waning in common law Canada probably even faster than in England': K. Mackenzie, 'Back to the Future: The Common Law and the *Charter*' (1993) 51 Advocate 927 at 929, 930. The US Supreme Court has never considered itself bound by its own decisions, though an initially rigorous concept of stare decisis for lower courts dictated the practice of per curiam decisions, in the name simply of the court. See, with further ref., H. P. Glenn, 'Sur l'impossibilité d'un concept de stare decisis' Rev. rech. jur. Droit prospectif 1993. 1073.

[88] See Goutal, 'Characteristics of Judicial Style' (1976), above, at 52, on computer search of case law in the US ('nothing normative in this process, no appeal to hierarchy or formal authority . . . without any hint of anything binding'). And for the common law consisting of 'rules that *would be* generated at the present moment by application of the institutional principle of adjudication', see Eisenberg, *Nature of Common Law* (1988) at 143 (emphasis added).

[89] See Langbein, 'Chancellor Kent and History of Legal Literature' (1993), above, at 567 ('we still for many purposes think of the English and American legal systems as comprising an inseparable entity called Anglo-American law'); Atiyah and Sommers, *Form and Substance* (1987) (commensurability of English and American law though profound differences).

judges'.[90] This is most evident in US constitutional law, where individual rights and judicial power have become the major and distinctive features of US government, though now often emulated abroad. Rights have changed in this process. From individual powers or potestas of private law they are now generalized, as simple 'interests' or political claims protected by law, capable of protection by the broad sweep of constitutional decision.[91] How this all came about is not entirely clear. From a legal perspective the US revolution is another historical accident, or chance, the precise explanation for which may always escape us. Some, running against the traditional 'nation-building' explanation, simply ascribe it to the stupidity of the English Colonial Office.[92] Yet the affirmative construction of US law seems more amenable to legal understanding. Compared to the Normans, US lawyers had an open field—or conceptually created one by marginalization of chthonic American law. So there was no need for restraint, to protect local sensibilities, no need to reflect local patterns of life, to legitimize a novel undertaking. Local patterns of life were to be created, and law was the instrument for doing so, according even to much (civil) law in the old world. The frontier was not only physical; it was also legal—uncharted legal land. To create the new national identity, the common law could not simply amble on; it had to be harnessed in much the same way law had been harnessed by the French kings. Law here fulfils a function of identifying people in the same way that it historically did for jewish and islamic people, though the identity is a new and secular one. The law may not be the common law as it has been, but the common law has always known a concept of change.

Elsewhere in the world a common law tradition continues to be shared amongst different countries, whose identities in law are thereby diluted, though without apparent prejudice to nation-state existence. Citation patterns indicate a high level of inter-jurisdictional use of precedent, of persuasive authority;[93] a shared notion of a common law has impeded federalization of court structures, either through maintenance in principle of a unitary court system, as in Canada, or through an 'autochthonous expedient' of leaving much federal-matter litigation to state courts, as in Australia.[94] There is in principle no federal common law in these countries, nor even state or provincial common law. The common law keeps on floating. It does so

[90] Gilmore, *Ages of American Law* (1977) at 10, 35.

[91] For the breadth of rights, see R. Dworkin, *Taking Rights Seriously* (Cambridge, Mass.: Harvard Univ. Press, 1978).

[92] See, e.g., D. Cook, *The Long Fuse: England and America, 1760–1785: a British Perspective on the American Revolution* (New York: Atlantic Monthly Press, 1995); and on the US revolution as 'one more English revolution', with the 'rhetoric of the revolution . . . borrowed from Europe and . . . [its] leaders . . . pursuing an old-world image of themselves', F. Fernández-Armesto, *Millennium* (London/New York: Bantam, 1995) at 325 (thus foreshadowing the derivative nature of many contemporary movements towards national statehood).

[93] See, with refs, Glenn, 'Common Law in Canada' (1995) at 283 ff. ('Patterns of common authority'); and more generally Glenn, 'Persuasive Authority' (1987).

[94] See H. P. Glenn, 'Divided Justice? Judicial Structures in Federal and Confederal States' (1995) 46 S. C. L. Rev. 819; and for recent Australian developments, B. Opeskin, 'Federal Jurisdiction in Australian Courts: Policies and Prospects' (1995) 46 S. C. L. Rev. 765.

in spite of some formal recognition of the idea of separate and distinct common laws in the Commonwealth,[95] so a common law tradition also has its 'these and these' logic,[96] its doctrine of ikhtilaf.[97] There is something beyond positive decisions which is constitutive of the common law.[98] Yet geography and professionalization of the judiciary have affected the status of the judges. Judicial discipline is now known in the common law world, both in the United States and elsewhere, and the notion of holding office during good behaviour has slowly become compatible with official reprimand.[99] The discipline of judges, however, is an affair of judges.

The identities of those who adhere to the common law are not well protected by it, though a concept of blasphemy has traditionally formed a part of the common law, protecting christianity in some measure though not other religions, or at least not islam.[100] Otherwise identity is protected only by national concepts of treason and sedition, as in the civil law world, while exit through change of nationality or, more easily, domicile (which attracts private law), is now commonplace, in spite of earlier common law notions of indefeasible allegiance (at least for purposes of military service). As in civil law countries, identity is now protected mostly by protection of national borders, and the state is as much an obstacle to liberty of movement in the common law world as in that of the civil law. Though the common law may float, statutory law does not, and access to it is strictly controlled. Human rights here do not prevail over their national, positive and territorial articulation. And as in states of the civil law tradition, recognition of distinct legal identities within national territory is problematical, except with respect to chthonic

---

[95]  See H. Marshall, 'The Binding Effect of Decisions of the Judicial Committee of the Privy Council' (1968) 17 Int. & Comp. Law Q. 60; J. Crawford, *Australian Courts of Law* (Melbourne: Oxford Univ. Press, 1982) at 171 ('The common law become not one but many'); Laskin, *British Tradition in Canadian Law* (1969) at 60.

[96]  See above, Ch. 4, *Of schools, traditions and movements*.

[97]  See above, Ch. 6, *Of schools and schism*.

[98]  See, e.g., K. M. Hogg, 'Negligence and Economic Loss in England, Australia, Canada and New Zealand' (1994) 43 Int. & Comp. Law Q. 116, notably at 117 ('divergence *in* the common law' [emphasis added]); A. Watson, 'The Future of the Common Law Tradition' (1984) 9 Dalhousie L. J. 67 at 84 ('many of the rules have a common origin which still influences the understanding of them, even if they have come to diverge from one another in the different jurisdictions'); and more generally Matson, 'The Common Law Abroad (1993) notably at 754 (date of formal reception of English law largely irrelevant); Harding (ed.), *Common Law in Singapore and Malaysia* (1985); yet for the inevitable particularity in the process, see, e.g., P. Girard, 'Themes and Variations in Early Canadian Legal Culture: Beamish Murdoch and his *Epitome of the Laws of Nova Scotia*' (1993) 11 Law & Hist. Rev. 101.

[99]  See, for a case of judicial discipline by way of criticism or reprimand of a high court judge, resulting in his resignation, 'Report and Record of the Committee of Investigation into the Conduct of the Hon. Mr Justice Berger and Resolution of the Canadian Judicial Council' (1983) 28 McGill L. J. 378; and for the growth of judicial disciplinary agencies, H. P. Glenn, 'La responsabilité des juges' (1983) 28 McGill L. J. 228, at 244 ff.

[100]  *R.* v. *Chief Metropolitan Stipendiary Magistrate*, ex parte *Choudhury* [1991] 1 QB 429 (common law offence of blasphemy for historical reasons restricted to scurrilous vilification of christian religion; *The Satanic Verses* of S. Rushdie therefore not blasphemous); for the 'fading away' of the the idea in the process of reception of the common law in the USA, however, see S. Banner, 'When Christianity Was Part of the Common Law' (1998) 16 Law & Hist. Rev. 27.

populations (in some instances) and through the operation of formal rules of private international law (which accommodate foreign status and foreign law only in cases of a significant 'foreign' connection).[101]

## THE PRACTICE OF COMPARISON

For most of its history the common law was in the *process* of becoming a common law, and its history is above all one of relations with other laws, themselves also common in considerable measure, both in England and in Europe. This was the case with chthonic law, its earliest and most significant interlocutor, and then with ecclesiastical law, once the ecclesiastical courts were up and running. In examining the growth of the common law we have necessarily spoken of unavoidable reciprocal influences and also, more interestingly, of the underlying harmony of this process. This came about because of common law judges coming from an ecclesiastical background, and exercising powers of review over feudal courts, and also because of shared perspectives on procedure and a refusal to give priority to fixed abstract rules or to uniformity of result. Rules are not seen as being in conflict if the rules count for less than the facts. And while roman law was not represented in England by means of particular courts, the same intellectual perspective has been found to exist towards roman law. Vinogradoff thus remarked that there can be no question of *measuring* the influence of roman law, institution by institution and reference by reference, on English law, but only of examining in a general manner the development of legal ideas.[102] Since the ideas floated, the law floated, and no one was very interested in tracking precise results (within certain pre-determined boundaries). The process was necessarily casuistic, since it disposed of cases, but cases did not make law and cases were therefore not in conflict. Beyond the common law, the same attitude appears to have prevailed in ecclesiastical law, and Maitland severely criticized the thesis of Stubbs that English ecclesiastical courts were best seen as acting in some kind of manner which was formally independent from the ecclesiastical courts of the continent.[103]

The process of nesting of general legal ideas in particular institutional and historical contexts is perhaps best seen in the development of the trust. Much

---

[101] On the debate concerning treatment of minorities adhering to other legal traditions, in both civil and common law traditions, see above, Ch. 3, *The state as middle ground* (chthonic), Ch. 4, *Talmudic retreat?*, Ch. 6, *The islamic diaspora*, and below Ch. 8, *Universal tolerance?* (hindu).

[102] Vinogradoff, *Roman Law in Medieval Europe* (1968), above, at 117, 118.

[103] See F. W. Maitland, 'Church, State and Decretals', in F. Maitland, *Roman Canon Law in the Church of England* (London: Methuen, 1898) at 51; van Caenegem, *Royal Writs* (1972), above, at 361, n. 2, with refs; C. Donahue, 'Roman Canon Law in the Medieval English Church: Stubbs vs. Maitland Re-Examined After 75 Years in the Light of Some Records from the Church Courts' (1974) 72 Mich. L. Rev. 647 at 700; S. Whittaker, 'An Historical Perspective to the "Special Equitable Action" in *Re Diplock*' (1983) 4 J. Legal Hist. 3 at 21–3; and more particularly on the influence of papal bulls in England, C. Duggan, *Canon Law in Medieval England* (London: Valorium Reprints, 1982) at 365 ff.; C. Duggan, *Twelfth-Century Decretal Collections and their Importance in English Legal History* (London: Athlone Press, 1963), notably at 146–55.

effort has been expended in attempting to ascertain a precise antecedent to the trust in other laws. So it has been seen as specifically derived from the roman fideicommissum, the germanic Salmann, and the islamic waqf (the Crusades again, reinforced by St Francis' visit to Egypt prior to the growth in England of gifts for pious purposes).[104] Yet all these arguments suppose the existence of rules of law as they are thought of today, and precise legal institutions, such as the trust, such that some kind of precise transfer could take place from one bounded legal 'system' to another. Earlier lawyers didn't, however, appear to think that way. So the trust may be seen as simply the crystallization of some rather large, legal ideas in the English context. The common law courts individualized the concept of property (in individualizing seisin, following the emerging civil and canon law teaching); the ecclesiastical courts, later followed by the Court of Equity, enforced chthonic and christian obligations which said that property is a shared concept, such that a legal owner can be obliged to an equitable owner.[105] The trust was patched together from a mix of legal ideas. It resulted from the practice of comparison.

Common law courts were so laid back in this process of reciprocal influence that after their creation other courts emerged in England, with deleterious effects on their jurisdiction. Commercial courts came to thrive, applying a borderless law merchant which included islamic notions of the cheque (sakk) and its endorsement (aval in French, from hawala)[106] and a range of security devices to which talmudic law greatly contributed.[107] The large and lucrative maritime practice was taken over by the Court of Admiralty, also applying a law drawn from largely continental sources and providing great advantages to the maritime community, beyond any-

---

[104] For the fideicommissum, see D. Johnston, *The Roman Law of Trusts* (Oxford: Oxford Univ. Press, 1988). The romanist thesis was opposed by Holmes, who saw germanic origins, in the Salmann or Treuhand. See O. W. Holmes, 'Early English Equity' (1885) 1 LQR 162, and for the debate, H. P. Glenn, 'Le *trust* et le *jus commune*' in P. Legrand (ed.), *Common Law d'un siècle l'autre* (Cowansville, Quebec: Yvon Blais, 1993) at 87, repr. in English as 'The Historical Origins of the Trust' in A. Rabello (ed.), *Aequitas and Equity: Equity in Civil Law and Mixed Jurisdictions* (Jerusalem: The Harry and Michael Sacher Institute for Legislative Research and Comparative Law, The Hebrew University of Jerusalem, 1997) at 749; R. Helmholz and R. Zimmermann (eds.), *Itinera Fiduciae: Trust and Treuhand in Historical Perspective* (Berlin: Duncker & Humblot, 1998). For the waqf, see H. Cattan, 'The Law of Waqf' in M. Khadduri and H. Liebesny, *Law in the Middle East*, vol. I, *Origin and Development of Islamic Law* (Washington, DC: The Middle East Institute, 1955) at 203, notably at 214, 215 (chronology 'favorable in support of the derivation of uses [and later trusts] from waqf'); for St Francis in Egypt, see Passant, 'Effects of Crusades' (1926), above, at 325; and for traces of him also in Sicily, where Arab thought contributed to a brilliant civilization, Norwich, *Normans in Sicily* (1992), above, at 5.

[105] For a detailed argument, see Glenn, '*Trust* et *jus commune*' (1993), above, and for the early work of the ecclesiastical courts in enforcing uses, R. Helmholz, 'Trusts in the English Ecclesiastical Courts 1300–1640', in Helmholz and Zimmermann (eds.), *Itinera Fiduciae* (1998), above, notably at 171 ('it *is* right to think that some of the elements of trust law in England were shaped by the *ius commune*. The process happened gradually and without much notice being taken of it').

[106] See J. Schacht, *An Introduction to Islamic Law* (Oxford: Clarendon Press, 1964) at 78.

[107] See Rabinowitz, 'Influence of Jewish Law on Common Law', (1960), above, at 823; and above, this Chapter, *The secreted law*.

thing the common law could offer.[108] More generally, the common law in its entirety became suject to an institutionalized, equitable shadow, in the Court of Equity. This came to exist only because of the limited character of the common law, as a result of seekers of justice returning to its source, the Crown, and seeing their complaints referred to the chancellor. The chancellor, a cleric and civilian by training, investigated complaints in the civilian, roman manner (using written pleadings and no jury) and decided them on the basis of general, substantive principles of law infused with morality, as in the civilian mode. Thus the chancellor, and the Court of Equity, came to enforce trust obligations on legal owners of land, to grant specific performance of contracts (under the writ of trespass, enlarged to contract, only damages could be given), to allow borrowers under a mortgage to recover their property even though the time for redemption had passed (the equitable right of redemption), to grant injunctions to prevent infliction of unjustifiable harm (Equity acts on the conscience, in personam) and to allow discovery as a means of investigation of fact.[109] In all of this, Equity 'followed the law' in the sense of acting only upon the conscience of a defendant and not replicating any of the remedies of the common law. Yet in following the common law, the chancellor necessarily knew the common law and the common lawyers eventually came to know very well the equitable principles being grafted upon their own law. Relations between the common law courts and the Court of Equity were the most stormy of those of the jurisdictions of England, but compromise, of sorts, was eventually reached in the seventeenth century.

For centuries, therefore, the common law existed in a kind of perpetual, institutional debate with other laws. The debate was facilitated by the practice of civilian lawyers testifying in common law courts as to civilian practice, and by the existence of a formal, civilian bar practising in the other courts, with a magnificent library in Doctors' Common, open to all.[110] It can therefore be said that the barristers of the common law were very open to the civil law and 'not at all unfamiliar' with it, though not at the level of actual practice.[111] What may therefore have been a (rela-

---

[108] Such as in rem proceedings, hypothecation of vessels and negotiable bills of exchange, as well as broad, civil law principles of contractual and delictual liability. For the early and full reception of the law merchant in Admiralty, contrasted with the common law courts, see *Select Pleas in the Court of Admiralty* (London: Selden Soc., 1894) at p. lxvii. As late as 1641 the complaint was heard that 'the common law doth not provide in all causes concerning maritime affairs'; see G. F. Steckley, 'Merchants and the Admiralty Court During the English Revolution' (1978) 22 Am. J. Legal Hist. 137 at 151; the 'imperfection of the common law system' was still the object of Admiralty complaint in the 19th century; see F. L. Wiswall, *The Development of Admiralty Jurisdiction and Practice since 1800: an English Study with American Comparisons* (Cambridge: Cambridge University Press, 1970) at 101.

[109] Later privatized, in its oral form, and entrusted to private counsel in the US, an essentially civilian investigative technique being used in support of deficient common law procedural method.

[110] See D. Coquillette, *Civilian Writers of Doctors' Commons* (1988), above; Levack, *Civil Lawyers in England* (1973), above.

[111] W. R. Prest, *The Rise of the Barristers: A Social History of the English Bar 1590–1640* (Oxford/New York: Clarendon Press/Oxford Univ. Press, 1986) at 191; and see R. Helmholz, 'Continental Law and Common Law: Historical Strangers or Companions' [1990] Duke L. J. 1207 at 1215 (libraries of common law lawyers showing large numbers of continental law books; also evidence of use in practice).

tively) harmonious and floating series of relationships between different laws began to change, however, apparently around the sixteenth century. This is the time, you may recall, when the Inns of Court began to think and teach law in a more detailed and even systematic manner.[112] From the sixteenth to the nineteenth centuries the common law moves into an aggressive mode, taking over defamation and bankruptcy from the ecclesiastical courts in the sixteenth century,[113] driving Admiralty jurisdiction back to the high seas, stopping Equity's expansion, and absorbing commercial law into itself in the eighteenth century, under the guidance of Lord Mansfield.[114] With the fundamental reforms of the common law in the nineteenth century, relations with other laws necessarily change, to their detriment. All the courts are fused; Equity and Admiralty disappear as such (though their law is retained, in priority to that of the common law), while ecclesiastical jurisdiction over civil law matters disappears. Doctors' Common is closed in 1858, its library dispersed. Yet given the new imperium of the common law, its old writs, recast substantively, cover relatively little ground. They notably provide few reasons for (substantive) judgment. So the successors of Cujas are prayed in aid; Pothier becomes a formal authority in the common law, 'the highest that can be had, next to a decision of a court of justice in this country',[115] and the process is replicated outside of the field of obligations.[116] There's lots of civil law information contained within common law information, if you look carefully, though it is often exported abroad in decanted, common law form. In England, however, they are now writing on the law of 'obligations'.[117]

This transfusion of foreign law into the common law occurred from the early nineteenth century. It was happening at the same time in US law, so there is a curious tracking of legal events beneath the creation of different (though parallel) political identities. By the late nineteenth century, however, stare decisis had set in, so the common law closed into itself, though now in its larger, Commonwealth existence. Comparative law came also to be recognized in more scientific form, though never acquiring the scientific character of its continental version.[118] The

---

[112] See above, this Chapter, *Changing thought.*

[113] R. H. Helmholz, *Canon Law and English Common Law* (London: Selden Soc., 1983) at 8–15.

[114] On an earlier, 15th century 'reception' of Italian mercantile law, however, see Plucknett, *Concise History of Common Law* (1956) at 663.

[115] Best J. in *Cox* v. *Troy* (1822), 5 B. and All. 474 at 481, 106 E. R. 1264 at 1266.

[116] See generally Simpson, 'Innovation in Nineteenth Century Contract Law' (1975), above; J. Gordley, *The Philosophical Origins of Modern Contract Doctrine* (Oxford: Clarendon Press, 1991) at 134 ff.; P. Birks, 'English and Roman Learning in *Moses* v. *Macferlan* (1984) Curr. Legal Problems 1 (restitution); P. Birks and G. McLeod, 'The Implied Contract Theory of Quasi-Contract: Civilian Opinion Current in the Century before Blackstone' (1986) 6 OJLS 46; B. Rudden, 'Comparative Law in England' in W. E. Butler and V. N. Kudriavtsev (eds.), *Comparative Law and Legal Systems: Historical and Socio-Legal Perspectives* (New York: Oceana, 1985) 79 at 81–3 (property).

[117] See P. J. Cooke and D. W. Oughton, *The Common Law of Obligations* (London: Butterworths, 1989); A. Tettenborn, *An Introduction to the Law of Obligations* (London/Toronto: Butterworths, 1984).

[118] See H. C. Gutteridge, *Comparative Law: an Introduction to the Comparative Method of Legal Study and Research*, 2nd edn. (Cambridge: Cambridge Univ. Press, 1949).

practice of comparison had been different from the science of comparison, at least for several centuries. Yet when the positive, systemic construction of English common law began, from the sixteenth century, the English practice differed from the continental only in its means and not in its end result. Comparative law in both cases had become constructive, an instrument for mining other law in the process of systematizing one's own. The process finished, closure followed, and comparativists began the often thankless task of attempting to illuminate the pools of national introspection. The closures of the nineteenth and twentieth centuries are now clearly drawing to an end, however, and the underlying commonalities becoming of prime importance. This is most evident in Europe, where civil and common laws now often work in tandem at the European level,[119] but also beyond the regional level, such that US law, which took so much from Europe, can now re-pay the compliment.[120] Commensurability is respectable again.

## WESTERN LAW IN THE WORLD

Western people have a tendency to think that colonialism is something which occurred in the eighteenth and nineteenth centuries and is now over. The rest of the world doesn't see things quite the same way. The Greeks went east; the Romans went in all directions;[121] the 'dark ages' were happy times for everybody else; it all started again with the Crusades, which went on for centuries in a highly military mode; then western expansion began on a more world-wide basis once the means existed, and continues today. Islam, as has been said, makes much of this, as did Lenin.[122] The Greek and Roman expansions were clearly military, as were the Crusades, even with their religious justification. Since then expansion of western people, and western tradition, has been much more subtle, overall, bringing many

---

[119] See Stein, 'Legal History', above, at 79 ('English developments are beginning to be seen, as Maitland suggested, in the light of contemporary movements in continental laws. Thus, in legal history at least, the splended isolation of the common law is beginning to disappear'); M. Delmas-Marty, *Pour un droit commun* (Paris: Seuil, 1994) at 82 (error to force distinction between common law and continental laws at level of European Court of Human Rights); Glenn, 'Civilization de common law' (1993) (with reservations, however, for differences in substantive law and role of judge); Lord Oliver of Aylmerton, 'Requiem for Common Law?' (1993) at 679–83 (relations with Europe 'a revolutionary change in the law and the legal system'); Irvine, 'Development of Human Rights', above, at 231 (in administrative law, 'it seems undeniable that the traditional common law concepts converge with their continental cousins'); J. Levitsky, 'The Europeanization of the British Legal Style' (1994) 42 Am. J. Comp. Law 347; Markesinis (ed.), *Gradual Convergence* (1994); and for the views of a contemporary English solicitor and a French avocat, both in active practice, see F. Neate, 'Mystification of the Law' (1997) 25, No. 1, Int. Bus. Lawyer 5 ('There is no difference between civil law and common law which matters'); A. de Foucaud, 'Civil Law and Common Law in Paris as in New York' (1997) 25, No. 1, Int. Bus. Lawyer 15 ('The differences of common law and civil law no longer create communication problems which are detrimental to the effectiveness of our representation of clients').

[120] V. W. Wiegand, 'The Reception of American Law in Europe' (1991) 39 Am. J. Comp. Law 229.

[121] On the influence of Roman notions of empire in subsequent western notions of expansion, see A. Pagden, *Lords of all the World: Ideologies of Empire in Spain, Britain and France* c. 1500–c. 1800 (New Haven/London: Yale Univ. Press, 1995), ch. 1 ('The Legacy of Rome').

[122] See above, Ch. 6, *Jihad*; and for the notion of legal imperialism, J. Schmidhauser, 'Legal Imperialism: Its Enduring Impact on Colonial and Post-Colonial Judicial System' (1992) 13 *Int. Pol. Sci. Rev.* 321.

different types of actors into play. There is a large question of the role of law in this, though lawyers could hardly be said to be on the leading edge of western exploration of the world.

On the other hand, western lawyers and western people in general see western thought and western law as essentially liberating and beneficial, capable of bringing about 'development' and well-being while overcoming oppression, discrimination and prejudice. It is not imposed but is simply there, as were the common laws of Europe, available by free choice as a means of liberation and relief.[123] This should not been seen as expansion, still less as imperialism, but rather as consensus on universally valid objectives. Once again, good arguments all, and there may never be a winner. But there may be more to be said on both sides.

Western expansion, whether rooted in common or civil law (which we have here to return to),[124] has come about through three essential techniques or concepts. Military means have supplemented them in case of need, but often there has been surprisingly little use of military force. The first is physical presence of western settlers, that is, private, non-governmental means of expansion of western people and western thought. Since the western churches are now seen as institutions functioning in the private sphere, missionary activities of the churches must also be seen as private. This is not to say that private settlers did not have government support; they often received substantial aid from the state, particularly when companies were given monopolies of settlement of new areas, as occurred under both British and French regimes in North America. When western settlement occurred in an area which had been previously settled, existing law was held to remain in force, though there were different techniques, as has been noted, for co-ordinating existing law and the law of the new settlers.[125] English technique generally involved a more hands-off approach, leaving existing law for existing people, new law for new people (and there were exceptions even to this). The French saw a more universal role for a more universal French law, so local people could opt for the new law. In both cases, however, western law could become clearly dominant, depending on the rate of western settlement (hindu and muslim law remained in force in India, but both have been profoundly affected by English law).[126] Otherwise, where settlement occurred in lands of no previous settlement (an interesting concept), western law

---

[123] On the 'voluntary' character of much current legal development work, often tied to financing by western or international financial institutions, see J. Reitz, 'Systems Mixing and in Transition: Import and Export of Legal Models', forthcoming in *General Reports* to the XVth International Congress of Comparative Law, Bristol, UK, 1998.

[124] From the brief discussion at the conclusion of Ch. 5, above, *Civil law in the world*.

[125] See above, Ch. 3, *The state as middle ground*.

[126] See above, Ch. 8, *Hindu law in India*. The Indian experience indicates that common law methods of cases (supported by stare decisis) and occasional legislation can be as effective a means of legal influence as flat-out legislation in the civilian manner. For one instance of reaction, see H. Pawlisch, *Sir John Davies and the Conquest of Ireland: A Study in Legal Imperialism* (Cambridge/New York: Cambridge Univ. Press, 1985). An historical overview of the process of western expansion is provided in W. J. Mommsen and J. A. de Moor (eds.), *European Expansion and Law: the Encounter of European and Indigenous Law in 19th-and 20th-Century*

was taken to be imported with the settlers themselves. This appears to have occurred throughout the Americas, so chthonic populations and chthonic law were essentially ignored, for purposes of creating a territorial law, by almost all European powers (including Spain, Portugal, Holland, France and England). The western law of 'reception' was profoundly rooted in western legal and political philosophy. If the human person exercised, as delegate, the dominium of God on earth, the earth was to be subdued. In the English-speaking world Locke said this most clearly, though he was clearly echoing civilian concepts of individualized property, which had since the fourteenth century been moving beyond chthonic concepts of sharing. Subduing the earth, for Locke, meant to 'improve it for the benefit of life and therein lay out something upon it that was his [the settler's] own, his labour'.[127] If there was resistance to this process, the military could be used (and was, perhaps most widely by Spain) but the principal means of lasting expansion were private.[128] So imperialism is not necessarily governmental in character and method; governments may sponsor and aid, and hold underlying title, but lasting impact is a matter of private enterprise. This has become more evident in recent times, as the process of western 'globalization' depends largely on corporate activities, technological support and the development of an informal and supranational lex mercatoria to which both civil and common law traditions have contributed.[129]

*Africa and Asia* (Oxford/New York: Berg Publishers, 1992); and for a marxist perspective on the entire process, A. Papachristos, *La réception des droits privés étrangers comme phénomène de sociologie juridique* (Paris: LGDJ, 1975). For the significance of implantation of western methods of education in this process, displacing chthonic ways, see E. Goldsmith, *The Way* (London: Rider, 1992) at 284, 285.

[127] J. Locke, *Two Treatises of Government*, ed. M. Goldie (London: J. M. Dent, 1993) at 130; and see J. Tully, *Strange Multiplicity: Constitutionalism in an age of diversity* (Cambridge: Cambridge Univ. Press, 1995) at 73–5 (hunting and gathering lands considered vacant, since title derived exclusively from labour in form of tilling, cultivating, improving; chthonic peoples will be better off as a result of assimilation since will share in greater abundance of commodities and employment). On the civilian move from chthonic to individual concepts of property, see above, Ch. 5, *The centrality of the person and the growth of rights*.

[128] For the inherently private character even of the Spanish conquista, the state essentially granting concessions, see N. Rouland, S. Pierré-Caps and J. Poumarède, *Droit des minorités et des peuples autochtones* (Paris: Presses universitaires de France, 1996) at 106.

[129] The extent of this globalization should not be exaggerated. The World Bank has concluded that the process of globalization 'has yet to touch a large chunk of the world economy. Roughly half of the developing world's people have been left out of the much-discussed rise in the volume of international trade and capital flows since the early 1980's.' See The World Bank, *World Development Report 1997: the State in a Changing World* (Oxford: Oxford Univ. Press, 1997) at 12; for criticism of the globalization process, P. Hirst and G. Thompson, *Globalization in Question* (Cambridge: Polity Press, 1996); D. Rodrik, *Has Globalization Gone Too Far?* (Washington DC: Institute for International Economics, 1997); and for different forms of 'globalization' in the world, above, Ch. 2, *Globalizations*. The lex mercatoria remains controversial. It would represent not a truly cosmopolitan legal development but a form of 'globalized localism', a creation of civilian theory and common law practice (though often resisted by common law practitioners, and lawyers from developing countries). B. de Sousa Santos, *Toward a New Common Sense: Law, Science and Politics in the Paradigmatic Transition* (New York/London: Routledge, 1995) at 293; and see O. Lando, 'The Lex Mercatoria in International Commercial Arbitration' (1985) 34 Int. & Comp. Law Q. 747; R. Goode, 'Usage and its Reception in Transnational Commercial Law' (1997) 46 Int. & Comp. Law Q. 1; B. Goldman, 'La lex mercatoria dans les contrats et l'arbitrage international: réalités et perspectives' J. dr. int., 1979. 475.

The second concept underlying western expansion is that of the state. The age of western imperialism coincided with that of the emergence of the nation-state, and it has been said that the 'building of nations was seen inevitably as a process of expansion'.[130] The process first occurred 'internally' as the states, in Europe, took into themselves diverse nations, with their own traditions, to be submerged, successfully or less successfully, into that of the particular state. It then occurred 'externally', first by Spain, then France, then the others, as the age of imperialism unfolded and foreign territory was acquired, as source of wealth and zone of expansion, through enlisting of private effort in the larger cause.[131] The process then replicated itself, as new states, themselves often the result of reaction to the old, imperial ones, themselves expanded, to carve out as much territory for themselves as possible. The 'frontier' is thus a national, not colonial phenomenon, but represents the same process at work.[132] The present division of most of the surface of the world into state territories (Antarctica has a particular status) is an indication of how powerful these ideas of formal organization and territorial control have been. The existence of states everywhere comes to be an argument, a beach-head, for the advancement of other western concepts of social organization. These represent the third technique of western expansion.

States themselves are the product of constructive human rationality, and rights are the crowning expression of the unique and God-given character of human rationality. Rights are instruments of liberty, so the process of improving the human condition in the world can easily be seen as necessarily following the European pattern, and necessarily taking up the European instruments. These are now those of the western world as a whole, as the new nations of America and Australasia add their great influence to those of Europe. To western people all of this has a certain self-evident character, and movement towards a western way of life is seen as an immense and largely irreversible process, which suffers occasional setbacks but which can probably only be stopped by some kind of global catastrophe. This was also the way things were seen in the nineteenth century, however, and colonialism and subjection of other peoples occurred during the time when European peoples themselves were beginning to enjoy the fruits of self-determination, liberty and, in some cases at least (England dissenting, as a matter of doctrine), rights.[133] So there were major discrepancies in the way in which western, liberal legal theory was

[130] E. Hobsbawm, *Nations and Nationalism since 1780: Programme, Myth, Reality* (Cambridge/New York: Cambridge Univ. Press, 1990) at 32.

[131] See P. McAuslan, 'Land Policy: A Framework for Analysis and Action' [1988] J. African Law 185 at 185 ('The scramble for Africa, the carve up of the Pacific, the settlement of Australasia were, at bottom, organized, governmentally sanctioned and ultimately directed, land grabbing exercises').

[132] See, e.g., R. Williams Jr., *The American Indian in Western Legal Thought: the Discourses of Conquest* (New York/Oxford: Oxford Univ. Press, 1990) at 249 ('Locke's Theory Applied: the Colonial Radicals' Praxis on the Indian Frontier').

[133] See H. von Senger, 'From the Limited to the Universal Concept of Human Rights: Two Periods of Human Rights' in W. Schmale (ed.), *Human Rights and Cultural Diversity* (Goldbach, Germany: Keip Publishing, 1993) 47 at 50–2.

applied in the world.[134] This was not entirely oversight or slippage; there were very clear doctrines of inherent human superiority reaching back (if perhaps not entirely faithfully) to Aquinas' notions of practical reason and some people enjoying 'superior intellect',[135] which gave rise to 'degrees of humanity' being enjoyed by different peoples.[136] The concept of 'civilization' was one of French procedure (moving from criminal to civil courts) until the mid-eighteenth century when it emerged as a process of universal history.[137] So liberalism *was* developing at the same time as colonialism (Lenin quietly nodding) and there really *was* a notion of the white man's (not woman's) burden.[138] J. S. Mill was 'pretty close to sharing the crude racism of his time',[139] and western anthropology carried the notion of 'primitive peoples' well into the twentieth century.[140] The legal reaction to all of this had occurred as early as the mid-sixteenth century in the writings of Francisco de Vitoria in Spain, for whom 'no business shocks me or embarrasses me more than the corrupt profits and affairs of the Indies. Their very mention freezes the blood in my veins.'[141] De Vitoria's writing is still the theoretical foundation of many chthonic legal claims in the world today,[142] and takes the difference between European and chthonic American people as due mainly to 'evil and barbarous education' which could in no way justify then current colonial practices.[143] De Vitoria's argument was taken up by Bartolomé de las Casas, for whom differences were due

---

[134] There were also discrepancies within western states, since women were consistently excluded from the ambit of rights declarations, both in formal enunciation and in actual entitlement. von Senger, 'From Limited to Universal Concept of Human Rights', above, at 53–5, on the 'patriarchal Enlightenment' and detailing 'meristic' manner of inclusion, reaching back to the Greek polity ('meros' meaning 'part'), according to which a definition includes one part defined as the whole, hypertrophied, while the other part is tacitly extirpated from the definition, thus disappearing. For the 18th-century struggle of French women against their exclusion from concepts of citizenship and human rights, see von Senger, above, this note; J. Scott, *Only Paradoxes to Offer: French Feminists and the Rights of Man* (Cambridge, Mass./London: Harvard Univ. Press, 1996), notably at 19 ff. on drafting by Olympe de Gouges of a Declaration of the Rights of Women and Citizen.

[135] M. van Gelderen, 'Vitoria, Grotius and Human Rights. The Early Experience of Colonialism in Spanish and Dutch Political Thought' in Schmale (ed.), *Human Rights and Cultural Diversity* (1993), above, 215 at 217.

[136] Ibid., at 218.

[137] F. Braudel, *A History of Civilizations*, trans. R. Mayne (New York: Penguin, 1993) at 3.

[138] See von Senger, 'From Limited to Universal Concept of Human Rights' (1993), above, at 65, 66, on the 'civilising mission' of 'superior races'.

[139] B. Parekh, 'Superior People: the narrowness of liberalism from Mill to Rawls' *TLS*, 25 Feb. 1994, at 11.

[140] For the history of the development and decline of the idea, see A. Kuper, *The Invention of Primitive Society: Transformations of an Illusion* (London/New York: Routledge, 1988); A. Pagden, *The Fall of Natural Man. The American Indian and the Origins of Comparative Ethnology* (Cambridge: Cambridge Univ. Press, 1986); and for current reaction, above, Ch. 2, in introductory text.

[141] F. de Vitoria, *Political Writings*, ed. A. Pagden (Cambridge: Cambridge Univ. Press, 1991) at 331; cited in M. van Gelderen, 'Vitoria, Grotius and Human Rights' (1993), above, 215 at 219.

[142] See, e.g., P. Cumming and N. Mickenberg, *Native Rights in Canada*, 2nd edn. (Toronto: General Publishing, 1972) at 14; and generally, above, Ch. 3, *The state as middle ground*.

[143] de Vitoria, *Political Writings* (1991), above, at 290, cited in van Gelderen, 'Vitoria, Grotius and Human Rights' (1993), above, at 220.

not to biological factors but to, among other things, 'adherence to different customs'.[144]

If the writings of de Vitoria and de las Casas did not markedly slow imperial expansion, they have, however, become fundamental in contemporary arguments in favour of universal human rights.[145] From a perspective internal to the western world, once the distinctions between peoples (long present in western thought) are eliminated, rights and human liberty become universal concepts, as they were originally conceived to be. As universal concepts, they prevail both within states and between them, such that national barriers to enforcement cannot be allowed to prevail. There are, of course, few effective means of international enforcement of human rights (the regional European Court of Human Rights being an exception, though constituting a form of collaborative, supra-national positivization of human rights standards), though the background human rights debate is of great importance for potentially shaping future institutions. Are human rights universal?

They are clearly not, though this should in no way stop the argument. Human rights are inextricably bound up with the western legal tradition and exist as such only within it. They exist because of two broad streams of western legal thought. One is derived from judaeo–christian–islamic religious tradition, which sees the human person in the image of God and as God's delegate on earth.[146] The other is derived from Greek (or Egyptian) rationality—not accepted, or not entirely accepted, by either talmudic or islamic legal thought—which allows the construction of legal systems, and concepts, required for the enforcement of rights.[147] Human rights are a very particular concept in the world, a 'contingent, mutable truth and not an eternal one',[148] and 'exist' only because of an extraordinary congruence of traditions, which occurred nowhere else in the world. They may also be seen as reactions within the west: reactions to medieval feudalism, to imperial

---

[144] Ibid., at 221.

[145] For partial treatment of this well-rehearsed subject, see Schmale (ed.), *Human Rights and Cultural Diversity* (1993), above, with extensive bibliography at 334 ff.; J. Waldron (ed.), *Theories of Rights* (Oxford: Oxford Univ. Press, 1984); A. A. An' Na'im and F. M. Deng (eds.), *Human Rights in Africa: Cross-Cultural Perspectives* (Washington, DC: Brookings Institution, 1990), with refs.; D. Little (ed.), *Human Rights and the Conflict of Cultures: Western and Islamic Perspectives on Religious Liberty* (Columbia, SC: Univ. of South Carolina Press, 1988); C. Welch Jr., and V. A. Leary, *Asian Perspectives on Human Rights* (Boulder, Colo./San Francisco: Westview Press, 1990); L. S. Rouner, *Human Rights and the World's Religions* (Notre Dame: Univ. of Notre Dame Press, 1988).

[146] See above, Ch. 5, *The centrality of the person and the growth of rights*.

[147] See above, Ch. 5, *Law as reason's instrument*.

[148] R. Blickle, 'Appetitus Libertatis. A Social Historical Approach to the Development of the Earliest Human Rights: The Example of Bavaria' in Schmale (ed.), *Human Rights and Cultural Diversity* (1993), above, 143 at 144; and see D. Lal, *Unintended Consequences: the Impact of Factor Endowment, Culture and Politics on Long-Run Economic Performance* (Cambridge, Mass./London: MIT Press, 1998) at 177 (contemporary notion of rights latecomer even in Western cosmology, 'nothing universal about the notion'); B. de Sousa Santos, *Toward New Common Sense* (1995), above, at 337 ('human rights are universal only when they are viewed from a Western standpoint'); the conclusion parallels that of important representatives of contemporary moral philosophy, which reject notions of final justice. See above, Ch. 2, Commensurability: Of Apples and Oranges.

racism, and more recently to precise national and international circumstances since World War II.[149]

This should not stop the argument, however, about application of notions of human rights outside western legal tradition. Traditions exchange information. The particular and contingent origin of human rights teaching should, however, inform the discussion. It may be that rights can be useful elsewhere. It may be, as well, that they are useless and even prejudicial elsewhere, notably if there is no legal structure and no (uncorrupted) judiciary capable of giving effect to them. It may be that peoples adhering to traditions which have explicitly rejected subjective definitions of law can rework their own traditions so as to provide results superior to those which any superficial grafting of rights doctrine might yield. The *results* of rights doctrines can be held up as examples; if other doctrines fall short of them they will be challenged, even internally. Insisting on the necessarily universal character of rights, however, is seen and will continue to be seen as a modern form of imperialism, using the same old private means. Universal rights are simply another form of universalizing the truths of a particular tradition. It is being illiberal about being liberal, forcing people to be free. Yet if people are all of equal potential, if all exercise human rationality (of one type or another) and if all, as human beings, are entitled to choose how they will live their lives, their choice must count. So rights doctrines eventually end up, as they should, being evaluated against other doctrines, in particular circumstances by particular people. More will have to be said about how such evaluations can be made.[150]

## WESTERN LAW AND CORRUPTION

If rights talk is the sunny side of western law, corruption is the dark side. There is no other tradition—outside that of the civil and common laws, now together looking out over the world—which so lends itself to corruption. There is not much to be corrupt about in the chthonic world; the rabbis were seen as corrupt, but mostly by the christians, who had other objectives than internal reform; islam provides few occasions for pecuniary or institutional corruption, though some, even within islams, would say that doctrinal non-endeavour is a form of corruption. Yet western legal tradition offers all of the prerequisites for all of the corrup-

---

[149] See W. Kymlicka, *Liberalism, Community and Culture* (Oxford: Oxford Univ. Press, 1989) at 213–15 (liberal theory compatible with variable treatment for national minorities until World War II; major effect on future UN policy of Nazi abuse of Minority Protection scheme, state of black–white race relations in USA in 1950s and 1960s). The human rights debate is thus of importance not only in terms of international relations, but for the possibility of differential treatment within states. See above, Ch. 2, *The view from somewhere else*, and the 4th section of each of the chapters on individual traditions, dealing with their relations with other traditions.

[150] See below, Ch. 10, Reconciling Traditions; and for alleged 'discordance between the West's—particularly America's—efforts to promote a universal Western culture and its declining ability to do so', describing the 1993 Vienna Human Rights Conference as a 'defeat for the West', S. Huntington, *The Clash of Civilizations and the Remaking of World Order* (New York: Simon & Schuster, 1996) at 183, 196.

tions. The situation is probably the least worrisome in matters of doctrinal corruption. Free doctrine is generally not corrupt, though it may be highly undisciplined.[151] Yet in creating large states, large corporate structures, large labour organizations, large legal professions—in short, large institutionalized élites in all directions, western law provides all the disadvantages of a large, wooden house in a warm, humid climate. It may be beautiful, and well-designed, but be subject to many forms of internal rot. To survive, it requires protection beyond the structure itself and if this is neglected, or impossible, the structure will not last.

Some forms of traditional corruption have been dealt with effectively in western law. The doctrinal corruption of racism, bereft of any scientific foundation, has now been at least marginalized in legal thought, though it remains still vigorous outside it. Judges who once bought their positions (as in France) or who sold minor positions and collected fees from litigants (as in England) have now been assured the means of financial security. Indeed, in some countries even a relatively underpaid judiciary has undertaken heroic and life-threatening work against combined traditions of governmental corruption and organized crime (as in Italy). So law can do much to prevent corruption in non-legal institutions, if legal institutions themselves remain free of corruption. The problem with this is that it is well known to forces of corruption, which often concentrate as much on legal institutions as on others.[152] And when the external forces of corruption are not at work, there remain the internal ones, the inherent pressure, on those in positions to profit, towards unjustifiable personal advantage. The problems of corruption are somewhat different in the countries of origin of western law from those which exist in the countries to which western law has been exported.

Within western countries, the problems are the (relatively) limited ones of maintaining the underlying ethic of the legal professions, the underlying ethic of other institutions, and having the legal professions (lawyers and judges) control the breakdowns. Generalized corruption is not encountered as much as it is elsewhere, though to the extent organized crime is more influential than in the past, this conclusion is a fragile one. Within the legal professions, there are differences within traditions. European professions (of both civil and common law varieties) were traditionally divided ones, and in the limitations of activity there were inherent ethical restraints.[153] The conceptual notion is that of incompatibilities, activities incompatible with the status of being a member of a particular profession. Acting as a notary or solicitor has been incompatible with acting as an advocate or barrister; acting as a barrister has been incompatible with other forms of commercial activity, or even entering into partnership; acting as an avocat, until very recently,

---

[151] See, on the multiplicity of traditions, below, Ch. 10.

[152] For the narco project of taking over the administration of justice in latin America, see J. Witke, 'Globalización, Estado y Derecho' (1995) 28 Bol. mex. der. comp. 341 at 350 ('un NarcoEstado') and 353 (emergence of informal, extra-constitutional law as means of dealing with corrupt state structures).

[153] See H. P. Glenn, 'Professional Structures and Professional Ethics' (1990) 35 McGill L. J. 424.

was incompatible with salaried employment, even by other avocats. There were limits on the trouble lawyers could get into, and structures of practice remained of limited size, and often purely individual, as with the barrister. North American professions have been less strictly defined (something about the needs of the frontier, most explanations go) and the notion of incompatibility is almost entirely unknown. No structural concepts exist to keep lawyers out of trouble. North American lawyers therefore exercise in a single, broad profession, as in the United States, or in fused (though still identifiable) professions, as in Canada. The result has been growth in firm size to meet the demands of corporate and large scale litigation practice, with the result that the lawyer in North America is now subject to structural loyalties (those of the large firm) which are not always consistent with the obligation of loyalty to the client. Many maintain in North America that the practice of law is a business, as such freed from any single and dominant obligation to come to the aid of those in need (advocare). There has been discussion of 'the lost lawyer', and by this is meant the lawyer who has lost sight of the primary obligation of service.[154] The growth of very large firms and internal work standards is now occurring in Europe as well, most notably in firms of solicitors in England, but also in large firms of Advokates and Rechtsanwälte in Holland and Germany.[155] Accompanying this process comes a necessary judicial control of conflicts of interest, as large firms act for innumerable clients whose relations may become conflictual, or as lawyers move from firm to firm in the course of particular law suits. This type of 'satellite litigation' has become a costly adjunct to litigation in much of the western world. To the extent the large firms become international in character, the control of ethical conduct is exacerbated. In Europe, as in the federations of the United States and Canada, trans-border codes of ethics have emerged, though often they have adopted the (ethically interesting) technique of choice-of-ethics rules, the submission of ethical problems to ethics rules of a particular jurisdiction on the basis of primarily geographical considerations. The juridification of professional ethics presents its own problems.

Where western law has been exported beyond its host jurisdictions, or those which have developed in close tandem with them, the problem of corruption has assumed massive proportions. There is above all no positive phenomenon of obedience to positive law, so one of the current doctrinal foundations for positive law in western thought is brutally removed (as it may now slowly be dissolving in the west).[156] It is simply thin, written law, controlled immediately by whoever is in authority in a particular state, having no greater social embedding. Its institutions

---

[154] A. Kronman, *The Lost Lawyer: Failing Ideals of the Legal Profession* (Cambridge, Mass./London: Belknap Press 1993); and see N. Bowie, 'The Law: From a Profession to a Business' (1988) 41 Vanderb. L. Rev. 741. The problems of ethical commitment would then be replicated within the firms themselves (the 'grabbing and leaving' problem).

[155] See Y. Dezalay, *Marchands de droit* (Paris: Fayad, 1992).

[156] See, for the basis of positive law being positive obedience, as simple fact, above, Ch. 5, *Positive law and positive science*, and for world decline in adherence to 'rational–legal authority,' above, Preface.

rest on no particular ethical tradition, and whatever ethical claims they may make may well conflict with others, such as loyalty to family or tribe.[157] The result is generalized corruption, 'ant' (hormiga) corruption as it is called in some countries, since all the ants in the pile are busily engaged in it, including, most importantly, all agents of police, who become often more feared and avoided than those whom they are meant to police. Judges and lawyers who dare to attempt to do something in such circumstances are often subject to fearful reprisals; the state itself will provide no protection to them.[158] Western development work has thus far been unable to overcome the problem of widespread corruption of western institutions and western law when it has been transplanted abroad, since there is no immediate way of reconstructing western ethical and intellectual supports for such a type of law abroad. There appears to be little difference between civil and common law traditions in this regard. So western doctrine often claims for itself a universal role; it is another thing to universalize the institutions needed for its effective implementation.

# GENERAL BIBLIOGRAPHY

Atiyah, P. S. and Sommers, R. S., *Form and Substance in Anglo-American Law* (Oxford: Clarendon Press, 1987).

Baker, J. H., 'English Law and the Renaissance' (1985) 44 Cambridge Law Journal 46.

—— *An Introduction to English Legal History*, 3rd edn. (London: Butterworths, 1990).

Berman, H., *Law and Revolution: The Formation of the Western Legal Tradition* (Cambridge, Mass: Harvard University Press, 1983).

Birks, P., 'Adjudication and interpretation in the common law: a century of change' (1994) 14 Legal Studies 156.

Buckland, W. and McNair, A. D., *Roman Law and Common Law: a Comparison in Outline*, 2nd edn. by F. H. Lawson (Cambridge: Cambridge University Press, 1965).

Cairns, J. W., 'Blackstone, an English Institutist: Legal Literature and the Rise of the Nation State' (1984) 4 Oxford Journal Legal Studies 318.

Cross, R. and Harris, J. W., *Precedent in English Law*, 4th edn. (Oxford: Clarendon Press, 1991).

David, R. and Brierley, J. E. C., *Major Legal Systems in the World Today*, 3rd edn. (London: Stevens, 1985), Pt Three ('The Common Law').

Dawson, J., *The Oracles of the Law* (Ann Arbor: The University of Michigan Law School, 1968), ch. 1 ('The Growth and Decline of English Case Law').

---

[157] See, above, Ch. 3, *Chthonic peoples, states and human rights*, on conflicts between institutional loyalty and societal loyalties in so-called developing countries; and on the problem of corruption generally, above, Ch. 1, Tradition and Corruption.

[158] See the valuable and chilling publications of the Centre for the Independence of Judges and Lawyers of the International Commission of Jurists, on *The Harassment and Persecution of Judges and Lawyers.*

Eisenberg, M., *The Nature of the Common Law* (Cambridge: Harvard University Press, 1988).

Farnsworth, A., *An Introduction to the Legal System of the United States*, 3rd edn. (Dobbs Ferry, NY: Oceana, 1996), published also in French under the title *Introduction au système juridique des États-Unis* (Paris: LGDJ, 1986).

Gilmore, G., *The Ages of American Law* (New Haven: Yale University Press, 1977).

Glendon, M. A., Gordon, M. and Osakwe, C., *Comparative Legal Traditions* (St Paul, Mich.: West Publishing, 1994), Pt three ('The Common Law Tradition').

Glenn, H. P., 'Persuasive Authority' (1987) 32 McGill Law Journal 261.

—— 'La civilization de la common law,' Revue internationale de droit comparé 1993. 559.

—— 'The Common Law in Canada' (1995) 74 Canadian Bar Review 261.

Goldstein, L. (ed.), *Precedent in Law* (Oxford: Clarendon Press, 1987).

Goodhart, A. L., 'The Migration of the Common Law' (1960) 76 Law Quarterly Review 39.

Gordley, J., 'Common Law und civil law: eine überholte Unterscheidung' (1993) Zeitschrift für europäisches Privatrecht 498.

Hand, G. and Bentley, D. (eds.), *Radcliffe and Cross: the English Legal System*, 6th edn. (London: Butterworths, 1977).

Harding, A. J., *The Common Law in Singapore and Malaysia* (Singapore: Butterworths, 1985).

Hart, H. L. A., *The Concept of Law*, 2nd edn. (Oxford/New York: Clarendon/ Oxford University Press, 1994).

Holdsworth, W. S., *A History of English Law* (London: Methuen, 1966).

Holmes, O. W., *The Common Law* (Cambridge, Mass.: Belknap Press, 1963).

Horowitz, M., *The Transformation of American Law, 1780–1860* (New York: Oxford University Press, 1992).

—— *The Transformation of American Law: the Crisis of Legal Orthodoxy, 1870–1960* (New York: Oxford University Press, 1992).

Hudson, J., *The Formation of the English Common Law: Law and Society in England from the Norman Conquest to Magna Carta* (London/New York: Longman, 1996).

Jolowicz, J. A., 'Les décisions de la Chambre des Lords', Revue internationale de droit comparé 1979. 521.

—— (ed.) *Droit anglais*, 2nd edn. (Paris: Dalloz, 1992).

Kiralfy, A. K. R., *Potter's Historical Introduction to English Law and its Institutions*, 4th edn. (London: Sweet and Maxwell, 1958).

Laskin, B., *The British Tradition in Canadian Law* (London: Stevens, 1969).

Lederman, W., 'The Independence of the Judiciary' (1956) 34 Canadian Bar Review 1139.

Levasseur, A., *droit des états-unis* (Paris: Dalloz, 1990).

Lieberman, D., *The Province of Legislation Determined: Legal Theory in Eighteenth-Century Britain* (Cambridge/New York: Cambridge University Press, 1989).

Lobban, M., *The Common Law and English Jurisprudence 1760–1850* (Oxford/New York: Clarendon Press, 1991).

Maitland, F. W., *The Forms of Action at Common Law* (Cambridge: Cambridge University Press, 1954).

Markesinis, B. (ed.), *The Gradual Convergence: Foreign Ideas, Foreign Influences, and English Law on the Eve of the 21st Century* (New York: Oxford University Press, 1994).

Matson, J. N., 'The Common Law Abroad: English and Indigenous Laws in the British Commonwealth' (1993) 42 International and Comparative Law Quarterly 753.

Milsom, S., *Historical Foundations of the Common Law*, 2nd edn. (Toronto: Butterworths, 1981).

Morrison, A., (ed.), *Fundamentals of American Law* (New York: Oxford University Press and New York University Law School, 1996).

Nelson, W. E., *Americanization of the Common Law: The Impact of Legal Change on Massachusetts Society, 1760–1830* (Cambridge, Mass.: Harvard University Press, 1975).

Oliver of Aylmerton, Lord, 'Requiem for the Common Law?' (1993) 67 Australian Law Journal 675.

Plucknett, T. F. T., *A Concise History of the Common Law*, 5th edn. (London: Little, Brown, 1956).

Pollock, F. and Maitland, F., *The History of English Law before the Time of Edward I*, 2nd edn., 2 vols. (London: Cambridge University Press, 1898).

Pringsheim, F., 'The Inner Relationship between English and Roman Law' (1935) 5 Cambridge Law Journal 347.

Sawer, G., 'The Western Conception of Law' in International Association of Legal Science (K. Zweigert and U. Drobnig, eds.), *International Encyclopedia of Comparative Law*, vol. II, ch. 1 (Tübingen/The Hague/Paris: J. C. B. Mohr (Paul Siebeck)/Mouton, 1975) at 14, notably s. D ('English Common Law') at 24.

Schauer, F., 'Is the Common Law Law?' (1989) 77 California Law Review 455.

van Caenegem, R. C., *The Birth of the English Common Law*, 2nd edn. (Cambridge: Cambridge University Press, 1988).

Weir, T., 'The Common Law System' in International Association of Legal Science (K. Zweigert and U. Drobnig, eds.), *International Encyclopedia of Comparative Law*, vol. II, ch. 2 (Tübingen/The Hague/Paris: J. C. B. Mohr (Paul Siebeck)/Mouton, 1974) at 77.

Zweigert, K. and Kötz, H., *Introduction to Comparative Law*, 3rd edn., trans. T. Weir (Oxford: Clarendon Press, 1998), ch. B.III ('The Anglo-American Legal Family').

# 8

# A HINDU LEGAL TRADITION: THE LAW AS KING, BUT WHICH LAW?

Beyond the Khyber Pass are the flat lands of Turkistan, cold in winter and torrid in summer. About 3,500 years ago (dates are not very precise, for reasons we will see but which you may already guess at), some of the people of Turkistan moved south and west, into what we know as Iran; others moved south and east, into what we know as India. These people were 'kin to the Hellenes, the Italiots, the Celts, the Germanic peoples and the Slavs'.[1] When they got to the southern plains, they called themselves aryan, or superior,[2] compared to the people they found there (it's a state of mind). We could probably think of both groups as variants of a chthonic world, yet the new arrivals appear to have brought with them a 'faded tradition'[3] of sacred knowledge or Veda (from the verb to see). So they have been known as 'Vedic-Aryans' to distinguish them from the 'aborigines' or 'pre-aryans', the descendants of whom still constitute the larger part of the population of India. The tradition of the new people gradually came into contact with those of the old people and there were many compromises in the process, as seems to happen. The Veda, moreover,

[1] F. Braudel, *A History of Civilizations*, trans. R. Mayne (New York: Penguin, 1993 (original French ed. 1963) at 219; on the various theories of the migration, and some contrasting views, see Pal, *History of Hindu Law* (1958) at 34–45; K. Klostermaier, *A Survey of Hinduism* (Albany: State Univ. of New York Press, 1994) at 34 ff.; and, suggesting movement not so much of an 'Aryan race' of people but of entry into India of an 'Indo-Aryan' language, R. Thapar, 'The First Millennium BC in Northern India' in R. Thapar (ed.), *Recent Perspectives of Early Indian History* (Bombay: Popular Prakashan, 1995) 80, at 85, 86.

[2] Venkataraman, *N. R. Raghavachariar's Hindu Law* (1987) at 19 ('the Vedic Aryans (Arya signifying superior culture, prestige)'). Iran is thus the 'land of the Aryans'. These people have been described elsewhere, '[t]otalitarian claims apart', as 'a vigorous and unsophisticated people full of the joy of life and . . . not much given to intellectual broodings'; Desai, *Mulla [on] Principles of Hindu Law* (1966) at 5. The word 'aryan' or 'arian' is derived from the Sanskrit 'arya' as indicating nobility or good family. Its primary scientific sense, however, is linguistic, referring to those who speak the aryan or indo-european languages. Cf., however, for its use in description of 'biological units', S. Molnar, *Human Variation: Races, Types, and Ethnic Groups*, 2nd edn. (Englewood Cliffs, NJ: Prentice-Hall, 1983) at 5. On the Harappan civilization (itself 'hardly likely to have been aboriginal') which the Vedic-Aryans encountered, see J. Lipner, *Hindus: their religious beliefs and practices* (London/New York: Routledge, 1994) at 28.

[3] Watts, *Philosophies of Asia* (1995) at 12; on the ancient religious tradition brought with the Vedic-Aryans, see Lipner, *Hindus* (1994), above, at 29; and on its written manifestation, below, *Of Vedas, sastras and commentaries*.

says a lot about toleration and multiple beliefs, so there were particular reasons for the process which here took place.[4]

When the Greeks came east (Alexander arrived in the fourth-century BC, not long after the Twelve Tables in Rome, and Greek communities stayed on for centuries), they couldn't be bothered sorting out all the local beliefs. They just called everybody indoi, as settled on the banks of what they called the Indus (from the original Sindhu).[5] So being hindu originally had to do with territory rather than belief, and shifted gradually to belief as the belief spread. This meant casting the poetic web of the Veda over many rich and varied forms of local life, so that all could see at least some of themselves in the new, complex, vedic teaching. Vedic law thus lived in close association with many, particular chthonic traditions, never purporting to abrogate them, and the importance of local tradition is an ongoing theme in hindu thought.[6] People remained governed by their old law until such time as they came to see the new vedic law more as their law than the old one. Neither law remained the same in this process, and people came to be identifiable as hindu as they came to subscribe to modified vedic law. If they did not, they remained a distinct community.[7] You find in the law books lists of peoples who have become hindu, which read rather like found poems:

> the Yadavas of Madura,
> the Ezhavas of Palghat,
> the Thiyyas of Malabar,
> the Marayars of Tinnevelly,
> the Santals of Assam,
> the Kurmi Mahtons of Chota Nagpur,
> the Raj Bansis of Bengal,
> the Boro Borokachari.[8]

The others, more or less recalcitrant, preserved their own ways or, more radically, originated new religions. Buddhism emerged this way from the sixth-century BCE,[9] essentially in protest against the (legal) 'formalism' of hindu teaching, and jainism and sikhism were also heterodox religions of protest. They were eventually brought back into the fold of hindu law, in India, but there were, and are, ongoing forms of reluctance. Now it is said that hinduism has lost in large

---

[4] On hinduism and tolerance, see below, *Time and Brahman*, and *Hindu identity*.

[5] Diwan, *Modern Hindu Law* (1958) at 1; Venkataraman, *N. R. Raghavachariar's Hindu Law* (1987) at 19 ('hindu' as 'foreign' expression).

[6] See below, *Sadachara and schools*.

[7] See *Mayne's Treatise* (1991) at 3,4.

[8] See Venkataraman, *N. R. Raghavachariar's Hindu Law* (1987) at 21 (citations omitted).

[9] The tradition in hindu legal literature is to use the christian measure of time. This says something both about notions of tolerance, and about colonial inheritance. By contrast, buddhist tradition, now largely outside India, prefers the designations BCE and CE (the commonalities are now multiplying, the common referent is christian). For BCE and CE in jewish–christian relations, see above, Ch. 4, in introductory text.

measure its 'credal' significance,[10] and nobody really knows what it means, except for its law.[11]

# A TRADITION OF DISTANT REVELATION

Gods appear reluctant to lay down the law. Detail never sounds divine, and they say that's where the devil is. So the Pentateuch and the Koran are the work of big thinkers—hedgehogs, not foxes, though of course they could be foxes if they wanted to be, at any time. Gods know all there is to know, and have learned to delegate. After the Pentateuch and the Koran came the Mishnah and the Sunna (the oral explications), and then the lawyers were called in, and we have the Talmud and the doctrinal ijma. You can see the same pattern in hindu legal tradition: a revelatory source (the Vedas); a first series of explications (the Smriti, and most notably the dharmasastras); then the detailed commentaries and digests, which come to play the largest, later role. Yet we are here dealing with perhaps the oldest of the non-chthonic legal traditions, which may go back 4,000 years or more, and allowances have to be made for time, and for the particularity of every tradition.[12] Moreover, if other laws are said to take the shape of pyramids, right-side-up or inverted,[13] nobody talks about pyramids in hindu law. It's more like a dirigible or montgolfier; you can tie it down, but its real mission in life is to float.

## OF VEDAS, SASTRAS AND COMMENTARIES

Most people say that around 1500 or 2000 B C, though some go back to 4000 B C, the Vedas (four books of Veda) came into being, beyond the Khyber.[14] The Vedas are

[10] Diwan, *Modern Hindu Law* (1958) at 1.

[11] The inherent ambiguity of the notion is reflected in contemporary Indian legislation and judicial pronouncement, where 'no precise definition' is available. Diwan, *Modern Hindu Law* (1958) at 1, and see below, *Hindu identity*.

[12] For views on duration see *Mayne's Treatise* (1991), Preface to the First Edition ('the oldest pedigree of any known system of jurisprudence'); Derrett, *Introduction to Modern Hindu Law* (1963) at 1 (law 'already at least two thousand years old', customs still older); Diwan, *Modern Hindu Law* (1958) at 26 ('Hindu law is about 6000 years old', 'remarkable durability').

[13] See above, Ch. 4, *The written words proliferate* (talmudic tradition); Ch. 6, *The shari'a: sources* (islamic tradition).

[14] On the Vedas, see generally Lingat, *Classical Law of India*, (1973) at 7 ff. Some of the hymns of the Vedas refer to events of the Vedic-Aryan migration, however, indicating subsequent redaction. The inherent vagueness of the tradition in matters of chronology has been said to be 'compounded' by the content of the scriptures being memorized and handed down orally for hundreds of years before being committed to writing. Watts, *Philosophies of Asia* (1995) at 12. Mayne spoke of a 'want of a reliable chronology', which made sequencing difficult: *Mayne's Treatise* (1991) at 15; and on the problems of dating, see Varadaghariar, *Hindu Judicial System* (1946) at 55 ff. We should therefore probably just forget about sequencing, at least for

also known as the Sruti, from the root sru, to hear, so they are that which was heard, or revealed, and there are many statements of their divine and revelatory character.[15] Like other revelations, they do not contain much which is recognizable as law, though there are many songs, prayers, hymns and sayings, all considered essential to a hindu way of life. What makes the Vedas different, as revelation (aside from their content), is that there is very little insistence on their author, or on their author's messenger. Some speak simply of revelation, others of gods, others again, as time went by, of God. And no one is identified as messenger, or prophet, or saviour. It is a clearer case of revelation coming to be recognized as revelation, but apparently over such a period of time that its manner of revelation just slipped away. Compared to the content, it wasn't worth memorizing. It has been said that '[t]he theory is that some one among us, our great rishis, had attained such spiritual heights that they could be in direct communion with God'.[16] The content appears to count most, rather than a kind of personal commitment to any One in particular (we will have to come back to the idea of One), which appears to free the content from any more precise commitment—to persons, particular authority, miracles or resurrection. It floats, and over many other more particular kinds of belief. More generally (and so we shouldn't be concerned with dates), '. . . the Vedas are not related to time and space. They are regarded as beginningless (anadi), self-existent and forever immanent.'[17]

Teaching the Vedas was the task of the Brahmans (from the Sanskrit root brh, to grow or expand, though Brahman is also the word for the concept of a supreme absolute, beyond particular, knowable gods), who did so largely from memory, and putting different constructions on the texts to suit local requirements.[18] They apparently taught through use of mnemonic devices in the form of sutras—maxim-like strings or chains of ideas, notions and rules, 'trapped in a very few words [which] together constituted a string as if beads were put together on a

the Vedas, which is what the teaching actually tells us we should do. See below, *Time and Brahman*. On later chronology, see Lingat, *Classical Law of India* (1973), Pt One, Appendix ('Some Reflections on the Chronology of the Dharma-Sastras') at 123.

[15] See Sen, *General Principle[s] of Hindu Jurisprudence* (1891–2) at 25 ('founded on direct revelation . . . not to be questioned or tested by the application of sceptical reasoning'); Venkataraman, *N. R. Raghavachariar's Hindu Law* (1987) at 3, 4 ('the very words of the Deity'); Diwan, *Modern Hindu Law* (1958) at 1, n. 2 ('of divine origin and therefore the legislature cannot change'); Markby, *Hindu and Mahommedan Law* (1906) at 13 ('of divine origin, and, therefore, fixed and immutable'); Watts *Philosophies of Asia* (1995) at 12.

[16] Diwan, *Modern Hindu Law* (1958) at 18. The Rishi have been described as persons of 'higher spiritual experience and knowledge'; see Pal, *History of Hindu Law* (1958) at 106. Use of the expression Sruti itself would indicate that the time of the ecstatic seers, who themselves might have 'seen', is over and the revelation complete. See J. C. Heesterman, *The Inner Conflict of Tradition: Essays in Indian Ritual, Kingship, and Society* (Chicago/London: Univ. of Chicago Press, 1985) at 97.

[17] Venkataraman, *N. R. Raghavachariar's Hindu Law* (1987) at 4. On a similar view of timeless revelation in talmudic tradition, see above, Ch. 4, *Talmud, the Divine Will and Change.*

[18] Sen, *General Principle[s] of Hindu Jurisprudence* (1984) at 31; Diwan, *Modern Hindu Law* (1958) at 28. On the consequences of this for subsequent schools of law, and diversity in general, see below, *Sadachara and schools.*

thread'.[19] The sutras were written from (about) 800 BC to 200 BC and have today lost much of their importance; they were simply the first manifestations of the written tradition developing.[20] This became known generally as the Smriti ('the remembered', the tradition, as distinct from 'the heard'),[21] and the tradition became more refined with the writing of the sastras, the textbooks, covering much of life, and more particularly the dharmasastras, the main legal texts (on dharma, more later). The sastras were written from about 200 BC to 400 AD, so their compilation occurred in large part during the classical period of roman law, and overlapped as well with the writing of the Mishnah and possibly the Jerusalem Talmud. There is little if any discussion of roman or talmudic influence on the writing of the Smriti, but it is inconceivable that these developments were unknown. The Greeks, at least, would have been messengers, though it is possible that the information went from east to west, and that the sutras influenced the early stages of roman law, and the early sastras the classical roman writers. The 'golden age' of hindu jurisprudence was a time of great development elsewhere, and this is at least a great coincidence.[22]

The dharmasastras, in their totality, dealt with more than law, strictly defined. They extended to religious observance and penance, or expiation, though in the later period there is a tendency to concentrate on what looks more today, in the west, like law. There are three great dharmasastras, though the greatest of all, and the earliest, is that of Manu, or at least the mythical Manu, since the true authorship is said to be unknown.[23] Manu, around 200 BC (possibly), answered the 'long-felt need of a legal treatise', and his text is described as a landmark in the history of India and hinduism, an enormous reservoir of legal concepts, rules and institutions.[24] In cases of later conflict of authority, Manu is always said to prevail, a hindu version of the law of citations (and perhaps prior to it), with Manu and Papinian

---

[19] Diwan, *Modern Hindu Law* (1958) at 28; and see *Mayne's Treatise* (1991) at 16; Venkataraman, *N. R. Raghavachariar's Hindu Law* (1987) at 4.

[20] See Lingat, *Classical Law of India* (1973) at 18 ff., and 71 ('the little treatises ... touch law properly speaking only in an indirect and accessory manner') though (at 28) their study is 'essential if we are to do justice to the atmosphere which surrounded the birth of law in India and which impregnated it for ever afterwards'.

[21] Lingat, *Classical Law of India* (1973) at 9 ff.

[22] The quoted expression is that of Diwan, *Modern Hindu Law* (1958) at 29. For the possibility of elements of hindu law being adopted by the Romans, 'through the Greek and Egyptian channels', see M. Sharan, *Court Procedure in Ancient India* (New Delhi: Abhinav Publications, 1978) at 2; for the 'legend' of the great spartan law-giver, Lycurgus (9th century, BC) going to India, see K. Assimakopoulou, 'Comparative Law in the History of Greek Law' (1986) 39 Rev. hell. dr. int. 323; for discussion of hindu law in the writing of Nearchus, a companion of Alexander in the 4th century, BC, E., Bevan, 'India in Early Greek and Latin Literature' in E. Rapson (ed.), *The Cambridge History of India*, vol. I, *Ancient India* (Cambridge; Cambridge Univ. Press, 1922) 391 at 413, 414; and more generally for Indian thought 'present in the fashionable intellectual circuit of ancient Athens', Klostermaier, *Survey of Hinduism* (1994), above, at 19.

[23] See E. W. Hopkins (ed.), *The Ordinances of Manu*, trans. and intro. by A. Burnell (London: Trübner & Co., 1884).

[24] Diwan, *Modern Hindu Law* (1958) at 32; on the Manusmriti generally and its origins, see Lingat, *Classical Law of India* (1973) at 77 ff.; and for its dating see *Mayne's Treatise* (1991) at 19, 20 (estimates from 5th century BC to as late as 150 BC).

playing the same role.[25] After Manu, around 300 AD, came Yajnavalkya, himself listing twenty sages, starting with Manu, and whose text shows knowledge of Greek astronomy.[26] Finally, of the great sastras, comes that of Narada, possibly in the fourth or fifth century AD, whose text is less obviously religious in character; is said to concentrate on civil law; and shows Narada as not hesitating to differ from the earlier sages.[27]

While the sastras are the great law books, they are law books of a particular kind. Derived from the teaching of the Brahmans, from the earliest times and as both recorded (by the sutras) and remembered, the sastras have authority equivalent to that of the Mishnah or the Sunna. Though human in production, they are derived from the original source and, revelation being a continuing process, enjoy supreme authority. They are themselves 'beyond dispute' (though there is always interpretation).[28] They are also, in the tradition of the Vedas, not written in just your ordinary, legal prose. They consist of metrical, continuous verse (or at least mixed verse and prose) and divide not into chapters and sections but, naturally, into verses.[29] Law is here poetic. This helps it float, and who but Brahman could make law into poetry?

If the time of the sastras represented the golden age of hindu law, that of the later commentaries and digests represented the period of critical enquiry, expansion and consolidation. The commentaries and digests went on for a millennium (from 700 to 1700 AD, and the dates may here be more precise).[30] Both commentaries and digests accepted the sastras, though the commentaries were on individual sastras (as glosses on the Digest, or Coke on Littleton). So there were, on Manu, Medhatihi (ninth century, as the door of ijtihad began to close), Govindaraja (eleventh or twelfth century, around the birth of the common law) and Kulluka (the most renowned, in the thirteenth century); then, on Yajnavalkya, the Balakrida by Vis-

---

[25] On the roman law of citations, preferring Papinian as ultimate author, see above, Ch. 5, *Substantive, secular law*; and on Manu's authority, *Mayne's Treatise* (1991) at 18, 19 with refs.; Venkataraman, *N. R. Raghavachariar's Hindu Law* (1987) at 5.

[26] *Mayne's Treatise* (1991) at 15, 20; Lingat, *Classical Law of India* (1973) at 97 ff. (Yajnavalkya also 'celebrated theologian' and credited with well known treatise on yoga); and on the relations between Manu and Yajnavalkya, see Jayaswal, *Manu and Yajnavalkya* (1930).

[27] Diwan, *Modern Hindu Law* (1958) at 31, 34; *Mayne's Treatise* (1991) at 21; Lingat, *Classical Law of India* (1973) at 100 ff., notably at 102 (citing Dareste on whether Narada influenced by Roman law).

[28] Venkataraman, *N. R. Raghavachariar's Hindu Law* (1987) at 4 ('emanated from the Deity . . . in the language of inspired men'); *Mayne's Treatise* (1991) at 29.

[29] More precisely, the 'typical thirty-two syllable distichs called sloka or anustbh,' characteristic also of learned treatises in fields such as architecture and medicine. See Rocher, 'Hindu Conceptions of Law' (1978) at 1290; E. W. Hopkins, 'Growth of Law and Legal Institutions' (1922), above; Lingat, *Classical Law of India* (1973) at 73. For Manu's dharmasastra as a 'versified recension of an older treatise in prose,' see Hopkins (ed.), *Ordinances of Manu* (1884), above, at p. xviii; also at p. xxi for traces of roman law in metrical form, notably the Twelve Tables. The metric style of the original sanskrit is less clearly evident in translation. Thus Manu I: 98: 'The birth of a Brahman is a perpetual incarnation of *dharma*: for he exists for the sake of *dharma*, and is for the existence of the Vedas.' Ibid., at 13. For another form of law in poetry, in the adat law of Asia, see below, Ch. 9, *Adat law and chthonic law*.

[30] See Lingat, *Classical Law of India* (1973) ch. 6 ('The Commentaries and the Digests').

varupa (ninth century), the more famous Mitakshara by Vijnanesvara (eleventh century) ('practically freeing Hindu Law from its religious fetters', in the interesting language of Mayne, and giving rise to a major school);[31] and, on Narada, Asahaya (as early as the seventh century). The digests generally came later, from the twelfth century, and attempted syntheses of the Smriti, with varying success.[32] There were also particular treatises and the most famous of these, the Dayabhaga by Jimutava-hana (on partition and succession, at the heart of hindu law) has given rise to a second major school of law.

These are many names, and there are many, many, more, so it is evident that there was here a written, legal tradition of enormous vitality and prestige, whose work was the principal source of law for a population which has always been one of the world's largest. The works are private ones, like those of the mufti, and they prevailed without judicial or legislative foundation. Hindu law is not official law, in its classic sources; nor did it tend to large institutions, or potentially corrupt institu-tions. This seems to be shared (in greater or less measure) by all explicitly religious legal traditions, regardless of their breadth of application. If they are to get the message through, it has to be done by the word.

## POETIC JUSTICE

Even private law, however, needs some forum for what is today called application. We don't know much, however, about early forms of hindu dispute resolution, nor about its 'judicial' philosophy.[33] It may be that a notion of applying law was seen as consistent with the written sources. Then again, poetry doesn't lend itself to appli-cation, so the general view may have been closer to the islamic one, of 'law-finding' as a collaborative effort of parties and adjudicators.[34] The Vedas do refer to some forms of communal organization. There was the Parishad, an assembly of advisers on questions of 'philosophy'; the Samiti, a general deliberative body on policy and the minor forms of legislation which existed; and the Sabha, a kind of village council which acted as the main agency of dispute resolution.[35] The Sabha was continued by all the Smriti authors. It functioned with a president, the pradvivaka, who might yield to the king as president, though the king would ordinarily accept

[31] *Mayne's Treatise* (1991) at 32.

[32] For exposition of the Krityakalpataru of Lakshmidhara, see Derrett and Iyer, 'Hindu Law' (1974) at 143 ff.

[33] Rocher, 'Hindu Conceptions of Law' (1978) at 1302 ('Next to nothing is known about actual legal practice in ancient India'). Cf., however, for what is known, Varadaghariar, *Hindu Judicial System* (1946); Sharan, *Court Procedure* (1978), above, notably ch. 2; and for progression of procedural rules from Manu through Narada, Desai, *Mulla [on] Principles of Hindu Law* (1966) at 24–6.

[34] See above, Ch. 6, *Qadi justice and mufti learning*; and on Dharmasastras regarding administration of justice not merely as matter of public order, but as sacred and religious duty, Varadaghariar, *Hindu Judicial System* (1946) at 122.

[35] Varadaghariar, *Hindu Judicial System* (1946) at 13; Pal, *History of Hindu Law* (1958) at 20, 99; Jayaswal, *Manu and Yajnavalkya* (1930) at 110 ff.

the opinion of Sabha members.[36] As things became inevitably more complicated, the Sabha, which functioned as the king's court, itself derived directly from the Vedas, became the summit of more specialized, people's courts. Thus there was the Puga, or most local of village courts, the Sreni or commercial court and the Kula or family court.[37] And, for the first time in religious legal thinking, and perhaps for the first time anywhere, there were appeals, and even a rather complicated structure of them. From the lowest court in the hierarchy (there was one), the Puga, you could appeal successively through the Sreni, the Kula and eventually to the king's court. At each level appeal was possible to the courts above, and each appeared to have unlimited appellate jurisdiction.[38] If this begins to sound 'modern' and western, it probably was not. There were no written records, no professional pleaders[39] and absolutely no concept of creating precedent by appellate or any other adjudicative decision. The notion of asking for a different result from a different court may have come from a fear of bias in going back to the same court. The notion of res judicata appears to have been recognized only by Narada in the fourth- or fifth-century AD.[40] This was very late; the burden of cases may have had something to do with it.

## POETIC LAW

The law of the sastras appears in no way to have suffered from its manner of expression. As early as Manu the oft-repeated eighteen titles of hindu law were listed: recovery of debt, deposit, sale without ownership (nemo dat is ever with us), partnership, resumption of gift, non-payment of wages, non-performance of agreements, rescission of sale and purchase, disputes between master and servant, boundary disputes, assault, defamation, theft, robbery and violence, adultery, mutual duties of husband and wife, partition and inheritance, and gambling and betting.[41] Here is 'every branch of jurisprudence',[42] though the centre of gravity appears to have been in the complex of family, property and succession law, which has also had the greatest ultimate power of survival.

Henry Maine drew the learning for his *Ancient Law* (and the famous evolution-

---

[36] Venkataraman, *N. R. Raghavachariar's Hindu Law* (1987) at 3. On the king's obligation to the sastras, see below, *Dharma and the king*.

[37] Venkataraman, *N. R. Raghavachariar's Hindu Law* (1987) at 3; *Mayne's Treatise* (1991) at 10, with references; Varadaghariar, *Hindu Judicial System* (1946) at 100; Desai, *Mulla [on] Principles of Hindu Law* (1966) at 37, 38; Sharan, *Court Procedure* (1978), above, at 25.

[38] Ibid.

[39] See L. Rocher, '"Lawyers" in Classical Hindu Law' (1968–9) 3 Law & Soc. Rev. 383, reproduced in V. Nanda and S. Sinha, *Hindu Law and Legal Theory* (New York: New York Univ. Press, 1996) at 141.

[40] Venkataraman, *N. R. Raghavachariar's Hindu Law* (1987) at 5. On the absence or weakness of res judicata in talmudic and islamic law, where return to the original court is often possible, see above, Ch. 4, *Applying divine law* and Ch. 6, *Qadi justice and mufti learning*.

[41] See Sen, *General Principle[s] of Hindu Jurisprudence* (1984) at 33, who recasts the hindu pattern into that of roman law (persons, things and actions).

[42] Derrett, *Introduction to Modern Hindu Law* (1963) at 7.

ary thesis of the person moving from status to contract) from hindu law, yet at the same time taught the resemblances between hindu family law and early European law.[43] In both there was concern with the large and enduring family, and property was used as a means of its support and survival. Marriage in hindu law was a profoundly religious institution, though the form of its celebration varied. There were eight ways of getting married, four approved, four 'unapproved', though all apparently resulted in marriage. The notion of gift or even sale of the bride by the father is present in some of them, and there was then clearly financial benefit involved. Minority was not a ground of invalidation.[44] Polygamy was permitted, 'though monogamy . . . recommended by the texts' and local tradition could operate to prevent a second marriage.[45] Once constituted, the family saw its patrimony protected by the absence of testamentary disposition and by the notion of joint family property, by virtue of which property vested in the family itself, necessitating formal measures of partition in the event of death of the father. This was not a minor and technical point of succession law; it brought about the great divide between the main schools of hindu law. The Mitakshara school considered sons co-owners with the father on their birth; the Dayabhaga delayed joint ownership until the father's death.[46] Women did not succeed. Private ownership of land was thus possible, though the transition from common tillage to private ownership appears to have occurred between Manu and Yajnavalkya (who speaks of transfer by sale).[47]

Yet much of the great corpus of hindu law is now said to be obsolete, and is even difficult to find. It was written in Sanskrit, now infrequently known in India, and translations brought about by the British were highly selective and at times 'of no value'.[48] Of the eighteen titles, sixteen are now said to be obsolete and replaced by Anglo-Indian law.[49] There have been profound changes in the remaining two titles,

---

[43] H. Maine, *Ancient Law: its connection with the early history of society and its relation to modern ideas*, 10th edn. (Boston: Beacon Press, 1963, 1st edn. 1861) at 165 ('the movement of the progressive societies has hitherto been a movement *from Status to Contract*'); and for Maine's comparison of early European (roman and germanic) and hindu law, see notably chs. 6 and 7 on the law of succession. Cf., for contemporary tendency of western law to return from contract to status, above, Ch. 5, *Law's expansion*.

[44] See Venkataraman, *N. R. Raghavachariar's Hindu Law* (1987) at 35 ff.; on the forms of marriage, also described as 'orthodox' and 'unorthodox', with different legal consequences attaching to each, see L. Sternbach, *Juridical Studies in Ancient Indian Law* (Delhi: Motilal Banarsidass, 1965) at 347; Lingat, *Classical Law of India* (1973) at 59, 60; and on the controversy surrounding bride sale, see Hopkins (ed.), *Ordinances of Manu* (1884), above, at 291.

[45] Venkataraman, *N. R. Raghavachariar's Hindu Law* (1987) at 33.

[46] Markby, *Hindu and Mahommedan Law* (1977) at 35, 36; Trevelyan, *Hindu Law as administered in British India* (1913) at 212, 213; Derrett and Iyer, 'Hindu Law' (1974) at 151; Lingat, *Classical Law of India* (1973) at 62.

[47] Markby, *Hindu and Mahommedan Law* (1977), at 18, 19; and see J. Derrett, 'The Development of the Concept of Property in India circa AD 800–1800' (1962) Zvgl Rwiss 15.

[48] The judgment is that of Mayne and Kuppuswami, *Mayne's Treatise* (1991) at 39.

[49] Markby, *Hindu and Mahommedan Law* (1977) at 17. There are vestiges of the old law in the Anglo-Indian law, though few. On survival of the damdupat rule (interest limited to a maximum of the capital owed) and the benami agreement, similar to fiducia and trusts (literally 'without name' or putting property in the name of another), see David and Brierley, *Major Legal Systems* (1985) at 490, 496, with refs.; Desai, *Mulla [on] Principles of Hindu Law* (1966) at 574–83; Derrett and Iyer, 'Hindu Law' (1974) at 153.

those of partition and inheritance and husband and wife, notably with regard to marriage. It can no longer be polygamous; the wife's consent is now required; divorce, originally precluded, is now authorized;[50] and nullity for lack of age is recognized. In short, the drama of hindu law is in knowing whether it is still alive, which is a very large question of the immediate relations between major, complex traditions.[51]

# KARMA, DHARMA AND THE KING

Hindu law has accumulated a vast literature, yet nests in a still larger field of thought, identifiable as hindu philosophy or hindu theology. This immediately tells us something about the place of law in this particular world, though it tells us little about the reasons for such a state of affairs, nor about the consequences. To understand why hindu law is the way it is, you have to ask questions about hindu thought in general, and then speculate in a way that modern hindu lawyers don't necessarily have to, to get their work done. If your speculation is wrong, it's probably all right, since the chances are good you're not hindu yourself, and even if you are, there is a lot of room for speculation.

## THE WEIGHT OF KARMA

Karma is what we do in life, and there are good karmas, which bring well-being and pleasure, and bad karmas, which bring sadness and suffering. Everbody knows that they have some responsibility for what they do in life, but hindu thought takes this beyond the other religions. The soul is immortal and simply lives in temporary shelters, those of human bodies. When a human body dies the soul does not simply float off to some stipulated, non-verifiable place. It must necessarily take shelter again, in another physical form, here on earth, which everyone knows and thinks they understand. And since it is the same soul, with the same history of karma, its past karma continues to have effect. Bad karmas will notably preclude salvation, becoming close to Brahman, so a new life is in no way a fresh start.[52] It's like succession without benefit of inventory, as the civilians say—the debts accumulate as well as the assets, and the new life is just a chance to pay them off.

---

[50] For the absence of divorce in hindu law yet borrowing of talaq from islamic law, see B. Jackson, 'Evolution and Foreign Influence in Ancient Law' (1968) 16 Am. J. Comp. Law 372 at 376; and for vedic notions of indissolubility of marriage, Pal, *History of Hindu Law* (1958) at 375; Jayaswal, *Manu and Yajnavalkya* (1930) at 229–31.

[51] See below, *Hindu law in India.*

[52] This extends, notably, to crime. See Rocher, 'Hindu Conceptions of Law' (1978) at 1287 ('Hindu crime extends beyond this life, and is linked to the theory of rebirth').

The teaching of karma comes from the Upanishads, which accompany the Vedas and have been around almost as long. They too are revelation—Sruti—and adhering to hindu faith in principle (the qualification is important) means adhering to Sruti. Since a hindu life is one of many, of the same soul, there are many consequences of present and future karma which you should bear in mind, and they are not just legal consequences. So when Manu wrote down eighteen titles of law, all of which look just like chapters in a western legal digest of some kind, he was reflecting a more limited concept of law than that which prevails in talmudic or islamic thought. This seems to flow—and this is speculation—from the ongoing effect of karma and the detailed teaching on the eternal nature of the soul. The lawyers didn't feel this was part of their job, and while Manu said a lot about things not strictly legal, by the time we get to Narada the theology or philosophy is largely left aside. If you are hindu, you have to know about it, but it can be learned from someone other than the lawyers. They never got to occupy the field, or didn't think they could, given the existence of the Upanishads. There is not even a direct equivalent, in Sanskrit, for the word 'law',[53] so the lawyers did a great deal without that much support. If the word 'law' was taken out of western languages, there would probably be a lot less said about it.

There is therefore a lot of hindu teaching outside the law books about how to live a life. There are other sutras and sastras, notably those of politics (arthasutras, arthasastras) and pleasure (kamasutras, kamasastras) and Manu admits that in terms of personal conduct a further criterion of a'tma tushti, or internal guidance, is recognized, an 'internal ethical standard' (living 'inside the law' again, though here perhaps having a larger place).[54] Yet it would not be faithful to the tradition to conclude that there is here a limited role of law and hence a separation of law and morals, in the western sense. Some western scholars have so argued, in concluding that the religious character of hindu law has been 'greatly exaggerated',[55] and they have prayed in aid distinctions made within hindu law itself, such as those between duties enforceable by secular authority (vyavahara) and those enforceable by conscience.[56] If there is a 'civil law' identifiable as such within hindu law, however, the same can be said about other religious laws, such as talmudic law and islamic law,

---

[53] Derrett, *Introduction to Modern Hindu Law* (1963) at 499; though see, for Sanskrit equivalent in word daya or rule, Derrett and Iyer, 'Hindu Conception of Law' (1975) at 110.

[54] On living inside the law, in talmudic tradition, see above, Ch. 4, *Halakhah and aggadah*, and for a similar idea in islamic tradition, above, Ch. 6, *Shari'a and kalam*.

[55] *Mayne's Treatise* (1991) at 12; Derrett, *Introduction to Modern Hindu Law* (1963) at 2 ('great mistake to suppose that it was founded or rooted in theology or philosophy'). Cf. Varadaghariar, *Hindu Judicial System* (1946) at 26 (view of Mayne 'difficult to take seriously', Mayne speaking with 'his usual contempt' of Brahminical India).

[56] Diwan, *Modern Hindu Law* (1958) at 20 (though Judicial Committee of the Privy Council largely converted into legal/moral, mandatory/directory distinctions). And on the notion of vyavahara as 'civil law', distinct from remaining religious (achara) and moral (prayaschitta) obligations of dharma, see *Mayne's Treatise* (1991) at 6, 11; S. Purohit, *Ancient Indian Legal Philosophy* (1994) at 84 ff.; and Kane, *History of the Dharmasastra*, vol. III (1973) at 242 ff.

and it is admitted there (except by those who believe that tradition counts for more than revelation) that all the law is infused by its religious source. You may wish to talk about law and morals, but the reason it *is* law is because of the (religious) morals, which infuse all types of obligation. So it has also been argued, from within and without the tradition, that speaking of a separation of law and morals would be to place 'foreign garb' on hindu law,[57] that separation might be possible but that the two can never be 'detached'.[58] We may end up with something which resembles the wavy, permeable line of talmudic/islamic law. It's all religious, all within revelation, but you can make out, if you want to, the halakhah, the shari'a, the vyavahara. In hindu law it may be a little easier, though, to make it out. Revelation is more distant, and less sharply defined; the weight of karma perhaps leaves a less total role for law (in contrast with other religious traditions); and the king has very specific legal duties, which we've finally reached.

## DHARMA AND THE KING

Everybody says that talmudic and islamic legal traditions are ones of obligation—obligation to God and ensuing obligations to study and to act towards others in accordance with God's will. Yet the notion of obligation in these traditions is a diffused one. It is everywhere but has never really crystallized into an abstract, general concept. This is what hindu thought has done, however, in originating the concept of dharma. Dharma is impossible to define, but comes from the root dhr, signifying that which sustains and upholds life. It is all the social glue, and sustains both individuals and community, and both material and spiritual life. It is a 'highly distinctive, extraordinarily stable grand idea'[59] (Brahman is a really big thinker) and exists in both grand, unbounded form and in particular, even minute, duties. It has been said that it can only be defined by its content,[60] yet its ultimate content may be as indeterminate as its general outline. Each of us, however, is capable of knowing our dharma (which is going to be determined in large measure by past karma) so the need for a general definition is only a systemic one, and we are again not here concerned with system. Dharma of course infuses hindu law, and also all other obligations of hindu tradition, and in a sense that which we can make out as law is a part, and part only, of dharma. Dharma runs through everything,

---

[57]   Sen, *General Principle[s] of Hindu Jurisprudence* (1984) at 7; Diwan, *Modern Hindu Law* (1958) at 21 ('does not conform to the Austinian view . . . moral aspect which pervades throughout the rules of law'); and see Lingat, *Classical Law of India* (1973) at p. xiii (hindu jurists must be concerned with many duties which cannot be object of external restraint, distinction between law and morals 'essential only for the western jurist').

[58]   Sen, *General Principle[s] of Hindu Jurisprudence* (1984) at 7.

[59]   C. Geertz, *Local Knowledge* (New York: Basic Books, 1983) at 195, 199.

[60]   *Mayne's Treatise* (1991) at 7; for notion of 'all righteousness', see Derrett and Iyer, 'Hindu Conception of Law' (1975) at 110; and for that of 'mystic force' which both pervades and regulates universe, Purohit, *Ancient Indian Legal Philosophy* (1994) at 35. Dharma may also be seen in other religious legal traditions; see T. Manickam, *Dharma according to Manu and Moses* (Bangalore: Dharmaram Publications, 1977).

however, so there is a specific, hindu reason why it is impossible to separate law from morals.

What is the relation between dharma and the king? In modern language a large, constitutional principle is involved, which has never received the same attention in other religious traditions. Nor has it always received the same solution in western legal tradition.[61] The principle is that the king's dharma is to enforce the dharma of others. Put traditionally, the law is king, or even king of kings, and the sastras make it clear that in the king's court it is the sastric law which the king is to apply.[62] The king's position as enforcer is thereby strengthened, since the king has the power of danda,[63] the secular instrument of enforcement (where the king uses it, things look very legal) yet is weakened at the same time, since the king is necessarily, and forever, subordinate to the law. Now, it may be said, it's all very well to announce a principle, but the key is in enforcement (a very western view), and it is true that hindu thought did not anticipate the ultimate role of some western courts. There was never a secular authority beyond the king, to ensure the king's compliance with law. Yet there was dharma, that of the king, and there was karma, such that a king who did not act according to law accumulated bad karma.[64] And that didn't just mean some distant, and potential, religious sanction. It meant living lives, life after life, in repayment of the bad karma. If you are a king, the idea of being other than king is a repugnant one, and bad karmas could mean much more than not being king, in the next life. They could mean very unfortunate forms of existence indeed, and those disgruntled litigants might well be still around. So ongoing karma could be spelt out in imaginative detail for the edification of secular authority, and this may have had something to do with the very articulation of the principle of the king's subservience to law. So kings could legislate, but in necessarily minor form,[65]

---

[61] Roman law taught that the ruler was not bound by the law. See Ulpian, Digest 1. 3. 31 ('The Emperor is free from the operation of the law'), in S. P. Scott, *The Civil Law*, vol. II. (Cincinatti: The Central Trust Co., 1932) at 225; *The Digest of Justinian*, trans. A. Watson, vol. I (Philadelphia: Univ. of Pennsylvania Press, 1985), 13. This was good news for the Crown in England in its struggle with Parliament, and one of the few temptations in roman law for French royal authority. The feudal equivalent was that of the Crown being incapable of wrongdoing, now most alive, however, in the republican jurisdiction of the USA, in the form of state immunity against tort claims. For the inevitable decline of the doctrine, see W. P. Keeton (ed.), *Prosser and Keeton on the Law of Torts*, 5th edn. (St. Paul, Mich.: West Publishing, 1984) ch. 25 (though it remains a vigorous means of state defence against liability created by federal law).

[62] See *Mayne's Treatise* (1991) at 11 (putting it in terms of the law book as a member of the king's court); Varadaghariar, *Hindu Judicial System* (1946) at 31, 87; Heesterman, *Inner Conflict of Tradition*, (1985), above, at 115; J. C. Heesterman, 'India and the Inner Conflict of Tradition' (1973) 102, No. 1 *Daedalus* 97, notably at 101 (on inner conflict in tradition between '"kingly" order immanent in social relations and the transcendent brahminical order'). The king's court itself, of course, is a consequence of the king's dharma to administer justice.

[63] Lingat, *Classical Law of India* (1973) at 214; Diwan, *Modern Hindu Law* (1958) at 32.

[64] See Lingat, *Classical Law of India* (1973) at 66, citing *Gaut.*, XII. 48 ('the guilt recoils onto him').

[65] Sen, *General Principle[s] of Hindu Jurisprudence* (1984) at 30; Diwan, *Modern Hindu Law* (1958) at 24; Lingat, *Classical Law of India* (1973) at 224 ff. Narada, however, would have given absolute authority to the king; the European debate was thus replicated to some extent, prior to it, in hindu law. Narada still enjoined the king to stay within the sacred law. Diwan, *Modern Hindu Law* (1958) at 34.

since the law was already there, in the sastras, and legislation in violation of it would be violation of the king's dharma, bad karma.

## FULFILLING DHARMA

For us ordinary people, there is not only the menace of accumulated bad karma, but also the secular power of the king, danda, to ensure our compliance with our own, individual dharma. Dharma for each of us is more than a general concept of doing good; it assigns to each of us a place in life and even specific obligations in the course of living that life. This is where the castes, or varna, come in, and they represent not just an arbitrary pattern of social class, or arbitrary feudal authority, but a perfectly logical consequence of everything hindu religious thought has developed. This is why castes continue to prevail today. They are an inherent element in a much larger tradition, and extracting them, to reform and eliminate them, is a very difficult enterprise. Hundreds of millions of people believe in them, as an inherent part of their larger faith. Maine talked of the transition from status to contract, but most people in India have never heard of Maine.[66]

Castes exist because they are dictated by accumulated karma, in previous lives.[67] If castes didn't exist, there would be no demonstrable evidence of the effect of bad karma, so castes must exist. They are a kind of necessary grouping or classing of the consequences of different kinds of previous lives, a consequence of the ongoing soul, and no historical work has been able to show them as a product of particular social circumstances in India at a particular time. So far as is known, they have existed since the Vedas became known, prior to the Smriti.[68] There are four castes or varnas, to which particular dharmas attach: the Brahmans (who teach), the Kshatriya (who protect, and are warriors and benefactors), the Vaishyas (who trade) and the Sudras (who are servants). In law there is no fifth class of untouchables, though popular conceptions of untouchables translate into Sudras.[69] There are large numbers of sub-classes, and duties attaching at different stages in the lives of all members of all classes. Now, if all of these ongoing souls are taken into account, there are problems in administering a caste structure. There could be billions of souls (depending on the point of departure) and only about a billion existing lives, though this problem may be solved by admitting new lives in non-human form, which has interesting consequences for hindu views of the natural world. There are also problems in reconciling the theory of karma with the now widespread view that caste is acquired by birth, and by virtue of one's parents' caste. Why should the sins of our parents be visited upon us? Should not good

[66] See above, *Poetic law*.

[67] Diwan, *Modern Hindu Law* (1958) at 16, 17; and on the development of notions of karma and rebirth, see Lipner, *Hindus* (1994), above, at 230 ff.

[68] Diwan, *Modern Hindu Law* (1958) at 28; and see Lingat, *Classical Law of India* (1973) at 30 for their being 'fully formulated' by the dharma-sutras.

[69] Derrett, *Introduction to Modern Hindu Law* (1963) at 28.

karma, as in classical theory, justify a varna higher than that previously enjoyed and somehow demonstrably so? This appears recognized, in the legal literature at least, as a conceptual and actual problem, a present vulnerability of the tradition. Thus, 'with the passage of time caste acquired significance as indicative of social status arising by virtue of birth only. The social inequality, if any, implied in the system does not appe[a]r to have led to ill will so long as it did not involve disparity in material advantages.'[70] Recent changes in conditions 'arising from the impact of the West and from the new methods of education and public administration have changed the out-look on the subject'.[71] Nor does the structure admit individual improvement of caste, as a palliative measure, though the possibility of change of an entire caste is apparently recognized.[72] Discrimination on the basis of caste has today been prohibited, in India, by the Indian Constitution. How the constitution of a modern nation-state can do this is a larger question, but the constitutional debate allows challenge to the caste tradition, there where it is vulnerable.[73] Since inequality of status is a fundamental feature of traditional hindu teaching, those suffering particular inequalities, such as women, are deprived in debate of the leverage of a general hindu principle of equality. As in islamic law, however, there are classic instances of beneficial change in the status of women, notably Narada's admission, about a millennium and a half ago, of women's rights to hold and inherit property,[74] a reform now consolidated by modern legislation.

Absent any general principle of equality in hindu society, and given the pervasive presence of dharma, the notion of rights, as individual power, or as anything else, is not inherent in hindu thought. As in islamic tradition, however, efforts are being made to reconcile hindu tradition with the teaching of rights and to justify disparity. Dharma would thus protect the weak (so the theory) and both freedom of movement and physical health would be implicit in a hindu world. The incorpor-

[70] Venkataraman, N. R. Raghavachariar's Hindu Law (1987) at 20.

[71] Ibid.

[72] See Derrett, Introduction to Modern Hindu Law (1963) at 28, 29. The change could be effectively opposed by another caste, however, and would require more than a majority of the changing caste to be brought about. On exit from hinduism entirely, however, see below, Hindu identity.

[73] See Galanter, Competing Equalities (1984); and on the growing influence of US legal scholarship in India, see R. Dhavan, 'Borrowed Ideas: On the Impact of American Scholarship on Indian Law' (1985) 33 Am. J. Comp. L. 505.

[74] Diwan, Modern Hindu Law (1958) at 35; though for ongoing gender inequalities in enjoyment of land, see B. Agarwal, A field of one's own: gender and land rights in South Asia (Cambridge: Cambridge Univ. Press, 1994), notably on the respective roles of 'customary' law, hindu law and contemporary laws. On the status of women generally in hindu tradition see J. O'Connor, 'Rereading, reconceiving and reconstructing traditions: feminist research in religion' (1989) 17 Women's St. 101 at 119, 120; Srivastava, Women and the Law (1985); A. S. Altekar, The Position of Women in Hindu Civilization: From Prehistoric Times to the Present Day, 2nd edn. (Delhi: Motilal Banarsidass, 1959); D. Mitter, The Position of Women in Hindu Law (New Delhi: Inter-India Publications, 1913, repr. 1984); Klostermaier, Survey of Hinduism (1994), above, ch. 23; and for colonial re-interpretation of hindu tradition (abolition of female infanticide and sati (widow burning)), see D. Engels, 'Wives, Widows and Workers: Women and the Law in Colonial India' in W. J. Mommsen and J. A. de Moor, European Expansion and Law: The Encounter of European and Indigenous Law in 19th- and 20th-Century Africa and Asia (Oxford/New York: Berg Publishers, 1992) at 159.

ation of rights into the Indian Constitution has accelerated this debate enormously. It is part of the entire process of defining, or attempting to define, the nature of Indian law today.[75]

Rationality in hindu legal tradition is also in function of dharma. The dharma of the Brahmans is to teach the law flowing from the Vedas. Where they got it from is an interesting question, and some answers are available, but there are no indications that they simply made it up, as rational construction. The Vedas and the sastras already tell us something about the rationality of hindu thought, by their metric form. This is not how deduction expresses itself, and Manu's eighteen titles of law demonstrate no impulse to systematize. So the place of reason is 'a circumscribed and limited one',[76] its realm 'granular',[77] though more liberty was later taken in the development of the commentaries and digests, and even in the later sastras (Narada, the 'progressive sage'). No doors were closed here, and much endeavour continued to be expended. Notions of change and tolerance of change are therefore vitally important in the ongoing life of hindu law.


## TOLERATING CHANGE


There is no trace in hindu law of procedural limits or institutional restraints, as were so important in the (slow) development of roman law and the common law. In this, hindu law parallels talmudic and islamic law in moving directly from chthonic to revealed substantive law, with courts and judges meant to give effect to it, in all its breadth. Like talmudic and islamic law, however, there are external restraints on change, in the form of primary sources which are themselves 'beyond dispute'.[78] Talmudic law admitted the possibility of change in the world, then smothered it with obligation. Islamic law went further, in explicitly encouraging knowledge, then deciding it had to shut the door on it. In both, an acknowledged concept of change went underground, into the dialogic form and the schools and movements of talmudic law, into the institutionalized diversity and subtlety of islamic law. Hindu law also recognizes the possibility of change, both of law and of the world, but its attitude towards it is perhaps closer to that of chthonic law than to any of the others. It just tolerates it, without in any way encouraging it, as something that's going to happen, but which shouldn't disturb the basic harmony of the world. If it does, it's bad karma, and this too will be dealt with. Thus, for a written tradition, hindu tradition is incredibly roomy. Toleration is not at the

---

[75] See below, *Hindu law in India*.
[76] Sen, *General Principle[s] of Hindu Jurisprudence* (1984) at 16.
[77] Geertz, *Local Knowledge* (1983), above, at 195.
[78] Above, this Chapter, *Of vedas, sastras and commentaries*.

perimeter of it, but at the centre. And toleration turns out to have its own kind of discipline.

## TIME AND BRAHMAN

The parallel between chthonic and hindu tradition is evident in the attitude of both towards time. In neither does it flow, from then to now and on to the beyond; it rather just comes around, again and again.[79] In the chthonic world it was not the year which ended but the world, which had to be revived and reborn, in an endless process of recycling which engaged the necessary collaboration of all. In the perpetuation of souls, hindu tradition individualizes this process, and it is a very realistic position. Nobody is ever going to go anywhere; we are all here, for the duration, and we can only hope to do better the next time around. But it's still the same soul, still the same place and still the same temptations. Things can be done differently, but the idea of change is a necessarily muted one in a permanent, recycling world.

It is also a world permanently infused with Brahman, who (or which) provides an underlying harmony in everything. This is not an easy idea to get hold of, particularly for those with western training. Hindu theology is not 'monarchical' in form, as are the religions which have so influenced western thought. In jewish, christian and islamic religions, God is up there, a kind of prefiguration of the Austinian sovereign, and we are all down here, expected to do as bidden. We also know what God looks like, a kind of wiser, older version of ourselves. God thus has a place, a person and a hierarchical function. If you want to believe in such a God in hinduism, you're perfectly entitled to, and hindus do subscribe to many gods, notably Vishnu and Shiva. Brahman, however, is beyond particular gods, however god-like they may be. Brahman has no particular person, no particular place, no particular, hierarchical function. Brahman is 'the actor of the world ... the actor who is playing all the parts at once'.[80] And each of us is God or Brahman, Brahman wearing our particular mask, and all beings and things are equally infused with this supreme form of being. Since each of us represents supreme being, each of us is fundamental. The self is of profound importance, hence the necessity of dharma as a means of bringing about our complete fulfillment, drawing near to the perfection of Brahman. So Brahman *dances* the whole universe, though is eventually and profoundly unknowable to us.[81] And since Brahman is common to all things, never dividing them, Brahman has to exist in non-dual (advita, from dva or duo) or, we would say today, non-binary form. Brahman cannot be thought of as one or as

[79] On the cyclical nature of hindu time, see Watts, *Philosophies of Asia* (1995) at 12; Sen, *General Principle[s] of Hindu Jurisprudence* (1984) at 9; Weggel, *Die Asiaten* (1989) at 200; but for variations in hindu conceptions of time, Lipner, *Hindus* (1994), above, at 251 ff.

[80] Watts, *Philosophies of Asia* (1995) at 6. Brahman, in the sense of the absolute, mystical power of the world, also must be distinguished from Brahma, a particular God, of creation.

[81] Watts, *Philosophies of Asia* (1995) at 14, 15.

many (either–or thinking); Brahman dances everyone and everything so you just cannot think in terms of opposites or dichotomies or boundaries. Brahman just *is*, here and everywhere, and only Brahman knows how to do it.

Hinduism therefore just *has* to be a 'commonwealth of all faiths' since that's how it sees the world, infused with a 'unity of Spirit under a plurality of forms'.[82] Each god is a manifestation of Brahman; in the ultimate world there are no differentiations of I and thou, subject and object. The self cannot exist, as self, without the other, as other, and thus both are fundamentally united. Losing sight of the fundamental unity of the world is to succumb to the illusion (maya) that opposites are really separate from each other.[83] Separation cannot really happen (Carlos Fuentes must know this teaching)[84] and change (going from one separate thing or form to another) is also necessarily illusion. What is most essential is getting to understand all of this. So hinduism has no particular, fixed dogmas or theories, no formal institutions, since it is most concerned with bringing about a transformation of everyday consciousness, a simple realization that 'this is the way things are'.[85]

Now, what would you like to change? You can of course change things, play the game of hide-and-seek. Those who have not seen the way things are will be doing so all the time, so there will be changes in the world, which must be tolerated. And even those who have understood, whose consciousness has been transformed, may prefer the world to take one particular shape rather than another, since it has to take, after all, some shape. Corruption may also be a reason for change, and the word comes up in discussion of hinduism,[86] though today in India it is more associated with the state, as elsewhere. So there are changes, which are not really encouraged, but are necessarily tolerated. And don't forget the bad karma; some changes are not wise ones.

### SADACHARA AND SCHOOLS

In a sense, hindu teaching makes a virtue of necessity. Like the Normans, the Vedic-Aryans faced a trop-plein of local ways of life on their arrival in the rich, southern lands. The explications of the Vedas had therefore to show why they should be accepted, and the surest way of doing so was to explain them largely in terms of

---

[82] Venkataraman, *N. R. Raghavachariar's Hindu Law* (1987) at 19, 20 ('Hinduism . . . a mass of fluctuating faiths and opinions . . . marvellously catholic and elastic . . . marked by eclecticism and tolerance and almost unlimited freedom of private worship'; even Charmans, who eat meat of dead animals, included within it); Diwan, *Modern Hindu Law* (1958) at 3 (hindu religion was able 'to restore all thoughts, ideas, dissentions, practices and professions in its fold and retained its basic unity'); Purohit, *Ancient Indian Legal Philosophy* (1994) at 9 (on logical consequences of concept of 'One Supreme God' on legal philosophy and 'great strength' of Vedas being avoidance of dominance of world by one god).

[83] Watts, *Philosophies of Asia* (1995) at 17, 28.

[84] See, for Fuentes on separation, above, Preface.

[85] Watts, *Philosophies of Asia* (1995) at 19.

[86] See Diwan, *Modern Hindu Law* (1958) at 3 ('Whenever a saint or religious reformer attempted the task of reforming Hindu religion and fought the irrational or corrupt practices which crept into it, a sect was born').

local practice.[87] In any event, the law which the Vedas themselves did not contain had to be drawn from somewhere, and there was no reason to be disruptive about its articulation. Local tradition, of the virtuous, could even be shown to have unsuspected, divine qualities. This must have been taken as good news. So, from Manu on, sadachara, that which has been handed down from time immemorial, by those who are virtuous, has also figured as a source of hindu law. In contemporary books it is usually referred to as 'custom' or 'usage' and we see here the same conversion of normative information into repetitive fact as has occurred in the west, yet the language of sadachara makes it clear that we are dealing with informal, local tradition.[88] What distinguishes hinduism from other traditions, religious and other, is that informal tradition is recognized generally as having priority even over the sacred texts.[89] This may appear astonishing, but you have to learn to be tolerant. If the sacred texts originally only acknowledged the teaching of the virtuous locals, they should continue to do so; if the teaching changes, the law should also change. It has to be within the requirements of dharma, but there are many ways of doing so, as there can be many gods. Later tradition is simply previously unrevealed revelation.[90] In the same way the later commentaries, as reflecting later forms of tradition, are taken as having priority over the earlier sastras, where conflict is seen (though, of course, often it is not seen).[91] There is therefore no obstacle to a people changing its law,[92] though of course there is no way of accomplishing this by individual will or formal act.

A commonwealth of faiths must lead to diversity in law, and hindu law has been diverse, apparently, from its origins. The Brahmans taught versions of the Vedas in different regions, in largely oral form, so the local traditions gained in status.[93] The sastras were more precise in law, but poetry doesn't nail much down, so diversity

---

[87] See Derrett, *Introduction to Modern Hindu Law* (1963) at 1; *Mayne's Treatise* (1991) at 7 (analogy with recording rules of grammar) and 27 (unstructured nature of Manu's 18 titles of law showing 'practical needs of society'); Venkataraman, *N. R. Raghavachariar's Hindu Law* (1987) at 2.

[88] See Lingat, *Classical Law of India* (1973) at 14 ('One must take care to avoid confusing this ideal "custom" with what *we* call custom ... *Sadacara* is a religious life ... It amounts to the practices observed from generation to generation by *sistas*, or those who are at once *instructed* and virtuous').

[89] See *Mayne's Treatise* (1991) at 44–6; Derrett, *Introduction to Modern Hindu Law* (1963) at 13; Venkataraman, *N. R. Raghavachariar's Hindu Law* (1987) at 14; Diwan, *Modern Hindu Law* (1958) at 23; Desai, *Mulla [on] Principles of Hindu Law* (1966) at 2; M. P. Jain, *Outlines of Indian Legal History* (1966) at 712; Trevelyan, *Hindu law as administered in British India* (1913) at 23; Purohit, *Ancient Indian Legal Philosophy* (1994) at 67 ff.; and generally Menski, 'Role of Custom in Hindu Law' (1992) notably at 323 (Smriti literature originally that of small élite, only slowly gaining larger influence); Kane, *History of Dharmasastra* (1968–77) at 825 ff. Cf. Sen, *General Principle[s] of Hindu Jurisprudence* (1984) at 16–20.

[90] Thus the explanation of Venkataraman, *N. R. Raghavachariar's Hindu Law* (1987) at 17. It follows that tradition cannot be extended by analogy. Ibid., at 15.

[91] See *Mayne's Treatise* (1991) at 29; Diwan, *Modern Hindu Law* (1958) at 39; Venkataraman, *N. R. Raghavachariar's Hindu Law* (1987) at 5. The 'social code' of hinduism can thus be seen as 'more stringent' than its religious teaching. This appears to be what the buddhists most objected to. See Venkataraman, *N. R. Raghavachariar's Hindu Law* (1987) at 19. On practices of interpretation, see below, this section.

[92] Markby, *Hindu and Mahommedan Law* (1977) at 15 ('no impediment to a gradual modification').

[93] Diwan, *Modern Hindu Law* (1958) at 28.

could just be there, with no one particularly concerned about it or even interested in it. Different folks in different regions had particular sastras, and the great sastras floated above them all. Some see 'schools' or sakhas in this,[94] but most see formal schools arising only with the arrival of the commentaries, from, say, the seventh to the twelfth centuries AD, when things to the west were beginning to get more formal as well. With fuller, prose statements of law, it becomes recognized as more specific, even in different form, though still united by the Sruti and Smriti. The two great schools are those of Mitakshara, from the commentary on Yajnavalkya, whose applications covers most of India outside Bengal, and Dayabhaga, from the text on inheritance and partition, which prevails for people of Bengal.[95] The schools were not static; their authors incorporated ongoing local information into their works; as expositors of a somewhat clearer notion of law they took greater liberty themselves in the process of exposition. All of hindu law is right, but you can be excused for thinking some of it is more right than the rest.[96] And since there's nothing wrong with diversity, since it's all united in the end, you can have even a little more diversity, and the Mitakshara (larger) school divides into sub-schools, each with its texts, and people take their school of law with them if they move (as in islam). Yet, as in islam, they can change their law as well, by moving to a new place and adopting the law of that place.[97] To solve a problem, you're therefore never very interested in hindu law in the abstract. You have to know the people, the place, the school and the local circumstances. It's all united, but it gets very specific.

With all the diversity, and with the need to reconcile the ancient, general texts with the newer, local texts, there has always been a great deal of interpretation, and interpretation in a way which minimized actual conflict. For the rules recognized as ritual alone, the method for dealing with conflicts was simple, that of option. For rules with sanctions, conflicts were minimized by concluding that only one rule was imperative; or that one of the rules dealt only with fact; or that each had separate spheres of application; or, ultimately, that Manu was to be preferred.[98]

## CHANGE THROUGH LAW

Hindu teaching was not opposed to the acquisition of knowledge, or its use. Hindu science made great advances in astronomy, mathematics in general (including dif-

---

[94] *Mayne's Treatise* (1991) at 16.

[95] See above, *Of Vedas, sastras and commentaries*; Derrett, *Introduction to Modern Hindu Law* (1963) at 22; *Mayne's Treatise* (1991) at 40; Venkataraman, *N. R. Raghavachariar's Hindu Law* (1987) at 6,7; Markby, *Hindu and Mahommedan Law* (1977) at 16; Trevelyan, *Hindu law as administered in British India* (1913) at 9–22 (with indications of principal authorities in schools and sub-divisions).

[96] On being righter than right, see Derrett, *Introduction to Modern Hindu Law* (1963) at 3 (on modification and development in hindu law) and 5 (on skillful interpretation by the authors); Sen, *General Principle[s] of Hindu Jurisprudence* (1984) at 22.

[97] Trevelyan, *Hindu law as administered in British India* (1913) at 22

[98] See Sen, *General Principle[s] of Hindu Jurisprudence* (1984) at 14; Lingat, *Classical Law of India* (1973) at 158, 159.

ferential calculus and trigonometry) and the development of 'arabic' numerals.[99] Yet the absence of rights and the transmission of karma places hinduism clearly on the side of the environment and the world of animals (hence the original holy cow). As in chthonic, talmudic and islamic traditions, there is no distinction between natural and legal orders, no neutral world of facts or objects. The objects may incorporate lives, ones filled with suffering, but lives none the less. This idea is profoundly rooted in hindu concepts of knowledge, which are directed not so much towards the how of things but towards the why, why one is oneself, why other beings and things are the way they are. It is a science which is more interested in the relations in the world than in the detail of things, more interested in specific functions in fulfilling dharma (the mathematics of temple-building) than in 'pure research'. It is very much related to the importance of self-discovery and discovery of what lies beyond the physical self, which has important consequences again for the notion of toleration. There is a story of a buddhist (a religion derived from hinduism) who, on meeting a starving lion, lay down to provide food. This may take us even beyond toleration.

# TOLERATING OTHERS

Hindu people know who they are, though hindu tolerance makes the inherent interdependence of group identities more pronounced than is usually the case. There is also, in hinduism, a certain disjunction between law and religion, such that hinduism in religion is not necessarily coterminous with hindu law, an idea not really welcomed in other religious legal traditions. Tolerance is also of obvious relevance to any measures taken for the protection of identity, and if such measures are difficult or impossible, there may be serious questions as to how a tradition of tolerance can survive. This observation may seem almost perverse when made with respect to one of the world's oldest legal traditions, but entropy doesn't go away, and then there are all the other truths, claiming their due.

## HINDU IDENTITY

Hindu religion includes many gods and many beliefs, such that it is difficult to define it inclusively. This is done, if necessary, by reference to acceptance of the authority of the Vedas and a corresponding belief in the unity of the spirit under a

[99] So called because Europe discovered them from the Arabs, who knew them as 'Indian (*Hindi*) numerals'. See Weggel, *Die Asiaten* (1989) at 51; R. Eaton, *Islamic History as Global History* (Washington, DC: Am. Hist. Assoc., 1990) at 25.

plurality of forms,[100] such that J. D. M. Derrett observed that '[p]erhaps the best test is whether people claim to be Hindus and are acknowledged as Hindus by their immediately contiguous society'.[101] Tolerance is not compatible with rigid tests or boundaries. Two conclusions seem to follow from this, in terms of hindu law. The first is that hindu law is now not a law of all hindus or of hindus alone.[102] Hindu law applies, at least in India, to buddhists, jainists and sikhs, whose religions have not developed law of general application.[103] And there are communities in India, religiously defined as hindu, to whose members particular, local legal traditions are applied, to the exclusion of hindu law.[104] So from the first conclusion appears to follow a second, that it is religion (in all its fluidity) which fulfils the primary function of identity, and not law. Yet some form of legal identity re-emerges within hindu law, in the form of the more precise, local variants of it, which the particular groups of hindu society retain 'tenaciously'.[105]

With all its tolerance, hinduism did not entirely renounce protection of hindu identity. Excommunication is known, though its practice is as debatable in function as it is elsewhere.[106] And some form of apostasy did exist, though abolished by legislation in the nineteenth century under the British, and entailing apparently only forfeiture of rights under hindu law rather than any more severe penalty, such as that of islamic law.[107] Exit, however, like adherence, is simply done, through adherence to another religion.[108] In the absence of formal conversion, hindu law will generally continue to apply to the non-conforming (witness buddhists, jains and sikhs) yet even this rule admits of exception. The 'renoncants of Pondicherry' are allowed to continue to adhere to French civil law, as they have since exercising their option under French law, during the time of French presence in India. If you *are* a

---

[100] See Venkatamaran, *N. R. Raghavachariar's Hindu Law* (1987) at 19, 20, with refs. ('But the people know the difference well and can easily tell who are Hindus and who are not'); Diwan, *Modern Hindu Law* (1958) at 2.

[101] Derrett, *Introduction to Modern Hindu Law* (1963) at 21.

[102] Venkataraman, *N. R. Raghavachariar's Hindu Law* (1987) at 32.

[103] This in spite of the opposition of these religions to hinduism and their development as alternatives to it. Jainism thus denies the authority of the Vedas but sees the law derived from them applied to its adherents. Local versions of hindu law may alleviate this considerably, however. On buddhism and law, see below, Ch. 9, *Limiting religion*; on sikhism see Juss, 'Constitution and Sikhs in Britain' (1995) (noting at 490 that it is 'their faith that stands them apart and defines them'). Legislation in India takes this principle still further in declaring hindu law applicable as well to 'any person who is not a Muslim, Christian, Parsi or Jew'. See Diwan, *Modern Hindu Law* (1958) at 1.

[104] Venkataraman, *N. R. Raghavachariar's Hindu Law* (1987) at 32 designating several communities.

[105] Derrett, *Introduction to Modern Hindu Law* (1963) at 26.

[106] See, for talmudic law, above, Ch. 4, *Talmudic law and jewish identity*.

[107] For its abolition, see Venkataraman, *N. R. Raghavachariar's Hindu Law* (1987) at 12, and for hinduism being 'not so much upset by heresy', see A. Sharma, 'Hinduism', in A. Sharma (ed.), *Our Religions* (San Francisco: Harper SanFrancisco, 1993) 1, at 5; cf., for various forms of hindu 'orthodoxy' and corresponding notions of 'heresy', though with few indications of sanction, Klostermaier, *Survey of Hinduism* (1994), above, at 49 ff., notably at 63 ('large potential of intolerance in today's political Hinduism'). For apostasy in islamic law, see above, Ch. 6, *The umma and its protection*.

[108] *Mayne's Treatise* (1991) at 65, 66; Diwan, *Modern Hindu Law* (1958) at 3; Venkataraman, *N. R. Raghavachariar's Hindu Law* (1987) at 22.

renoncant of Pondicherry, it is law which defines who you are, though you might, apparently, still be a hindu.

## HINDU LAW IN INDIA

As chthonic legal structures offered relatively little resistance to western expansion, so hindu law has folded back into itself when faced with external pressure. This may be one of the burdens of tolerance, or pluralism, as a central philosophy. Hindu teaching could offer itself to the chthonic people of India, and be largely accepted by them, but on the arrival of the muslims, around the eleventh century, hindu law was gradually supplanted by islamic law as the law of the land, though it probably retained some application in local hindu dispute resolution.[109] Digests continued to be written through the arrival of the British, and it is unlikely they were purely literary exercises. The arrival of the British was to supplant both hindu and islamic law as territorial law and to convert both to special status, as personal laws of hindu and islamic people. In this the Indian experience parallels that of western expansion in many areas of the world, with indigenous law being either replaced entirely by state law or reduced to a particular status, depending on the particular philosophy of the colonial power. The displacement of hindu law, however, like that of islamic law, is a particular case. It is a written law, of great breadth, and as written law meant to be applied, in courts. Its displacement as written law by another written law greatly reduces the prospect for its continuing vitality, as a way of life. That which is written may be more fragile than that which is not. The prospects for hindu law are presently not clear. The law of India has been described as 'palpably foreign' to its inhabitants,[110] the arrival of the British 'fatal' to hindu law.[111] Yet hindu law is remarkably resilient, and time has always been on its side. We may see things more clearly in a few hundred years.

The British arrived with other colonial powers in the seventeenth century, not 'to conquer the country, but to trade'.[112] The Factory system was installed in some ports and by the eighteenth century officers of the East India Company 'began to take an active part in native politics'.[113] Soon sovereignty 'fell' into the hands of the servants of the company, and new territories were then acquired by 'cession and conquest'.[114] The British Crown took over the governing of India from the mid-nineteenth cen-

---

[109] On islamic expansion into India, see above, Ch. 6, *The islamic diaspora*.

[110] See Galanter, *Law and Society in Modern India* (1989) at 15 (also 'notoriously incongruent with the attitudes and concerns of much of the population' and 'extremely small' likelihood of return to hindu law).

[111] David and Brierley, *Major Legal Systems* (1985) at 491.

[112] Markby, *Hindu and Mahommedan Law* (1977) at 3; on the justice of the companies, see H.-J. Leue, 'Legal Expansion in the Age of Companies: Aspects of the Administration of Justice in the English and Dutch Settlements of Maritime Asia, c. 1600–1750' in Mommsen and de Moor, *European Expansion and Law* (1992), above, at 129; and on the early English charters, M. P. Jain, *Outlines of Indian Legal History* (1966) at 7–11.

[113] M. P. Jain, *Outlines of Indian Legal History* (1966) at 5.

[114] Ibid., at 9.

tury. Now, British colonial policy was to retain existing law in force in the case of acquisition of settled territory, and there was no denying the settlement of India. So hindu law here got a shot in the arm, becoming officially recognized law for at least the hindu population, a status it had not enjoyed for centuries. Official status meant official sources, so formal translations were effected of classic hindu texts, notably the Mitakshara and the Dayabhaga, rescuing in some measure hindu law from its status as the 'imagination of hindu lawyers with no sanskrit'.[115] Pundits were also commissioned to assist the judiciary in application and interpretation of the revived law. The effect of English law on hindu law was therefore not immediate and abrupt, nor did it prejudice the legitimacy and availability of classic hindu sources. The change was more subtle, and would become more evident over time. It consisted in a gradual 'expropriation' of law,[116] the gradual ascendancy of state institutions, legislative or judicial, as sources of law, to the detriment of the classic, private, revelatory sources of hindu (and islamic) law. Legislation and judicial decisions simply became recognized as sources of law, since they were taught as such and came to be accepted as such—western law as slow-moving juggernaut (the word is from the temple car of Jagannatha). This was greatly facilitated by secular legal education, and the Indian legal professions now number, in absolute terms, amongst the largest of the world.[117]

Under British rule the primacy of official law was perhaps most evident in terms of case law. Hindu law came to be, under the appellation Anglo-Indian law, 'not the sastraic law but the law as declared by the courts themselves'.[118] So decisions became win–lose, their result was seen as law, clarity (the 'death-sickness')[119] replaced imprecision, custom became difficult to establish, differences between schools became differences in formal law, decisions became over-reported and the role of traditional tribunals declined. There could well be parity of decision in many areas

[115] Venkataraman, *N. R. Raghavachariar's Hindu Law* (1987) at 14, attributing the remark to J. H. Nelson. On the quality of some of the translation, however, see above, *Poetic law*; and on the process of translation, involving search for a fixed body of law, see B. Cohen, 'The Command of Language and the Language of Command' in R. Guha (ed.), *Subaltern Studies IV: Writings on South Asian History and Society* (Delhi/Oxford/New York: Oxford Univ. Press, 1985) 276, notably at 290–5.

[116] Galanter, *Law and Society* (1989) at 17; and on the entire process of the 'rise of the common law', see M. Setalvad, *The Common Law in India* (London: Stevens, 1960), ch. 1; A. Gledhill, 'The Influence of Common Law and Equity on Hindu Law since 1800' (1954) 3 Int. & Comp. Law Q. 576, reproduced in Nanda and Sinha, *Hindu Law and Legal Theory* (1996) at 279.

[117] On the profession, however, as undertaking an 'inner colonialization' of hindu tradition, see Weggel, *Die Asiaten* (1989) at 123.

[118] Venkataraman, *N. R. Raghavachariar's Hindu Law* (1987) at 19. And see, for authority of judicial decisons as 'permanent', Markby, *Hindu and Mahommedan Law* (1977) at 16 (this in 1906); and on the doctrine of precedent being 'woven into the fabric of the Indian legal system,' M. P. Jain, *Outlines of Indian Legal History* (1966) at 727.

[119] J. Derrett, 'Sanskrit Legal Treatises Compiled at the Instance of the British' (1961) 63 ZvglRwiss 72 at 112, cited by Galanter, *Law and Society* (1989) at 24. The notion of decision according to 'justice, equity and good conscience', a civilian concept, also became current, yet subject itself to the ongoing effect of precedent. H. Liebesny, 'English Common Law and Islamic Law in the Middle East and South Asia: Religious Influences and Secularization' (1985–6) 34 Clevel. St. L. Rev. 19 at 27.

of the common law and hindu law, yet the nature of the law, the nature of the tradition, was being radically transformed. The growth of legislation in common law tradition also became evident in legislative practice in India. The kings of India had always possessed some regulatory or legislative power, though it is doubtful if this traditional authority could be squared with its new exercise. Most notably, in the nineteenth century, the entire hindu law of contract and transfer of property was replaced by statute and there was 'virtually complete codification of all fields of commercial, criminal and procedural law'.[120] What remained, two of Manu's famous eighteen titles, was the law of family and succession. Even this, however, became touched by the legislative hand on Indian independence, Indian legislators not repealing the old law but recasting it in what is known as the Hindu Code. The law of the sastras is now legislation, meant to establish a single, *common* statutory standard for all hindus. And beyond the legislation is now the Constitution, stating the constitutional rights of Indian people, hindu, islamic or other. The full panoply of civil and common laws is now available in India—substantive law, rights, case law, legislation, codes and judicial review. It looks a lot like US law, yet there remain profound differences.

The main difference is in the population to which the law applies. It is not a western population and it remains a profoundly rural population. The sub-strata of religious, political and legal thought which gives western law whatever normativity it has in western jurisdictions is here lacking. The local tradition says different things, and they are profound things relating to life and death and personal responsibility, which have been passed on for millennia. There is no widespread, positive phenomenon of obedience to law which is simply enacted or judicially stated. Already, within a half-century of the Hindu Code's creation, it is being pointed out that older notions of legality still persist—caste autonomy, accepted forms of deviance, evasion or ignorance of the law. The traditional society also uses the formal law for its own ends (as in Africa and latin America).[121] So we may see the Hindu Code, like Maimonides' code,[122] pulled back to the people, surrounded by

---

[120] Galanter, *Law and Society* (1989) at 18. The court system was also rationalized in 1860. For tables of repealing legislation, see Venkataraman, *N. R. Raghavachariar's Hindu Law* (1987) at 12, 13; and for the entire process and justification of codification, see M. P. Jain, *Outlines of Indian Legal History* (1966) at 600 ff., notably at 603 (only through codification that homogeneity of law could be achieved, that law could be 'systematised' and made 'somewhat clear and precise'). On hindu contract law, see Jayaswal, *Manu and Yajnavalkya* (1930) at 175 ff. ('Void and voidable contracts—Public Policy—Definiteness—Acts of God and State—Debts—Interest . . . Rule of Priority—Bonds—novation—attestation and registration . . .').

[121] Galanter, *Law and Society* (1989) at 33, 49 (villages 'bi-legal' in picking and choosing amongst official and indigenous laws; U. Baxi, 'People's Law in India, The Hindu Society' in M. Chiba, *Asian Indigenous Law in Interaction with Received Law* (London/New York: KPI, 1986) at 216; B. Cohn, 'Some Notes on Law and Change in North India' in B. Cohn, *An Anthropologist among the Historians and Other Essays* (Delhi: Oxford Univ. Press, 1987) 554 at 568–71 (effect of caste differences on litigation in which parties presumed equal); and for the phenomenon of picking and choosing law in Africa and latin America, see above, Ch. 3, *The state as middle ground.*

[122] See above, Ch. 4, *The style of reason.*

commentary, subject to ongoing, revelatory development of tradition. If the law is king, hindu law has long taught that it is the people who decide which law.

## UNIVERSAL TOLERANCE?

Hindu law could be exported, and universalized, in one or more of its many variants, yet this would somehow seem contrary to the point of it. If there are many manifestations of supreme being, in law as in all else, why go to special efforts to displace those which already exist abroad, in favour of one developed at home? And which of those developed at home should it be? Diversity is here not just a way of managing resistance and local circumstance; it is fundamental. It is all the masks of the greatest of actors, and the greatness is in the multiplicity of the masks. Another way of thinking it is that everybody is already hindu, though in different states of awareness. There has thus been great influence of hindu thought and hindu law, notably in south-east Asia, where Manu was long cited as persuasive authority and where hindu ideas are found in adat law, yet there have been no major or particular efforts to impose or territorially expand the law.[123] Hindu law is also widely applied abroad, where it is formally recognized as a personal law, as in states in east Africa,[124] or in western states where hindu people persist in following, to the extent possible, their traditional law. There is also an English hindu law, as there is an English shari'a, both the result of the combined application of two traditions, one local and one distant, by people who adhere to them both.[125] The combination occurs whether it is authorized by law or not; it is simply how all the information comes to be used, by particular people.

# GENERAL BIBLIOGRAPHY

Agarwal, D. N., *Hindu Law* (Allahabad: University Book Agency, 1993).
Carman, J. B., 'Duties and Rights in Hindu Society' in L. S. Rouner (ed.), *Human Rights and the World's Religions* (Notre Dame: University of Notre Dame Press, 1988) at 113.

---

[123] M. B. Hooker, *A Concise Legal History of South-East Asia* (Oxford: Clarendon Press, 1978), ch. 1 ('The Indian Legal World: The Law Texts of Burma, Thailand, Champa and Cambodia, and Java'); Weggel, *Die Asiaten* (1989) at 260, 264, 265 (also rejecting commercial or military reasons for hindu influence, in favour of expertise of Brahmans in many fields of life); below, Ch. 9, *Limiting religion.*

[124] For application of hindu law in the world (citing jurisdictions, in some cases as they then were, of India, Pakistan, Burma, Malaya, Singapore, Aden, Tanzania, Kenya, Uganda, Surinam, British West Indies, Nepal), see Derrett and Iyer, 'Hindu Conception of Law' (1975) at 107.

[125] See, e.g., W. Menski, 'Legal pluralism in the Hindu marriage' in R. Burghard (ed.), *Hinduism in Great Britain; the perpetuation of religion in an alien cultural milieu* (London: Tavistock, 1987) 180; S. Poulter, *English Law and Ethnic Minority Customs* (London: Butterworths, 1986).

David, R. and Brierley, J. E. C., *Major Legal Systems in the World Today*, 3rd edn. (London: Stevens and Sons, 1985), Pt Four, Title II ('Law of India').

Derrett, J., *Introduction to Modern Hindu Law* (Oxford: Oxford University Press, 1963).

—— *Essays in Classical and Modern Hindu Law*, 4 vols. (Leiden: E. J. Brill, 1976–8).

—— 'Das Dilemma des Rechts in der traditionellen indischen Kultur' in W. Fikentscher, H. Franke and O. Köhler (eds.), *Entstehung und Wandel rechtlicher Traditionen* (Freiburg/Munich: Verlag Karl Alber, 1980) at 497.

—— and Iyer, T. 'Hindu Law' in International Association of Legal Science (K. Zweigert and U. Drobnig, eds.), *International Encyclopedia of Comparative Law*, vol. II, ch. 2 (Tübingen/The Hague/Paris: J. C. B. Mohr (Paul Siebeck)/Mouton, 1974) 143.

—— —— 'The Hindu Conception of Law' in International Association of Legal Science (K. Zweigert and U. Drobnig, eds.), *International Encyclopedia of Comparative Law*, vol. II, ch. 1 (Tübingen/The Hague/Paris: J. C. B. Mohr (Paul Siebeck)/Mouton, 1975) 107.

Desai, S., *Mulla [on] Principles of Hindu Law*, 13th edn. (Bombay: N. M. Tripathi, 1966).

Diwan, P., *Modern Hindu Law: Codifed and Uncodified*, 1st edn. (Allahabad: Allahabad Law Agency, 1958) (now available in 9th edn. by P. Diwan and P. Diwan, 1993).

Ebert, K., *Rechtsvergleichung: Einführing in die Grundlagen* (Berne: Verlag Stämpfli and Cie AG, 1978), ch. 11 ('Der Rechtskreis des Hindu-Rechts') at 124.

Galanter, M., *Competing Equalities: Law and the Backward Classes in India* (Berkeley: University of California Press, 1984).

—— *Law and Society in Modern India* (Delhi/Bombay/Calcutta/Madras: Oxford University Press, 1989).

Hopkins, E. W., 'The Growth of Law and Legal Institutions' in E. J. Rapson (ed.), *The Cambridge History of India*, vol. I, *Ancient India* (Cambridge: Cambridge University Press, 1922) at 277.

Jain, M. P., *Outlines of Indian Legal History*, 2nd edn. (Bombay: N. M. Tripathi, 1966).

Jain, M. S., 'The Law of Contract before the Codification' (1972) Journal of the Indian Law Institute 178.

Jayaswal, K., *Manu and Yajnavalkya—A Comparison and a Contrast: A Treatise on the Basic Hindu Law* (Calcutta: Butterworth, 1930).

Juss, S., 'The Constitution and Sikhs in Britain' [1995] Brigham Young University Law Review 481.

Kane, P. V., *History of Dharmasastra (Ancient and Medieval Religions and Civil Law in India)*, 5 vols., 2nd edn. (Poona: Bhandarkar Oriental Research Institute, 1968–77), notably vol. III.

Lingat, R., *The Classical Law of India*, trans. J. D. M. Derrett (Berkeley/Los Angeles/London: University of California Press, 1973).

*Laws of Manu*, trans. W. Doniger and B. Smith (London/New York: Penguin, 1991).

Markby, W., *Hindu and Mahommedan Law* (Delhi: Inter-India Publications, 1906, 1st repr. 1977).

Marsh, N. (ed.), *Some Aspects of Indian Law Today* (London: British Institute of International and Comparative Law, 1964).

May, R., *Law and Society, East and West. Dharma, Li, and Nomos: Their Contribution to Thought and to Life* (Wiesbaden: Franz Steiner Verlag, 1985).

*Mayne's Treatise on Hindu Law and Usage*, 13th edn. rev. by A. Kuppuswami (New Delhi: Bharat Law House, 1991).

Menski, W., 'The Role of Custom in Hindu Law', in (1992) 53 *Recueils de la Société Jean Bodin pour l'Histoire Comparative des Institutions, Custom* (Brussels: De Boeck University, 1992) at 311.

Nanda, V. P. and Sinha, S. P. (eds.), *Hindu Law and Legal Theory* (New York: New York University Press, 1996).

Pal, R., *The History of Hindu Law in the Vedic Age and in Post-Vedic Times down to the Institutes of Manu* (Calcutta: University of Calcutta, 1958).

Purohit, S., *Ancient Indian Legal Philosophy: Its Relevance to Contemporary Jurisprudential Thought* (New Delhi: Deep and Deep, 1994).

Rocher, L., 'Hindu Conceptons of Law' (1978) 29 Hastings Law Journal 1283.

Sen, P. N., *General Principle[s] of Hindu Jurisprudence* (Allahabad: Allahabad Law Agency, 1891–92 Tagore Law Lectures, 1984 repr.).

Setalvad, M. C. *The Role of English Law in India* (Jerusalem: Magnes Press, Hebrew University, 1966).

—— *The Common Law in India*, 2nd edn. (Bombay: N. M. Tripathi, 1970).

Srivastava, T. N., *Women and the Law* (New Delhi: Intellectual Publishing House, 1985).

Sternbach, L., *Juridical Studies in Ancient Indian Law* (Delhi: Motilal Banarsidass, 1965).

Trevelyan, E., *Hindu Law as administered in British India* (Calcutta/Simla/London: Thacker, 1913).

Varadaghariar, S., *The Hindu Judicial System* (Lucknow: Lucknow University, 1946).

Venkata Subbarao, G. C., 'Influence of Western Law on the Indian Law of Trusts' (1957) Revista del Instituto de derecho comparado 108.

Venkataraman, S., 'Influence of the Common Law and Equity on the Personal Law of the Hindus' (1957) Revista del Instituto de derecho comparado 156.

—— *N. R. Raghavachariar's Hindu Law: Principles and Precedents*, 8th edn. (Madras: Madras Law Journal Office, 1987)

Watts, A., *The Philosophies of Asia* (Boston/Rutland, Vt./Tokyo: Charles E. Tuttle Co., 1995), ch. 2 ('The Mythology of Hinduism').

Weggel, O., *Die Asiaten*, (C. H. Beck: Munich, 1989).

Zweigert, K. and Kötz, H., *Introduction to Comparative Law*, 3rd edn., trans. T. Weir (Oxford: Clarendon Press, 1998), ch. 23 ('Hindu Law').

# 9

# AN ASIAN LEGAL TRADITION: MAKE IT NEW (WITH MARX?)

Asia may exist more in western thinking than in Asian, and the diversity of Asia is perhaps greater today than it ever has been. Yet there apppear to be underlying, common attitudes towards law throughout much of Asia—attitudes which are compatible with local, intellectual, and spiritual diversity—and there have been many recent statements, in Asia, as to how Asian legal thought is different from western legal thought. Pursuit of an Asian legal tradition may therefore be a justifiable activity though, since we are now dealing with more than half of the world's population, we may have to climb rather high to see common features. We should also keep in mind that Asia is a big place, extending from Moscow (say) in the west (and, further south, Turkey, Israel and Saudi Arabia), through Pakistan and India, to Japan and the Philippines in the east. So it has historically included some particular legal traditions we have already looked at (chthonic, talmudic, islamic, hindu) and is now picking and choosing from civil and common law sources. Yet beyond these particular traditions there are also attitudes which appear more distinctively Asian, representing a kind of Asian default position, which must necessarily address all the particular traditions which the people of Asia have known.

How this is done may appear rather miraculous, though Asian religions (other than talmudic, islamic and hindu ones) have chosen not to be very interested in law. It may therefore just be the result of the accumulated cunning[1] of some of the world's oldest civilizations, which have survived so long only by somehow getting above the flak. We are therefore dealing both with great age and great diversity, and that which is very old turns out to be most supportive of immediate diversity. MAKE IT NEW, wrote Ezra Pound,

> Day by day make it new
> cut underbrush,
> pile the logs
> keep it growing

citing a Ch'ing emperor who was concerned, not with the new, but with revivifying the old, with keeping the massive, old tradition alive and well, by constant,

---

[1] C. Geertz, *Local Knowledge* (New York: Basic Books, 1983) at 233.

contemporary labour.[2] So it has been said that in China the creation of formal law is much easier than its application, since informal legal traditions continue to dominate modern, formal ones,[3] and many strong arguments are made that this is the only way in which really large populations can be held together. Yet the old traditions in Asia are challenged by perhaps the most aggressive of the new, in the forms of Chinese and Vietnamese communism, and we see once again, as with hindu law and common law, one of the oldest legal traditions of the world subject to immediate and powerful challenge.

# A TRADITION OF PERSUASION

Religion and revelation have little place in Asian legal tradition. In this, Asian law is perhaps closer to western law than it is to explicitly religious legal traditions, though you can perhaps find religion everywhere if you look hard enough. In both Asia and the west, however, there is no explicit reliance on religion or revelation as an immediate source of law. Probably the greatest traditional source of normativity in Asia is confucianism, which is not a religion, while Asian religions, such as buddhism, taoism or shintoism, have concerns which are largely other than legal. At the same time, Asian legal tradition differs from western legal tradition, at least since the thirteenth century (or thereabouts), in refusing to root normativity in formal structures and sanctions. You are left with pure tradition—not present positivism and not revealed truth—and tradition which seeks primarily to persuade and not oblige. It is a tradition of great and friendly persuasion, just based on all of us. This is what has to be made NEW. It has no transcendent existence, and cannot be simply laid down. There is something of the chthonic in it, yet Asia has greatly refined the chthonic.[4]

---

[2] E. Pound, *The Cantos of Ezra Pound*, rev. edn. (London: Faber & Faber, 1975) at 265, cited in R. Hughes, *Culture of Complaint* (New York/Oxford: Oxford Univ. Press/The New York Public Library, 1993) at 110. On tradition's designation as hadith, or what is new, in islamic thought, see above, Ch. 6, *The shari'a: sources*.

[3] J. Sagot and H. Xie, 'La Chine: Etat de droit? Etat de non droit?', Gaz. Pal., 2–4 July 1995, 6 at 7; on the exceptional force of informal tradition in China, resting on some 5,000 years of civilization, see A. Chen, *Introduction to Legal System* (1992) at 1; and for a vivid illustration in the field of intellectual property law, see W. Alford, *To Steal a Book is an Elegant Offense: Intellectual Property Law in Chinese Civilization* (Stanford: Stanford Univ. Press, 1995 (noting, at 25, that in China 'the need to interact with the past sharply curtailed the extent to which it was proper for anyone other than persons acting in a fiducial capacity to restrict access to its expression').

[4] For the parallel with chthonic law, and admission of both chthonic and asian informal normativity as law, see R. Sacco, M. Guadagni, R. Aluffi Beck-Peccoz and L. Castellani, *Il diritto africano* (Turin: UTET, 1995) at 21, 22.

## ADAT LAW AND CHTHONIC LAW

Much of Asian life remains chthonic in character, and there is the same overlay in Asia of chthonic tradition by other traditions as exists in Africa, the Americas or the south Pacific. Inuit people in Siberia share much of the way of life of Inuit people in Canada or northern Scandinavia, and face similar problems in obtaining recognition of chthonic norms.[5] Elsewhere in Asia, however, chthonic law appears to have an easier time of it, and this may be related to the persuasive character of Asian tradition. This is reflected in the existence of adat law in south-east Asia (notably in Indonesia and Malaysia) and in the ongoing relationship between chthonic tradition and confucianism.

Adat law is chthonic law, at least in origin.[6] Adat is a word derived from the Arabic ada, to return to or repeat, and we see here the notions of both tradition (that which is returned to) and custom (repetitive action). Clifford Geertz has written, echoing (relatively rare) statements in western legal theory,[7] that adat law is not custom, custom being a concept which would reduce to potentially mindless habit that which is outlook or propriety, something between social consensus and 'moral style'.[8] Adat law is thus information or content and people repeat their adherence to its injunctions, or not, depending on their evaluation of its continuing relevance, to them. Like other forms of chthonic law, it is vulnerable, with few explicit means of defence and little tendency to universalize. Yet it has survived in Asia even in jurisdictions whose people have largely accepted islamic law, so we may see here yet another, gentler, form of islam, one which is able to leave a place even to people not of the book.[9] This may be because of the influence of broader Asian traditions; it may also have something to do with recent forms of crystallization of

[5] On chthonic peoples of northern Asia, including peoples of Siberia and the Ainu of Hokkaido (Japan), see I. Schulte-Tenckhoff, La question des peuples autochtones (Brussels/Paris: Bruylant/LGDJ 1997) at 81 ff.

[6] See Geertz, Local Knowledge (1983), above, at 208 ('discovered lying about amid the common routines of village life'); Weggel, Die Asiaten (1989) at 119, 120 (notably on patriarchal or matriarchal character; communal and agricultural character; and influence of hindu tradition); M. B. Hooker, Adat Law in Modern Indonesia (Kuala Lumpur/New York: Oxford Univ. Press, 1978) (notably on diversity of adat law within itself and, at 34–9, on combination of kinship and territory as defining adat groups); M. B. Hooker, Adat Laws in Modern Malaya: Land Tenure, Tradition Government, and Religion (Kuala Lumpur/New York: Oxford Univ. Press, 1972); and for the 'traditional verse form' of adat law, M. B. Hooker, Islamic Law in South-East Asia (Singapore: Oxford Univ. Press, 1984) at 162.

[7] See above, Ch. 3, Law and the cosmos.

[8] Geertz, Local Knowledge (1983), above, at 185, 210 ('volksgedachte not volksgebruik'), citing F. von Benda-Beckmann, Property in Social Continuity: Continuity and Change in the Maintenance of Property Relationships through Time in Manangkabau, West Sumatra (The Hague: Martinus Nijhoff, 1979) at 113, 114, and noting Arabic word 'urf' as closer to custom in western sense; also evoking notion, at 213, of truth-finding, 'truth at once of circumstances and of principle'. On concepts of urf and truth-finding in islamic tradition, see above, Ch. 6, Qadi justice and mufti learning and Subtle change; and for administrative divisions within the Indonesian Supreme Court between 'unwritten civil law' (adat law) and 'written civil law', see Ali Budiardjo, Nugroho, Reksodiputro, Diagnostic Assessment of Legal Development in Indonesia, vol. I (Jakarta: 1997) at 129.

[9] On the privileged position of other religions of the book in islamic thought, see above, Ch. 6, Jihad; and on the influence on Asian islamic law of sufi 'mystics', see Hooker, Concise Legal History of South-East Asia (1978) at 48, 49, 61, 62; yet for incorporation of muslim law into adat law, see above, Ch. 6, The islamic diaspora.

adat law itself, with its becoming more formal in expression under the influence of western colonialization.[10] This may not make it more resistant; it does make it more visible.

Adat law thus represents a particular, Asian exemplification of chthonic law, and its survival in Asia tells us a great deal of the value attached to informal tradition. Another form of chthonic law could be found in Chinese feudalism, which may be seen as the original source of the normativity developed by, and derived from, the man known in the west as Confucius.

## ON LI AND FA

Master K'ong (K'ong fou-tseu), taught in the sixth and fifth centuries BC, in a time of great social upheaval. It was a time of dissolution of the old feudal order, roughly comparable to the end of the middle ages in Europe, though a millennium or two earlier.[11] People were saying it was time to take things in hand by creating formal laws which would establish a uniform and egalitarian order in a new, centralized structure. Their arguments were extensive, and were made with great vigour, and we will have to return to them. With the benefit of hindsight, however, we now see that they served perhaps most of all to incite Master K'ong and his many disciples to develop a social and moral philosophy which sought to induce and persuade, rather than command and punish. It was as though, in Europe, a great, secular philosopher resurrected all that was harmonious and good in medieval times, in a way that permanently stalled (perhaps) the enlightenment, rights, and the development of positive law. That would have been quite a philosopher, and the west didn't produce one, though it may have had something to do with the nature of European feudalism and the virtues (or lack of them) which it generated. Confucius managed this in China, however, both through subtle continuation of existing, feudal tradition and through brilliant reformulation and reconstruction of it. He is the philosopher of the li,[12] which means many things but most of all means denial

---

[10] On the struggle around adat law, largely between those who would discard it and those who would develop it (into a form of 'homespun corpus juris'), see Geertz, *Local Knowledge* (1983), above, at 208; Weggel, *Die Asiaten* (1989) at 119; C. Fasseur, 'Colonial Dilemma: Van Vollenhoven and the Struggle Between Adat Law and Western Law in Indonesia' in W. J. Mommsen and J. A. de Moor, *European Expansion and Law: the Encounter of European and Indigenous Law in 19th- and 20th-Century Africa and Asia* (Oxford/New York: Berg Publishers, 1992) at 237.

[11] On the comparability of European and Chinese feudalism (under the Chou dynasty, 11th–3rd centuries BC), see Bodde and Morris, *Law in Imperial China* (1967) at 15; and on the variety of pre-Confucian Chinese law and its development into written form see Liu, *Origins of Chinese Law* (1998).

[12] On the measure in which Confucius continued older teaching or reformed it (there are 2 traditions as to his contribution) see M. Kaltenmark, *La philosophie chinoise*, 2nd edn. (Paris: Presses universitaires de France, 1980) at 12; Liu, *Origins of Chinese Law* (1998) at 101. Classic books, or king, existed prior to Confucius, so there is clearly 'no creation myth here, no Genesis'; see de Bary, *Trouble with Confucianism* (1991) at 2, 3 (Confucius as transmitter of tradition); Schwartz, *World of Thought in Ancient China* (1985) at 66, 67 (Confucius as 'transmitter' yet still innovator). On the belief of confucians that li was created by ancient sages; that contemporary disorder results from failure to understand it; that a prime confucian duty is to study and

of the lasting and effective normativity of formal law and formal sanctions. There is therefore little place for describing the detail of confucian regulation of society. You are supposed to understand its *general* teaching (which we will get to) and once you understand that you will no longer be concerned with the detail of formal law.

There is, however, a long tradition of formal law and formal sanctions, or fa, in China, though it has played a subordinate role to the li, or persuasion, of the confucians. In western discussion those who argued the case for fa in China are known as legalists (and sometimes realists) and they have been making the case since before Confucius, at least since the eighth century BC, which was about two centuries before the Twelve Tables and around the time of the early dharmasutras.[13] Myth has it that fa was invented by a 'barbarian people' (the confucians have had something to do with the myth), the Miao, who flourished around 2300 BC, even before Hammurabi.[14] At some point the word fa, originally model, pattern or standard, was taken over to mean an imposed standard, closely associated with criminal conduct and conduct repugnant to established order.[15] With all the troubles of declining feudalism and warring states the legalists got a real boost, and did their part to show why things had to change. There is much here which recalls the debate between rationalizing lawyers ('Juristen, bösen Christen') and others, less impressed with formal law, in late medieval Europe. The work of Confucius must have done a lot to hold things together, but from at least the later sixth century the first formal books of punishment begin to appear.[16] Political structures continued to deteriorate, however, with everyone blaming everyone else until, in a cataclysmic moment, the Chinese (internal) empire crystallized in 221 BC, under the Ch'in. The legalists appear in reality to have had a lot to do with this, as the lawyers had a lot to do with the emergence of states in Europe, but the Chinese story thereafter is a very different one from the European one. The Ch'in empire was to be one of fa, and the notion of fa was a key idea in its creation. Law was seen here not as a means of regulation of private, economic activity, nor as a means of upholding religious values, but rather as an instrument of politics and public

interpret li to make it meaningful for the present day, made to LIVE, see Bodde and Morris, *Law in Imperial China* (1967) at 19.

[13] Kaltenmark, *Philosophie chinoise*, above, at 54, and see generally Vandermeersch, *La formation du Légisme* (1965); Ch'u, *Law and Society in Traditional China* (1965) at 241 ff. (insisting on legalist concern with equality of citizens); Ren, *Tradition of Law and Law of Tradition* (1997) at 19–22 (also on notion of equality); Schwartz, *World of Thought in Ancient China* (1985) ch. 8 ('Legalism: the Behavioral Science'); B. Zhengyuan Fu, *China's Legalists: the Earliest Totalitarians and Their Art of Ruling* (Armonk, NY/London: M. E. Sharpe, 1996); Liu, *Origins of Chinese Law* (1998), chs. 6 and 7, notably at 179 ('real purpose . . . to justify contemporary rulers' absolute power of legislation').

[14] Bodde and Morris, *Law in Imperial China* (1967) at 13; and for intervening visibility of legalism, see Folsom, Minan & Otto, *Law and Politics* (1992) at 5.

[15] Bodde and Morris, *Law in Imperial China* (1967) at 11.

[16] See, with some variations in dates, A. Chen, *Introduction to Legal System* (1992) at 8; Kaltenmark, *Philosophie chinoise*, above, at 54; Bodde and Morris, *Law in Imperial China* (1967) at 15. None of the early codes has survived.

order.[17] It is known as rule *by* law,[18] and much flows from these simple phrases. Fa is thus concerned with criminal conduct and administrative regulation; it is primarily directed not to the people, but to administrative officials;[19] it was closely associated with militarism ('enrich the state; reinforce the army'); and in practice exhibited a measure of doctrinal intolerance which matched that known in the west, including burning of the books of confucianism.[20] For many of these reasons, and also for brutal repression above and beyond the rule by law, the Ch'in empire was of short duration, collapsing after fourteen years. Since that time (peoples have long memories) fa has been labouring under a heavy load, and has essentially never recovered the credibility it might then have had. It's a bit like the notion of a 'gouvernement des juges' in France; shorthand for a massive amount of social resistance. With the new regime, that of the Han, confucianism became the official doctrine of the new empire, so it became a question of how confucianism could be used in a new political order, which was rapidly losing its feudal characteristics. It turned out that confucianism needed help, and from the lawyers.

When confucianism became official doctrine of the empire sometime in the late third century BC, books of punishment had existed for some four centuries. The confucians could argue for their abolition, and seek to abolish what had become at least a minor tradition, or live with them and use them, seeking to have them adapted to confucian teaching. They of course chose to do the latter; it was safer, smart politics, and consistent with the eclectic mix of thought which confucianism represented.[21] The tradition of criminal/administrative codes thus continued, and through to the last of the dynasties, that of the Ch'ing, which terminated in 1911. The codes became sophisticated documents, often treated as near-sacred in character, and eventually became greatly admired in eighteenth and nineteenth century Europe, where their ultimate versions were translated into French, Russian and English.[22] From the legalist perspective this can been seen as a kind of vindication;

[17] Bodde and Morris, *Law in Imperial China* (1967) at 11.

[18] von Senger, *Einführung in das chinesische Recht* (1994) at 20.

[19] Tay, 'Struggle for Law in China' (1987) at 563; Folsom et al.,*Law and Politics* (1992) at 7; Weggel, *Die Asiaten* (1989) at 115; and see Ren, *Tradition of Law and Law of Tradition* (1997) at 24 ('two Chinese make a family; three Chinese make a bureaucracy').

[20] Bodde and Morris, *Law in Imperial China* (1967) at 27; de Bary, *Trouble with Confucianism* (1991) at 46 (legalist prime minister declaring that those referring to the past to criticize the present to be put to death); for burning of books of law in the west, notably those of the talmudic tradition, see above, Ch. 4, *Talmudic law and jewish identity.*

[21] On confucianism not as 'one immutable body of thinking but an evolving one, split into many schools, developed through time and in response to various stimuli' (including buddhism and western philosophy), see M. Ng, 'Are Rights Culture-bound' in M. Davis, *Human Rights and Chinese Values: Legal, Philosophical and Political Perspectives* (Hong Kong/Oxford/New York: Oxford Univ. Press, 1995) 59 at 66.

[22] Tay, 'Struggle for Law in China' (1987) at 563; and see generally Bodde and Morris, *Law in Imperial China* (1967) at 7 (on full record which codes provide, more extensive than that of comparable period in Europe); P. Keller, 'Sources of Order in Chinese Law' (1994) 42 Am. J. Comp. Law 711 at 715 (near-sacred character of codes giving rise to subordinate forms of law, phenomenon continued into period of communist government); G. MacCormack, *Spirit of Traditional Chinese Law* (1996), notably at 27–31, 33, 34.

their programme was (only) one of criminal and administrative law, supportive of governmental order, and it was preserved within the broader context of confucian teaching. Yet the cause of fa was irreparably damaged by the failure of the Ch'in dynasty. It could never expand beyond its criminal and administrative beginnings. Much of the field of private law was closed to it, now the privileged field of confucian li.[23] And the confucians were hard at work within the codes, generating the process known as confucianization, by which the relational principles of confucian society became integrated into legalist statements of positive law.[24]

## IMPERIAL INSTITUTIONS

Chinese society thus became a combination of stick and carrot, the stick always available but the carrot enjoying the theoretical advantage. Rulers were therefore never considered as having an absolute right to rule, though legalist fa would have so decreed.[25] The confucians were weak, however, on the controls which could be exercised over a despotic ruler, and tended to talk about their own disapproval, or refusal to visit and counsel the despot.[26] Despots weren't much impressed, and there seems to have been a lot of them. In the absence of any clear notion of separation of powers, the despot's orders were to be applied by magistrates who exercised both of what we call today administrative and judicial functions.[27] The magistrates were clearly not independent officials. They were held strictly to the text

[23] For codification of important elements of family law, however (notably divorce by mutual consent), see MacCormack, *Spirit of Traditional Chinese Law* (1996) at 88–91 (measures of family law often, however, penally sanctioned); M. Palmer, 'The Re-emergence of Family Law in Post-Mao China: Marriage, Divorce and Reproduction' in Lubman (ed.), *China's Legal Reforms* (1996) at 110; and for archival evidence suggesting resort to courts in family matters was more frequent, at least in recent centuries, than confucian theory would suggest, see K. Bernhardt and P. Huang (eds.), *Civil Law in Qing and Republican China* (Stanford: Stanford Univ. Press, 1994); M. Allee, *Law in Local Society in Late Imperial China: Northern Taiwan in the Nineteenth Century* (Stanford: Stanford Univ. Press, 1994); P. Huang, *Civil Justice in China* (Stanford: Stanford Univ. Press, 1996) (with useful discussion of individual cases); cf. M. Bastid-Bruguière, 'L'esprit de la codification chinoise', Droits 1998. 129 (codification, in spite of existence of private interests in litigation, remained instrument of administrative power); Epstein, 'Codification of Civil Law in People's Republic of China' (1998) at 159 (some principles of civil law codified but criminalized as with other clearly public offences) and 161 ('no autonomous discourse of Chinese civil law ever emerged').

[24] On the confucian notions incorporated into positive law, see below, *Confucianization*.

[25] See Folsom et al., *Law and Politics* (1992) at 16; Kaltenmark, *Philosophie chinoise*, (1980), above, at 55.

[26] See de Bary, *Trouble with Confucianism* (1991) at 16 (and noting that confucianism placed responsibility entirely on single, noble ruler, while judaism places responsibility on entire people); and on the (highly exceptional) duty of opposition to tyranny, see von Senger, *Chinesische Recht* (1994) at 19; Folsom et al., *Law and Politics* (1992) at 13; Bunger, 'Entstehen und Wandel des Rechts in China' (1980) at 457 (constant refs. to precedent meant to hold emperor in check, idea of state not absolutist). The emperor's obligation was rooted in the concept of minben or the people-as-the-basis. A. Chen, *Introduction to Legal System* (1992) at 10; R. Ames, 'Rites and Rights' (1988) at 206.

[27] Bodde and Morris, *Law in Imperial China* (1967) at 5 (magistrates also lacking formal legal training); L. Vandermeersch, 'An Enquiry into the Chinese Conception of the Law' in Schram, *Scope of State Power in China* (1985) at 5; Folsom et al., *Law and Politics* (1992) at 7; A. Chen, *Introduction to Legal System* (1992) at 13.

of the codes; questions of interpretation were to be referred to the government.[28] To ensure correctness of decision, a carefully defined system of appeals existed,[29] and erring magistrates could be subjected to administrative or even criminal punishment.[30] The legal side of the function was clearly neglected, and there is talk of deliberate toleration of corruption. The result was many maxims, of the type 'Win a lawsuit and lose a friend', 'Better to be vexed to death than bring a lawsuit', 'Litigation ultimately ends in disaster'. The confucians preferred conciliation; if legal complaint was possible it was to be deterred by all possible means. Don't even think about a legal profession, though over time informal advisers inevitably developed, for those unfortunately caught in legal machinery.[31] Absent a profession, the magistrate did everything—investigating, prosecuting, interrogating, judging.[32] The expression 'inquisitorial' may here be justifiable.

## LI IN ASIA

China, by its great size, influences everthing in Asia, but the confucian teaching of li has been variously received. Its influence has perhaps been greatest in Korea[33] and Japan,[34] though both of these have seen (different) processes of recognition of formal sources of law. Japan too had its feudal structures, and shoguns, with heavy reliance on established roles and practices. Again, no lawyers. The land of the rising sun (as seen from China) was also to receive the buddhism which influenced China from the first century AD This too was a tradition which reinforced legal reticence, for reasons we will see. To the south, confucianism is currently being taught officially in Singapore. Its influence is reduced in the islamic lands of Indonesia and Malaysia, where islam has its own ways of dealing with those who would make their own law. In the other southern countries it is the religion of buddhism which has

[28] Bunger, 'Wandel des Rechts' (1980) at 456; Huang, *Civil Justice in China* (1996), above, at 107, 108.

[29] Bodde and Morris, *Law in Imperial China* (1967) at 5; Folsom et al., *Law and Politics* (1992) at 9; and generally on the lack of independence of adjudicators, de Bary, 'Neo-Confucianism and Human Rights' (1988) 183 at 187.

[30] Folsom et al., *Law and Politics* (1992) at 9.

[31] von Senger, *Chinesische Recht* (1994) at 22, on 'Winkelkonsultenten'; A. Chen, *Introduction to Legal System* (1992) at 14 (informal legal consultants not considered respectable, 'sometimes punished for stirring up litigation or drafting inaccurate pleadings'); MacCormack, *Spirit of Traditional Chinese Law* (1996) at 25 ('litigation tricksters', 'pettifoggers').

[32] Folsom et al., *Law and Politics* (1992) at 7; Bodde and Morris, *Law in Imperial China* (1967) at 5: Mac-Cormack, *Spirit of Traditional Chinese Law* (1996) at 146 (no history of 'irrational' means of proof in China, magistrate having task of ascertaining truth from parties, witnesses); Wang Chenguang, 'Introduction: An Emerging Legal System' in Wang Chenguang and Zhang Xianchu, *Introduction to Chinese Law* (Hong Kong/Singapore: Sweet & Maxwell, 1997) at 6 (absence of judicial impartiality in China has contributed to distrust of formal judicial system, practice of seeking justice from intelligent, individual officials).

[33] See C. Shin-yong (ed.), *Legal System of Korea* (Seoul: The Si-sa-yong-o-san Publishers, 1982) at 13–8, 203–7 (reception of Chinese laws, confucianism); S. Song (ed.), *Introduction to the Law and Legal System of Korea* (Seoul: Kyung Mun Sa Publishing, 1983) at 43–5, 112–40.

[34] Noda, *Introduction to Japanese Law* (1976) at 22, 23, 25 (though confucian ideal 'neglected' by 9th century).

by and large prevailed over confucianism.[35] As in Japan, this does little to reinforce the role of formal law, and does much for an Asian tradition of persuasion.

## ASIAN WAYS

Though Asian legal tradition is similar to that of the west (in its secularity) and to legal traditions which are religiously inspired (in its rejection in principle of formal structures and sanctions), it remains profoundly different from them, precisely because of this combination. It is law which is secular in origin, yet greatly limited, in its formal version, in its reach and effect. In China the limits are the secular ones of confucianism; elsewhere Asian religions have done the same work of limiting the role of the lawyers. Everywhere in the Asian tradition we are here discussing, however, there is denial of the primary role of secular law-makers and denial of the idea of a sweeping religious law. In short, there is denial everywhere of a primary role for what is usually known as law. It is a secular, largely informal, legal tradition, though informed by great learning. In spite of the accumulated experience, the argument goes on as to whether such a tradition is even possible.

### LI'S DOMAIN

If you are coming to Asian law for the first time you may be puzzled at how it could consist in principle only of penal and administrative law. What about everything else? How could there be regulation of some things but not of others, equally important in daily life? How could there be little or no family law, no generally applicable law of civil wrongs or obligations or contracts, no law of farming? It is true that a western concept of civil or private law was largely absent from Asian tradition, which tended, at least visibly, to operate vertically rather than horizontally.[36] In the absence of formal, private law, however, it does not appear strictly

---

[35] See below, *Limiting religion*. Confucianism and the Chinese-style codes were very influential, however, in Vietnam. See Hooker, *Concise Legal History of South-East Asia* (1978) at 73 ff., notably at 79 (chinese form of texts and confucianism); N. Huy and T. Tài, 'The Vietnamese Texts' in M. B. Hooker (ed.), *Laws of South-East Asia*, vol. I, *The Pre-Modern Texts* (Singapore: Butterworths, 1986) 435 at 450 ('Confucianization of law').

[36] Bodde and Morris, *Law in Imperial China* (1967) at 4 (complaints against other individuals, if to be dealt with by law, directed to state authorities); A. Chen, *Introduction to Legal System* (1992) at 20, 21 (for absence of commercial law in traditional China); cf., however, for archaeological evidence of written contract being practised in China at least by 3rd century BC, Sagot and Xie, 'La Chine: Etat de droit? Etat de non droit?' (1995), above, at 6; for means of enforcement of commercial contract under the Han dynasty (of the first 2 centuries AD), in spite of confucian resistance, H. Scogin, 'Between Heaven and Man: Contract and the State in Han Dynasty China' (1990) 63 S. Calif. L. Rev. 1326; and for the view that '[a]lthough written contracts were used to express transactional terms and conditions, these generally did not receive formal recognition from the state but were supported by private guarantees enforced through informal organizations centered on the family and guild', see P. Potter, *The Economic Contract Law of China* (Seattle/London: Univ. of Washington Press, 1992) at 9, 10.

accurate to say that everything else was simply left to 'free enterprise', with the connotation that there was here a true, market-driven society.[37] We rather have to think, again, of law in a different manner. We have to think of law as li, a learned, even written, but informal tradition of normativity, whose persuasiveness was so great that it could effectively control all those areas of life which were not given over to the formal world of fa-edicted sanction. So it is possible to speak both of the 'normative richness' of life in China while at the same time taking note of the episodic and unreliable character of Chinese (formal) laws, and this in very recent times as well as in the most ancient.[38] The normative world of China, and Asia, is as complete as any other in which people live together in large numbers. It is, however, a pluralist form of legal order, in which different forms of normativity co-exist and even constantly rub against one another, each being recognized by the other as necessary yet each busily pushing at the boundary which separates them.[39]

The domain of li is thus greater than the domain of law, at least as it is understood in the west. It is also normal that li is difficult to define, just as no one has been able to successfully and conclusively define law. The narrowest definition of li is unfortunately one you will see most often, defining it in terms of rites or ceremonial practices. Li certainly includes rites, but it has been said that li 'does not carry the pejorative connotations such as superficiality, formalism and irrationality often associated with the Western understanding of ritual. Li is not passive deference to external patterns. It is a *making* of society that requires the investment of oneself and one's own sense of importance.'[40] Broader, more accurate statements of the nature of li can be thus be found and, as with chthonic law, you can get an understanding of informal normativity once you are over the initial limits of western teaching. Li has been variously defined, in its totality, as 'moral law',[41] as 'customary, uncodified law, internalized by individuals',[42] as 'the concrete institutions and the accepted modes of behaviour in a civilized state',[43] as the 'moral and social rules of conduct',[44] as 'propriety',[45] and as the 'courtesy, customs and traditions we

---

[37] Cf. de Bary, *Trouble with Confucianism* (1991) at 48 (much left in private hands, which today 'might be called free enterprise').

[38] Keller, 'Sources of Order' (1994) at 711 (noting western need for formal Chinese law to deal with Chinese; less need within China itself).

[39] On the variety of Asian normativity see Folsom et al., *Law and Politics* (1992) at 6; Weggel, *Die Asiaten* (1989) at 115 (on 'Sittenordnung'); R. Sacco, 'Mute Law' (1995) 43 Am. J. Comp. Law 455.

[40] Ames, 'Rites and Rights' (1988) at 200, 203 (English term 'ritual' often negative and formal while Chinese counterpart 'li' generally not); and for an earlier distinction between li as natural morality and yi as ritual, overlooked by confucians themselves, Liu, *Origins Chinese Law* (1998) at 78 ff.

[41] D. Tan, 'Judicial Independence in the People's Republic of China: Myth or Reality' (1994) 68 Aust. L. J. 660 at 663.

[42] J. Ching, 'Human Rights: A Valid Chinese Concept?' in W. de Bary and Tu Weiming, *Confucianism and Human Rights* (New York: Columbia Univ. Press, 1998) 67 at 74.

[43] Bodde and Morris, *Law in Imperial China* (1967) at 19.

[44] A. Chen, *Introduction to Legal System* (1992) at 8.

[45] Bunger, 'Wandel des Rechts' (1980) at 449; de Bary, *Trouble with Confucianism* (1991) at 33; Ames, 'Rites and Rights' (1988) at 200 (also 'making community one's own').

come to share ... following the human Way'.[46] In Japan li becomes giri, often translated as an omnipresent obligation of thanks or loyalty.[47] Confucianism thus stands somewhere between religious norm and positive law, necessarily defending itself in both directions.


## LIMITING FA

From the west it is the opposition between confucian li and legalist fa which appears most evident, an opposition thrown into greater relief (as will be seen) by importation of different varieties—both capitalist and communist—of western law. The debate, however, is a very old one within Asia, and western models serve largely to illustrate theoretical positions which have long been staked out and even implemented (at least partially) at various times in the past. So confucian reticence towards positive legal models is not based on lack of familiarity or ignorance; it is rather profoundly principled and rational in character, though the rationality has pointed in a direction other than towards rational law.

Underlying the confucian position is a fundamentally positive view of human nature, the basic virtues of which can be refined and heightened by persuasion and example, or li.[48] Li is profoundly relational, and the fulfilment of personal life is seen as fulfilment of role, whether familial, professional or political. Since li is not sovereign command (though may be written down, even in book form) it may be flexibly interpreted, in a consensual manner, such that harmony in society is preserved through mutual reinforcement of norms rather than dispute over their content. This is how li is an enterprise of *creating* a society, in which all must share, so that even formal ritual becomes an expression and affirmation of underlying objectives, and of the importance of each of the participants in it, at whatever level of society. And since li is flexible it allows personal variation, such that it may be poetical and beautiful in expression, never being rendered uniform and monotonous in its precise detail.[49] Li, in short, is an instrument of aspiration.[50] Business relations are therefore best not reduced to written form and should be seen as ongoing, harmonious relationships of mutual advantage. If one of the parties insists on formal documentation of the terms of an initial agreement, the writing should not impede adjustments necessary for ongoing harmonious relationships. All claims are thus personalized, contextualized, and placed within their ongoing,

---

[46] H. Rosemont Jr., 'Why Take Rights Seriously? A Confucian Critique' in Rouner (ed.), *Human Rights and World's Religions* (1988), above, at 167.

[47] G. Rahn, 'Rechtsverständnis' in W. Fikentscher et al. (eds.), *Entstehung und Wandel rechtlicher Traditionen* (1980) 473 at 486; Noda, *Introduction to Japanese Law* (1976) at 174 ff.; Noda, 'Far Eastern Conception of Law' (1975) at 134, 135; M. Chiba, 'Three Level Structure of Law in Contemporary Japan, the Shinto Society' in Chiba, *Asian Indigenous Law* (1986) at 301.

[48] Bodde and Morris, *Law in Imperial China* (1967) at 21; Weggel *Die Asiaten* (1989) at 188.

[49] Bodde and Morris, *Law in Imperial China* (1967) at 21.

[50] Ames, 'Rites and Rights' (1988) at 202.

supportive, human frame of reference. A kind of 'fireside equity'[51] smothers any sharp, textually driven differences. All parties should be driven by the long term; the exemplary person seeks harmony rather than agreement on immediate detail, the small person does the opposite.[52]

Since the short-lived triumph of the legalists in the third century BC, the confucians have not held to their programme as a complete and exhaustive one, and have even buttressed it with fa as required, to deal with the really incorrigible types. This has served to reinforce confucian conviction, since li can now be made operative where it *must* be effective, on those capable of being led to higher things. The persistence of the legalists and westerners, in arguing for a larger role for fa, is thus seen as a fundamentally misconceived position, mistaking a minimalist position of human good—that which can be obtained through formal means and force—for a maximalist (confucian) one. A confucian society, in short, is one which does what it says should be done, leaving no gap between formal law and actual behaviour, no slippage between formal equality and massive social discrepancy. Formal laws, in contrast, induce no higher form of behaviour, leading only to manipulation of texts, litigation and over-regulation.[53] Laws cannot stand alone, say the confucians; absent the appropriate human support, they simply disappear.

## LIMITING RELIGION

As a secular, rational philosophy confucianism also stands opposed to normativity rooted in religion, though Confucius himself made imprecise references to a distant heaven.[54] From a confucian perspective, religion tends to develop along one of two undesirable paths—either as a complex, written law (talmudic, islamic, hindu traditions) or as a preoccupation with an immortal soul, to the detriment of daily life and present human relations (christianity, buddhism, taoism, shintoism). From its

---

[51] Tay, 'Struggle for Law in China' (1987) at 562. Great reliance is thus placed on personal, mutual respect and good faith. In terms of roman law, the old maxim of rebus sic stantibus (in these circumstances) prevails over that of pacta sunt servanda (agreements are binding). For the emergence of 'Sinocized' contracts, with shorter sentences and fewer words, see Y. Dezalay and B. Garth, *Dealing in Virtue: International Commercial Arbitration and the Construction of a Transnational Legal Order* (Chicago/London: Univ. of Chicago Press, 1996) at 262; and for contractual relations in Japan being seen as analogous to matrimonial relations, see G. F. Margadant S., *El derecho japonés actual* (Mexico City: Fondo de cultura económica, 1993) at 280.

[52] Ames, 'Rites and Rights' (1988) at 201.

[53] Bodde and Morris, *Law in Imperial China* (1967) at 17 (citing arguments used in confucian opposition to the first codes of the 6th century, BC).

[54] See Kaltenmark, *Philosophie chinoise* (1980), above, at 14; and see de Bary, *Trouble with Confucianism* (1991) at 10–12 for distinction between confucianism and religion (confucianism no established priesthood, no personal God, no sense of a people's response to heaven as a given people, no prospect of final fulfilment or reward, no final judgment; though noble person bearing some resemblance to prophet); and for confucianism distinguished from a Chinese rationalist perspective of natural order (Huang-Lao, having clear parallels with western natural law tradition), see R. Peerenboom, *Law and Morality in Ancient China: the Silk Manuscripts of Huang-Lao* (Albany: State Univ. of New York Press, 1993), noting at 253 ff. the decline of this perspective in the face of confucianism.

base in China, confucianism provided little resistance to the growth of talmudic, islamic and hindu traditions far to the west, and did not prevail against the sweep of islam into south-east Asia, notably in Indonesia and Malaysia. It has stood more firmly against the other religions, Asian ones, though the results have been mixed, depending on both time and territory.

Buddhism had its origins in India, in reaction to hinduism.[55] The Buddha, or awakened one (in real life Gautama Siddhartha) came from Nepal and lived in the sixth century, BCE (even before the dharmasastras, or legal textbooks). The Buddha objected to a great deal of hinduism—its formalism (as he saw it), its revelation, its structure of castes—and proposed a different vision of the world which has come to be seen, by many, as religious in character. Buddhism teaches many things and has been described as 'the most mature and really intelligent theory of human life and of the cosmos that man has ever devised'.[56] This is quite a claim, and it wasn't made by someone thinking about law, since the Buddha had other than legal things in mind. Some are now saying, however, that his teaching has legal implications not yet understood.

Buddhism is profoundly egalitarian as a philosophy[57] and its egalitarianism extends to all forms of existence. Its egalitarianism flows from the unreal character which it assigns to the physical world, including the human one. Human beings do not stand in some privileged position as observers of everything else.[58] They themselves are as unreal as everything else, and the real aim of buddhism is therefore to bring about a realization, an appreciation, of the truly ephemeral character of ourselves and all that surrounds us. When this happens, when we achieve

---

[55] See Watts, *Philosophies of Asia* (1995), ch. 6; and more generally P. Harvey, *Introduction to Buddhism: Teachings, History, and Practices* (Cambridge: Cambridge Univ. Press, 1990); R. Gethin, *The Foundations of Buddhism* (Oxford/New York: Oxford Univ. Press, 1998). For buddhist criticism of hinduism (castes, élitism), see R. Thapar, 'Society and Law in the Hindu and Buddhist Traditions' in R. Thapar, *Ancient Indian Social History* (New Delhi: Orient Longman, 1978) 26, notably at 32, 33

[56] Watts, *Philosophies of Asia* (1995) at 82. While buddhism does not involve belief in a creator god, it would be religious in providing a 'practical way of dealing with the reality of suffering', using devotional practices and ritual to this end. Gethin, *Foundations of Buddhism* (1998), above, at 64, 65.

[57] Some forms of zen (or in China tch'an) buddhism even deny explicit teaching, leaving the discovery of truth to the individual. The teacher will teach that there is nothing to be taught and there will have to be discussion of the nothingness which cannot be taught. On buddhism as dialogue or method rather than doctrine, in which books are only the 'opening gambit' see Watts, *Philosophies of Asia* (1995) at 77, 80.

[58] On the Buddhahood of mountains, rivers, grass and trees, see T. Unno, 'Personal Rights and Contemporary Buddhism' in Rouner (ed.), *Human Rights and World's Religions* (1988), above, 129 at 138; and on the notion that 'The world exists, but it is not real', see A. David-Neel, *Buddhism* (1977) at 134–8; and for evident parallels between buddhist teaching on the nature of physical reality and contemporary western quantum theory, see G. Zukav, *The Dancing Wu Li Masters: an Overview of the New Physics* (New York: William Morrow & Co., 1979), notably at 32 (li here as 'universal order' or 'universal law' (showing how far it can be distanced from 'ritual') and wu as matter or energy, yielding the Chinese word for physics, wu li, or 'patterns of organic energy'), 212 (modern science, parallelling buddhism, concluding no 'ultimate stuff' of universe, only energy), 253–6 (western scientific support for buddhist views that all reality 'virtual' and that the appearance of physical 'reality' dependent on the interdependence of all things).

enlightenment (nirvana), we will come to see as ego-less persons,[59] and the world we see will be an interdependent world, one in which the relationship between the one and the many, between contradictory but necessary opposites, will be finally understood.[60] It is a world characterized by what has been described as the 'Middle Way', not one of moderation but one of the bringing together of opposites.[61] Once nirvana has been achieved you can return to the world of objects and things, or the game of dealing with them, but you will now understand their character and your relationship to them, and you will act in a different manner. You will, among other things, be an extremely tolerant person, even mystical, even other-worldly.

Because of buddhist teaching there aren't many lawyer buddhists, though buddhism spread into China, Korea and Japan in the north and, even more strongly and in a different variant, into Burma, Cambodia, Laos, Sri Lanka, Thailand and Vietnam in the south. It did so, however, in a non-political, non-institutional way, just telling people about the way of the world and achieving some kind of political consensus only in Tibet.[62] Generally, it was only within the communities of buddhist monks that some type of formal order developed, leaving external societies free to drift or even to enact positive (though necessarily unreal) law.[63] The confu-

---

[59] On the not-self teaching, which describes the human person as a collection of interacting mental and physical processes, see Harvey, *Introduction to Buddhism* (1990), above, at 50–3; Gethin, *Foundations of Buddhism* (1998), above, at 133–57; Unno, 'Personal Rights and Contemporary Buddhism' (1988), above, at 130, 133.

[60] Unno, 'Personal Rights and Contemporary Buddhism' (1988), above, at 140; and on the impossibility of concluding as to the existence of a precise, single being without comparing and contrasting with what is external to the being, see Watts, *Philosophies of Asia* (1995) at 44–7, 59 (contrasting yoga, being joined or connected, with myopic sense of separateness (sakyadrishti) felt by most people considered civilized).

[61] Watts, *Philosophies of Asia* (1995) at 82.

[62] On the general lack of success of buddhism at the level of the political, legal and economic (how could it be otherwise?), see R. Thurman, 'Social and Cultural Rights in Buddhism' in Rouner (ed.), *Human Rights and World's Religions* (1988), above, 148 at 148; de Bary, *Trouble with Confucianism* (1991) at 58 (buddhists could be discounted as viable political force by asking 'Where is their alternative to the civil service?'); and (on monastic institutions becoming the central power in Tibet), Thurman, 'Social and Cultural Rights in Buddhism' (1988), above, at 160. For Tibetan law, profoundly inspired by buddhism, see R. French, *The Golden Yoke: the Legal Cosmology of Buddhist Tibet* (Ithaca, NY/London: Cornell Univ. Press, 1995), notably at 13–15 (Tibetan community divided between monks or spiritual seekers and spiritual supporters), 41–4 (genesis of Tibetan law codes), 64 (principle of non-duality or elimination of binary opposites), 72 (multiple concepts of time but generally no sequential counting of it in Tibetan law, delays of little consequence, no limitation periods, causation not requiring temporal proximity, emphasis on 'what' and 'how' rather than 'when'), 134 (rolling dice accepted means of dispute resolution where parties unclear and evidence insufficient, with invocation of deity), 344, 345 (lack of finality or closure, no concepts of stare decisis, res judicata, necessity of calming mind before dispute considered over). For the buddhist monastic code of discipline see Harvey, *Introduction to Buddhism* (1990), above, at 224–9.

[63] The notion of 'buddhist law' is most frequently encountered in Myanmar (Burma), where there has been a process of conversion of hindu dharmasastras and fusion with local, informal tradition. See O. Lee, *Legal and Moral Systems in Asian Customary Law: the Legacy of the Buddhist Social Ethic and Buddhist Law* (San Francisco: Chinese Materials Center, 1978) at pp. xx, xxi, 151, 169; R. Okudaira, 'The Burmese Dhammathat' in Hooker, *Laws of South-East Asia* (1986) at 23, notably at 55 (buddhist scriptures not used in compilation of texts, probably because of absence of specific legal rules, law of Manu still considered applicable); and for a similar process of re-working of hindu texts in Thailand, P. Kovilaikool, 'The Legal System of Thailand' in ASEAN Law Association, *ASEAN Legal Systems* (Singapore/Malaysia/Hong Kong: Butterworths Asia, 1995) 383 at 384; S. Sucharitkul, 'Thai Law and Buddhist Law' (1998) 46 Am. J. Comp. Law (Suppl.) 69.

cians made much of the 'emptiness' of buddhism,[64] in contrast to the solid, this-worldliness of confucianism, and they largely displaced buddhism from the prominent role it once played in China (from about the first century, CE), while reducing its influence in Korea, Japan and Vietnam. Yet in spite of this long animosity, confucianism and buddhism unite in refusing to take positive law very seriously. They are part of a larger Asian tradition.

Other Asian religions reinforce this larger tradition. Taoism, the other great religion of China, has historically been linked with buddhism in its disdain for worldly concerns.[65] It propounds the philosophy of doing nothing (wu-wei), inevitably attractive for many, and gives profound and succint reasons for doing so. Tao teaching says that 'the more laws are promulgated, the greater the number of thieves' and, still more pithily,

> Governing a large nation
> is like cooking little fish.[66]

We should therefore not exalt cleverness, so as to stop people contending, and not put high prices on hard-to-get goods, so as to stop stealing. You can see how dangerous this all is, and it is accompanied by buddhist-like notions of interdependence and reconciliation of opposites:

> So being and nonbeing produce each other
> difficulty and ease complement each other
> long and short shape each other
> high and low contrast with each other
> voice and echoes conform to each other
> before and after go along with each other.[67]

Tao means path, or principle or doctrine, so it too purports to present a large vision of the world and everything in it, though there is little place for law in the world of tao. Laws are seen as simply advancing the position of interest groups,[68] so the principle of doing nothing is not only the least harmful course of action but also the most likely to reap positive benefit. The reactions of the confucians to taoism was essentially the same as their reaction to buddhism. Something is better than nothing, and in place of positive law or emptiness they offer li, social construction through harmonious consensus.

[64] de Bary, 'Neo-Confucianism and Human Rights' (1988) at 188.
[65] See Watts, *Philosophies of Asia* (1995) ch. 7; Kaltenmark, *Philosophie chinoise* (1980), above, 33–47; Noda, 'Far Eastern Conception of Law' (1975) at 121, 122.
[66] See T. Cleary, trans., *The Essential Tao* (San Francisco: Harper, 1993) at 44, 46.
[67] Ibid., at 9.
[68] This appears to be put forward by taoists as a result of simple intuition, though more explicit foundations have been argued in recent US legal writing. See, e.g., R. Posner, *Economic Analysis of Law*, 4th edn. (Boston/Toronto: Little, Brown, 1992) §§ 19. 3 ('That [legislative] process creates a market for legislation in which legislators "sell" legislative protection to those who can help their electoral prospects with money or votes').

In Japan, shintoism parallels buddhism and taoism for its lack of immediate social direction,[69] such that confucian-inspired notions of social harmony can remain significant, in particular Japanese variants. An Asian default position is thus maintained in a large range of religious and secular views throughout Asia, and they are all directed, explicitly or implicitly, against formal legality. This is not in any way to suggest a high level of Asian social uniformity. The differences in religion or philosophy may explain much in different underlying social attitudes,[70] yet there is also an underlying common theme, that persuasion and models are the only viable means of social cohesion. This is reflected in the manner of expression of the law which exists, and in the informal norms which are expected to dominate the formal law.

## CONFUCIANIZATION

Confucianism manifests itself most obviously in li and the primacy which it accords to human relations, but there has also been a process in which the formal law which exists—the fa—has been confucianized. In both these forms of normativity the notion of abstract rules and abstract, individual persons is absent. In all cases, according to confucian teaching, li and law must speak to individuals in the relationship in which they find themselves, in sufficient detail for them to recognize the information needed for guidance. So the language of li is precise and concrete and there is an evident parallel with both talmudic and islamic law, which seek to regulate a similar range of conduct, through written texts.[71] Li is thus expressed in concepts which people know and recognize—'walnuts and mulberry leaves' rather than things and property[72]—and the criminal, written texts are characterized by a high level of casuistry. There is not a single crime of homicide, but twenty of them, differentiated according to status of criminal and victim (within, without the family; privileged, non-privileged people) and the manner of perpetration.[73] Li also requires many exceptions, so the apparent harshness of the definitions of crime and sanction could be tempered by consideration of all and any mitigating factors. The formal process of adjudication thus shades into the informal process of dispute resolution, since in both it is the particularity of the specific events and

[69] Rahn, ' Rechtsverständnis' (1980), above, at 479, 481 (shintoism a combination of animism and polytheism, reaching back to beginnings of Japan).

[70] On different buddhist and confucian perspectives on economic activity (buddhism less economically driven, confucianism emphasizing saving, competition, corporativity) see Weggel, *Die Asiaten* (1989) at 153, 155, 160, 170 and 177 (no single culture providing overarching recipe for development; no single 'eastern model'; motto 'look east' should be replaced with 'look around').

[71] On the style of expression of talmudic and islamic law, see above, Ch. 4, *The style of the text*, and Ch. 6, *Islamic texts and islamic reason: the role of ijtihad*.

[72] Weggel, *Die Asiaten* (1989) at 117.

[73] Bodde and Morris, *Law in Imperial China* (1967) at 29; von Senger, *Chinesische Recht* (1994) at 20; and generally on confucianization, Ch'u, *Law and Society in Traditional China* (1965) at 267 ff.; Ren, *Tradition of Law and Law of Tradition* (1997) at 22, 23.

specific relations which are considered primary, rather than any notion of normativity above and beyond the human relations examined. Models are preferred to
rules; teaching to sanctions; symbols to concepts; and even fa is expected to change
its nature, to increase its efficiency and contribute to the greater aspirational
objective.

The rationality inherent in this entire confucian process, which disdains the
'mysticism' of religions, particularly Asian ones, is mistrustful of universals. That
there *is* a rationality, both in terms of worked-out objectives and detailed methods,
seems clear enough, though it is a rationality of social conduct and not a rationality
of enquiry. So China, in its confucian mode and until very recently, had no concept
of philosophy, in the wide, western, sweeping sense.[74] It had only *a* philosophy,
which concentrated on the concrete, the particular, the dynamic, the practical, and
this for a single objective, the harmonious survival of social relations, necessarily
lasting over millennia.[75] Rationality here emerges out of and is defended by 'appeal
to concrete historical instances of reasonableness' and morality is 'articulated
through analogy with particular historical exemplars'.[76] Particularity is here conscious of its particularity, rejecting the idea of getting beyond it, concerned with
extracting the maximum of instruction from it, concerned with making it NEW.

In one important sense, however, confucian rationality comes close to that of the
buddhist or taoist. In seeking social harmony, buddhism and taoism teach the ego-
less self or the virtue of doing nothing as means of understanding the interdependent character of the world. In its attention to detail, particularity and relations,
confucianism comes close to the same result. The buddhist may see and admit
opposites, which are related and connected; the confucian may see only infinite
gradations of reality, all harmoniously linked, none so discordant as to bring about
rupture.[77] Day begins in the heart of night. Are they necessarily related opposites?
Or ongoing, varying shades of one another? In neither case can they be separated.
The underlying harmony should preclude conflictual views of apparent reality.
Formal law, with its formal boundaries and conflicts, has an unfortunate tendency
to mask the underlying harmony.

## LI, SOCIAL HARMONY AND RIGHT

From what has been said thus far, you get a sense of the importance of social
harmony and social relations in most variants of Asian tradition. Their importance
leads to an informal concept of normativity, a de-emphasis on punishment and
sanction, an entire style or manner of deontological and legal expression. The

[74] Kaltenmark, *Philosophie chinoise* (1980), above, at 6; Noda, 'Far Eastern Conception of Law' (1975) at 123
('Confucianists are rationalists').

[75] Weggel, *Die Asiaten* (1989) at 213.

[76] Ames, 'Rites and Rights' (1988) at 207.

[77] Ding, *Understanding Confucius* (1997) at 201–3 (harmony, like cuisine and music, dependent on diversity;
all things in universe inter-connected in one way or another).

current western view is that it also leads to the submergence of the individual and a decline in human values and human worth. Yet confucianism doesn't somehow just flow from these given notions of li and harmony; they themselves have to be constructed and defended, notably against competing notions of human nature (as darkly described by proponents of fa) and against notions of individual autonomy and freedom (now largely coming from western theory but also from indigenous voices within Asia). The confucians haven't, however, just started to worry about these things. Confucianism is the response which has been made to them over thousands of years, and is above all an attempt to integrate claims of freedom and self, taken as given, into a larger, accommodating cadre. Confucianism does not seek to deny, but to integrate, in the manner, apparently, of complex traditions everywhere.

Early Chinese tradition, to which Confucius was sensible, appears clearly chthonic in character, in simply integrating human beings into a larger, cyclical cosmos, which both required support and wreaked vengeance when it did not receive it.[78] Confucianism developed, however, by articulating a specific and detailed social philosophy which departed from chthonic tradition, constituting a larger and identifiable body of teaching as Chinese society grew in complexity. Since maintaining harmony in the universe was becoming overshadowed in importance by the task of maintaining harmony in the warring kingdoms, it was necessary to concentrate more specifically on the human means for doing so. These were found in recognized forms of human relations—and this theme has not lost its currency[79]—below the level of formal state or national structures. There are many such relationships: family, guild, employment, age, village, friendship—all of which contain implicit or even explicit information as to their own maintenance and survival. So the confucians essentially say that social harmony has to come from the society itself, without being laid upon it, and that there is no way of creating social harmony which does not to a considerable degree already exist. The work of the confucians, and the lawyers that might be necessary, is to facilitate and recognize the means of social harmony which presently prevail. This includes the recognition and fostering of individual human aspiration, since all institutions and relations which exist are necessarily composed of individuals. There is proclamation of the primacy of communities and relations within which individuals can easily recognize themselves, while individual worth and aspiration are recognized and praised in the maintenance and prospering of these communities and relations. The individual is not meant to be left out of this reasoning, but rather swept up in it. It is all part of the inseparable, interdependent world. You can no more separate individuals from

---

[78] See Bodde and Morris, *Law in Imperial China* (1967) at 4; David and Brierley, *Major Legal Systems* (1985) at 518.

[79] On notions of informal communities in current western legal and political theory, see the symposium *Individualism and Communitarianism in Contemporary Legal Systems: Tensions and Accomodations* [1993] Brigham Young U. L. Rev. 385–741.

the relations in which they exist than you can separate day from night, yet this in no way denigrates day or night, or individual people.

Guanxi or relations are thus the key intermediaries between the individual and larger harmonious groupings, and remain so throughout Asia today. Grounded in natural human affections, the entire society is meant to have a dynamic of its own, requiring little external intervention or threat of force to make it coherent.[80] Outside of China, even buddhism became a means of justification of social ordering, as in Japan where the notion of kaisha or large family has largely controlled corporate life.[81] Confucianized fa went to considerable lengths to reinforce the intermediate communities, even to the prejudice of more direct forms of social control. Thus punishment was merited for denouncing a member of one's own family for a crime, and this even if the accusation were true.[82]

Asian tradition thus did not generate a notion of individual rights or 'droits subjectifs' and it has even been said that the notion of individual autonomy, unresponsiveness to others, is suggestive of 'idiocy or immorality'.[83] It is too radical a proposition for human ordering to be successful over an extended period of time, implicitly denied by the non-transcendental character of Asian moral philosophy and by the refusal to conceptualize individuals in any way other than relational—as children, parents, friends, lovers, youngsters, oldsters, employees, employers and on and on.[84] Yet confucianism denies that it is at the collective end of a spectrum between collectivity and individualism and has, particularly in its modern variants, sought to ensure individual values within the relational cadre it proposes. Inequality is recognized as necessarily existing in society, but is either justified or to be corrected. It is justified where it is simply forbearance, to allow people and things to be themselves, a kind of co-ordinated diversity.[85] Justification may also exist where privileges and duties even up, equitably, over time, as where the duties of the child become the rights or privileges of the parent.[86] It may not be justified when the virtues of saving and competition are pushed to the extreme, such that the accumu-

---

[80] de Bary, 'Neo-Confucianism and Human Rights' (1988) at 185, 186; and on the importance of notions of guanxi for western societies, see J.-M. Ghéhenno, La fin de la démocratie (Paris: Flammarion, 1995) at 43–6 (on lack of social grounding of western notions of contract), 84, 85 (on relational logic) and 107–9 (on social control by society itself, through guanxi) (published in English as The End of the Nation State, trans. V. Elliott (London/Minneapolis: Univ. of Minnesota Press, 1995).

[81] Weggel, Die Asiaten (1989) at 162; Rahn, 'Rechtsverständnis' (1980), above, at 480, 484.

[82] Bodde and Morris, Law in Imperial China (1967) at 40.

[83] Ames, 'Rites and Rights' (1988) at 200; and for parallels between roman and chinese law in insisting on role and proportionality, as opposed to equality and rights, Li, 'L'esprit du droit chinois' notably at 33, 35.

[84] On individuals not playing such roles, but being them, see Rosemont, 'Why Take Rights Seriously?' (1988), above, at 175; and on the different conception of the self generally, see T. Metzger, 'Continuities between Modern and Premodern China: Some Neglected Methodological and Substantive Issues' in P. Cohen and M. Goldman (eds.), Ideas Across Culture: Essays on Chinese Thought in Honor of Benjamin I. Schwartz (Cambridge, Mass.: Council on East Asian Studies, Harvard Univ., 1990) 263 at 267 ('inner transcendence').

[85] Ames, 'Rites and Rights' (1988) at 208 (emphasizing equivocal nature of notions of equality, consisting either of sameness between things or forbearance to allow things to be themselves).

[86] de Bary, 'Neo-Confucianism and Human Rights' (1988) at 186; Ames, 'Rites and Rights' (1988) at 208.

lation of wealth generates social inequities and ill will.[87] Inequality may also be corrected by specific means, such as the democratization of teaching[88] or the use of competitive examinations for changes of employment.[89] And within the disparate roles which society will inevitably contain, the individual person is to be praised in all contributions which are made. The entire confucian structure rests on a notion of underlying human good, which the relational structure is meant to facilitate and serve. It is self-cultivation which is the key to governance,[90] collapsing the means-end distinction so that each person is both an end in themselves and a means for everyone else.[91] Li is a means of registering one's importance, leaving a mark on the tradition, in the same way as each is a *creator* of the talmudic tradition. It is possible to write a book on *The Liberal Tradition in China*.[92] And if you are still suspicious, think of the Chinese stratagems, all the wiles for getting where you need to be, for circumventing the bureaucracy, for achieving personal goals against all odds. Always kill with a borrowed knife.[93] It's not exactly confucian, but it's part of the entire tradition.

## CHANGE AND THE ETERNAL EMPIRE

In a confucian society motivated by a sense of loyalty to human relations there is no major impetus to change. Nor is there much point, from a buddhist perspective, in expending major energy in changing what is unreal. For the taoist, doing nothing

---

[87] On inherent limits on making of profit, not in itself excluded, see von Senger, *Chinesische Recht* (1994) at 18.

[88] Kaltenmark, *Philosophie chinoise* (1980), above, at 13; Ding, *Understanding Confucius* (1997) at 34, 63 ('teaching everyone without making distinctions').

[89] R. Ingelhardt, 'Changing values, economic development and political change' (1995) 47 Int. Soc. Sci. J. 379 at 382; A. Cotterell and D. Morgan, *China's Civilization: a Survey of its History, Arts, and Technology* (New York: Praeger Publishers, 1975) at 56, 57 (noting adoption of the idea in 19th-century Europe); Zweigert and Kötz, *Introduction to Comparative Law* (1998) at 290; H. McAleavy, 'Chinese Law' (1968) at 111 (examination system facilitated by introduction of printing as early as 9th century); T. Huff, *The rise of early modern science: Islam, China, and the West* (Cambridge: Cambridge Univ. Press, 1993) at 275 ff.

[90] de Bary, *Trouble with Confucianism* (1991) at 55.

[91] Ames, 'Rites and Rights' (1988) at 201; on the 'common gender prejudice of placing women in a subordinate position far beyond the common economic and political causes', however, see Ren, *Tradition of Law and Law of Tradition* (1997) at 27.

[92] de Bary, *Liberal Tradition in China* (1983); and see Schwartz, *World of Thought in Ancient China* (1985) at 113 ('If "individualism" refers to something like Kantian moral autonomy, something of it can certainly be found here'); Ren, *Tradition of Law and Law of Tradition* (1997) at 27 (Chinese 'nation of individualists', 'family-minded, not social-minded', 'family mind is only a form of magnified selfishness', citing Lin Yu-tang).

[93] See H. von Senger, 'Chinese Culture and Human Rights' in W. Schmale (ed.), *Human Rights and Cultural Diversity* (Goldbach, Germany: Keip Publishing, 1993) 281 at 305 (on underlying Chinese self-esteem, use of stratagems); H. von Senger, *The Book of Stratagems: Tactics for Triumph and Survival*, trans. M. Gubitz (New York: Viking Penguin, 1991) at 41 ff. (Stratagem No. 3).

presents positive advantages. Asian secularity and Asian religions thus come together in asking very large questions of those who would undertake major initiatives. They also apply a great deal of pressure, through the influence of those they have persuaded, against rash or imprudent conduct. There are here different, Asian reasons for muting a concept of change, though there are also different, Asian reasons for accommodating it.

## ASIAN TIME AND SPACE

Chthonic and hindu notions of time have been seen as largely circular—everything just keeps coming around—and there is much in Asian thinking of time which is close to that of chthonic and hindu tradition. Now, it may be that Asian concepts of time are derived from the necessary stability of social relations, which must be constantly recycled within a time which is therefore stabilized, or it may be that the stability of relations is itself derived from an overarching sense of time, within which human existence is essentially fixed. The question is not answered in discussion of Asian law, and may never be answered. There is insistence everywhere, however, on the absence of any linear view of history, any possibility of an 'apocalyptic finale'.[94] The inherent confucian view of time is reinforced, moreover, by buddhist notions of the recycling soul (maintaining this link with hinduism) and of the primacy of seeing the world as it is, in each moment in which it is. The buddhist sees the world (interdependent, though unreal) in the spring and then, again, in the summer, and each moment is what is essential, and not some kind of progression in the state of the world itself.[95] As for taoists, time cannot be anything which accommodates change, from then to now, since nobody is supposed to change anything anyway.

   Living in stable time has as a consequence that one is living in the same time as those who live before or after oneself, such that Asian views of time coincide with those of the chthonic and hindu world in extending the benefits of human relations to the inter-generational community.[96] This explains the place of elders in Asian society and even the principle of seniority in many industrial organizations. Some say it also extends to a certain detachment in commercial matters; if you don't sign the contract it is quite possible your descendants will, and this amounts to essentially the same thing. In an interdependent world there is also necessary concern for non-human beings. They are far from being descartian soulless machines, though they have not been imbued with the sacred, godlike character which they have attained in hinduism. Asian sympathy towards the natural world is also replicated

---

[94] de Bary, *Trouble with Confucianism* (1991) at 13; N. Tarling, *Nations and States in Southeast Asia* (Cambridge: Cambridge Univ. Press, 1998) at 121, 122; and see Weggel, *Die Asiaten* (1989) at 205 (little resulting place for 'progress' or 'future'; old valuable as such).

[95] Watts, *Philosophies of Asia* (1995) at 102, citing 13th-century buddhist teaching on time.

[96] See Rosemont, 'Why Take Rights Seriously?' (1988), above, at 177.

in Asian attitudes towards space. It is particularized, not seen as abstract zones or areas ready to be appropriated but rather as the environment in which human relations flourish.[97] So empty land in a sense just disappears, whereas the town centre is *where* things really happen, where the space is.

Confucianism is, however, a learned tradition, in which learning is said to occupy a place almost equal to that of li and its underlying (Asian) humanism.[98] So confucianism is to be learned, as are the essentials of various human relations, and all else which will contribute to the objectives of social harmony. There has even been a confucian school of 'Evidential Research'.[99] As in hinduism, there has therefore been great intellectual development, and ensuing initiatives and change, and it is said that until at least the thirteenth century China was the most intellectually and technologically advanced place in the world. Yet, as in hinduism, the spirit of enquiry is here a functional one, limited to what is compatible with confucian teaching and not free and boundless in scope. Learning is a moral and practical undertaking, with integration its primary objective.[100] In buddhism it is essentially rejected, with bookish learning seen as largely irrelevant to the process of awakening. Early on, China developed paper, the compass, gunpowder (only), porcelain, silk, printing, the wheelbarrow (unknown in the west until the thirteenth century)[101] and acupuncture, and then seems to have decided, in a consensual, non-formal way, that that was probably about as far as things should go. This really follows from the nature of li, so the humanism which develops a rational view of social harmony is also one which develops necessary and rational limits on human change. You don't presume to change the world and its relations very much; it follows that you don't change the li and the law very much either. And historically the great codes of fa lasted for centuries without change, coming to be seen themselves as perpetual and near-sacred in character.

---

[97] Weggel, *Die Asiaten* (1989) at 206; N. Tarling, *Nations and States* (1998), above, at 47 (concept of frontier uncommon in south-east Asia; emphasis rather on allegiance); and for the introduction of western notions of mapping into Asia, see B. Anderson, *Imagined Communities*, rev. edn. (London/New York: Verso Editions, 1991) at 171–3.

[98] de Bary, *Trouble with Confucianism* (1991) at 45, 91 (also on difficulty of implementing educational aims beyond basic level of family and those of ruling élites); and for learning as the key to knowledge and tolerance in confucian thought, D. Gangjian and S. Gang, 'Relating Human Rights to Chinese Culture: The Four Paths of the Confucian Analects and the Four Principles of a New Theory of Benevolence' in Davis (ed.), *Human Rights and Chinese Values* (1995) 35 at 43.

[99] de Bary, *Trouble with Confucianism* (1991) at 84; and for the creation of the Poh Shih Kuan, or Imperial University, in the 2nd century BC, many centuries before the appearance of universities in islamic or western worlds, see Cotterell and Morgan, *China's Civilization* (1975), above, at 56. Cf., above, Ch. 7, *Of judges and judging.*

[100] Kaltenmark, *Philosophie chinoise* (1980), above, at 6 (humanist character of thought but close link to natural world); Weggel, *Die Asiaten* (1989) at 50. For the great accomplishments of Chinese science, however, see J. Needham, *Science and Civilisation in China*, vols. I–VI (Cambridge: Cambridge Univ. Press, 1954 to date, ongoing); Huff, *Rise of early modern science* (1993), above.

[101] Cotterell and Morgan, *China's Civilization* (1975), above, at 56; for the transmission of paper via islamic jurisdictions to Europe, see R. Eaton, *Islamic History as Global History* (Washington, DC: Am. Hist. Assoc., 1990) at 22.

## ASIAN CORRUPTION

Confucianism presents the great advantage, shared with talmudic, islamic and hindu traditions, of calling for no large, institutional priesthood or bureaucracy for purposes of implementation. The corruption which can affect it is somehow outside itself, to be found in a turning away from its objectives by those who have no *institutional* obligation, as confucians, of loyalty and trust. Ideally, there is no confucian state, no confucian structure to corrupt. Yet Asia is no more immune to corruption than any other place, and appears even to have developed, from its particularity, some particular forms of corruption.

Ritual may become corrupt or formalized, as it is often thought of in the west, such that the most elusive form of corruption, the intellectual, may easily affect forms of conduct expected to control entire populations. Confucianism has long struggled with the problem of simplifying and revivifying its teaching, struggling against the tendency toward vulgar, popular custom.[102] The bureacracy of the world of fa, accepted by the confucians, is also one which offers all the temptations of large organizations, and confucians themselves, it is said, have long tolerated corruption of the judiciary and judicial system. Most importantly, a society of relations, of guanxi, may easily slide towards cronyism, the ongoing cultivation of reciprocal, unjustified advantage, to the exclusion of considerations of the outside world.[103] Confucianism is necessarily weak on this; its control of crime is harsh, but is not itself free of corruption, and loyalty is a thing which in principle is to be nurtured and promoted, not prosecuted. It becomes difficult to distinguish the loyalties which are rooted and justifiable, even though less responsive to outside need, from those which are transient or parasitic, designed simply to leach away the resources of the outside world.

## ASIA AS CENTRE OF THE WORLD

Tradition has it in Asia that Asia, or even China, is the centre of the world. The rest is periphery. This comes from the age and development of Asian tradition, from the size and density of the population, and from underlying (though not ostentatious)

---

[102] de Bary, *Trouble with Confucianism* (1991) at 43.

[103] In contemporary form, in China, see Folsom et al., *Law and Politics* (1992) at 391 ('trading through the back door'); H. Kolenda, 'One Party, Two Systems: Corruption in the People's Republic of China and Attempts to Control It' (1990) 4 J. Chinese Law 187, notably at 203 (notion of 'two-hatted officials', holding posts both in government and commerce) and 220 (on whether Party members subject to less severe standards); and for the process of western lex mercatoria becoming 'guanxified' in its application in China, see B. de Sousa Santos, *Toward a New Common Sense: Law, Science and Politics in the Paradigmatic Transition* (New York/London: Routledge, 1995) at 294. Singapore, however, would be the 4th least corrupt country in the world as result of its anti-corruption measures (including large street signs indicating directions to the Corrupt Practices Investigation Bureau); *The Economist*, 3 Oct., 1998, at 120.

notions of self-esteem. It is therefore not China which should be seen as having been relatively isolated for much of history, but everyone else,[104] living in relatively underpopulated cultural backwaters until (perhaps) the last few centuries. China had thus argued out, or discovered, or refused to discover, most things well before anyone else even stumbled upon them. And today China and Asia are so large that almost everything can be discovered within them, thriving in one way or another, whereas elsewhere it has been possible to channel and direct human thought and activity in a way impossible to conceive in Asia. There is no ideological or legal or political vacuum in China today, as some have contended. There is rather a surfeit of competing ideologies and legal and political philosophies, such that no one is able to nail down any one of them as that which necessarily prevails. The old pluralism continues, and the religious, political and legal preoccupation with pluralism continues as well.

## ASIAN IDENTITIES

In an interdependent world identities cannot be too sharply drawn. There is something of the new blur of Europe in Asian identities; they exist, but often in multiple form and with a recurrent phenomenon of overlap. Loyalties are multidirectional and even the most affirmative forms of political direction and identity cannot eradicate the informal, boundary-dissolving, groupings. This is most evident in religion, where belonging to two religions, or moving back and forth between them, is seen as entirely normal, a reflection of the big tent of hinduism. Being shinto or buddhist in Japan is said to present as much social interest as one's blood type.[105] This doesn't yield religious wars, while the secularity of confucianism is compatible with most religious outlooks, including western ones.[106] Identities do emerge from this,[107] but they are the result of a combination of religion, social philosophy (confucianism), geography (the people of that place of the rising sun) and, not to be

[104] See Cotterell and Morgan, *China's Civilization* (1975), above, at 65, 66 ('Discovery of the West', 'cities, mansions and houses as in China'), 188 (Europe still 'narrow, closed world' at time of Marco Polo in 13th century).

[105] Weggel, *Die Asiaten* (1989) at 52, contrasting, however, other Asian religions with islam, which would display a concern with boundaries and exclusivity of belief which is more western in character; and on historical religious overlapping in China and Japan, F. Braudel, *A History of Civilizations*, trans. R. Mayne (New York: Penguin, 1993) at 171 and 283 (notion of shingon, in which shintoism and buddhism virtually fused into one, local gods becoming particular and temporary manifestations of buddhist gods).

[106] See Watts, *Philosophies of Asia* (1995) at 92 (first jesuit missionary to China, Matteo Ricci—he of the memory palace, see above, Ch. 1, *Presence*—finding no belief or commitment of confucianism which would be in conflict with catholic faith); cf., however, on the 'Chinese rites' controversy of the 17th and 18th centuries, J. Taylor, 'Canon Law in the Age of the Fathers' in J. Hite and D. Ward, *Readings, Cases, Materials in Canon Law* (Collegeville, Minn.: The Liturgical Press, 1990) 43 at 69; and on the same debate, from the Chinese side, as the 'Catholic Crisis', Shen Fuwei, *Cultural Flow Between China and Outside World Throughout History*, trans. Wu Jingshu (Beijing: Foreign Languages Press, 1996) at 256 ff.

[107] See, for shintoism as emotional bond of Japanese people from early time, Rahn, 'Rechtsverständnis' (1980), above, at 48.

forgotten, state politics. Law here is clearly not the identifying agency it is in other traditions, whether talmudic, islamic, civil or common law, or even chthonic or hindu. Persuasion resists boundaries, and tends to jump over them.

Given overlapping identities, protection of any one of them is problematical. It is very difficult to find discussion of heresy or apostasy or even of dissent in Asian thought and literature. Most people don't, of course, engage in it. They have been brought on board, most notably by the idea of not forcing people to do things.[108] The absence of a doctrine of heresy is evident from the flourishing of both religion and legalism, bracketing main line confucianism in China. Buddhism and taoism, moreover, could hardly take a notion of heresy seriously. Treason, however, was another matter, long viewed in China as one of the ten (criminal) 'Abominations', along with killing a close relative or scolding a parent. Legalism was here clearly influential, resorting to notions of group or family responsibility and requiring divulgation of treason even when committed by members of one's own family. '[W]hen the confucian state felt its existence to be *really* threatened, it was willing to forgo its confucian precepts.'[109] This was, however, the confucian *state*, so treason is here much as it is everywhere in the world.

## LAYERED TRADITION

China has exercised its influence everywhere in Asia, yet has itself been greatly influenced—most notably, historically, by buddhism coming from India since the first century CE. Chinese goods were known in India in the fourth century BCE, so there remain traces of still earlier physical contact, even if the trail of ideas is harder to follow. East Asian contact with the west was either through the south (the South China Sea and around the corner to the Indian Ocean) or through the flat lands to the west of China, the origins of the Vedic-Aryans, via Tashkent.[110] The notion of isolation of east Asia from the rest of the world is thus very difficult to sustain, though China has been able to put its own, particular, spin on many things.[111] Elsewhere in Asia the layering of traditions is perhaps even more evident than in

[108] See von Senger, *Chinesische Recht* (1994) at 18.

[109] See Bodde and Morris, *Law in Imperial China* (1967) at 29, 41; more generally MacCormack, *Spirit of Traditional Chinese Law* (1996) at 109, 110; and for legalist attachment to notions of heresy, Z. Fu, *China's Legalists* (1996), above, at 116, 117.

[110] On Chinese expeditions to the west, from at least the 2nd century BC, see Cotterell and Morgan, *China's Civilization* (1975), above, at 19–21, 65, 66 (extending to the east coast of Africa); B. Lewis, *The Middle East: 2000 years of History from Rise of Christianity to the Present Day* (London: Weidenfeld & Nicolson, 1995) at 40 (control of inner Asian silk route extending to present territories of Uzbekistan and 'western neighbours'); for Chinese records of relations extending to at least the 6th century, BCE, see Shen Fuwei, *Cultural Flow* (1996), above, at 3–34; and generally J. Roberts, *History of the World* (London/New York: Penguin, 1995) at 306 ('Yet the insulation of one civilization from another was never absolute; there was always some physical and mental interaction going on').

[111] Braudel, *History of Civilizations* (1993), above, at 171 ('Nor, despite appearances, was it closed to the outside world').

China and it has been said of Indonesia that '[t]here is hardly a form of legal sensibility (African, perhaps, and Eskimo) to which it has not been exposed',[112] while the same sort of layering ('Verschichtung',[113] 'driving in two [legal] lanes'[114]) has been commented on in Malaysia. What is remarkable here is not the coming together or encounter of traditions, but their simultaneous preservation, layered in time but without prejudice to the survival of all. Receptions here don't end, don't become history. There have been many of them, and they just keep going on. The most recent in time have been those of western law and of socialist law. As in all receptions, however, the process is never a linear and unidirectional one.

## WESTERN LAW IN ASIA

Western colonialism in Asia, as elsewhere, left a legacy of western law. Legal accidents, such as the second world war, also have been influential, notably through expanding the influence of US law, particularly in Japan. In south-east Asia, Dutch, French and English laws were formally received in the colonialization process and continue their influence today, with varying degrees of intensity and visibility. In other instances the process of 'westernization' of Asian law was undertaken domestically as a means of reducing or eliminating western presence (then guaranteed by treaty), and to provide legal stability for ongoing western (private) investment.[115] Japan led this process in the late nineteenth century and French and German codification models jostled one another for influence (the German ultimately prevailing),[116] an early example of the struggle for prestige and influence

---

[112] Geertz, *Local Knowledge* (1983), above, at 226 (citing early austronesian arrivals (from today's China and Vietnam), indic state building ('Borobudur and all that'), islamic missionary activity, Dutch and English colonization ('bringing eminent domain and left-side driving'), Japanese occupation and being 'intruded upon' by more recent western and eastern interests, including those of the former Soviet Union); and see generally Hooker, *Legal Pluralism* (1975); Hooker, *Concise Legal History* (1978) and Hooker, *Islamic Law in South-East Asia* (1984), above.

[113] Weggel, *Die Asiaten* (1989) at 11.

[114] D. Horowitz, 'The Qur'an and the Common Law: Islamic Law Reform and the Theory of Legal Change' (1994) 42 Am. J. Comp. Law 233 (I), 543 (II) at 578, 579.

[115] For Japan, see K. Igarashi, *Einführung in das japanische Recht* (Darmstadt: Wissenschaftliche Buchgesellschaft, 1990) at 2; Rahn, 'Rechtsverständnis' (1980), above, 473 at 489; for China, A. Chen, *Introduction to Legal System* (1992) at 20, 21.

[116] On the process see Igarashi, *Japanische Recht* (1990), above, at 3 (various schools of law in Japan; French and progressive Japanese schools favouring implementation of French-inspired code drafted by Boissonade; opposed by English and conservative Japanese schools; delay leading to redrafting according to German model; original code a combination of German BGB (civil code) with long-standing Japanese family law, though latter revised substantially in later years; some French principles remaining, such as transfer of property by simple consent); M. Ishimoto, 'L'influence du Code civil français sur le droit civil japonais' 6 Rev. int. dr. comp. 1954. 744; Rahn, 'Rechtsverständnis' (1980), above, at 475; Noda, *Introduction to Japanese Law* (1976) 41–58; Z. Kitagawa, *Rezeption und Fortbildung des europäischen Zivilrechts in Japan* (Frankfurt: A. Metzner, 1970); A Katsuta, 'Japan: A Grey Legal Culture', in E. Örücü, E. Attwooll and S. Coyle (eds.), *Studies in Legal Systems: Mixed and Mixing* (The Hague/London/Boston: Kluwer, 1996) at 249; Tanaka, 'Role of Law in Japanese Society' (1985).

of western versions of legal rationality (such as is now occurring in eastern Europe and Russia). Following adoption of the German-model code, a 'theory reception' of German doctrine also occurred ('Was nicht deutsches Recht ist, ist kein Recht') which placed Japanese law, from a western perspective, firmly in the orbit of civilian thinking.[117] Yet even with the arrival of western law two offsetting and related phenomena became visible. The first was the making-over ('Japanisierung') of western models in their actual operation;[118] the second was the nesting of the entire concept of formal, civil law in the larger context of informal Japanese normativity. So you have today a civil code in Japan with very few lawyers, very few judges and very few lawsuits, comparatively speaking. The restraint is clearly informal.[119] Western legal structures now provide no means of restraint, other than cost, and are everywhere sagging under the burden of formalized disputes. The influence of US law following the second world war (notably in areas of constitutional law, labour law, criminal procedure and commercial law) thus occurred in a crowded, normative field. It remains today largely a beach-head.

China followed Japan's lead in following western legal models, in some measure, as a means of obtaining relief from western, treaty-guaranteed presence. The turn to western law began in the last years of the Ch'ing empire, which even established a minister for law reform from 1900–10.[120] There was of course opposition, itself also swept away with the fall of the empire in 1911 and the installation of the nationalist, Guomintang regime, which proceeded to codify large areas of law (the Six Codes), using mainly Japanese and German models.[121] The Six Codes remained essentially paper law. To the inherent resistance of Chinese society to formal normativity was now added the resistance of Chinese communism, itself politically successful in 1949.

Elsewhere in Asia the pattern of reliance on western law has been varied. The French law of Indo-China suffered division and decline on the creation of the independent states of Cambodia, Laos and Vietnam (then North and South), though there is now a French 'Maison du droit' established in Hanoi in the effort to

---

[117] Rahn, 'Rechtsverständnis' (1980), above, at 475; Igarashi, *Japanische Recht* (1990), above, at 6 (citing notions of Treu und Glauben, culpa in contrahendo).

[118] See generally H. Coing et al., *Die Japaniesierung des westlichen Rechts* (Tübingen: J. C. B. Mohr (Paul Siebeck) 1990), and notably Z. Kitagawa, 'Von der Japanisierung zur Entjapanisierung' at 441, 444 on multiple levels or layering (Mehrschichtigkeit) of Japanese law. The process appears one of constructive reception, i. e., what happened to roman law in France or civil law in the USA, an initial borrowing followed by subsequent, exclusivist domestication.

[119] K. Pistor and P. Wellons, *The Role of Law and Legal Institutions in Asian Economic Development 1960–1995* (New York/Hong Kong: Oxford Univ. Press, 1999) at 17, 18, 229–32; cf., however, for instances of legal response to conflict in Japan, and governmental efforts to restrain litigation, F. K. Upham, *Law and Social Change in Postwar Japan* (Cambridge, Mass./London: Harvard Univ. Press, 1987).

[120] See A. Chen, *Introduction to Legal System* (1992) at 21.

[121] Notably civil, criminal and commercial law, the law of courts, as well as civil and criminal procedure. See generally Tay, 'Struggle for Law in China' (1987) at 564 (Swiss law also used in codifying civil law; Austrian for civil procedure; US-type constitution contemplated). The Six Codes remain the fundamental basis of the law of Taiwan.

regain legal influence and revive legal ties.[122] Dutch law has largely faded from view.[123] The common law is perhaps most visible of western laws, in Singapore, Malaysia and Brunei,[124] though it is common law institutions (judges and barristers) which are most evident, rather than a pervasive presence of common law principle in daily existence. The least persistent of the western legal traditions, at least in its English mode, the common law in some ways parallels Asian thinking in limiting its own ambit of application. US common law thinking has also been influential in the Philippines, overlaying Spanish-derived civil law.[125]

## SOCIALIST LAW IN ASIA

It has been argued that socialist law constitutes a young or recent tradition in the world,[126] yet the argument suffered a terrible blow with the disintegration of the legal order of the former Soviet Union.[127] So the tradition of socialist law, in its

[122] The new Civil Code of the Socialist Republic of Vietnam (in force 1 July, 1996) is also a code more in the continental tradition (838 articles, divided into seven Parts) than in that of the General Principles of socialist tradition (fewer than 200 articles; for China see below, *Socialist law in Asia*).

[123] See S. Gautama and R. Hornick, *An Introduction to Indonesian Law: Unity in Diversity* (Bandung: Alumni Press, 1974) at 7 (Dutch civil code amended by legislation since Indonesian independence in 1945; no longer clear which provisions in force since new legislation does not explicitly repeal affected texts; no 'authoritative edition' of code in force in 1974); Hooker, *Concise Legal History* (1978) at 212, 213 ('effective codification in practice . . . based upon the old Civil Code'); W. Aun, *An Introduction to the Malaysian Legal System*, 2nd edn. (Kuala Lumpur/Singapore/Hong Kong: Heinemann Educational Books (Asia), 1978) at 3 (few records in Malaysia of Dutch occupation, 1641–1807, nor of earlier Portuguese occupation, 1511–1641); S. Hartono, 'The Legal System of Indonesia. Chapter 1—Historical Overview' in ASEAN Law Association *ASEAN Legal Systems* (1995) 17 at 21 ('now incorrect to say that Indonesian law is the same as Dutch law').

[124] See A. J. Harding (ed.), *The Common Law in Singapore and Malaysia* (Singapore: Butterworths, 1985); M. Rutter, *The Applicable Law in Singapore and Malaysia* (Singapore: Butterworths, 1989); A. Leong, *The Development of Singapore Law: Historical and Socio-Legal Perspectives* (Singapore: Butterworths, 1990); K. Tan (ed.), *The Singapore Legal System*, 2nd edn. (Singapore: Singapore Univ. Press, 1999); Horowitz, 'Qur'an and Common Law' (1994), above; Aun, *Introduction to Malaysian Legal System* (1978), above (for succession by English common law to Dutch law in Malaysia); Hooker, *Concise Legal History* (1978) (ch. 5, 'The English Legal World: The Straits Settlements [including Singapore], Federated and Unfederated Malay States, British Borneo, and Burma').

[125] Hooker, *Concise Legal History* (1978) ch. 8 ('The Spanish-American Legal World: The Philippines') (though both overlaying pre-Spanish islamic law and non-islamic 'native custom' (quotations in original, at 214)); M. Feliciano, 'The Legal System of the Philippines' in ASEAN Law Association, *ASEAN Legal Systems* (1995) 141 at 141, 142 (detail of received Spanish law, overlaying prior barangays).

[126] See above, Ch. 1, *Pastness*.

[127] As to which see W. E. Butler, *Soviet Law*, 2nd edn. (London: Butterworths, 1988); O. Ioffe and P. Maggs, *Soviet Law in Theory and Practice* (London/Rome/New York: Oceana, 1983); F. J. M. Feldbrugge (ed.), *Encyclopedia of Soviet Law*, 2nd edn. (Dordrecht: Martinus Nijhoff, 1985); J. Hazard, W. Butler and P. Maggs, *The Soviet Legal System: The Law in the 1980s* (New York/London/Rome: Parker School of Foreign and Comparative Law of Columbia Univ./Oceana, 1984); J. Bellon, *Le droit soviétique* (Paris: Presses universitaires de France, 1967); David and Brierley, *Major Legal Systems* (1985) Pt Two ('Socialist Laws'); Zweigert and Kötz, *Introduction to Comparative Law*, 2nd edn. (1987) vol. I, sect. 5 ('The Socialist Legal Family'); I. Szabó, 'The Socialist Conception of Law' in International Association of Legal Science (K. Zweigert and U. Drobnig, eds.), *International Encyclopedia of Comparative Law*, vol. II, ch. 2 (Tübingen/The Hague/Paris: J. C. B. Mohr (Paul Siebeck)/Mouton, 1974) at 49; V. Tschchikvadze and S. Zivs, 'The System of Socialist Law' in International Association of Legal Science, *International Encyclopedia of Comparative Law*, above, this note, at 115. On the transition of socialist

Soviet or European variant, has gone into a state of suspended animation, surviving only in partial or attenuated form in currently communist-governed or communist-influenced jurisdictions such as Cuba, North Korea, Vietnam, or Tanzania. If you are a western lawyer with no previous experience of Soviet or socialist law, there are no major conceptual problems in understanding it. Simply assume a hyper-inflated public law sector in the jurisdiction in which you presently function. Historical fields of private law such as contract, commercial law, civil responsibility or torts, property, bankruptcy or competition simply shrink away to relatively insignificant proportions, to be replaced by public law variants or replacements. State contracts (of innumerable agencies and units of production) largely displace private contracts; private commercial law and bankruptcy become essentially irrelevant; public compensation regimes replace, almost totally, court-ordered compensation; land is made public or collectivized. There need not be repeal of existing private law; it simply finds little future application. This public law regime relies intensely on formal law, which is even more visible than in non-socialist western law. It is formal law with a difference, however, since its application is entirely in the hands of the guardian of socialist legality, the communist party, which exercises its influence through an entire network of organizations, shadowing those of the state and the courts. Judicial decisions, of allegedly independent judges, are subject to party control and revision. The inherent western tendency to corruption, through the creation of large, instrumental bureaucracies, is exacerbated enormously. The Soviet regime fell in part because nobody could possibly believe in its formal, state institutions. To reverse a communist legal order you simply reverse the process; the problems are those of implementation (massive though they are), not of fundamental concepts.[128] Who gets the new private property? How do you avoid corruption in the process of allocation? How do you convert corrupt institutions to ones of integrity? How do you keep the mob, with its own informal tradition, from profiting from the transition?

Soviet communism, however, was formal communism, heavily influenced by western ideas and western concepts of law. Socialist law in Asia is different, neces-

jurisdictions to non-socialist law, see F. J. M. Feldbrugge, *Russian Law: The End of the Soviet System and the Role of Law* (Dordrecht/Boston: Martinus Nijhoff, 1993); G. Ginsburgs, D. Barry and W. Simons, *The Revival of Private Law in Central and Eastern Europe: Essays in Honour of F. J. M. Feldbrugge* (The Hague/Boston: Martinus Nijhoff, 1996); G. Ajani, *Diritto dell'Europa Orientale* (Turin: UTET, 1996).

[128] On civil law and civil society in Russia, see B. Rudden, 'Civil Law, Civil Society and the Russian Constitution' (1994) 110 LQR 56; G. Ajani, 'By Chance and Prestige: Legal Transplants in Russia and Eastern Europe' (1995) 43 Am. J. Comp. Law 93; and on the process of recodification of civil law in Russia, driven by the dedicated work of the Centre of Private Law reporting to the President of the Russian Federation, see *The Civil Code of the Russian Federation* (with introductory commentary by A. Makovsky and S. Khokhlov), trans. P. Maggs and A. Zhiltsov (Armonk, NY/London: M. E. Sharpe, 1997); E. A. Sukhanov, 'Russia's New Civil Code' (1994) 1 Parker Sch. J. East Eur. Law 619; L. Blumenfeld, 'Russia's New Civil Code: The Legal Foundation for Russia's Emerging Market Economy' (1996) 30 Int. Lawyer 477; H. P. Glenn, 'The Grounding of Codification' (1998) 31 U. Calif. Davis L. Rev. 765; Special Issue on Russian Law Reform (1999) 44, No. 2, McGill L. J.

sarily a kinder, gentler form of communism, though of course equally savage when necessary. Asian communism is different because Asia is different, and there is less place for formal law in it, whether of socialist or capitalist tendency. The Chinese communists originally followed Soviet models, for about a decade from 1949, until they realized how different things were and how they just couldn't make Soviet institutions function in Chinese society.[129] The break with formal communism occurred in 1957, coinciding with a ferocious campaign against 'rightists' (legalists) and landlords, and great efforts were made, at great cost, towards bringing about an egalitarian, commmunist society by informal, educational means. Confucianism was in no way seen as an ally in this process, being historically linked with hierarchical relationships, not all of which were familial or affectionate.[130] The disaster of this effort to somehow steer an informal type of communism came to an end with that of the political careers of its main proponents, and since the late 1970s there has been re-emergence of traditional Chinese teaching, still within a cadre of communist government. Confucianism, if not explicitly resurrected, has become an ally in the effort to generate loyalty and preserve structures.[131]

With the revival of confucianism has come a (limited) rebirth of its old nemesis and necessary ally, fa, now expanded under western and Guomintang influence to many aspects of private law, at least with respect to legal relations with the west. The new socialist legislation looks in many instances just like western legislation.[132] It

[129] For the turbulent legal history of China since 1949, see Tay, 'Struggle for Law in China' (1987); A. Chen, *Introduction to Legal System* (1992) at 24–30; Keller, 'Sources of Order' (1994) at 720–3; Folsom et al., *Law and Politics* (1992) at 25–46.

[130] On the attempted conversion, by Mao Tse-tung, of confucianism into a 'museum piece' (or artefact), see de Bary, *Trouble with Confucianism* (1991) at 45.

[131] On the revivification of confucianism in China, see ibid. at 108, 109 (confucianism, not marxist revolutionary morality, will guard gates against western decadence); von Senger, *Chinesische Recht* (1994) at 25 (confucian tradition making China more receptive to communism than western states; communist party can play cosmic role); H. von Senger, 'Recent Developments in the Relations between State and Party Norms in the People's Republic of China' in Schram, *Scope of State Power in China* (1985) 188 at 200 (comparing statements of communist party with legalist statements of 7th century BC; return of pendulum towards rule by law); Keller, 'Sources of Order' (1994) at 755 (dominant theme maintained of law's contextual character, influenced by external order); Bunger, 'Wandel des Rechts' (1980), above, at 458 (large areas free of legal influence, partly explainable by resistance of rural population to direct regulation); A. Chen, *Introduction to Legal System* (1992) at 38 (marxism and confucianism converging in distrust of rule of law); Ren, *Tradition of Law and Law of Tradition* (1997) at 48 (marxism and confucianism sharing underlying secularity); Gregg, 'Law in China' (1995), notably at 76 ('Communist China inherited and never rejected this Confucian-based antilegalism'); D. Clarke, 'Dispute Resolution in China' (1991) 15 J. Chinese Law 245 at 285–8 (on Mao Zedong's teaching that 'the people' be regulated by education and persuasion; enemies by dictatorship and compulsion); and for recent incorporation of confucianism into primary and secondary education and academic activities in China, see J. Chan, 'A Confucian Perspective on Human Rights for Contemporary China' in J. Bauer and D. A. Bell, *The East Asian Challenge for Human Rights* (Cambridge: Cambridge Univ. Press, 1999) 212 at 214.

[132] On the 'chronic disorder' of Chinese legislation, however, see Keller, 'Sources of Order' (1994) at 711; and for a recent 2,208–page compendium, clearly designed for external use, *A Guide to the Latest Foreign Economic Law and Regulations of the People's Republic of China (Chinese and English Version)* (Beijing: Publishing House of Law, 1995).

doesn't, however, do the same work, nesting as it does in deeper forms of normativity and subject to the pushing and shoving of the communist party.[133] Just as communism had to bend to deep-rooted Asian thought, however, so too is western-style law clearly the object of confucianization, as filtered through communist authority. There is now civil law, and even a type of codification of it, in the form of the General Principles of Civil Law, as was the case in the former Soviet Union.[134] In the Soviet Union, similar Fundamental Principles were fleshed out by more detailed legislation at the level of the republics, but no similar extensive codification has yet occurred in China (though there are reports of its ongoing preparation). If you are going to have formal law, you have to be wary of having too much of it. And as in more explicitly confucian times, litigation has been a last, derided resort. There are

---

[133] On the perennial communist problem of separating government from party, and the difficulty of speaking of any rule of law (though rule *by* law would remain as operative as it has been for thousands of years) see S. Lubman, 'Studying Contemporary Chinese Law: Limits, Possibilities and Strategy' (1991) 39 Am. J. Comp. Law 316 at 317 (China no legal *system*; separation of party and government not seriously undertaken; party still dominating work of courts); Ames, 'Rites and Rights' (1988) at 209, 210 (no effective means of enforcement of claims against state); Z. Hairong, 'The Re-establishment of the Chinese Legal System: Achievements and Disappointments' (1991) 10 CJQ 44 at 47 (urgent need to limit and define scope and application of party policy); von Senger, 'Recent Developments in Relations between State and Party Norms' (1985), above, at 190 (difficulty of democratizing state without democratization of party); Keller, 'Sources of Order' (1994) at 747 (Administrative Litigation Law introduced in late 1980s to permit suit against state, replicating similar measure in Soviet perestroika); J. Liang, 'Nouveau développement du droit administratif en Chine' (1996) 37 Cahiers de Droit 707; R. Keith, *China's Struggle for the Rule of Law* (New York: St. Martin's Press, 1994) notably at 80, 81, on the Administrative Litigation Law of 1989; P. Potter, 'The Administrative Litigation Law of the PRC: Judicial Review and Bureaucratic Reform' in P. Potter (ed.), *Domestic Law Reforms in Post-Mao China* (Armonk, NY/London: M. E. Sharpe, 1994) at 270; Lin Feng, 'Administrative Law' in Wang Chenguang and Zhang Xianchu, *Introduction to Chinese Law* (1997), above, at 75 ff. As part of the current law reform process in China, however, the Minister of Justice has recently stated that promoting the 'rule of law' will be a guiding principle in future years. 'Minister: Promoting "rule of law"', *China Daily*, 27 Apr. 1998, 1.

[134] For the General Principles see W. Gray and H. Zheng, 'General Principles of Civil Law of the People's Republic of China' (1986) 34 Am. J. Comp. Law 715; and for discussion, H. Zheng, 'China's New Civil Law' (1986) 34 Am. J. Comp. Law 669; Epstein, 'Evolution of General Principles' (1986); Epstein, 'Codification of Civil Law in People's Republic of China' (1998) (notably on influence of German Pandectist thought on Chinese legislation); von Senger, *Chinesische Recht* (1994) at 129–32; K. Lei, 'Les principes généraux du droit civil chinois' Gaz. Pal., 2–4 July 1995, at 26; B. Xu, 'Les principes généraux du droit civil en Chine' Rev. int. dr. comp. 1989. 125 (noting at 128 that it is, however, the state which orients, aids and controls the economy, by administrative measures); Lubman, 'Studying Contemporary Chinese Law' (1991), above, at 329; X. Tong, 'Le droit chinois de contrats: sa codification, ses sources, ses champs d'application et ses caractéristiques' (1996) 37 Cahiers de Droit 715; J. Chen, *From Administrative Authorisation to Private Law: a Comparative Perspective of the Developing Civil Law in the People's Republic of China* (Dordrecht/Boston/London: Martinus Nijhoff, 1995); and for detailed regulation of specific contracts, important for western trading, see H. Leclercq, *Introduction au droit chinois des contrats* (Paris: GLN Joly Editions, 1994); Keller, 'Sources of Order' (1994) at 740, 741 (governmental departmental structure having effect of fragmenting legislation along departmental lines). A new codification of contract law was, however, enacted in China in 1999, preliminary comment suggesting it represents a turn toward the 'contractual' and away from the 'administrative'. See Liu Lan, 'Brèves réflexions sur le droit chinois des contrats et ses perspectives d'évolution', Rev. int. dr. comp. 1996. 865; and for the text, *Contract Law of the People's Republic of China* (Beijing: China Legal System Publishing House, 1999).

some signs of change, at the legislative level,[135] but mediation remains where it's at;[136] courts exist, but are notoriously unwelcoming (the story goes that an agricultural creditor recently tied ten (live) bulls to a courthouse in an effort to file a claim);[137] judges are subject to the 'telephone law' (telefonnoe pravo, as it was known in the Soviet Union) of the party;[138] lawyers have been state workers of low status, even after their revival;[139] case reporting is deliberately bad, much worse (even) than in civil law countries;[140] precedents are nowhere to be found. You can guess at traditional criminal procedure, under the influence of militarily conditioned fa and notions of communist legality. Confessions and re-education

[135] See, for recent procedural reforms in China, R. Brown, *Understanding Chinese Courts and Legal Process: Law with Chinese Characteristics* (The Hague/London/Boston: Kluwer, 1997), notably at 3 (litigation increasing 16% annually), 8 ff. (reviews of recent reforms of civil and criminal procedure, law of judges). For the possible emergence of class actions in Chinese civil procedure, see Note, 'Class Action Litigation in China' (1998) 111 Harv. L. Rev. 1523 (many cases, however, appearing to involve joinder of known claimants as opposed to representation of unknown claimants).

[136] See J. Cohen, 'Chinese Mediation on the Eve of Modernization' (1966) 54 Calif. L. Rev. 1201; B. Jia, 'Du système de médiation populaire de la Chine' (1996) 37 Cahiers de Droit 739; Folsom et al., *Law and Politics* (1992) at 45 (preference for li manifested in neighbourhood mediation committees); von Senger, *Chinesische Recht* (1994) at 26, 134 (for full range of non-conflictual dispute resolution activities); and for the growing importance of arbitration in China for international disputes, Cheng Dejun, M. Moser and Wang Shengchang, *International Arbitration in the People's Republic of China* (Hong Kong/Singapore/Malaysia: Butterworths Asia, 1995).

[137] Z. Hairong, 'Re-establishment of Chinese Legal System' (1991), above, at 53, 54 (notably on lack of legal or even higher education of judiciary); and for the institutional weakness of Chinese courts, see Gregg, 'Law in China' (1995) at 76.

[138] R. Szawloski, 'Reflections on "The Laws of the People's Republic of China, 1979–1986"' (1989) 38 Int. & Comp. Law Q. 197 at 206; and on party control of judges and courts see generally M. Y. K. Woo, 'Adjudication Supervision and Judical Independence in the P. R. C.' (1991) 39 Am. J. Comp. Law 95; von Senger, 'Recent Developments in Relations between State and Party Norms', above, at 196; Keller, 'Sources of Order' (1994) at 752–4; Hairong, 'Re-establishment of Chinese Legal System' (1991), above, at 54, 55 (judge 'totally surrenders' powers to adjudicate to trial committee; trial degenerates into 'theatrical event'); Tan, 'Judicial Independence in People's Republic of China' (1994), above, at 667, 668; Lubman, 'Studying Contemporary Chinese Law' (1991), above, at 320; Vandermeersch, 'Enquiry into Chinese Conception of Law' (1985), above, at 20, 24; Ren, *Tradition of Law and Law of Tradition* (1997) ch. 3, at 47 ff.; and on Vietnam's version of the problem, M. Sidel, 'The Re-emergence of Legal Discourse in Vietnam' (1994) 43 Int. & Comp. Law Q. 163 at 169–71 ('Judicial independence and the struggle for the courts').

[139] Szawloski, 'Reflections' (1989), above, at 203, 204 (judicial decisons may be recorded before lawyer consulted); M. Levitz, 'The Criminal Justice System of China: The Role of the Judge, Prosecutor and Defence' (1989) 47 The Advocate 89 at 95; von Senger, 'Recent Developments in Relations between State and Party Norms' (1985), above, at 188; Tay, 'Struggle for Law in China' (1987) at 579 (lawyer also to 'propagate the socialist rule of law'); W. Alford, 'Tasselled Loafers for Barefoot Lawyers: Transformation and Tension in the World of Chinese Legal Workers' in Lubman, *China's Legal Reforms* (1996) at 22; and for historic social antagonism to 'litigation masters', M. Macauley, *Social Power and Legal Culture: Litigation Masters in Late Imperial China* (Stanford: Stanford Univ. Press, 1998) notably at 325 ('"Lawyer" Bashing and Litigation Loathing'); a new law on lawyers which came into force in 1997 has, however, opened the possibility of private practice; see C. Sari, 'La nouvelle loi sur la profession d'avocat en Chine' Gaz. Pal. 14–6 Dec. 1997, 24, 25; Brown, *Understanding Chinese Courts and Legal Process* (1997), above, at 24–8, 115–17 and 335 (for text of law).

[140] X. Tong, *Fondements et formation des contrats en droit chinois*, (doctoral thesis, Laval University, Quebec, 1994) at 4 (cases difficult to obtain, pre-selected, cannot tell if majority or minority jurisprudence).

are important (this is confucian); if they are not forthcoming, watch out.[141] Defence counsel have been expected to produce proof of guilt;[142] judgments in cases of serious crime have been given without citing the accused, without announcing the trial and without communication of the act of accusation.[143] Major legislative changes which came into effect in 1997, however, may be of major benefit to accused persons (who would no longer be referred to as 'offenders').[144] Criminal law has also extended, beyond treason, to counter-revolutionary acts and violation of the socialist economic order.[145] Confucianism is meant to provide justice without laws; communist fa gives rise to discussion of laws without justice. You also can't forget about corruption. Communism in China has always tended to the dogmatic, without leading theoreticians. And the communist bureacracy is even larger than the ancient ones, multiplying the potential effect of gratifying relationships.[146] There's lots to think about in socialist Asia; and then there are the western critics.

## RIGHTS AND ASIAN TRADITION

An explicit concept of rights is not found either in indigenous Asian thought or in Asian concepts of communism, and it has been said that it became known only on

[141] On the confucian principle of voluntariness, as applied to confessions, see Ren, *Tradition of Law and Law of Tradition* (1997), ch. 6, at 115 ff. ('a means of allowing humanitarian leniency to those who choose to comply with the authorities', as (perhaps) in common law plea bargaining, though here extending, historically, to torture).

[142] Folsom et al., *Law and Politics* (1992) at 44; H. Koguchi, 'The Role of Lawyers in the People's Republic of China' in Institute of Comparative Law, Waseda University, *Law in East and West* (Tokyo: Waseda Univ. Press, 1988) 167 at 168.

[143] K. Weissberg and P. Kemayou, 'Le Code pénal et la procédure pénale' Gaz. Pal., 2–4 July 1995. 23 at 25; on parallels with classic fa procedures see Bodde and Morris, *Law in Imperial China* (1967) at 28; A. Chen, *Introduction to Legal System* (1992) at 14; and for severity of Asian criminal law generally, see Weggel, *Die Asiaten* (1989) at 124 (notably on high level of death sentences in Japan); Gregg, 'Law in China' (1995) at 72.

[144] See H. Fu, 'The Right to a Fair Trial in China: The New Criminal Procedure Law' in A. Byrnes (ed.), *The Right to Fair Trial in International Comparative Perspective* (Hong Kong Centre for Comparative and Public Law, Univ. of Hong Kong, 1997) at 78 (new law recognizes presumption of innocence, would prevent court from adjudication prior to trial; no remedies provided, however, for breach of these principles; no power to exclude evidence unlawfully obtained; no elimination of police power to summarily adjudicate and punish); H. Fu, 'Criminal Procedure Law' in Wang Chenguang and Zhang Xianchu, *Introduction to Chinese Law* (1997), above, at 129 ff.

[145] Tay, 'Struggle for Law in China' (1987) at 577, 578; Szawloski, 'Reflections' (1989), above, at 201; Weissberg and Kemayou, 'Le Code pénal et la procédure pénale' (1995), above, at 23, 24; Ren, *Tradition of Law and Law of Tradition* (1997), ch. 5, at 87 ff. ('Punishing for Thought: Counterrevolutionary Crime in Chinese Law'). The 1997 amendments to the Criminal Law revised, however, the crime of 'counter-revolutionary activity' to that of 'jeopardizing state security'. See State Council Information Office, 'Progress in China's Human Rights Cause in 1996', *Beijing Review* 21–27 Apr. 1997, at 11.

[146] On inherent tendencies to corruption in confucianism, see above, *Asian corruption*; on corruption as a major factor in economic development in China, see Folsom et al., *Law and Politics* (1992) at 39.

its arrival from the west in the nineteenth century.[147] There were of course obligations in Asian society, but it is important that they were conceptualized from the
perspective of the debtor, never from that of the creditor as an abstract, subjective
advantage. So it is beside the point to say there must have been rights since there
were obligations; development of the notion of rights and a subjective view of legal
relations is precisely what is being rejected by the ongoing insistence on obligations
rooted in human relations. Confucian thought was not naive about individuality. It
deployed many devices to both overcome and co-opt it.[148] Communism grew out of
opposition to rights and to the bourgeois society they were said to represent. The
communists have also heard most of the arguments; they just don't agree with
them. The debate about human rights in China and Asia is therefore a very deeply
rooted one, and it is multi-faceted. If you are a westerner arguing the human rights
case, you will be met by opposition which is either confucian, or communist, or
both subtly combined. You may also find a surprising amount of agreement on
what you are arguing for.

Since confucianism is based on the idea of the innate goodness of human nature,
it cannot be said to be opposed to the value of human life. Its basic premises have
been said to be 'somewhat akin' to those of the 'inherent dignity of man' and the
'intrinsic worth of the individual'.[149] In 1948 Chinese (non-communist) representatives to the United Nations could argue, along with those of India, that the principle
of respect for human life and innate human virtues was accepted in their countries.[150] More recently, sinologists have pleaded for the underlying compatibility of
China's tradition with that of human rights.[151] Recent confucian criticism of rights
doctrine, however, echoes that of talmudic tradition in denying that rights can
provide what they promise. They would dehumanize and compromise our ability
to define appropriate conduct and ultimately prove incompatible with the goal of
protection of human dignity.[152] Communist rights critique has been directed only
towards the individualistic or subjective definition of rights. If rights are seen as
collective (they can be seen many ways), then rights of development, self-

---

[147] von Senger, 'Chinese Culture and Human Rights' (1993), above, at 303 (originally translated as quanli, an
old Chinese word meaning power and material benefit).

[148] See above, *Li, social harmony and right.*

[149] de Bary, 'Neo-Confucianism and Human Rights' (1988) at 188.

[150] J. Rüsen, 'Human Rights from the Perspective of a Universal History' in W. Schmale (ed.), *Human Rights
and Cultural Diversity* (1993), above, 28 at 39; and see Gangjian and Gang, 'Relating Human Rights to Chinese
Culture' (1995), above, at 36, 37 ('ample room within the traditional dictates of Chinese culture for a form of
constitutional government which embodies a strong commitment to modern human rights values', need to
identify 'the elements in classical Confucian thought that bear comparison to modern principles of human
rights').

[151] See the views of H. Roetz, University of Frankfurt, in *Neue Züricher Zeitung* 17. Jan. 96, at 13 (confucian
tradition no more distant from fundamental values of rights than western tradition; confucian thought
directed more to concept of moral person than to subjective right); and similar views expressed by a number
of authors in de Bary and Weiming, *Confucianism and Human Rights* (1998), above.

[152] Ames, 'Rites and Rights' (1988) at 212, 213 and for similar statements relying on talmudic tradition, see
above, Ch. 4, *Talmudic example?*

determination, peace and racial equality are to be strongly supported.[153] Even individually defined rights can be accepted, as in the General Principles of Civil Law, if they are seen as societally derived and in no way as pre-existing.[154] China has signed, it is said, as many human rights conventions as the United States of America and vigorously defends its human rights record. Its ultimate response is in the form of a question, addressed to particular western countries raising human rights issues: 'How many tens of millions of Chinese will you accept in your country to improve their human rights?' This has stilled some western voices.[155]

## EASTERNIZATION?

Asian representatives are now declaring that 'Asia can say no' to various forms of 'western predatory imperialism' and western 'hyperindividualism'. Many western countries, moreover, would constitute NDCs—the Newly Decaying Countries. This is the language of political hyperbole, and it would not adequately reflect many features of Asian economic growth, but it is noteworthy for its essentially defensive character. It is not itself the language of imperialism, nor even of universalizing theory. There should be some relation between this and the fundamental tolerance of Asian beliefs. Buddhism and taoism display little interest in controlling a single territory or state; there is no incentive in aggregating them. Confucianism accepts institutional construction and constraint only with reluctance, and for domestic purposes. It could scarcely become a major instrument of confucian expansion. So China has been, Tibet notwithstanding, a remarkably restrained political community, and the world has never seen a form of Asian expansion similar to that of Europe.[156]

---

[153] von Senger, *Chinesische Recht* (1994) at 156.

[154] For cases in China awarding damages for unauthorized use of personal photographs, going beyond some western jurisdictions in protection of 'rights of personality', see R. Szawloski, 'Reflections' (1989), above, n. 17. And on rights as contingent 'goals to be reached', rather than prerogatives of personhood, see Lubman, 'Studying Contemporary Chinese Law' (1991), above, at 325; von Senger, *Chinesische Recht* (1994) at 149.

[155] For particulars of the debate amongst western and Chinese leaders, see von Senger, *Chinesische Rechts* (1994) at 163 (Chinese population and human rights problems could be resolved by inviting 300 million Chinese to USA, 200 million to Europe, a further 50 million each to Canada, Australia, Siberia); and for the general debate, see J. Copper, F. Michael and Y.-L Yu, *Human Rights in Post-Mao China* (Boulder, Colo.: Westview Press, 1985): R. Edwards, L. Henkin and A. J. Nathan (eds.), *Human Rights in Contemporary China* (New York: Columbia Univ. Press, 1986); A. Kent, *Between Freedom and Subsistence: China and Human Rights* (Hong Kong/Oxford/New York: Oxford Univ. Press, 1993), notably at 222 on human rights debate within China and the Chinese government; N. Rouland, 'La doctrine juridique chinoise et les droits de l'homme' (1998) 10 Rev. univ. dr. de l'homme 1 (with current position of government of China, outline of Chinese doctrinal rights debate, Chinese ratification of some 15 human rights conventions (at n. 197)); Davis, *Human Rights and Chinese Values* (1995) notably Pt. IV ('Contemporary Practices'); and for a recent statement of the Chinese position, State Council Information Office, 'Progress in China's Human Rights Cause in 1996', Beijing Review, 21–7 April 1977, at 11. (1997), above. On the human rights discussion in Singapore, see S. Tay, 'Human Rights, Culture, and the Singapore Example' (1996) 41 McGill L.J. 743.

[156] See W. Schmale, 'Human Rights from the Perspective of a Universal History' in Schmale (ed.), *Human Rights and Cultural Diversity* (1993), above, 3 at 13 (though individual Asian states may have undertaken

The notion of 'easternization' therefore has to be understood differently from 'westernization'.[157] It does not imply constraint (public or private), or even vigorous private pursuit of social dominance (though markets may be another thing). Confucianism and buddhism are both undergoing revivals, within Asia and beyond,[158] but they remain necessarily what they have always been—major human efforts to explain, reconcile and persuade, in which dominance, over persons or things, is either uninteresting, or unreal, or both. So you will be easternized neither by force nor by insidious and persistent efforts of acculturation. You can be easternized, however, if you think about it.

# GENERAL BIBLIOGRAPHY

Alford, W., 'Of Arsenic and Old Lace: Looking Anew at Criminal Justice in Late Imperial China' (1984) 72 California Law Review 1180.

Ames, R., 'Rites and Rights: The Confucian Alternative' in L. Rouner (ed.), *Human Rights and the World's Religions* (Notre Dame: University of Notre Dame Press, 1988) 199.

ASEAN Law Association, *ASEAN Legal Systems* (Singapore/Malaysia/Hong Kong: Butterworths Asia, 1995).

Bauer, J. R. and Bell, D. A., *The East Asian Challenge for Human Rights* (Cambridge: Cambridge University Press, 1999).

Blet, R., *La justice en Chine: des cent fleurs aux cent codes* (Paris: PCM, 1979).

Bodde, D. and Morris, C., *Law in Imperial China: Exemplified by 190 Ch'ing Dynasty Cases* (Cambridge Mass.: Harvard University Press, 1967).

Brady, J. P., *Justice and Politics in People's China: Legal Order or Continuing Revolution?* (New York: Academic Press, 1982).

Bunger, K. 'Entstehen und Wandel des Rechts in China' in W. Fikentscher, H. Franke and O. Köhler (eds.) *Entstehung und Wandel rechtlicher Traditionen* (Freiburg/Munich: Verlag Karl Alber, 1980) 439.

military expansion); and see N. Rouland, S. Pierré-Caps and J. Poumarède, *Droit des minorités et des peuples autochtones* (Paris: Presses universitaires de France, 1996) at 138, for Chinese incursions into Turkistan; and F. Fernández-Armesto, *Millennium* (London/New York: Bantam, 1995) at 240–2, for China's conquest of her own 'wild west', Sinkiang. Chinese control over Vietnam was lost in the 10th century.

[157] For the notion, usually encountered in management circles, see R. Kaplinsky and A. Posthuma, *Easternization: The Spread of Japanese Management Techniques to Developing Countries* (Ilford/ Portland, Oreg.: F. Cass, 1994); T. Elger and C. Smith (eds.), *Global Japanization? The Transnational Transformation of the Labor Process* (New York: Routledge, 1994); J. Fallows, *Looking at the Sun: The Rise of the New East Asian Economic and Political System* (New York: Pantheon Books, 1994); and for the notion of informal sub-state social groupings (guanxi) achieving greater world-wide importance, J. -M. Ghéhenno, *Fin de la démocratie* (1995), above, notably at 105–21.

[158] W. Reed and R. Little, *The Confucian Renaissance* (Annandale, NSW: Federation Press, 1989); de Bary, *Trouble with Confucianism* (1991) at p. x; and for growing influence of buddhism in the USA, Unno, 'Personal Rights and Contemporary Buddhism' (1988), above, at 146 (greater concern with social issues such as role of women, poverty and hunger, desire for peace, respect for animals).

Chan, S. F., 'Role of Lawyers in the Chinese Legal System' (1983) 13 Hong Kong Law Journal 157.

Chen, A., *An Introduction to the Legal System of the People's Republic of China* (Singapore/ Malaysia/Hong Kong: Butterworths Asia, 1992).

Chen, P. W., *Law and Justice: The Legal System in China: 2400 BC to 1960 AD* (New York: Dunellen, 1973).

Chiba, M., *Asian Indigenous Law in Interaction with Received Law* (London/New York: KPI, 1986).

Ch'u, T., *Law and Society in Traditional China* (Paris/La Haye: Mouton & Co., (1965).

Cohen, J., Edwards, R. and Chen, F. (eds), *Essays on China's Legal Tradition* (Princeton: Princeton University Press, 1980).

Confucius, *The Analects of Confucius*, trans. S. Leys (London: W. W. Norton, 1997).

Copper, J. F., Michael, F. and Wu, Y.-L., *Human Rights in Post-Mao China* (Boulder, Colo.: Westview Press, 1985).

Creel, H. G., *What is Taoism?* (Chicago: University of Chicago Press, 1970).

David, R. and Brierley, J. E. C., *Major Legal Systems in the World Today*, 3rd edn. (London: Stevens, 1985), Pt 4, Title III ('Laws of the Far East').

David-Neel, A., *Buddhism: its doctrines and its methods*, trans. H. Hardy and B. Miall (London/Sydney/Toronto): The Bodley Head, 1977).

Davis, M. C., 'Anglo-American Constitutionalism with Chinese Characteristics' (1988) 36 American Journal of Comparative Law 761.

—— (ed.), *Human Rights and Chinese Values: Legal, Philosophical, and Political Perspectives* (Hong Kong/Oxford/New York: Oxford University Press, 1995).

de Bary, W., *The Liberal Tradition in China* (Hong Kong: Chinese University Press, 1983).

—— 'Neo-Confucianism and Human Rights' in L. Rouner (ed.), *Human Rights and the World's Religions* (Notre Dame: University of Notre Dame Press, 1988) 183.

—— *The Trouble with Confucianism* (Cambridge, Mass. /London: Harvard University Press, 1991).

—— Chan, W. and Watson, B. (eds.), *Sources of Chinese Tradition* (New York: Columbia University Press, 1960).

Ding, W., *Understanding Confucius* (Beijing: Chinese Literature Press, 1997).

Donahue, E., 'The Promise of Law for the Post-Mao Leadership in China' (1989) 44 Stanford Law Review 21.

*Droit chinois* (1996) 37 (No. 3) Cahiers de Droit 595–906.

Edwards, R., Henkin, L. and Nathan, A. (eds.), *Human Rights in Contemporary China* (New York: Columbia University Press, 1986).

Epstein, E. J., 'The Evolution of China's General Principles of Civil Law' (1986) 34 American Journal of Comparative Law 705.

—— 'Codification of Civil Law in the People's Republic of China: Form and Substance in the Reception of Concepts and Elements of Western Law' (1998) 32 University of British Columbia Law Review 153.

Escara, J., *Le droit chinois: conception et évolution. Institutions législatives et judiciaires. Science et enseignement.* (Beijing/Paris: Henri Veitch/Sirey, 1936).

Etiemble, *Confucius* (Paris: Gallimard, 1966).

Folsom, R., Minan, J. and Otto L., *Law and Politics in the People's Republic of China* (St. Paul, Mich.: West Publishing, 1992).

Fujikura, K., *Japanese Law and Legal Theory* (Aldershot/Singapore/Sydney: Dartmouth, 1996).

Goldman, M., 'Human Rights in the People's Republic of China' (1983) 12 *Daedalus* 43.

Goossen, R. J., 'An Introduction to Chinese Law: Does it Exist? What is it? How is it Interpreted?' (1989) 27 Osgoode Hall Law Journal 93.

Granet, M., *La pensée chinoise* (Paris: A. Michel, 1968).

Gray, W. and H. Zeng, trans., 'General Principles of Civil Law in the People's Republic of China' (1986) 34 American Journal of Comparative Law 715.

Gregg, B., 'Law in China: The Tug of Tradition, the Push of Capitalism' (1995) 21 Review of Central and East European Law 65.

Han, D. and Kanter, S., 'Legal Education in China' (1984) 32 American Journal of Comparative Law 543.

Hooker, M., *Legal Pluralism: An Introduction to Colonial and Neo-Colonial Law* (Oxford/New York: Clarendon/Oxford University Press, 1975).

—— *A Concise Legal History of South-East Asia* (Oxford/New York: Clarendon/Oxford University Press, 1978)

——(ed.), *Laws of South East Asia*, 2 vols. (Singapore: Butterworths, 1986 & 1988).

Journal of Chinese Law (New York: Columbia University School of Law & Parker School of Foreign and Comparative Law, vol. I, 1987 onwards).

Keller, P., 'Sources of Order in Chinese Law' (1994) 42 American Journal of Comparative Law 711.

Kent, A., *Between Freedom and Subsistence: China and Human Rights* (Hong Kong/Oxford/New York: Oxford University Press, 1993).

Kim, H. I., *Fundamental Legal Concept of China and the West: A Comparative Study* (London: Kennikat Press, 1981).

Li, V. H., *Law Without Lawyers: A Comparative View of Law in China and the United States* (Boulder, Colo.: Westview Press, 1978).

Li, X., 'L'esprit du droit chinois: perspectives comparatives' Revue internationale de droit comparé 1997. 1.

Liu, Y., *Origins of Chinese Law: Penal and Administrative Law in its Early Development* (Hong Kong/Oxford/New York: Oxford University Press, 1998).

Lubman, S., *China's Legal Reforms* (New York: Oxford University Press, 1996).

McAleavy, H., 'Chinese Law' in J. Derrett, *An Introduction to Legal Systems* (London: Sweet & Maxwell, 1968) 105.

MacCormack, G., *The Spirit of Traditional Chinese Law* (Athens, Ga./London: University of Georgia Press, 1996).

Noda, Y., 'The Far Eastern Conception of Law' in International Association of Legal Science (K. Zweigert and U. Drobnig (eds.), *International Encyclopedia of Comparative Law*, vol. II, ch. 1 (Tübingen/The Hague/Paris: J. C. B. Mohr (Paul Siebeck)/Mouton, 1975) 120.

—— *Introduction to Japanese Law*, trans. A. Angelo (Tokyo: University of Tokyo Press, 1976).

Pitney, H., 'The Role of Legal Practitioners in the People's Republic of China' (1988) 24 Stanford Journal of International Law 323.

Ren, X., *Tradition of the Law and Law of the Tradition: Law, State and Social Control in China* (Westport, Conn./London: Greenwood Press, 1997).

Schram, S., *The Scope of State Power in China* (London/Hong Kong: European Science

Foundation/School of Oriental and African Studies/Chinese University Press/St Martin's Press, 1985).

Schwartz, B., *The World of Thought in Ancient China* (Cambridge, Mass./London: Harvard University Press, 1985) notably chs 3 ('Confucius'), 6 ('Taoism') and 8 ('Legalism').

Tanaka, H., 'The Role of Law in Japanese Society: Comparisons with the West' (1985) 19 University of British Columbia Law Review 375, and repr. in Fujikura, above.

Tay, A. E. S., 'Law, Legal Theory and Legal Education in the People's Republic of China' (1986) 7 New York Law School of International and Comparative Law 1.

—— 'The Struggle for Law in China' (1987) 21 University of British Columbia Law Review 561.

Vandermeersch, L., *La formation du Légisme: recherche sur la constitution d'une philosophie politique caractéristique de la Chine ancienne* (Paris: École française d'Extrême-Orient, 1965).

van der Sprenkel, S., *Legal Institutions in Manchu China* (London: Athlone Press, 1977).

von Mehren, A. (ed.), *Law in Japan: the Legal Order in a Changing Society* (Cambridge, Mass.: Harvard University Press, 1963).

von Senger, H., *Einführung in das chinesische Recht* (Munich: C. H. Beck, 1994).

Watts, A., *The Philosophies of Asia* (Boston/Rutland, Vt./Tokyo: Charles E. Tuttle Co., 1995).

Weggel, O., *Die Asiaten* (C. H. Beck, Munich, 1989).

Zheng. H., 'China's New Civil Law' (1986) 34 American Journal of Comparative Law 669.

Zweigert, K. and Kötz H., *Introduction to Comparative Law*, 3rd edn., trans. T. Weir (Oxford: Clarendon Press, 1998), chs. 20, 21 ('Law in the Far East').

# 10
# RECONCILING LEGAL TRADITIONS: SUSTAINABLE DIVERSITY IN LAW

The legal traditions of the world thus contain very large amounts of information relating to human conduct. They also contain, however, a large amount of theory, or at least second-order information, about themselves and the relations which each of them has with other traditions. A theory of traditions might then be a difficult thing to construct, from scratch, but it turns out that you can learn a lot of theory relating to traditions from the traditions themselves. This would include the (very) theoretical teaching on tradition being developed in the west, but also the more grounded teaching of each tradition on how it gets on with the rest of the world. So we may end up, as did Professor Popper, only working 'towards' a theory of tradition,[1] but this is how the traditions would have it. There is just too much diversity out there to conclude on any given single answer, or theory. We should be on the watch, though, for commonalities which advance the project of thinking multiple traditions.

## THE MULTIPLICITY OF TRADITIONS

In looking at (only) seven legal traditions of the world, it has been impossible to avoid the existence of other recognizable legal traditions. Some might say the other legal traditions are minor ones, which complement or oppose the traditions which have been examined. This may or may not be accurate, since there are no well established criteria for distinguishing major from minor traditions, in law or in any other field of endeavour. If the traditions in law which have been examined here (chthonic, talmudic, civil, islamic, common, hindu and asian) appear presently as the major ones of the world, it may be that this is only a conclusion of first impression, and that there are other legal traditions—of thought, of expression, or

[1] Above, Ch. 1, A Theory of Tradition?

of sources—which are still more profound and which await investigation, and recognition, as being of primary importance. Recognition of any legal tradition thus involves choice (hairesis)—choice of the defining elements of the tradition, choice in evaluating its importance and the extent of adherence to it, choice in determining its origins (or decline and disappearance). Isolating a tradition in this way means attempting to separate it from others, and once this effort has been made all that which has been separated out is free to reconstitute itself as support- ing, or complementary, or opposing, tradition. So the separation we seek to bring about, for purposes of clarity and recognition, is immediately challenged by infor- mation which is inconsistent with the separation we have chosen. This process may not be as random or as arbitrary as it may initially appear. There do appear to be commonalities. They relate first of all to the manner in which traditions, in law, multiply. They appear to do so both within the context of other, established traditions, and also in a way which is lateral or pan-traditional, recognizable in a discernible way in whatever other traditional context they may be found.

## INTERNAL TRADITIONS

Some very old, long-recognized traditions exist within other (major) traditions. There are endless, particular, chthonic legal traditions, as varied as the means of living harmoniously with the world. They have names, which are the names of chthonic peoples, such as Iroquois, or Aztec, or Masai. Talmudic law knows, among others, sephardic and ashkenazi traditions, and the traditions of orthodox, con- servative and reform jewry. The civil law has known traditions of the jus civile, of the jus gentium, of Bartolus, of Cujas, of rhetoric, of constructive rationality, of dissent, of the nation-states which have each given to civil law a particular form of expression. Islamic law has its islams—sunni and shi'ite—and its schools—the Hanafi, Maliki, Shafi and Hanbali, and there are the regional variants, the accommodation—even incorporation—of local, informal, tradition. The common law has had its 'customs', its writs, its now-incorporated Equity, its tradition of judicial restraint (or activism, if you prefer) and now extends in diverse national form to many different societies. Hindu law too has its sadachara (the practice of virtue) and its schools—the Mitakshara and the Dayabhaga—and continues to float over, and govern, those who have their particular ways. Asia knows both li *and* fa, and neither of these places a premium on uniformity of execution; they appear compatible to some extent with both buddhist and taoist attitudes to legal ordering.

These are all traditions internal to one of those we have examined, in some cases supporting, in others opposing, the leading or primary version of the larger, or major, tradition. They are forms of internal dialogue or argument, known so long that they have become identifiable by name—shorthand references to whole bundles of argument (as with the maxims of Equity) which achieve some form of incorporation into the larger tradition. Even when they contradict the larger tradition they have become in most cases indispensable parts of it, providing correction judged necessary or variation judged unavoidable. There are many internal traditions, in law, other than these historically recognizable ones. There are others less recognized, and you will know, whatever your legal tradition, of other principles and institutions which have earned adherence over time and performed valuable service, for some or many. These too are forms of tradition—of information adhered to over time—and there is no way of limiting the notion of tradition to any definitive list of those which are somehow established. There is no hierarchy and no canon, only hierarchies and canons, and resistance.

There are also, arguably, the 'young traditions', the goslings of the traditional world, those which may (already) have been originated but which lack the accumulated 'pastness' which allows us to verify their staying power. These young, internal traditions seem to appear most often in traditions which value effort, originality or ijtihad, often along with aristotelian forms of logic. So we have the current shi'ite efforts to create a doctrine of the islamic state, or a contemporary legal cadre for islamic banking. The civil law world has known movements of 'libre recherche scientifique',[2] of 'Freirecht'[3] (both perhaps expired), of interest analysis ('Interessenjurisprudenz')[4] and of 'alternative' forms of thinking law and commenting on law.[5] In the effervescent common/civil law world which is the United States of America there are many movements in law, which may be a sign of intellectual strength or a sign of intellectual weakness. There is a movement which would analyse law in terms of its positive and utilitarian characteristics (law and economics);[6] another

---

[2] See F. Gény, *Méthode d'interprétation et sources en droit privé positif: essai critique*, 2nd edn. (Paris: LGD J, 1919).

[3] See E. Bodenheimer, *Jurisprudence: the Philosophy and Method of the Law*, rev. edn. (Cambridge, Mass./London: Harv. Univ. Press, 1974) at 115, with references; J. Herget and S. Wallace, 'The Free Law Movement as the Source of American Legal Realism' (1987) 73 Va L. Rev. 399.

[4] See M. Schoch (trans. and ed.), *The Jurisprudence of Interests* (Cambridge, Mass.: Harv. Univ. Press, 1948). Interest analysis has also been influential in the United States, in various forms.

[5] R. Wassermann (ed.), *Reihe Alternativkommentar zum Bürgerlichen Gesetzbuch*, mult. vols. (Neuwied: Verlag Luchterhand, 1980–90).

[6] See R. Posner, *Economic Analysis of Law*, 4th edn. (Boston: Little, Brown, 1992); much of the economic analysis of law stems from the basic theme, developed in R. Coase, 'The Problem of Social Cost' (1960) 3 J. Law & Econs. 1, that any initial assignment of a patrimonial or property right will not affect its ultimate use, which will in principle (the costs of transactions aside) devolve to the person for whom it represents the greatest value. Efficiency would then dictate assignment of rights according to such value. For the extension of this idea to comparative law and the process of judging national solutions, while still recognizing that '[t]raditional or cultural factors may be construed as real-world transaction costs . . . that resist the evolution toward efficiency', see U. Mattei, *Comparative Law and Economics* (Ann Arbor: Univ. of Michigan Press, 1997) notably at 121. For criticism of economic analysis of law, however, as failing to acknowledge the importance of a prior legal order in which assignments can predictably be made, see C. Goodhart, 'Economics and Law: Too Much One-Way Traffic' (1997) 60 MLR 1; and for continental European echos of economic analysis of law, A. Stray Ryssdal, *Legal Realism and Economics as Behaviour: A Scandinavian Look at Economic Analysis of Law* (Oslo: Jur. Forlag, 1995); H.-B. Schäfer and C. Ott, *Lehrbuch der ökonomischen Analyse des Zivilrechts*, 2nd edn. (Berlin/Heidelberg: Springer, 1995); and the symposium on law and economics in civil law countries (1991) 11 Int. Rev. of Law & Econs. 261–342.

which would subject it to feminist thought (feminist legal theory);[7] another which would unmask its arbitrary and indeterminate methods (critical legal studies);[8] another which would unearth its empirical assises (law and society);[9] another which would situate it generally in postmodern society (postmodernism and law).[10] Are these traditions *in* law, legal traditions, or do they represent something eventually antithetical to law, at least as it has (traditionally) been thought? We may eventually know. They are in any event presently internal to western law, though there are reflections of all of them (in varying strengths) in both common and civil law traditions.

## LATERAL TRADITIONS

There are also further, recognizable traditions which are not particular or internal to any given, larger tradition but which seem to run across many larger traditions. Casuistry is one such tradition, with deep and explicit roots in roman, talmudic, islamic and common laws (and perhaps hindu law, though there is the poetry). Nor would chthonic ways or asian li stand opposed to casuistic thinking, though neither would track its exercise. Analogical reasoning or qyas is also fundamental and explicit in traditions which seek to limit, subtly, judicial creativity (as in talmudic, islamic and common laws). Notions of inter-generational equity are very present in chthonic, hindu and asian law, while contemporaneous notions of equity are explicit in both civil and common law, talmudic law ('acting inside the law') and islamic law. There is a tradition of constructive rationality in law, of ijtihad, most marked in western law (civil and common), the object of passionate debate in islamic law, of incredulity and scepticism elsewhere. Fundamentalism is a lateral tradition, in the name of particular gods, particular texts, particular principles (such as rights). There are also traditions of professional role—those of the adjudicator (decisor, iudex, judge, qadi) or, less frequently, of counsel (advocate, barrister,

---

[7] See F. Olsen, *Feminist Legal Theory* (Aldershot/Singapore: Dartmouth, 1995); D. Kelly Weisberg, *Feminist Legal Theory: Foundations* (Philadelphia: Temple Univ. Press, 1993). Much (though certainly not all) feminist legal theory is derived from an epistemological position described as feminist which insists on contextual, local, fact-specific analysis, which would exhibit a high level of tolerance for ambiguity, ambivalence, and multiple voices, while questioning exclusive resort to 'bright-line rules' (inadequate in their correspondence with life situations). These views, most notably articulated by C. Gilligan, *In a Different Voice: Psychological Theory and Women's Development*, 2nd edn. (Cambridge, Mass.: Harvard Univ. Press, 1993), have much in common with many legal traditions of the world.

[8] R. Bauman, *Critical Legal Studies: a Guide to the Literature* (Oxford: Westview Press, 1996); R. Unger, 'Critical Legal Studies' (1983) 96 Harv. L. Rev. 561.

[9] See Law and Society Rev.

[10] See G. Minda, *Postmodern Legal Movements: Law and Jurisprudence at Century's End* (New York: New York Univ. Press, 1995); C. Douzinas and R. Warrington, *Postmodern Jurisprudence: The Law of Text in the Texts of Law* (London/New York: Routledge, 1991).

attorney or simple adviser).[11] And there are the undefended, but practised, traditions, of racism, of crime, of unthinking and spontaneous antagonism to the other, however defined.

There are two other large, important lateral traditions. One of these is a tradition of universalism, or universalizing. It may take the form of a particularly aggressive form of fundamentalism; it may be more subtle and insinuating. In all cases it is characterized by an ineluctable pressure to spread and solidify particular teachings, which themselves are formulated, or capable of being formulated, in universal terms. Peace, God, rights, understanding, metaphysics, are all capable of universal formulation, indeed may only be capable of universal formulation. There may be no major legal tradition (even that of hindu law) which is free of universalizing tendencies. The other tradition is one which has been referred to throughout the discussion thus far as a tradition of tolerance. There is a problem of language here, which will have to be returned to, but it is evident that a tradition of tolerance of other traditions will exist in constant tension with a tradition of universalism, and that both will exist in varying degrees within a particular major tradition as well as existing across all traditions. If major legal traditions are to co-exist in the world, without themselves contributing in a major way to violence, imperialism and suppression, it therefore seems necessary to examine somewhat more closely the teaching of different traditions with respect to universalism and what is known in the west as tolerance.

# RECONCILING TRADITIONS

Traditions appear to differ amongst themselves with respect to whether they must be universalized. Some traditions appear more aggressive than others with respect to their own expansion. This may flow from what a tradition explicitly teaches, or from what its adherents, or some of them, take to be its implicit teaching. At the core of the universalizing tendency of any tradition is necessarily its normativity. If it makes no claim to normativity, it will have little claim to universality. Binding no one can scarcely give rise to a claim to bind everyone. The nature of the normativity of each tradition is therefore an essential feature of its potential universality. Whether a given tradition is universalizing, however, will be a question of how it reconciles its own normativity with its own tolerance of other traditions. This latter question raises the general issue of the complexity of traditions, of how traditions

---

[11] See H. P. Glenn, 'Professional Structures and Professional Ethics' (1990) 35 McGill L. J. 424. Within the field of professional traditions, there are of course sub-traditions: of ethics of role, instructive in how to act ('God loveth adverbs') and ethics of situation, instructive in what to do; and of countries and regions (North American vs. European professional models, though the contrast may now be declining).

manage their relations with other traditions. Here as well there appear to be commonalities.

## THE NORMATIVITY OF TRADITION

Western theory of tradition teaches that all tradition is normative, that is, that it provides a model, drawn from the past, as to how one should act. Legal traditions, of all traditions, should not depart from this general phenomenon, since law is perhaps the most normative of human endeavours. There are clear differences, however, amongst legal traditions in terms of the extent to which they claim to regulate human conduct. Chthonic law doesn't appear to regulate much, yet in proscribing all conduct incompatible with a recycling cosmos its normativity is unquestionable. Talmudic and islamic law regulate most of life; they are normative in all directions. The civil and common laws are laws of liberty; both have existed as optional, suppletive forms of social regulation, allowing some form of escape from congealed, chthonic patterns. In modern guise, they would both to some extent deny the normativity of their own pasts (reconstructed as fact), both directing attention to a more limited form of present law. Yet underlying notions of intellectual liberty, rights and institutional integrity are inherent and highly normative features of both, however notions of liberty and rights may contribute to present disruption. Hindu law allows a lot of choice, both individually and in terms of multiple informal traditions, yet no one who is hindu would escape some form of law recognized as hindu. Asian tradition rejects much formal law, but does so in favour of another type of normativity, one profoundly anchored, informally, in the past.

So in spite of some confusing signals, normativity is a constant feature of these legal traditions. Even in the western ones, where liberty is most prized, it is often constrained, and where it is not it assumes its own normativity—the obligation to be free and to exercise one's rights. The indecision of relativism is a problem external to these traditions; they do not acknowledge it. Relativism would be a problem, however, where legal traditions meet. It could be avoided by universalism—by insisting on the normativity in all cases of one's own tradition. If one refuses universalism, in the name of some form of tolerance, how does one avoid the indecision of relativism? How is this question dealt with, in the traditions?

## COMPLEX TRADITIONS

The legal traditions which have been examined all contain sub-traditions, either purely internal ones or lateral traditions. This appears to be another perspective on the multiplicity of traditions; they nest (like Russian dolls) within one another, such that the largest can even be said to be composed of a series of supporting, complementing, even recalcitrant, sub-traditions. *The largest, major traditions would therefore be large and major because of their complexity.* They succeed in bringing together, in the name of some important principle or being, a number of identifiable other traditions, providing some form of overarching cohesion. This notion of a complex tradition has been identified in western literature.[12] The study of complex legal traditions may add to its understanding.

How are major legal traditions complex and how do they explain their own complexity? They are complex in incorporating multiple internal and lateral traditions which are not consistent with each other and which may not even be consistent with the leading version of the major tradition. Complex traditions thus reach the stage of complexity, and of being major traditions, because of their ability to deal with diversity, contradiction and demands for what is usually known as change. They are epistemologically complex. The theoretical recognition of tradition as a factor of change[13] would thus be a recognition of the underlying complexity of major traditions, which are constantly in the process of reconciling sub-traditions of stability and innovation, or sub-traditions opposing one another on other grounds.

The complexity of major legal traditions, moreover, is a fundamental part of their own teaching, of their own understanding of themselves. Chthonic tradition allows great diversity within itself, giving quiet approval to all chthonic ways, and even change of them, on condition of ongoing respect for the natural world.[14] Talmudic law knows its principle of 'These and these', which both, though contradictory, represent the word of God,[15] and in the ongoing, often contradictory, talmudic debate, there is constant re-affirmation of the larger synthesis of the Perfect Author. The civil law has always known multiple, and contradictory, versions of itself—from the jus civile and jus gentium of Roman times and the later tension

---

[12] See D. Armstrong, 'The Nature of Tradition' in D. Armstrong, *The Nature of Mind* (Ithaca, NY: Cornell Univ. Press, 1981) 89 at 102 (complex traditions, such as western academic tradition or tradition of English novel, 'are some sort of fused mass of simple traditions . . . the set of simple traditions that make up the complex tradition will have a certain unity . . . at any given moment in the history of a complex tradition, a large number of the simple traditions that it involves will be secure, although others are in the process of being modified, abandoned, or created. In this way, a complex tradition is well suited to meeting demands both for continuity and change in society'); M. Krygier, 'Law as Tradition' (1986) 5 Law & Philos. 237 at 254 ('Any complex tradition, such as law, itself is likely to be made up of different sorts of traditions'); D. Pearce, *Roads to Commensurability* (Dordrecht: D. Reidel, 1987) at 10 ('The guiding principle is to represent a research tradition as a structured family of interrelated theories'). On modern (western) theory of complexity, see M. Gell-Mann, *The Quark and the Jaguar: Adventures in the Simple and the Complex* (New York: W. H. Freeman, 1994); P. Coveney and R. Highfield, *Frontiers of Complexity: the Search for Order in a Chaotic World* (New York: Fawcett Columbine, 1995); J. Horgan, 'From Complexity to Perplexity' *Scientif. Am.*, June 1995 at 104 (on challenge to the idea of a 'unified theory' of complex systems; competing view of complexity of discrete fields of science); and on the need for contemporary havens for 'complex memes' (or bodies of information), D. C. Dennett, *Darwin's Dangerous Idea: Evolution and the Meanings of Life* (New York: Simon & Schuster, 1995) at 519.

[13] See above, Ch. 1, The Changing Presence of the Past.

[14] See above, Ch. 3, Change and the Natural World.

[15] See above, Ch. 4, *Of schools, traditions and movements.*

between local, chthonic ways and the ius commune, through emergent then flour-ishing national legislation, to the 'fuzzy' relations emerging within the European Union.[16] Islam has its ikhtilaf, the doctrine of diversity (the trees and branches, the rivers and seas, the threads and garments) and an entire hadith, that 'Difference of opinion . . . is a sign of the bounty of God'.[17] The common law co-opted local diversity, leaving juries to their own devices, then, as 'chaos with an index', accom-modated, then integrated, ecclesiastical, Admiralty and Equity courts and case law, before going on to its present, trans-oceanic diversity.[18] Hindu law gives pride of place to local law, since Brahman infuses all, never dividing, never separating, essentially advita (non-dual) and allowing hinduism to be a 'Commonwealth of all faiths', an illustration of the fundamental unity of the world.[19] Asian normativity knows the 'middle way' of buddhism; the infinite, related, gradations of confucian-ism; the massive effort of intellectual integration—of individuals and groups, of relations and autonomy, of self-worth and common effort.[20]

All of these complex, major traditions thus achieve complexity because of their proven ability to hold together mutually inconsistent sub-traditions. They all involve a particular way of thinking, which has become explicit in some of them though remaining implicit in others. It is a way of thinking which has been described as multivalent,[21] as opposed to bivalent, because sub-traditions are not either right or wrong but may be right in different, multiple (inconsistent) ways. The traditions are hence multivalued. Multivalent logic has traditionally been associated with hindu and other asian thinking, bivalent thinking with western thinking, yet all major legal traditions, asian, western and other, appear built on multivalent thought. What characterizes multivalent thinking and how is it distinct from bivalent thinking?

## BIVALENCE AND MULTIVALENCE

Bivalent thought involves the proposition that you can't have your cake and eat it too. Most people say the idea is aristotelian (though others, before Aristotle, must have known about it if they disagreed with it) and involves a formal, logical rule: that of the excluded middle. Between two mutually inconsistent things, there is no middle ground (no buddhist middle way). In formal language, it is always '[A] or [not A]'. '[A] and [not A]' would be asserting inconsistency.[22] It would be trying to

---

[16] See above, Ch. 5, *European identities.*
[17] See above, Ch. 6, *Of schools and schism.*
[18] See above, Ch. 7, *Common law and nation-states* and *The practice of comparison.*
[19] See above, Ch. 8, *Time and Brahman* and *Sadachara and schools.*
[20] See above, Ch. 9, *Limiting religion, Confucianization* and *Li, social harmony and right.*
[21] From the Latin valentia, meaning vigour or capacity, hence more generally power, importance or value.
[22] For Artistotle's formulation, see his *Metaphysica,* IV 3 1005b 18–37, 1006 1–5, IV 6 1011b 12–25. Aristotle acknowledged, however, that 'it will not be possible to be and not to be the same thing, *except in virtue of an ambiguity'* (emphasis added). Ibid. IV 4 1006b 18,19.

have your cake and eat it too. Bivalent thought thus implies clear boundaries between distinct and separate concepts, and prevents mixing and confusion over the boundaries, once they are created. It is very logical, in the way western people have been trained to be logical. Much east and south Asian thinking, however, has never been very impressed with the idea of a world divided into distinct and separate, often inconsistent, elements. This thinking would challenge, not the idea of inconsistency, so much, as the process of drawing boundaries or separating distinct units of whatever is being discussed. It would say separation is artificial and ignores the complexity of the real world, where everything is really a matter of degree rather than of sharp boundaries.

The Greek philosophers knew there was a problem here, and treated it as a paradox (which is what you do when you can't explain something important). One of the examples of the paradox was that of a pile of sand. If you withdraw a grain of sand at a time from the pile, at what point do you no longer have a pile? To use a (slightly) newer example, at what point, exactly, did Rembrandt become old? Well, you might say, these are vague categories so of course you can't escape some of these paradoxes, which will exist whenever your categories are inherently vague. The challenge of multivalence, however, is a very large one. It asserts that *all* categories are vague and that all efforts of separation are arbitrary and artificial. This would even extend to the physical world, where sharp, physical boundaries are now dissolving under the close inspection of quantum physics. *Everything* would be a matter of degree. You *can* have your cake and eat it too, if you eat only half of it (though we'd better say some of it, since we can't be sure where the half-way point would be).

Bivalent logic is behind much of the construction of the western world (and is ferociously defended), but various forms of multivalent logic are now being taken seriously in western theoretical thinking. In the early twentieth century a philosopher, Pierce, argued for 'many-valued' or 'triadic' logic (true, false or somewhere in between), and philosophy is now taking seriously, and very precisely, the problem of vagueness.[23] In mathematics, the theory of sets would now recognize partial membership in one or more sets at the same time, a phenomenon giving rise to 'fuzzy' sets and more generally to 'fuzzy' logic, as it has come to be known in English, though the appellation would have something still rather pejorative about it.[24] In technology, multivalent logic would allow smoother machines (such as air conditioners which don't go clunk in the night as they move across the excluded middle between different commands).[25] There has been some recognition of the

[23] See T. Williamson, *Vagueness* (London/New York: Routledge, 1994), citing a 1909 Pierce ms (unpub.) at 102. The question, as formulated by Williamson, would be whether vagueness flows 'from the failure of the statement to be true or false, or simply from our inability to find out which' (at 2). He defends the latter.

[24] Williamson, *Vagueness* (1994), above, at 120, citing notably the work of Lofti Zadeh and the *International Journal of Fuzzy Sets and Systems*. The initial article of Zadeh is 'Fuzzy Sets' (1965) 8 *Information and Control* 338.

[25] See B. Kosko, *Fuzzy Thinking: the New Science of Fuzzy Logic* (New York: Hyperion, 1993).

idea in law, in the 'fuzzy' legal relations of national laws under pan-European norms,[26] and in some areas of substantive law, such as security interests.[27] In all of these cases there is recognition of a once-excluded middle. The middle becomes recognizable once you recognize the real subtlety of the world, once you recognize the detailed information which the hasty drawing of boundaries, the separation, would exclude. The more information you have, the less separation, the less potential conflict there is. Multivalent logic is not really fuzzy. It is very precise, very informed, and highly particular. It insists on more information. There is something of the casuistic in it, in its methodological insistence on detail.[28]

Casuistic legal traditions thus have the potential to become major and complex legal traditions, and some of them have made this transition, using their own casuistry to move above and beyond competing, internal sub-traditions. Other major legal traditions, such as those of the civil and common law, have recently placed less emphasis on casuistry in their internal workings (particularly within nation-states). Yet in their full dimensions, modern civil and common laws are necessarily complex. They must reconcile different rules, different solutions within a single, transnational tradition. Casuistry, particularity, greater and more detailed information: all become essential in this process. Civil and common law lawyers have been multivalent without talking much about it. The major, complex traditions of the civil and common laws are the proof of it. They both display a great deal of internal tolerance, as do other major, complex, legal traditions. Or is tolerance really the right expression?

## BEYOND TOLERANCE?

You could say that complex traditions are by nature tolerant ones, but there seems to be something slightly bizarre about using the idea of tolerance *within* a tradition. It's a little like saying, whether you are left-handed or right-handed, that you *tolerate* that other hand. Toleration, it seems, should be reserved for that which is really external, different, strange, even radically wrong or, for some, evil. And most

[26]   Above, Ch. 5, *European identities*. Fuzzy logic would be most apt as a means of organizing a plurality of simultaneously applicable normative ensembles, without suppression of any of them. See M. Delmas-Marty, *Le flou du droit* (Paris: Presses universitaires de France, 1986) at 269.

[27]   This is not to say that multivalent logic is necessarily preferable in all fields of law. For attempts in application, see E. Adams, S. Nickles and T. Ressler, 'Wedding Carlson and Schwartz: Understanding Secured Credit and a Fuzzy System' (1994) 80 Va L. Rev. 2233 (being secured or not a matter of degree, forcing judge to seek more facts, and to seek intersections of agreement); J. Williams, 'The Fallacies of Contemporary Fraudulent Transfer Models as Applied to Intercorporate Guaranties: Fraudulent Transfer Law as a Fuzzy System' (1994) 15 Cardozo L. Rev. 1403; and for fuzzy logic in legal theory, E. Adams and T. Spaak, 'Fuzzifying the Natural Law—Legal Positivist Debate' (1995) 43 Buff. L. Rev. 85.

[28]   For use of 'if, then' language, as opposed to more apodictic styles of expression ('it is forbidden', 'do this'), in both fuzzy logic and casuistic legal styles, see Adams, Nickles and Ressler, 'Wedding Carlson and Schwartz' (1994), above, 2241; R. Westbrook, 'Biblical Law' in N. Hecht, B. Jackson, S. Passamaneck, D. Piattelli and A. Rabello (eds.), *An Introduction to the History and Sources of Jewish Law* (Oxford: Clarendon Press, 1996) 1 at 6.

teaching about toleration, in the west, says essentially that. The idea of toleration seems to have been developed as a result of western religious conflicts, and eventually came to say that even though other beliefs were profoundly wrong, even evil, there were reasons for not attempting to stamp them out, such as the sincerity of those who held them (Locke's argument), or the personal autonomy of belief (an enlarged, liberal view) or the need to suppress violence.[29] So the western idea of tolerance is ultimately a very unstable one (some would say an impossible one) since it teaches that we may continue to detest, though we value autonomy more.[30] It turns out to be a very western idea (not articulated as such elsewhere), and it has been said, for example, that 'it is very misleading to transfer a concept that is indigenous to eighteenth-century Europe to India and say that Indians believed in toleration'.[31]

So toleration doesn't seem to be the right word, or right concept, in describing the complexity of major legal traditions. They are complex, not because they are tolerant, but because they build real bridges. They don't just tolerate, they accept, in spite of difference. They are genuinely multivalent in refusing to categorically condemn and exclude. They construct a middle ground for the tradition, one which allows ongoing reconciliation of its inconsistent poles, themselves taken as exclusive and categorical by those we designate as fundamentalists (of all traditions). The better notion seems to be one of interdependence,[32] or of non-separation, and this emerges as the most fundamental idea in the existence of major, complex, legal traditions. It is the fundamental, underlying characteristic of multivalence.

The notion of interdependence between elements of complex traditions also tells us something about commensurability and relativism. If there is interdependence, and hence sharing, there is commensurability. Incommensurability has no place, if

---

[29] On Locke, see J. Tulley, 'Toleration, Skepticism and Rights: John Locke and Religious Toleration' in E. Furcha (ed.), *Truth and Tolerance* (Montreal: Faculty of Religious Studies, McGill Univ., 1990) 13. For toleration as a (value-laden) characteristic of liberalism, see J. Horton, 'Toleration as a Virtue' in D. Heyd (ed.), *Toleration: an Elusive Virtue* (Princeton: Princeton Univ. Press, 1996) 28 at 36 (toleration only a temporary expedient on way to larger liberal goals); and for the 'Hobbesian equilibrium' of toleration, see B. Williams, 'Toleration: An Impossible Virtue?' in Heyd (ed.), *Toleration* (1996), above, at 21; I. Berlin, 'The Originality of Machiavelli' in H. Hardy (ed.), *Against the Current: Essays in the History of Ideas* (New York: Viking Press, 1979) 25 at 78.

[30] Williams, 'Toleration' (1996), above, at 18 (toleration required only for the intolerable) (other group 'blasphemously, disastrously, obscenely wrong'), 26; B. Herman, 'Pluralism and the Community of Moral Judgment' in Heyd (ed.), *Toleration* (1996), above, 60 at 61 (toleration not neutral response since permits 'continued private moral hostility'). Christians, it is therefore often said (and the remark is attributed to many), want to be accepted, not tolerated.

[31] A. T. E. Embree, 'Introduction, Part III: The Hindu Way of Life' in A. T. E. Embree (ed.), *Sources of Indian Tradition*, 2nd edn. (New York: Columbia Univ. Press, 1988) at 205.

[32] For the importance of interdependence in contemporary world trade, see J. H. Jackson, *The World Trading System: Law and Policy of International Economic Relations*, 2nd edn. (Cambridge, Mass./London: MIT Press, 1997), notably at 6 ('The Meaning of Interdependence'), 79 and ff. ('Interrelationship of National and International Institutions').

it has a place anywhere, within complex traditions. They *are* complex traditions because of their ability to overcome arguments of incommensurability, and to hold the larger tradition together. And if there is no incommensurability within a tradition, if all of its elements are constantly engaged with one another—in conversation, dialogue or argument—then there is no place for the indecision of relativism. Complex traditions do not allow you to say, 'I cannot choose between these two irreconcilable, incommensurable positions'. The complex tradition tells you they are not irreconcilable; that they both have a claim to your loyalty; and that there are a large number of reasons (which you must consider as an adherent to the complex tradition) for deciding in a way which may favour one or the other of them, in the circumstances of your case. Complex traditions thus do not acknowledge relativism because they cannot. Their whole structure is one which multiplies the arguments and means of decision-making, given the existence of differing views, internal to the tradition. Traditions are normative; complex traditions are irresistibly normative. There is still a problem, however, in terms of the relations of complex traditions between themselves.

## RECONCILING COMPLEX TRADITIONS

A tradition which is internally complex nevertheless maintains some form of external coherence. This is what allows us to identify a complex legal tradition, such as those examined in this book. So if complex legal traditions overcome questions of incommensurability or conflict within themselves, these same questions of incommensurability or conflict may arise between complex traditions. They have identities, or boundaries, and it is perhaps possible to exclude any middle ground between them, as in saying, for example, that a religious legal tradition is incompatible or incommensurable with a secular legal tradition. To what extent does the nature of a complex legal tradition speak to the relations between complex traditions? What do the traditions tell us?

The first thing they appear to tell us is that their identities are not mutually exclusive ones. The boundaries which define them are not impregnable. The proof of this would be in the lateral traditions which are recognizable, in nearly identical form, in multiple, complex traditions. Traditions of casuistry, or intergenerational equity, or equity tout court, or professional role, unite their adherents across the complex traditions which they may see as their primary traditions. The lateral traditions thus constitute a kind of horizontal webbing, through and across the complex traditions, such that the complex traditions themselves nourish and support certain forms of their own interdependence. The lateral traditions are of course in no way limited to those identified here. They exist in general and detailed form across the entire range of what we know as private or public law.

There is, however, a larger and more important way in which the nature of a complex tradition affects the relations between complex traditions. The theoretical teaching of tradition in the west has already stated that any contact between traditions involves exchange of information. If something is known to be out there, it is already in here.[33] The simple existence of information derived from another complex tradition thus blurs the boundary between the two traditions. Moreover, if the information is in here, it becomes subject to the multivalent, bridging, complexity of the receiving tradition. It must be dealt with. It may be the object of rejection (requiring reasons), limitation, accommodation or even adoption. The complexity and multivalence of the receiving tradition prevent the information from being somehow, simply, walled off or cabined.

What this means is that complexity and interdependence is not a phenomenon which is simply internal to complex traditions. Complexity and interdependence necessarily characterize the relations between complex traditions as well. How can a complex tradition, composed of multiple, competing sub-traditions, informed by lateral traditions shared with other traditions, and existing as a complex tradition only because of its ability to bridge multiple, simple traditions, somehow renounce its complexity in favour of a single, universal truth? This is what fundamentalists seek to do (in all traditions). They elevate one truth, or one tradition, to exclusive status, and seek to impose it.[34] Fundamentalists may thus act in an imperial or aggressive or violent manner. In so doing, they do not reflect the entirety of their own tradition. Nor do they represent a truth which has the potential of becoming a major tradition in the world. It is, as interpreted, insufficiently complex to attract support across the wide range of human opinion. Complex traditions are therefore by their nature, and in their leading versions, non-universal and non-universalizing. They offer many grounds of accommodation with other complex traditions. The larger and more complex the tradition, the less dangerous it is for others. Fundamentalism is always, and necessarily, a limited phenomenon and a limited threat.

The interdependence of complex traditions is evident both from the difficulty in defining the starting points of major legal traditions (even the prophets retain much of previous law, now revealed) and by the ongoing, major forms of communication and debate between complex traditions. Chthonic law is used to criticize civil and common law dealing with the environment. Islamic law criticizes civil and common law jurisdictions for their treatment of the poor and the persecuted; western lawyers criticize islamic criminal sanctions and its limits on human expression and speech. Talmudic law knows that the law of the state is law, and may even incorporate some of it, while itself being cited as a different (and perhaps better) model of law than state law. Civil and common law jurisdictions 'borrow' from one

---

[33] Above, Ch. 2, Tradition and Identity.
[34] See J. Kekes, *The Morality of Pluralism* (Princeton: Princeton Univ. Press, 1993) at 3 ('the terrible simplicities of fundamentalists of various persuasions').

another, or create 'mixed' jurisdictions,[35] and these processes now appear as western and formalized versions of the exchange of information between complex traditions which has always gone on, in a massive way. Hindu and asian law exist as layered traditions, those which have developed indigenously and those which have been developed in some manner from western models. Where is the core of any of these major traditions which could supplant all the law of the rest of them? The answer would appear to be that there is no such universalizable core. This is good news for the sustainability of the major, complex, legal traditions of the world.

## SUSTAINABLE DIVERSITY IN LAW

The multivalence of major, complex legal traditions, and the interdependence between them, has necessary consequences for their ongoing survival. There is, of course, no guarantee of survival, and there are concerns within some major legal traditions as to their ongoing identity or viability. There are certainly highs and lows, moreover, in the persuasive power of each tradition, as lives go on. Yet multivalence provides an ongoing stability for major traditions which is lacking in the case of simple or minor ones, or in the case of various legal 'movements'. Multivalence allows for movement within the tradition itself, such that disaffection in one of its branches does not imply exit on the part of those disaffected, or an overall loss in adherence to the major tradition. It is the advantage of the big tent.

Multivalence within a tradition is also an inherent limit on its external expansion. Internal ambiguity creates doubts about external expansion. What, exactly, is to be expanded? Why is it necessarily superior to competing internal views, and to competing external views? These doubts—which multivalence welcomes—are reinforced in the case of relations between major legal traditions by the strength of the arguments which each of them raises. They all represent truths—ecological ones, religious ones, ethical ones, rational ones—and each represents enormous effort over a very long period of time to give effect in human lives to these truths. So each major, complex legal tradition provides something to the world which the others do not, and probably cannot, and each eventually comes to recognize this. There may therefore be, after several thousand years of legal history, some (general)

---

[35] See, e.g., M. Meston, W. Sellar and Lord Cooper, *The Scottish Legal Tradition*, new edn. (Edinburgh: The Saltire Society and The Stair Society, 1991); R. Evan-Jones (ed.), *The Civil Law Tradition in Scotland* (Edinburgh: The Stair Society, 1995); R. Zimmermann, *Das römisch-hollandische Recht in Südafrika* (Darmstadt: Wissenschaftliche Buchgesellschaft, 1983); R. Zimmermann and D. Visser (eds.), *Southern Cross: Civil Law and Common Law in South Africa* (Oxford: Clarendon Press, 1996); J. Brierley and R. Macdonald (eds.), *Quebec Civil Law: an Introduction to Quebec Private Law* (Toronto: Emond Montgomery, 1993); H. P. Glenn (ed.), *Droit français et droit québécois: communauté, autonomie, concordance* (Cowansville, Quebec: Yvon Blais, 1993).

point of stabilization of major legal traditions.[36] There have to be legal traditions which are major, since there are major themes for such traditions. Since the themes persist, the major traditions persist. They each remind us of something important; they each must qualify and limit their own teaching (the cost of complexity); they each provide social ordering in the world which the other traditions may be unable to provide.[37] So legal diversity looks like it will be with us for a long time. It is sustainable, and perhaps there should even be efforts to sustain it.

## SUSTAINING DIVERSITY

If diversity in law, on a large scale, is compatible with all major legal traditions, and is perhaps even inevitable or natural (though this would be a very large claim, not explicitly found in the traditions themselves), then there might be no point in efforts to sustain it. It would just happen, in spite of anything we did. So we could all be free to be universalizers, or imperialists, since we wouldn't succeed and we would know what to believe in, in the meantime. Two answers seem possible to this argument.

The first is that the case for natural, harmonious diversity might be overcome, if enough people decide to act on contrary assumptions. Then it is likely that a great deal of damage would be done, in order to ensure the eventual dominance of a single tradition in the world. There is, moreover, considerable learning (survival of the fittest, competition theory) which suggests that we are all constantly in the process of attack or self-defence and that some form of lasting dominance may be possible.[38] And it may be, if everyone decided to act as aggressively as possible in pursuit of a single truth, that a world of ongoing violent conflict, interspersed by periods of hegemony, could be brought about. So resisting diversity in order to rule the world might turn out to be a strategy some would call correct, and harmonious diversity could be overcome. If this is the case, then the reasons for acting in a way

---

[36] This would not control, of course, their precise relations at any time.

[37] For the importance of intellectual or 'cultural' diversity, as well as natural diversity, see, e. g., D. J. Anton, *Diversity, Globalization and the Ways of Nature* (Ottawa: International Development Research Centre, 1995) notably at 198, 200 ('Diversity is the main resource of life. The future of living systems is a result of multiple current options. Diversity provides flexibility . . . Diversity is life; uniformity is death'), 201–9.

[38] Cf., however, for a biologist's view that 'cultural evolution' must be distinguished from genetic evolution, notably by human capacity for 'genuine, disinterested, true altruism', R. Dawkins, *The Selfish Gene* (Oxford: Oxford Univ. Press, 1976), at 205, 215; views further elaborated in Dennett, *Darwin's Dangerous Idea* (New York: Simon and Schuster, 1995), above, ch. 16 ('On the Origin of Morality'), notably at 461 ('entirely natural—it wasn't supernatural—for us to step out of the state of nature and adopt a host of societal practices for our mutual benefit'), 473 (memes, i.e., ideas or information, 'can redirect our underlying genetic proclivities'); and see L. Wieseltier, *Kaddish* (New York: Alfred A. Knopf, 1998) at 269 ('The reproduction of tradition is not like the reproduction of genes. Strictly speaking, tradition is not replicated, since it is never transmitted exactly as it was received. More important, the spiritual legacy and the biological legacy differ in their reasons for survival. The former promises more than itself: the true, the good, the beautiful. The latter promises only itself. Genes survive so that genes will survive. In this respect they are profoundly inhuman, even if they are the physical history of humanity').

which supports sustainable diversity in law are the reasons for avoiding the pursuit of, and the installation of, world hegemony. They are reasons relating to the cost and suffering of world conflict; to the difficulty in maintaining any sort of world hegemony (as shown by the survival of traditions); and to the ultimate benefits of sustainable diversity.

The second answer is perhaps more realistic. It says that there will be sustainable diversity in law in the world, and that all the efforts of all the universalizers (of all traditions) will now not succeed in disrupting it. So the argument says you should go with the flow. Running against it will cause damage (major damage, though perhaps not global damage) and will bring only minor and temporary gains. In contrast, working within the cadre of diverse legal traditions, and knowing how to do so, can provide equal or greater benefits to whatever cause is being advanced. Traditions are agents or factors of change and innovation. They provide all the levers which are necessary.

So there are reasons for acting positively, for sustaining diversity, and not simply allowing diversity to sustain itself, as it might.[39] Sustaining diversity means accepting (not tolerating) the major, complex legal traditions of the world (all of them). It means seeing them as mutually interdependent, such that the loss of any of them would be a loss to all the others, which would then lose a major source of support, or at least of self-interrogation. It means seeing all traditions as one's own, in some measure, since each is dependent on the others. It means seeing dominance, and efforts to obtain dominance, as a form of corruption of all major legal traditions, which exist as varying forms of equilibrium. It also means seeing your own, particular tradition (or at least the tradition or traditions to which you are most attached) as secure, as beyond repression by any means which could be successful in any lasting, meaningful way. It's not just the others' ways of thought which are secured. It's also your own. So western, bivalent thinking does not somehow have to be abandoned, within western legal traditions.[40] There need simply be recognition that multivalent thinking also exists, in other legal traditions and even as a major, constitutive element of western legal traditions themselves.

Acting positively to sustain diversity in law should improve communication between lawyers of the world. It should enhance the prospect for peaceful settlement of disputes, enhance the legal mission. Individualistic traditions may borrow, and use, informal notions of normativity to complement themselves. Collectivist traditions may borrow, and use, instruments of self-empowerment, again to com-

---

[39] See M. Walzer, *On Toleration* (New Haven/London: Yale Univ. Press, 1997) at 92 ('some mix of curiosity and enthusiasm is necessary').

[40] In any event, '[m]ultivalence reduces to bivalence in extreme cases', i.e., if you look to either end of the middle ground, you find extreme positions which are bivalent. Adams, Nickles and Ressler, 'Wedding Carlson and Schwartz' (1994), above, at 2236; and for resort to different types of logic in science, see Pearce, *Roads to Commensurability* (1987), above, at 9 ('one may . . . recognise that different types of logic and semantics may be appropriate in different contexts and for different theories').

plement themselves. All in the limits they judge acceptable. All according to the constraints of context.

Recognition and acceptance of the diverse legal traditions of the world has implications for the identities which people in the world give themselves. Recognition of other traditions as partially your own means adhering, however partially, to those traditions. It means identifying with them in some measure. Identity then becomes less clear than it was before (partial) adherence to another tradition. Identity is fuzzier, more multivalent; there are more loyalties claiming your attention. At the same time, in accepting more traditions there is more awareness of them, of their detail and variation, such that the other is less obviously and clearly the other. There are certainly others, yet they appear in greater variety and it becomes less easy to group them in monolithic blocks. Large forms of animosity become more conceptually difficult. There are too many groups out there, too much variety. How do you keep track of it all? How do you conceptually deal with ongoing diversity?

### THE WAYS OF DIVERSITY

Multivalent thinking tells you to keep in mind the sources of conflict, that is, the large, inconsistent principles, the sources of alleged incommensurability, the ideas which people use to (differently) identify themselves. This is not hard to do, since these are the terms by which conflict is usually defined, and the parties to disputes will often want to talk about little else. Multivalent thinking tells you, however, that these opposing principles really only serve to define the field of play. They tell you where to find the middle ground, and there is always a middle ground. To find the middle ground you need more information. You need the detailed information which disintegrates boundaries (it's just like quantum physics).

There are two valuable sources of further information. One is within the conflicting traditions themselves. They do not themselves solve disputes by invoking world views. They are complex legal traditions because they succeed in reconciling different theoretical views in the cadre of ongoing, specific dispute resolution. So what nuances do they themselves allow in application of their most important principles? What sources of differentiation are possible, since they are already recognized in the sources of the present antagonism? If you are in a mediating position, you may have to do this research yourself. Those engaged in a dispute, in advancing a position, will not voluntarily and immediately advance a range of fall-back positions. They may not themselves have come to recognize them, in the rush to present a united front. The second source of information comes from what western lawyers call the facts. In other legal traditions there are no facts, just sacred or vital ways of life, which have their own, internal normativity. If you know enough of what went on, goes the argument, a solution will eventually suggest itself. The solution will be for *this case*, which will have inspired its own form of resolution. So the more you know about your dispute, the more you will be able to map where it is in the middle ground and the closer you will be to having the parties recognize the middle ground. They will be better informed. Increasing the information means reducing the conflict.

If you are a lawyer you will probably recognize this technique of dispute resolution. Its use indicates the extent of multivalence which already characterizes your legal practice, even if the legal theory of your tradition tells you that cases are decided by application of a single, pre-established rule. An example of multivalent practice at the level of different legal traditions may, however, be useful.

There is an ongoing, international debate about whether parties to contracts (usually international ones) are free to choose the law applicable to their contract. Some say it is the parties who make contracts (the law follows the deal, as in many of the traditions examined here) so party choice should be allowed.[41] Others say it is the state which gives binding effect to contracts, so no contract is above or beyond state law, and any choice expressed by the parties is only one factor in a process of objectively deciding which state law must govern the contract.[42] These are two, large, opposing principles. In the European Common Market, now the European Union, it was decided that there should be a common law which determines the law applicable to contracts. The resulting Rome Convention on the Law Applicable to Contractual Obligations is an example of a multivalent international convention.[43] It explicitly recognizes the validity of the two opposing principles, and directs attention to the criteria for resolving individual cases in the middle ground.[44] Neither opposing principle is dispositive of any individual case. To resolve an individual case, imprecise (even fuzzy) standards are set out, the application of which requires detailed information on the circumstances of the individual case. Parties to the Convention will exchange further information by way of persuasive authority on how they have resolved particular disputes in the middle ground. The Rome Convention has naturally been influential elsewhere in law reform. It is a Convention which accepts (not just tolerates) opposing views and defines the information needed to function in the middle ground. It is an instrument which deals, not with the conflict of laws (they are disintegrated), but with the conciliation of laws, conciliation being a primary feature of multivalence.

Some other fields of application of multivalent thinking—the ways of

---

[41] The argument dates from at least Dumoulin in 16th century France, who sought to free contractual obligations from the grip of regional 'customs'. As the grip of the 'customs' weakened, however, that of the state strengthened, so party autonomy met powerful, ongoing resistance. In some areas of the world, such as latin America, it was almost eliminated in the 19th century.

[42] The argument is perhaps most famously put in H. Batiffol, 'Subjectivisme et objectivisme dans le droit international privé des contrats' in *Mélanges Maury* (Paris: Dalloz & Sirey, 1960) at 53.

[43] For details of the Convention, with references, see L. Collins (ed.), *Dicey and Morris on the Conflict of Laws*, 12th edn. (London: Sweet & Maxwell, 1993), vol. II, at 1187 ff.

[44] Art. 3 thus provides that a contract is governed by the law chosen by the parties. Yet art. 7 of the Convention provides that nothing in the Convention shall restrict the application of rules of the law of the forum which are 'mandatory'. State control thus exists for states which wish to affirm it and state control will prevail in an individual case whenever a state law is 'mandatory' (the fuzzy standard).

diversity—may be suggested. The international debate over human rights can be framed as one of the validity, or not, of the idea of human rights. This is related to the idea of their universality. Yet rights in western thought are not absolute, are often denied (as in English common law), are frequently expressed as group rights, and vary in their national or regional implementation (the nuances internal to the traditions).[45] So the debate about whether human rights are respected can take as a given that human rights exist, and other legal traditions now do so in formulating their own versions of human rights. It must also be a given in such debates, however, that there are alternatives to rights in other traditions, which are advanced with as much persuasion and as much intensity, as means of advancing human dignity.

A former President of the Federal Republic of Germany has argued the case for multivalent thinking in the international human rights debate. All major human traditions, has said Roman Herzog, have an 'ethic of humanity'.[46] In resolving debates about the treatment of human beings we must carry forward, not relativize, the human rights debate, but the most effective technique is that of examination of particular problems in detail and given the circumstances of each country. What is the most effective, general idea in the circumstances in which decisions must be made? How is human dignity advanced, in this case, by invocation of general concepts? The same technique of multivalence is said to prevail in the (regional) jurisprudence of the European Court of Human Rights, where the notion of human rights as variable standards, capable of violation *in varying degrees* is increasingly said to be recognized.[47] The international regime of human rights may

[45] See, for the historical ambivalence of western thought concerning rights, J. Coleman, 'Medieval Discussion of Human Rights' in W. Schmale (ed.), *Human Rights and Cultural Diversity* (Goldbach, Germany: Keip Publishing, 1993) 103 at 106 (prior to current liberal theory all rights theorists viewed holders of rights only 'in relation to other humans as bearers of rights and recognizers of the rights of others'); and for current practice, E. Wise, 'Legal Tradition as a Limitation on Law Reform' (1978) 26 Am. J. Comp. Law (Suppl.) 1 at 10 ('Prevailing modes of constitutional adjudication require either passionate assertion of inflexible, abstract imperatives standing outside of time, or (more commonly these days) a rationalistic calculation in largely contemporary terms of the point of balance between the interests of government and a merely *prima facie* commitment to respect the individual rights in question').

[46] R. Herzog, 'Die Rechte des Menschen,' *Die Zeit*, 13 Sept. 1996, 3; and see S. Sinha, 'Human Rights: A Non-Western Viewpoint' (1981) 67 Archiv für Rechts- und Sozialphilosophie 76 at 89 ('What is required is a redefinition of the problem of human rights which would focus not so much upon a particular way of human emancipation but at the very issue of that emancipation, recognizing the fact that there [is] more than one way of achieving such emancipation ... The universal part consists of the imperative that there must be a minimization of injustice ... acccountability in terms of the condition of [each] society'); and on an underlying notion of the dignity of the human person, see V. Saint-James, 'Réflexions sur la dignité de l'être humain en tant que concept juridique du droit français' Dalloz 1997. I. 61; M. -L. Pavia and T. Revet, *La dignité de la personne humaine* (Paris: Economica, 1999) (dignity as 'young old idea', at p. vi); and for application in the context of French–Chinese legal dialogue, M. Delmas-Marty and Gao Mingxuan, *Criminalité économique et atteintes à la dignité de la personne* (Paris: Éditions de la Maison des sciences de l'homme, 1997).

[47] M. Delmas-Marty, *Pour un droit commun* (Paris: Seuil, 1994) at 119, 120 (content of human rights 'faiblement déterminées'), 161 (notion of extent or degree of violation of human rights); F. Ost, 'La jurisprudence de la Cour européenne des droits de l'homme: amorce d'un nouveau "jus commune"?' in B. de Witte and C. Forder (eds.), *The common law of Europe and the future of legal education* (Deventer, Netherlands: Kluwer, 1992) 683 notably at 701 ('la marge d'appréciation nationale') and 717 ('une logique polyphonique').

be seen, moreover, as a *complex* regime, the theory of international regimes now being advanced as a supple, inclusive, conciliatory technique for ongoing resolution of international disputes.[48]

International development is also a field in which multivalent thinking has recently been urged, though perhaps not explicitly. Multivalent thinking is implicit, however, in the entire school of thought which has developed in recent decades and which advocates limits on notions of growth (in accordance with local tradition), and means of strengthening local societal structures (including legal ones) as a means of providing the ongoing structures necessary for development. Traditions here are layered, and western ones, to the extent they are received, are adjusted to those which exist already.[49] Markets are not absolute. They cannot be made absolute without elimination of the traditions which limit them, and these are many, if not most, of the legal traditions of the world. Western teaching, moreover (or some of it) acknowledges the existence of legal structures as an essential pre-condition to the functioning of markets.[50] The legal structures cannot be identical in the world; this would imply elimination of other major, complex legal traditions. Sustaining legal traditions means restraining market activity, where different legal traditions require restraint. Markets exist, but they are more or less free. It is, again, a question of degree.

Multivalence also appears useful in thinking about contemporary, complex societies, where multiple claims of (legal) recognition are made on behalf of different groups within states, often relying on some form of international or regional

[48] See, e.g., S. Krasner (ed.), *International Regimes* (Ithaca, NY: Cornell Univ. Press, 1983; O. Young, 'International Regimes: Toward a New Theory of Institutions' (1986) 39 *World Politics* 104.

[49] See O. Weggel, *Die Asiaten* (Munich: C. H. Beck, 1989) at 331; H. von Senger, *Einführung in das chinesische Recht* (Munich: C. H. Beck) at 9, with refs.; S. Abou, *Culture et droits de l'homme* (Paris: Hachette, 1992) at 126 (notion of 'développement intégré'); J. Brohman, *Popular Development: Rethinking the Theory and Practice of Development* (Oxford: Blackwell, 1996), notably ch. 11 ('Indigenization of Development'); A. Sen, *Resources, Values and Development* (Oxford: Basil Blackwell, 1984), notably at 489 (need to consider passions as well as interests), 495 (economic growth no more than means to other objectives) and 504 (need to consider 'Political Complexities'); Anton, *Diversity, Globalization, and Ways of Nature* (1995), above, at 150–2 (failure of colonial, socialist and capitalist productivist models will promote search for new models based on indigenous resources and cultures); Mattei, *Comparative Law and Economics* (1997), above, notably at 239 (law and economics in best position to see that 'transaction costs of substituting modern solutions to traditional ones are just too high').

[50] C. Goodhart, 'Economics and Law' (1997), above, with refs.; D. Campbell and S. Picciotto, 'Exploring the interaction between law and economics: the limits of formalism' (1998) 18 Legal St. 249, notably at 253 ('all transactions, can take place only within constitutive social relations . . . If one really took away all the costs of exchanging, the exchange would not take place cost free, it would not take place at all') and 264 ('the point is not *whether* to regulate markets, for they cannot exist without regulation, but *how* to regulate them'); and see 'It's the government, stupid', *The Economist*, 28 June, 1997 at 71, reporting on the World Bank, *World Development Report 1997* (Oxford: Oxford Univ. Press, 1997), notably at 41 ('Markets rest on a foundation of institutions'); M. Mahmoud, 'L'économie de marché et les droits de l'homme' Rev. int. dr. éc. 1996. 159, notably at 162; D. Lal, *Unintended Consequences: the Impact of Factor Endowment, Culture and Politics on Long-Run Economic Performance* (Cambridge, Mass./London: MIT Press, 1998), notably at 44, 174 on the importance of 'cosmological beliefs' in determining economic outcomes. Absence of appropriate legal structures encourages parasitic, criminal traditions (gangs and mobs) in all social contexts.

guarantee of minority rights. Legal traditions and identities here overlap in very close proximity, and different states respond in different fashion (none is immune from the process). Again, there are conflicting principles, and much of the theoretical debate is in terms of these conflicting principles. On the one hand there is a notion of citizenship which would demand exclusive loyalty to the state and which would relegate other legal traditions, if recognized at all, to the realm of a purely private sphere. On the other hand there is the model of 'personal laws', representing co-existence of different legal traditions and groups, which would (perhaps fatally) weaken the structure of the modern state. In the law of the states of the world, solutions are usually found between these two poles. There are many places in the middle ground, most of which accept the continuing relevance of both state citizenship and personal, non-state, legal allegiances. Multivalence in law is the order of the day, whether recognized in political or state theory or not. Recognition of many legal traditions is facilitated, moreover, by their non-legislative character; they do not purport to occupy the legislative field of state law.

There are of course important differences between states. States such as the United States of America and France have (traditionally) placed greatest emphasis on exclusivity of citizenship and loyalty to the state. US law recognizes much chthonic law, however ('tribal sovereignty'), and the well known separation of church and state in US law has been described as a 'blurred, indistinct and variable barrier depending on all the circumstances of a particular relationship'.[51] In France the principle of secularity is nevertheless compatible both with the wearing of religious garb in schools (providing public order—a fuzzy standard—is not violated) and judicial orders designed to compel the granting of talmudic divorces.[52] In jurisdictions which recognize personal laws—the application of non-state legal traditions to many questions of personal status, family law and succession—the state, somehow, persists. There are many structures and solutions available, and multivalent thought facilitates the non-violent adoption of them.

---

[51]   *Lemon* v. *Kurtzman*, 403 US 602 at 614 (1971) (Burger CJ).

[52]   For the wearing of a veil, see above, Ch. 6, *The islamic diaspora*; and for measures compelling the granting of religious divorce, Civ. 13 Dec. 1972, D. 1973. 493.

# Index

INDEX

363

Prophet, the, *see Muhammad*
prophet(s) 330
  in talmudic tradition 87 n.
property
  in chthonic tradition 62–3, 67, 79–80
  in civil law tradition 131, 152–3, 168
  in common law tradition 168, 212–4, 218, 222,
    236
  concepts of, in colonization process 241
  and ejido 63
  in hindu tradition 258–9
  in islamic tradition 168–9
  in roman legal tradition 120, 214
  in socialist law 307
  in talmudic tradition 92–4
proselytizing, *see* universalizing
public international law 50 n.
public law
  in Asian tradition 285, 307–9
  in chthonic tradition 60
  in civil law tradition 118, 134, 148, 150
  in common law tradition 220, 234
  in hindu tradition 263–4
  in islamic tradition 192–4
  private/public law distinction 217 n.
  in roman law tradition 118
  in talmudic tradition 13 n.
  *see also* administrative law, constitutional law
public policy (order) 181 n., 338
Pufendorf 132
Puga 258
pundits 274
punishment
  and Asian legal tradition 282, 283, 284, 297
pyramids of law 140 n.
  in hindu tradition (no) 253
  in islamic legal tradition (inverted) 159
  in talmudic tradition (inverted) 91
  in theory of H. Kelsen 140 n.

qadi 163–5, 172, 193, 321
quaestiones disputatae 123, 185 n.
quantum physics 326, 334
  and buddhism 291 n.
quasi-contract
  in roman law 120
qyas 162, 175–6, 183, 185, 321

rabbi(s) 91
race, racisim 30 n., 33–5, 246, 313, 322
  and chthonic tradition 74, 75
  construction of idea in west 34 n.
rationality, *see* tradition (of rationality)
Rawls, J. 42 n.

ra'y 161–2, 173, 176
reading
  interactive, in talmudic tradition 98
  silent, in western tradition 98
rebus sic stantibus 290 n.
reception
  of civil law
    in Asia 304–6
    in Russia 307 n.
  of common law 228–35, 306
  of Greek philosophy 133 n.
  of Italian mercantile law, in England 238 n.
  of roman law 123–4, 140, 151–2, 305 n.
  of western law in colonialism 239–45, 337
reform movement (in judaism) 105–6, 110–11, 319
refugees 153
  in islamic tradition 196
regime theory (international) 337
regionalization 49, 194
reincarnation 260–1, 264–6, 267
relativism 30 n., 323, 328–9
religion 47, 153, 188, 331
  and Asian tradition 279–80, 290, 294, 295
  buddhism as 291 n.
  in chthonic tradition 58, 66, 68
  in civil law tradition 127, 130–3
  in common law tradition 221, 226
  in hindu tradition 253–5, 258, 260–2, 272
  in islamic tradition
    no compulsion in 192, 199, 201
  in talmudic tradition 95–6, 103
  in western law 192 n.
religious courts, in western jurisdictions
  shari'a courts 198
  talmudic courts 92
renaissance 61, 122, 136, 208, 221, 226
Renan 51 n.
renoncants of Pondicherry 272–3
requenoissants (recognitions) 209 n.
res judicata
  in common law tradition 219
  in hindu tradition 258
  in islamic tradition 164
  in talmudic tradition 93
reservations (for chthonic peoples) 78
resistance 320
responsa
  in talmudic tradition 90–1, 93
Restatements (US) 161 n.
revelation 9, 116, 207, 213
  and Asian tradition 280
  in hindu tradition 254, 256, 262, 269, 276, 291
  in islamic tradition 158, 160, 171–8, 189, 190, 191,
    196